The Handbook of Traditional and Alternative Investment Vehicles

The Frank J. Fabozzi Series

The Handbook of Traditional and Alternative Investment Vehicles

Investment Characteristics and Strategies

MARK J. P. ANSON
FRANK J. FABOZZI
FRANK J. JONES

WILEY

John Wiley & Sons, Inc.

For general information on our other products and services or for technical support, please contact our Customer Care Department within the United States at (800) 762-2974, outside the United States at (317) 572-3993, or fax (317) 572-4002.

Wiley also publishes its books in a variety of electronic formats. Some content that appears in print may not be available in electronic books. For more information about Wiley products, visit our web site at www.wiley.com.

ISBN: 978-0-470-60973-6 (cloth); 978-1-118-00868-3 (ebk); 978-1-118-00869-0 (ebk)

10 9 8 7 6 5 4 3 2 1

MJPA
To my wife Mary,
my children Madeleine and Marcus,
and our two cats, Scout and Fuffy—
two important members of our family

FJF
To my wife Donna
and my children Patricia, Karly, and Francesco

FJJ
To my wife Sally for her good humor and patience

Contents

Preface

The financial industry has grown tremendously in terms of size and sophistication over the last 30 years. The great bull stock market that began in the early 1980s combined with the birth of enormous computing power led to a growth in the financial markets that no one could have predicted. So, it was a bit of a daunting task to produce a one-volume handbook to the financial instruments that exist in the global marketplace.

At the outset of this book, we decided to take a pragmatic approach—mixing a little theory with a lot of real world examples. As authors, we thought it better to provide you with a user-friendly reference guide than to provide you with a theoretical treatise. Not that we are beyond being academic—indeed we have all been professors at one point in our careers. However, we thought a better approach would be to dazzle the reader less with our academic credentials and instead, to provide a more descriptive textbook.

In this book we provide a "soup to nuts" approach to describing the various financial instruments there are in the marketplace. We start with the basics: commons stock and basic bonds. We then move on to municipal bonds, agency passthrough securities, collateralized mortgage obligations, and the more specialized structured products in the credit industry. We also cover the fastest growing part of the asset management industry: exchange-traded funds. Over the past decade, exchange-traded funds have grown at a cumulative average growth rate of over 40% per year—stronger growth than the alternative asset market.

This brings us to the next part of the book. We provide an in depth review of the major segments of the alternative asset market. We start with real estate and then move on to publicly traded real estate investment trusts. We then venture into the world of hedge funds, providing both a descriptive overview of the many types and styles of hedge funds as well as providing a "how to" guide to investing in these vehicles. We also cover the world of private equity—dedicating a chapter to each of the four parts of the private equity world: leveraged buyouts, venture capital, mezzanine debt, and distressed debt. Last, we include commodities. Over the last 20 years, commodities have developed as an investable asset class.

In summary, our goal in this book is not to display our command of the arcane nomenclature associated with the financial markets, but instead, to provide the reader with a thoughtful guide to financial instruments. If you pull this book down from your bookshelf from time to time to consult how the market works for a particular financial instrument, we consider this a successful effort.

Mark J. P. Anson
Frank J. Fabozzi
Frank J. Jones

About the Authors

Mark Anson is the Chief Investment Officer and Managing Partner for Oak Hill Investments, a wealth advisory firm serving high net worth clients. Prior to joining OHIM, Mark was President and Executive Director of Investment Services at Nuveen Investments, an asset management firm with $150 billion assets under management. Prior to Nuveen, Mark served as Chief Executive Officer of Hermes Pensions Management Ltd., an institutional asset management company based in London, where he was also the Chief Executive Officer of the British Telecom Pension Scheme, the largest pension fund in the United Kingdom and the sole owner of Hermes. Prior to joining Hermes, he served as the Chief Investment Officer of the California Public Employees' Retirement System, the largest pension fund in the United States. Mark is the former Chairman of the Board of the International Corporate Governance Network. He also has served on the advisory boards for the New York Stock Exchange, NYSE/Euronext, MSCI-Barra, The Dow Jones-UBS Commodity Index, and the International Association of Financial Engineers. Currently, he is a member of the Board of Governors of the CFA Institute and the SEC Advisory Committee to SEC Chairwoman Mary Schapiro. He has published over 100 research articles in professional journals, has won two Best Paper Awards, is the author of four financial textbooks including the *Handbook of Alternative Assets*, which is the primary textbook used for the Chartered Alternative Investment Analyst program, and sits on the editorial boards of several financial journals. Mark earned a B.A. in Economics and Chemistry from St. Olaf College, a J.D. from Northwestern University School of Law, and a Masters and a Ph.D. in Finance from Columbia University Graduate School of Business, all with honors. In addition, Mark has earned the Chartered Financial Analyst, Chartered Alternative Investment Analyst, Certified Public Accountant, Certified Management Accountant, and Certified Internal Auditor professional designations.

Frank J. Fabozzi, Ph.D., CFA, CPA is Professor in the Practice of Finance in the Yale School of Management. Prior to joining the Yale faculty, he was a Visiting Professor of Finance in the Sloan School at MIT. Frank is a Fellow of the International Center for Finance at Yale University and on the Advisory Council for the Department of Operations Research and Financial

Engineering at Princeton University. He is the editor of the *Journal of Portfolio Management* and an associate editor of the *Journal of Fixed Income* and the *Journal of Structured Finance*. He is a trustee for the BlackRock family of closed-end funds. In 2002, Frank was inducted into the Fixed Income Analysts Society's Hall of Fame and is the 2007 recipient of the C. Stewart Sheppard Award given by the CFA Institute. He has authored numerous books in investment management and structured finance. Frank earned a doctorate in economics from the City University of New York in 1972 and earned the designation of Chartered Financial Analyst and Certified Public Accountant.

Frank J. Jones is a Professor of Finance and Accounting at San Jose State University. He is also the Chairman of the Investment Committee of Private Ocean Wealth Management, a wealth management advisory firm serving high net worth clients. Frank served on the Board of Directors of the International Securities Exchange for 10 years until 2010 where he was alternately Chairman and Vice-Chairman and was on the Executive Committee, IPO Committee, and Finance and Audit Committee. Prior to returning to academia, he was the Executive Vice President and Chief Investment Officer of the Guardian Life Insurance Company; President of the Park Avenue Portfolio, a mutual fund company; Director of Global Fixed Income Research and Economics at Merrill Lynch and Company; and Senior Vice President at the New York Stock Exchange. Frank has been on the Graduate Faculty of Economics at the University of Notre Dame; an Adjunct Professor of Finance at the New York University Stern School of Business; and a Lecturer at the Yale University School of Management. He is on the Editorial Board of the *Journal of Investment Management*. He received a Doctorate from the Stanford University Graduate School of Business and a Masters of Science in Nuclear Engineering from Cornell University. He is the author of several books, chapters in books, and articles in investments and finance.

CHAPTER 1

Introduction

There is a wide range of financial instruments. The most general classification of financial instruments is based on the nature of the claim that the investor has on the issuer of the instrument. When the contractual arrangement is one in which the issuer agrees to pay interest and repay the amount borrowed, the financial instrument is said to be a *debt instrument*. In contrast to a debt instrument, an *equity instrument* represents an ownership interest in the entity that has issued the financial instrument. The holder of an equity instrument is entitled to receive a pro rata share of earnings, if any, after the holders of debt instruments have been paid. Common stock is an example of an equity claim. A partnership share in a business is another example.

Some financial instruments fall into both categories in terms of their attributes. Preferred stock, for example, is an equity instrument that entitles the investor to receive a fixed amount of earnings. This payment is contingent, however, and due only after payments to holders of debt instrument are made. Another hybrid instrument is a convertible bond, which allows the investor to convert a debt instrument into an equity instrument under certain circumstances. Both debt instruments and preferred stock are called *fixed income instruments*.

In this chapter, we'll provide some basics about financial instruments, the general types of risks associated with investing, and characteristics of asset classes.

RISKS ASSOCIATED WITH INVESTING

There are various risks associated with investing and these will be described throughout the book. Here we will provide a brief review of the major risks associated with investing.

Total Risk

The dictionary defines risk as "hazard, peril, exposure to loss or injury." With respect to investing, investors have used a variety of definitions to describe risk. Today, the most commonly accepted definition of risk is one that involves a well-known statistical measure known as the variance and is referred to as the *total risk*. The variance measures the dispersion of the outcomes around the expected value of all outcomes. Another name for the expected value is the average value.

In applying this statistical measure to the returns for a financial instrument, which we refer to as an asset for our discussion here, the observed returns on that asset over some time period are first obtained. Appendix A explains how returns for an asset are calculated. From those observed returns, the average return (which is the average or mean value) can be computed and using that average value, the variance can be computed. The square root of the variance is the standard deviation.

Despite the dominance of the variance (or standard deviation) as a measure of total risk, there are problems with using this measure to quantify the total risk for many of the assets we describe in this book. The first problem is that since the variance measures the dispersion of an asset's return around its expected value, it considers the possibility of returns above the expected return and below the average return. Investors, however, do not view possible returns above the expected return as an unfavorable outcome. In fact, such outcomes are viewed as favorable. Because of this, it is argued that measures of risk should not consider the possible returns above the expected return. Various measures of downside risk, such as risk of loss and value at risk, are currently being used by practitioners.

The second problem is that the variance is only one measure of how the returns vary around the expected return. When a probability distribution is not symmetrical around its expected return, then another statistical measure known as *skewness* should be used in addition to the variance. Skewed distributions are referred to in terms of *tails* and *mass*. The tails of a probability distribution for returns is important because it is in the tails where the extreme values exist. An investor should be aware of the potential adverse extreme values for an investment and an investment portfolio. The statistical measures important for understanding risk, skewness and kurtosis, are explained in Appendix B.

Diversification

One way of reducing the total risk associated with holding an individual asset is by diversifying. Often, one hears financial advisors and professional money managers talking about diversifying their portfolio. By this it is meant the construction of a portfolio in such a way as to reduce the port-folio's total risk without sacrificing expected return. This is certainly a goal that investors should seek. However, the question is, how does one do this in practice?

Some financial advisors and the popular press might say that a port-folio can be diversified by including assets across all asset classes. (We'll explain in more detail what we mean by an asset class below.) Although that might be reasonable, two questions must be addressed in order to construct a diversified portfolio. First, how much of the investor's wealth should be invested in each asset class? Second, given the allocation, which specific assets should the investor select?

Some investors who focus only on one asset class such as common stock argue that such portfolios should also be diversified. By this they mean that an investor should not place all funds in the stock of one company, but rather should include stocks of many companies. Here, too, several questions must be answered in order to construct a diversified portfolio. First, which companies should be represented in the portfolio? Second, how much of the portfolio should be allocated to the stocks of each company?

Prior to the development of portfolio theory by Harry Markowitz in 1952,[1] while financial advisors often talked about diversification in these general terms, they never provided the analytical tools by which to answer the questions posed here. Markowitz demonstrated that a diversification strategy should take into account the degree of correlation (or covariance) between asset returns in a portfolio. The correlation of asset returns is a measure of the degree to which the returns on two assets vary or change together. Correlation values range from –1 to +1.

Indeed, a key contribution of what is now popularly referred to as "Markowitz diversification" or "mean-variance diversification" is the for-mulation of an asset's risk in terms of a portfolio of assets, rather than the total risk of an individual asset. Markowitz diversification seeks to combine assets in a portfolio with returns that are less than perfectly positively cor-related in an effort to lower the portfolio's total risk (variance) without sacrificing return. It is the concern for maintaining expected return while lowering the portfolio's total risk through an analysis of the correlation between asset returns that separates Markowitz diversification from other approaches suggested for diversification and makes it more effective.

The principle of Markowitz diversification states that as the correlation between the returns for assets that are combined in a portfolio decreases, so does the variance of the portfolio's total return. The good news is that

---

[1]Harry M. Markowitz, "Portfolio Selection," *Journal of Finance* 7, no. 1 (1952): 77–91.

investors can maintain expected portfolio return and lower portfolio total risk by combining assets with lower (and preferably negative) correlations. However, the bad news is that very few assets have small to negative correlations with other assets. The problem, then, becomes one of searching among a large number of assets in an effort to discover the portfolio with the minimum risk at a given level of expected return or, equivalently, the highest expected return at a given level of risk. Such portfolios are called *efficient portfolios*.

The recent financial market crisis has taught an important lesson about constructing efficient portfolios and what to expect from them. Specifically, when constructing a portfolio based on the historical correlations observed, there is no assurance that those correlations may not adversely change over time, particularly in stressful periods in financial markets. By "adversely change" it is meant that correlations that may be considerably less than one when designing a diversified portfolio might move closer to one. This is because during such times there are typically massive sell offs of all assets because of the concerns of a systemic threat to the financial markets throughout the world.

Systematic vs. Unsystematic Risk

The total risk of an asset or a portfolio can be divided into two types of risk: systematic risk and unsystematic risk. William Sharpe defined *systematic risk* as the portion of an asset's variability that can be attributed to a common factor.[2] It is more popularly referred to as *market risk*. Because in the models developed to explain how total risk can be partitioned, the Greek letter beta was used to represent the quantity of systematic risk associated with an asset or portfolio, the term "beta" or "beta risk" has been used to mean market risk.

Systematic risk is the minimum level of risk that can be attained for a portfolio by means of diversification across a large number of randomly chosen assets. As such, systematic risk is that which results from general market and economic conditions that cannot be diversified away. For this reason the term *undiversifiable risk* is also used to describe systematic risk.

Sharpe defined the portion of an asset's return variability (i.e., total risk) that can be diversified away as *unsystematic risk*. It is also called *diversifiable risk*, *unique risk*, *residual risk*, *idiosyncratic risk*, or *company-specific risk*. This is the risk that is unique to a company, such as an employee strike, the outcome of unfavorable litigation, or a natural catastrophe.

---

[2]William F. Sharpe, "Capital Asset Prices," *Journal of Finance* 19, no. 3 (1963): 425–442.

EXHIBIT 1.1 Systematic and Unsystematic Portfolio Risk

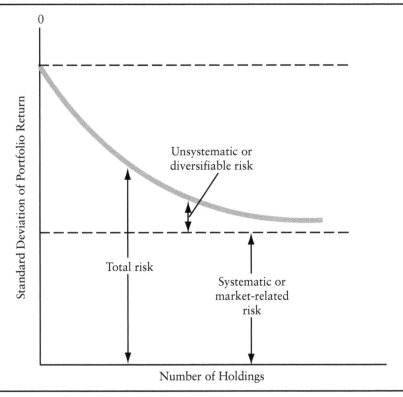

How diversification reduces unsystematic risk for portfolios is illustrated in Exhibit 1.1. The vertical axis shows the standard deviation of a portfolio's total return. The standard deviation represents the total risk for the portfolio (systematic plus unsystematic). The horizontal axis shows the number of holdings of different assets (e.g., the number of common stock held of different companies). As can be seen, as the number of asset holdings increases (assuming that the assets are less than perfectly correlated as discussed below), the level of unsystematic risk is almost completely eliminated (that is, diversified away). The risk that remains is systematic risk. Studies of different asset classes support this. For example, for common stock, several studies suggest that a portfolio size of about 20 randomly selected companies will completely eliminate unsystematic risk leaving only systematic risk.

The relationship between the movement in the price of an asset and the market can be estimated statistically. There are two products of the estimated relationship that investors use. The first is the beta of an asset.

Beta measures the sensitivity of an asset's return to changes in the market's return. Hence, beta is referred to as an index of systematic risk due to general market conditions that cannot be diversified away. For example, if an asset has a beta of 1.5, it means that, on average, if the market changes by 1%, the asset's return changes by about 1.5%. The beta for the market is one. A beta that is greater than one means that systematic risk is greater than that of the market; a beta less than one means that the systematic risk is less than that of the market. Brokerage firms, vendors such as Bloomberg, Yahoo! Finance, and online Internet services provide information on beta for common stock.

The second product is the ratio of the amount of systematic risk relative to the total risk. This ratio, called the coefficient of determination or R-squared, varies from zero to one. A value of 0.8 for a portfolio means that 80% of the variation in the portfolio's return is explained by movements in the market. For individual assets, this ratio is typically low because there is a good deal of unsystematic risk. However, as shown in Exhibit 1.1, through diversification the ratio increases as unsystematic risk is reduced.

Inflation or Purchasing Power Risk

Inflation risk, or *purchasing power risk*, is the potential erosion in the value of an asset's cash flows due to inflation, as measured in terms of purchasing power. For example, if an investor purchases an asset that produces an annual return of 5% and the rate of inflation is 3%, the purchasing power of the investor has not increased by 5%. Instead, the investor's purchasing power has increased by 2%.

Different asset classes have different exposure to inflation risk. As explained in later chapters, there are some financial instruments specifically designed to adjust for the rate of inflation.

Credit Risk

The typical definition of *credit risk* is that it is the risk that a borrower will fail to satisfy its financial obligations under a debt agreement. The securities issued by the U.S. Department of the Treasury are viewed as free of credit risk. (Whether this remains true in the future will depend on the U.S. government economic policies.) An investor who purchases an asset not guaranteed by the U.S. government is viewed as being exposed to credit risk. Actually, there are several forms of credit risk: default risk, downgrade risk, and spread risk. We describe these various risks in Chapter 4 and we will see that the definition of credit risk given above is for that of default risk.

Liquidity Risk

When an investor wants to sell an asset, he or she is concerned whether the price that can be obtained is close to the true value of the asset. For example, if recent trades in the market for a particular asset have been between $40 and $40.50 and market conditions have not changed, an investor would expect to sell the asset in that range.

Liquidity risk is the risk that the investor will have to sell an asset below its true value where the true value is indicated by a recent transaction. The primary measure of liquidity is the size of the spread between the bid price (the price at which a dealer is willing to buy an asset) and the ask price (the price at which a dealer is willing to sell an asset). The wider the bid-ask spread, the greater the liquidity risk.

Exchange Rate or Currency Risk

An asset whose cash flows are not in the investor's domestic currency has unknown cash flows in the domestic currency. The cash flows in the investor's domestic currency are dependent on the exchange rate at the time the payments are received from the asset. For example, suppose an investor's domestic currency is the U.S. dollar and that the investor purchases an asset whose payments are in euros. If the euro depreciates relative to the U.S. dollar at the time a euro payment is received, then fewer U.S. dollars will be received.

The risk of receiving less of the domestic currency than is expected at the time of purchase when an asset makes payments in a currency other than the investor's domestic currency is called *exchange rate risk* or *currency risk*.

ASSET CLASSES

In most developed countries, the four major asset classes are (1) common stocks, (2) bonds, (3) cash equivalents, and (4) real estate. Why are they referred to as asset classes? That is, how do we define an *asset class*? There are several ways to do so. The first is in terms of the investment attributes that the members of an asset class have in common. These investment characteristics include

- The major economic factors that influence the value of the asset class and, as a result, correlate highly with the returns of each member included in the asset class.
- Risk and return characteristics that are similar.
- A common legal or regulatory structure.

Based on this way of defining an asset class, the correlation between the returns of two different asset classes—the key statistical measure for successful diversification—would be low.

Mark Kritzman offers a second way of defining an asset class based simply on a group of assets that is treated as an asset class by asset managers.[3] He writes:

> some investments take on the status of an asset class simply because the managers of these assets promote them as an asset class. They believe that investors will be more inclined to allocate funds to their products if they are viewed as an asset class rather than merely as an investment strategy. (p. 79)

Kritzman then goes on to propose criteria for determining asset class status which includes the attributes that we mentioned above and that will be described in more detail in later chapters.

Based on these two ways of defining asset classes, the four major asset classes above can be extended to create other asset classes. From the perspective of a U.S. investor, for example, the four major asset classes listed earlier have been expanded as follows by separating foreign securities from U.S. securities: (1) U.S. common stocks, (2) non-U.S. (or foreign) common stocks, (3) U.S. bonds, (4) non-U.S. bonds, (5) cash equivalents, and (6) real estate.

Common stocks and bonds are commonly further partitioned into more asset classes. For U.S. common stocks (also referred to as U.S. equities), asset classes are based on market capitalization and style (growth versus value).

The *market capitalization* of a firm, commonly referred to as "market cap," is the total market value of its common stock outstanding. For example, suppose that a corporation has 400 million shares of common stock outstanding and each share has a market value of $100. Then the market capitalization of this company is $40 billion (400 million shares times $100 per share). The categories of common stock based on market capitalization are *mega-cap* (greater than $200 billion), *large cap* ($10 billion to $200 billion), *mid-cap* ($1 billion to $10 billion), *small cap* ($300 million to $1 billion), *micro-cap* ($50 million to $300 million), and *nano-cap* (less than $50 million).

While the market cap of a company is easy to determine given the market price per share and the number of shares outstanding, how does one define "value" and "growth" stocks? We describe how this done in Chapter 3.

For U.S. bonds, also referred to as fixed income securities, the following are classified as asset classes: (1) U.S. government bonds, (2) corporate bonds, (3) U.S. municipal bonds (i.e., state and local bonds), (4) residential

---

[3]Mark Kritzman, "Toward Defining an Asset Class," *Journal of Alternative Investments* 2, no. 1 (1999): 79–82.

mortgage-backed securities, (5) commercial mortgage-backed securities, and (6) asset-backed securities. In turn, several of these asset classes are further segmented by the credit rating of the issuer. For example, for corporate bonds, investment-grade (i.e., high credit quality) corporate bonds and non-investment grade corporate bonds (i.e., speculative quality) are treated as two asset classes.

For non-U.S. stocks and bonds, the following are classified as asset classes: (1) developed market foreign stocks, (2) developed market foreign bonds, (3) emerging market foreign stocks, and (4) emerging market foreign bonds. The characteristics that market participants use to describe emerging markets is that the countries in this group:

- Have economies that are in transition but have started implementing political, economic, and financial market reforms in order to participate in the global capital market.
- May expose investors to significant price volatility attributable to political risk and the unstable value of their currency.
- Have a short period over which their financial markets have operated.

Loucks, Penicook, and Schillhorn describe what is meant by an emerging market as follows:[4]

Emerging market issuers rely on international investors for capital. Emerging markets cannot finance their fiscal deficits domestically because domestic capital markets are poorly developed and local investors are unable or unwilling to lend to the government. Although emerging market issuers differ greatly in terms of credit risk, dependence on foreign capital is the most basic characteristic of the asset class. (p. 340)

The asset classes above are referred to as *traditional asset classes*. Other asset classes are referred to as *nontraditional asset classes* or *alternative asset classes*. They include hedge funds, private equity, and commodities and are discussed later.

Real Estate

Before we discuss alternative asset classes, we provide a brief digression to consider where real estate belongs in our classification scheme. Real estate

---

[4]Maria Mednikov Loucks, John A. Penicook, and Uwe Schillhorn, "Emerging Markets Debt," Chapter 31 in *Handbook of Finance: Vol. I, Financial Markets and Instruments*, edited by Frank J. Fabozzi (Hoboken, N.J.: John Wiley & Sons, 2008).

is a distinct asset class, but is it an alternative asset class? There are three reasons why we do not consider real estate to be an alternative asset class.

First, real estate was an asset class long before stocks and bonds became the investment of choice. In fact, in times past, land was the single most important asset class. Kings, queens, lords, and nobles measured their wealth by the amount of property that they owned. "Land barons" were aptly named. Ownership of land was reserved only for the wealthiest of society. However, over the past 200 years, our economic society changed from one based on the ownership of property to the ownership of legal entities. This transformation occurred as society moved from the agricultural age to the industrial age. Production of goods and services became the new source of wealth and power.

Stocks and bonds evolved to support the financing needs of new enterprises that manufactured material goods and services. In fact, stocks and bonds became the "alternatives" to real estate instead of vice versa. With general acceptance of owning equity or debt stakes in companies, it is sometimes forgotten that real estate was the original and primary asset class of society. In fact, it was less than 30 years ago that in the United States real estate was the major asset class of most individual investors. This exposure was the result of owning a primary residence. It was not until around 1983 that investors began to diversify their wealth into the "alternative" assets of stocks and bonds.

Second, given the long-term presence of real estate as an asset class, models have been developed based on expected cash flows for valuing real estate.

Finally, real estate is not an alternative to stocks and bonds—it is a fundamental asset class that should be included within every diversified portfolio. The alternative assets that we describe in this book are meant to diversify the stock-and-bond holdings within a portfolio context.

What Is an Alternative Asset Class?

Part of the difficulty of working with alternative asset classes is defining them. Are they a separate asset class or a subset of an existing asset class? Do they hedge the investment opportunity set or expand it? That is, in terms of Markowitz diversification, do they improve the efficient portfolio for a given level of risk? This means that for a given level of risk, do they allow for a greater expected return than by just investing in traditional asset classes? Are they listed on an exchange or do they trade in the over-the-counter market?

In most cases, alternative assets are a subset of an existing asset class. This may run contrary to the popular view that alternative assets are separate asset classes. However, we take the view that what many consider separate "classes" are really just different investment strategies within an existing asset class. In most cases, they expand the investment opportunity set, rather than hedge it. Finally, alternative assets are generally purchased in the private markets, outside of any exchange. While hedge funds and private equity meet these criteria, commodity futures prove to be the exception to these general rules.

Alternative assets, then, are just alternative investments within an existing asset class. Specifically, most alternative assets derive their value from either the debt or equity markets. For instance, most hedge fund strategies involve the purchase and sale of either equity or debt securities. Additionally, hedge fund managers may invest in derivative instruments whose value is derived from the equity or debt market.

SUPER ASSET CLASSES

Although we have defined the general attributes of an asset class, it would help clarify alternative assets if we first define a super asset classes. There are three super asset classes: capital assets, assets that are used as inputs to creating economic value, and assets that are a store of value.[5]

Capital Assets

Capital assets are defined by their claim on the future cash flows of an enterprise. They provide a source of ongoing value. As a result, capital assets may be valued based on discounted cash flow models; that is, models that compute the present of the expected cash flow from a capital asset.

Corporate financial theory demonstrates that the value of the firm is dependent on its cash flows. How those cash flows are divided up between shareholders and bondholders in a perfect capital market is irrelevant to firm value.[6] Capital assets, then, are distinguished not by their possession of physical assets, but rather, by their claim on the cash flows of an underlying enterprise. Hedge funds and private equity funds, for example, fall within the super asset class of capital assets because the value of their funds are all determined by the present value of expected future cash flows from the assets in which the fund manager invests.

Consequently, we can conclude that it is not the types of assets in which they invest that distinguish alternative asset classes such as hedge funds and

---

[5]Robert Greer, "What is an Asset Class Anyway?" *Journal of Portfolio Management* **23**, no. 2 (1997): 83–91.

[6]This is the well-known Modigliani-Miller theory of capital structure. See Franco Modigliani and Merton Miller, "The Cost of Capital, Corporation Finance, and the Theory of Investment," *American Economic Review* 48, no. 3 (1958): 433–443.

private equity funds from traditional asset classes. Rather, it is the alternative investment strategies that are pursued by the managers of these asset classes that distinguish them from traditional asset classes such as stocks and bonds.

Assets that Can be Used as Economic Inputs

Certain assets can be consumed as part of the production cycle. Consumable or transformable assets can be converted into another asset. Generally, this class of asset consists of the physical commodities: grains, metals, energy products, and livestock. These assets are used as economic inputs into the production cycle to produce other assets, such as automobiles, skyscrapers, new homes, and appliances.

These assets generally cannot be valued using the traditional discounted cash flow approaches used for common stocks and bonds. For example, a pound of copper, by itself, does not yield an economic stream of revenues. Nor does it have much value for capital appreciation. However, the copper can be transformed into copper piping that is used in an office building or as part of the circuitry of an electronic appliance.

While consumable assets cannot produce a stream of cash flows, this asset class has excellent diversification properties for an investment portfolio. In fact, the lack of dependency on future cash flows to generate value is one of the reasons why commodities have important diversification potential vis-à-vis capital assets.

Assets that Are a Store of Value

Art is considered the classic asset that stores value. It is not a capital asset because there are no cash flows associated with owning a painting or a sculpture. Consequently, art cannot be valued using a discounted cash flow analysis. It is also not an asset that is used as an economic input because it is a finished product. Instead, art requires ownership and possession. Its value can be realized only through its sale and transfer of possession. In the meantime, the owner retains the artwork with the expectation that it will yield a price at least equal to that which the owner paid for it.

There is no rational way to gauge whether the price of art will increase or decrease because its value is derived purely from the subjective (and private) visual enjoyment that the right of ownership conveys. Therefore, to an owner, art is a store of value. It neither conveys economic benefits nor is used as an economic input, but retains the value paid for it.

Gold and precious metals are another example of a store-of-value asset. In the emerging parts of the world, gold and silver are a significant means of maintaining wealth. In these countries, residents do not have access to the same range of financial products that are available to residents of more developed economies. Consequently, they accumulate their wealth through a tangible asset as opposed to a capital asset.

However, the lines between the three super classes of assets can become blurred. For example, gold can be leased to jewelry and other metal manufacturers. Jewelry makers lease gold during periods of seasonal demand, expecting to purchase the gold on the open market and return it to the lessor (i.e., owner of the gold) before the lease term ends. The gold lease provides a stream of cash flows that can be valued using discounted cash flow analysis.

Precious metals can also be used as a transformable/consumable asset because they have the highest level of thermal and electrical conductivity among the metals. Silver, for example, is used in the circuitry for most telephones and light switches. Gold is used in the circuitry for televisions, cars, airplanes, and computers.

STRATEGIC VS. TACTICAL ALLOCATIONS

Alternative assets should be used in a tactical rather than strategic allocation. Strategic allocation of resources is applied to fundamental asset classes such as equity, fixed income, cash, and real estate. These are the basic asset classes that should be held within a diversified portfolio.

Strategic asset allocation is concerned with the long-term asset mix. The strategic mix of assets is designed to accomplish an investor's long-term goal. For trustees of defined benefit pension plans, the long-term goal is to meet the long-term liabilities. Risk aversion is considered when deciding the strategic asset allocation, but current market conditions are not. In general, policy targets are set for strategic asset classes, with allowable ranges around those targets. Allowable ranges are established to allow flexibility in the management of the investment portfolio.

Tactical asset allocation is short-term in nature. This strategy is used to take advantage of current market conditions that may be more favorable to one asset class over another. The goal of funding long-term liabilities has been satisfied by the target ranges established by the strategic asset allocation. The goal of tactical asset allocation is to maximize return.

Tactical allocation of resources depends on the ability to diversify within an asset class. This is where alternative assets have the greatest ability to add value. Their purpose is not to hedge the fundamental asset classes, but rather to expand them. Consequently, alternative assets should be considered as part of a broader asset class.

EFFICIENT VS. INEFFICIENT ASSET CLASSES

Another way to distinguish alternative asset classes from traditional asset classes is based on the efficiency of the marketplace in which the assets trade. The U.S. public stock-and-bond markets are generally considered to be the most price efficient marketplaces in the world. Often, these markets are referred to as "semistrong efficient." As explained in Chapter 3, this means that all publicly available information regarding a publicly traded corporation, both past information and present, is fully digested into the price of that company's traded securities.

Yet inefficiencies exist in all markets, both public and private. If there were no informational inefficiencies in the public equity market, there would be no case for pursuing a strategy that seeks to outperform the market. Such strategies are referred to as *active management strategies*. Nonetheless, whatever inefficiencies do exist, they are small and fleeting. The reason is that information is easy to acquire and disseminate in the publicly traded securities markets. Top-quartile[7] active managers in the public equity market earn returns in excess of their benchmark of approximately 1% a year.

In contrast, with respect to alternative assets, information is very difficult to acquire. Most alternative assets (with the exception of commodities) are privately traded. This includes private equity and hedge funds. The difference between top-quartile and bottom-quartile performance in private equity can be as much as 25%.

Consider venture capital, one subset of the private equity market. Investments in start-up companies require intense research into the product niche the company intends to fulfill, the background of the management of the company, projections about future cash flows, exit strategies, potential competition, beta testing schedules, and so forth. This information is not readily available to the investing public. It is time consuming and expensive to accumulate. Furthermore, most investors do not have the time or the talent to acquire and filter through the rough data regarding a private company. One reason why alternative asset managers charge large management and incentive fees is to recoup the cost of information collection.

This leads to another distinguishing factor between alternative asset classes and traditional asset classes: the investment intermediary. Continuing with our venture capital example, most investments in venture capital are made through limited partnerships, limited liability companies, or special-purpose vehicles. It is estimated that 80% of all private equity investments in the United States are funneled through a financial intermediary.

Investments in alternative assets are less liquid than their public market counterparts. Investments are closely held and liquidity is minimal.

---

[7]We explain what is meant by a quartile in Appendix B.

Furthermore, without a publicly traded security, the value of private securities cannot be determined by market trading. The value of the private securities must be estimated by book value or appraisal, or determined by a cash flow model.

BETA AND ALPHA DRIVERS

Two terms bandied about in asset management are "beta drivers" and "alpha drivers." To understand these terms, we must understand what is meant by a *market risk premium*. A market (or systematic) risk premium for an asset class is the difference in the return on an asset class and the return offered on a risk-free asset such as a U.S. Treasury security. Investors seek to capture that risk. An *excess return* is the return earned on an asset class that exceeds the return on a risk-free asset.

In constructing a portfolio, an investor seeks the most efficient trade-off between risk and return given a mix of asset classes. In the context of Markowitz diversification discussed earlier in this chapter, an efficient portfolio is sought—the portfolio that maximizes the expected portfolio return for a given level of risk. In this sense, the basic asset allocation is all about capturing the market risk premiums that exist for investing in different asset classes. However, if additional asset classes can be added to the mix of potential investment opportunities in which an investor may invest, the efficient frontier can be improved so as to provide a greater range of risk and return opportunities for an investor. Recall that in our earlier description of an asset class, we explained that it had a low correlation of returns with other asset classes.

Beta drivers capture market risk premiums in an efficient manner. We have already discussed the notion or beta or systematic risk. In contrast, *alpha drivers* seek pockets of excess return often without regard to benchmarks.

It is useful to think of traditional and alternative assets within the context of beta and alpha drivers. Alternative assets represent an alternative source of beta that is different from the mixture of traditional assets— stocks and bonds. Access to alternative assets can provide new systematic risk premiums that are distinctly different than that obtained from stocks and bonds. Commodities are a good example—they provide a different risk exposure than stocks or bonds. Consequently, the risk premium associated with commodities is less than perfectly correlated with the markets for traditional asset classes.[8]

Alternative assets fall squarely into the category of alpha drivers. Alpha drivers seek excess return or added value. They tend to seek sources of

---

[8]This is a form of what is popularly referred to as "alternative beta."

return less correlated with traditional asset classes, which reduces risk in the entire portfolio via the process as we explained earlier in this chapter when we discussed diversification.

Financial Instruments and Concepts Introduced in this Chapter (in Order of Presentation)

Debt instrument
Equity instrument
Fixed income instruments
Total risk
Skewness
Tails
Mass
Efficient portfolios
Systematic risk
Market risk
Undiversifiable risk
Unsystematic risk
Diversifiable risk
Unique risk
Residual risk
Idiosyncratic risk
Company-specific risk
Inflation risk
Purchasing power risk
Credit risk
Liquidity risk
Exchange rate risk

Currency risk
Liquidity risk
Asset class
Market capitalization
Mega-cap
Large cap
Mid-cap
Small cap
Micro-cap
Nano-cap
Traditional asset classes
Nontraditional asset classes
Alternative asset classes
Capital assets
Strategic asset allocation
Tactical asset allocation
Active management strategies
Market risk premium
Excess return
Beta drivers
Alpha drivers

Investing in Common Stock

Common stocks are also called *equity securities*. Equity securities represent an ownership interest in a corporation. Holders of equity securities are entitled to the earnings of the corporation when those earnings are distributed in the form of dividends; they are also entitled to a pro rata share of the remaining equity in case of liquidation.

Common stock is only one type of equity security. Another type is preferred stock. The key distinction between the two forms of equity securities is the degree to which their holders may participate in any distribution of earnings and capital and the priority given to each class in the distribution of earnings. Typically, preferred stockholders are entitled to a fixed dividend, which they receive before common stockholders may receive any dividends. Therefore, we refer to preferred stock as a senior corporate security, in the sense that preferred stock interests are senior to the interests of common stockholders.

What determines the market price of a share of common stock? Like anything else, price depends on what people are willing to pay. The price of a share of stock today depends on what investors believe is today's value of all the cash flows that will accrue in the future from that share of stock. In other words, investors are not going to pay more today for a share of stock than they think it is worth—based on what they get out of it in terms of future cash flows. What people are willing to pay for a share of stock today determines its market value. This theory of stock prices makes sense. If we could accurately forecast a company's cash flows in the future, we could determine the value of the company's stock today and determine whether the stock is over- or under-valued by the market. But forecasting future cash flows is difficult. As an alternative, what is typically done is to examine the historical and current relation between stock prices and some fundamental value, such as earnings or dividends, using this relation to estimate the value of a share of stock.

In this chapter and the next, we look at common stock as an investment. We explain the fundamental factors of earnings and dividends and their relations with share price as expressed in such commonly-used ratios as the price-earnings ratio and the dividend yield, where stocks are traded, the mechanics of stock trading, and trading costs. In the next chapter we focus on common stock portfolio strategies.

EARNINGS

A commonly used measure of a company's performance over a period of time is its *earnings*, which is often stated in terms of a return—that is, earnings scaled by the amount of the investment. But earnings can really mean many different things depending on the context. If a common stock analyst is evaluating the performance of a company's operations, the focus is on the operating earnings of the company—its *earnings before interest and taxes*, EBIT. If the analyst is evaluating the performance of a company overall, the focus is upon net income, which is essentially EBIT less interest and taxes. If the analyst is evaluating the performance of the company from a common shareholder's perspective, the earnings are the earnings available to common shareholders—EBIT less interest, taxes, and preferred stock dividends. Finally, if the analyst is forecasting future earnings and cash flows, the focus is on earnings from continuing operations. Therefore, it is useful to be very specific in the meaning of "earnings."

There is a possibility that reported financial information may be managed by the judicious choice of accounting methods and timing employed by management. In particular, earnings can be managed using a number of accounting devices. There are many pressures that a company may face that affect the likelihood of earnings management. These pressures include executive compensation based on earnings targets, reporting ever-increasing earnings (especially when the business is subject to variations in the business cycle), and meeting or beating analyst forecasts.

Earnings targets comes in various forms, but typically schemes on earnings targets provide for a bonus if earnings meet or exceed a specified target such as a return on equity. One-sided incentives such as this—rewards for beating the target return, but no penalty for not making the target—create problematic situations. Combine this with the tendency of stock prices to be affected by whether or not analysts' forecasts are met or beat, and there is significant potential for problems. If, for example, management knows that the earnings target cannot be met in a period, there may be an incentive to either (1) manage earnings, through such mechanics as accruals, changes in estimates, or changes in accounting method, or (2) take large write-offs in that period, increasing chances of making earnings targets in future periods—referred to as taking a "big bath."

Meeting analysts' forecasts presents still another pressure for the management of earnings. We know from the wealth of empirical evidence that stock prices react to earnings surprises, where surprises are defined as the difference between expected and actual earnings. Because there is a market reaction to surprises—negative for earnings less than expected and positive for earnings better than expected—companies have an incentive to manage earnings to meet or exceed forecasted earnings. The pressure to report constant or constantly increasing earnings may also result in earnings management, manipulation, or, in extreme cases, even fraud.

Evidence suggests that there is a strong incentive to meet analysts' forecasts. More companies meet or beat earnings forecasts than miss these forecasts.[1] Stock prices are sensitive to whether earnings meet analysts' forecasts.[2] Finally, management is more likely to sell their shares of the company's stock after meeting or beating forecasts, than if the company fails to meet forecasts.[3] As a result of these incentives, investors should not only look for unusual patterns in earnings, but also earnings that are perhaps *too* predictable.

Is there a relation between earnings and stock value? The research into the relation between earnings and value concludes the following. First, stock prices change in response to an announcement of unexpected earnings. Second, accounting earnings are correlated with stock returns, especially returns measured over a long horizon following the release of earnings.[4] The strong relation between earnings and stock prices may be due to reported earnings being strongly correlated with true earnings (that is, earnings in the absence of earnings management). Or the earnings–stock price relation may be due to the valuation of stocks being dependent on reported earnings.

Earnings Per Share

Earnings per share (EPS) is earnings available for common shareholders, divided by the number of common shares outstanding:

---

[1]See Carla Hayn, "The Information Content of Losses," *Journal of Accounting and Economics,* 20, no. 2 (1995): 125–153; and Sarah McVay, Venky Nagar, and Vivki Tang, "Trading Incentives to Meet Earnings Thresholds," Working Paper, University of Michigan, January 2005.

[2]See E. D. Bartov, D. Givoly, and Carla Hayn, "The Rewards to Meeting or Beating Earnings Expectations," *Journal of Accounting and Economics* 33, no. 2 (2002): 173–204.

[3]McVay, Nagar, and Tang, "Trading Incentives to Meet Earnings Thresholds."

[4]See, for example, Peter D. Easton, Trevor S. Harris, and James A. Ohlson, "Aggregate Accounting Earnings Can Explain Most of Security Returns," *Journal of Accounting and Economics* 15 (1992): 119–142.

Earnings per share

$$= \frac{\text{Earnings available to common stockholders}}{\text{Weighted average number of common shares outstanding}}$$

This ratio indicates each share's portion of how much is earned by the company in a given accounting period.

The EPS doesn't tell us anything about the preferred shareholders. And that's acceptable because preferred shareholders, in most cases, receive a fixed dividend amount. Because the common shareholders are the residual owners of the firm—they are the last ones in line after creditors and preferred shareholders—we are interested in seeing just what is left over for them.

When we see an amount given for EPS, we have to be sure we know what it really means. But what is there to interpret? Net income available to common shares is pretty clear-cut (with some exceptions). What about the number of common shares outstanding? Can that change during the period of time under consideration? It can, affecting the calculated value of earnings per share. The number of common shares outstanding can change for two reasons. First, net income is earned over a specific period of time, yet the number of shares outstanding may change over this period. This is the reason why the weighted average number of shares over the time period is used in the denominator of the EPS calculation. Second, the company may have securities outstanding that can be converted into common stock or employee stock options and warrants that may be exercisable, so the number of shares of common that potentially may share in this net income is greater than the number reported as outstanding. These securities are referred to as *dilutive securities*.

For a company with securities that are dilutive—meaning they could share in net income—there are two earnings per share amounts that are reported in financial statements. *Basic earnings per share* are earnings (minus preferred dividends), divided by the average number of shares outstanding. *Diluted earnings per share* is earnings (minus preferred dividends), divided by the number of shares outstanding considering all dilutive securities. Companies that report earnings per share for any prior period must restate these amounts in terms of the new basic and diluted calculations. Accounting principles require that the diluted earnings per share may never be reported as greater than basic earnings per share.

Price-Earnings Ratio

Many investors are interested in how the earnings are valued by the market. A measure of how these earnings are valued is the *price-earnings ratio*

(P/E). This ratio compares the price per common share with earnings per common share:

$$\text{Price-earnings ratio} = \frac{\text{Market price per share}}{\text{Earnings per share}}$$

The result is a multiple—the value of a share of stock expressed as a multiple of earnings per share.

The inverse of this measure is referred to as the *earnings yield*, or E/P. Studies have found that E/P is one of the factors that explains stock returns.[5]

Because investors are forward-looking in their valuation, earnings in this ratio represent the expected normal earnings per share for the stock. If the market value of the stock represents today's forecast of future earnings to common shareholders and if current earnings are an indication of future earnings, this ratio tells us that each dollar of earnings has a value equal to some multiple today. For this reason, the P/E ratio is also referred to as the *multiple*. P/E ratios vary over time for the S&P 500, typically ranging from 8 to 20 times, averaging around 14.2 times, though there have been recent years where the P/E has gone out of these bounds, reaching up towards record-breaking highs toward 45 times.

An interesting issue arises in deciding the appropriate inputs to this ratio. The numerator is rather straightforward: use a recent market price per share. The denominator presents a number of issues. Aside from the issue of whether the denominator is the basic or diluted earnings per share, an important issue is over what period to measure earnings per share. At any point in time, the most recently ending annual period or quarter's earnings may not usually be available. Further muddying the waters is whether the P/E ratio should be measured over an historical period (backward-looking) or measured using forecasted earnings (forward-looking). There are several approaches that are used: (1) the sum of the latest available four reported quarters, (2) estimated earnings for the next fiscal year, and (3) earning per share averaged over several historical, annual periods. The first approach results in what is referred to as the *trailing P/E ratio*. The second approach is referred to as the *forward P/E ratio*. The last approach, suggested by Graham and Dodd whose investment philosophy we discuss in the next chapter, uses an EPS that is the average of EPS for "not less than five years, preferably seven or ten years."[6] Yahoo! Finance, for example, reports the

---

[5]See as an example, Sanjoy Basu, "The Relationship Between Earnings Yield, Market Value, and Return for NYSE Common Stocks: Further Evidence," *Journal of Financial Economics* 12, no. 1 (1983): 129–156.

[6]Benjamin Graham and David L. Dodd, *Security Analysis*, 1st ed. (New York: McGraw-Hill, 1934): 452.

forward P/E it obtains from Capital IQ which, in turn, is based on the projected 12-month EPS.

DIVIDENDS

A *dividend* is the cash, stock, or any type of property a corporation distributes to its shareholders. The board of directors may declare a dividend at any time, but dividends are not a legal obligation of the corporation—it is the choice of the board of directors. Unlike interest on debt securities, if a corporation does not pay a dividend, there is no violation of a contract, nor any legal recourse for shareholders.

When the board of directors declares a distribution, it specifies the amount of the distribution, the date on which the distribution is paid, and the *date of record*, which determines who has the right to the distributions. Because shares are traded frequently and it takes time to process transactions, the exchanges have devised a way of determining which investors receive the dividend: the exchanges take the record date, as specified by the board of directors, and identify the *ex-dividend date*, which is two business days prior to the record date. The ex-dividend date is often referred to simply as the *ex-date*.

Therefore, there are four key dates in a distribution:

1. The *declaration date*, which is the date the board declares the distribution.
2. The *ex-dividend date*, which is the date that determines which investors receive the dividend. Any investor who owns the stock the day before the ex-date receives the forthcoming dividend. Any investor who buys the stock on the ex-date does not receive the dividend.
3. The *date of record*, which is specified by the board of directors as the date that determines who receives the dividend.
4. The *payment date*, which is the day the distribution is made.

Most dividends are in the form of cash. Cash dividends are payments made directly to shareholders in proportion to the shares they own. When cash dividends are paid, they are paid on all outstanding shares of a class of stock.[7] A few companies pay *special dividends* or *extra dividends* occasionally—identifying these dividends apart from their regular dividends.

The cash dividends that a corporation pays is described in terms of *dividend per share*, calculated as follows:

---

[7]Therefore, a corporation may pay dividends on its preferred stock, but not on its common stock.

$$\text{Dividend per share} = \frac{\text{Cash dividends paid to common stockholders}}{\text{Number of common shares outstanding}}$$

Another way of describing cash dividends is in terms of the percentage of earnings paid out in dividends, which we refer to as the *dividend payout ratio*. We can express the dividend in terms of the proportion of earnings over a fiscal period:

$$\text{Dividend payout ratio} = \frac{\text{Cash dividends paid to common stockholders}}{\text{Earnings available to common shareholders}}$$

Alternatively, the dividend payout ratio can be calculated as follows:

$$\text{Dividend payout ratio} = \frac{\text{Dividend per share}}{\text{Earnings per share}}$$

The dividend payout ratio is the complement of the *retention ratio*, also referred to as the *plowback ratio*:

$$\text{Retention ratio}$$
$$= \frac{\text{Earnings available to common shareholders} - \text{Cash dividends}}{\text{Earnings available to common shareholders}}$$
$$= 1 - \text{Dividend payout ratio}$$

The retention ratio is the proportion of earnings that the company retains, that is, the proportion of earnings reinvested back into the company.

Corporations have different dividend policies. A dividend policy is a corporation's decision about the payment of cash dividends to shareholders. There are several basic ways of describing a corporation's *dividend policy*: (1) no dividends, (2) constant growth in dividends per share, (3) constant payout ratio, and (4) low regular dividends with periodic extra dividends.

The corporations that typically do not pay dividends are those that are generally viewed as younger, faster growing companies. For example, Microsoft Corporation was founded in 1975 and went public in 1986, but it did not pay a cash dividend until January 2003.

A common pattern of cash dividends tends to be the constant growth of dividends per share. Another pattern is the constant payout ratio. Many companies in the food processing industry, such as Kellogg and Tootsie Roll Industries, pay dividends that are a relatively constant percentage of earnings. Some companies display both a constant dividend payout and a constant growth in dividends. This type of dividend pattern is characteristic of large, mature companies that have predictable earnings growth—the dividends growth tends to mimic the earnings growth, resulting in a constant payout.

U.S. corporations that pay dividends tend to pay either constant or increasing dividends per share. Dividends tend to be lower in industries that have many profitable opportunities in which to invest their earnings. But as a company matures and finds fewer and fewer profitable investment opportunities, it generally pays out a greater portion of its earnings in dividends.

Many corporations are reluctant to cut dividends because the corporation's share price usually falls when a dividend reduction is announced. For example, the U.S. auto manufacturers cut dividends during the recession in the early 1990s. As earnings per share declined the automakers did not cut dividends until earnings per share were negative—and in the case of General Motors, not until it had experienced two consecutive loss years. But as earnings recovered in the mid-1990s, dividends were increased. (General Motors increased dividends until cutting them once again in 2006 as it incurred substantial losses.)

Because investors tend to penalize companies that cut dividends, corporations tend to only raise their regular quarterly dividend when they are sure they can keep it up in the future. By giving a special or extra dividend, the corporation is able to provide more cash to the shareholders without committing itself to paying an increased dividend each period into the future.

Dividends and Stock Prices

By buying common stock, an investor obtains a financial position that represents an ownership interest in the corporation. Shares of common stock are a perpetual security—there is no maturity. The investor who owns shares of common stock has the right to receive a certain portion of any dividends—but dividends are *not* a sure thing. Whether a firm will pay dividends is up to its board of directors—the representatives of the common shareholders. Typically we see some pattern in the dividends companies pay: Dividends per share are either constant or grow at a constant rate. But there is no guarantee that dividends will be paid in the future.

It is reasonable to assume that what an investor pays for a share of stock should reflect what in the aggregate investors expect to receive from it—return on investment. What an investor receives are cash dividends in the future. How can we relate that return to what a share of common stock is worth? Well, the value of a share of stock should be equal to the present value of all the future cash flows investors expect to receive from that share. Because common stock never matures, today's value is the present value of an infinite stream of cash flows. And also, common stock dividends are not fixed. Not knowing the amount of the dividends—or even if there will be future dividends—makes it difficult to determine the value of common stock.

So what are investors to do? They can grapple with the valuation of common stock by looking at its current dividend and making assumptions about any future dividends the company may pay. This is the basic idea behind the financial models used to value common stock. Because these models involve the discounting of future earnings, they are called *dividend discount models.* A discussion of these models is beyond the scope of this chapter.

Dividend Reinvestment Plans

Many U.S. corporations allow shareholders to reinvest automatically their dividends in the shares of the corporation paying them. A *dividend reinvestment plan* (DRP or DRIP) is a program that allows shareholders to reinvest their dividends, buying additional shares of stock of the company instead of receiving the cash dividend. A DRP offers benefits to both shareholders and the corporation. First, shareholders can buy shares without transactions costs—brokers' commissions—and at a discount from the current market price. Second, the corporation retains cash without the cost of a new stock issue.

There is one drawback, however. Dividends are taxed as income before they are reinvested, even though shareholders never receive the dividend. The result is similar to a dividend cut, but with a tax consequence for the shareholders: The cash flow that would have been paid to shareholders is plowed back into the corporation.

Stock Distributions

In addition to cash dividends, a corporation may provide shareholders with dividends in the form of additional shares of stock or, rarely, some types of property owned by the corporation. When dividends are not in cash, they are usually additional shares of stock. Additional shares of stock can be distributed to shareholders in two ways: paying a stock dividend and splitting the stock.

A *stock dividend* is the distribution of additional shares of stock to shareholders. Stock dividends are generally stated as a percentage of existing share holdings. If a corporation pays a stock dividend, it is not transferring anything of value to the shareholders. The assets of the corporation remain the same and each shareholder's proportionate share of ownership remains the same. All the corporation is doing is cutting its equity "pie" into more slices and at the same time cutting each shareholder's portion of that equity into more slices.

A stock split is something like a stock dividend. A *stock split* splits the number of existing shares into more shares. For example, in a 2:1 split—

referred to as "two for one"—each shareholder gets two shares for every one owned. If an investor owns 1,000 shares and the stock is split 2:1, the investor then owns 2,000 shares after the split. Has the portion of the investor's ownership in the company changed? No, the investor now simply owns twice as many shares—and so does every other shareholder. If the investor owned 1% of the corporation's stock before the split, the investor still owns 1% after the split.

A *reverse stock split* is similar to a stock split, but backwards: a 1:2 reverse stock split reduces the number of shares of stock such that a shareholder receives half the number of shares held before the reverse stock split. A stock split in which more shares are distributed to shareholders is sometimes referred to as a *forward stock split* to distinguish it from a reverse stock split. Similar to both the stock dividend and the stock split, there is no actual distribution or contribution made, but simply a division of the equity pie—in this case, into fewer pieces.

Stock distributions, similar to cash dividends, are a decision of the board of directors, but in this case the "payment" date is similar when the additional shares are provided to shareholders, or shares exchanged, in the case of a forward or a reverse stock split.

There are a couple of reasons for paying dividends in the form of stock dividends. One is to provide information to the market. A company's management may want to communicate good news to shareholders without paying cash. For example, if the corporation has an attractive investment opportunity and needs funds for it, paying a cash dividend doesn't make any sense—so the corporation pays a stock dividend instead. But is this an effective way of communicating good news to shareholders? It costs very little to pay a stock dividend—just minor expenses for record keeping, printing, and distribution. But if it costs very little, do investors really trust it as a signal?

Another reason given for paying a stock dividend is to reduce the price of the stock. If the price of a stock is high relative to most other stocks, there may be higher costs related to investors' transactions of the stock, as in a higher broker's commission. By paying a stock dividend—which slices the equity pie into more pieces—the price of the stock should decline. Let's see how this works. Suppose an investor owns 1,000 shares, each worth $50 per share, for a total investment of $50,000. If the corporation pays the investor a 5% stock dividend, the investor then owns 1,050 shares after the dividend. Is there is any reason for the investor's holdings to change in value? Nothing economic has gone on here—the company has the same assets, the same liabilities, and the same equity—total equity is just cut up into smaller pieces. There is no reason for the value of the portion of the equity this investor owns to change. But the price per share should decline: from $50 per share to $47.62 per share. The argument for reducing the share price only works if the market brings down the price substantially, from an unattractive trading range to a more attractive trading range in terms of reducing brokerage commissions and enabling small investors to purchase even lots of 100 shares.

So why split? Like a stock dividend, the split reduces the trading price of shares. If an investor owns 1,000 shares of the stock trading for $50 per share prior to a 2:1 split, the shares should trade for $25 per share after the split.

Aside from a minor difference in accounting, stock splits and stock dividends are essentially the same. The stock dividend requires a shift within the stockholders' equity accounts, from retained earnings to paid-in capital, for the amount of the distribution; the stock split requires only a memorandum entry. A 2:1 split has the same effect on a stock's price as a 100% stock dividend, a 1.5 to 1 split has the same effect on a stock's price as a 50% stock dividend, and so on. The basis of the accounting rules is related to the reasons behind the distribution of additional shares. If companies want to bring down their share price, they tend to declare a stock split; if companies want to communicate news, they often declare a stock dividend.

Companies tend to reverse stock split when the stock's price is extremely low, so low that they are at risk of being delisted from an exchange. A low stock price is a function of how many shares are outstanding, but mostly a function of poor performance, which has led to a low share price.

How can investors tell what the motivation is behind stock dividends and splits? They cannot, but they can get a general idea of how investors interpret these actions by looking at what happens to the corporation's share price when a corporation announces its decision to pay a stock dividend or split its stock, or reverse split. If the share price tends to go up when the announcement is made, the decision is probably good news; if the price tends to go down, the stock dividend is probably bad news. This is supported by evidence that indicates corporation's earnings tend to increase following stock splits and dividends.[8]

The share price of companies announcing stock distributions and forward stock splits generally increase at the time of the announcement. The stock price typically increases by 1% to 2% when the split or stock dividend is announced. When the stock dividend is distributed or the split is effected (on the "ex" date), the share's price typically declines according to the amount of the distribution. Suppose a company announces a 2:1 split. Its share price may increase by 1% to 2% when this is announced, but when the shares are split, the share price will go down to approximately half of its pre-split value. The most likely explanation is that this distribution is interpreted as good news—that management believes that the future prospects

[8]See, for example, Maureen McNichols and Ajay Dravid, "Stock Dividends, Stock Splits, and Signaling," *Journal of Finance* 45, no. 3 (1990): 857–879.

of the company are favorable or that the share price is more attractive to investors.

STOCK REPURCHASES

Corporations have repurchased their common stock from their shareholders. A corporation repurchasing its own shares is effectively paying a cash dividend, with one important difference: taxes. Cash dividends are ordinary taxable income to the shareholder. A company's repurchase of shares, on the other hand, results in a capital gain or loss for the shareholder, depending on the price paid when they were originally purchased. If the shares are repurchased at a higher price, the difference may be taxed as capital gains, which may be taxed at rates lower than ordinary income.

A number of studies have looked at how the market reacts to such repurchase announcements. In general, the share price goes up when a company announces it is going to repurchase its own shares. It is difficult to identify the reason the market reacts favorably to such announcements since so many other things are happening at the same time. By piecing bits of evidence together, however, we see that it is likely that investors view the announcement of a repurchase as good news—a signal of good things to come.

Methods of Repurchasing Stock

The company may repurchase its own stock by any of three methods: (1) a tender offer, (2) open market purchases, and (3) a targeted block repurchase. A *tender offer* is an offer made to all shareholders, with a specified deadline and a specified number of shares the corporation is willing to buy back. The tender offer may be a fixed price offer, where the corporation specifies the price it is willing to pay and solicits purchases of shares of stock at that price.

A tender offer may also be conducted as a *Dutch auction* in which the corporation specifies a minimum and a maximum price, soliciting bids from shareholders for any price within this range at which they are willing to sell their shares. After the corporation receives these bids, they pay all tendering shareholders the maximum price sufficient to buy back the number of shares they want. A Dutch auction reduces the chance that the company pays a price higher than needed to acquire the shares.

Biogen, a biotechnology company, announced a Dutch auction tender offer in May 2007 for shares of its common stock. The offer was for up to 57 million shares of stock, at a price not less than $47 per share and not more than $53 per share. Biogen accepted 56,424,155 shares at $53.00 per share, or 16.4% of its shares outstanding at the time of the offer.

A corporation may also buy back shares directly in the open market. This involves buying the shares through a broker. A corporation that wants to buy shares may have to spread its purchases over time so as not to drive the share's price up temporarily by buying large numbers of shares.

The third method of repurchasing stock is to buy it from a specific shareholder. This involves direct negotiation between the corporation and the shareholder. This method is referred to as *targeted block repurchase* because there is a specific shareholder (the "target") and a large number of shares (a "block") to be purchased at one time. Targeted block repurchases, also referred to as "greenmail," were used in the 1980s to fight corporate takeovers.

THE U.S. EQUITY MARKETS

The U.S. equity markets have undergone considerable change in recent years. Traditionally, the U.S. markets have been driven by two exchanges, the New York Stock Exchange (also called "the Big Board") and Nasdaq (originally the National Association of Securities Dealers Automated Quotation System).

An *exchange* is typically defined as a market where intermediaries meet to deliver and execute customer orders. There are, however, some off-exchange markets that perform this function. In the U.S., exchanges must be registered by the Securities and Exchange Commission (SEC). The U.S. markets have been based on two different market models. The first model is "order-driven," in which public participants who are owners of securities meet and provide buy and sell orders ("orders") and via an auction system establish market prices at which other public participants can trade. This mechanism is an *auction-based, order-driven market*. The second model involves intermediaries, referred to as market makers or dealers, who provide quotes (bid quotes to buy and offer quotes to sell) at which market participants can trade. This mechanism is a *dealer-based, quote-driven market*.

The NYSE has been mainly an order-driven, auction market. The NYSE has not, however, been purely an order-driven market because it provides "specialists" for each stock who function as dealers for their allocated stocks and buy or sell these stocks for their own account to maintain "orderly markets." The NYSE is often called a *specialist system*. Nasdaq has always (since it was founded in 1971) been a pure quote-driven, dealer market. The American Stock Exchange (Amex) has been a third, much smaller, national exchange that functions like the NYSE. There have also been regional stock exchanges in Chicago, Philadelphia, Boston, San Francisco, and other cities that have functioned similarly to the NYSE.

Off-exchange markets (also called *alternative electronic markets*) have also evolved. There are two major types. The first and most important is *electronic communication networks* (ECNs) that are direct descendents of Nasdaq. Archipelago ("Arca") and Instinet are early and important examples of ECNs. The second type is, in general, *alternative trading systems* (ATS) that involve the direct trading of stock between two customers without an intermediary, either a broker or an exchange. An ATS is essentially for-profit broker's brokers that match investor orders. There are two types of ATS. The first type is a *crossing network* that is an electronic venue that do not display quotes but simply anonymously match (or cross) large institutional customer orders. The second type is a *dark pool*. A dark pool is a neutral gathering place that provides private crossing networks where participants submit orders to cross trades at externally specified prices. No quotes are involved, only orders at externally determined prices. Dark pools, thus, provide anonymous sources of liquidity (hence the name "dark").

In addition to the development of off-exchange markets, the two major exchanges, particularly the NYSE, have transformed themselves since 2000. During December 2005, the NYSE acquired Archipelago, a leading ECN and a public company. This permitted the NYSE to both become a public company and also become a hybrid of an order-driven auction (specialist) market and a quote-driven (dealer) market (called electronic trading) (initially named the NYSE Hybrid Market). Since then, however, the new electronic trading component of NYSE has dominated the traditional specialist trading component. In fact, during early 2006, the NYSE closed one of its traditional trading rooms. During April 2007, the NYSE acquired Euronext, the trans-European fully electronic stock exchange, making NYSE the first transatlantic stock exchange. The current name of the exchange is NYSE Euronext, Inc. During October 2008, the NYSE acquired the Amex.

Nasdaq was also very acquisitive and transformative. During July 2002, Nasdaq bought a controlling interest in OMX, a Nordic-based exchange that operated eight stock exchanges in Europe. At the same time, on July 2, 2002, Nasdaq publicly listed its own stock. Its name is the Nasdaq OMX Group, Inc. In April 2005 (two days after NYSE acquired Archipelago), Nasdaq acquired Instinet, the largest and oldest ECN. During 2007, Nasdaq also acquired the Philadelphia Stock Exchange and the Boston Stock Exchange.

As of mid-2010, there had been two recent changes in the composition of stock exchanges. The first was the disappearance of regional stock exchanges due to their acquisitions by the NYSE and Nasdaq. The second trend was the formation of new independent exchanges from previous ECNs. The major new exchanges formed in this way were BATS (an acronym for Better Alternative Trading System) and Direct Edge. BATS was founded in June 2005 as an ECN and by early 2009 was the third largest stock exchange in the world, after the NYSE and Nasdaq. Direct Edge, an ECN that had previously operated as a stock exchange using the International Securities Exchange (ISE) stock platform, was approved by the SEC as a stock exchange in March 2010. Direct Edge is the fourth largest U.S. stock exchange.

TRADING MECHANICS

Now let's look at the key features involved in trading stocks by individuals. There are special trading arrangements (block trades and program trades) that developed specifically for coping with the trading needs of institutional investors but they will not be discussed here.

Types of Orders

When an investor wants to buy or sell a share of common stock, the price and conditions under which the order is to be executed must be communicated to a broker. The simplest type of order is the *market order*, an order to be executed at the best price available in the market. If the stock is listed and traded on an organized exchange, the best price is assured by the exchange rule that when more than one order on the same side of the buy/sell transaction reaches the market at the same time, the order with the best price is given priority. Thus, buyers offering a higher price are given priority over those offering a lower price; sellers asking a lower price are given priority over those asking a higher price.

The danger of a market order is that an adverse move may take place between the time the investor places the order and the time the order is executed. To avoid this danger, the investor can place a *limit order* that designates a price threshold for the execution of the trade. A *buy limit order* indicates that the stock may be purchased only at the designated price or lower. A *sell limit order* indicates that the stock may be sold at the designated price or higher. The key disadvantage of a limit order is that there is no guarantee that it will be executed at all; the designated price may simply not be reached.

The limit order is a *conditional order*: It is executed only if the limit price or a better price can be obtained. Another type of conditional order is the *stop order*, which specifies that the order is not to be executed until the market moves to a designated price, at which time it becomes a market order. A *buy stop order* specifies that the order is not to be executed until the market rises to a designated price, that is, until it trades at or above, or is bid at or above, the designated price. A *sell stop order* specifies that the order is not to be executed until the market price falls below a designated price—that is, until it trades at or below, or is offered at or below, the designated price. A stop order is useful when an investor cannot watch the market constantly. Profits can be preserved or losses minimized on a stock position by allowing market movements to trigger a trade. In a sell (buy) stop order, the designated price is lower (higher) than the current market price of the stock. In a sell (buy) limit order, the designated price is higher (lower) than the current market price of the stock.

There are two dangers associated with stop orders. Stock prices sometimes exhibit abrupt price changes, so the direction of a change in a stock price may be quite temporary, resulting in the premature trading of a stock. Also, once the designated price is reached, the stop order becomes a market order and is subject to the uncertainty of the execution price noted earlier for market orders.

A *stop-limit order*, a hybrid of a stop order and a limit order, is a stop order that designates a price limit. In contrast to the stop order, which becomes a market order if the stop is reached, the stop-limit order becomes a limit order if the stop is reached. The stop-limit order can be used to cushion the market impact of a stop order. The investor may limit the possible execution price after the activation of the stop. As with a limit order, the limit price may never be reached after the order is activated, which therefore defeats one purpose of the stop order—to protect a profit or limit a loss.

An investor may also enter a *market if touched order*. This order becomes a market order if a designated price is reached. A market if touched order to buy becomes a market order if the market falls to a given price, while a stop order to buy becomes a market order if the market rises to a given price. Similarly, a market if touched order to sell becomes a market order if the market rises to a specified price, while the stop order to sell becomes a market order if the market falls to a given price. We can think of the stop order as an order designed to get out of an existing position at an acceptable price (without specifying the exact price), and the market if touched order as an order designed to get into a position at an acceptable price (also without specifying the exact price).

Orders may be placed to buy or sell at the open or the close of trading for the day. An *opening order* indicates a trade to be executed only in the opening range for the day, and a *closing order* indicates a trade is to be executed only within the closing range for the day.

An investor may enter orders that contain order cancellation provisions. A *fill or kill order* must be executed as soon as it reaches the trading floor or it is immediately canceled. Orders may designate the time period for which the order is effective—a day, week, or month, or perhaps by a given time within the day. An *open order* or *good till canceled order* is good until the investor specifically terminates the order.

Orders are also classified by their size. One *round lot* is typically 100 shares of a stock. An *odd lot* is defined as less than a round lot. A *block trade* is defined on the NYSE as an order of 10,000 shares of a given stock or a total market value of $200,000 or more. Both the major national stock exchanges and the regional stock exchanges have systems for routing orders of a specified size (that are submitted by brokers) through a computer directly to the specialists' posts where the orders can be executed.

Short Selling

Short selling involves the sale of a security not owned by the investor at the time of sale. The investor can arrange to have a broker borrow the stock from someone else, and the borrowed stock is delivered to implement the sale. To cover the short position, the investor must subsequently purchase the stock and return it to the party that lent the stock.

Let us look at an example of how this is done in the stock market. Suppose Ms. Stokes believes that Wilson Steel common stock is overpriced at $20 per share and wants to be in a position to benefit if her assessment is correct. Ms. Stokes calls her broker, Mr. Yats, indicating that she wants to sell 100 shares of Wilson Steel. Mr. Yats will do two things: (1) sell 100 shares of Wilson Steel on behalf of Ms. Stokes, and (2) arrange to borrow 100 shares of that stock to deliver to the buyer. Suppose that Mr. Yats is able to sell the stock for $20 per share and borrows the stock from Mr. Jordan. The shares borrowed from Mr. Jordan will be delivered to the buyer of the 100 shares. The proceeds from the sale (ignoring commissions) will be $2,000. However, the proceeds do not go to Ms. Stokes because she has not given her broker the 100 shares. Thus, Ms. Stokes is said to be "short 100 shares."

Now, let's suppose one week later the price of Wilson Steel stock declines to $15 per share. Ms. Stokes may instruct her broker to buy 100 shares of Wilson Steel. The cost of buying the shares (once again ignoring commissions) is $1,500. The shares purchased are then delivered to Mr. Jordan, who lent 100 shares to Ms. Stokes. At this point, Ms. Stokes has sold 100 shares and bought 100 shares. So, she no longer has any obligation to her broker or to Mr. Jordan—she has covered her short position. She is entitled to the funds in her account that were generated by the selling and buying activity. She sold the stock for $2,000 and bought it for $1,500. Thus, she realizes a profit before commissions of $500. From this amount, commissions are subtracted.

Two more costs will reduce the profit further. First, a fee will be charged by the lender of the stock and we will discuss this shortly. Second, if there are any dividends paid by Wilson Steel while the stock is borrowed, Ms. Stokes must compensate Mr. Jordan for the dividends he would have been entitled to.

If, instead of falling, the price of Wilson Steel stock rises, Ms. Stokes will realize a loss if she is forced to cover her short position. For example, if the price rises to $27, Ms. Stokes will lose $700, to which must be added commissions and the cost of borrowing the stock (and possibly dividends).

Margin Transactions

Investors can borrow cash to buy securities and use the securities themselves as collateral. For example, suppose Mr. Boxer has $10,000 to invest and is considering buying Wilson Steel, which is currently selling for $20 per share. With his $10,000, Mr. Boxer can buy 500 shares. Suppose his broker can arrange for him to borrow an additional $10,000 so that Mr. Boxer can buy an additional 500 shares. Thus, with a $20,000 investment, he can purchase a total of 1,000 shares. The 1,000 shares will be used as collateral for the $10,000 borrowed, and Mr. Boxer will have to pay interest on the amount borrowed.

A transaction in which an investor borrows to buy shares using the shares themselves as collateral is called *buying on margin*. By borrowing funds, an investor creates financial leverage. Note that Mr. Boxer, for a $10,000 investment, realizes the consequences associated with a price change of 1,000 shares rather than 500 shares. He will benefit if the price rises but be worse off if the price falls (compared to borrowing no funds).

To illustrate, we now look at what happens if the price subsequently changes. If the price of Wilson Steel rises to $29 per share, ignoring commissions and the cost of borrowing, Mr. Boxer will realize a profit of $9 per share on 1,000 shares, or $9,000. Had Mr. Boxer not borrowed $10,000 to buy the additional 500 shares, his profit would be only $4,500. Suppose, instead, the price of Wilson Steel stock decreases to $13 per share. Then, by borrowing to buy 500 additional shares, he lost $7 per share on 1,000 shares instead of $7 per share on just 500 shares.

The funds borrowed to buy the additional stock will be provided by the broker, and the broker gets the money from a bank. The interest rate that banks charge brokers for these funds is the *call money rate* (also referred to as the *broker loan rate*). The broker charges the borrowing investor the call money rate plus a service charge.

Margin Requirements

The brokerage firm is not free to lend as much as it wishes to the investor to buy securities. The Securities Exchange Act of 1934 prohibits brokers from lending more than a specified percentage of the market value of the securities. The *initial margin requirement* is the proportion of the total market value of the securities that the investor must pay as an equity share, and the remainder is borrowed from the broker. The 1934 act gives the Board of Governors of the Federal Reserve (the Fed) the responsibility to set initial margin requirements. The initial margin requirement has been below 40%, and is 50% as of this writing.

The Fed also establishes a *maintenance margin requirement*. This is the minimum proportion of the equity in the investor's margin account to the total market value. If the investor's margin account falls below the minimum maintenance margin (which would happen if the share price fell), the investor is required to put up additional cash. The investor receives a margin call from the broker specifying the additional cash to be put into the investor's margin account. If the investor fails to put up the additional cash, the broker has the authority to sell the securities in the investor's account.

Let us illustrate a maintenance margin. Assume an investor buys 100 shares of stock at $60 per share for $6,000 on 50% margin and the maintenance margin is 25%. By purchasing $6,000 of stock on 50% margin, the investor must put up $3,000 of cash (or other equity) and therefore borrows $3,000 (referred to as the debit balance). The investor, however, must maintain 25% of margin. To what level must the stock price decline to hit the maintenance margin level? The price is $40. At this price, the stock position has a value of $4,000 ($40 × 100 shares). With a loan of $3,000, the equity in the account is $1,000 ($4,000 − $3,000), or 25% of the account value ($1,000/$4,000 = 25%). If the price of the stock decreases below $40, the investor must deposit more equity to bring the equity level up to 25%. In general, if the maintenance margin is 25%, the account level has to decrease to 4/3 times the amount borrowed (the debit balance) to reach the minimum maintenance margin level.

There are also margin requirements for short selling. Consider a similar margin example for a short position. An investor shorts (borrows and sells) 100 shares of stock at $60 for total stock value of $6,000. With an initial margin of 50%, the investor must deposit $3,000 (in addition to leaving the $6,000 from the sale in the account). This leaves the investor with a *credit balance* of $9,000 (which does not change with the stock price since it is in cash). However, the investor owes 100 shares of the stock at the current market price. To what level must the stock price increase to hit the maintenance margin level, assumed to be 30% (which is the equity in the account as a percentage of the market value of the stock)? The answer is $69.23, for a total stock value of $6,923. If the stock is worth $6,923, there is $2,077 of equity in the account ($9,000 – $6,923),which represents 30% of the market value of the stock ($2,077/$6,923 = 30%). If the maintenance margin is 30%, the value of the stock that triggers the maintenance level is calculated by multiplying the credit balance by 10/13 (10/13 × $9,000 = $6,923).

Stock Lending

An investor who shorts a stock must be able to borrow that stock in order to deliver it to the buyer of the stock. A short seller can use a mechanism called *stock lending* to borrow the stock. The two parties in a stock lending transaction are the owner of a stock who agrees to lend that stock to the party that sold the stock short. In a stock lending transaction, the former party is referred to as the *stock lender* or the *beneficial owner*. The second party is the entity that agrees to borrow the stock, called the *stock borrower*. Hence, a stock lending transaction is one in which the stock lender loans the requested stock to the stock borrower at the outset and the stock borrower agrees to return the same stock to the stock lender at some time in the future. The loan may be terminated by the stock lender upon notice to the stock borrower.

To protect against credit (counterparty) risk, the stock lender will require that the stock borrower provide collateral. Typically the collateral is cash that is equal to at least the value of the stock lent. The stock lender must pay the stock borrower a fee and this fee is called a *rebate*. Effectively, the stock borrower has provided a loan to the stock lender, charging the stock lender the rebate. The cash received by the stock lender is then invested. The stock lender faces all the risks associated with investing that cash received from the stock borrower. The stock lender only earns a profit if the amount earned on investing the cash collateral exceeds the rebate. In fact, if the amount earned is less than the rebate, the stock lender incurs this cost.

Institutional investors with a stock portfolio to lend can either (1) lend directly to counterparties that need stocks, (2) use the services of an intermediary, or (3) employ a combination of (1) and (2). If a party decides to lend directly, it must have the in-house capability of assessing counterparty risk. When an intermediary is engaged, the intermediary receives a fee for its services and can guarantee against counterparty risk. Moreover, when cash is reinvested, a stock lender must decide whether it will reinvest the cash or use the services of an external money manager to invest the funds. As noted earlier, stock lenders may realize a return on the cash collateral that is less than the rebate. Reinvesting cash collateral requires an understanding of the risks associated with investing.

TRADING COSTS

Trading is an integral component of the investment process. A poorly executed trade can eat directly into investment returns. This is because financial markets are not frictionless and transactions have a cost associated with them. Costs are incurred when buying or selling securities.

Probably the easiest way to describe transaction costs is to classify them in terms of fixed versus variable transaction costs, and explicit versus implicit transaction costs.

Fixed transaction costs are independent of factors such as trade size and market conditions. In contrast, variable transaction costs depend on some or all of these factors. In other words, although fixed transaction costs are "what they are," investors can seek to reduce, optimize, and efficiently manage variable transaction costs.

Explicit transaction costs are those costs that are observable and known upfront such as commissions, fees, and taxes. Implicit transaction costs, in contrast, are unobservable and not known in advance. Examples of transaction costs that fall into this category are market impact and opportunity cost. In general, the implicit costs make up the dominant part of the total transaction costs.

Trading commissions and fees, taxes, and bid-ask spreads are explicit transaction costs. Explicit transaction costs are also referred to as observable transaction costs. These costs include commissions, fees, taxes, and bid-ask spreads. Fees include custodial fees (fees charged by an entity that holds the securities in safekeeping for an investor) and transfer fees (fees charged when ownership of a stock is transferred). The most common taxes are *capital gains taxes*, if applicable. The *bid-ask spread* is the difference between the quoted sell and buy order and represents the immediate transaction cost that the market charges anyone for the privilege of trading. High immediate liquidity is synonymous with small spreads.

Investment delay, market impact cost, and market timing cost are implicit transaction costs. Implicit transaction costs are also referred to as unobservable transaction costs. Normally, there is a delay between the time when an investor makes a buy/sell decision of a stock and when the actual trade is brought to the market. If the price of the stock changes during this time, the price change (possibly adjusted for general market moves) represents the *investment delay cost*, or the cost of not being able to execute immediately. The *market impact cost* of a transaction, also referred to as *price impact cost*, is the deviation of the transaction price from the market (mid) price that would have prevailed had the trade not occurred.

The market timing costs are due to the movement in the price of a stock at the time of the transaction that can be attributed to other market participants or general market volatility.

Financial Instruments and Concepts Introduced in this Chapter (in Order of Presentation)

Equity securities	Exchange
Earnings	Auction-based, order-driven market
Earnings before interest and taxes	Dealer-based, quote-driven market
Earnings per share	Specialist system
Dilutive securities	Off-exchange markets
Basic earnings per share	Alternative electronic markets
Diluted earnings per share	Electronic communication networks
Price-earnings ratio	Alternative trading systems
Earnings yield	Crossing network
Multiple	Dark pool
Trailing P/E ratio	Market order
Forward P/E ratio	Limit order
Dividend	Buy limit order
Date of record	Sell limit order
Ex-dividend date	Conditional order
Ex-date	Stop order
Declaration date	Buy stop order
Date of record	Sell stop order
Payment date	Stop-limit order
Special dividends	Market if touched order
Extra dividends	Opening order
Dividend per share	Closing order
Dividend payout ratio	Fill or kill order
Plowback ratio	Open order
Dividend policy	Good till canceled order
Dividend discount models	Round lot
Dividend reinvestment plan	Block trade
Stock dividend	Short selling
Stock split	Buying on margin
Reverse stock split	Call money rate
Forward stock split	Broker loan rate
Tender offer	Initial margin requirement
Dutch auction	Maintenance margin requirement
Targeted block repurchase	Stock lending

Stock lender
Beneficial owner
Stock borrower
Rebate
Capital gains taxes

Bid-ask spread
Investment delay cost
Market impact cost
Price impact cost

CHAPTER 3

More on Common Stock

In the previous chapter we described the fundamental characteristics of common stocks, where stocks trade, trading mechanics, and trading costs. In this chapter, we look at in more detail various topics associated with investing in this asset class: the pricing efficiency of the stock market and its implications for investing, stock market indicators, risk factors, and tracking error. Several of these topics apply equally to other asset classes. We conclude the chapter with a description of popular common stock investment strategies.

PRICING EFFICIENCY OF THE STOCK MARKET

Investors do not like risk and they must be compensated for taking on risk—the larger the perceived risk, the more the compensation. An important question about financial markets, which has implications for the different strategies that investors can pursue (as explained in this chapter), is: Can investors earn a return in financial markets beyond that necessary to compensate them for the risk? Economists refer to this excess compensation as an *abnormal return*. Whether this can be done in the stock market is an empirical question. If a strategy is identified that can generate abnormal returns, the attributes that lead one to implement such a strategy is referred to as a *market anomaly*.

This issue of how efficiently a financial market prices the assets traded in that market is referred to as *market pricing efficiency*. An *efficient market* is defined as a financial market where asset prices rapidly reflect all available information. This means that all available information is already impounded in an asset's price, so that investors should expect to earn a return necessary to compensate them for their opportunity cost, anticipated inflation, and risk. That would seem to preclude abnormal returns. But according to Eugene Fama,[1] there are the following three levels of efficiency: weak form efficient, semistrong form efficient, and strong form efficient.

---

[1] Eugene F. Fama, "Efficient Capital Markets: A Review of Theory and Empirical Work," *Journal of Finance* 25, no. 2 (1970): 383–417.

In the *weak form of market efficiency*, current asset prices reflect all past prices and price movements. In other words, all worthwhile information about previous prices of the stock has been used to determine today's price; the investor cannot use that same information to predict tomorrow's price and still earn abnormal returns. Empirical evidence from the U.S. stock market suggests that this market is weak-form efficient. In other words, you cannot outperform ("beat") the market by using information on past stock prices.

In the *semistrong form of market efficiency*, the current asset prices reflect all publicly available information. The implication is that if investors employ investment strategies based on the use of publicly available information, they cannot earn abnormal returns. This does not mean that prices change instantaneously to reflect new information, but rather that information is impounded rapidly into asset prices. Empirical evidence supports the view that the U.S. stock market is for the most part semistrong efficient. This, in turn, implies that careful analysis of companies that issue stocks cannot consistently produce abnormal returns.

In the *strong form of market efficiency*, asset prices reflect all public and private information. In other words, the market (which includes all investors) knows everything about all financial assets, including information that has not been released to the public. The strong form implies that investors cannot generate abnormal returns from trading on inside information, where inside information is information that is not yet public.[2] In the U.S. stock market, this form of market efficiency is not supported by empirical studies. In fact, we know from many well publicized events reported by the media that the opposite is true; gains are available from inside information. Thus, the U.S. stock market, the empirical evidence suggests, is essentially semistrong efficient but not efficient in the strong form.

STOCK MARKET INDICATORS

Stock market indicators perform a variety of functions, from serving as benchmarks for evaluating the performance of professional money managers to answering the question "How did the market do today?" Exhibits 3.1 and 3.2 provide a list of the various stock indexes in the United States.

In general, stock market indexes rise and fall in fairly similar patterns. The indexes do not move in exactly the same ways at all times. The differences in movement reflect the different ways in which the indexes are constructed. Three factors enter into that construction:

---

[2]There is no exact definition of "inside information" in law. Laws pertaining to insider trading remain a gray area, subject to clarification mainly through judicial interpretation.

EXHIBIT 3.1 U.S. Stock Market Indexes

Exchange-Provided Indexes	
New York Stock Exchange	
NYSE Composite Index	NYSE World Leaders Index
NYSE U.S. 100 Index	NYSE TMT Index
Nasdaq	
Nasdaq Composite Index	Nasdaq Bank Index
Nasdaq National Market Composite Index	Nasdaq Computer Index
Nasdaq-100 Index	Nasdaq Health Care Index
Nasdaq-100 Equal Weighted Index	Nasdaq Industrial Index
Nasdaq-100 Technology Sector Index	Nasdaq National Market Industrial Index
Nasdaq-100 Ex-Tech Sector Index	
Nasdaq Financial-100 Index	Nasdaq Insurance Index
Nasdaq Biotechnology Index	Nasdaq Other Finance Index
Nasdaq Biotechnology Equal Weighted Index	Nasdaq Telecommunications Index
	Nasdaq Transportation Index

- The universe of stocks represented by the sample underlying the index.
- The relative weights assigned to the stocks included in the index.
- The method of averaging across all the stocks in the index.

The stocks included in a stock market index must be combined in certain proportions, and each stock must be given a weight. The three main approaches to weighting are (1) weighting by the market capitalization of the stock's company, which is the value of the number of shares multiplied by the price per share; (2) weighting by the price of the stock; and (3) equal weighting for each stock, regardless of its price or market capitalization. With the exception of the Dow Jones averages and the Value Line Composite Index, all the most widely used indexes are market-value weighted and the Value Line Composite Index is a equal-weighted index. The Dow Jones Industrial Average (DJIA) is a price-weighted average.

Stock market indicators can be classified into three groups:

1. Those produced by stock exchanges based on all stocks traded on the exchanges.
2. Those produced by organizations that subjectively select the stocks to be included in indexes.
3. Those where stock selection is based on an objective measure, such as the market capitalization of the company.

The first group, exchange-provided indexes, are shown in Exhibit 3.1. The New York Stock Exchange Composite Index and, although it is not an exchange, the Nasdaq Composite Index, fall into this category. Indexes that fall into the second group are shown in Exhibit 3.2. The two most popular stock market indicators in the second group are the Dow Jones Industrial Average (DJIA) and the Standard & Poor's 500 (S&P 500). The DJIA is constructed from 30 of the largest and most widely held U.S. companies. The companies included in the average are those selected by Dow Jones & Company, publisher of the *Wall Street Journal*. The S&P 500 represents stocks chosen from the New York Stock Exchange and the over-the-counter market. The stocks in the index at any given time are determined by a committee of the Standard & Poor's Corporation, which may occasionally add or delete individual stocks or the stocks of entire industry groups. The aim of the committee is to capture present overall stock market conditions as reflected in a broad range of economic indicators. The Value Line Composite Index, produced by Value Line Inc., covers a broad range of widely held and actively traded NYSE, Nasdaq, and Toronto Stock Exchange issues selected by Value Line.

Some indexes represent a broad segment of the stock market while others represent a particular sector such as technology, oil and gas, and financial. In addition, because the notion of an equity investment style (which we discuss later in this chapter) is widely accepted in the investment community, early acceptance of equity style investing (in the form of growth versus value and small market capitalization versus large capitalization) led to the creation and proliferation of published *style indexes*. Both the broad and the style indexes are shown in Exhibit 3.2.

In the third group, also shown in Exhibit 3.2, we have the Wilshire indexes produced by Wilshire Associates (Santa Monica, California) and the Russell indexes produced by the Frank Russell Company (Tacoma, Washington), a consultant to pension funds and other institutional investors. The criterion for inclusion in each of these indexes is solely a firm's market capitalization. The most comprehensive index is the Wilshire 5000, which actually includes more than 6,700 stocks now, up from 5,000 at its inception. The Wilshire 4500 includes all stocks in the Wilshire 5000 except for those in the S&P 500. Thus, the shares in the Wilshire 4500 have smaller capitalization than those in the Wilshire 5000. The Russell 3000 encompasses the 3,000 largest companies in terms of their market capitalization. The Russell 1000 is limited to the largest 1,000 of those, and the Russell 2000 has the remaining smaller firms.

The MSCI (Morgan Stanley Capital International) indexes are U.S. capitalization-weighted stock indexes that have received increased acceptance.

EXHIBIT 3.2 Nonexchange Indexes

Dow Jones & Co.

Dow Jones Average–30 Industrial	Dow Jones Average–15 Utilities
Dow Jones Average–20 Transportation	Dow Jones Average–65 Composite

Wilshire Associates

Wilshire 5000 Total Market Index	Wilshire Large Cap 750 Index
Wilshire 4500 Completion Index	Wilshire Mid-Cap 500 Index
Wilshire U.S. Large-Cap Index	Wilshire Small Cap 1750 Index
Wilshire U.S. Mid-Cap Index	Wilshire Micro-Cap Index
Wilshire U.S. Small-Cap Index	Wilshire Large Value Index
Wilshire U.S. Micro-Cap Index	Wilshire Large Growth Index
Wilshire U.S. Large-Cap Value Index	Wilshire Mid-Cap Value Index
Wilshire U.S. Large-Cap Growth Index	Wilshire Mid-Cap Growth Index
Wilshire U.S. Mid-Cap Value Index	Wilshire Small Value Index
Wilshire U.S. Mid-Cap Growth Index	Wilshire Small Growth Index
Wilshire U.S. Small-Cap Value Index	Wilshire All Value Index
Wilshire U.S. Small-Cap Growth Index	Wilshire All Growth Index
Wilshire U.S. 2500 Index	The Wilshire Small Cap 250

Standard & Poor's

S&P Composite 1500 Index	S&P MidCap 400 Index
S&P 100 Index	S&P SmallCap 600 Index
S&P 500 Index	

Frank Russell

Russell 3000 Index	Russell 2000 Growth
Russell 2000 Index	Russell 2000 Value
Russell 1000 Index	Russell 1000 Growth
Russell 3000 Growth	Russell 1000 Value
Russell 3000 Value	Russell–Midcap Index

Value Line

Value Line Composite Index

MSCI BARRA

MSCI BARRA	MSCI US Investable Market Energy Index
MSCI US Broad Market Index	MSCI US Investable Market Financials Index
MSCI US Prime Market 750 Index	MSCI US Investable Market Health Care
MSCI US Prime Market Value Index	Index
MSCI US Prime Market Growth Index	MSCI US Investable Market Industrials Index
MSCI US Mid Cap 450 Index	MSCI US Investable Market Information
MSCI US Small Cap 1750 Index	Technology Index
MSCI US Small Cap Value Index	MSCI US Investable Market Materials Index
MSCI US Small Cap Growth Index	MSCI US Investable Market Telecommunica-
MSCI US Investable Market Consumer	tions Index
Discretionary Index	MSCI US Investable Market Utilities Index
MSCI US Investable Market Consumer	
Staples Index	

RISK FACTORS

In well-functioning capital markets, an investor should be rewarded for accepting the various risks associated with investing in an asset. Risks are also referred to as "risk factors" or "factors." We can express an *asset pricing model* in general terms based on N risk factors as follows:

$$E(R_i) = f(F_1, F_2, ..., F_N)$$

where $E(R_i)$ denotes the expected return for asset i and F_k denotes risk factor k.

In words, the asset pricing model says that the expected return is a function of N risk factors. The challenge in investing in any asset class is to figure out what the risk factors are and to specify the precise relationship between expected return and the risk factors.

We can fine-tune the asset pricing model above by thinking about the minimum expected return we would want from investing in an asset. There are securities issued by the U.S. Department of the Treasury that offer a known return if held over some period of time. The expected return offered on such securities is called the *risk-free return* or the *risk-free rate* because there is believed to be no default risk. By investing in an asset other than such securities, investors will demand a premium over the risk-free rate. That is, the expected return that an investor will require is

$$E(R_i) = R_f + \text{Risk premium}$$

where R_f is the risk-free rate.

The *risk premium* or additional return expected over the risk-free rate depends on the risk factors associated with investing in the asset. Thus, the general form of the asset pricing model can be rewritten as follows:

$$E(R_i) = R_f + f(F_1, F_2, ..., F_N)$$

Systematic vs. Nonsystematic Risk

Risk factors can be divided into two general categories. The first category is risk factors that cannot be diversified away. That is, no matter what the investor does, the investor cannot eliminate these risk factors. These risk factors are referred to as *systematic risk factors* or *nondiversifiable risk factors*. The second category is risk factors that can be eliminated via diversification. These risk factors are unique to the asset and are referred to as *unsystematic risk factors* or *diversifiable risk factors*.

Capital Asset Pricing Model

Probably the most well-known asset pricing model is the Capital Asset Pricing Model (CAPM) given by

$$E(R_i) = R_f + \beta_i [E(R_M) - R_f]$$

where $E(R_M)$ represents the expected return on the "market" and β_i is the quantity of risk for asset i. The only risk factor in the CAPM is the movement in the market. That is, market is the only systematic risk factor in the CAPM.

Note that in this model that the relationship between the sensitivity of an asset's expected return to a risk factor is denoted by the Greek letter beta (β). It is for this reason that the financial community has adopted the term "beta" to describe the quantity of a risk factor.

The expected return for an asset i according to the CAPM is equal to the risk-free rate plus a risk premium. The risk premium is

$$\text{Risk premium in the CAPM} = \beta_i [E(R_M) - R_f]$$

First look at *beta* (β_i) in the risk premium component of the CAPM. Beta is a measure of the sensitivity of the return of asset i to the return of the market portfolio. A beta equal to one means that the asset has the same quantity of risk as the market. A beta greater than one means that the asset has more market risk than the market portfolio, and a beta less than one means that the asset or portfolio has less market risk than the market portfolio. The second component of the risk premium in the CAPM is the difference between the expected return on the market portfolio, $E(R_M)$, and the risk-free rate. It measures the potential reward for taking on the risk of the market above what can earned by investing in an asset that offers a risk-free rate. Taken together, the risk premium is a product of the quantity of market risk (as measured by beta) and the potential compensation of taking on market risk (as measured by $[E(R_M) - R_f]$).

In applying the CAPM to common stocks, beta is typically estimated using time series data of historical returns. The statistical model used is the single index market model or simply market model that is estimated by simple linear regression analysis. There are various ways to do this. One way is to calculate the price change of a particular company's relative to the price change of some representative stock market index. The price changes can be calculated weekly or monthly. Then in regression analysis the price of the stock is the dependent variable and the price change of the stock market index is the independent variable. The coefficient of the independent variable is the estimated beta used in the CAPM. The second way is to calculate the difference between the price change for the stock and the risk-free rate and the difference between the price change for the stock market index and the risk-free rate. The former is then the dependent variable in the regression and the latter the independent variable. When estimated over the same period of time, the difference in the beta estimates for the two methods is typically small.

In practice, the proxy used for the market in the market model is typically the S&P 500 stock index. Usually, monthly or weekly returns are used to calculate the price changes.

Yahoo! Finance provides estimates for beta for stocks employing the first method.[3] Monthly price changes are used for 36 months. The S&P 500 is used as the market index. The beta for six companies as reported by Yahoo! Finance on June 10, 2010 is given below:

Company	Beta
Kellogg	0.50
3M	0.80
Microsoft	0.99
Google	1.07
Goldman Sachs	1.34
Caterpillar	1.82

The beta of a portfolio of stocks is equal to the weighted average of the stocks comprising the portfolio. The weight assigned to each beta is the percentage of the market value of the portfolio that the stock makes up. For example, suppose a portfolio consists of the six stocks whose beta is listed above. Suppose further that the first two stocks each represent 22% of the portfolio and the other four stocks 14%. The beta for this hypothetical portfolio would be

$$\text{Portfolio beta} = 0.22(0.50) + 0.22(0.80) + 0.14(0.99) + 0.14(1.07) + 0.14(1.34) + 0.14(1.82) = 1.02$$

Multifactor Models

It is well recognized that despite its popularity, CAPM is not adequate for describing asset returns given that it assumes there is only one risk factor, market risk. Instead, today there are more sophisticated empirical models that have identified risk factors that can better explain observed asset

---

[3]The estimated are obtained by Yahoo! Finance from Capital IQ, a Standard & Poor's business.

returns. These models are called *multifactor models* or simply *factor models*. As in the CAPM, in the mathematical presentation of these models, the Greek letter beta is used to measure the systematic risk of a risk factor.

There are several companies that sell such models. One popular model is that of MSCI Barra. This multifactor model is called a fundamental factor model because it uses company and industry attributes to create risk factors. Examples of the attributes used in the model are earnings/price ratios, book/ price ratios, estimated earnings growth, and trading activity. The estimation of a fundamental factor model begins with an analysis of historical stock returns and descriptors about a company. In the MSCI Barra model, for example, the process of identifying the risk factors begins with monthly returns for hundreds of stocks that the descriptors must explain. Descriptors are not the "risk factors." They are the candidates for risk factors.

The descriptors are selected in terms of their ability to explain stock returns. That is, all of the descriptors are potential risk factors but only those that appear to be important in explaining stock returns are used in constructing risk factors.

Once the descriptors that are determined to be statistically important in explaining stock returns are identified, they are grouped into "risk indexes" or "factors" to capture related company attributes. For example, descriptors such as market leverage, book leverage, debt-to-equity ratio, and company's debt rating are combined to obtain a risk index or factor referred to as "leverage." Thus, a risk index is a combination of descriptors that captures a particular attribute of a company. One version of the MSCI Barra fundamental factor model has 13 risk indexes and 55 industry groups.

TRACKING ERROR

The risk of a common stock portfolio can be measured by the standard deviation of portfolio returns. This statistical measure provides a range around the average return of a portfolio within which the actual return over a period is likely to fall with some specific probability. The mean return and standard deviation (or volatility) of a portfolio can be calculated over a period of time.

The standard deviation or volatility of a common stock portfolio or a market index is an absolute number. A portfolio manager or client can also ask what the variation of the return of a portfolio is relative to a specified benchmark. Such variation is called the portfolio's *tracking error*. Specifically, tracking error measures the dispersion of a portfolio's returns relative to the returns of its benchmark. That is, tracking error is the standard deviation of the portfolio's *active return*, where active return is defined as:

Active return = Portfolio's actual return − Benchmark's actual return

A portfolio created to match the benchmark index (that is, an index fund) that regularly has zero active returns (that is, always matches its benchmark's actual return) would have a tracking error of zero. But a portfolio that is actively managed that takes positions substantially different from the benchmark would likely have large active returns, both positive and negative, and thus would have an annual tracking error of, say, 5% to 10%.

To find the tracking error of a portfolio, it is first necessary to specify the benchmark. The tracking error of a portfolio, as indicated, is its standard deviation relative to the benchmark, not its total standard deviation. Exhibit 3.3 presents the information used to calculate the tracking error for a hypothetical portfolio and benchmark using 30 weekly observations. The fourth column in the exhibit shows the active return for the week. It is from the data in this column that the tracking error is computed. As reported in the exhibit, the standard deviation of the weekly active returns is 0.54%. This value is then annualized by multiplying by the square root of 52—52 representing the number of weeks in a year. This gives a value of 3.89%. If the observations were monthly rather than weekly, the monthly tracking error would be annualized by multiplying by the square root of 12.

Given the tracking error, a range for the possible portfolio active return and corresponding range for the portfolio can be estimated assuming that the active returns are normally distributed. For example, assume the following:

Benchmark = S&P 500
Active return relative to the S&P 500 = 10%
Tracking error relative to S&P 500 = 2%

then to simplify the analysis, assuming that the tracking error is normally distributed:

Number of Standard Deviations	Range for Portfolio Active Return	Corresponding Range for Portfolio Return	Probability
1	±2%	8%–12%	67%
2	±4%	6%–14%	95%
3	±6%	4%–16%	99%

Tracking error decreases as the portfolio progressively includes more of the stocks that are in the benchmark index. This general effect is illustrated in Exhibit 3.4, which shows the effect of portfolio size for a large-cap portfolio benchmarked to the S&P 500. Notice that an optimally chosen portfolio of just 50 stocks can track the S&P 500 within 2.3%. For mid-cap

EXHIBIT 3.3 Data and Calculation of Active Return, Alpha, and Information Ratio

Week	Weekly Return (%)		
	Portfolio	Benchmark	Active
1	3.69	3.72	–0.02
2	–0.56	–1.09	0.53
3	–1.41	–1.35	–0.06
4	0.96	0.34	0.62
5	–4.07	–4.00	–0.07
6	1.27	0.91	0.37
7	–0.39	–0.08	–0.31
8	–3.31	–2.76	–0.55
9	2.19	2.11	0.09
10	–0.02	–0.40	0.37
11	–0.46	–0.42	–0.05
12	0.09	0.71	–0.62
13	–1.93	–1.99	0.06
14	–1.91	–2.37	0.46
15	1.89	1.98	–0.09
16	–3.75	–4.33	0.58
17	–3.38	–4.22	0.84
18	0.60	0.62	–0.02
19	–10.81	–11.60	0.79
20	6.63	7.78	–1.15
21	3.52	2.92	0.59
22	1.24	1.89	–0.66
23	–0.63	–1.66	1.03
24	3.04	2.90	0.14
25	–1.73	–1.58	–0.15
26	2.81	3.05	–0.23
27	0.40	1.64	–1.23
28	1.03	1.03	0.01
29	–0.94	–0.95	0.00
30	1.45	1.66	–0.21

Average of active returns = 0.04%; Standard deviation of active returns = 0.54%
Annualizing
Annual average = Weekly average × 52
Annual variance = Weekly variance × 52
Annual std dev = Weekly std dev × $(52^{0.5})$

EXHIBIT 3.4   Typical Tracking Error vs. Number of Benchmark Stocks in Portfolio for S&P 500

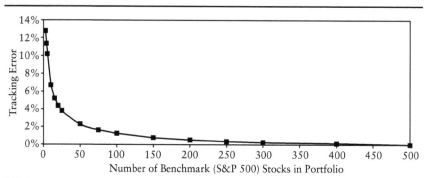

and small-cap stocks, one study found that the tracking errors are 3.5% and 4.3%, respectively.[4] In contrast, tracking error increases as the portfolio progressively includes more stocks that are not in the benchmark.

Forward-Looking vs. Backward-Looking Tracking Error

In Exhibit 3.3 the tracking error of the hypothetical portfolio is shown based on the active returns reported. However, the performance shown is the result of the portfolio manager's decisions during those 30 weeks with respect to portfolio positioning issues such as beta, sector allocations, style tilt (that is, value versus growth), stock selections, and so on. Hence, we can call the tracking error calculated from these trailing active returns a *backward-looking tracking error*. It is also called the *ex post tracking error*.

One problem with a backward-looking tracking error is that it does not reflect the effect of current decisions by the portfolio manager on the future active returns and hence the future tracking error that may be realized. If, for example, the manager significantly changes the portfolio beta or sector allocations today, then the backward-looking tracking error that is calculated using data from prior periods would not accurately reflect the current portfolio risks going forward. That is, the backward-looking tracking error will have little predictive value and can be misleading regarding portfolio risks going forward.

The portfolio manager needs a forward-looking estimate of tracking error to accurately reflect the portfolio risk going forward. This is done in practice by using the services of a commercial vendor that has a multi-factor risk model, that has defined the risks associated with a benchmark

---

[4]Raman Vardharaj, Frank J. Fabozzi, and Frank J. Jones, "Determinants of Tracking Error For Equity Portfolios," *Journal of Investing* 13, no. 2 (2004): 37–47.

index. Statistical analysis of the historical return data of the stocks in the benchmark index are used to obtain the factors and quantify their risks. (This involves the use of variances and correlations.) Using the portfolio manager's current portfolio holdings, the portfolio's current exposure to the various factors can be calculated and compared to the benchmark's exposures to the factors. Using the differential factor exposures and the risks of the factors, a *forward-looking tracking error* for the portfolio can be computed. This tracking error is also referred to as the *predicted tracking error* or *ex ante tracking error*.

There is no guarantee that the forward-looking tracking error at the start of, say, a year would exactly match the backward-looking tracking error calculated at the end of the year. There are two reasons for this. The first is that as the year progresses and changes are made to the portfolio, the forward-looking tracking error estimate would change to reflect the new exposures. The second is that the accuracy of the forward-looking tracking error depends on the extent of the stability in the variances and correlations that were used in the analysis. These problems notwithstanding, the average of forward-looking tracking error estimates obtained at different times during the year will be reasonably close to the backward-looking tracking error estimate obtained at the end of the year.

Each of these estimates has its use. The forward-looking tracking error is useful in risk control and portfolio construction. The portfolio manager can immediately see the likely effect on tracking error of any intended change in the portfolio. Thus, she can do a what-if analysis (commonly called sensitivity analysis) of various portfolio strategies and eliminate those that would result in tracking errors beyond her tolerance for risk. The backward-looking tracking error can be useful for assessing actual performance analysis, such as the information ratio discussed next.

Information Ratio

Alpha is the average active return over a time period. Since backward-looking tracking error measures the standard deviation of a portfolio's active return, it is different from alpha. A portfolio does not have backward-looking tracking error simply because of outperformance or underperformance. For instance, consider a portfolio that outperforms (or underperforms) its benchmark by exactly 10 basis points (bps) every month. This portfolio would have a backward-looking tracking error of zero and a positive (negative) alpha of 10 bps. In contrast, consider a portfolio that outperforms its benchmark by 10 bps during half the months and underperforms by 10 bps during the other months. This portfolio would have a backward-looking tracking error that is positive but an alpha equal to zero.

The *information ratio* combines alpha and tracking error as follows:

$$\text{Information ratio} = \frac{\text{Alpha}}{\text{Backward-looking tracking error}}$$

The information ratio is essentially a reward-risk ratio. The reward is the average of the active return, that is, alpha. The risk is the standard deviation of the active return, the tracking error, and, more specifically, backward-looking tracking error. The higher the information ratio, the better the investor or portfolio manager performed relative to the risk assumed.

To illustrate the calculation of the information ratio, consider the active returns for the hypothetical portfolio shown in Exhibit 3.3. The weekly average active return is 0.04%. Annualizing the weekly average active return by multiplying by 52 results in an alpha of 1.83%. Since the backward-looking tracking error is 3.89%, the information ratio is 0.47 (1.83%/3.89%).

COMMON STOCK INVESTMENT STRATEGIES

Common stock investment strategies can be classified as active and passive. The selection of a strategy depends on the risk tolerance of the investor and the investor's view of the efficiency of the stock market. Investors who believe the stock market is efficient would tend to favor a passive strategy such as indexing; investors who believe the stock market is inefficient will embrace an active strategy.

Throughout the history of the stock market, there have been numerous strategies suggested on how to "beat the market." A useful way of thinking about active versus passive management is in terms of the following three activities performed by investors: (1) stock selection (deciding on stocks to buy and sell), (2) trading of securities, and (3) portfolio monitoring.[5] Generally, investors pursuing active strategies devote the majority of their time to stock selection and portfolio allocation. In contrast, with passive strategies such as indexing, investors devote significantly less time to this activity. Below we provide an overview of active common stock portfolio strategies.

Fundamental Versus Technical Analysis

In active management there are two schools as to what information is useful in the selection of stocks and the timing of the purchase of stocks. These two schools are the fundamental analysis school and the technical analysis school.

[5]Jeffrey L. Skelton, "Investment Opportunities with Indexing," in *Equity Markets and Valuation Methods*, edited by Kathrina F. Sherrerd, pp. 47–50 (Charlottesville, VA: The Institute of Chartered Financial Analysts, 1988).

Fundamental analysis involves the analysis of a company's operations to assess its future economic prospects. The analysis begins with the company's financial statements in order to investigate earnings, cash flow, profitability, and debt burden. Advocates of fundamental analysis will look at a company's major product lines, the economic outlook for the products (including existing and potential competitors), and the industries in which the company operates. The results of this analysis will be an assessment of the future growth prospects of earnings. Based on the growth prospects of earnings, a follower of fundamental analysis attempts to determine the fair value of the stock using one or more common stock valuation models. The estimated fair value is then compared to the market price to determine if the stock is fairly priced in the market, cheap (a market price below the estimated fair value), or rich (a market price above the estimated fair value). The father of traditional fundamental analysis is Benjamin Graham, who espoused this analysis in his classic book *Security Analysis.*[6]

Technical analysis ignores company specific information of the firm. Instead, technical analysis focuses on price and/or trading volume of individual stocks, groups of stocks, and the overall market resulting, for example, from shifting supply and demand, and changes in market sentiment. This type of analysis is not only used for the analysis of common stock, but it is also a tool used in the trading of commodities, bonds, futures contracts, and other securities.

Fundamental analysis and technical analysis can certainly be integrated within one overall strategy. Specifically, an investor can use fundamental analysis to identify stocks that are candidates for purchase or sale and employ technical analysis to time the trade entry or exit points.

Strategies Based on Technical Analysis

Various common stock strategies that involve only historical price movement, trading volume, and other technical indicators have been suggested since the beginning of stock trading in the United States. Many of these strategies involve investigating patterns based on historical trading data (past price data and trading volume) to forecast the future movement of individual stocks or the market as a whole. Based on observed patterns, mechanical trading rules indicating when a stock should be bought, sold, or sold short are developed. Thus, no consideration is given to any factor other than the specified technical indicators.

---

[6]Benjamin Graham and Sidney Cottle, *Security Analysis*, 1st ed. (New York: Whitlesey House, 1934); and Benjamin Graham, David I. Dodd, and Sidney Cottle, *Security Analysis: Principles and Technique*, 4th ed. (New York: McGraw-Hill, 1962).

As we explained earlier, this approach to active management is called technical analysis. Because some of these strategies involve the analysis of charts that plot price and volume movements, investors who follow a technical analysis approach are referred to as *chartists*. The overlying principle of these strategies is to detect changes in the supply of and demand for a stock and capitalize on the expected changes.

Dow Theory   The father of the technical analysis school is Charles Dow. During his tenure as the first editor of the *Wall Street Journal* from July 1889 to December 1902, his editorials speculated on the future direction of the stock market. This body of writing, now referred to as the *Dow Theory*, rests on two basic assumptions. First, according to Charles Dow:

> Because they reflect the combined market activities of thousands of investors, including those possessed of the greatest foresight and the best information on trends and events, the averages in their day-to-day fluctuations discount everything known, everything foreseeable, and every condition which can affect the supply of or the demand for corporate securities. Even unpredictable natural calamities, when they happen, are quickly appraised and their possible effects discounted.

This assumption sounds very much like the efficient market theory. But there's more. The second basic assumption is that the stock market moves in trends—up and down—over periods of time. According to Charles Dow, it is possible to identify these stock price trends and predict their future movement.

According to the Dow Theory, there are three types of trends or market cycles. The primary trend is the long-term movement in the market. Primary trends are basically four-year trends in the market. From the primary trend, a trend line showing where the market is heading can be derived. The secondary trend represents short-run departures of stock prices from the trend line. The third trend involves short-term fluctuations in stock prices. Charles Dow believed that upward movements in the stock market were tempered by fallbacks that lost a portion of the previous gain. A market turn occurred when the upward movement was not greater than the last gain.

In assessing whether or not a gain did in fact occur, he suggested examining the co-movements in different stock market indexes such as the Dow Jones Industrial Average and the Dow Jones Transportation Average. One of the averages is selected as the primary index and the other as the confirming index. If the primary index reaches a high above its previous high, the increase is expected to continue if it is confirmed by the other index also reaching a high above its previous high.

Simple Filter Rules The simplest type of technical strategy is to buy and sell on the basis of a predetermined movement in the price of a stock. The rule is if the stock increases by a certain percentage, the stock is purchased and held until the price declines by a certain percentage, at which time the stock is sold. The percentage by which the price must change is called the "filter." Every investor pursuing this technical strategy decides his or her own filter.

Moving Averages Some technical analysts make decisions to buy or sell a stock based on the movement of a stock over an extended period of time (e.g., 200 days). An average of the price over the time period is computed, and a rule is specified that if the price is greater than some percentage of the average, the stock should be purchased; if the price is less than some percentage of the average, the stock should be sold. The simplest way to calculate the average is to calculate a simple moving average. Assuming that the time period selected by the technical analyst is 200 days, then the average price over the 200 days is determined. A more complex moving average can be calculated by giving progressively greater weight to recent prices.

Advance/Decline Line On each trading day, some stocks will increase in price or "advance" from the closing price on the previous trading day, while other stocks will decrease in price or decline from the closing price on the previous trading day. It has been suggested by some market observers that the cumulative number of advances over a certain number of days minus the cumulative number of declines over the same number of days can be used as an indicator of short-term movements in the stock market and a predictor of future movements. If the *advance/decline line* is positive, it is presumed that the market will trend upward. Conversely, if the advance/decline line is negative, it is presumed that the market will decline.

Relative Strength The *relative strength* of a stock is measured by the ratio of the stock price to some price index. The ratio indicates the relative movement of the stock to the index. The price index can be the index of the price of stocks in a given industry or a broad-based index of stocks. If the ratio rises, it is presumed that the stock is in an uptrend relative to the index; if the ratio falls, it is presumed that the stock is in a downtrend relative to the index. Similarly, a relative strength measure can be calculated for an industry group relative to a broad-based index. Relative strength is also often referred to as price momentum or price persistence.

Price and Trading Relationship One popular Wall Street adage is that "It takes volume to make price move." This suggests a price-volume relationship as a signal for detecting the price movement of a stock used in some technical analyses. The argument put forth by technical analysts is that a rise in both trading volume and price signals investor interest in the stock, and this interest should be sustained. In contrast, a rise in price accompanied by a decline in trading volume signals a subsequent decline in the price of the stock.

Short Interest Ratio   Some technical analysts believe that the ratio of the number of shares sold short relative to the average daily trading volume is a technical signal that is valuable in forecasting the market. This ratio is called the *short interest ratio*. However, the economic link between this ratio and stock price movements can be interpreted in two ways. On one hand, some market observers believe that if this ratio is high, this is a signal that the market will advance. The argument is that short sellers will have to eventually cover their short position by buying the stocks they have shorted and, as a result, market prices will increase. On the other hand, there are some market observers who believe this is a bearish signal being sent by market participants who have shorted stocks in anticipation of a declining market.

Linear and Nonlinear Dynamic Models   Some market observers believe that stock price behavior is more complex and that patterns of prices follow dynamic mathematical models. A dynamic mathematical model is a relationship between prices, returns, and eventually other variables at different points in time. Future prices and returns are believed to be determined, for example, by past prices, returns, and possibly other variables. Though a mathematical model allows predicting the future at least in a probabilistic sense, it does not imply that prices follow visually recognizable patterns.

There are many types of mathematical models. The simplest are linear probabilistic models. A linear probabilistic model is a model where future prices or returns are a weighted average of past prices, returns, and other variables plus a random disturbance. Models of this type supply probabilistic forecasts because of the presence of random disturbances. Given a linear probabilistic model of prices, we cannot predict future prices but we can predict their expectations (that is, their averages) in a statistical sense.

Nonlinear models are predicated on a belief that the relationships between different variables at different points in time are not linear, that is, not simple proportionality relationships. Nonlinear models might exhibit very complex behavior. The behavior of a nonlinear model might be so complex that it appears random even if the model does not include a random term or random disturbance.

Nonlinear models that originate apparently random behavior are called chaotic models. The theory of these phenomena is called *chaos theory*. If stock prices follow a nonlinear chaotic model, their fluctuations might appear random even if there is a precise relationship between past and present prices.

A distinctive feature of chaotic models is that they are so sensitive to the known data that predictions are possible only over very short time periods. An example is weather forecasting. Models of weather developed by meteorologists can be viewed as nonlinear chaotic models. As a consequence, reliable forecasts over long periods of time are impossible. However, chaotic models exhibit reliable statistical behavior in the very long run. Thus, if we let a weather model run for a long time, we gain an insight of the statistical behavior of weather.

Nonlinear dynamic models have been suggested for analyzing stock price patterns. There have been several empirical studies that suggest that stock prices exhibit the characteristics of a nonlinear dynamic model. The particular form of nonlinear dynamic model that has been suggested is chaos theory. At this stage, the major insight provided by chaos theory is that stock price movements that may appear to be random may in fact have a structure that can be used to generate abnormal returns.

Market Overreaction To benefit from favorable news or to reduce the adverse effect of unfavorable news, investors must react quickly to new information.[7] Cognitive psychologists have shed some light on how people react to extreme events. In general, people tend to overreact to extreme events. People tend to react more strongly to recent information and they tend to heavily discount older information.

Do investors follow a uniform pattern? That is, do investors overreact to the same events? The overreaction hypothesis suggests that when investors react to unanticipated news that will benefit a company's stock, the price rise will be greater than it should be given that information, resulting in a subsequent decline in the price of the stock. In contrast, the overreaction to unanticipated news that is expected to adversely affect the economic well-being of a company will force the price down too much, followed by a subsequent correction that will bolster the price.

When the market overreacts, investors may be able to exploit this to realize positive abnormal returns if they can (1) identify an extreme event and (2) determine when the effect of the overreaction has been impounded in the market price and is, therefore, ready to reverse. Investors who are capable of doing this will pursue the following strategies: When positive news is identified, buy the stock and sell it before the correction to the underreaction. In the case of negative news, short the stock and then buy it back to cover the short position before the correction to the overreaction.

Market overreaction is one part of an area of what is called *behavioral finance*. This theory of finance believes that in addition to market

---

[7]Werner DeBondt and Richard Thaler, "Does the Market Overreact? *Journal of Finance* 40, no. 3 (1985): 793–805.

fundamentals, stock prices are affected by the emotional behavior of market participants. Overreaction is one example of behavior affecting stock prices in addition to economic data. Other forms of behavioral finance include over confidence, herding, and regret. These behavioral patterns can affect the value of a common stock in addition to fundamental data.

Strategies Based on Fundamental Analysis

As explained earlier, fundamental analysis involves an economic analysis of a firm with respect to earnings growth prospects, ability to meet debt obligations, competitive environment, and the like. We discuss a few of these strategies later when we cover equity style management.

Proponents of semistrong market efficiency argue that strategies based on fundamental analysis will not produce abnormal returns in the long run. Semistrong-form efficiency means that the price of the security fully reflects all public information (which, of course, includes but is not limited to, historical price and trading patterns).[8] The reason is simply that there are many independent analysts undertaking basically the same sort of analysis, with the same publicly available data, so that the price of the stock reflects all the relevant factors that determine value.

A fundamental tenet of finance theory is that there is a relationship between risk and return. Risk itself cannot be eliminated. If there were no risk, finance theory would be reduced to accounting. Abnormal returns always have to be compared to the inherent risk. One cannot simply say that a given level of return is abnormal unless the relative amount of risk is given. Stated differently, even in an efficient market we can still make forecasts, but we have to consider the risk associated with our forecasts.

The focus of strategies based on fundamental analysis is on the earnings of a company and the expected change in the earnings. In fact, a study in the early 1980s found that two of the most important measures used by analysts are short-term and long-term changes in earnings.[9]

Earnings Surprises   Studies have found that it is not merely the absolute change in earnings that is important. The reason is that analysts have a consensus forecast of a company's expected earnings. What might be expected to generate abnormal returns is the extent to which the market's forecast of future earnings differs from actual earnings that are subsequently announced. The divergence between the actual earnings announced and the

---

[8]Eugene F. Fama, "Efficient Capital Markets: A Review of Theory and Empirical Work," *Journal of Finance* 24, no. 2 (1970): 383–417.
[9]Lal C. Chugh and Joseph W. Meador, "The Stock Valuation Process: The Analysts' View," *Financial Analysts Journal* 40 (November–December 2004): 41–48.

forecasted earnings by the consensus of analysts is called an *earnings surprise*. When the actual earnings exceed the market's forecast, then this is a positive earnings surprise; a negative earnings surprise arises when the actual earnings are less than the market's forecast.

There have been numerous studies of earnings surprises. These studies seem to suggest that identifying stocks that may have positive earnings surprises and purchasing them may generate abnormal returns. Of course, the difficulty is identifying such stocks.

Low Price-Earnings Ratio The legendary Benjamin Graham proposed a classic investment model in 1949 for the "defensive investor"—one without the time, expertise, or temperament for aggressive investment. The model was updated in each subsequent edition of his book, *The Intelligent Investor,* first published in 1949. Some of the basic investment criteria outlined in the 1973 edition are representative of the approach:

1. A company must have paid a dividend in each of the past 20 years.
2. Minimum size of a company is $100 million in annual sales for an industrial company and $50 million for a public utility.
3. Positive earnings must have been achieved in each of the past 10 years.
4. Current price should not be more than 1.5 times the latest book value.
5. Market price should not exceed 15 times the average earnings for the past three years.

Graham considered the P/E ratio as a measure of the price paid for value received. He viewed high P/Es with skepticism and as representing a large premium for difficult-to-forecast future earnings growth. Hence, lower-P/E companies were viewed favorably as having less potential for earnings disappointments and the resulting downward revision in price.

While originally intended for the defensive investor, numerous variations of Graham's low-P/E approach are currently followed by a number of professional investment advisors.

Market-Neutral Long-Short Stratregy An active strategy that seeks to capitalize on the ability of an investor to select stocks is a market-neutral long-short strategy. The basic idea of this strategy is as follows. First, a quantitative model is used to analyze the expected return of individual stocks within a universe of stocks. Based on this analysis, the stocks analyzed are classified as either "high-expected return stocks" or "low-expected return stocks." Based on this classification of each stock, one of the following strategies is pursued: (1) purchase only high-expected return stocks, (2) short low-expected return stocks, or (3) simultaneously purchase high-expected return stocks and short low-expected return stocks.[10]

The problem with the first two strategies is that general movements in the market can have an adverse affect. For example, suppose an investor selects high-expected return stocks and the market declines. Because of the positive correlation between the return on all stocks and the market, the drop in the market will produce a negative return even though the investor may have indeed been able to identify high-expected return stocks. Similarly, if an investor shorts low-expected return stocks and the market rallies, the portfolio will realize a negative return. This is because a rise in the market means that the investor must likely cover the short position of each stock at a higher price than which a stock was sold.

Let's look at the third alternative—simultaneously purchasing stocks with high-expected returns and shorting those stocks with low-expected returns. Consider what happens to the long and the short positions when the market in general moves. A drop in the market will hurt the long position but benefit the short position. A market rally will hurt the short position but benefit the long position. Consequently, the long and short positions provide a hedge against each other.

While the long-short position provides a hedge against general market movements, the degree to which one position moves relative to the other is not controlled by simply going long the high-expected return stocks and going short the low-expected return stocks. That is, the two positions do not neutralize the risk against general market movements. However, the long and short positions can be created with a market exposure that neutralizes any market movement. Specifically, long and short positions can be constructed to have the same beta and, as a result, the beta of the collective long-short position is zero. For this reason, this strategy is called a *market-neutral long-short strategy*. If, indeed, an investor is capable of identifying high- and low-expected return stocks, then neutralizing the portfolio against market movements will produce a positive return whether the market rises or falls.

Market Anomaly Strategies

While there are investors who are skeptical about technical analysis and others who are skeptical about fundamental analysis, some investors believe that there are pockets of pricing inefficiency in the stock market. That is, there are some investment strategies that have historically produced statistically significant positive abnormal returns. Some examples of these anomalies are the small-firm effect, the low-price-earnings ratio effect, the

---

[10]Bruce L. Jacobs and Kenneth N. Levy, "The Long and Short on Long-Short," *Journal of Investing* 6, no. 1 (Spring 1997): 78–88.

neglected-firm effect, and various calendar effects. There are also strategies based on following the trading transactions of the insiders of a company.

Some of these anomalies are a challenge to the semistrong form of market efficiency. This includes the small-firm effect and the low price-earnings effect. The calendar effects are a challenge to the weak form of pricing efficiency. Following insider activities with regard to buying and selling the stock of their company is a challenge to both the weak and strong forms of pricing efficiency. (Recall that weak-form efficiency means that the price of the security reflects the past price and trading history of the security; strong-form efficiency exists in a market where the price of a security reflects all information, whether it is publicly available or known only to insiders such as the firm's managers or directors.) The challenge to the weak form is that, as will be explained shortly, information on *insider activity* is publicly available and, in fact, has been suggested as a technical indicator. Thus, the question is whether "outsiders" can use information about trading activity by insiders to generate abnormal returns. The challenge to the strong form of pricing efficiency is that insiders are viewed as having special (insider) information and therefore based on this information they may be able to generate abnormal returns from their special relationship with the firm.

Small-Firm Effect   The *small-firm effect* emerges in several studies that have shown that portfolios of small firms (in terms of total market capitalization) have outperformed large firms. Because of these findings, there has been increased interest in stock market indicators that monitor small-capitalization firms. We will describe this more fully when we discuss equity style management.

Low P/E Effect   Earlier we discussed Benjamin Graham's strategy for defensive investors based on low P/Es. The *low P/E effect* is supported by several studies showing that portfolios consisting of stocks with a low P/E have outperformed portfolios consisting of stocks with a high P/E. However, other studies found that after adjusting for the transaction costs necessary to rebalance a portfolio, as prices and earnings change over time, the superior performance of portfolios of low-P/E stocks no longer holds. An explanation for the presumably superior performance is that stocks trade at low P/Es because they are temporarily out of favor with market participants. As fads change, companies not currently in vogue will rebound at some time in the future.

Neglected-Firm Effect   Not all firms receive the same degree of attention from security analysts. One school of thought is that firms that are essentially neglected by security analysts will outperform firms that are the subject of considerable attention. One study has found that an investment strategy based on the level of attention devoted by security analysts to different stocks may lead to positive abnormal returns. This market anomaly is referred to as the *neglected-firm effect*.

Calendar Effects   While some empirical work focuses on selected firms according to some criterion such as market capitalization, P/E, or degree of analysts' attention, the calendar effect looks at the best time to implement strategies. Examples of *calendar anomalies*, as these strategies are referred to, are the January effect, month-of-the-year effect, day-of-the-week effect, and holiday effect. It seems from the empirical evidence that there are times when the implementation of a strategy will, on average, provide a superior performance relative to other calendar time periods.

Following Insider Activity   While the U.S. Securities and Exchange Commission (SEC) has a more comprehensive definition of an insider, we can think of insiders of a corporation as the corporate officers, directors, and holders of large amounts of a company's common stock. The SEC requires that all trading activity by insiders be reported by the 10th of the month following the trade. The SEC then releases this information in a report called the *SEC Insider Transaction Report*. Thus, after a time lag, the information is made publicly available. Studies have found that insiders have been able to generate abnormal returns using their privileged position. However, when outsiders use this information, one study found that after controlling for the other anomalies discussed above and transaction costs, outsiders cannot benefit from this information. In other words, insider activity information published by the SEC is not a useful technical indicator for generating abnormal returns.

One of the difficulties with assessing all of the strategies described here is that the factors that are believed to generate market anomalies are interrelated. For example, small firms may be those that are not given much attention by security analysts and that therefore trade at a low P/E. Even a study of insider activity must carefully separate abnormal returns that may be the result of a market anomaly having nothing to do with insider activity. For example, one study that found no abnormal returns from following insiders also found that if there are any abnormal returns they are due to the size and low P/E effects. There have been many attempts to disentangle these effects.

Equity Style Management

Several academic studies found that there were categories of stocks that had similar characteristics and performance patterns. Moreover, the returns of these stock categories performed differently than other categories of stocks.

That is, the returns of stocks within a category were highly correlated and the returns between categories of stocks were less correlated. The first such study was by James Farrell,[11] who labeled these categories of stocks "clusters." He found that for stocks there were at least four such categories or clusters—growth, cyclical, stable, and energy. The latter half of the 1970s saw studies that suggested even a simpler categorization by size (as measured by market capitalization) produced different performance patterns.

Practitioners began to view these categories or clusters of stocks with similar performance as a "style" of investing. Some managers, for example, held themselves out as "growth stock managers" and others as "cyclical stock managers." Using size as a basis for categorizing style, some managers became "large-cap" (cap refers to market capitalization) investors while others became "small-cap" investors. Moreover, there was a commonly held belief that a manager could shift "styles" to enhance performance return.

Today, the notion of an equity investment style is widely accepted in the investment community. Next we look at the popular style types and the difficulties of classifying stocks according to style.

Types of Equity Styles

Stocks can be classified by style in many ways. The most common is in terms of one or more measures of "growth" and "value." Within a growth and value style, there is a substyle based on some measure of size. The most plain vanilla classification of styles is as follows: (1) large-cap value, (2) large-cap growth, (3) small-cap value, and (4) small-cap growth.

The motivation for the value/growth style categories can be explained in terms of the most common measure for classifying stocks as growth or value—the price-to-book ratio (P/B). Earnings growth will increase the book value per share. Assuming no change in the P/B, a stock's price will increase if earnings grow. An investor who is growth oriented is concerned with earnings growth and seeks those stocks from a universe of stocks that have higher relative earnings growth. The risks faced by a growth investor are that growth in earnings will not materialize and/or that the P/B will decline.

For a *value investor*, concern is with the price component rather than with the future earnings growth. Stocks would be classified as *value stocks* within a universe of stocks if they are viewed as cheap in terms of their P/B. By cheap, it is meant that the P/B is low relative to the universe of stocks or to a specified peer group. The expectation of the investor who follows a value style is that the P/B will return to some normal level and thus even with book value constant, the price will rise.

---

[11]James L. Farrell, Jr. "Homogeneous Stock Groupings: Implications for Portfolio Management," *Financial Analysts Journal* 31, no. 3 (May–June 1975): 50–62.

Within the value and growth categories, there are three basic substyles. In the value category, there are three basic substyles: low P/E, contrarian, and yield.[12] The low-P/E manager concentrates on companies trading at low prices to their earnings. The P/E can be defined as the current P/E, a normalized P/E, or a ratio using discounted future earnings. The contrarian investor looks at the book value of a company and focuses on those companies that are selling at a low valuation relative to book value. The companies that fall into this category are typically depressed cyclical stocks or companies that have little or no current earnings or dividend yields. The expectation is that the stock is on a cyclical rebound or that the company's earnings will turn around. Both of these occurrences are expected to lead to substantial price appreciation. The most conservative value investors are those that focus on companies with above-average dividend yields and are expected to be capable of increasing, or at least maintaining, those yields. This style is followed by a manager who is referred to as a yield investor.

A *growth investor* seeks companies with above-average growth prospects. In the growth style category, there tends to be two major substyles. The first is a growth investor who focuses on high-quality companies with consistent growth. An investor who follows this substyle is referred to as a "consistent growth investor." The second growth substyle is followed by an "earnings momentum growth investor." In contrast to a growth investor, an earnings momentum growth investor prefers companies with more volatile, above-average growth. Such an investor seeks to buy companies in expectation of an acceleration of earnings.

There are some investors who follow both a growth and value investing style but have a bias (or tilt) in favor of one of the styles. The bias is not sufficiently identifiable to categorize the investor as a solely growth or value manager. Most investors who fall into this hybrid style look for companies that are forecasted to have above-average growth potential selling at a reasonable value (commonly referred to as GARP or growth at a reasonable price).

Strategies Based on Mathematical Models

A number of active strategies are based on mathematical models of prices and returns.[13] Perhaps the most widely applied models are linear regressions

---

[12]See Jon A. Christopherson and C. Nola Williams, "Equity Style: What it is and Why it Matters," in *The Handbook of Equity Style Management*, 2nd ed., edited by T. Daniel Coggin, Frank J. Fabozzi, and Robert D. Arnott, pp. 1–20 (Hoboken, N.J.: John Wiley & Sons, 1997).

[13]For a review of these models, see Sergio M. Focardi, Petter N. Kolm, and Frank J. Fabozzi, "New Kids on the Block: Trends in Quantitative Finance and Their Impact on Investment Management," *Journal of Portfolio Management* 30, no. 5 (Fall 2004): 42–54.

on a number of predictors. This means that prices and returns are forecasted as weighted averages of a number of past variables that are considered to be predictors. Predictors might also include prices and returns themselves.

There are many varieties of these models. First, the choice of predictors typically reflects the economic views of the modeler. Given that linear regressions are relatively simple mathematical constructs and that a vast body of commercially available software exists, the choice of predictors is effectively the most critical element of this type of model.

Families of strategies that have gained popularity are *momentum strategies* and *reversal strategies*. Momentum and reversal strategies are based on the empirical fact that large ensembles of stock prices exhibit a pattern of persistence and reversals of returns. Persistence of returns means that those stocks that had the highest returns in a given period will likely continue to exhibit high returns in the future. Conversely, those stocks that had the lowest returns in a given period will likely continue to exhibit low returns in the future.

Reversals mean that those stocks that had the highest returns in given time windows will exhibit low returns in the future, while those stocks that had the lowest returns in given time windows will exhibit high returns in the future.

The important, and somewhat surprising, fact is that there seems to be stable patterns of both momentum and reversals in the stock market. Indeed, stock prices exhibit reversals over short time windows, from a few days to one month, momentum in medium time periods from six to 12 months, and reversals over long periods, from two to five years. It has been empirically found that these patterns have remained stable for several decades in the United States and Europe. Some studies, however, seem to conclude that as of the early 2000s, it has become more difficult in some markets to profit from patterns of momentum and reversals.

Financial Instruments and Concepts Introduced in this Chapter (in Order of Presentation)

Abnormal return
Market anomaly
Market pricing efficiency
Efficient market
Weak form of market efficiency
Semistrong form of market efficiency
Strong form of market efficiency
Style indexes
Asset pricing model
Risk-free return

Risk-free rate
Risk premium
Systematic risk factors
Nondiversifiable risk factors
Unsystematic risk factors
Diversifiable risk factors
Capital Asset Pricing Model
Beta
Multifactor models
Simply factor models

Tracking error
Active return
Ex post tracking error
Backward-looking tracking error
Forward-looking tracking error
Predicted tracking error
Ex ante tracking error
Alpha
Information ratio
Fundamental analysis
Technical analysis
Chartists
Dow Theory
Advance/decline line
Relative strength
Short interest ratio

Chaos theory
Nonlinear dynamic models
Earnings surprise
Market overreacton
Behavioral finance
Market-neutral long-short strategy
Insider activity
Small-firm effect
Low P/E effect
Neglected-firm effect
Calendar anomalies
Value investor
Growth investor
Momentum strate
Reversal strategies

CHAPTER 4

Bond Basics

In its simplest form, a bond is a financial obligation of an entity that promises to pay a specified sum of money at specified future dates. The payments are made up of two components: (1) the repayment of the amount of money borrowed and (2) interest. The entity that promises to make the payment is called the issuer of the security or the borrower. We provide the basic features of bonds and the risks associated with investing in this asset class in this chapter. In subsequent chapters we provide details on specific sectors of the bond market.

FEATURES OF BONDS

In the following sections, we describe the basic features of bonds.

Maturity

Unlike common stock, which has a perpetual life, bonds have a date on which they mature. The number of years over which the issuer has promised to meet the conditions of the obligation is referred to as the *term to maturity*. The *maturity* of a bond refers to the date that the debt will cease to exist, at which time the issuer will redeem the bond by paying the amount borrowed. The maturity date of a bond is always identified when describing a bond. For example, a description of a bond might state "due 12/15/2025."

The maturity of a bond is used for classifying two sectors of the market. Debt instruments with a maturity of one year or less are referred to as *money market instruments* and trade in the *money market*. What we typically refer to as the "bond market" includes debt instruments with a maturity greater than one year. The bond market is then categorized further based on the bond's term to maturity: short-term, intermediate-term, and long-term. The classification is somewhat arbitrary and varies amongst market participants. A common classification is that *short-term bonds* have a maturity of from one to five years, *intermediate-term bonds* have a maturity from five to 12 years, and *long-term bonds* have a maturity that exceeds 12 years.

The term to maturity of a bond is important for two reasons in addition to indicating the time period over which the bondholder can expect to receive interest payments and the number of years before the amount borrowed will be repaid in full. The first reason is that the yield on a bond depends on it. At any given point in time, the relationship between the yield and maturity of a bond indicates how bondholders are compensated for investing in bonds with different maturities. The second reason is that the price of a bond will fluctuate over its life as interest rates in the market change. The degree of price volatility of a bond is dependent on its maturity. More specifically, all other factors constant, the longer the maturity of a bond, the greater the price volatility resulting from a change in interest rates.

Par Value

The *par value* of a bond is the amount that the issuer agrees to repay the bondholder by the maturity date. This amount is also referred to as the *principal, face value, redemption value,* or *maturity value.*

Because bonds can have a different par value, the practice is to quote the price of a bond as a percentage of its par value. A value of 100 means 100% of par value. So, for example, if a bond has a par value of $1,000 and is selling for $850, this bond would be said to be selling at 85. If a bond with a par value of $100,000 is selling for $106,000, the bond is said to be selling for 106.

Coupon Rate

The annual interest rate that the issuer agrees to pay each year is called the *coupon rate.* The annual amount of the interest payment made to bondholders during the term of the bond is called the *coupon* and is determined by multiplying the coupon rate by the par value of the bond. For example, a bond with a 6% coupon rate and a par value of $1,000 will pay annual interest of $60.

When describing a bond issue, the coupon rate is indicated along with the maturity date. For example, the expression "5.5s of 2/15/2024" means a bond with a 5.5% coupon rate maturing on February 15, 2024.

For bonds issued in the United States, the usual practice is for the issuer to pay the coupon in two semiannual installments. Mortgage-backed securities and asset-backed securities, that we cover in later chapters, typically pay interest monthly. For bonds issued in some markets outside the United States, coupon payments are made only once per year.

In addition to indicating the coupon payments that the investor has contractually agreed to accept over the term of the bond, the coupon rate also affects the bond's price sensitivity to changes in market interest rates. All other factors constant, the higher the coupon rate, the less the price will change in response to a change in market interest rates.

There are bonds that have a coupon rate that increases over time according to a specified schedule. These bonds are called *step-up notes* because the coupon rate increases over time.

Not all bonds make periodic coupon payments. *Zero-coupon bonds,* as the name suggests, do not make periodic coupon payments. Instead, the holder of a zero-coupon bond realizes interest at the maturity date. The aggregate interest earned is the difference between the maturity value and the purchase price. For example, if an investor purchases a zero-coupon bond for 63, the aggregate interest at the maturity date is 37, the difference between the par value (100) and the price paid (63). The reason why certain investors like zero-coupon bonds is that they eliminate one of the risks that we will discuss later, reinvestment risk. The two disadvantages of a zero-coupon bond are that (1) the accrued interest earned each year is taxed despite the fact that no actual cash payment is made and (2) they exhibit greater price volatility when interest rates change than coupon-paying bonds with the same maturity.

There are issues whose coupon payment is deferred for a specified number of years. That is, there is no coupon payment for the deferred period and then at some specified date coupon payments are made until maturity. These securities are referred to as *deferred interest securities.*

A coupon-bearing security need not have a fixed interest rate over the term of the bond. There are bonds that have an interest rate that is variable. These bonds are referred to as *floating rate securities.* In fact, another way to classify bond markets is the *fixed rate bond market* and the *floating rate bond market.* Typically, the interest rate is adjusted on specific dates, referred to as the *coupon reset date.* There is a formula for the new coupon rate, referred to as the *coupon reset formula,* that has the following generic formula:

$$\text{Coupon reset formula} = \text{Reference rate} + \text{Quoted margin}$$

The quoted margin is the additional amount that the issuer agrees to pay above the reference rate. The most common reference rate is the London Interbank Offered Rate (LIBOR). LIBOR is the interest rate at which major international banks offer each other on Eurodollar certificates of deposit with given maturities. The maturities range from overnight to five years. Suppose that the reference rate is one-month LIBOR and the quoted margin is 80 basis points.[1] Then the coupon reset formula is

$$\text{1-month LIBOR} + 80 \text{ basis points}$$

So, if one-month LIBOR on the coupon reset date is 4.6%, the coupon rate is reset for that period at 5.4% (4.6% plus 80 basis points).

While the reference rate for most floating rate securities is an interest rate or an interest rate index, there are some issues where this is not the case. Instead, the reference rate can be some financial index such as the return on the Standard & Poor's 500 index or a nonfinancial index such as the price of a commodity or the consumer price index.

Typically, the coupon reset formula on floating rate securities is such that the coupon rate increases when the reference rate increases, and decreases when the reference rate decreases. There are issues whose coupon rate moves in the opposite direction from the change in the reference rate. Such issues are called *inverse floaters* or *reverse floaters*.

A floating rate security may have a restriction on the maximum coupon rate that will be paid at a reset date. The maximum coupon rate is called a *cap*. Because a cap restricts the coupon rate from increasing, a cap is an unattractive feature for the investor. In contrast, there could be a *floor* that is the minimum coupon rate specified and this is an attractive feature for the investor.

Accrued Interest

In the United States, coupon interest is typically paid semiannual for government bonds, corporate, agency, and municipal bonds. In some countries, interest is paid annually. For mortgage-backed and asset-backed securities, interest is usually paid monthly. The coupon interest payment is made to the bondholder of record. Thus, if an investor sells a bond between coupon payments and the buyer holds it until the next coupon payment, then the entire coupon interest earned for the period will be paid to the buyer of the bond since the buyer will be the holder of record.

The seller of the bond gives up the interest from the time of the last coupon payment to the time until the bond is sold. The amount of interest over this period that will be received by the buyer even though it was earned by the seller is called *accrued interest* In the United States and in many countries, the bond buyer must compensate the bond seller for the accrued interest. The amount that the buyer pays the seller is the agreed-upon price

---

[1] A basis point is equal to 0.0001 or 0.01%. Thus, 100 basis points are equal to 1%.

for the bond plus accrued interest. This amount is called the *full price*. The agreed-upon bond price without accrued interest is called the *clean price*.

A bond in which the buyer must pay the seller accrued interest is said to be trading *cum*-coupon. If the buyer must forgo the next coupon payment, the bond is said to be trading *ex*-coupon. In the United States, bonds are always traded *cum*-coupon. There are bond markets outside the United States where bonds are traded *ex*-coupon for a certain period before the coupon payment date.

There are exceptions to the rule that the bond buyer must pay the bond seller accrued interest. The most important exception is when the issuer has not fulfilled its promise to make the periodic payments. In this case, the issuer is said to be in default. In such instances, the bond's price is sold without accrued interest and is said to be traded *flat*.

Provisions for Paying Off Bonds

The issuer of a bond agrees to repay the principal by the stated maturity date. The issuer can agree to repay the entire amount borrowed in one lump sum payment at the maturity date. That is, the issuer is not required to make any principal repayments prior to the maturity date. Such bonds are said to have a *bullet maturity*.

Bonds backed by pools of loans (mortgage-backed securities and asset-backed securities) often have a schedule of principal repayments. Such bonds are said to be *amortizing securities*. For many loans, the payments are structured so that when the last loan payment is made, the entire amount owed is fully paid off. Another example of an amortizing feature is a bond that has a *sinking fund provision*. As explained next, this provision for repayment of a bond may be designed to liquidate all of an issue by the maturity date, or it may be arranged to repay only a part of the total by the maturity date.

A bond issue may have a call provision granting the issuer an option to retire all or part of the issue prior to the stated maturity date. Some issues specify that the issuer must retire a predetermined amount of the issue periodically. These provisions are discussed next.

Call and Refunding Provisions

An issuer generally wants the right to retire a bond issue prior to the stated maturity date because it recognizes that at some time in the future the general level of interest rates may fall sufficiently below the issue's coupon rate so that redeeming the issue and replacing it with another issue with a lower coupon rate would be economically beneficial. This right is a disadvantage to the bondholder since proceeds received must be reinvested at a lower interest rate. As a result, an issuer who wants to include this right as part of a bond offering must compensate the bondholder when the issue is sold by offering a higher coupon rate, or equivalently, accepting a lower price than if the right is not included.

The right of the issuer to retire the issue prior to the stated maturity date is referred to as a *call provision* and is more popularly referred to as a *call option*. A bond with this provision is referred to as a *callable bond*. If an issuer exercises this right, the issuer is said to "call the bond." The price that the issuer must pay to retire the issue is referred to as the *call price*. There may not be a single call price but, instead, a *call schedule* that sets forth a call price based on when the issuer may exercise the option to call the bond.

When a bond is issued, the issuer may be restricted from calling the bond for a number of years. In such situations, the bond is said to have a *deferred call*. The date at which the bond may first be called is referred to as the *first call date*. However, not all issues have a deferred call. If a bond issue does not have any protection against early call, then it is said to be a *currently callable issue*. But most new bond issues, even if currently callable, usually have some restrictions against certain types of early redemption. The most common restriction is that prohibiting the refunding of the bonds for a certain number of years. *Refunding* a bond issue means redeeming bonds with funds obtained through the sale of a new bond issue.

Call protection is much more absolute than refunding protection. While there may be certain exceptions to absolute or complete call protection in some cases, it still provides greater assurance against premature and unwanted redemption than does refunding protection. Refunding prohibition merely prevents redemption only from certain sources of funds, namely the proceeds of other debt issues sold at a lower cost of money. The bondholder is only protected if interest rates decline, and the borrower can obtain lower-cost money to pay off the debt.

Bonds can be called in whole (the entire issue) or in part (only a portion). When less than the entire issue is called, the specific bonds to be called are selected randomly or on a pro rata basis. Generally, the call schedule is such that the call price at the first call date is a premium over the par value and scaled down to the par value over time. The date at which the issue is first callable at par value is referred to as the *first par call date*. However, not all issues have a call schedule in which the call price starts out as a premium over par. There are issues where the call price at the first call date and subsequent call dates is par value. In such cases, the first call date is the same as the first par call date.

The call prices in a call schedule are referred to as the *regular* or *general redemption prices*. There are also *special redemption prices* for debt redeemed through the sinking fund and through other provisions, and the proceeds from the confiscation of property through the right of eminent domain. The special redemption price is usually par value.

Prepayments

Amortizing securities backed by loans have a schedule of principal repayments. However, individual borrowers typically have the option to pay off all or part of their loan prior to the scheduled principal repayment date. Any principal repayment prior to the scheduled date is called a *prepayment*. The right of borrowers to prepay is called the *prepayment option*. Basically, the prepayment option is the same as a call option. However, unlike a call option, there may not be a call price that depends on when the borrower pays off the issue. Typically, the price at which a loan is prepaid is at par value.

Sinking Fund Provision

A *sinking fund provision* included in a bond indenture requires the issuer to retire a specified portion of an issue each year. Usually, the periodic payments required for sinking fund purposes will be the same for each period. There are bond issues that permit variable periodic payments, where payments change according to certain prescribed conditions set forth in the bond's indenture. The alleged purpose of the sinking fund provision is to reduce credit risk. This kind of provision for bond principal repayment may be designed to liquidate all of a bond issue by the maturity date, or it may be arranged to pay only a part of the total by the end of the term. If only a part is paid, the remainder is referred to as a *balloon maturity*. Many indentures include a provision that grants the issuer the option to retire more than the amount stipulated for the scheduled sinking fund retirement. This is referred to as an *accelerated sinking fund provision*.

To satisfy the sinking fund requirement, an issuer is typically granted one of following choices: (1) make a cash payment of the face amount of the bonds to be retired to the trustee, who then calls the bonds for redemption using a lottery; or (2) deliver to the trustee bonds purchased in the open market that have a total par value equal to the amount that must be retired. If the bonds are retired using the first method, interest payments stop at the redemption date.

Usually the sinking fund call price is the par value if the bonds were originally sold at par. When issued at a price in excess of par, the call price generally starts at the issuance price and scales down to par as the issue approaches maturity.

There is a difference between the amortizing feature for a bond with a sinking fund provision, and the regularly scheduled principal repayment for a mortgage-backed and an asset-backed security. The owner of a mortgage-backed security and an asset-backed security knows that assuming no default that there will be principal repayments. In contrast, the owner of a bond with a sinking fund provision is not assured that his or her particular holding will be called to satisfy the sinking fund requirement.

Options Granted to Bondholders

A provision in the indenture could grant the bondholder and the issuer an option to take some action against the other party. The most common type of option embedded in a bond is a call option discussed already. This option is granted to the issuer. There are two options that can be granted to the bondholder: the right to put the issue and the right to convert the issue to the issuer's common stock.

A bond with a put provision grants the bondholder the right to sell the bond (that is, force the issuer to redeem the bond) at a specified price on designated dates. A bond with this provision is referred to as a *putable bond*. The specified price is called the *put price*. Typically, a bond is putable at par value if it is issued at or close to par value. For a zero-coupon bond, the put price is below par. The advantage of the put provision to the bondholder is that if after the issue date market rates rise above the issue's coupon rate, the bondholder can force the issuer to redeem the bond at the put price and then reinvest the proceeds at the prevailing higher rate.

A *convertible bond* is an issue giving the bondholder the right to exchange the bond for a specified number of shares of the issuer's common stock. Such a feature allows the bondholder to take advantage of favorable movements in the price of the issuer's common stock. An *exchangeable bond* allows the bondholder to exchange the issue for a specified number of shares of common stock of a corporation different from the issuer of the bond. Convertible bonds are described in Chapter 7.

Currency Denomination

The payments that the issuer makes to the bondholder can be in any currency. For bonds issued in the United States, the issuer typically makes both coupon payments and principal repayments in U.S. dollars. However, there is nothing that forces the issuer to make payments in U.S. dollars. The indenture can specify that the issuer may make payments in some other specified currency. For example, payments may be made in euros or yen.

An issue in which payments to bondholders are in U.S. dollars is called a *dollar-denominated issue*. A *nondollar-denominated issue* is one in which payments are not denominated in U.S. dollars. There are some issues whose coupon payments are in one currency and whose principal payment is in another currency. An issue with this characteristic is called a *dual-currency issue*.

Some issues allow either the issuer or the bondholder the right to select the currency in which a payment will be paid. This option effectively gives the party with the right to choose the currency the opportunity to benefit from a favorable exchange rate movement.

YIELD MEASURES AND THEIR LIMITATIONS

Frequently, investors assess the relative value of a bond by some yield measure. There are various yield measures that are quoted in the bond market. These measures are based on assumptions that limit their use to gauge relative value. In this section, the various yield measures and their limitations are explained.

Sources of Return

When an investor purchases a fixed income security, he or she can expect to receive a dollar return from one or more of the following sources:[2]

1. The coupon interest payments made by the issuer.
2. Any capital gain (or capital loss minus a negative dollar return) when the security matures, is called, or is sold.
3. Income from reinvestment of the interim cash flows.

Any yield measure that purports to measure the potential return from a bond should consider all three sources of return described above.

Coupon Interest Payments

The most obvious source of return is the periodic coupon interest payments. For zero-coupon instruments, the return from this source is zero, although

---

[2]The classification of the sources of return in our discussion in this chapter is different from the treatment under the U.S. tax code. For example, for zero-coupon instruments purchased at issuance, the tax code treats the difference between the par value and the purchase price as interest income. More specifically, the discount from par value is called an *original interest discount*. In our discussion in this chapter, it would be classified as a capital gain. As a second example, the tax code has rules for the treatment of what it defines as a bond purchased below par value because of changes in market interest rates. The difference between the par value and market price is called a *market discount* and is treated as interest income under the tax code. In our discussion we would define the difference as a capital gain.

the investor is effectively receiving interest by purchasing a security below its par value and realizing interest at the maturity date when the investor receives the par value.

Capital Gain or Loss

When the proceeds received when a bond matures, is called, or is sold are greater than the purchase price, a capital gain results. For a bond held to maturity, there will be a capital gain if the bond is purchased below its par value. A bond purchased below its par value is said to be purchased at a *discount*. For example, a bond purchased for $94.17 with a par value of $100 will generate a capital gain of $5.83 ($100 − $94.17) if held to maturity. For a callable bond, a capital gain results if the price at which the bond is called (i.e., the call price) is greater than the purchase price. For example, if the bond in our previous example is callable and subsequently called at $100.5, a capital gain of $6.33 ($100.5 − $94.17) will be realized. If the same bond is sold prior to its maturity or before it is called, a capital gain will result if the proceeds exceed the purchase price. So, if our hypothetical bond is sold prior to the maturity date for $103, the capital gain would be $8.83 ($103 − $94.17).

A capital loss is generated when the proceeds received when a bond matures, is called, or is sold are less then the purchase price. For a bond held to maturity, there will be a capital loss if the bond is purchased for more than its par value. A bond purchased for more than its par value is said to be purchased at a premium. For example, a bond purchased for $102.5 with a par value of $100 will generate a capital loss of $2.5 ($102.5 − $100) if held to maturity. For a callable bond, a capital loss results if the price at which the bond is called is less than the purchase price. For example, if the bond in our previous example is callable and subsequently called at $100.5, a capital loss of $2 ($102.5 − $100.5) will be realized. If the same bond is sold prior to its maturity or before it is called, a capital loss will result if the sale price is less than the purchase price. So, if our hypothetical bond is sold prior to the maturity date for $98.5, the capital loss would be $4 ($102.5 − $98.5).

Reinvestment Income

With the exception of zero-coupon instruments, fixed income securities make periodic payments of interest that can be reinvested until the security is removed from the portfolio. There are also instruments in which there are periodic principal repayments that can be reinvested until the security is removed from the portfolio. Repayment of principal prior to the maturity date occurs for amortizing instruments such as mortgage-backed securities and asset-backed securities. The interest earned from reinvesting the interim cash flows (interest and/or principal payments) until the security is removed from the portfolio is called *reinvestment income.*

Yield Measures

There are several yield measures cited in the bond market. These include current yield, yield to maturity, yield to call, yield to put, yield to worst, and cash flow yield.

Current Yield

The current yield relates the annual dollar coupon interest to the market price. The formula for the current yield is:

$$\text{Current yield} = \frac{\text{Annual dollar coupon interest}}{\text{Price}}$$

For example, the current yield for a 7% 8-year bond whose price is $94.17 is 7.43% as shown below:

Annual dollar coupon interest = $0.07 \times \$100 = \$7$

Price = $94.17

$$\text{Current yield} = \frac{\$7}{\$94.17} = 0.0743 \text{ or } 7.43\%$$

The current yield will be greater than the coupon rate when the bond sells at a discount; the reverse is true for a bond selling at a premium. For a bond selling at par, the current yield will be equal to the coupon rate.

The drawback of the current yield is that it considers only the coupon interest and no other source that will impact an investor's return. No consideration is given to the capital gain that the investor will realize when a bond is purchased at a discount and held to maturity; nor is there any recognition of the capital loss that the investor will realize if a bond purchased at a premium is held to maturity.

Yield to Maturity

The most popular measure of yield in the bond market is the yield to maturity. The *yield to maturity* is the interest rate that will make the present value of the cash flows from a bond equal to its market price plus accrued interest. Calculation of the yield to maturity of a bond is the reverse process of calculating the price of a bond. To find the price of a bond we determine the cash flows and the required yield, then we calculate the present value of the cash flows to obtain the price. To find the yield to maturity, we first determine the cash flows. Then we search by trial and error for the interest rate that will make the present value of the cash flows equal to the market price plus accrued interest. Software and financial calculators are available for computing a bond's yield to maturity.

The following relationships between the price of a bond, coupon rate, current yield, and yield to maturity hold:

Bond selling at	Relationship
Par	Coupon rate = Current yield = Yield to maturity
Discount	Coupon rate < Current yield < Yield to maturity
Premium	Coupon rate > Current yield > Yield to maturity

The yield to maturity considers not only the coupon income but also any capital gain or loss that the investor will realize by holding the bond to maturity. The yield to maturity also considers the timing of the cash flows. It does consider reinvestment income; however, it assumes that the coupon payments can be reinvested at an interest rate equal to the yield to maturity. So, if the yield to maturity for a bond is 8%, for example, to earn that yield the coupon payments must be reinvested at an interest rate equal to 8%.

Thus, an investor will only realize the yield to maturity that is stated at the time of purchase if (1) the coupon payments can be reinvested at the yield to maturity and (2) the bond is held to maturity. With respect to the first assumption, the risk that an investor faces is that future interest rates will be less than the yield to maturity at the time the bond is purchased. This risk is referred to as reinvestment risk. If the bond is not held to maturity, it may have to be sold for less than its purchase price, resulting in a return that is less than the yield to maturity. The risk that a bond will have to be sold at a loss is referred to as interest rate risk.

There are two characteristics of a bond that determine the degree of reinvestment risk. First, for a given yield to maturity and a given coupon rate, the longer the maturity the more the bond's total dollar return is dependent on reinvestment income to realize the yield to maturity at the time of purchase (i.e., the greater the reinvestment risk). The implication is that the yield to maturity measure for long-term coupon bonds tells little about the potential yield that an investor may realize if the bond is held to maturity. For long-term bonds, in high interest rate environments the reinvestment income component may be as high as 70% of the bond's potential total dollar return.

The second characteristic that determines the degree of reinvestment risk is the coupon rate. For a given maturity and a given yield to maturity, the higher the coupon rate, the more dependent the bond's total dollar return will be on the reinvestment of the coupon payments in order to produce the yield to maturity at the time of purchase. This means that holding maturity and yield to maturity constant, premium bonds will be more dependent on reinvestment income than bonds selling at par. In contrast, discount bonds will be less dependent on reinvestment income than bonds selling at par. For zero-coupons bonds, none of the bond's total dollar return is dependent on reinvestment income. So, a zero-coupon bond has no reinvestment risk if held to maturity.

Yield to Call

When a bond is callable, the practice has been to calculate a *yield to call* as well as a yield to maturity. A callable bond may have a call schedule. The yield to call assumes that the issuer will call the bond at some assumed call date and the call price is then the call price specified in the call schedule.

Typically, investors calculate a *yield to first call* or *yield to next call*, a *yield to first par call*, and *yield to refunding*. The yield to first call is computed for an issue that is not currently callable, while the yield to next call is computed for an issue that is currently callable.

The procedure for calculating any yield to call measure is the same as for any yield calculation: Determine the interest rate that will make the present value of the expected cash flows equal to the price plus accrued interest. In the case of yield to first call, the expected cash flows are the coupon payments to the first call date and the call price. For the yield to first par call, the expected cash flows are the coupon payments to the first date at which the issuer can call the bond at par and the par value. For the yield to refunding, the expected cash flows are the coupon payments to the first refunding date and the call price at the first refunding date.

Let's take a closer look at the yield to call as a measure of a bond's potential return. The yield to call does consider all three sources of potential return from owning a bond. However, as in the case of the yield to maturity, it assumes that all cash flows can be reinvested at the yield to call until the assumed call date. As we just explained, this assumption may be inappropriate. Moreover, the yield to call assumes that (1) the investor will hold the bond to the assumed call date and (2) the issuer will call the bond on that date.

These assumptions underlying the yield to call are often unrealistic. They do not take into account how an investor will reinvest the proceeds if the issue is called. For example, consider two bonds, M and N. Suppose that the yield to maturity for bond M, a 5-year noncallable bond, is 7.5%, while for bond N the yield to call assuming the bond will be called in three years is 7.8%. Which bond is better for an investor with a 5-year investment horizon? It's not possible to tell for the yields cited. If the investor intends to hold the bond for five years and the issuer calls bond N after three years, the total dollars that will be available at the end of five years will depend on the interest rate that can be earned from investing funds from the call date to the end of the investment horizon.

Yield to Put

When a bond is putable, the yield to the first put date is calculated. The *yield to put* is the interest rate that will make the present value of the cash flows to the first put date equal to the price plus accrued interest. As with all yield measures (except the current yield), yield to put assumes that any interim coupon payments can be reinvested at the yield calculated. Moreover, the yield to put assumes that the bond will be put on the first put date.

Yield to Worst

A yield can be calculated for every possible call date and put date. In addition, a yield to maturity can be calculated. The lowest of all these possible yields is called the *yield to worst*. For example, suppose that there are only four possible call dates for a callable bond and that a yield to call assuming each possible call date is 6%, 6.2%, 5.8%, and 5.7%, and that the yield to maturity is 7.5%. Then the yield to worst is the minimum of these values, 5.7% in our example.

The yield to worst measure holds little meaning as a measure of potential return.

Cash Flow Yield

As we explain in later chapters in this book, mortgage-backed securities and asset-backed securities are backed by a pool of loans. The cash flows for these securities include principal repayment as well as interest. The complication that arises is that the individual borrowers whose loans make up the pool typically can prepay their loan in whole or in part prior to the scheduled principal repayment date. Because of prepayment, in order to project the cash flows it is necessary to make an assumption about the rate at which prepayments will occur. This rate is called the *prepayment rate* or *prepayment speed*.

Given the cash flows based on the assumed prepayment rate, a yield can be calculated. The yield is the interest rate that will make the present value of the projected cash flows equal to the price plus accrued interest. A yield calculated is commonly referred to as a *cash flow yield*.

As we have noted, the yield to maturity has two shortcomings as a measure of a bond's potential return: (1) It is assumed that the coupon payments can be reinvested at a rate equal to the yield to maturity, and (2) it is assumed that the bond is held to maturity. These shortcomings are equally present in application of the cash flow yield measure: (1) The projected cash flows are assumed to be reinvested at the cash flow yield, and (2) the mortgage-backed or asset-backed security is assumed to be held until the final payoff of all the loans based on some prepayment assumption. The importance of reinvestment risk—the risk that the cash flows will be reinvested at a rate less than the cash flow yield—is particularly important for mortgage-backed and asset-backed securities since payments are typically monthly and include principal repayments (scheduled and prepayments), as well as interest. Moreover, the cash flow yield is dependent on realization of the projected cash flows according to some prepayment rate. If actual prepayments differ significantly from the prepayment rate assumed, the cash flow yield will not be realized.

INTEREST RATE RISK

The price of a typical bond will change in the opposite direction from a change in interest rates. That is, when interest rates rise, a bond's price will fall; when interest rates fall, a bond's price will rise. For example, consider a 6%, 20-year bond. If the yield investors require to buy this bond is 6%, the price of this bond would be $100. However, if the required yield increases to 6.5%, the price of this bond would decline to $94.45. Thus, for a 50 basis point increase in yield, the bond's price declines by 5.55%. If, instead, the yield declines from 6% to 5.5%, the bond's price will rise by 6.02% to $106.02.

The reason for this inverse relationship between price and changes in interest rates or changes in market yields is as follows. Suppose investor X purchases our hypothetical 6% coupon 20-year bond at par value ($100). The yield for this bond is 6%. Suppose that immediately after the purchase of this bond two things happen. First, market interest rates rise to 6.50% so that if an investor wants to buy a similar 20-year bond, a 6.50% coupon rate would have to be paid by the bond issuer in order to offer the bond at par value. Second, suppose investor X wants to sell the bond. In attempting to sell the bond, investor X would not find an investor who would be willing to pay par value for a bond with a coupon rate of 6%. The reason is that any investor who wanted to purchase this bond could obtain a similar

20-year bond with a coupon rate 50 basis points higher, 6.5%. What can the investor do? The investor cannot force the issuer to change the coupon rate to 6.5%. Nor can the investor force the issuer to shorten the maturity of the bond to a point where a new investor would be willing to accept a 6% coupon rate. The only thing that the investor can do is adjust the price of the bond so that at the new price the buyer would realize a yield of 6.5%. This means that the price would have to be adjusted down to a price below par value. The new price must be $94.45. While we assumed in our illustration an initial price of par value, the principle holds for any purchase price. Regardless of the price that an investor pays for a bond, an increase in market interest rates will result in a decline in a bond's price.

Suppose instead of a rise in market interest rates to 6.5%, they decline to 5.5%. Investors would be more than happy to purchase the 6% coupon, 20-year bond for par value. However, investor X realizes that the market is only offering investors the opportunity to buy a similar bond at par value with a coupon rate of 5.5%. Consequently, investor X will increase the price of the bond until it offers a yield of 5.5%. That price is $106.02.

Since the price of a bond fluctuates with market interest rates, the risk that an investor faces is that the price of a bond held in a portfolio will decline if market interest rates rise. This risk is referred to as *interest rate risk* and is a major risk faced by investors in the bond market.

Bond Features that Affect Interest Rate Risk

The degree of sensitivity of a bond's price to changes in market interest rates depends on various characteristics of the issue, such as maturity and coupon rate. Consider first maturity. All other factors constant, the longer the maturity, the greater the bond's price sensitivity to changes in interest rates. For example, we know that for a 6%, 20-year bond selling to yield 6%, a rise in the yield required by investors to 6.5% will cause the bond's price to decline from $100 to $94.45, a 5.55% price decline. For a 6%, five-year bond selling to yield 6%, the price is $100. A rise in the yield required by investors from 6% to 6.5% would decrease the price to $97.89. The decline in the bond's price is only 2.11%.

Now let's turn to the coupon rate. A property of a bond is that all other factors constant, the lower the coupon rate, the greater the bond's price sensitivity to changes in interest rates. For example, consider a 9%, 20-year bond selling to yield 6%. The price of this bond would be $112.80. If the yield required by investors increases by 50 basis points to 6.5%, the price of this bond would fall by 2.01% to $110.53. This decline is less than the 5.55% decline for the 6%, 20-year bond selling to yield 6%. An implication is that zero-coupon bonds have greater price sensitivity to interest rate changes than same-maturity bonds bearing a coupon rate and trading at the same yield.

Because of default risk (discussed later), different bonds trade at different yields, even if they have the same coupon rate and maturity. How, then, holding other factors constant, does the level of interest rates affect a bond's price sensitivity to changes in interest rates? As it turns out, the higher the level of interest rates that a bond trades, the lower the price sensitivity.

To see this, we can compare a 6%, 20-year bond initially selling at a yield of 6%, and a 6%, 20-year bond initially selling at a yield of 10%. The former is initially at a price of $100, and the latter carries a price of $65.68. Now, if the yield on both bonds increases by 100 basis points, the first bond trades down by $10.68 (10.68% decline). After the assumed increase in yield, the second bond will trade at a price of $59.88, for a price decline of only $5.80 (or 8.83%). Thus, we see that the bond that trades at a lower yield is more volatile in both percentage price change and absolute price change, as long as the other bond characteristics are the same. An implication of this is that, for a given change in interest rates, price sensitivity is lower when the level of interest rates in the market is high, and price sensitivity is higher when the level of interest rates is low.

We can summarize these three characteristics that affect the bond's price sensitivity to changes in market interest rates as follows:

Characteristic 1. For a given maturity and initial yield, the lower the coupon rate the greater the bond's price sensitivity to changes in market interest rates.

Characteristic 2. For a given coupon rate and initial yield, the longer the maturity of a bond the greater the bond's price sensitivity to changes in market interest rates.

Characteristic 3. For a given coupon rate and maturity, the lower the level of interest rates the greater the bond's price sensitivity to changes in market interest rates.

A bond's price sensitivity will also depend on any options embedded in the issue. This is explained below when we discuss call risk.

Measuring Interest Rate Risk

Investors are interested in knowing the price sensitivity of a bond to changes in market interest rates. The measure commonly used is duration. *Duration* gives the approximate percentage price change for a 100 basis point change in interest rates.

For example, the duration for the 6% coupon, five-year bond trading at par to yield 6% is 4.27. Thus, the price of this bond will change by approximately 4.27% if interest rates change by 100 basis points. For a 50 basis point change, this bond's price will change by approximately 2.14% (4.27% divided by 2). As previously explained, this bond's price would actually change by 2.11%. Thus, duration does a good job of telling an investor the approximate percentage price change attributable to interest rate changes.

It turns out that the approximation is good the smaller the change in interest rates. The approximation is not as good for a large change in interest rates.[3] Nevertheless, it is a good approximation that the investor can use to get a feel for the exposure of a bond or even a bond a portfolio to a change in interest rates. For example, if a bond portfolio has a duration of 5, this means that for a 100 basis point change in interest rates, the value of this portfolio will change by approximately 5%.

As another example, there are mutual funds (the subject of Chapter 12) that indicate in their prospectus that the portfolio will have a duration of between 1 and 3. Using the upper duration value, this means that for a 100 basis point change in interest rates, the fund shares will change by approximately 3%. In the early 1990s, there were so-called limited duration funds in which the fund's manager thought that the fund had a limited duration but that was far from the portfolio's actual duration. An investor in such funds could have realized this (although it took a long time for regulators to do so) by understanding this simple duration concept. Such funds appreciated in the double digit range when interest rates declined by 100 basis points. Eventually, only when interest rates increased and the value of the fund shares declined dramatically did investors begin to appreciate the importance of understanding the concept of duration.

CALL AND PREPAYMENT RISK

As explained earlier, a bond may include a provision that allows the issuer to retire or call all or part of the issue before the maturity date. From the investor's perspective, the following are the disadvantages to call provisions:

- The cash flow pattern of a callable bond is not known with certainty.
- Because the issuer will call the bonds when interest rates have dropped, the investor is exposed to *reinvestment risk*. This is the risk that the investor will have to reinvest the proceeds when the bond is called at a lower interest rate.

---

[3]For explanation of why, see Frank J. Fabozzi, *Bond Markets, Analysis, and Strategies* (Upper Saddle River, N.J.: Prentice Hall, 2009).

■ The price appreciation potential of a bond when market interest rates decline will be reduced because a callable bond's price may not rise much above the price at which the issuer is entitled to call the bond. This property of a callable bond is referred to as *price compression*.

Because of these attributes, a callable bond is said to expose the investor to *call risk*. This risk applies to even a simple debt-type instrument such as an FDIC-insured bank certificate of deposit (CD). For example, on 6/26/2008, MidFirst Bank of Oklahoma issued a callable CD with a coupon interest rate of 5% maturing on 12/26/2013. On 6/26/2009 (one year after issuance), the CD was called at par value. At the time it was called, CDs maturing on 12/26/2013 (i.e., 4.5-year CDs) were offering an interest rate of 2.8%. Hence, the proceeds received from the called CD had to be reinvested at a lower interest rate if the target maturity date for the original investment was 12/26/2013. This is not to say that the investor in this CD was unfairly disadvantaged at the time the callable CD was purchased. The investor received compensation for call risk because a CD maturing around 12/26/2013 offered on 6/26/2009 a rate of about 40 basis points less.

The same disadvantages apply to bonds that can prepay such as mortgage-backed securities and certain asset-backed securities. In this case, call risk is referred to as *prepayment risk*.

CREDIT RISK

While investors commonly refer to *credit risk* as if it is one dimensional, there are actually three forms of this risk. *Default risk* is the risk that the issuer will fail to satisfy the terms of the obligation with respect to the timely payment of interest and repayment of the amount borrowed. To gauge default risk, investors rely on analysis performed by nationally recognized statistical rating organizations (i.e., more popularly known as rating agencies) that perform credit analysis of bond issues and issuers and express their conclusions in the form of a *credit rating*. *Credit spread risk* is the loss or underperformance of an issue or issues due to an increase in the credit spread. *Downgrade risk* is the risk that an issue or issuer will be downgraded, resulting in an increase in the credit spread.

Default Risk

We begin our discussion of default risk with an explanation of credit ratings and the factors used by rating agencies in assigning a credit rating. We then discuss the rights of creditors in a bankruptcy in the United States and why the actual outcome of a bankruptcy typically differs from the theoretical credit protection afforded under the bankruptcy laws. Finally, we look at corporate bond *default rates* and *recovery rates* in the United States.

Credit Ratings

The prospectus or offer document for an issue provides investors with information about the issuer so that credit analysis can be performed on the issuer before the bonds are placed. Credit assessments take time, however, and also require the specialist skills of credit analysts. Large institutional investors do in fact employ such specialists to carry out credit analysis; however, often it is too costly and time consuming to assess every issuer in every debt market. Therefore, investors often rely on credit ratings.

A credit rating is a formal opinion given by a rating agency of the default risk faced by investing in a particular issue of debt securities. For long-term debt obligations, a credit rating is a forward-looking assessment of the probability of default and the relative magnitude of the loss should a default occur. For short-term debt obligations, a credit rating is a forward-looking assessment of the probability of default.

The three major rating agencies include Moody's Investors Service, Standard & Poor's Corporation (S&P), and Fitch Ratings. On receipt of a formal request, the rating agencies will carry out a rating exercise on a specific debt issue. The request for a rating comes from the organization planning the issuance of bonds. Although ratings are provided for the benefit of investors, the issuer must bear the cost. However, it is in the issuer's interest to request a rating as it raises the profile of the bonds; moreover, investors may refuse to buy a bond that is not accompanied by a recognized rating.

Although the rating exercise involves credit analysis of the issuer, the rating is applied to a specific debt issue. This means that, in theory, the credit rating is applied not to an organization itself, but to specific debt securities that the organization has issued or is planning to issue. In practice, it is common for the market to refer to the creditworthiness of organizations themselves in terms of the rating of their debt. A highly rated company, for example, may be referred to as a "triple-A rated" company, although it is the company's debt issues that are rated as triple A.

The rating systems of the three rating agencies use similar symbols. Separate categories are used by each rating agency for short-term debt (with original maturity of 12 months or less) and long-term debt (over one year original maturity). Exhibit 4.1 shows the long-term debt ratings. In all rating systems the term "high grade" means low credit risk or, conversely, high probability of future payments. The highest-grade bonds are designated by Moody's by the letters Aaa, and by the others as AAA. The next highest

EXHIBIT 4.1   Summary of Long-Term Bond Rating Systems and Symbols

Fitch	Moody's	S&P	Summary Description
Investment Grade			
AAA	Aaa	AAA	Gilt edged, prime, maximum safety, lowest risk, and when sovereign borrower considered "default-free"
AA+	Aa1	AA+	
AA	Aa2	AA	High grade, high credit quality
AA–	Aa3	AA–	
A+	A1	A+	
A	A2	A	Upper-medium grade
A–	A3	A–	
BBB+	Baa1	BBB+	
BBB	Baa2	BBB	Lower-medium grade
BBB–	Baa3	BBB–	
Speculative Grade			
BB+	Ba1	BB+	
BB	Ba2	BB	Low grade; speculative
BB–	Ba3	BB–	
B+	B1		
B	B	B	Highly speculative
B–	B3		
Predominantly Speculative, Substantial Risk, or in Default			
CCC+		CCC+	
CCC	Caa	CCC	Substantial risk, in poor standing
CC	Ca	CC	May be in default, very speculative
C	C	C	Extremely speculative
		CI	Income bonds—no interest being paid
DDD			
DD			Default
D		D	

grade is designated as Aa by Moody's, and by the others as AA; for the third grade, all rating agencies use A. The next three grades are Baa (Moody's) or BBB, Ba (Moody's) or BB, and B, respectively. There are also C grades. S&P and Fitch use plus and minus signs to provide a narrower credit quality breakdown within each class. Moody's uses 1, 2, or 3 for the same purpose. Bonds rated triple A (AAA or Aaa) are said to be "prime"; double A (AA or Aa) are of "high quality"; single A issues are called "upper medium grade"; and triple B are "medium grade." Lower-rated bonds are said to have "speculative" elements or be "distinctly speculative."

Bond issues that are assigned a rating in the top four categories are referred to as *investment-grade bonds*. Bond issues that carry a rating below the top four categories are referred to as *noninvestment-grade bonds* or more popularly as *high-yield bonds* or *junk bonds*. Thus, the bond market can be divided into two sectors: the *investment-grade sector* and the *noninvestment-grade sector*. *Distressed debt* is a subcategory of noninvestment-grade bonds. These bonds may be in bankruptcy proceedings, may be in default of coupon payments, or may be in some other form of distress. We discussed investing in distressed bonds in Chapter 21.

Factors Considered by Rating Agencies

In conducting its examination of corporate bond issues, the rating agencies consider the "four Cs of credit": character, capacity, collateral, and covenants. The meaning of each is as follows:

- *Character* includes the ethical reputation as well as the business qualifications and operating record of the board of directors, management, and executives responsible for the use of the borrowed funds and repayment of those funds.
- *Capacity* is the ability of an issuer to repay its obligations.
- *Collateral* is looked at not only in the traditional sense of assets pledged to secure the debt, but also to the quality and value of those unpledged assets controlled by the issuer. In both senses, the collateral is capable of supplying additional aid, comfort, and support to the debt and the debt holder. Assets form the basis for the generation of cash flow, which services the debt in good times as well as bad.
- *Covenants* set forth restrictions on how management operates the company and conducts its financial affairs. Covenants can restrict management's discretion. A default or violation of any covenant may provide a meaningful early warning alarm enabling investors to take positive and corrective action before the situation deteriorates further. Covenants have value as they play an important part in minimizing

risk to creditors. They help prevent the unconscionable transfer of wealth from debt holders to equity holders.

Character analysis involves the analysis of the quality of management. Moody's, for example, assesses management quality by looking at the business strategies and policies formulated by management. Following are factors that are considered: (1) strategic direction, (2) financial philosophy, (3) conservatism, (4) track record, (5) succession planning, and (6) control systems.[4] In assessing the ability of an issuer to pay, an analysis of the financial statements is undertaken. In addition to management quality, Moody's, for example, looks at (1) industry trends, (2) the regulatory environment, (3) basic operating and competitive position, (4) financial position and sources of liquidity, (5) company structure (including structural subordination and priority of claim), (6) parent company support agreements, and (7) special event risk.

Covenants deal with limitations and restrictions on the borrower's activities. *Affirmative covenants* call on the debtor to make promises to do certain things. *Negative covenants* are those that require the borrower not to take certain actions. Negative covenants are usually negotiated between the borrower and the lender or their agents. Borrowers want the least restrictive loan agreement available, while lenders should want the most restrictive that is consistent with sound business practices. But lenders should not try to restrain borrowers from accepted business activities and conduct. A borrower might be willing to include additional restrictions (up to a point) if it can get a lower interest rate on the debt obligation. When borrowers seek to weaken restrictions in their favor, they are often willing to pay more interest or give other consideration.

Bankruptcy and Creditor Rights in the United States

The holder of a corporate debt instrument has priority over the equity owners in the case of bankruptcy. There are creditors who have priority over other creditors. Here, we will provide an overview of the bankruptcy process and then look at what actually happens to creditors in bankruptcies. More details about the bankruptcy process is explained in Chapter 21 where we cover investing in distressed bond.

There is a federal law governing bankruptcies in the United States and this law is amended periodically. One purpose of the bankruptcy law is to set forth the rules for a corporation to be either liquidated or reorganized. The *liquidation* of a corporation means that all the assets will be distributed

---

[4] "Industrial Company Rating Methodology," *Global Credit Research*, Moody's Investor Service, July 1998.

to the holders of claims of the corporation and no corporate entity will survive. In a *reorganization*, a new corporate entity will result. Some holders of the claim of the bankrupt corporation will receive cash in exchange for their claims, others may receive new securities in the corporation that results from the reorganization, and others may receive a combination of both cash and new securities in the resulting corporation.

Another purpose of the bankruptcy law is to give a corporation time to decide whether to reorganize or liquidate and then the necessary time to formulate a plan to accomplish either a reorganization or liquidation. This is achieved because when a corporation files for bankruptcy, the law grants the corporation protection from creditors who seek to collect their claims. The petition for bankruptcy can be filed either by the company itself, in which case it is called a *voluntary bankruptcy*, or be filed by its creditors, in which case it is called an *involuntary bankruptcy*. A company that files for protection under the bankruptcy act generally becomes a *debtor-in-possession* (DIP), and continues to operate its business under the supervision of the court.

The bankruptcy law is comprised of 15 chapters, each covering a particular type of bankruptcy. Of particular interest here are two of the chapters, Chapter 7 and Chapter 11. Chapter 7 deals with the liquidation of a company; Chapter 11 deals with the reorganization of a company.

When a company is liquidated, creditors receive distributions based on the "absolute priority rule" to the extent assets are available. The absolute priority rule is the principle that senior creditors are paid in full before junior creditors are paid anything. For secured creditors and unsecured creditors, the absolute priority rule guarantees their seniority to equity holders.

In liquidations, the absolute priority rule generally holds. In contrast, there is a good body of literature that argues that strict absolute priority has not been upheld by the courts or the Securities and Exchange Commission (SEC). Studies of actual reorganizations under Chapter 11 have found that the violation of absolute priority is the rule rather the exception.

Consequently, while investors in the debt of a corporation may feel that they have priority over the equity owners and priority over other classes of debtors, the actual outcome of a bankruptcy may be far different from what the terms of the debt agreement state.

Default and Recovery Rates

There is a good deal of research published on default rates by rating agencies and academicians. From an investment perspective, default rates by themselves are not of paramount significance: It is perfectly possible for a portfolio of corporate bonds to suffer defaults and to outperform Treasuries at the same time, provided the yield spread of the portfolio is sufficiently high to offset the losses from defaults. Furthermore, because holders of defaulted bonds typically recover a percentage of the face amount of their investment, the *default loss rate* can be substantially lower than the default rate. The default loss rate is defined as follows:

$$\text{Default loss rate} = \text{Default rate} \times (100\% - \text{Recovery rate})$$

For instance, a default rate of 5% and a recovery rate of 30% means a default loss rate of only 3.5% (70% of 5%).

Therefore, focusing exclusively on default rates merely highlights the worst possible outcome that a diversified portfolio of corporate bonds would suffer, assuming all defaulted bonds would be totally worthless.

Several studies have found that the recovery rate is closely related to the bond's seniority. However, seniority is not the only factor that affects recovery values. In general, recovery values will vary with the types of assets and competitive conditions of the firm, as well as the economic environment at the time of bankruptcy. In addition, recovery rates will also vary across industries. For example, some manufacturing companies, such as petroleum and chemical companies, have assets with a high tangible value, such as plant, equipment, and land. These assets usually have a significant market value, even in the event of bankruptcy. In other industries, however, a company's assets have less tangible value, and bondholders should expect low recovery rates.

Credit Spread Risk

The *credit spread* is the premium over the government or risk-free rate required by the market for taking on a certain assumed credit exposure. The higher the credit rating, the smaller the credit spread to the benchmark rate all other factors constant. Credit spread risk is the risk of financial loss resulting from changes in the level of credit spreads used in the marking-to-market of a debt instrument. Changes in market credit spreads affect the value of the portfolio and can lead to losses for traders or underperformance relative to a benchmark for portfolio managers.

As explained earlier, duration is a measure of the change in the value of a bond when interest rates change. The interest rate that is assumed to change is the benchmark rate. For credit-risky bonds, the yield is equal to the benchmark rate plus the credit spread. A measure of how a credit-risky bond's price will change if the credit spread sought by the market changes is called "spread duration." For example, a spread duration of 2 for a credit-risky bond means that for a 100 basis point increase in the credit spread (holding the benchmark rate constant), the bond's price will decline by approximately 2%.

Downgrade Risk

As explained earlier, market participants gauge the credit default risk of an issue by looking at the credit ratings assigned to issues by the rating agencies. Once a credit rating is assigned to a debt obligation, a rating agency monitors the credit quality of the issuer and can reassign a different credit rating. An improvement in the credit quality of an issue or issuer is rewarded with a better credit rating, referred to as an *upgrade*; a deterioration in the credit rating of an issue or issuer is penalized by the assignment of an inferior credit rating, referred to as a *downgrade*. The actual or anticipated downgrading of an issue or issuer increases the credit spread and results in a decline in the price of the issue or the issuer's bonds. This risk is referred to as downgrade risk and is closely related to credit spread risk. A rating agency may announce in advance that it is reviewing a particular credit rating, and may go further and state that the review is a precursor to a possible downgrade or upgrade. This announcement is referred to as "putting the issue under credit watch."

Occasionally, the ability of an issuer to make interest and principal payments changes seriously and unexpectedly because of an unforeseen event. This can include any number of idiosyncratic events that are specific to the corporation or to an industry, including a natural or industrial accident, a regulatory change, a takeover or corporate restructuring, or even corporate fraud. This risk is referred to generically as *event risk* and will result in a downgrading of the issuer by the rating agencies. Because the price of the entity's securities will typically change dramatically or jump in price, this risk is sometimes referred to as *jump risk*.

The rating agencies periodically publish, in the form of a table, information about how issues that they have rated have changed over time. This table is called a *rating migration table* or *rating transition table*. The table is useful for investors to assess potential downgrades and upgrades. A rating migration table is available for different lengths of time. Exhibit 4.2 shows a hypothetical rating migration table for a one-year period. The first column shows the ratings at the start of the year, and the first row shows the ratings at the end of the year.

Let's interpret one of the numbers. Look at the cell where the rating at the beginning of the year is AA and the rating at the end of the year is AA. This cell represents the percentage of issues rated AA at the beginning of the year that did not have their rating change over the year. As can be seen, 92.75% of the issues rated AA at the start of the year were rated AA at the end of the year. Now look at the cell where the rating at the beginning of

EXHIBIT 4.2   Hypothetical One-Year Rating Migration Table

Rating at Start of Year	Rating at End of Year								
	AAA	AA	A	BBB	BB	B	CCC	D	Total
AAA	93.20	6.00	0.60	0.12	0.08	0.00	0.00	0.00	100
AA	1.60	92.75	5.07	0.36	0.11	0.07	0.03	0.01	100
A	0.18	2.65	91.91	4.80	0.37	0.02	0.02	0.05	100
BBB	0.04	0.30	5.20	87.70	5.70	0.70	0.16	0.20	100
BB	0.03	0.11	0.61	6.80	81.65	7.10	2.60	1.10	100
B	0.01	0.09	0.55	0.88	7.90	75.67	8.70	6.20	100
CCC	0.00	0.01	0.31	0.84	2.30	8.10	62.54	25.90	100

the year is AA and at the end of the year is A. This shows the percentage of issues rated AA at the beginning of the year that were downgraded to A by the end of the year. In our hypothetical one-year rating migration table, this percentage is 5.07%. One can view this figure as a probability. It is the probability that an issue rated AA will be downgraded to A by the end of the year.

A rating migration table also shows the potential for upgrades. Again, using Exhibit 4.2, look at the row that shows issues rated AA at the beginning of the year. Looking at the cell shown in the column AAA rating at the end of the year, there is the figure 1.60%. This figure represents the percentage of issues rated AA at the beginning of the year that were upgraded to AAA by the end of the year.

In general, the following hold for actual rating migration tables. First, the probability of a downgrade is much higher than for an upgrade for investment-grade bonds. Second, the longer the migration period, the lower the probability that an issuer will retain its original rating. That is, a one-year rating migration table will have a lower probability of a downgrade for a particular rating than a five-year rating migration table for that same rating.

Financial Instruments and Concepts Introduced in this Chapter (in Order of Presentation)

Term to maturity
Maturity
Money market instruments
Money market
Short-term bonds
Intermediate-term bonds
Long-term bonds
Par value

Principal
Face value
Redemption value
Maturity value
Coupon rate
Coupon
Step-up notes
Zero-coupon bonds

Deferred interest securities
Floating rate securities
Fixed rate bond market
Floating rate bond market
Coupon reset date
Coupon reset formula
Inverse floaters
Reverse floaters
Cap
Floor
Accrued interest
Full price
Clear price
Flat
Bullet maturity
Amortizing securities
Sinking fund provision
Call provision
Call option
Callable bond
Call price
Call schedule
Deferred call
First call
Currently callable issue
Refunding
First par call date
Regular redemption prices
General redemption prices
Special redemption prices
Prepayment
Prepayment option
Sinking fund provision
Balloon maturity
Accelerated sinking fund provision
Putable bond
Put price
Convertible bond
Exchangeable bond
Dollar-denominated issue
Nondollar-denominated issue
Dual-currency issue
Reinvestment income
Yield to maturity
Yield to call
Yield to first call

Yield to next call
Yield to first par call
Yield to refunding
Yield to put
Yield to worst
Prepayment rate
Prepayment speed
Cash flow yield
Interest rate risk
Duration
Reinvestment risk
Price compression
Prepayment risk
Credit risk
Default risk
Credit rating
Credit spread risk
Downgrade risk
Default rates
Recovery rates
Investment-grade bonds
Noninvestment-grade bonds
High-yield bonds
Junk bonds
Investment-grade sector
Noninvestment-grade sector
Distressed debt
Character
Capacity
Collateral
Covenants
Affirmative covenants
Negative covenants
Liquidation
Reorganization
Voluntary bankruptcy
Involuntary bankruptcy
Debtor-in-possession
Default loss rate
Credit spread
Upgrade
Downgrade
Event risk
Jump risk
Rating migration table
Rating transition table

U.S. Treasury and Federal Agency Securities

The securities issued by the U.S. Department of the Treasury (U.S. Treasury hereafter) are called *Treasury securities, Treasuries,* or *U.S. government securities*. Because they are backed by the full faith and credit of the U.S. government, market participants throughout the world view them as having no credit risk. Hence, the interest rates on Treasury securities are the benchmark default-free interest rates.

In this chapter, the different types of marketable Treasury securities are explained. In addition, we describe securities issues by federal agencies, entities chartered by Congress to provide funding support for the housing and agricultural sectors of the U.S. economy and specific funding projects of the U.S. government. The largest issuers are also known as government-sponsored enterprises (GSEs). GSEs are either public or government owned shareholder corporations (Fannie Mae, Freddie Mac, and Tennessee Valley Authority) or the funding entities of federally chartered bank lending systems (Federal Home Loan Banks and the Federal Farm Credit Banks). The debt of the GSEs is not guaranteed by the U.S. government.

TREASURY SECURITIES

Treasury securities are classified as nonmarketable and marketable securities. The former securities include savings bonds that are sold to individuals and state and local government series (SLGS) securities that are sold to state and local government issuers of tax-exempt securities. There are two types of marketable Treasury securities issued: fixed-principal securities and inflation-indexed securities.

Advantages of investing in Treasury securities in addition to their minimal credit risk (assuming the U.S. government action in the future does not alter this perception) is that they are highly liquid and the interest paid is exempt from state and local income taxes.

Fixed Principal Treasury Securities: Treasury Bills

The U.S. Treasury issues two types of *fixed principal securities:* discount securities and coupon securities. Discount securities are called Treasury bills; coupon securities are called Treasury notes and Treasury bonds.

Treasury bills are issued at a discount to par value, have no coupon rate, and mature at face value. As of mid-2010, the practice of the U.S. Treasury is to issue Treasury bills with maturities of four weeks, 13 weeks, 26 weeks, and 52 weeks (one year). The one-year Treasury bill is issued every four weeks and the other Treasury bills are issued weekly.

As discount securities, Treasury bills do not pay coupon interest. Instead, Treasury bills are issued at a discount from their face value; the return to the investor is the difference between the face value and the purchase price.

Treasury bills prices are quoted on a *bank discount basis* using the following formula:

$$\text{Annualized yield on a bank discount basis}$$
$$= (\text{Dollar discount / Face value}) \times (360 / \text{Days to maturity})$$

where dollar discount is the difference between the face value and the price.

As an example, consider a Treasury bill with 43 days to maturity, a face value of $1 million, and selling for $993,908.33. The dollar discount is $6,091.67. The annualized yield on a bank discount basis is then

$$\text{Yield on a bank discount basis} = (\$6,091 / \$1,000,000) \times (360 / 43) = 5.1\%$$

The price of a Treasury bill can be determined from the yield on a bank discount basis by using the following formula:

$$\text{Price} = \text{Face value} - [\text{Yield on a bank discount basis}$$
$$\times \text{Face value} \times (\text{Days to maturity} / 360)]$$

For example, consider again the 43-day Treasury bill. If the yield on a bank discount basis is 5.1%, then the price is

$$\text{Price} = \$1,000,000 - [0.051 \times \$1,000,000 \times (43 / 360)] = \$993,908.33$$

As a yield measure, the yield on a bank discount basis is flawed for two reasons. First, the measure is based on a face-value investment rather than on the actual dollar amount invested. Second, the yield is annualized according to a 360-day rather than a 365-day year, making it difficult to compare Treasury bill yields with Treasury notes and bonds, which pay interest on a 365-day basis. The use of 360 days for a year is a money market convention. Despite its shortcomings as a measure of return, this is the method that dealers have adopted to quote Treasury bills.

The yield measure employed by market participants to make the quotes on Treasury bills comparable to Treasury notes and bonds that we discuss next is called the *bond-equivalent yield*. The *CD equivalent yield,* also called the *money market equivalent yield,* makes the quoted yield on a Treasury bill more comparable to yield quotations on other money market instruments that pay interest on a 360-day basis. This is achieved by taking into consideration the price of the Treasury bill rather than its face value. The formula for the CD equivalent yield is

$$\text{CD equivalent yield} = \frac{360 \times \text{Yield on a bank discount basis}}{360 - (\text{Days to maturity} \times \text{Yield on a bank discount basis})}$$

As an illustration, consider a 123-day Treasury bill with a face value of $1 million, selling for $982,916.67, and offering a yield on a bank discount basis of 5%. Then

$$\text{CD equivalent yield} = \frac{360 \times 0.05}{360 - (123 \times 0.05)} = 5.09\%$$

Fixed Principal Treasury Securities: Treasury Notes and Bonds

The U.S. Department of theTreasury issues securities with initial maturities of two years or more as coupon securities. Treasury coupon securities are issued at approximately par and, in the case of fixed principal securities, mature at par value. They are not callable. *Treasury notes* are coupon securities issued with original maturities of more than two years but no more than 10 years. As of mid-2010, the U.S. Treasury issues 2-, 3-, 5-, 7-, and 10-year notes.

Treasuries with original maturities greater than 10 years are called *Treasury bonds*. As of mid-2010, the U.S. Department of the Treasury issues a 30-year bond.

Treasury Inflation-Protected Securities

The U.S. Treasury issues coupon securities that provide inflation protection. They do so by having the principal increase or decrease based on the rate of inflation such that when the security matures, the investor receives the greater of the principal adjusted for inflation or the original principal. These Treasury securities are called *Treasury inflation-protected securities* (TIPS).

As of mid-2010, the U.S. Department of the Treasury issues TIPS with a maturities of five, 10-year, and 30-years.

TIPS work as follows. The coupon rate on an issue is set at a fixed rate, the rate being determined via the auction process described later in this chapter. The coupon rate is referred to as the *real rate* because it is the rate that the investor ultimately earns above the inflation rate. The inflation index used for measuring the inflation rate is the nonseasonally adjusted U.S. City Average All Items Consumer Price Index for All Urban Consumers (CPI-U).

The adjustment for inflation is as follows: The principal that the U.S. Treasury will base both the dollar amount of the coupon payment and the maturity value on is adjusted semiannually. This is called the *inflation-adjusted principal*. For example, suppose that the coupon rate for a TIPS is 3.5% and the annual inflation rate is 3%. Suppose further that, on January 1, an investor purchases $100,000 par value (principal) of this issue. The semiannual inflation rate is 1.5% (3% divided by 2). The inflation-adjusted principal at the end of the first six-month period is found by multiplying the original par value by one plus the semiannual inflation rate. In our example, the inflation-adjusted principal at the end of the first six-month period is $101,500. It is this inflation-adjusted principal that is the basis for computing the coupon interest for the first six-month period. The coupon payment is then 1.75% (one-half the real rate of 3.5%) multiplied by the inflation-adjusted principal at the coupon payment date ($101,500). The coupon payment is therefore $1,776.25.

Let's look at the next six months. The inflation-adjusted principal at the beginning of the period is $101,500. Suppose that the semiannual inflation rate for the second six-month period is 1%. Then the inflation-adjusted principal at the end of the second six-month period is the inflation-adjusted principal at the beginning of the six-month period ($101,500) increased by the semiannual inflation rate (1%). The adjustment to the principal is $1,015 (1% times $101,500). So, the inflation-adjusted principal at the end of the second six-month period (December 31 in our example) is $102,515 ($101,500 + $1,015). The coupon interest that will be paid to the investor at the second coupon payment date is found by multiplying the inflation-adjusted principal on the coupon payment date ($102,515) by one-half the real rate (i.e., one-half of 3.5%). That is, the coupon payment will be $1,794.01.

As can be seen, part of the adjustment for inflation comes from the coupon payment since it is based on the inflation-adjusted principal. However, the U.S. government has decided to tax the adjustment each year. This feature reduces the attractiveness of TIPS as investments in accounts of tax-paying entities.

Because of the possibility of disinflation (that is, price declines), the inflation-adjusted principal at maturity may turn out to be less than the original par value. However, the Treasury has structured TIPS so that they are redeemed at the greater of the inflation-adjusted principal and the original par value.

An inflation-adjusted principal must be calculated for a settlement date if an issue is sold prior to maturity. The inflation-adjusted principal is defined in terms of an index ratio, which is the ratio of the reference CPI for the settlement date to the reference CPI for the issue date. The reference CPI is calculated with a three-month lag. For example, the reference CPI for May 1 is the CPI-U reported in February. The U.S. Department of the Treasury publishes and makes available on its web site a daily index ratio for an issue.

Treasury Auction Process

Treasury securities are sold in the primary market through an auction process. Each auction is announced several days in advance by means of a Treasury Department press release or press conference. The announcement provides details of the offering, including the offering amount and the term and type of security being offered, and describes some of the auction rules and procedures. Treasury auctions are open to all entities.

The U.S. Treasury makes the determination of the procedure for auctioning new Treasury securities, when to auction them, and what maturities to issue. There are periodic changes in the auction cycles and the maturity of the issues auctioned.

While the Treasury regularly offers new securities at auction, it often offers additional amounts of outstanding securities. This is referred to as a *reopening of an issue.* The Treasury has established a regular schedule of reopenings for certain maturities. To maintain the sizes of its new issues and help manage the maturity of its debt, the Treasury launched a debt buyback program. Under the program, the Treasury redeems outstanding unmatured Treasury securities by purchasing them in the secondary market through reverse auctions.

The auction for Treasury securities is conducted on a competitive bid basis. There are two types of bids that may be submitted by a bidder: noncompetitive bids and competitive bids. A *noncompetitive bid* is submitted by an entity that is willing to purchase the auctioned security at the yield that is determined by the auction process. When a noncompetitive bid is submitted, the bidder specifies only the quantity sought. The quantity in a noncompetitive bid may not exceed a specified amount. A *competitive bid* specifies both the quantity sought and the yield at which the bidder is willing to purchase the auctioned security.

The auction results are determined by first deducting the total noncompetitive tenders and nonpublic purchases (such as purchases by the Federal

Reserve) from the total securities being auctioned. The remainder is the amount to be awarded to the competitive bidders. The competitive bids are then arranged from the lowest yield bid to the highest yield bid submitted. (This is equivalent to arranging the bids from the highest price to the lowest price that bidders are willing to pay.) Starting from the lowest yield bid, all competitive bids are accepted until the amount to be distributed to the competitive bidders is completely allocated. The highest yield accepted by the Treasury is referred to as the *stop-out yield*. Bidders whose bid is higher than the stop-out yield are not distributed any of the new issue (that is, they are unsuccessful bidders). Bidders whose bid was the stop-out yield (that is, the highest yield accepted by the Treasury) are awarded a proportionate amount for which they bid. For example, suppose that $4 billion was tendered for at the stop-out yield, but only $1 billion remains to be allocated after allocating to all bidders who bid lower than the stop-out yield. Then each bidder who bid the stop-out yield will receive 25% of the amount for which they tendered. So, if an entity tendered for $12 million, then that entity would be awarded only $3 million.

The results announced by the U.S Treasury include the stop-out yield, the associated price, and the proportion of securities awarded to those investors who bid exactly the stop-out yield. Also announced is the quantity of noncompetitive tenders, the median-yield bid, and the ratio of the total amount bid for by the public to the amount awarded to the public (called the *bid-to-cover ratio*). For notes and bonds, the announcement includes the coupon rate of the new security. The coupon rate is set to be that rate (in increments of one-eighth of 1%) that produces the price closest to, but not above, par when evaluated at the yield awarded to successful bidders.

Now we know how the winning bidders are determined and the amount that successful bidders will be allotted, the next question is the yield at which they are awarded the auctioned security. All U.S. Treasury auctions are *single-price auctions*. In a single-price auction, all bidders are awarded securities at the highest yield of accepted competitive tenders (that is, the high yield). This type of auction is called a *Dutch auction*.

Secondary Market

The secondary market for Treasury securities is an over-the-counter (OTC) market where a group of U.S. government securities dealers offers continuous bid and ask prices on outstanding Treasuries. There is virtual 24-hour trading of Treasury securities. The three primary trading locations are New York, London, and Tokyo. The normal settlement period for Treasury securities is the business day after the transaction day ("next day" settlement).

The most recently auctioned issue is referred to as the *on-the-run issue* or the *current issue*. A security that is replaced by the on-the-run issue is called an *off-the-run issue*. At a given point in time there may be more than one off-the-run issue with approximately the same remaining maturity as the on-the-run issue. Treasury securities are traded prior to the time they are issued by the Treasury. This component of the Treasury secondary market is called the *when-issued market,* or WI market. When-issued trading for both bills and coupon securities extends from the day the auction is announced until the issue day.

Stripped Treasury Securities

The U.S. Department of theTreasury does not issue zero-coupon notes or bonds. However, because of the demand for zero-coupon instruments with no credit risk, the private sector has created such securities using a process called *coupon stripping*.

To illustrate the process, suppose that $2 billion of a 10-year fixed principal Treasury note with a coupon rate of 5% is purchased by a dealer firm to create zero-coupon Treasury securities. The cash flow from this Treasury note is 20 semiannual payments of $50 million each ($2 billion times 0.05 divided by 2) and the repayment of principal of $2 billion 10 years from now. As there are 21 different payments to be made by the U.S. Department of the Treasury for this note, a security representing a single payment claim on each payment is issued, which is effectively a zero-coupon Treasury security. The amount of the maturity value or a security backed by a particular payment, whether coupon or principal, depends on the amount of the payment to be made by the U.S. Department of the Treasury on the underlying Treasury note. In our example, 20 zero-coupon Treasury securities each have a maturity value of $50 million, and one zero-coupon Treasury security, backed by the principal, has a maturity value of $2 billion. The maturity dates for the zero-coupon Treasury securities coincide with the corresponding payment dates by the U.S. Department of the Treasury.

Zero-coupon Treasury securities are created as part of the U.S. Treasury's *Separate Trading of Registered Interest and Principal of Securities* (STRIPS) program to facilitate the stripping of designated Treasury securities. Today, all Treasury notes and bonds (fixed principal and inflation-indexed) are eligible for stripping. The zero-coupon Treasury securities created under the STRIPS program are direct obligations of the U.S. government.

A disadvantage to a taxable investor investing in stripped Treasury securities is that the accrued interest is taxed each year even though interest is not paid. Thus, these instruments are negative cash flow instruments until the maturity date. They have negative cash flow because tax payments on interest earned but not received in cash must be made.

FEDERAL AGENCY SECURITIES

Federal agency securities can be classified by the type of issuer—federally related institutions and government-sponsored enterprises (GSEs). Federal agencies that provide credit for certain sectors of the credit market issue two types of securities: debentures and mortgage-backed securities. Our focus here is on the former securities. We discuss the latter in Chapters 8 and 9.

Federally Related Institutions

Federally related institutions are arms of the federal government and generally do not issue securities directly in the marketplace. They include the Export-Import Bank of the United States, the Tennessee Valley Authority, the Commodity Credit Corporation, the Farmers Housing Administration, the General Services Administration, the Government National Mortgage Association, the Maritime Administration, the Private Export Funding Corporation, the Rural Electrification Administration, the Rural Telephone Bank, the Small Business Administration, and the Washington Metropolitan Area Transit Authority.

With the exception of securities issued by the Tennessee Valley Authority and the Private Export Funding Corporation, the securities are backed by the full faith and credit of the U.S. government. Interest income on securities issued by federally related institutions is exempt from state and local income taxes.

Since the federally related institution that has issued securities in recent years is the Tennessee Valley Authority, we discuss these securities.

Tennessee Valley Authority

The *Tennessee Valley Authority* (TVA) is the largest public power system in the United States. The TVA issues a variety of debt securities in U.S. dollars and other currencies (British pounds and euros). TVA debt obligations are not guaranteed by the U.S. government. However, the securities are rated triple-A by Moody's and Standard & Poor's. The rating is based on the TVA's status as a wholly owned corporate agency of the U.S. government and the view of the rating agencies of the TVA's financial strengths.

There are issues targeted to individual investors (retail debt offerings) and institutional investors (nonretail offerings). For retail offerings, there are standard callable bonds and these have an interesting investment feature, the *estate feature*. This feature allows the estate of the bondholder to redeem the issue at par value plus accrued interest upon the death of the bondholder. The Putable Automatic Rate Reset Securities (PARRS) bonds (1999 Series A and 1998 Series D) are noncallable but have two interesting features. First, they have a fixed coupon rate for the first five years. Then there is an annual reset provision that provides for a reduction in the issue's coupon rate under certain conditions. The reduction is tied to the 30-year Treasury Constant Maturity (CMT). Second, the bondholder has the right to put the bond at par value plus accrued interest if and when the coupon rate is reduced. More recently, the TVA has issued "electronotes." The retail bonds (as well as electronotes) just described are referred to as "power bonds." There are retail bonds that are "subordinated debt." That is, they are subordinated to the power bonds. The only outstanding issue is the 1996 Series A Quarterly Income Debt Securities (QIDS).

Government-Sponsored Enterprises

Government-sponsored enterprises (GSEs) are privately owned, publicly chartered entities. They were created by Congress to reduce the cost of capital for certain borrowing sectors of the economy deemed to be important enough to warrant assistance.

There are five GSEs that currently issue debentures: Freddie Mac, Fannie Mae, Federal Home Loan Bank System, Federal Farm Credit System, and the Federal Agricultural Mortgage Corporation. Fannie Mae, Freddie Mac, and Federal Home Loan Bank are responsible for providing credit to the housing sectors. The Federal Agricultural Mortgage Corporation provides the same function for agricultural mortgage loans. The Federal Farm Credit Bank System is responsible for the credit market in the agricultural sector of the economy.

In addition to the debt obligations issued by these five GSEs, there are issues outstanding by one-time GSE issuers that have been dismantled. These GSEs include the Financing Corporation, Resolution Trust Corporation, and the Farm Credit Assistance Corporation. One former GSE, Student Loan Marketing Association (Sallie Mae), elected to alter its status.

Description of GSEs and Securities Issued

The five GSEs that currently issue securities are discussed next. In general, GSEs issue two types of debt: debentures and discount notes. Debentures can be either notes or bonds. GSE-issued notes, with minor exceptions, have 1- to 20-year maturities and bonds have maturities longer than 20 years.

There are issues with bullet maturities and those with call provisions. GSEs also issue structured notes that we will describe in Chapter 7. Discount notes are short-term obligations with maturities ranging from overnight to 360 days. As with Treasury bills, no coupon interest is paid. Instead, the investor earns interest by buying the note at a discount.

GSEs have programmatic platforms for issuing securities to introduce greater transparency in their funding programs and to promote greater liquidity for the securities that they issue debt. These programmatic platforms involve preannounced funding calendars and large minimum sized issues. Fannie Mae issues Benchmark Bills, Notes, and Bonds in this way and Freddie Mac issues Reference Bills, Notes and Bonds. The Federal Home Loan Banks and the Federal Farm Credit Banks, through their respective funding entities—the Federal Home Loan Banks Office of Finance and the Federal Farm Credit Funding Corporation—have a programmatic debt platform.

Fannie Mae

The residential mortgage debt market in the United States represents the largest mortgage debt market in the world. The problem the U.S. government faces is to attract investors to invest in residential mortgages. At one time, savings and loan associations were the primary investors, especially with special inducements the government provided. But since there was not an active market where these debt instruments traded, mortgages were illiquid and financial institutions that invested in them were exposed to liquidity risk. *Fannie Mae*, previously called the Federal National Mortgage Association, was created in 1930 to provide liquidity to the housing finance market.

Fannie Mae issues Benchmark Bills, Benchmark Notes and Benchmark Bonds, Callable Benchmark Notes, Subordinated Benchmark Notes, Investment Notes, callable securities, and structured notes. Benchmark Notes and Benchmark Bonds are noncallable instruments. Fannie Mae issues securities with maturities of 2, 3, 5, 10, and 30 years.

Due to the major downturn in the housing and credit markets beginning in 2007, in September 2008 the entity that regulates Fannie Mae, as well as Freddie Mac, the Federal Housing Finance Agency (FHFA), placed these two GSEs in conservatorship. This meant that the FHFA had complete control over the operations and assets of these two GSEs. The FHFA suspended all dividend payments. Because of the concern by the federal government that the failure of these two GSEs would cause the housing finance market to dry up and cause severe disruptions in the global financial market due to the wide holding of the securities of these two GSEs, the U.S. Department of the Treasury put in place financing agreements to ensure that these two entities could continue to satisfy the debt obligations that they issued as well as those that guaranteed securities that we will discuss in Chapters 8 and 9).

Freddie Mac

Freddie Mac (at one time called the Federal Home Loan Mortgage Corporation) was created in 1970 to provide further support for the housing finance market.

Freddie Mac issues Reference Bills, discount notes, medium-term notes, Reference Notes and Bonds, Callable Reference Notes, Euro Reference Notes (debt denominated in euros) and global bonds. Reference Bills and discount notes are issued with maturities of one year or less. Reference Notes and Bonds have maturities of 2 to 30 years and Callable Reference Notes have maturities of 2 to 10 years. Freddie Mae will issue and/or reopen Reference Bills, Reference Notes, 30-year Reference Bonds, and Euro Reference Notes according to a published issuance calendar and within minimum issue size guidelines. Freddie Mac Reference Notes and Reference Bonds are eligible for stripping.

Both Freddie Mac and Fannie Mae issue bullet and callable medium-term notes (discussed in Chapter 7) and structured notes, which are customized based on demand from institutional investors. The structured notes issued have been various floating rate, zero-coupon, and step-up securities. There are securities denominated in U.S. dollars as well as issues denominated in a wide range of foreign currencies.

Federal Home Loan Bank System

The *Federal Home Loan Bank System* (FHL Banks) consists of the 12 district Federal Home Loan Banks and their member banks. The major source of debt funding for the Federal Home Loan Banks is the issuance of consolidated debt obligations, which are joint and several obligations of the 12 Federal Home Loan Banks. Consolidated FHL Bank discount notes with maturities from one to 360 days are issued daily. Discount notes are also auctioned twice weekly in 4-, 9-, 13-, and 26-week maturities. Because FHL Bank bond issuance is directly related to member bank needs, there is no debt calendar in the traditional sense. Bullets, callables, and floaters are issued on a daily basis.

The FHL-Banks have several programs to facilitate the issuance of certain bond types. The TAP Issue program aggregates FHL Bank demand for six common (1.5-, 2-, 3-, 5-, 7-, and 10-year) bullet maturities, and then offers them daily through competitive auctions. These issues feature standardized terms and are reopened via auction for three-month periods, enabling them to reach multibillion dollar size. TAP Issues can also be reopened as they roll down the curve. Callable bonds are issued daily, primarily as customized issues from reverse inquiry of institutional investors. The FHL Bank Global Bond Program will periodically offer larger sized ($1 billion minimum for callable and $3 billion minimum for bullet maturities) with standardized term and are targeted to foreign investors in either U.S. dollars or other currencies.

The Federal Agricultural Mortgage Corporation

The *Federal Agricultural Mortgage Corporation (Farmer Mac)* provides a secondary market for first mortgage agricultural real estate loans. It was created by Congress in 1998 to improve the availability of mortgage credit to farmers, ranchers, and rural homeowners, businesses, and communities. It does so by purchasing qualified loans from lenders in the same way as Freddie Mac and Fannie Mae.

Farmer Mac raises funds by selling debentures and mortgage-backed securities backed by the loans purchased. The latter securities are called *agricultural mortgage-backed securities* (AMBSs). The debentures that are issued include discount notes and medium-term notes.

Federal Farm Credit Bank System

The purpose of the *Federal Farm Credit Bank System* (FFCBS) is to facilitate adequate, dependable credit and related services to the agricultural sector of the economy. The Farm Credit System consists of three entities: the Federal Land Banks, Federal Intermediate Credit Banks, and Banks for Cooperatives. All financing for the FFCBS is arranged through the Federal Farm Credit Banks Funding Corporation (FFCBFC), which issues consolidated obligations.

The FFCBFC issues debt through five formats. Discount notes are offered daily through posted rates. Calendar Bonds of three- and six-month maturities are offered monthly. Designated Bonds of typically two-year maturities can be offered twice monthly as either a new issue ($1 billion minimum) or reopening ($100 million minimum). Unscheduled bonds are issued throughout the month in varying sizes and structures either by competitive bidding or negotiated reverse inquiry by institutional investors. FFCB Master Notes are issued as individually tailored daily investment agreements usually designed for a single investor.

Financial Instruments and Concepts Introduced in this Chapter (in Order of Presentation)

Treasury securities
Treasuries
U.S. governsecurities
Fixed-principal securities
Bank discount basis
Bond-equivalent yield
CD equivalent yield
Money market equivalent yield
Treasury notes
Treasury bonds
Treasury inflation-protected securities
Real rate
Inflation-adjusted principal
Reopening of an issue
Noncompetitive bid
Competitive bid
Stop-out yield
Bid-to-cover ratio
Single-price auctions

Dutch auction
On-the-run issue
Current issue
Off-the-run issue
When-issued market
Coupon stripping
Separate Trading of Registered Interest
  and Principal of Securities
Federal agency securities
Federally related institutions
Tennessee Valley Authority
Estate feature
Government-sponsored enterprises
Fannie Mae
Freddie Mac
Federal Home Loan Bank System
Federal Agricultural Mortgage
  Corporation
Federal Farm Credit Bank System

CHAPTER 6

Municipal Securities

Debt obligations issued by state and local governments (municipalities, counties, and townships) and by entities that they establish are generically referred to as *municipal securities* or *municipal bonds*. The primary attractiveness of municipal bonds is that the interest earned is exempt from federal income taxation. While not all municipal securities are exempt from federal income taxation, tax-exempt municipal bonds are the largest component of the market. However, in 2009 the federal government introduced a new type of taxable bond, Build America Bonds, that significantly increased the size of the taxable sector of the municipal bond market.

In this chapter, we discuss the types of debt obligations issued by states, municipal governments, and public agencies and their instrumentalities, and the investment characteristics of these financial instruments.

TAX-EXEMPT AND TAXABLE MUNICIPAL SECURITIES

There are both tax-exempt and taxable municipal securities. "Tax-exempt" means that interest on a municipal security is exempt from federal income taxation. The tax exemption of municipal securities applies to interest income, not capital gains. The exemption may or may not extend to taxation at the state and local levels. The state tax treatment depends on (1) whether the issue from which the interest income is received is an "in-state issue" or an "out-of-state issue," and (2) whether the investor is an individual or a corporation. The treatment of interest income at the state level will be one of the following:

1. Taxation of interest from municipal issues regardless of whether the issuer is in state or out of state.
2. Exemption of interest from all municipal issues regardless of whether the issuer is in state or out of state.
3. Exemption of interest from municipal issues that are in state but some form of taxation where the source of interest is an out-of-state issuer.

Because most municipal securities that have been issued are tax-exempt, municipal securities are commonly referred to as *tax-exempt securities*.

There are other types of tax-exempt bonds. These include bonds issued by nonprofit organizations. Such organizations are structured so that none of the income from the operations of the organization benefit an individual or private shareholder. The designation of a nonprofit organization must be obtained from the Internal Revenue Service (IRS). Since the tax-exempt designation is provided pursuant to Section 501(c)(3) of the Internal Revenue Code, the tax-exempt bonds issued by such organizations are referred to as 501(c)(3) obligations. Museums and foundations fall into this category.

Tax-exempt obligations also include bonds issued by the District of Columbia and any possession of the United States—Puerto Rico, the U.S. Virgin Islands, Guam, American Samoa, and the Northern Mariana Islands. The interest income from securities issued by U.S. territories and possessions is exempt from federal, state, and local income taxes in all 50 states.

Tax Provisions Affecting Municipal Securities

Federal tax rates and the treatment of municipal interest at the state and local levels affect municipal security values and strategies employed by investors. There are provisions in the Internal Revenue Code that investors in municipal securities should recognize. These provisions deal with original issue discounts, the alternative minimum tax, and the deductibility of interest expense incurred to acquire municipal securities.

Treatment of Original-Issue Discount

If at the time of issuance the original-issue price is less than its maturity value, the bond is said to be an *original-issue discount* (OID) *bond*. The difference between the par value and the original-issue price represents tax-exempt interest that the investor realizes by holding the issue to maturity.

For municipal bonds there is a complex treatment that investors must recognize when purchasing OID municipal bonds. The Revenue Reconciliation Act of 1993 specifies that any capital appreciation from the sale of a municipal bond that was purchased in the secondary market after April 30, 1993, could be either (1) free from any federal income taxes, (2) taxed at the capital gains rate, (3) taxed at the ordinary income rate, or (4) taxed at a combination of the two rates.

The key to the tax treatment is the *rule of de minimis* for any type of bond. The rule states that a bond is to be discounted up to 0.25% from the par value for each remaining year of a bond's life before it is affected by ordinary income taxes. The discounted price based on this rule is called the *market discount cutoff price.* The relationship between the market price at which an investor purchases a bond, the market discount cutoff price, and the tax treatment of the capital appreciation realized from a sale is as follows:

- If the bond is purchased at a market discount, but the price is higher than the market discount cutoff price, then any capital appreciation realized from a sale will be taxed at the capital gains rate.
- If the purchase price is lower than the market discount cutoff price, then any capital appreciation realized from a sale may be taxed as ordinary income or a combination of the ordinary income rate and the capital gains rate. (Several factors determine what the exact tax rate will be in this case.)

The market discount cutoff price changes over time because of the rule of de minimis. The price is revised. An investor must be aware of the revised price when purchasing a municipal bond because this price is used to determine the tax treatment.

Alternative Minimum Tax

Alternative minimum taxable income (AMTI) is a taxpayer's taxable income with certain adjustments for specified tax preferences designed to cause AMTI to approximate economic income. For both individuals and corporations, a taxpayer's liability is the greater of (1) the tax computed at regular tax rates on taxable income and (2) the tax computed at a lower rate on AMTI. This parallel tax system, the *alternative minimum tax* (AMT), is designed to prevent taxpayers from avoiding significant tax liability as a result of taking advantage of exclusions from gross income, deductions, and tax credits otherwise allowed under the Internal Revenue Code.

One of the tax preference items that must be included is certain tax-exempt municipal interest. Under the current tax code, there are municipal issues that are subject to the AMT and others that are not. For the former issues, the value of the tax-exempt feature is therefore reduced. An implication is that those issues that are subject to the AMT will trade at a higher yield than those exempt from the AMT.

For investors in mutual funds that invest in municipal bonds, the prospectus will disclose whether the fund's manager is permitted to invest in AMT bonds and if it is permitted, the maximum percentage allowed. Usually, when a mutual fund allows investments in AMT bonds, the maximum is 20%. The year-end 1099 form provided to investors in mutual funds will show the percentage of the income of the fund that must be included in AMTI.

Deductibility of Interest Expense Incurred to Acquire Municipals

Ordinarily, the interest expense on borrowed funds to purchase or carry investment securities is tax deductible. There is one exception that is relevant to investors in municipal bonds. The Internal Revenue Code specifies that interest paid or accrued on "indebtedness incurred or continued to purchase or carry obligations, the interest on which is wholly exempt from taxes," is not tax deductible. It does not make any difference if any tax-exempt interest is actually received by the taxpayer in the taxable year. In other words, interest is not deductible on funds borrowed to purchase or carry tax-exempt securities.

TYPES OF MUNICIPAL SECURITIES

Municipal securities are issued for various purposes. Short-term notes typically are sold in anticipation of the receipt of funds from taxes or receipt of proceeds from the sale of a bond issue, for example. Proceeds from the sale of short-term notes permit the issuing municipality to cover seasonal and temporary imbalances between outlays for expenditures and inflows from taxes. Municipalities issue long-term bonds as the principal means for financing both (1) long-term capital projects such as schools, bridges, roads, and airports; and (2) long-term budget deficits that arise from current operations.

An *official statement* describing the issue and the issuer is prepared for new offerings. Municipal securities have legal opinions that are summarized in the official statement. The importance of the legal opinion is twofold. First, bond counsel determines if the issue is indeed legally able to issue the securities. Second, bond counsel verifies that the issuer has properly prepared for the bond sale by having enacted various required ordinances, resolutions, and trust indentures and without violating any other laws and regulations.

There are basically two types of municipal security structures: tax-backed debt and revenue bonds. We describe each type, as well as variants.

Tax-Backed Debt

Tax-backed debt obligations are secured by some form of tax revenue. The broadest type of tax-backed debt obligation is the general obligation debt. Other types that fall into the category of tax-backed debt are appropriation-backed obligations, debt obligations supported by public credit enhancement programs, and short-term debt instruments.

General Obligation Debt

General obligation debt includes unlimited and limited tax general obligation debt. The stronger form is the unlimited tax general obligation debt because it is secured by the issuer's unlimited taxing power and is said to be secured by the full faith and credit of the issuer. A limited tax general obligation debt is a limited tax pledge because for such debt there is a statutory ceiling on the tax rates that may be levied to service the issuer's debt.

There are general obligation bonds that are secured not only by the issuer's general taxing powers to create revenues accumulated in a general fund, but also secured by designated fees, grants, and special charges from outside the general fund. Due to the dual nature of the revenue sources, bonds with this security feature are referred to as "double-barreled in security." As an example, special purpose service systems issue bonds that are secured by a pledge of property taxes, a pledge of special fees/operating revenue from the service provided, or a pledge of both property taxes and special fees/operating revenues.

Appropriation-Backed Obligations

Bond issues of some agencies or authorities carry a potential state liability for making up shortfalls in the issuing entity's obligation. While the appropriation of funds must be approved by the issuer's state legislature, and hence they are referred to as appropriation-backed obligations, the state's pledge is not binding. Because of this nonbinding pledge of tax revenue, such issues are referred to as *moral obligation bonds*. The reason for the moral obligation pledge is to enhance the creditworthiness of the issuing entity.

Another type of appropriation-backed obligation is lease-backed debt. There are two types of leases. One type is basically a secured long-term loan disguised as lease. The "leased" asset is the security for the loan. In the case of a bankruptcy, the court would probably rule such an obligation as the property of the user of the leased asset and the debt obligation of the user. In contrast, the second type of lease is a true lease in which the user of the leased asset (called the "lessee") makes periodic payments to the leased asset's owner (called the "lessor") for the right to use the leased asset. For true leases, there must be an annual appropriation by the municipality to continue making the lease payments.

Dedicated Tax-Backed Obligations

States and local governments have issued bonds where the debt service is to be paid from so-called dedicated revenues such as sales taxes, tobacco settlement payments, fees, and penalty payments. Many are structured to mimic asset-backed securities that we describe in Chapter 10.

Let's look at one type of such security. Tobacco settlement revenue bonds are backed by the tobacco settlement payments owed to the state or local entity resulting from the master settlement agreement between most of the states and the four major U.S. tobacco companies (Philip Morris Inc., R. J. Reynolds Tobacco Co., Lorillard Tobacco Co., and Brown & Williamson Tobacco Corp.) in November 1998. The states that are parties to the settlement have subsequent to the settlement issued $36.5 billion of tax-exempt revenue bonds. There are unique risks associated with TSR bonds having to do with structural risk, the credit risk of the four tobacco companies, cash flow risk, and litigation risk.

Debt Obligations Supported by Public Credit Enhancement Programs

Unlike a moral obligation bond, there are bonds that carry some form of public credit enhancement that is legally enforceable. This occurs when there is a guarantee by the state or a federal agency or when there is an obligation to automatically withhold and deploy state aid to pay any defaulted debt service by the issuing entity. It is the latter form of public credit enhancement that is employed for debt obligations of a state's school systems.

Short-Term Debt Instruments

Short-term debt instruments issued by municipalities include notes, commercial paper, variable rate demand obligations, and a hybrid of the last two products.

Municipal Notes   Usually, *municipal notes* are issued for a period of 12 months, although it is not uncommon for such notes to be issued for periods as short as three months and for as long as three years. Municipal notes include bond anticipation notes (BANs) and cash flow notes. BANs are issued in anticipation of the sale of long-term bonds. The issuing entity must obtain funds in the capital market to pay off the obligation.

Cash flow notes include tax anticipation notes (TANs) and revenue anticipation notes (RANs). TANs and RANs (also known as TRANs) are issued in anticipation of the collection of taxes or other expected revenues. These are borrowings to even out irregular flows into the treasury of the issuing entity. The pledge for cash flow notes can be either a broad general obligation pledge of the issuer or a pledge from a specific revenue source. The lien position of cash flow noteholders relative to other general obligation debt that has been pledged the same revenue can be either (1) a first lien on all pledged revenue, thereby having priority over general obligation debt that has been pledged the same revenue; (2) a lien that is in parity with general obligation debt that has been pledged the same revenue; or (3) a lien that is subordinate to the lien of general obligation debt that has been pledged the same revenue.

Commercial Paper   Commercial paper is issued by municipalities to raise funds on a short-term basis ranging from one day to 270 days. There are two types of commercial paper issued, unenhanced and enhanced. Unenhanced commercial paper is a debt obligation issued based solely on the issuer's credit quality and liquidity capability. Enhanced commercial paper is a debt obligation that is credit enhanced with bank liquidity facilities (e.g., a letter of credit), insurance, or a bond purchase agreement. The role of the enhancement is to reduce the risk of nonrepayment of the maturing commercial paper by providing a source of liquidity for payment of that debt in the event no other funds of the issuer are currently available.

Provisions in the 1986 tax act restricted the issuance of tax-exempt commercial paper. Specifically, the act limited the new issuance of municipal obligations that are tax exempt, and as a result, every maturity of a tax-exempt municipal issuance is considered a new debt issuance. Consequently, very limited issuance of tax-exempt commercial paper exists. Instead, issuers use one of the next two products to raise short-term funds.

Variable Rate Demand Obligations   *Variable rate demand obligations* (VRDOs) are floating rate obligations that have a nominal long-term maturity but have a coupon rate that is reset either daily or every seven days. The investor has an option to put the issue back to the trustee at any time with seven days notice. The put price is par plus accrued interest. As with commercial paper, there are unenhanced and enhanced VRDOs.

Commercial Paper/VRDO Hybrid   The commercial paper/VRDO hybrid is a product that is customized to meet the investor's cash flow needs. There is flexibility in structuring the maturity as with commercial paper because there is a remarketing agent who establishes interest rates for a range of maturities. While there may be a long stated maturity for such issues, they contain a put provision as with a VRDO. The range of the put period can be from one day to more than 360 days. On the put date, the investor has two choices. The first is to put the bonds to the issuer; by doing so, the investor receives principal and interest. The second choice available to the investor is to extend the maturity at the new interest rate and put date posted by the remarketing agent at that time.

Revenue Bonds

Revenue bonds are the second basic type of security structure found in the municipal bond market. These bonds are issued for enterprise financings that are secured by the revenues generated by the completed projects themselves, or for general public-purpose financings in which the issuers pledge to the bondholders the tax and revenue resources that were previously part of the general fund. This latter type of revenue bond is usually created to allow issuers to raise debt outside general obligation debt limits and without voter approval.

The trust indenture for a municipal revenue bond details how revenue received by the enterprise will be distributed. This is referred to as the *flow-of-funds structure*. In a typical revenue bond, the revenue is first distributed into a revenue fund. It is from that fund that disbursements for expenses are made. The typical flow-of-funds structure provides for payments in the following order into other funds: operation and maintenance fund, sinking fund, debt service reserve fund, renewal and replacement fund, reserve maintenance fund, and surplus fund.

Revenue bonds can be classified by the type of financing. These include utility revenue bonds, transportation revenue bonds, housing revenue bonds, higher education revenue bonds, health care revenue bonds, seaport revenue bonds, sports complex and convention center revenue bonds, and industrial development revenue bonds. We discuss these revenue bonds as follows. Revenue bonds are also issued by Section 501(c)3 entities (museums and foundations).

Utility Revenue Bonds

Utility revenue bonds include water, sewer, and electric revenue bonds. Water revenue bonds are issued to finance the construction of water treatment plants, pumping stations, collection facilities, and distribution systems. Revenues usually come from connection fees and charges paid by the users of the water systems. Electric utility revenue bonds are secured by revenues produced from electrical operating plants. Some bonds are for a single issuer who constructs and operates power plants and then sells the electricity. Other electric utility revenue bonds are issued by groups of public and private investor-owned utilities for the joint financing of the construction of one or more power plants.

Also included as part of utility revenue bonds are resource recovery revenue bonds. A resource recovery facility converts refuse (solid waste) into commercially saleable energy, recoverable products, and residue to be landfilled. The major revenues securing these bonds usually are (1) fees paid by those who deliver the waste to the facility for disposal; (2) revenues from steam, electricity, or refuse-derived fuel sold to either an electric power company or another energy user; and (3) revenues from the sale of recoverable materials such as aluminum and steel scrap.

Transportation Revenue Bonds

Included in the category of transportation revenue bonds are toll road revenue bonds, highway user tax revenue bonds, airport revenue bonds, and mass transit bonds secured by fare-box revenues. For toll road revenue bonds, bond proceeds are used to build specific revenue-producing facilities such as toll roads, bridges, and tunnels. The pledged revenues are the monies collected through tolls. For highway-user tax revenue bonds, the bondholders are paid by earmarked revenues outside of toll collections, such as gasoline taxes, automobile registration payments, and driver's license fees. The revenues securing airport revenue bonds usually come from either traffic-generated sources—such as landing fees, concession fees, and airline fueling fees—or lease revenues from one or more airlines for the use of a specific facility such as a terminal or hangar.

Housing Revenue Bonds

There are two types of housing revenue bonds: single-family mortgage revenue bonds and multifamily housing revenue bonds.

Single-family revenue bonds are issued by state and local housing finance agencies in order to obtain funds to assist low- to middle-income individuals purchase their first home. This assistance is accomplished by using the proceeds from the bond sale to acquire the newly originated mortgages and pooling them. More specifically, the loans are one-to-four-single-family home, 30-year fixed rate mortgages. While the primary source of repayment for these bonds is the mortgage payments on the pool of loans, there are several other layers of credit protection. These include (1) overcollateralization of the loan pool (that is, from 102% to as much as 110% of the bonds outstanding); (2) for loans in the pool with a loan-to-value ratio of 80% or greater, primary mortgage insurance is required (either Federal Housing Administration or Veteran's Administration or private mortgage insurance with a rating of at least double A); and (3) the housing finance agency of many states will provide their general obligation pledge.

As with mortgage-backed securities issued in the taxable sector, investors in single-family mortgage revenue bonds are exposed to prepayment risk (see Chapter 8). This is the risk that borrowers in the mortgage pool will prepay their loans when interest rates decline below their loan rate. The disadvantage to the investor as explained in Chapter 4 is twofold. First, the proceeds received from the prepayments must be reinvested at a lower rate. Second, a property of bonds with prepayment or call options is that their price performance is adversely affected when interest rates decline compared to noncallable bonds.

Multifamily revenue bonds are usually issued for a variety of housing projects involving tenants who qualify as low-income families and senior citizens. There are various forms of credit enhancement for these bonds. Some of these are what is found in commercial mortgage-backed securities where the underling is multifamily housing: overcollateralization, senior-subordinated structure, private and agency mortgage insurance (state insurance for some issues), bank letters of credit, and cross-collateralization and cross default provisions in pools. In addition, there may be credit enhancement in the form of moral obligations or an appropriation obligation of the state or city issuing the bonds.

Higher Education Revenue Bonds

There are two types of higher education revenue bonds: college and university revenue bonds and student loan revenue bonds. The revenues securing public and private college and university revenue bonds usually include dormitory room rental fees, tuition payments, and sometimes the general assets of the college or university. For student loan revenue bonds, the structures are very similar to what is found in the student loan sector of the taxable asset-backed securities market covered in Chapter 10.

Health Care Revenue Bonds

Health care revenue bonds are issued by private, not-for-profit hospitals (including rehabilitation centers, children's hospitals, and psychiatric institutions) and other health care providers such as health maintenance organizations (HMOs), continuing care retirement communities and nursing homes, cancer centers, university faculty practice plans, and medical specialty practices. The revenue for health care revenue bonds usually depends on federal and state reimbursement programs (such as Medicaid and Medicare), third-party commercial payers (such as Blue Cross, HMOs, and private insurance), and individual patient payments.

Seaport Revenue Bonds

The security for seaport revenue bonds can include specific lease agreements with the benefiting companies or pledged marine terminal and cargo tonnage fees.

Special Bond Structures

Some municipal securities have special security structures. These include *insured bonds, bank-backed municipal bonds*, and *refunded bonds*. We describe these three special security structures as follows.

Insured Bonds

Municipal bonds can be credit enhanced by an unconditional guarantee of a commercial insurance company. The insurance cannot be canceled and typically is in place for the term of the bond. The insurance provides for the insurance company writing the policy to make payments to the bondholders of any principal and/or coupon interest that is due on a stated maturity date but that has not been paid by the bond issuer. The insurer's payment is not an advance of the payments due by the issuer but is rather made according to the original repayment schedule obligation of the issuer.

The track record on municipal bonds is unblemished. Since the first introduction of municipal bond insurance in 1971, no insurer had failed to make payments on any insured municipal bond as of year end 2007. That said, starting in early 2008, the major bond insurers were either downgraded or faced potential downgrading because of their commitments in the subprime mortgage market, not their involvement in the municipal bond market. As a result, their financial guarantee became a concern.

Bank-Backed Bonds

Municipal issuers have increasingly used various types of facilities provided by commercial banks to credit enhance and thereby improve the marketability of issues. There are three basic types of bank support: letter of credit, irrevocable line of credit, and revolving line of credit.

A *letter of credit* (LOC) is the strongest type of support available from a commercial bank. The parties to a LOC agreement are (1) the bank that issues the LOC (that is, the LOC issuer); (2) the municipal issuer who is requesting the LOC in connection with a security (the LOC-backed bonds); and (3) the LOC beneficiary who is typically the trustee. The municipal issuer is obligated to reimburse the LOC issuer for any funds it draws down under the agreement.

There are two types of LOCs: direct-pay LOC and standby LOC. With a direct-pay LOC, typically the issuer is entitled to draw upon the LOC in order to make interest and principal payment if a certain event occurs. The LOC beneficiary receives payments from the LOC issuer with the trustee having to request a payment. In contrast, with a standby LOC, the LOC beneficiary typically can only draw down on the agreement if the municipal issuer fails to make interest and/principal payments at the contractual due date. The LOC beneficiary must first request payment from the municipal issuer before drawing upon the LOC. When a LOC is issued by a smaller local bank, there may be a second LOC in place issued by a large national bank. This type of LOC is called a confirming LOC and is drawn upon only if the primary LOC issuer (the smaller local bank) fails to pay a draw request.

An irrevocable line of credit is not a guarantee of the bond issue, though it does provide a level of security. A revolving line of credit is a liquidity-type credit facility that provides a source of liquidity for payment of maturing debt in the event no other funds of the issuer are currently available. Because a bank can cancel a revolving line of credit without notice if the issuer fails to meet certain covenants, bond security depends entirely on the creditworthiness of the municipal issuer.

Refunded Bonds

Municipal bonds are sometimes refunded. An issuer may refund a bond issue for the same reasons that a corporate treasurer may seek to do so: (1) reducing funding costs after taking into account the costs of refunding; (2) eliminating burdensome restrictive covenants; and (3) altering the debt maturity structure for budgetary reasons.

Often, a refunding takes place when the original bond issue is escrowed or collateralized by direct obligations guaranteed by the U.S. government. By this it is meant that a portfolio of securities guaranteed by the U.S. government is placed in a trust. The portfolio of securities is assembled such that the cash flows from the securities match the obligations that the issuer must pay. Once this portfolio of securities whose cash flows match those of the municipality's obligation is in place, the refunded bonds are no longer general obligation or revenue bonds. Instead, the issue is supported by the cash flows from the securities in the escrow fund. Such bonds, if escrowed with securities guaranteed by the U.S. government, have little, if any, credit risk and are therefore the safest municipal bonds available.

The escrow fund for a refunded municipal bond can be structured so that the refunded bonds are to be called at the first possible call date or a subsequent call date established in the original bond indenture. Such bonds are known as prerefunded municipal bonds. While refunded bonds are usually retired at their first or subsequent call date, some are structured to match the debt obligation to the retirement date. Such bonds are known as "escrowed-to-maturity bonds."

Floating Rate Municipal Securities

As in the taxable bond market, municipal bonds may have a fixed or floating interest rate. There are two types of floating rate municipal bonds. The first has the traditional floating rate formula that calls for the resetting of the issue's coupon rate based on a reference rate plus a quoted margin. The quoted margin is fixed over the life of the bond issue. In the municipal bond market, the reference rate is typically some percentage of a taxable reference rate (e.g., 75% of six-month LIBOR) or a standard industry reference rate such as the Securities Industry and Financial Markets Association (SIFMA) Municipal Swap Index (formerly The Bond Market Association/PSA Municipal Swap Index). The index is calculated weekly.

The other type of floating rate municipal bond is an inverse floating rate bond or *inverse floater.* For an inverse floater the coupon rate changes in the direction that is opposite of the change in interest rates. That is, if interest rates increase (decrease) since the previous reset of the coupon rate, the new coupon rate decreases (increase).

Inverse floaters in the municipal market are created by a sponsor who deposits a fixed rate municipal security into a trust. The trust then creates two classes of floating rate securities. The first is a short-term floating rate security. This floating rate security can be tendered for redemption at par value on specified dates (typically every week) and are referred to as *tender option bonds* (TOBs). The interest on the TOBs is determined through an auction process that is conducted by a remarketing agent. The second bond class created is the inverse floater. The interest paid to this bond class is the residual interest from the fixed rate municipal bonds placed in the trust after paying the floating rate security bondholders and the expenses of the trust. For this reason, the inverse floater is sometimes called the *residual.* When reference rates rise (fall) and the floating rate security receives a greater (lesser) share of the interest from the fixed rate municipal security in the trust, the inverse floater investor receives less (more) interest. The holders of the inverse floater have the option to collapse the trust. They can do so by requiring the trustee to pay off the floating rate securities outstanding and instructing the trustee to give them the fixed rate securities placed in the trust.

TAX-EXEMPT MUNICIPAL BOND YIELDS

Interest rates on municipal bonds reflect not only the risks associated with corporate bonds but also reflect the tax advantage of tax-exempt municipal bonds, including the impact of the AMT and state and local tax treatment. A commonly used yield measure when comparing the yield on a tax-exempt municipal bond with a comparable taxable bond is the *equivalent taxable yield* and is computed as follows:

Equivalent taxable yield = Tax-exempt yield / (1 – Effective marginal tax rate)

The equivalent taxable yield shows the approximate yield that an investor would have to earn on a taxable bond in order to realize the same yield after taxes.

The *effective marginal tax rate* must take into account both the exemption of interest income from federal income taxes and the effective tax rate applied at the state level if one applies. In computing the effective state marginal tax rate, consideration is given to the deductibility of state taxes for determining federal income taxes. To do so, the following formula can be used to calculate the effective state marginal tax rate:

Effective state marginal tax rate

= (1 – Federal marginal tax rate) × State marginal tax rate

For example, in 2009 the Pennsylvania tax rate was flat at 3.07% for a taxpayer who does not reside in the city of Philadelphia. Thus, the state marginal tax rate is 3.07%. Assuming an investor faces a 35% federal marginal tax rate, then the effective state marginal tax rate is

$$(1 - 0.35) \times (0.0307) = 0.019955 \text{ or roughly } 2\%$$

In a state that does not tax municipal interest from either in-state or out-of-state issuers, the state marginal tax rate is obviously zero. In comparing the yield offered on in-state and out-of-state issuers, this adjustment is important.

The federal marginal tax rate in the above formula is the benefit received from being able to deduct state taxes in determining federal income taxes. For investors who do not itemize deductions or whose income is such that state tax deductions have minimal value, the effective state marginal tax rate is therefore the state marginal tax rate.

The effective marginal tax rate that is used in the formula for the equivalent-taxable yield is then the sum of the federal marginal tax rate plus the effective state marginal tax rate. In our example, an investor facing a 35% federal marginal tax rate and an effective state marginal tax rate of 2% would have an effective marginal tax rate of 37%. Suppose, for example, a yield on a municipal bond being considered for acquisition is 3%. Then the equivalent taxable yield is 3%/(1 – 0.37) = 4.76%.

A convention in the bond market is to quote yields on municipal bonds relative to some benchmark taxable bond yield such as a comparable maturity Treasury security or as a percentage of the London Interbank Offered Rate (LIBOR) from the swap yield curve. This ratio is referred to as the *yield ratio*, and it is normally less than 100% because municipal bonds offer a yield that is less than the yield on a comparable taxable bond.

RISKS ASSOCIATED WITH INVESTING IN MUNICIPAL BONDS

Investors in municipal bonds face the typical risks associated with investing in bonds that we described earlier in this book: credit risk, interest rate risk, call risk, and liquidity risk.

Credit risk includes credit default risk, credit spread risk, and downgrade risk. Credit default risk is gauged by the ratings assigned by Moody's, Standard & Poor's, and Fitch. Interest rate risk is typically measured by the duration of a bond: the approximate percentage price change of a bond for a 100-basis-point change in interest rates. Call risk arises for callable bonds and the adverse consequences associated when interest rates decline. An investor in single-family housing revenue bonds is exposed to a form of call risk, prepayment risk.

There are two risks that are to some extent unique to investors in the municipal bond market. The first is *structure risk*. This is the risk that the security structure may be legally challenged. This may arise in new structures, with the best example being the Washington Public Supply System (WPPS) bonds in the 1980s.

The second risk is *tax risk*. This risk comes in two forms. The first is the risk that the federal income tax rate will be reduced. To understand this risk, note that in the formula for the equivalent taxable yield, the yield is lower the smaller the effective marginal tax rate. A reduction in the effective marginal tax rate therefore reduces the equivalent taxable yield and, so that the yield on municipal bonds can stay competitive with taxable bonds, the price of municipal bonds will decline. The second type of tax risk is related to legal risk. The IRS may declare a bond issued as tax exempt as taxable. This may be the result of the issuer not complying with IRS regulations. A loss of the tax-exemption feature will cause the municipal bond to decline in value in order to provide a yield comparable to similar taxable bonds.

BUILD AMERICA BONDS

Thus far our focus has been on tax-exempt municipal securities. Because of the financial difficulties faced by state and local governments and their agencies in recent years, Congress authorized the issuance of a new type of taxable bond under the American Recovery and Investment Act of 2009. These bonds, dubbed *Build America Bonds* (BABs), come in two forms.

The first type, called a *direct payment BAB*, is a taxable municipal bond. However, the issuer is subsidized for the higher cost of issuing a taxable bond rather than a tax-exempt bond in the form of a payment from the U.S. Department of the Treasury. The payment is equal to 35% of the interest payments.

The second type of BAB is one in which a taxable municipal bond is issued but the bondholders receive a tax credit against their federal income taxes equal to 35% of the interest payment. This form of BAB is called a *tax credit BAB*.

The U.S. Department of the Treasury reported that between the time the program was launched in April 2009 and the end of May 2010, there were 1,306 separate issuances of BABs by state and local government in 49 states, the District of Columbia, and two U.S. territories. Total issuance was $106 billion. As a result, within the 13-month period since the launch of this new type of municipal bond, BABs constituted 21% of the municipal bond market.

Financial Instruments and Concepts Introduced in this Chapter (in Order of Presentation)

Municipal securities
Municipal bonds
Tax-exempt securities
Original-issue discount bond
Rule of de minimis
Market discount cutoff price
Alternative minimum taxable income
Alternative minimum tax
Official statement
Tax-backed debt obligations
General obligation debt
Moral obligation bonds
Tobacco settlement revenue bonds
Municipal notes
Variable rate demand obligations
Revenue bonds
Flow-of-funds structure

Single-family revenue bonds
Multifamily revenue bonds
Insured bonds
Bank-backed municipal bonds
Refunded bonds
Letter of credit
Inverse floater
Tender option bonds
Residual
Equivalent taxable yield
Effective marginal tax rate
Yield ratio
Structure risk
Tax risk
Build America Bonds
Direct payment BAB
Tax credit BAB

CHAPTER 7

Corporate Fixed Income Securities

Corporations are classified into five general categories by bond information services: utilities, transportations, industrials, banks, and finance (nonbanks). Within these five general categories, finer breakdowns are often made to create more homogeneous groupings. For example, utilities are subdivided into electric power companies, gas distribution companies, water companies, and communication companies. Transportations are divided further into airlines, railroads, and trucking companies. Industrials are the catchall class and the most heterogeneous of the groupings with respect to investment characteristics because this category includes all kinds of manufacturing, merchandising, and service companies.

Corporations issue several types of fixed income securities. These include debt instruments and preferred stock. Debt instruments that are issued include corporate bonds, medium-term notes, commercial paper, and asset-backed securities. In Chapter 10, we explain asset-backed securities. In this chapter, we will describe the general characteristics of the other debt instruments as well as preferred stock. A key investment attribute of corporate securities is their credit risk. In Chapter 4 we described the various aspects of credit risk and the credit ratings assigned to corporate debt obligations. We'll have more to say on other types of corporate bond issues in later chapters. More specifically, we cover investing in mezzanine debt and distressed debt in Chapters 19 and 20, respectively.

CORPORATE BONDS

While the prospectus may provide most of the needed information about a bond issue and information about the issuer, the indenture is the more important document. The *indenture* sets forth in great detail the promises of the issuer. Here we look at what indentures of corporate bond issues contain.

Secured Debt and Unsecured Debt

A corporate bond can be secured or unsecured. Below we describe each type.

Secured Debt

By secured debt it is meant that some form of collateral is pledged to ensure repayment of the debt. Debt secured by real property such as plant and equipment is called a *mortgage bond*. The largest issuers of mortgage bonds are electric utility companies. Mortgage bonds go by many different names such as *first mortgage bonds* or *first refunding mortgage bonds*. There are instances when a company might have two or more layers of mortgage debt outstanding with different priorities. This situation usually occurs because the companies cannot issue additional first mortgage debt (or the equivalent) under the existing indentures. Often, this secondary debt level is called *general and refunding mortgage bonds*. In reality, this is mostly second mortgage debt.

Today, nonutility companies do not offer much mortgage debt. Instead, the preferred form of debt financing is unsecured. In the broad classification of industrial companies, only a few have first mortgage bonds outstanding. While electric utility mortgage bonds generally have a lien on practically all of the company's property, mortgage debt of industrials has more limited liens. Some mortgage bonds issued by industries are secured by a lien on a specific property rather than on most of a company's property, as in the case of an electric utility.

Debt can be secured by many different assets. For example, a debt issue can be secured by a first-priority lien on substantially all of the issuer's real property, machinery, and equipment, and by a second-priority lien on its inventory, accounts receivables, and intangibles. *Collateral trust bonds* and notes are secured by financial assets such as cash, receivables, other notes, debentures, or bonds, and not by real property. They have been issued by companies engaged in vehicle leasing.

Railroads and airlines have financed much of their rolling stock and aircraft with secured debt. The securities go by various names such as *equipment trust certificates* (ETCs), in the case of railroads, and secured equipment certificates, guaranteed loan certificates, and loan certificates in the case of airlines. The structure of the financing usually provides for periodic retirement of the outstanding certificates. The most common form of ETC is the serial variety. It is usually issued in 15 equal maturities, each one coming due annually in years 1 through 15. There are single-maturity (or "bullet-maturity") ETCs. There are also sinking-fund equipment trust certificates where the ETCs are retired through the operation of a normal sinking fund, one-fifteenth of the original amount issued per year.

The standing of railroad or common carrier ETCs in bankruptcy is of vital importance to the investor. Because the equipment is needed for operations, the bankrupt railroad's management will more than likely reaffirm the lease of the equipment because, without rolling stock, it is out of business. Cases of disaffirmation of equipment obligations are very rare indeed, but if equipment debt were to be disaffirmed, the trustee could repossess and then try to re-lease or sell it to others. Any deficiency due the equipment debtholders would still be an unsecured claim against the bankrupt railway company. Standard-gauge, nonspecialized equipment should not be difficult to re-lease to another railroad.

Airline equipment debt has some of the special status that is held by railroad equipment trust certificates. The equipment is an important factor. If the airplanes are of recent vintage, well-maintained, fuel efficient, and relatively economical to operate, it is more likely that a company in distress and seeking to reorganize would assume the equipment lease. However, if the outlook for reorganization appears dim from the outset and the airplanes are older and less economical, the airline could very well disaffirm the lease. In this case, re-leasing the aircraft or selling it at rents and prices sufficient to continue the original payments and terms to the security holders might be difficult. Of course, the resale market for aircraft is on a plane-by-plane basis and highly subject to supply and demand factors. Multimillion-dollar airplanes have a somewhat more limited market than do boxcars and hopper cars in the case of railroad leases.

Unsecured Debt

We have discussed the features common of secured debt. Remove the collateral, and we have unsecured debt.

Unsecured debt, like secured debt, comes in several different layers or levels of claim against the corporation's assets. But in the case of unsecured debt, the nomenclature attached to the debt issues sounds less substantial. For example, "general and refunding mortgage bonds" may sound more important than "subordinated debentures," even though both are basically second claims on the issuing corporation. In addition to the normal debentures and notes, there are junior issues representing the secondary and tertiary levels of the capital structure. The difference in the case of a high-grade issuer may be considered insignificant as long as the issuer maintains its quality. But in cases of financial distress, the junior issues usually fare worse than the senior issues. Only in cases of very well-protected junior issues will investors come out whole—in which case, so would the holders of senior indebtedness. Thus, many investors are more than willing to take junior debt of high-grade companies. Investors who take such a view believe that the minor additional risk, compared to that of the senior debt of lower-rated issuers, may well be worth the incremental income.

Credit Enhancements

Some debt issuers have other companies guarantee their debt. This is normally done when a subsidiary issues debt and the investors want the added protection of a third-party guarantee. The use of guarantees makes it easier and more convenient to finance special projects and affiliates, although guarantees are extended to operating company debt.

Another credit-enhancing feature is the letter of credit (LOC) issued by a bank. A LOC requires the bank to make payments to the trustee when requested so that monies will be available for the bond issuer to meet its interest and principal payments when due. Thus, the credit of the bank under the LOC is substituted for that of the debt issuer. Monoline insurance companies also lend their credit standing to corporate debt, both new issues and outstanding secondary market issues.

While a guarantee or other type of credit enhancement may add some measure of protection to a debtholder, rating agencies perform an analysis of both the issuer and the guarantor. In many cases, only the latter is needed if the issuer is merely a financing conduit without any operations of its own. However, if both concerns are operating companies, it may very well be necessary for the rating agency to analyze both because the timely payment of principal and interest ultimately will depend on the stronger party. A downgrade of the enhancer's claims-paying ability reduces the value of the bonds.

Speculative-Grade Bonds

Speculative-grade bonds are those rated below investment grade by the rating agencies (that is, BBB– and lower by Standard & Poor's and Fitch Ratings and Baa3 and lower by Moody's). They may also be unrated, but not all unrated debt is speculative. They are also known as *high-yield bonds* and *junk bonds.*

Several types of issuers fall into the less-than-investment-grade highyield category. These include original issuers, fallen angels, and restructuring and leveraged buyouts.

Original issuers may be young, growing corporations lacking the stronger balance sheet and income statement profile of many established corporations, but often with lots of promise. Also called venture capital situations or growth or emerging market companies, the debt is often sold with a story projecting future financial strength. From this we get the term "story bond." There are also the established operating firms with financials neither measuring up to the strengths of investment-grade corporations nor possessing the weaknesses of companies on the verge of bankruptcy. Subordinated debt of investment-grade issuers may be included here. A bond rated at the bottom rung of the investment-grade category (Baa and BBB) or at the top end of the speculative-grade category (Ba and BB) is known as a "businessman's risk."

Fallen angels are formerly companies with investment-grade-rated debt that have come upon hard times with deteriorating balance sheet and income statement financial parameters.[1] They may be in default or near bankruptcy. In these cases, investors are interested in the workout value of the debt in a reorganization or liquidation, whether within or without the bankruptcy courts. Some refer to these issues as "special situations." Over the years they have fallen on hard times; some have recovered and others have not. General Motors Corporation and Ford Motor Company are examples of fallen angels. From 1954 to 1981, General Motors Corp. was rated AAA by S&P; Ford Motor Co. was rated AA by S&P from 1971 to 1980. In August 2005, Moody's lowered the rating on both automakers to junk bond status.

Restructurings and leveraged buyouts are companies that have deliberately increased their debt burden with a view toward maximizing shareholder value. The shareholders may be the existing public group to which the company pays a special extraordinary dividend, with the funds coming from borrowings and the sale of assets. Cash is paid out, net worth decreased and leverage increased, and ratings drop on existing debt. Newly issued debt gets junk bond status because of the company's weakened financial condition.

In a leveraged buyout (LBO), a new and private shareholder group owns and manages the company. The debt issue's purpose may be to retire other debt from commercial and investment banks and institutional investors incurred to finance the LBO. The debt to be retired is called bridge financing because it provides a bridge between the initial LBO activity and the more permanent financing. We discuss these bonds further in Chapter 18.

Often actions that are taken by management that result in the assignment of a non-investment-grade bond rating result in a heavy corporate interest payment burden. This places severe cash flow constraints on the firm. To reduce this burden, firms involved with heavy debt burdens have issued bonds with deferred coupon structures that permit the issuer to avoid using cash to make interest payments for a period of three to seven years. There are three types of deferred coupon structures: deferred-interest securities, step-up bonds, and payment-in-kind bonds. We described the first two types of coupon structures in Chapter 4. A *payment-in-kind* (PIK) *bond*

[1]Companies that have been upgraded to investment-grade status are referred to as rising stars.

gives the issuer an option to pay cash at a coupon payment date or give the bondholder a similar bond (that is, a bond with the same coupon rate and a par value equal to the amount of the coupon payment that would have been paid). The period during which the issuer can make this choice varies from five to 10 years.

An *extendible reset bond* structure allows the issuer to reset the coupon rate so that the bond will trade at a predetermined price. The coupon rate may reset annually or even more frequently, or reset only one time over the life of the bond. Generally, the coupon rate at the reset date will be the average of rates suggested by two investment banking firms. The new rate will then reflect (1) the level of interest rates at the reset date and (2) the credit spread the market wants on the issue at the reset date. Notice the difference between an extendible reset bond and a floating rate issue. In a floating rate issue, the coupon rate resets according to a fixed spread over the reference rate, with the index spread specified in the indenture. The amount of the index spread reflects market conditions at the time the issue is offered. The coupon rate on an extendible reset bond, in contrast, is reset based on market conditions (as suggested by several investment banking firms) at the time of the reset date. Moreover, the new coupon rate reflects the new level of interest rates and the new spread that investors seek. The advantage to investors of extendible reset bonds is that the coupon rate will reset to the market rate—both the level of interest rates and the credit spread—in principle keeping the issue at par value.

MEDIUM-TERM NOTES

A *medium-term note* (MTN) is a corporate debt instrument with the unique characteristic that the notes are offered continuously to investors by an agent of the issuer. Investors can select from several maturity ranges: nine months to one year, more than one year to 18 months, more than 18 months to two years, and so on up to 30 years. An MTN is registered with the SEC under Rule 415 (the shelf registration rule), which gives a corporation the maximum flexibility for issuing securities on a continuous basis.

The term "medium-term note" to describe this corporate debt instrument is misleading. Traditionally, the term "note" or "medium-term note" was used to refer to debt issues with a maturity greater than one year but less than 15 years. Certainly, this is not a characteristic of MTNs because they have been sold with maturities from 9 months to 30 years and even longer. For example, in July 1993, Walt Disney Corporation issued a security with a 100-year maturity off its MTN shelf registration. General Motors Acceptance Corporation first used MTNs in 1972 to fund automobile loans with maturities of five years and less. The purpose of the MTN was to fill the funding gap between commercial paper and long-term bonds. It is for this reason that they are referred to as "medium term." MTNs were issued directly to investors without the use of an agent.

An MTN differs from a corporate bond in the manner in which it is distributed to investors when it is initially sold. Most investment-grade corporate bond issues are underwritten by investment bankers. Traditionally, an MTN is distributed on a best-efforts basis by either an investment banking firm or other broker/dealers acting as agents. Another difference between a corporate bond and an MTN when they are offered is that an MTN is usually sold in relatively small amounts on a continuous or an intermittent basis, whereas a corporate bond issue is sold in large, discrete offerings.

A corporation that wants an MTN program will file a shelf registration with the SEC for the offering of securities. Once approved, the issuer posts rates over a range of maturities: for example, nine months to one year, one year to 18 months, 18 months to two years, and annually thereafter. This is called the *rate offering schedule*. Usually, an issuer will post rates as a spread over a Treasury security of comparable maturity.

The issuer's agents will then make the offering rate schedule available to their investor base interested in MTNs. An investor who is interested in the offering will contact the agent. In turn, the agent contacts the issuer to confirm the terms of the transaction. Because the maturity range in the offering rate schedule does not specify a specific maturity date, the investor can choose the final maturity subject to approval by the issuer. The minimum size that an investor can purchase of an MTN offering typically ranges from $1 million to $25 million.

Structured MTNs

Some MTN issuers couple an offering with transactions in the derivative markets (options, futures/forwards, swaps, caps, and floors) in order to create debt obligations with risk-return features unavailable in the corporate bond market. Specifically, an issue can be floating rate over all or part of the life of the security, and the coupon reset formula can be based on a benchmark interest rate, equity index or individual stock price, a foreign exchange rate, or a commodity index. Inverse floaters (that is, floaters whose coupon moves in the opposite direction of the change of a reference interest rate) are created in the structured MTN market. MTNs can have various embedded options included.

An MTN created when the issuer simultaneously transacts in the derivative markets is called a *structured note*. By using the derivative markets in combination with an offering, borrowers are able to create investment vehicles that are more customized for institutional investors to satisfy their investment objectives. Moreover, it allows institutional investors who are restricted to investing in investment-grade debt issues the opportunity to participate in other asset classes to make a market play. For example, an investor who buys an MTN whose coupon rate is tied to the performance of the S&P 500 is participating in the equity market without owning common stock. If the coupon rate is tied to a foreign stock index, the investor is participating in the equity market of a foreign country without owning foreign common stock. In exchange for creating/issuing a structured note, borrowers can reduce their funding costs.

COMMERCIAL PAPER

A corporation that needs long-term funds can raise those funds in either the bond or equity markets. Alternatively, if a corporation needs short-term funds, it may attempt to acquire funds via bank borrowing. One close substitute to bank borrowing for larger corporations with strong credit ratings is commercial paper. *Commercial paper* is a short-term promissory note issued in the open market as an obligation of the issuing entity.

The maturity of commercial paper is typically less than 270 days; a typical issue matures in less than 45 days. The combination of its short maturity and low credit risk make commercial paper an ideal investment vehicle for short-term funds. Most investors in commercial paper are institutional investors.

The market for commercial paper is a wholesale market and transactions are typically sizeable. The minimum round-lot transaction is $100,000. Some issuers will sell commercial paper in denominations of $25,000.

Commercial paper is classified as either direct paper or dealer paper. *Direct paper* is sold by an issuing firm directly to investors without using a securities dealer as an intermediary. The vast majority of the issuers of direct paper are financial firms. Because financial firms require a continuous source of funds in order to provide loans to customers, they find it cost effective to have a sales force to sell their commercial paper directly to investors. Direct issuers post rates at which they are willing to sell commercial paper with financial information vendors such as Bloomberg, Reuters, and Telerate. In the case of dealer placed commercial paper, the issuer uses the services of a securities firm to sell its paper. Commercial paper sold in this manner is referred to *as dealer paper.*

There is relatively little trading in the commercial paper secondary market. The reason is that most investors in commercial paper follow a "buy-and-hold" strategy. This is to be expected because investors purchase

EXHIBIT 7.1   Ratings of Commercial Paper

	Fitch	Moody's	S&P
Superior	F1-/F1	P1	A1-/A1
Satisfactory	F2	P2	A2
Adequate	F3	P3	A3
Speculative	F4	NP	B, C
Defaulted	F5	NP	D

commercial paper that matches their specific maturity requirements. Any secondary market trading is usually concentrated among institutional investors in a few large, highly rated issues. If investors wish to sell their commercial paper, they can usually sell it back to the original seller either dealer or issuer.

All investors in commercial paper are exposed to credit risk. Exhibit 7.1 presents the commercial paper ratings from Fitch, Moody's, and Standard & Poor's.

The risk that the investor faces is that the borrower will be unable to issue new paper at maturity. This risk is referred to as *rollover risk*. As a safeguard against rollover risk, commercial paper issuers secure backup lines of credit sometimes called "liquidity enhancement." Most commercial issuers maintain 100% backing because the rating agencies usually require a bank line of credit as a precondition for a rating. However, some large issues carry less than 100% backing. Backup lines of credit typically contain a "material adverse change" provision that allows the bank to cancel the credit line if the financial condition of the issuing firm deteriorates substantially.

The commercial paper market is divided into tiers according to credit risk ratings. The "top top tier" consists of paper rated A1-/P1/F1-. "Top tier" is paper rated A1/P1, F1. Next, "split tier" issues are rated either A1/P2 or A2/P1. The "second tier" issues are rated A2/P2.

PREFERRED STOCK

Unlike a corporate bond, MTN, and commercial paper, a *preferred stock* is a class of stock. It is classified on the balance sheet as equity. An investor in preferred stock is entitled to dividends just like the investor in common stock. However, unlike common stock, there is a specified dividend rate. The dividend amount is the product of the dividend rate and the par value of the preferred stock. The dividend rate can be a fixed rate or it can be a floating rate.

While there are occasionally exceptions, preferred stock limits the investor to the dividend amount as specified by the contractual dividend rate. That is, the investor can earn no more than this amount in the form of dividends. Thus, most preferred stock is *nonparticipating preferred stock*. Historically, there have been issues entitling the investor in preferred stock to participate in earnings distribution beyond the specified amount (based on some formula). Preferred stock with this feature is referred to as *participating preferred stock*.

It is because most preferred stock is of the nonparticipating variety that we classify preferred stock as a fixed income security. Thus, we can see that not all fixed income securities are debt obligations.

Dividend payments to preferred stockholders have priority over the payment to common stockholders but are paid after debt holders. A company usually has outstanding several preferred stock issues. In such cases, one of the issues is typically designated as having priority in the case of dividends payments over the others and is called *prior preferred stock*. The other preferred stock issues are called *preference preferred stock*. Hence, prior preferred stock has less risk than preference preferred stock and therefore offers a lower yield in the market.

If the issuer fails to make a preferred stock dividend payment, the preferred stockholders cannot force the issuer into bankruptcy. This is an attribute that preferred stock shares with common stock. When a preferred stock dividend payment is missed, the treatment of the unpaid dividend depends on whether the preferred stock is cumulative preferred stock or noncumulative preferred stock. With *cumulative preferred stock,* the dividend payment accrues until it is fully paid. Preferred stock of this variety shares this feature with a debt obligation. In the case of *noncumulative preferred stock,* the dividend payment is lost and is no longer the obligation of the issuer, as is the case with common stock. Regardless if the issue is cumulative or noncumulative, the failure to make dividend payments may result in preferred stockholders being given temporary voting rights and in the imposition of certain restrictions on certain activities of management.

In the liquidation of a corporation, the distribution of corporate assets to preferred stockholders comes after all debt holders are paid off. Preferred stockholders, as well as debt holders, can only recover up to their par value. Preferred stockholders are preferred to common stockholders in the distribution of corporate assets in a liquidation. As noted earlier, there is usually prior preferred stock and preference preferred stock in a corporation's capital structure. Not only does the former have priority over the latter with respect to dividend payments, but also in the case of a liquidation. Because preferred stock exposes an investor to credit risk, they are rated by the rating agencies.

Almost all preferred stock has a sinking-fund provision. Preferred stock may have a conversion feature that allows the investor to convert shares into common stock. Issues with this feature are called *convertible preferred stock.*

Preferred stock may be issued without a maturity date. This type of preferred stock is called *perpetual preferred stock.* There are putable and callable preferred stock issues.

As noted earlier, there are different types of preferred stock that have a floating or adjustable dividend rate. They include adjustable-rate preferred stock, auction rate preferred stock, and remarketed preferred stock. For *adjustable rate preferred stock,* the rate is determined by a formula. For *auction rate preferred stock,* the dividend rate is reset based on the results of an auction. Participants in the auction consist of current holders and potential buyers. The dividend rate that participants are willing to accept reflects current market conditions. In the case of *remarketed preferred stock,* the dividend rate is determined periodically by a remarketing agent, who resets the dividend rate so that any preferred stock can be tendered at par and be resold (remarketed) at the original offering price. The risks associated with remarked preferred stock is that that there is no assurance that the auction will succeed and that any holder will be able to sell their holdings at par value. Consequently, investors are exposed to liquidity risk. This is, in fact, what happened in August 2007. As of this writing, the auctions have continued to fail.

Payments made to preferred stockholders are treated as a distribution of earnings. Hence, unlike interest payments that are treated as business expenses by a corporation and therefore tax deductible in determining earnings, preferred stock dividend payments are not. While this raises the after-tax cost of funds if a corporation issues preferred stock rather than issuing debt or borrowing via bank loans, there is a provision in the tax code that makes the holding of preferred stock more appealing to treasurers of other corporations and thereby allows a corporation to issue preferred stock at a reduced cost. This provision is the *intercorporate tax dividend exclusion* which exempts a statutory percentage of qualified dividends from federal income taxation if the recipient is a qualified corporation. For example, assuming a dividend exclusion rate of 80%, if Corporation A owns the preferred stock of Corporation B, for each $1 million of dividends received by A, only 20% or $200,000 will be taxed at Corporation A's marginal tax rate. The purpose of this provision is to mitigate the effect of double taxation of corporate earnings. This tax provision is the chief reason that the major buyers of preferred stock are corporations who are seeking tax-advantaged investments.

CONVERTIBLE SECURITY

A *convertible security* is issued by a corporaton that gives the investor the option to convert into a specified number of shares of the issuer's common stock. A convertible security, or simply a *convertible*, can be a convertible bond or a convertible preferred stock. In our discussion of convertibles, we will focus on convertible bonds.

Convertible bonds issued today typically possess more than one embedded option in that they can be callable and putable. Accordingly, the value of a convertible bonds depends on: (1) how interest rate changes impact the bond's expected future cash flows via call and/or put options; (2) how creditworthiness of the underlying company impacts expected future cash flows; (3) how changes in the issuer's common stock price impact the value of the conversion feature; and (4) how volatile the common stock price is.

In its most basic form, there are two equivalent ways to describe a convertible bond. First, a convertible bond represents the combination of an option-free bond and call option on the common stock. However, unlike the exercise price of a call option, which is fixed, the value of the bond is surrendered to obtain a predetermined number of shares of common stock. Second, a convertible bond is a combination of common stock and a put option, which gives the bondholder the right to sell the stock back to the issuer with an exercise price equal to the market value of the convertible. If the investor chooses not to convert, this decision effectively exercises the put and thereby the investor keeps receiving the bond's cash flows.

Closely related to a convertible bond is an exchangeable bond. An exchangeable bond gives the bondholder the right, but not the obligation, to exchange the bond for the common stock of a firm other than the bond issuer. For example, in April 2007, UBS AG issued 6% six-month notes that were exchangeable into a fixed number of shares of Honda Motor Corporation. The same guidance in assessing the appeal of a convertible bond applies to an exchangeable bond. Hence our discussion below focuses on convertible bonds.

General Characteristics of Convertible Bonds

Let's use an actual convertible bond to explain the characteristics of this security. The convertible bond we will use is the 3.5% convertible issued by United Auto Group in April 2006 and matures April 1, 2026. The conversion privilege gives the bondholder the right to convert at any time up to the maturity date into a predetermined number of shares of the issuer's common stock. The predetermined number of shares is called the *conversion ratio*. This ratio is always adjusted proportionally for stock splits and stock dividends. For the

United Auto Group convertible, the conversion ratio is 42.2052 shares. Accordingly, the bondholder at a time may surrender the $1,000 maturity value bond for 42.2052 shares of United Auto Group common stock.

From the conversion ratio and the bond's price, the effective price per share the bondholder will pay by purchasing the bond at issuance and immediately converting it can be calculate. This effective price, referred to as the *conversion price*, is calculated by dividing the bond's price by the conversion ratio. If the United Auto Group bond is converted, the investor will receive 42.2052 shares of its common stock. Assuming that the bond's issuance price is $1,000, the conversion price per share is found by dividing $1,000 by the conversion ratio of 42.2052. Thus the convertible's conversion price is $23.69 per share.

Purchasing the common stock with a convertible security requires that the investor pay a premium over the current share price. This premium, which for the most part reflects the value of the conversion privilege and is called the *conversion premium*, is measured in percentage terms. When the United Auto Group bonds were issued, for example, the stock price was $18.95 and the conversion price was $23.69, so the initial conversion premium was therefore 25%

Virtually all convertible bonds are callable, giving the issuer the right to buy the bond back at a given price (that is, the call price) before maturity. The United Auto Group bond has a five-year call protection period such that the first call date is April 6, 2011, and gives the issuer the option to buy the bonds back before maturity at a call price of 100.

Many convertible bonds also possess a put feature. This feature gives the bondholder the right but not the obligation to sell the bond back to the issuer at par value before the maturity date. The United Auto Group bond is putable at par value commencing five years after issuance. Put features may be classified as either a hard part or a soft put. The difference is form of the payment the issuer makes to the bondholder when the put is exercised. A *hard put* requires the convertible to be redeemed for cash; a *soft put* permits the issuer to select the form of payment, which may be cash, common stock, subordinated debt, or some combination of the three.

The Traditional Approach for Assessing Convertibles

There are two approaches to assessing convertible. The first is the traditional approach and the one we discuss here. The second uses sophisticated modeling to value the embedded options in a convertible (the conversion and call options, as well as the put option if it is present). We will not discuss this second approach because it requires a thorough understanding of option pricing.

Conversion Value vs. Straight Value

The traditional approach to the valuation of convertible bonds begins with the determination of two values—conversion and straight. A bond's *straight value* is found by valuing the bond as if the conversion feature does not exist. The *conversion value* is the security's value if it is converted immediately. Specifically,

Conversion value = Conversion ratio × Market price of common stock

At any time prior to maturity, a convertible bond must be worth at least as much as the greater of the conversion value and the straight value. This is an arbitrage-enforced result. To see this, suppose the conversion value is greater than the straight value and the convertible bond's price is equal to its straight value. To exploit this arbitrage opportunity, an investor would buy the convertible and immediately convert. These actions enable the investor to capture the difference between the conversion value and the straight value less transaction costs. Suppose the opposite is true: The straight value is greater than the conversion value and the bond trades at its conversion value. If this occurs, the investor will be holding a bond that is undervalued relative to an otherwise similar straight bond.

Market Conversion Price

By taking a position in a convertible bond, an investor is acquiring the upside potential driven by the common stock's price with the downside protection of the straight bond. Accordingly, investors are willing to pay a premium over the current share price to purchase the common stock using the convertible. The price paid per share if the convertible is purchased and then converted is called the *market conversion price*.[2] The market conversion price is computed as follows:

$$\text{Market conversion price} = \frac{\text{Market price of convertible security}}{\text{Conversion ratio}}$$

The market conversion price can be viewed as a "break-even price" because if the price of the share of the issuer's common stock rises to this level, it just equals the price at which the investor effectively purchased the shares by buying the convertible.

---

[2]Note that the conversion price is the effective purchase price at the time of issuance, in contrast to the market conversion price where the effective purchase price is based on the prevailing price of the convertible.

The premium paid for buying the shares by exercising the convertible can be recast in terms of the value of a call option. This is true because the conversion feature allows for upside share price appreciation with a limited downside. This is done by calculating the market conversion premium per share as follows:

Market conversion premium per share

= Market conversion price − Current share price

The market conversion premium per share can be viewed as the value of the call option on the common stock underlying the convertible. An important difference between a call option on the stock and the conversion position is the downside risk exposure. The downside risk of the investor who purchases a call position on the common stock is limited to the price paid for the call option. In the case of a convertible, the downside risk exposure is the convertible's straight value that serves as a floor for the convertible's value. The floor, however, is not fixed. It can go up or down. This is true because the straight bond's value is a function of the level of interest rates, credit risk, and the like.

The market conversion premium per share can also be expressed as a percentage of the current share price. Specifically, the *market conversion premium ratio* is computed as follows:

$$\text{Market conversion premium ratio} = \frac{\text{Market conversion premium per share}}{\text{Market price of common stock}}$$

To illustrate, consider a 4.5% convertible issued by Ford Motor Company (Ford) in December 2006, matures in December 2036, and has a conversion ratio of 108.6957. The convertible current market value was at one time $1,113.80. The market conversion price was then

$$\text{Market conversion price} = \frac{\$1,113.80}{108.6957} = \$10.247$$

Accordingly, the investor is paying $10.247 a share for Ford's common stock. Suppose the current market share price for Ford is $8.01. The market conversion premium per share is computed as follows:

Market conversion premium per share = $10.247 − $8.01 = $2.24

This number tells us that if an investor purchases Ford common stock via the convertible, a premium of $2.24 a share is paid as opposed to buying the stock at the prevailing market price.

Finally, the market conversion premium ratio is computed as follows:

$$\text{Market conversion premium ratio} = \frac{\$2.24}{8.01} = 0.2793 = 27.93\%$$

This percentage means that the investor is paying a premium of 27.93% to purchase the Ford common stock through the convertible.

Measuring the Convertible's Income Advantage

Assuming that the issuer does not default on its debt, convertible bonds usually generate more in coupon interest than dividend income received from a number of common shares equal to the conversion ratio. This income advantage serves to mitigate the adverse effect of having to pay the premium for common stock purchased via the convertible bond.

To assess the convertible's income advantage, investors often compute a measure called the *premium payback period* (also called the *break-even time*). The premium payback period measures how long it takes to pay for the market conversion premium per share with the convertible's income advantage. The premium payback period is computed as follows:

$$\text{Premium payback period} = \frac{\text{Market conversion premium per share}}{\text{Favorable income differential per share}}$$

where the favorable income differential per share is computed as follows:

$$\frac{\text{Coupon interest} - (\text{Conversion ratio} \times \text{Common stock dividend per share})}{\text{Conversion ratio}}$$

There are two components to this ratio. The first component (the numerator) is the favorable income differential that is simply the coupon interest paid by the convertible less the dividend income forgone by not converting. The second component (denominator) is just the conversion ratio and puts the income advantage on a per share basis. Accordingly, the premium payback period answers the question: How long must one hold the convertible bond with its favorable income differential until the premium per share for buying the common stock via the convertible is recovered? Although this measure is useful, it is important to note that that this measure does not take into consideration either future dividend changes or the time value of money.

Let's use the Ford convertible to illustrate this measure. The favorable income differential per share is found as follows:

$$\text{Coupon interest from Ford bond} \quad = 0.045 \times \$1,000$$
$$= \$45.00$$
$$\text{Conversion ratio} \times \text{dividend per share} \quad = 108.6957 \times 0.05$$
$$= \$5.435$$

Accordingly,

$$\text{Favorable income differential per share} \ = \frac{\$45.00 - \$5.435}{108.6957}$$
$$= \$0.36$$

Therefore, the

$$\text{Premium payback period} = \frac{\$2.24}{\$0.36} = 6.2 \text{ years}$$

This number tells us that ignoring dividend changes and the time value of money, it will take approximately 6.2 years for the higher income of the convertible bond versus holding the common stock to recover the market conversion premium per share.

Measuring the Convertible Bond's Downside Risk

One might think about a convertible's straight value as the floor for the bond's value. Following this line of reasoning, the distance between the current market price and the straight value can be viewed as a measure of the investor's downside risk exposure. Formally, the downside risk is measured as a percentage of the straight value (that is, the floor), referred to as the *premium over straight value*. It is calculated using the following formula:

$$\text{Premium over straight value} = \frac{\text{Market price of convertible bond}}{\text{Straight value}} - 1$$

Holding all other factors constant, the greater the premium over the straight value, the greater the investor's exposure to downside risk.

We illustrate this measure using the Ford convertible assuming that the current market value for the convertible is $1,112.80:

$$\text{Premium over straight value} \ = \frac{\$1,112.80}{\$922.40} - 1 = 0.2064$$
$$= 20.64\%$$

The flaw in this measure is that the straight value is mistakenly viewed as a fixed and an immoveable barrier. The straight value depends on the level of yields and will move inversely to changes in those yields. The "floor" is a moving target.

Convertible Bonds as an Investment

A convertible is a hybrid financial instrument that combines elements of a position in a fixed income security and a position in the underlying common stock. The relative importance of each component is driven primarily by the financial performance of the underlying company that is ultimately reflected in the stock price. The relationship between the convertible bond price and the underlying stock price can be described as a continuum.

At one end of the continuum, the stock price is relatively low, such that the straight value of the convertible is considerably higher than the conversion value. When this occurs, convertibles have a low sensitivity to the underlying stock price because the conversion option is deep out-of-the-money and will trade like a high-yield straight bond. A convertible in such circumstances is referred to as a *fixed income equivalent* or *busted convertible*.

At the opposite end of the continuum, the stock price is relatively high, such that the conversion value is considerably higher than the straight value. The convertible bond will be highly responsive to changes in the stock price and possess a low conversion premium. When this occurs, the convertible bond will trade much like a common stock. The convertible under these conditions is said to be a *common stock equivalent*.

At prices in between, the convertible trades like a hybrid security possessing the characteristics of both a bond and a stock.

Other Types of Convertibles

There are two prominent variants of the traditional convertible bond—mandatory convertibles and reverse convertibles.

Mandatory convertibles are equity-linked hybrid securities that convert automatically at maturity into shares of the issuer's common stock. This automatic conversion differs from convertible bonds where conversion is optional. Mandatory convertibles offer higher coupon payments relative to the dividend income from holding the common stock directly. To glean these benefits, investors in mandatory convertibles pay a premium for the shares to be acquired at maturity. Moreover, these securities provide investors with limited upside participation in the underlying common stock. Mandatory convertibles are known by other trade names, including debt exchangeable for common stock (DECS).

One appealing feature of a regular convertible bond is the downside protection of the bond component. If the underlying common stock price performance is anemic and the conversion feature has no value, investors still have the bond. Due to the automatic conversion at expiration, a mandatory convertible has no bond floor and offers no downside protection.

The major difference between a regular convertible and reverse convertible turns on who owns the conversion option. The position of an investor in a *reverse convertible* can be thought of as the combination of the ownership of an option-free bond and the writing of a put option on the common stock. The issuer of the reverse convertible owns the put option and has the right but not the obligation to exercise its option to sell the common stock to the convertible owner. If the price of the issuer's common stock is below the exercise price at the exercise date, the bondholder receives a fixed number of shares of stock. The investor is obligated in effect to purchase shares above its market value. Conversely, if the stock price is above the exercise price at expiration, the bondholder receives the bond's maturity value.

Financial Instruments and Concepts Introduced in this Chapter (in Order of Presentation)

Indenture
Mortgage bond
First mortgage bonds (or first refunding mortgage bonds)
General and refunding mortgage bonds
Collateral trust bonds
Equipment trust certificates
Speculative-grade bonds
High-yield bonds
Junk bonds
Payment-in-kind bond
Extendible reset bond
Medium-term note
Rate offering schedule
Structured note
Commercial paper
Direct paper
Dealer paper
Rollover risk
Preferred stock
Nonparticipating preferred stock
Participating preferred stock

Prior preferred stock
Preference preferred stock
Cumulative preferred stock
Noncumulative preferred stock
Convertible preferred stock
Perpetual preferred stock
Adjustable rate preferred stock
Auction rate preferred stock
Remarketed preferred stock
Intercorporate tax dividend exclusion
Convertible security (convertible)
Conversion ratio
Conversion price
Conversion premium
Hard put
Soft put
Straight value
Conversion value
Market conversion price
Market conversion premium ratio
Premium payback period
Break-even time

Premium over straight value

Fixed income equivalent

Busted convertible

Common stock equivalent

Mandatory convertibles

Reverse convertible

CHAPTER 8

Agency Mortgage Passthrough Securities

Mortgage-backed securities are securities backed by a pool (collection) of mortgage loans. While any type of mortgage loans, residential or commercial, can be used as collateral for a mortgage-backed security, most are backed by residential mortgages. *Mortgage-backed securities* include the following securities: (1) mortgage passthrough securities, (2) collateralized mortgage obligations, and (3) stripped mortgage-backed securities. The latter two mortgage-backed securities are referred to as *derivative mortgage-backed securities* because they are created from mortgage passthrough securities. In this chapter we describe mortgage passthrough securities and stripped mortgage-backed securities. More specifically, we look at those securities either guaranteed by the full faith and credit of the U.S. government or guaranteed by a government-sponsored enterprise. Such mortgage-backed securities are called *agency mortgage-backed securities*. In Chapter 10, we look at nonagency mortgage-backed securities.

MORTGAGES

We begin our discussion with the raw material for a mortgage-backed security (MBS)—the mortgage loan. A *mortgage loan*, or simply mortgage, is a loan secured by the collateral of some specified real estate property, which obliges the borrower to make a predetermined series of payments. The mortgage gives the lender the right if the borrower defaults (i.e., fails to make the contracted payments) to "foreclose" on the loan and seize the property in order to ensure that the debt is paid off. The interest rate on the mortgage loan is called the *mortgage rate* or *contract rate*. Our focus is on residential mortgage loans.

When the lender makes the loan based on the credit of the borrower and on the collateral for the mortgage, the mortgage is said to be a *conventional mortgage.* The lender also may take out mortgage insurance to guarantee the fulfillment of the borrower's obligation. Some borrowers can qualify for mortgage insurance, which is guaranteed by one of three U.S. government agencies: the Federal Housing Administration (FHA), the Veteran's Administration (VA), and the Rural Housing Service (RHS). There are also private mortgage insurers.

There are many types of mortgage designs available in the United States. A *mortgage design* is a specification of the interest rate, term of the mortgage, and manner in which the borrowed funds are repaid. We describe the most popular mortgage design below: the fixed rate, level payment, fully amortized mortgage.

Fixed Rate, Level Payment, Fully Amortized Mortgage

The basic idea behind the design of the fixed rate, level payment, fully amortized mortgage is that the borrower pays interest and repays principal in equal installments over an agreed-upon period of time, called the *maturity* or *term* of the mortgage. The frequency of payment is typically monthly. Each monthly mortgage payment for this mortgage design is due on the first of each month and consists of:

1. Interest of one-twelfth of the annual interest rate times the amount of the outstanding mortgage balance at the beginning of the previous month.
2. A repayment of a portion of the outstanding mortgage balance (principal).

The difference between the monthly mortgage payment and the portion of the payment that represents interest equals the amount that is applied to reduce the outstanding mortgage balance. The monthly mortgage payment is designed so that after the last scheduled monthly payment of the loan is made, the amount of the outstanding mortgage balance is zero (i.e., the mortgage is fully repaid or amortized).

To illustrate this mortgage design, consider a 30-year (360-month) $100,000 mortgage with a mortgage rate of 8.125%. The monthly mortgage payment would be $742.50. Exhibit 8.1 shows for selected months how each monthly mortgage payment is divided between interest and repayment of principal. At the beginning of month 1, the mortgage balance is $100,000, the amount of the original loan. The mortgage payment for month 1 includes interest on the $100,000 borrowed for the month. Since the interest rate is 8.125%, the monthly interest rate is 0.0067708 (0.08125 divided by 12). Interest for month 1 is therefore $677.08 ($100,000 times 0.0067708). The $65.42 difference between the monthly mortgage payment

EXHIBIT 8.1 Amortization Schedule for a Fixed Rate, Level Payment, Fully Amortized Mortgage
Mortgage loan: $100,000
Mortgage rate: 8.125%
Monthly payment: $742.50
Term of loan: 30 years (360 months)

Month	Beginning Mortgage Balance ($)	Monthly Payment ($)	Monthly Interest ($)	Scheduled Principal Repayment ($)	Ending Mortgage Balance ($)
1	100,000.00	742.50	677.08	65.42	99,934.58
2	99,934.58	742.50	676.64	65.86	99,868.72
3	99,868.72	742.50	676.19	66.31	99,802.41
25	98,301.53	742.50	665.58	76.91	98,224.62
26	98,224.62	742.50	665.06	77.43	98,147.19
27	98,147.19	742.50	664.54	77.96	98,069.23
74	93,849.98	742.50	635.44	107.05	93,742.93
75	93,742.93	742.50	634.72	107.78	93,635.15
76	93,635.15	742.50	633.99	108.51	93,526.64
141	84,811.77	742.50	574.25	168.25	84,643.52
142	84,643.52	742.50	573.11	169.39	84,474.13
143	84,474.13	742.50	571.96	170.54	84,303.59
184	76,446.29	742.50	517.61	224.89	76,221.40
185	76,221.40	742.50	516.08	226.41	75,994.99
186	75,994.99	742.50	514.55	227.95	75,767.04
233	63,430.19	742.50	429.48	313.02	63,117.17
234	63,117.17	742.50	427.36	315.14	62,802.03
235	62,802.03	742.50	425.22	317.28	62,484.75
289	42,200.92	742.50	285.74	456.76	41,744.15
290	41,744.15	742.50	282.64	459.85	41,284.30
291	41,284.30	742.50	279.53	462.97	40,821.33
321	25,941.42	742.50	175.65	566.85	25,374.57
322	25,374.57	742.50	171.81	570.69	24,803.88
323	24,803.88	742.50	167.94	574.55	24,229.32
358	2,197.66	742.50	14.88	727.62	1,470.05
359	1,470.05	742.50	9.95	732.54	737.50
360	737.50	742.50	4.99	737.50	0.00

of $742.50 and the interest of $677.08 is the portion of the monthly mortgage payment that represents repayment of principal. The $65.42 in month 1 reduces the mortgage balance.

The mortgage balance at the end of month 1 (beginning of month 2) is then $99,934.58 ($100,000 minus $65.42). The interest for the second monthly mortgage payment is $676.64, the monthly interest rate (0.0067708) times the mortgage balance at the beginning of month 2 ($99,934.58). The difference between the $742.50 monthly mortgage payment and the $676.64 interest is $65.86, representing the amount of the mortgage balance paid off with that monthly mortgage payment. Notice that the last mortgage payment in month 360 is sufficient to pay off the remaining mortgage balance.

As Exhibit 8.1 clearly shows, the portion of the monthly mortgage payment applied to interest declines each month, and the portion applied to reducing the mortgage balance increases. The reason for this is that as the mortgage balance is reduced with each monthly mortgage payment, the interest on the mortgage balance declines. Since the monthly mortgage payment is fixed, an increasingly larger portion of the monthly payment is applied to reduce the principal in each subsequent month.

Servicing Fee and the Cash Flows

Every mortgage loan must be serviced. Servicing of a mortgage loan involves collecting monthly payments and forwarding proceeds to owners of the loan; sending payment notices to mortgagors; reminding mortgagors when payments are overdue; maintaining records of principal balances; administering an escrow balance for real estate taxes and insurance purposes; initiating foreclosure proceedings if necessary; and furnishing tax information to mortgagors when applicable.

The servicing fee is a portion of the mortgage rate. If the mortgage rate is 8.125% and the servicing fee is 50 basis points, then the investor receives interest of 7.625%. The interest rate that the investor receives is said to be the *net interest* or *net coupon*. The servicing fee is commonly called the *servicing spread*.

The dollar amount of the servicing fee declines over time as the mortgage amortizes. This is true for not only the mortgage design that we have just described, but for all mortgage designs.

Prepayments and Cash Flow Uncertainty

Our illustration of the cash flows from a fixed rate, level payment, fully amortized mortgage assumes that the homeowner does not pay off any portion of the mortgage balance prior to the scheduled due date. But homeowners do pay off all or part of their mortgage balance prior to the maturity date. Payments made in excess of the scheduled principal repayments are called *prepayments*. We'll look more closely at the factors that affect prepayment behavior later in this chapter.

The effect of prepayments is that the amount and timing of the cash flows from a mortgage are not known with certainty. This risk is referred to as *prepayment risk*. For example, all that the investor in a $100,000, 8.125% 30-year FHA-insured mortgage knows is that as long as the loan is outstanding, interest will be received and the principal will be repaid at the scheduled date each month; then at the end of the 30 years, the investor would have received $100,000 in principal payments. What the investor does not know—the uncertainty—is for how long the loan will be outstanding, and therefore what the timing of the principal payments will be. This is true for all mortgage loans, not just fixed rate, level payment, fully amortized mortgages.

MORTGAGE PASSTHROUGH SECURITIES

Investing in mortgages exposes an investor to default risk and prepayment risk. A more efficient way is to invest in a *mortgage passthrough security*. This is a security created when one or more holders of mortgages form a pool (collection) of mortgages and sell shares or participation certificates in the pool. A pool may consist of several thousand or only a few mortgages. When a mortgage is included in a pool of mortgages that is used as collateral for a mortgage passthrough security, the mortgage is said to be securitized.

The cash flows of a mortgage passthrough security depend on the cash flows of the underlying mortgages. As explained in the previous section, the cash flows consist of monthly mortgage payments representing interest, the scheduled repayment of principal, and any prepayments.

Payments are made to securityholders each month. Neither the amount nor the timing, however, of the cash flows from the pool of mortgages is identical to that of the cash flows passed through to investors. The monthly cash flows for a passthrough are less than the monthly cash flows of the underlying mortgages by an amount equal to servicing and other fees. The other fees are those charged by the issuer or guarantor of the passthrough for guaranteeing the issue. The coupon rate on a passthrough, called the *passthrough coupon rate*, is less than the mortgage rate on the underlying pool of mortgage loans by an amount equal to the servicing fee and guarantee fee. The latter is a fee charged by an agency for providing one of the guarantees discussed later.

The timing of the cash flows is also different. The monthly mortgage payment is due from each mortgagor on the first day of each month, but there is a delay in passing through the corresponding monthly cash flow to the securityholders. The length of the delay varies by the type of passthrough security.

Not all of the mortgages that are included in a pool of mortgages that are securitized have the same mortgage rate and the same maturity. Consequently, when describing a passthrough security, a weighted average coupon rate and a weighted average maturity are determined. A *weighted average coupon rate*, or WAC, is found by weighting the mortgage rate of each mortgage loan in the pool by the amount of the mortgage balance outstanding. A *weighted average maturity*, or WAM, is found by weighting the remaining number of months to maturity for each mortgage loan in the pool by the amount of the mortgage balance outstanding.

TYPES OF AGENCY MORTGAGE PASSTHROUGH SECURITIES

There are three types of agency passthrough securities backed by residential mortgages: Ginnie Mae, Freddie Mac, and Fannie Mae.

Government National Mortgage Association ("Ginnie Mae") passthroughs are guaranteed by the full faith and credit of the U.S. government. Therefore, Ginnie Mae passthroughs are viewed as risk-free in terms of default risk, just like Treasury securities. The security guaranteed by Ginnie Mae is called a *Ginnie Mae mortgage-backed security*.

The Federal Home Loan Mortgage Corporation (now officially known as Freddie Mac) is a government-sponsored enterprise (GSE) that issues a passthrough security that is called a *Freddie Mac participation certificate* (PC). Although a guarantee of Freddie Mac is not a guarantee by the U.S. government, at one time most market participants viewed Freddie Mac PCs as similar, although not identical, in credit worthiness to Ginnie Mae passthroughs. As explained in Chapter 5, Freddie Mac (as well as Fannie Mae described next) have been placed in conservatorship. Although there is an agreement with the federal government for Freddie Mac to borrow from the U.S. Department of the Treasury, there is still no assurance that the potential funding will assure that it will be able to satisfy its guarantees.

The passthrough issued by the Federal National Mortgage Association (now officially known as Fannie Mae) is called a *Fannie Mae mortgage-backed security*. Like a Freddie Mac PC, a Fannie Mae MBS is not the obligation of the U.S. government since Fannie Mae is a GSE and the risk that the guarantees on its securities will not be satisfied is the same as with Freddie Mac.

PREPAYMENT CONVENTIONS AND CASH FLOWS

In order to value a passthrough security, it is necessary to project its cash flows. The difficulty is that the cash flows are unknown because of prepayments. The only way to project cash flows is to make some assumptions about the prepayment rate over the life of the underlying mortgage pool. The prepayment rate is sometimes referred to as the *prepayment speed*. Two conventions have been used as a benchmark for prepayment rates: conditional prepayment rate and Public Securities Association prepayment benchmark.

Conditional Prepayment Rate

One convention for projecting prepayments and the cash flows of a passthrough assumes that some fraction of the remaining principal in the pool is prepaid each month for the remaining term of the mortgage. The prepayment rate assumed for a pool, called the *conditional prepayment rate* (CPR), is based on the characteristics of the pool (including its historical prepayment experience) and the current and expected future economic environment.

The CPR is an annual prepayment rate. To estimate monthly prepayments, the CPR must be converted into a monthly prepayment rate, commonly referred to as the *single-monthly mortality rate* (SMM). A formula can be used to determine the SMM for a given CPR:

$$SMM = 1 - (1 - CPR)^{1/12}$$

Suppose that the CPR used to estimate prepayments is 6%. The corresponding SMM is

$$SMM = 1 - (1 - 0.06)^{1/12} = 1 - (0.94)^{0.08333} = 0.005143$$

An SMM of $w\%$ means that approximately $w\%$ of the remaining mortgage balance at the beginning of the month, less the scheduled principal payment, will prepay that month. That is,

Prepayment for month t = SMM
$\times$ (Beginning mortgage balance for month t
– Scheduled principal payment for month t)

For example, suppose that an investor owns a passthrough in which the remaining mortgage balance at the beginning of some month is \$290 million. Assuming that the SMM is 0.5143% and the scheduled principal payment is $3 million, the estimated prepayment for the month is

$$0.005143 \times (\$290,000,000 - \$3,000,000) = \$1,476,041$$

PSA Prepayment Benchmark

The *Public Securities Association prepayment benchmark* (or simply *PSA benchmark*) is expressed as a monthly series of CPRs.[1] The PSA benchmark assumes that prepayment rates are low for newly originated mortgages and then will speed up as the mortgages become seasoned.

The PSA benchmark assumes the following prepayment rates for 30-year mortgages:

1. A CPR of 0.2% for the first month, increased by 0.2% per year per month for the next 30 months when it reaches 6% per year.
2. A 6% CPR for the remaining years.

This benchmark is referred to as "100% PSA" or simply "100 PSA." Mathematically, 100 PSA can be expressed as follows:

If $t \leq 30$, then CPR $= \dfrac{6\% t}{30}$

If $t > 30$, then CPR $= 6\%$

where t is the number of months since the mortgage originated.

Slower or faster speeds are then referred to as some percentage of PSA. For example, 50 PSA means one-half the CPR of the PSA benchmark prepayment rate; 150 PSA means 1.5 times the CPR of the PSA benchmark prepayment rate; 300 PSA means three times the CPR of the benchmark prepayment rate. A prepayment rate of 0 PSA means that no prepayments are assumed.

The CPR is converted to an SMM using the formula given above. For example, the SMMs for month 5, month 20, and months 31 through 360 assuming 100 PSA are calculated as follows:

For month 5:
    CPR = 6% (5/30) = 1% = 0.01

---

[1] This benchmark is commonly referred to as a prepayment model, suggesting that it can be used to estimate prepayments. Characterization of this benchmark as a prepayment model is inappropriate. It is simply a market convention describing the behavior pattern of prepayments.

$$SMM = 1 - (1 - 0.01)^{1/12}$$
$$= 1 - (0.99)0.083333 = 0.000837$$

For month 20:
$$CPR = 6\% \ (20/30) = 4\% = 0.04$$
$$SMM = 1 - (1 - 0.04)^{1/12}$$
$$= 1 - (0.96)0.083333 = 0.003396$$

For months 31 to 360:
$$CPR = 6\%$$
$$SMM = 1 - (1 - 0.06)^{1/12}$$
$$= 1 - (0.94)0.083333 = 0.005143$$

The SMMs for month 5, month 20, and months 31 through 360 assuming 165 PSA are computed as follows:

For month 5:
$$CPR = 6\% \ (5/30) = 1\% = 0.01$$
$$165 \ PSA = 1.65 \ (0.01) = 0.0165$$
$$SMM = 1 - (1 - 0.0165)^{1/12}$$
$$= 1 - (0.9835)0.083333 = 0.001386$$

For month 20:
$$CPR = 6\% \ (20/30) = 4\% = 0.04$$
$$165 \ PSA = 1.65 \ (0.04) = 0.066$$
$$SMM = 1 - (1 - 0.066)^{1/12}$$
$$= 1 - (0.934)0.083333 = 0.005674$$

For months 31 to 360:
$$CPR = 6\%$$
$$165 \ PSA = 1.65 \ (0.06) = 0.099$$
$$SMM = 1 - (1 - 0.099)^{1/12}$$
$$= 1 - (0.901)0.083333 = 0.00865$$

Notice that the SMM assuming 165 PSA is not just 1.65 times the SMM assuming 100 PSA. It is the CPR that is a multiple of the CPR assuming 100 PSA.

Illustration of Monthly Cash Flow Construction

We now show how to construct a monthly cash flow for a hypothetical passthrough given a PSA assumption. For the purpose of this illustration, the underlying mortgages for this hypothetical passthrough are assumed to be fixed rate, level payment, fully amortized mortgages with a weighted average coupon (WAC) rate of 8.125%. It will be assumed that the passthrough rate is 7.5% with a weighted average maturity (WAM) of 357 months.

Exhibit 8.2 shows the cash flow for selected months assuming 100 PSA. The cash flow is broken down into three components: (1) interest (based on the passthrough rate), (2) the regularly scheduled principal repayment, and (3) prepayments based on 100 PSA.

Let's walk through Exhibit 8.2 column by column.

Column 1: This is the month.

Column 2: This column gives the outstanding mortgage balance at the beginning of the month. It is equal to the outstanding balance at the beginning of the previous month reduced by the total principal payment in the previous month.

Column 3: This column shows the SMM for 100 PSA. Two things should be noted in this column. First, for month 1, the SMM is for a passthrough that has been seasoned 3 months. That is, the CPR is 0.8% for the first month. This is because the WAM is 357. Second, from month 27 on, the SMM is 0.00514, which corresponds to a CPR of 6%.

Column 4: The total monthly mortgage payment is shown in this column. Notice that the total monthly mortgage payment declines over time as prepayments reduce the mortgage balance outstanding. There is a formula to determine what the monthly mortgage balance will be for each month given prepayments.[2]

Column 5: The monthly interest paid to the passthrough investor is found in this column. This value is determined by multiplying the outstanding mortgage balance at the beginning of the month by the passthrough rate of 7.5% and dividing by 12.

Column 6: This column gives the regularly scheduled principal repayment. This is the difference between the total monthly mortgage payment [the amount shown in column (4)] and the gross coupon interest for the month. The gross coupon interest is 8.125% multiplied by the outstanding mortgage balance at the beginning of the month, then divided by 12.

---

[2]The formula is presented in Chapter 20 of Frank J. Fabozzi, *Fixed Income Mathematics: Analytical and Statistical Techniques* (Chicago: Probus Publishing, 1993).

EXHIBIT 8.2 Monthly Cash Flow for a $400 Million Passthrough with a 7.5% Passthrough Rate, a WAC of 8.125%, and a WAM of 357 Months Assuming 100 PSA

(1)	(2)	(3)	(4)	(5)	(6)	(7)	(8)	(9)
Month	Outstanding Balance	SMM	Mortgage Payment	Net Interest	Scheduled Principal	Prepayment	Total Principal	Cash Flow
1	$400,000,000	0.00067	$2,975,868	$2,500,000	$267,535	$267,470	$535,005	$3,035,005
2	399,464,995	0.00084	2,973,877	2,496,656	269,166	334,198	603,364	3,100,020
3	398,861,631	0.00101	2,971,387	2,492,885	270,762	400,800	671,562	3,164,447
4	398,190,069	0.00117	2,968,399	2,488,688	272,321	467,243	739,564	3,228,252
5	397,450,505	0.00134	2,964,914	2,484,066	273,843	533,493	807,335	3,291,401
6	396,643,170	0.00151	2,960,931	2,479,020	275,327	599,514	874,841	3,353,860
7	395,768,329	0.00168	2,956,453	2,473,552	276,772	665,273	942,045	3,415,597
8	394,826,284	0.00185	2,951,480	2,467,664	278,177	730,736	1,008,913	3,476,577
9	393,817,371	0.00202	2,946,013	2,461,359	279,542	795,869	1,075,410	3,536,769
10	392,741,961	0.00219	2,940,056	2,454,637	280,865	860,637	1,141,502	3,596,140
11	391,600,459	0.00236	2,933,608	2,447,503	282,147	925,008	1,207,155	3,654,658
12	390,393,304	0.00254	2,926,674	2,439,958	283,386	988,948	1,272,333	3,712,291
13	389,120,971	0.00271	2,919,254	2,432,006	284,581	1,052,423	1,337,004	3,769,010
14	387,783,966	0.00288	2,911,353	2,423,650	285,733	1,115,402	1,401,134	3,824,784
15	386,382,832	0.00305	2,902,973	2,414,893	286,839	1,177,851	1,464,690	3,879,583
16	384,918,142	0.00322	2,894,117	2,405,738	287,900	1,239,739	1,527,639	3,933,378
17	383,390,502	0.00340	2,884,789	2,396,191	288,915	1,301,033	1,589,949	3,986,139
18	381,800,553	0.00357	2,874,992	2,386,253	289,884	1,361,703	1,651,587	4,037,840
19	380,148,966	0.00374	2,864,730	2,375,931	290,805	1,421,717	1,712,522	4,088,453
20	378,436,444	0.00392	2,854,008	2,365,228	291,678	1,481,046	1,772,724	4,137,952
21	376,663,720	0.00409	2,842,830	2,354,148	292,503	1,539,658	1,832,161	4,186,309
22	374,831,559	0.00427	2,831,201	2,342,697	293,279	1,597,525	1,890,804	4,233,501
23	372,940,755	0.00444	2,819,125	2,330,880	294,005	1,654,618	1,948,623	4,279,503
24	370,992,132	0.00462	2,806,607	2,318,701	294,681	1,710,908	2,005,589	4,324,290
25	368,986,543	0.00479	2,793,654	2,306,166	295,307	1,766,368	2,061,675	4,367,841
26	366,924,868	0.00497	2,780,270	2,293,280	295,883	1,820,970	2,116,852	4,410,133
27	364,808,016	0.00514	2,766,461	2,280,050	296,406	1,874,688	2,171,094	4,451,144
28	362,636,921	0.00514	2,752,233	2,266,481	296,879	1,863,519	2,160,398	4,426,879
29	360,476,523	0.00514	2,738,078	2,252,978	297,351	1,852,406	2,149,758	4,402,736
30	358,326,766	0.00514	2,723,996	2,239,542	297,825	1,841,347	2,139,173	4,378,715
100	231,249,776	0.00514	1,898,682	1,445,311	332,928	1,187,608	1,520,537	2,965,848
101	229,729,239	0.00514	1,888,917	1,435,808	333,459	1,179,785	1,513,244	2,949,052
102	228,215,995	0.00514	1,879,202	1,426,350	333,990	1,172,000	1,505,990	2,932,340
103	226,710,004	0.00514	1,869,538	1,416,938	334,522	1,164,252	1,498,774	2,915,712
104	225,211,230	0.00514	1,859,923	1,407,570	335,055	1,156,541	1,491,596	2,899,166
105	223,719,634	0.00514	1,850,357	1,398,248	335,589	1,148,867	1,484,456	2,882,703
200	109,791,339	0.00514	1,133,751	686,196	390,372	562,651	953,023	1,639,219
201	108,838,316	0.00514	1,127,920	680,239	390,994	557,746	948,740	1,628,980
202	107,889,576	0.00514	1,122,119	674,310	391,617	552,863	944,480	1,618,790
203	106,945,096	0.00514	1,116,348	668,407	392,241	548,003	940,243	1,608,650
204	106,004,852	0.00514	1,110,607	662,530	392,866	543,164	936,029	1,598,560
205	105,068,823	0.00514	1,104,895	656,680	393,491	538,347	931,838	1,588,518

EXHIBIT 8.2   (Continued)

(1)	(2)	(3)	(4)	(5)	(6)	(7)	(8)	(9)
Month	Outstanding Balance	SMM	Mortgage Payment	Net Interest	Scheduled Principal	Prepayment	Total Principal	Cash Flow
300	$32,383,611	0.00514	$676,991	$202,398	$457,727	$164,195	$621,923	$824,320
301	31,761,689	0.00514	673,510	198,511	458,457	160,993	619,449	817,960
302	31,142,239	0.00514	670,046	194,639	459,187	157,803	616,990	811,629
303	30,525,249	0.00514	666,600	190,783	459,918	154,626	614,545	805,328
304	29,910,704	0.00514	663,171	186,942	460,651	151,462	612,113	799,055
305	29,298,591	0.00514	659,761	183,116	461,385	148,310	609,695	792,811
350	4,060,411	0.00514	523,138	25,378	495,645	18,334	513,979	539,356
351	3,546,432	0.00514	520,447	22,165	496,435	15,686	512,121	534,286
352	3,034,311	0.00514	517,770	18,964	497,226	13,048	510,274	529,238
353	2,524,037	0.00514	515,107	15,775	498,018	10,420	508,437	524,213
354	2,015,600	0.00514	512,458	12,597	498,811	7,801	506,612	519,209
355	1,508,988	0.00514	509,823	9,431	499,606	5,191	504,797	514,228
356	1,004,191	0.00514	507,201	6,276	500,401	2,591	502,992	509,269
357	501,199	0.00514	504,592	3,132	501,199	0	501,199	504,331

Note: Since the WAM is 357 months, the underlying mortgage pool is seasoned an average of 3 months. Therefore, the CPR for month 27 is 6%.

Column 7: The prepayment for the month is reported in this column. The prepayment is found as follows:

$$\text{SMM} \times (\text{Beginning mortgage balance for month } t - \text{Scheduled principal payment for month } t)$$

For example, in month 100, the beginning mortgage balance is $231,249,776, the scheduled principal payment is $332,298, and the SMM at 100 PSA is 0.00514301 (only 0.00514 is shown in the exhibit to save space). Therefore, the prepayment is

$$0.00514301 \times (\$231,249,776 - \$332,928) = \$1,187,608.$$

Column 8: The total principal payment, which is the sum of columns (6) and (7), is shown in this column.

Column 9: The projected monthly cash flow for this passthrough is shown in this last column. The monthly cash flow is the sum of the interest paid to the passthrough investor [column (5)] and the total principal payments for the month [column (8)].

EXHIBIT 8.3 Monthly Cash Flow for a $400 Million Passthrough with a 7.5% Passthrough Rate, a WAC of 8.125%, and a WAM of 357 Months Assuming 165 PSA

(1)	(2)	(3)	(4)	(5)	(6)	(7)	(8)	(9)
Month	Outstanding Balance	SMM	Mortgage Payment	Net Interest	Scheduled Principal	Prepayment	Total Principal	Cash Flow
1	$400,000,000	0.00111	$2,975,868	$2,500,000	$267,535	$442,389	$709,923	$3,209,923
2	399,290,077	0.00139	2,972,575	2,495,563	269,048	552,847	821,896	3,317,459
3	398,468,181	0.00167	2,968,456	2,490,426	270,495	663,065	933,560	3,423,986
4	397,534,621	0.00195	2,963,513	2,484,591	271,873	772,949	1,044,822	3,529,413
5	396,489,799	0.00223	2,957,747	2,478,061	273,181	882,405	1,155,586	3,633,647
6	395,334,213	0.00251	2,951,160	2,470,839	274,418	991,341	1,265,759	3,736,598
7	394,068,454	0.00279	2,943,755	2,462,928	275,583	1,099,664	1,375,246	3,838,174
8	392,693,208	0.00308	2,935,534	2,454,333	276,674	1,207,280	1,483,954	3,938,287
9	391,209,254	0.00336	2,926,503	2,445,058	277,690	1,314,099	1,591,789	4,036,847
10	389,617,464	0.00365	2,916,666	2,435,109	278,631	1,420,029	1,698,659	4,133,769
11	387,918,805	0.00393	2,906,028	2,424,493	279,494	1,524,979	1,804,473	4,228,965
12	386,114,332	0.00422	2,894,595	2,413,215	280,280	1,628,859	1,909,139	4,322,353
13	384,205,194	0.00451	2,882,375	2,401,282	280,986	1,731,581	2,012,567	4,413,850
14	382,192,626	0.00480	2,869,375	2,388,704	281,613	1,833,058	2,114,670	4,503,374
15	380,077,956	0.00509	2,855,603	2,375,487	282,159	1,933,203	2,215,361	4,590,848
16	377,862,595	0.00538	2,841,068	2,361,641	282,623	2,031,931	2,314,554	4,676,195
17	375,548,041	0.00567	2,825,779	2,347,175	283,006	2,129,159	2,412,164	4,759,339
18	373,135,877	0.00597	2,809,746	2,332,099	283,305	2,224,805	2,508,110	4,840,210
19	370,627,766	0.00626	2,792,980	2,316,424	283,521	2,318,790	2,602,312	4,918,735
20	368,025,455	0.00656	2,775,493	2,300,159	283,654	2,411,036	2,694,690	4,994,849
21	365,330,765	0.00685	2,757,296	2,283,317	283,702	2,501,466	2,785,169	5,068,486
22	362,545,596	0.00715	2,738,402	2,265,910	283,666	2,590,008	2,873,674	5,139,584
23	359,671,922	0.00745	2,718,823	2,247,950	283,545	2,676,588	2,960,133	5,208,083
24	356,711,789	0.00775	2,698,575	2,229,449	283,338	2,761,139	3,044,477	5,273,926
25	353,667,312	0.00805	2,677,670	2,210,421	283,047	2,843,593	3,126,640	5,337,061
26	350,540,672	0.00835	2,656,123	2,190,879	282,671	2,923,885	3,206,556	5,397,435
27	347,334,116	0.00865	2,633,950	2,170,838	282,209	3,001,955	3,284,164	5,455,002
28	344,049,952	0.00865	2,611,167	2,150,312	281,662	2,973,553	3,255,215	5,405,527
29	340,794,737	0.00865	2,588,581	2,129,967	281,116	2,945,400	3,226,516	5,356,483
30	337,568,221	0.00865	2,566,190	2,109,801	280,572	2,917,496	3,198,067	5,307,869

Exhibit 8.3 shows selected monthly cash flow for the same passthrough assuming 165 PSA.

FACTORS AFFECTING PREPAYMENT BEHAVIOR

The factors that affect prepayment behavior are (1) prevailing mortgage rate, (2) characteristics of the underlying mortgage pool, (3) seasonal factors, and (4) general economic activity.

EXHIBIT 8.3 (Continued)

(1)	(2)	(3)	(4)	(5)	(6)	(7)	(8)	(9)
Month	Outstanding Balance	SMM	Mortgage Payment	Net Interest	Scheduled Principal	Prepayment	Total Principal	Cash Flow
100	$170,142,350	0.00865	$1,396,958	$1,063,390	$244,953	$1,469,591	$1,714,544	$2,777,933
101	168,427,806	0.00865	1,384,875	1,052,674	244,478	1,454,765	1,699,243	2,751,916
102	166,728,563	0.00865	1,372,896	1,042,054	244,004	1,440,071	1,684,075	2,726,128
103	165,044,489	0.00865	1,361,020	1,031,528	243,531	1,425,508	1,669,039	2,700,567
104	163,375,450	0.00865	1,349,248	1,021,097	243,060	1,411,075	1,654,134	2,675,231
105	161,721,315	0.00865	1,337,577	1,010,758	242,589	1,396,771	1,639,359	2,650,118
200	56,746,664	0.00865	585,990	354,667	201,767	489,106	690,874	1,045,540
201	56,055,790	0.00865	580,921	350,349	201,377	483,134	684,510	1,034,859
202	55,371,280	0.00865	575,896	346,070	200,986	477,216	678,202	1,024,273
203	54,693,077	0.00865	570,915	341,832	200,597	471,353	671,950	1,013,782
204	54,021,127	0.00865	565,976	337,632	200,208	465,544	665,752	1,003,384
205	53,355,375	0.00865	561,081	333,471	199,820	459,789	659,609	993,080
300	11,758,141	0.00865	245,808	73,488	166,196	100,269	266,465	339,953
301	11,491,677	0.00865	243,682	71,823	165,874	97,967	263,841	335,664
302	11,227,836	0.00865	241,574	70,174	165,552	95,687	261,240	331,414
303	10,966,596	0.00865	239,485	68,541	165,232	93,430	258,662	327,203
304	10,707,934	0.00865	237,413	66,925	164,912	91,196	256,107	323,032
305	10,451,827	0.00865	235,360	65,324	164,592	88,983	253,575	318,899
350	1,235,674	0.00865	159,202	7,723	150,836	9,384	160,220	167,943
351	1,075,454	0.00865	157,825	6,722	150,544	8,000	158,544	165,266
352	916,910	0.00865	156,460	5,731	150,252	6,631	156,883	162,614
353	760,027	0.00865	155,107	4,750	149,961	5,277	155,238	159,988
354	604,789	0.00865	153,765	3,780	149,670	3,937	153,607	157,387
355	451,182	0.00865	152,435	2,820	149,380	2,611	151,991	154,811
356	299,191	0.00865	151,117	1,870	149,091	1,298	150,389	152,259
357	148,802	0.00865	149,809	930	148,802	0	148,802	149,732

Note: Since the WAM is 357 months, the underlying mortgage pool is seasoned an average of 3 months. Therefore, the CPR for month 27 is 1.65 × 6%.

Prevailing Mortgage Rate

The single most important factor affecting prepayments because of refinancing is the current level of mortgage rates relative to the borrower's contract rate. The more the contract rate exceeds the prevailing mortgage rate, the greater the incentive to refinance the mortgage loan. For refinancing to make economic sense, the interest savings must be greater than the costs associated with refinancing the mortgage. These costs include legal expenses, origination fees, title insurance, and the value of the time associated with obtaining another mortgage loan. Some of these costs, such as title insurance and origination points, will vary proportionately with the amount to be financed. Other costs, such as the application fee and legal expenses, are typically fixed.

Historically, it has been observed that when mortgage rates fall to more than 200 basis points below the contract rate, prepayment rates increase. However, the creativity of mortgage originators in designing mortgage loans such that the refinancing costs are folded into the amount borrowed has changed the view that mortgage rates must drop dramatically below the contract rate to make refinancing economic. Moreover, mortgage originators now do an effective job of advertising to make homeowners cognizant of the economic benefits of refinancing.

The historical pattern of prepayments and economic theory suggests that it is not only the level of mortgage rates that affects prepayment behavior but also the path that mortgage rates take to get to the current level.

To illustrate why, suppose the underlying contract rate for a pool of mortgage loans is 11% and that three years after origination, the prevailing mortgage rate declines to 8%. Let's consider two possible paths of the mortgage rate in getting to the 8% level. In the first path, the mortgage rate declines to 8% at the end of the first year, then rises to 13% at the end of the second year, and then falls to 8% at the end of the third year. In the second path, the mortgage rate rises to 12% at the end of the first year, continues its rise to 13% at the end of the second year, and then falls to 8% at the end of the third year.

If the mortgage rate follows the first path, those who can benefit from refinancing will more than likely take advantage of this opportunity when the mortgage rate drops to 8% in the first year. When the mortgage rate drops again to 8% at the end of the third year, the likelihood is that prepayments because of refinancing will not surge; those who can benefit by taking advantage of the refinancing opportunity will have done so already when the mortgage rate declined the first time. This prepayment behavior is referred to as *refinancing burnout* (or simply, *burnout*).

In contrast, the expected prepayment behavior when the mortgage rate follows the second path is quite different. Prepayment rates are expected to be low in the first two years. When the mortgage rate declines to 8% in the third year, refinancing activity and therefore prepayments are expected to surge. Consequently, burnout is related to the path of mortgage rates.

Our focus so far has been on the factors that affect prepayments caused by refinancing. Prepayments also occur because of housing turnover. The level of mortgage rates affects housing turnover to the extent that a lower rate increases the affordability of homes.

Seasonality

There is a well-documented seasonal pattern in prepayments referred to as *seasonality*. This pattern is related to activity in the primary housing market, with home buying increasing in the spring and gradually reaching a peak in the late summer. Home buying declines in the fall and winter. Mirroring this activity are the prepayments that result from the turnover of housing as home buyers sell their existing homes and purchase new ones. Prepayments are low in the winter months and begin to rise in the spring, reaching a peak in the summer months. However, probably because of delays in passing through prepayments, the peak may not be observed until early fall.

PREPAYMENT MODELS

A *prepayment model* is a statistical model that is used to forecast prepayments. It begins by modeling the statistical relationships among the factors that are expected to affect prepayments. These factors are then combined into one model.

Wall Street firms report their projections for different types of passthroughs in their publications. In addition to reports to their clients, MBS dealers provide their prepayment projections to sources such as Bloomberg, Reuters, and Telerate.

YIELD

Given the projected cash flows based on some prepayment speed and the market price of a passthrough, its yield can be calculated. The yield is the interest rate that will make the present value of the expected cash flows equal to the price. A yield computed in this manner is called a *cash flow yield*.

Although the cash flow yield on passthrough securities of all three agencies is published in financial publications and web sites, there is too often no information about what prepayment assumption is made. Any cash flow yield must be qualified by an assumption concerning prepayments. Without information about the prepayment speed, the cash flow yield is meaningless.

In addition of the cash flow yield, there may be two spread measures are reported: nominal spread and *option-adjusted spread* (OAS). The *nominal spread* is the difference between the cash flow yield and the yield on a comparable duration Treasury security. The OAS is the estimated spread over a comparable duration after adjusting for the option granted to the homeowners. That is, the OAS adjusts the spread for the prepayment risk faced by the investor.

Even with specification of the prepayment assumption, the yield number is meaningless in terms of the potential return from investing in a passthrough. For an investor to realize the cash flow yield based on some PSA assumption, a number of conditions must be met: (1) the investor must reinvest all the cash flows at the calculated yield; (2) the investor must hold the passthrough security until all the mortgages have been paid off; and (3) the assumed prepayment rate must actually occur over the life of the passthrough. We highlighted the limitations of any yield measure due to the first two conditions in Chapter 4. The third condition is unique to a mortgage-backed security.

What can be stated with a high degree of confidence is that the yield that an investor will realize will not be the cash flow yield calculated at the time of purchase.

Comparison to Treasuries

While we have explained that it is not possible to calculate a yield with certainty, it has been stated that passthrough securities offer a higher yield than Treasury securities. Typically, the comparison is between Ginnie Mae passthrough securities and Treasuries, for both are free of default risk. Presumably, the difference between the two yields primarily represents compensation for prepayment risk.

When we speak of comparing the yield of a mortgage passthrough security to a comparable Treasury, what does "comparable" mean? The stated maturity of a mortgage passthrough security is an inappropriate measure because of principal repayments over time. Instead, market participants calculate an average life for a mortgage-backed security.

The *average life* of a mortgage-backed security is the average time to receipt of principal payments (scheduled principal payments and projected prepayments), weighted by the amount of principal expected. Specifically, the average life is found by first calculating:

$$1 \times (\text{Projected principal received in month 1})$$
$$+ \, 2 \times (\text{Projected principal received in month 2})$$
$$+ \, 3 \times (\text{Projected principal received in month 3})$$
$$\cdots$$
$$\frac{+ \, T \times (\text{Projected principal received in month } T)}{\text{Weighted monthly average of principal received}}$$

where T is the last month that principal is expected to be received. Then the average life is found as follows:

$$\text{Average life} = \frac{\text{Weighted monthly average of principal received}}{12(\text{Total principal to be received})}$$

The average life of a passthrough depends on the PSA prepayment assumption. To see this, the average life is shown below for different prepayment speeds for the passthrough we used to illustrate the cash flows for 100 PSA and 165 PSA in Exhibits 8.2 and 8.3:

PSA speed	50	100	165	200	300	400	500	600	700
Average life	15.11	11.66	8.76	7.68	5.63	4.44	3.68	3.16	2.78

A CLOSER LOOK AT PREPAYMENT RISK

An investor who owns passthrough securities does not know what the cash flows will be because that depends on prepayments. As noted earlier, this risk is called prepayment risk.

Contraction Risk and Extension Risk

To understand the significance of prepayment risk, suppose an investor buys a 7.5% coupon Ginnie Mae at a time when mortgage rates are 7.5%. Let's consider what will happen to prepayments if mortgage rates decline to, say, 5%. There will be two adverse consequences. First, a basic property of fixed income securities is that the price of an option-free bond will rise. But in the case of a passthrough security, the rise in price will not be as large as that of an option-free bond because a fall in interest rates will give the borrower an incentive to prepay the loan and refinance the debt at a lower rate. Thus, the upside price potential of a passthrough security is truncated because of prepayments. The second adverse consequence is that the cash flows must be reinvested at a lower rate. These two adverse consequences when mortgage rates decline are referred to as *contraction risk*.

Now let's look at what happens if mortgage rates rise to 10%. The price of the passthrough, like the price of any bond, will decline. But again it will decline more because the higher rates will tend to slow down the rate of prepayment, in effect increasing the amount invested at the coupon rate, which is lower than the market rate. Prepayments will slow down because homeowners will not refinance or partially prepay their mortgages when mortgage rates are higher than the contract rate of 7.5%. Of course this is just the time when investors want prepayments to speed up so that they can reinvest the prepayments at the higher market interest rate. This adverse consequence of rising mortgage rates is called *extension risk*.

Therefore, prepayment risk encompasses contraction risk and extension risk. Prepayment risk makes passthrough securities unattractive for certain individuals and financial institutions to hold for purposes of accomplishing their investment objectives. Some individuals and institutional investors are concerned with extension risk and others with contraction risk when they purchase a passthrough security. Is it possible to alter the cash flows of a passthrough to reduce the contraction risk and extension risk for institutional investors? This can be done, as explained in the next chapter.

Prepayments: Friend Or Foe?

The investor does not know precisely what the monthly prepayments will be when purchasing a passthrough security. A certain prepayment speed is assumed when a passthrough is purchased. Actual prepayments will usually differ from prepayments that were anticipated at the time of purchase.

Prepayments above or below the amount anticipated may be good or bad depending on the purchase price. If an investor purchases a passthrough at a premium above par value, then actual prepayments greater than anticipated prepayments will hurt the investor for two reasons. First, there will be a loss since only par is returned, and second, the proceeds must be reinvested at a lower rate. The opposite is true for an investor who purchases a passthrough at a discount. The investor realizes a gain (since par is received but less than par was paid), and the investor can reinvest the proceeds at a higher rate.

TRADING AND SETTLEMENT PROCEDURES FOR AGENCY PASSTHROUGHS

Agency passthroughs are identified by a pool prefix and pool number provided by the agency. The prefix indicates the type of passthrough. For example, a pool prefix of "20" for a Freddie Mac PC means that the underlying pool consists of conventional mortgages with an original maturity of 15 years. A pool prefix of "AR" for a Ginnie Mae MBS means that the underlying pool consists of adjustable rate mortgages. The pool number indicates the specific mortgages underlying the passthrough and the issuer of the passthrough.

There are specific rules established by the Securities Industry and Financial Markets Association, SIFMA, (formerly the Public Securities Association and the Bond Market Association) for the trading and settlement of mortgage-backed securities. Our discussion here is limited to agency passthrough securities.

Many trades occur while a pool is still unspecified, and therefore no pool information is known at the time of the trade. This kind of trade is known as a "TBA" (to be announced) trade. In a *TBA trade*, the two parties agree on the agency type, the agency program, the coupon rate, the face value, the price, and the settlement date. The actual pools underlying the agency passthrough are not specified in a TBA trade. However, this information is provided by the seller to the buyer before delivery, as explained as follows. There are trades where more specific requirements are established for the securities to be delivered (e.g., a Freddie Mac Gold with a coupon rate of 8.5% and a WAC between 9.0% and 9.2%). There are also *specified pool trades* wherein the actual pool numbers to be delivered are specified.

Passthroughs are quoted in the same manner as U.S. Treasury coupon securities. A quote of 94-05 means 94 and $5/32$nds of par value, or 94.15625% of par value. The price that the buyer pays the seller is the agreed-upon sale price plus accrued interest. Given the par value, the dollar price (excluding accrued interest) is affected by the amount of the pool mortgage balance outstanding. The *pool factor* indicates the percentage of the initial mortgage balance for the pool still outstanding. So, a pool factor of 90 means that 90% of the original mortgage pool balance is outstanding. The pool factor is reported by the issuing agency each month.

The dollar price paid for just the principal is found as follows given the agreed-upon price, par value, and the month's pool factor provided by the issuing agency:

$$\text{Price} \times \text{Par value} \times \text{Pool factor}$$

For example, if the parties agree to a price of 92 for $1 million par value for a passthrough with a pool factor of 85, then the dollar price paid by the buyer in addition to accrued interest is

$$0.92 \times \$1,000,000 \times 0.85 = \$782,000$$

Trades settle according to a delivery schedule established by the SIFMA. This schedule is published quarterly by the BMA with information regarding delivery for the next 6 months. Each agency and program settles on a different day of the delivery month. There is also a distinction made in the delivery schedule by coupon rate.

By 3 P.M. eastern standard time two business days before the settlement date, the seller must furnish information to the buyer about pools that will be delivered. This is called the *48-hour rule*. The date that this information must be given is called the *notification date* or *call-out date*. Two parties can agree to depart from BMA guidelines and settle at any time.

When an investor purchases, say, $1 million Ginnie Mae 8s on a TBA basis, the investor can receive up to three pools. Three pools can be delivered because the BMA has established guidelines for standards of delivery and settlement of mortgage-backed securities, under which our hypothetical TBA trade permits three possible pools to be delivered. The option of what pools to deliver is left to the seller, as long as selection and delivery satisfy the BMA guidelines.

There are many seasoned issues of the same agency with the same coupon rate outstanding at a given point in time. For example, there are more than 30,000 pools of 30-year Ginnie Mae MBSs outstanding with a coupon rate of 9%. One passthrough may be backed by a pool of mortgage loans in which all the properties are located in California, while another may be backed by a pool of mortgage loans in which all the properties are in Minnesota. Yet another may be backed by a pool of mortgage loans in which the properties are from several regions of the country. So which pool is a dealer referring to when that dealer talks about Ginnie Mae 9s? The dealer is not referring to any specific pool but instead to a generic security, although the prepayment characteristics of passthroughs with underlying pools from different parts of the country are different. Thus, the projected prepayment rates for passthroughs reported by dealer firms are for generic passthroughs. A particular pool purchased may have a materially different prepayment speed from the generic. Moreover, when an investor purchases a passthrough without specifying a pool number, the seller can deliver the worst-paying pools as long as the pools delivered satisfy good delivery requirements.

STRIPPED MORTGAGE-BACKED SECURITIES

A mortgage passthrough security distributes the cash flow from the underlying pool of mortgages on a pro rata basis to the securityholders. A *stripped mortgage-backed security* is created by altering that distribution of principal and interest from a pro rata distribution to an unequal distribution. The result is that the securities created will have a price/yield relationship that is different from the price/ yield relationship of the underlying passthrough security.

In the most common type of stripped mortgage-backed securities, all the interest is allocated to one class (called the *interest-only class* or IO class) and all the principal to the other class (called the *principal-only class* or PO class). The IO class receives no principal payments.

Principal-Only Securities

The PO security, also called a *principal-only mortgage strip*, is purchased at a substantial discount from par value. The return an investor realizes depends on the speed at which prepayments are made. The faster the prepayments, the higher the investor's return. For example, suppose there is a mortgage pool consisting only of 30-year mortgages, with $400 million in principal, and that investors can purchase POs backed by this mortgage pool for $175 million. The dollar return on this investment will be $225 million. How quickly that dollar return is recovered by PO investors determines the actual return that will be realized. In the extreme case, if all homeowners in the underlying mortgage pool decide to prepay their mortgage loans immediately, PO investors will realize the $225 million immediately. At the other extreme, if all homeowners decide to remain in their homes for 30 years and make no prepayments, the $225 million will be spread out over 30 years, which would result in a lower return for PO investors.

Let's look at how the price of the PO would be expected to change as mortgage rates in the market change. When mortgage rates decline below the contract rate, prepayments are expected to speed up, accelerating payments to the PO holder. Thus, the cash flow of a PO improves (in the sense that principal repayments are received earlier). The cash flow will be discounted at a lower interest rate because the mortgage rate in the market has declined. The result is that the PO price will increase when mortgage rates decline. When mortgage rates rise above the contract rate, prepayments are expected to slow down. The cash flow deteriorates (in the sense that it takes longer to recover principal repayments). Couple this with a higher discount rate, and the price of a PO will fall when mortgage rates rise.

Interest-Only Securities

An IO, also called an *interest-only mortgage strip*, has no par value. In contrast to the PO investor, the IO investor wants prepayments to be slow because the IO investor receives interest only on the amount of the principal outstanding. When prepayments are made, less dollar interest will be received as the outstanding principal declines. In fact, if prepayments are too fast, the IO investor may not recover the amount paid for the IO even if the security is held to maturity.

Let's look at the expected price response of an IO to changes in mortgage rates. If mortgage rates decline below the contract rate, prepayments are expected to accelerate. This would result in a deterioration of the expected cash flow for an IO. While the cash flow will be discounted at a lower rate, the net effect typically is a decline in the price of an IO. If mortgage rates rise above the contract rate, the expected cash flow improves, but the cash flow is discounted at a higher interest rate. The net effect may be either a rise or fall for the IO.

Thus, we see an interesting characteristic of an IO: its price tends to move in the same direction as the change in mortgage rates (1) when mortgage rates fall below the contract rate and (2) for some range of mortgage rates above the contract rate. Both POs and IOs exhibit substantial price volatility when mortgage rates change. The greater price volatility of the IO and PO compared to the passthrough from which they were created is because the combined price volatility of the IO and PO must be equal to the price volatility of the passthrough.

An average life for a PO can be calculated based on some prepayment assumption. However, an IO receives no principal payments, so technically an average life cannot be computed. Instead, for an IO a "cash flow average life" is computed, using the projected interest payments in the average life formula instead of principal.

Trading and Settlement Procedures

The trading and settlement procedures for stripped mortgage-backed securities are similar to those set for agency passthroughs described in the previous section. The specifications are in the types of trades (TBA versus specified pool), calculations of the proceeds, and the settlement dates.

IOs and POs are extreme premium and discount securities and consequently are very sensitive to prepayments, which are driven by the specific characteristics (WAC, WAM, geographic concentration, average loan size) of the underlying loans. The TBA delivery option on IOs and POs is of too great an economic value, and this value is hard to quantify. Therefore, almost all secondary trades in IOs and POs are on a specified pool basis rather than on a TBA basis.

All IOs and POs are given a trust number. Since the transactions are on a specified trust basis, they are also done based on the original face amount. For example, suppose a portfolio manager agrees to buy $10 million original face of Trust 23 PO for August settlement. At the time of the transaction, the August factor need not be known; however, there is no ambiguity in the amount to be delivered because the seller does not have any delivery option. The seller has to deliver $3 million current face amount if the August factor turns out to be 0.30, and the seller needs to deliver $2.5 million current face amount if the August factor turns out to be 0.25.

The total proceeds of a PO trade are calculated the same way as with a passthrough trade except that there is no accrued interest. For example, suppose a buyer and a seller agree to trade $10 million original face of Trust

23 PO at 75-08 for settlement on August 25. The proceeds for the trade are calculated as follows assuming an August trust factor of 0.25:

$$
\underset{\text{price}}{75.08} \times \underset{\text{original face value}}{\$10,000,000} \times \underset{\text{pool factor}}{0.25} = \underset{\text{proceeds}}{\$1,881,250}
$$

The market trades IOs based on notional principal. The proceeds include the price on the notional amount and the accrued interest. For example, suppose a buyer and a seller agree to trade $10 million original notional face of Trust 23 IO at 33-20 for settlement on August 25. The proceeds for the trade are calculated as follows assuming an August factor of 0.25:

$$
\underset{\text{price}}{(0.33625 +} \underset{\text{coupon}}{0.10} \times \underset{\text{days accrued interest}}{24 \text{ days}/360 \text{ days})} \times \underset{\text{orig. notional}}{\$10,000,000} \times \underset{\text{factor}}{0.25} = \underset{\text{proceeds}}{\$857,292}
$$

As explained earlier, agency passthrough trades settle according to a delivery schedule established by the SIFMA. Stripped mortgage-backed securities trades follow the same delivery schedule according to their underlying mortgages. Any other nonstandard settlement dates can be agreed upon between the buyer and the seller.

Financial Instruments and Concepts Introduced in this Chapter (in Order of Presentation)

Mortgage-backed securities
Derivative mortsecurities
Agency mortgage-backed securities
Mortgage loan
Mortgage rate
Contract rate
Conventional mortgage
Mortgage design
Net interest
Net coupon
Servicing spread
Prepayments
Prepayment risk
Mortgage passthrough security
Passthrough coupon rate
Weighted average coupon rate
Weighted average maturity
Ginnie Mae mortgage-backed security
Freddie Mac participation certificate

Fannie Mae mortgage-backed security
Prepayment speed
Conditional prepayment rate
Single-monthly mortality rate
Public Securities Association prepayment benchmark
PSA benchmark
Refinancing burnout
Burnout
Sasonality
Prepayment model
Cash flow yield
Option-adjusted spread
Nominal spread
Average life
Contraction risk
Extension risk
TBA trade
Specified pool trades

Pool factors
48-hour rule
Notification date
Call-out date
Stripped mortgage-backed security

Interest-only class
Principal-only class
Principal-only mortgage strip
Interest-only mortgage strip

CHAPTER 9

Agency Collateralized Mortgage Obligations

Agency passthrough securities can be used as collateral to create a collateralized mortgage obligation (CMO). Most investors who follow the bond market have read about this product, and, more than likely, the statements about the product have been unfavorable. CMO products have been responsible for many reported (and unreported) financial debacles. It is not uncommon, for example, for reporters to state that CMOs are the riskiest type of mortgage-backed securities product while mortgage passthrough securities are the safest. This statement, however, is incorrect, as we shall see in this chapter as we explore the world of CMOs.

THE BASIC PRINCIPLE OF CMOs

As explained in the previous chapter, an investor in a mortgage passthrough security is exposed to prepayment risk. Furthermore, prepayment risk can be divided into extension risk and contraction risk. Some investors are concerned with extension risk and others with contraction risk when they invest in a passthrough. An investor may be willing to accept one form of prepayment risk but seek to avoid the other. For example, an investor who seeks a short-term security is concerned with extension risk. An investor who seeks a long-term security, and wants to avoid reinvesting unexpected principal prepayments should interest rates drop, is concerned with contraction risk.

By redirecting how the cash flows of passthrough securities are paid to different bond classes that are created, securities can be created that have different exposure to prepayment risk. When the cash flows of mortgage-related products are redistributed to different bond classes, the resulting securities are called *collateralized mortgage obligations*. The creation of a CMO cannot eliminate prepayment risk; it can only redistribute the two forms of prepayment risk among different classes of bondholders.

The basic principle is that redirecting cash flows (interest and principal) to different bond classes, called *tranches*, mitigates different forms of prepayment risk. It is never possible to eliminate prepayment risk. If one tranche in a CMO structure has less prepayment risk than the mortgage passthrough securities that are collateral for the structure, then another tranche in the same structure has greater prepayment risk than the collateral. Consequently, the statement that CMOs have greater prepayment risk than passthroughs is incorrect.

CMOs are referred to as paythroughs or multiclass passthroughs. (As will be explained later in this chapter, CMOs are also referred to as REMICs.) A security structure in which collateral is carved into different bond classes is not uncommon. We will see similar paythrough or multiclass passthrough structures when we cover asset-backed securities in Chapter 10.

AGENCY CMOs

Issuers of CMOs are the same three entities that issue agency passthrough securities: Freddie Mac, Fannie Mae, and Ginnie Mae. There has been little issuance of Ginnie Mae CMOs. However, Freddie Mac and Fannie Mae have used Ginnie Mae passthroughs as collateral for their own CMOs. CMOs issued by any of these entities are referred to as *agency CMOs*.

When an agency CMO is created, it is structured so that even under the worst circumstances regarding prepayments, the interest and principal payments from the collateral will be sufficient to meet the interest obligation of each tranche and pay off the par value of each tranche. Defaults are ignored because the agency that has issued the passthroughs used as collateral is expected to make up any deficiency. Thus, the credit risk of agency CMOs is minimal. However, as noted in the previous chapter, the guarantee of a government-sponsored enterprise does not carry the full faith and credit of the U.S. government. Fannie Mae and Freddie Mac CMOs created from Ginnie Mae passthroughs effectively carry the full faith and credit of the U.S. government.

CMO STRUCTURES

There is a wide range of CMO structures. We review these structures as follows. Rather than just provide a definition, it is useful to see how the various types of CMOs are created. In an actual CMO structure, the information regarding the rules for distributing interest and principal to the bond classes is set forth in the prospectus.

Sequential Pay Tranches

The first CMO was structured so that each class of bond would be retired sequentially. Such structures are referred to as *sequential pay* CMOs.

To illustrate a sequential pay CMO, we discuss CMO-01, a hypothetical deal made up to illustrate the basic features of the structure. The collateral for this hypothetical CMO is a hypothetical passthrough with a total par value of $400 million and the following characteristics: (1) the passthrough coupon rate is 7.5%, (2) the weighted average coupon (WAC) is 8.125%, and (3) the weighted average maturity (WAM) is 357 months. This is the same passthrough that we used in the previous chapter to describe the cash flows of a passthrough based on some PSA assumption.

From this $400 million of collateral, four bond classes or tranches are created. Their characteristics are summarized in Exhibit 9.1. The total par value of the four tranches is equal to the par value of the collateral (i.e., the passthrough security). In this simple structure, the coupon rate is the same for each tranche and also the same as the collateral's coupon rate. There is no reason why this must be so, and, in fact, typically the coupon rate varies by tranche.

Now remember that a CMO is created by redistributing the cash flow—interest and principal—to the different tranches based on a set of payment rules. The payment rules at the bottom of Exhibit 9.1 set forth how the monthly cash flow from the passthrough (i.e., collateral) is to be distributed

EXHIBIT 9.1 CMO-01: A Hypothetical Four-Tranche Sequential Pay Structure

Tranche	Par Amount	Coupon Rate (%)
A	$194,500,000	7.5
B	36,000,000	7.5
C	96,500,000	7.5
D	73,000,000	7.5
Total	$400,000,000	

Payment rules:

1. *For payment of periodic coupon interest:* Disburse periodic coupon interest to each tranche on the basis of the amount of principal outstanding at the beginning of the period.

2. *For disbursement of principal payments:* Disburse principal payments to tranche A until it is completely paid off. After tranche A is completely paid off, disburse principal payments to tranche B until it is completely paid off. After tranche B is completely paid off, disburse principal payments to tranche C until it is completely paid off. After tranche C is completely paid off, disburse principal payments to tranche D until it is completely paid off.

to the four tranches. There are separate rules for the payment of the coupon interest and the payment of principal, the principal being the total of the regularly scheduled principal payment and any prepayments.

In CMO-01, each tranche receives periodic coupon interest payments based on the amount of the outstanding balance. The disbursement of the principal, however, is made in a special way. A tranche is not entitled to receive principal until the entire principal of the tranche before it has been paid off. More specifically, tranche A receives all the principal payments until the entire principal amount owed to that bond class, $194,500,000, is paid off; then tranche B begins to receive principal and continues to do so until it is paid the entire $36,000,000. Tranche C then receives principal, and when it is paid off, tranche D starts receiving principal payments.

While the payment rules for the disbursement of the principal payments are known, the precise amount of the principal in each period is not. This will depend on the cash flow, and therefore principal payments, of the collateral, which depends on the actual prepayment rate of the collateral. An assumed PSA speed allows the monthly cash flow to be projected. Exhibit 8.2 in the previous chapter shows the monthly cash flow (interest, regularly scheduled principal repayment, and prepayments) assuming 165 PSA. Assuming that the collateral does prepay at 165 PSA, the cash flows available to all four tranches of CMO-01 will be precisely the cash flows shown in Exhibit 8.2 of the previous chapter.

To demonstrate how the payment rules for CMO-01 work, Exhibit 9.2 shows the cash flow for selected months assuming the collateral prepays at 165 PSA. For each tranche, the exhibit shows (1) the balance at the end of the month, (2) the principal paid down (regularly scheduled principal repayment plus prepayments), and (3) interest. In month 1, the cash flow for the collateral consists of a principal payment of $709,923 and interest of $2.5 million (0.075 times $400 million divided by 12). The interest payment is distributed to the four tranches based on the amount of the par value outstanding. So, for example, tranche A receives $1,215,625 (0.075 times $194,500,000 divided by 12) of the $2.5 million. The principal, however, is all distributed to tranche A. Therefore, the cash flow for tranche A in month 1 is $1,925,548. The principal balance at the end of month 1 for tranche A is $193,790,076 (the original principal balance of $194,500,000 less the principal payment of $709,923). No principal payment is distributed to the three other tranches because there is still a principal balance outstanding for tranche A. This will be true for months 2 through 80.

After month 81, the principal balance will be zero for tranche A. For the collateral the cash flow in month 81 is $3,318,521, consisting of a principal payment of $2,032,196 and interest of $1,286,325. At the beginning of month 81 (end of month 80), the principal balance for tranche A is

EXHIBIT 9.2 Monthly Cash Flow for Selected Months for CMO-01 Assuming 165 PSA

	Tranche A			Tranche B		
Month	Balance	Principal	Interest	Balance	Principal	Interest
1	194,500,000	709,923	1,215,625	36,000,000	0	225,000
2	193,790,077	821,896	1,211,188	36,000,000	0	225,000
3	192,968,181	933,560	1,206,051	36,000,000	0	225,000
4	192,034,621	1,044,822	1,200,216	36,000,000	0	225,000
5	190,989,799	1,155,586	1,193,686	36,000,000	0	225,000
6	189,834,213	1,265,759	1,186,464	36,000,000	0	225,000
7	188,568,454	1,375,246	1,178,553	36,000,000	0	225,000
8	187,193,208	1,483,954	1,169,958	36,000,000	0	225,000
9	185,709,254	1,591,789	1,160,683	36,000,000	0	225,000
10	184,117,464	1,698,659	1,150,734	36,000,000	0	225,000
11	182,418,805	1,804,473	1,140,118	36,000,000	0	225,000
12	180,614,332	1,909,139	1,128,840	36,000,000	0	225,000
75	12,893,479	2,143,974	80,584	36,000,000	0	225,000
76	10,749,504	2,124,935	67,184	36,000,000	0	225,000
77	8,624,569	2,106,062	53,904	36,000,000	0	225,000
78	6,518,507	2,087,353	40,741	36,000,000	0	225,000
79	4,431,154	2,068,807	27,695	36,000,000	0	225,000
80	2,362,347	2,050,422	14,765	36,000,000	0	225,000
81	311,926	311,926	1,950	36,000,000	1,720,271	225,000
82	0	0	0	34,279,729	2,014,130	214,248
83	0	0	0	32,265,599	1,996,221	201,660
84	0	0	0	30,269,378	1,978,468	189,184
85	0	0	0	28,290,911	1,960,869	176,818
95	0	0	0	9,449,331	1,793,089	59,058
96	0	0	0	7,656,242	1,777,104	47,852
97	0	0	0	5,879,138	1,761,258	36,745
98	0	0	0	4,117,880	1,745,550	25,737
99	0	0	0	2,372,329	1,729,979	14,827
100	0	0	0	642,350	642,350	4,015
101	0	0	0	0	0	0
102	0	0	0	0	0	0
103	0	0	0	0	0	0
104	0	0	0	0	0	0
105	0	0	0	0	0	0

EXHIBIT 9.2   (Continued)

Month	Tranche C			Tranche D		
	Balance	Principal	Interest	Balance	Principal	Interest
1	96,500,000	0	603,125	73,000,000	0	456,250
2	96,500,000	0	603,125	73,000,000	0	456,250
3	96,500,000	0	603,125	73,000,000	0	456,250
4	96,500,000	0	603,125	73,000,000	0	456,250
5	96,500,000	0	603,125	73,000,000	0	456,250
6	96,500,000	0	603,125	73,000,000	0	456,250
7	96,500,000	0	603,125	73,000,000	0	456,250
8	96,500,000	0	603,125	73,000,000	0	456,250
9	96,500,000	0	603,125	73,000,000	0	456,250
10	96,500,000	0	603,125	73,000,000	0	456,250
11	96,500,000	0	603,125	73,000,000	0	456,250
12	96,500,000	0	603,125	73,000,000	0	456,250
95	96,500,000	0	603,125	73,000,000	0	456,250
96	96,500,000	0	603,125	73,000,000	0	456,250
97	96,500,000	0	603,125	73,000,000	0	456,250
98	96,500,000	0	603,125	73,000,000	0	456,250
99	96,500,000	0	603,125	73,000,000	0	456,250
100	96,500,000	1,072,194	603,125	73,000,000	0	456,250
101	95,427,806	1,699,243	596,424	73,000,000	0	456,250
102	93,728,563	1,684,075	585,804	73,000,000	0	456,250
103	92,044,489	1,669,039	575,278	73,000,000	0	456,250
104	90,375,450	1,654,134	564,847	73,000,000	0	456,250
105	88,721,315	1,639,359	554,508	73,000,000	0	456,250
175	3,260,287	869,602	20,377	73,000,000	0	456,250
176	2,390,685	861,673	14,942	73,000,000	0	456,250
177	1,529,013	853,813	9,556	73,000,000	0	456,250
178	675,199	675,199	4,220	73,000,000	170,824	456,250
179	0	0	0	72,829,176	838,300	455,182
180	0	0	0	71,990,876	830,646	449,943
181	0	0	0	71,160,230	823,058	444,751
182	0	0	0	70,337,173	815,536	439,607
183	0	0	0	69,521,637	808,081	434,510
184	0	0	0	68,713,556	800,690	429,460
185	0	0	0	67,912,866	793,365	424,455
350	0	0	0	1,235,674	160,220	7,723
351	0	0	0	1,075,454	158,544	6,722
352	0	0	0	916,910	156,883	5,731
353	0	0	0	760,027	155,238	4,750
354	0	0	0	604,789	153,607	3,780
355	0	0	0	451,182	151,991	2,820
356	0	0	0	299,191	150,389	1,870
357	0	0	0	148,802	148,802	930

$311,926. Therefore, $311,926 of the $2,032,196 of the principal payment from the collateral will be disbursed to tranche A. After this payment is made, no additional principal payments are made to this tranche because the principal balance is zero. The remaining principal payment from the collateral, $1,720,271, is disbursed to tranche B. According to the assumed prepayment speed of 165 PSA, tranche B then begins receiving principal payments in month 81.

Exhibit 9.2 shows that tranche B is fully paid off by month 100, when tranche C now begins to receive principal payments. Tranche C is not fully paid off until month 178, at which time tranche D begins receiving the remaining principal payments. The maturity (i.e., the time until the principal is fully paid off) for these four tranches assuming 165 PSA is 81 months for tranche A, 100 months for tranche B, 178 months for tranche C, and 357 months for tranche D.

The *principal pay down window* for a tranche is the time period between the beginning and the ending of the principal payments to that tranche. So, for example, for tranche A, the principal pay down window would be month 1 to month 81 assuming 165 PSA. For tranche B it is from month 81 to month 100. The window is also specified in terms of the length of the time from the beginning of the principal pay down window to the end of the principal pay down window. For tranche A, the window would be stated as 81 months, for tranche B 20 months. In confirmation of trades involving CMOs, the principal pay down window is specified in terms of the initial month that principal is expected to be received to the final month that principal is expected to be received.

Let's look at what has been accomplished by creating the CMO. First, in the previous chapter we saw that the average life of the passthrough is 8.76 years, assuming a prepayment speed of 165 PSA. Exhibit 9.3 reports the average life of the collateral and the four tranches, assuming different prepayment speeds. Notice that the four tranches have average lives that are both shorter and longer than the collateral, thereby attracting investors who have a preference for an average life different from that of the collateral.

There is still a major problem: there is considerable variability of the average life for the tranches. We see how this can be tackled later on. However, there is some protection provided for each tranche against prepayment risk. This is because prioritizing the distribution of principal (i.e., establishing the payment rules for principal) effectively protects the shorter-term tranche A in this structure against extension risk. This protection must come from somewhere, so it comes from the three other tranches. Similarly, tranches C and D provide protection against extension risk for tranches A and B. At the same time, tranches C and D benefit because they are provided protection against contraction risk, the protection coming from tranches A and B.

EXHIBIT 9.3   Average Life for the Collateral and the Four Tranches of CMO-01

Prepayment Speed (PSA)	Average Life for				
	Collateral	Tranche A	Tranche B	Tranche C	Tranche D
50	15.11	7.48	15.98	21.02	27.24
100	11.66	4.90	10.86	15.78	24.58
165	8.76	3.48	7.49	11.19	20.27
200	7.68	3.05	6.42	9.60	18.11
300	5.63	2.32	4.64	6.81	13.36
400	4.44	1.94	3.70	5.31	10.34
500	3.68	1.69	3.12	4.38	8.35
600	3.16	1.51	2.74	3.75	6.96
700	2.78	1.38	2.47	3.30	5.95

Accrual Tranches

In CMO-01, the payment rules for interest provide for all tranches to be paid interest each month. In many sequential pay CMO structures, at least one tranche does not receive current interest. Instead, the interest for that tranche would accrue and be added to the principal balance. Such a bond class is commonly referred to as an *accrual tranche* or a *Z bond* (because the bond is similar to a zero-coupon bond). The interest that would have been paid to the accrual bond class is then used to speed up pay down of the principal balance of earlier bond classes.

To see this, consider CMO-02, a hypothetical CMO structure with the same collateral as CMO-01 and with four tranches, each with a coupon rate of 7.5%. The difference is in the last tranche, Z, which is an accrual tranche. The structure for CMO-02 is shown in Exhibit 9.4.

Exhibit 9.5 shows the cash flow for selected months for tranches A and B. Let's look at month 1 and compare it to month 1 in Exhibit 9.2. Both cash flows are based on 165 PSA. The principal payment from the collateral is $709,923. In CMO-01, this is the principal pay down for tranche A. In CMO-02, the interest for tranche Z, $456,250, is not paid to that tranche but instead is used to pay down the principal of tranche A. So, the principal payment to tranche A in Exhibit 9.5 is $1,166,173, the collateral's principal payment of $709,923 plus the interest of $456,250 that was diverted from tranche Z.

The expected final maturity for tranches A, B, and C has shortened as a result of the inclusion of tranche Z. The final payout for tranche A is 64

EXHIBIT 9.4 CMO-02: A Hypothetical Four-Tranche Sequential Pay Structure with an Accrual Bond Class

Tranche	Par Amount	Coupon rate (%)
A	$194,500,000	7.5
B	36,000,000	7.5
C	96,500,000	7.5
Z (accrual)	73,000,000	7.5
Total	$400,000,000	

Payment rules:
1. *For payment of periodic coupon interest:* Disburse periodic coupon interest to tranches A, B, and C on the basis of the amount of principal outstanding at the beginning of the period. For tranche Z, accrue the interest based on the principal plus accrued interest in the previous period. The interest for tranche Z is to be paid to the earlier tranches as a principal pay down.
2. *For disbursement of principal payments:* Disburse principal payments to tranche A until it is completely paid off. After tranche A is completely paid off, disburse principal payments to tranche B until it is completely paid off. After tranche B is completely paid off, disburse principal payments to tranche C until it is completely paid off. After tranche C is completely paid off, disburse principal payments to tranche Z until the original principal balance plus accrued interest is completely paid off.

months rather than 81 months; for tranche B it is 77 months rather than 100 months; and for tranche C it is 112 months rather than 178 months.

The average lives for tranches A, B, and C are shorter in CMO-02 compared to CMO-01 because of the inclusion of the accrual bond. For example, at 165 PSA, the average lives are as follows:

Structure	Tranche A	Tranche B	Tranche C
CMO-02	2.90	5.86	7.87
CMO-01	3.48	7.49	11.19

The reason for the shortening of the nonaccrual tranches is that the interest that would be paid to the accrual tranche is being allocated to the other tranches. Tranche Z in CMO-02 will have a longer average life than tranche D in CMO-01.

Thus, shorter-term tranches and a longer-term tranche are created by including an accrual bond. The accrual bond has appeal to investors who are concerned with reinvestment risk. Since there are no coupon payments to reinvest, reinvestment risk is eliminated until all the other tranches are paid off.

EXHIBIT 9.5 Monthly Cash Flow for Selected Months for Tranches A and B of CMO-02 Assuming 165 PSA

	Tranche A			Tranche B		
Month	Balance	Principal	Interest	Balance	Principal	Interest
1	194,500,000	1,150,965	972,500	36,000,000	0	195,000
2	193,349,035	1,265,602	966,745	36,000,000	0	195,000
3	192,083,433	1,379,947	960,417	36,000,000	0	195,000
4	190,703,486	1,493,906	953,517	36,000,000	0	195,000
5	189,209,581	1,607,383	946,048	36,000,000	0	195,000
6	187,602,197	1,720,286	938,011	36,000,000	0	195,000
7	185,881,911	1,832,519	929,410	36,000,000	0	195,000
8	184,049,392	1,943,990	920,247	36,000,000	0	195,000
9	182,105,402	2,054,604	910,527	36,000,000	0	195,000
10	180,050,798	2,164,271	900,254	36,000,000	0	195,000
11	177,886,528	2,272,897	889,433	36,000,000	0	195,000
12	175,613,631	2,380,393	878,068	36,000,000	0	195,000
60	16,303,583	3,079,699	81,518	36,000,000	0	195,000
61	13,223,884	3,061,796	66,119	36,000,000	0	195,000
62	10,162,088	3,044,105	50,810	36,000,000	0	195,000
63	7,117,983	3,026,624	35,590	36,000,000	0	195,000
64	4,091,359	3,009,352	20,457	36,000,000	0	195,000
65	1,082,007	1,082,007	5,410	36,000,000	1,910,280	195,000
66	0	0	0	34,089,720	2,975,428	184,653
67	0	0	0	31,114,292	2,958,773	168,536
68	0	0	0	28,155,519	2,942,321	152,509
69	0	0	0	25,213,198	2,926,071	136,571
70	0	0	0	22,287,128	2,910,020	120,722
71	0	0	0	19,377,107	2,894,169	104,959
72	0	0	0	16,482,938	2,878,515	89,283
73	0	0	0	13,604,423	2,863,057	73,691
74	0	0	0	10,741,366	2,847,794	58,182
75	0	0	0	7,893,572	2,832,724	42,757
76	0	0	0	5,060,849	2,817,846	27,413
77	0	0	0	2,243,003	2,243,003	12,150
78	0	0	0	0	0	0
79	0	0	0	0	0	0
80	0	0	0	0	0	0

Floating Rate Tranches

A floating rate tranche can be created from a fixed rate tranche by creating a floater and an inverse floater. We illustrate the creation of a floating rate and an inverse floating rate bond class using the hypothetical CMO structure CMO-02, which is a four-tranche sequential pay structure with an accrual bond. We can select any of the tranches from which to create a floating rate and an inverse floating rate tranche. In fact, we can create these two securities for more than one of the four tranches or for only a portion of one tranche.

In this case, we create a floater and an inverse floater from tranche C. The par value for this tranche is $96.5 million, and we create two tranches that have a combined par value of $96.5 million. We refer to this CMO structure with a floater and an inverse floater as CMO-03. It has five tranches, designated A, B, FL, IFL, and Z, where FL is the floating rate tranche and IFL is the inverse floating rate tranche. Exhibit 9.6 describes CMO-03. Any reference rate can be used to create a floater and the corresponding inverse floater. The reference rate selected for setting the coupon rate for FL and IFL in CMO-03 is 1-month LIBOR.

The amount of the par value of the floating rate tranche will be some portion of the $96.5 million. There are an infinite number of ways to cut up the $96.5 million between the floater and inverse floater, and final partitioning will be driven by the demands of investors. In the CMO-03 structure, we made the floater from $72,375,000, or 75% of the $96.5 million. The coupon rate on the floater is set at 1-month LIBOR plus 50 basis points. So, for example, if LIBOR is 3.75% at the coupon reset date, the coupon rate on the floater is 3.75% + 0.5%, or 4.25%. There is a cap on the coupon rate for the floater (discussed later).

Unlike a floating rate note whose principal is unchanged over the life of the instrument, the floater's principal balance declines over time as principal repayments are made. The principal payments to the floater are determined by the principal payments from the tranche from which the floater is created. In our CMO structure, this is tranche C.

Since the floater's par value is $72,375,000 of the $96.5 million, the balance is the inverse floater. Assuming that 1-month LIBOR is the reference rate, the coupon reset formula for an inverse floater takes the following form:

$$K - L \times (\text{1-month LIBOR})$$

In CMO-03, K is set at 28.50% and L at 3. Thus, if 1-month LIBOR is 3.75%, the coupon rate for the month is

$$28.50\% - 3 \times (3.75\%) = 17.25\%$$

EXHIBIT 9.6   CMO-03: A Hypothetical Five-Tranche Sequential Pay Structure with Floater, Inverse Floater, and Accrual Bond Classes

Tranche	Par Amount	Coupon Rate
A	$194,500,000	7.50%
B	36,000,000	7.50%
FL	72,375,000	1-mo. LIBOR + 0.50
IFL	24,125,000	28.50 – 3 × (1-mo. LIBOR)
Z (accrual)	73,000,000	7.50%
Total	$400,000,000	

Payment rules:

1. *For payment of periodic coupon interest:* Disburse periodic coupon interest to tranches A, B, FL, and IFL on the basis of the amount of principal outstanding at the beginning of the period. For tranche Z, accrue the interest based on the principal plus accrued interest in the previous period. The interest for tranche Z is to be paid to the earlier tranches as a principal pay down. The maximum coupon rate for FL is 10%; the minimum coupon rate for IFL is 0%.

2. *For disbursement of principal payments:* Disburse principal payments to tranche A until it is completely paid off. After tranche A is completely paid off, disburse principal payments to tranche B until it is completely paid off. After tranche B is completely paid off, disburse principal payments to tranches FL and IFL until they are completely paid off. The principal payments between tranches FL and IFL should be made in the following way: 75% to tranche FL and 25% to tranche IFL. After tranches FL and IFL are completely paid off, disburse principal payments to tranche Z until the original principal balance plus accrued interest is completely paid off.

K is the cap or maximum coupon rate for the inverse floater. In CMO-03, the cap for the inverse floater is 28.50%.

The L or multiple in the coupon reset formula for the inverse floater is called the *coupon leverage*. The higher the coupon leverage, the more the inverse floater's coupon rate changes for a given change in 1-month LIBOR. For example, a coupon leverage of 3 means that a 1 basis point change in 1-month LIBOR will change the coupon rate on the inverse floater by 3 basis points.

As in the case of the floater, the principal pay down of an inverse floater will be a proportionate amount of the principal pay down of tranche C.

Because 1-month LIBOR is always positive, the coupon rate paid to the floating rate tranche cannot be negative. If there are no restrictions placed on the coupon rate for the inverse floater, however, it is possible for the coupon rate for that tranche to be negative. To prevent this, a floor, or minimum, can be placed on the coupon rate. In many structures, the floor is set at zero. Once a floor is set for the inverse floater, a cap or ceiling is imposed on the floater. In CMO-03, a floor of zero is set for the inverse floater. The floor results in a cap or maximum coupon rate for the floater of 10%.

Planned Amortization Class Tranches

A *planned amortization class* (PAC) bond is one in which a schedule of principal of payments is set forth in the prospectus. The PAC bondholders have priority over all other bond classes in the structure with respect to the receipt of the scheduled principal payments. While there is no assurance that the principal payments will be actually realized so as to satisfy the schedule, a PAC bond is structured so that if prepayment speeds are within a certain range, the collateral will throw off sufficient principal to meet the schedule of principal payments.

The greater certainty of the cash flow for the PAC bonds comes at the expense of the non-PAC classes, called the *support bonds* or *companion bonds*. These tranches absorb the prepayment risk. Because PAC bonds have protection against both extension risk and contraction risk, they are said to provide two-sided prepayment protection.

To illustrate how to create a PAC bond, we use as collateral the $400 million passthrough with a coupon rate of 7.5%, an 8.125% WAC, and a WAM of 357 months. From this collateral a PAC bond with a par value of $243.8 million will be created. The second column of Exhibit 9.7 shows the principal payment (regularly scheduled principal repayment plus prepayments) for selected months assuming a prepayment speed of 90 PSA, and the next column shows the principal payments for selected months assuming that the passthrough prepays at 300 PSA.

The last column of Exhibit 9.7 gives the minimum principal payment if the collateral speed is 90 PSA or 300 PSA for months 1 to 349. (After month 349, the outstanding principal balance will be paid off if the prepayment speed is between 90 PSA and 300 PSA.) For example, in the first month, the principal payment would be $508,169.52 if the collateral prepays at 90 PSA and $1,075,931.20 if the collateral prepays at 300 PSA. Thus, the minimum principal payment is $508,169.52, as reported in the last column of Exhibit 9.7. In month 103, the minimum principal payment is also the amount if the prepayment speed is 90 PSA, $1,446,761, compared to $1,458,618.04 for 300 PSA. In month 104, however, a prepayment speed of 300 PSA would produce a principal payment of $1,433,539.23, which is less than the principal payment of $1,440,825.55 assuming 90 PSA. So, $1,433,539.23 is reported in the last column of Exhibit 9.7. In fact, from month 104 on, the minimum principal payment is the one that would result assuming a prepayment speed of 300 PSA.

EXHIBIT 9.7 Monthly Principal Payment for $400 Million Par 7.5% Coupon Passthrough with an 8.125% WAC and a 357 WAM Assuming Prepayment Rates of 90 PSA and 300 PSA

	Principal Payment		Minimum Principal Payment
Month	At 90% PSA	At 300% PSA	PAC Schedule
1	$508,169.52	$1,075,931.20	$508,169.52
2	569,843.43	1,279,412.11	569,843.43
3	631,377.11	1,482,194.45	631,377.11
4	692,741.89	1,683,966.17	692,741.89
5	753,909.12	1,884,414.62	753,909.12
6	814,850.22	2,083,227.31	814,850.22
7	875,536.68	2,280,092.68	875,536.68
8	935,940.10	2,474,700.92	935,940.10
9	996,032.19	2,666,744.77	996,032.19
10	1,055,784.82	2,855,920.32	1,055,784.82
11	1,115,170.01	3,041,927.81	1,115,170.01
12	1,174,160.00	3,224,472.44	1,174,160.00
13	1,232,727.22	3,403,265.17	1,232,727.22
14	1,290,844.32	3,578,023.49	1,290,844.32
15	1,348,484.24	3,748,472.23	1,348,484.24
16	1,405,620.17	3,914,344.26	1,405,620.17
17	1,462,225.60	4,075,381.29	1,462,225.60
18	1,518,274.36	4,231,334.57	1,518,274.36
101	1,458,719.34	1,510,072.17	1,458,719.34
102	1,452,725.55	1,484,126.59	1,452,725.55
103	1,446,761.00	1,458,618.04	1,446,761.00
104	1,440,825.55	1,433,539.23	1,433,539.23
105	1,434,919.07	1,408,883.01	1,408,883.01
211	949,482.58	213,309.00	213,309.00
212	946,033.34	209,409.09	209,409.09
213	942,601.99	205,577.05	205,577.05
346	618,684.59	13,269.17	13,269.17
347	617,071.58	12,944.51	12,944.51
348	615,468.65	12,626.21	12,626.21
349	613,875.77	12,314.16	3,432.32
350	612,292.88	12,008.25	0
351	610,719.96	11,708.38	0
352	609,156.96	11,414.42	0
353	607,603.84	11,126.28	0
354	606,060.57	10,843.85	0
355	604,527.09	10,567.02	0
356	603,003.38	10,295.70	0
357	601,489.39	10,029.78	0

Actually, if the collateral prepays at any speed between 90 PSA and 300 PSA, the minimum principal payment would be the amount reported in the last column of Exhibit 9.7. For example, if we had included principal payment figures assuming a prepayment speed of 200 PSA, the minimum principal payment would not change: from month 11 through month 103, the minimum principal payment is that generated from 90 PSA, but from month 104 on, the minimum principal payment is that generated from 300 PSA.

This characteristic of the collateral allows for the creation of a PAC bond, assuming that the collateral prepays over its life at a constant speed between 90 PSA and 300 PSA. A schedule of principal repayments that the PAC bondholders are entitled to receive before any other tranche in the CMO is specified. The monthly schedule of principal repayments is as specified in the last column of Exhibit 9.7, which shows the minimum principal payment. While there is no assurance that the collateral will prepay at a constant rate between these two speeds, a PAC bond can be structured assuming that it will.

Exhibit 9.8 shows a CMO structure, CMO-04, created from the $400 million 7.5% coupon passthrough with a WAC of 8.125% and a WAM of 357 months. There are just two tranches in this structure: a 7.5% coupon PAC bond created assuming 90 to 300 PSA with a par value of $243.8 million and a support bond with a par value of $156.2 million. The two speeds used to create a PAC bond are called the *initial PAC collars* (or *initial PAC bands*). For CMO-04, 90 PSA is the lower collar and 300 PSA the upper collar.

EXHIBIT 9.8   CMO-04 CMO Structure with One PAC Bond and One Support Bond

Tranche	Par Amount	Coupon Rate (%)
P (PAC)	$243,800,000	7.5
S (support)	156,200,000	7.5
Total	$400,000,000	

Payment rules:

1. *For payment of periodic coupon interest:* Disburse periodic coupon interest to each tranche on the basis of the amount of principal outstanding at the beginning of the period.
2. *For disbursement of principal payments:* Disburse principal payments to tranche P based on its schedule of principal repayments. Tranche P has priority with respect to current and future principal payments to satisfy the schedule. Any excess principal payments in a month over the amount necessary to satisfy the schedule for tranche P are paid to tranche S. When tranche S is completely paid off, all principal payments are to be made to tranche P regardless of the schedule.

EXHIBIT 9.9   Average Life for PAC Bond and Support Bond in CMO-04 Assuming Various Prepayment Speeds

Prepayment Rate (PSA)	PAC Bond (P)	Support Bond (S)
0	15.97	27.26
50	9.44	24.00
90	7.26	18.56
100	7.26	18.56
150	7.26	12.57
165	7.26	11.16
200	7.26	8.38
250	7.26	5.37
300	7.26	3.13
350	6.56	2.51
400	5.92	2.17
450	5.38	1.94
500	4.93	1.77
700	3.70	1.37

Exhibit 9.9 reports the average life for the PAC bond and the support bond in CMO-04 assuming various actual prepayment speeds. Notice that between 90 PSA and 300 PSA, the average life for the PAC bond is stable at 7.26 years. However, at slower or faster PSA speeds, the schedule is broken and the average life changes, lengthening when the prepayment speed is less than 90 PSA and shortening when it is greater than 300 PSA. Even so, there is much greater variability for the average life of the support bond.

A Series of PAC Bonds

Most CMO PAC structures have more than one class of PAC bonds. Exhibit 9.10 shows six PAC bonds created from the single PAC bond in CMO-04. We will refer to this CMO structure as CMO-05. Information about this CMO structure is provided in Exhibit 9.10. The total par value of the six PAC bonds is equal to $243.8 million, which is the amount of the single PAC bond in CMO-04.

Exhibit 9.11 shows the average life for the six PAC bonds and the support bond in CMO-05 at various prepayment speeds. From a PAC bond in CMO-04 with an average life of 7.26, we have created six PAC bonds with an average life as short as 2.58 years (P-A) and as long as 16.92 years (P-F) if prepayments stay within 90 PSA and 300 PSA.

EXHIBIT 9.10 CMO-05 CMO Structure with Six PAC Bonds and One Support Bond

Tranche	Par amount	Coupon rate (%)
P-A	$85,000,000	7.5
P-B	8,000,000	7.5
P-C	35,000,000	7.5
P-D	45,000,000	7.5
P-E	40,000,000	7.5
P-F	30,800,000	7.5
S	156,200,000	7.5
Total	$400,000,000	

Payment rules:

1. *For payment of periodic coupon interest:* Disburse periodic coupon interest to each tranche on the basis of the amount of principal outstanding at the beginning of the period.

2. *For disbursement of principal payments:* Disburse principal payments to tranches P-A to P-F based on their respective schedules of principal repayments. Tranche P-A has priority with respect to current and future principal payments to satisfy the schedule. Any excess principal payments in a month over the amount necessary to satisfy the schedule for tranche P-A are paid to tranche S. Once tranche P-A is completely paid off, tranche P-B has priority, then tranche P-C, etc. When tranche S is completely paid off, all principal payments are to be made to the remaining PAC tranches in order of priority regardless of the schedule.

As expected, the average lives are stable if the prepayment speed is between 90 PSA and 300 PSA. Notice that even outside this range the average life is stable for several of the PAC bonds. For example, PAC P-A is stable even if prepayment speeds are as high as 400 PSA. For the PAC P-B, the average life does not vary when prepayments are between 90 PSA and 350 PSA. Why is it that the shorter the PAC, the more protection it has against faster prepayments?

To understand why this is so, remember that there are $156.2 million in support bonds that are protecting the $85 million of PAC P-A. Thus, even if prepayments are faster than the initial upper collar, there may be sufficient support bonds to assure the satisfaction of the schedule. In fact, as can be seen from Exhibit 9.11, even if prepayments are at 400 PSA over the life of the collateral, the average life is unchanged.

Now consider PAC P-B. The support bonds are providing protection for both the $85 million of PAC P-A and $93 million of PAC P-B. As can be seen from Exhibit 9.11, prepayments could be 350 PSA and the average life

EXHIBIT 9.11 Average Life for the Six PAC Bonds in CMO-05 Assuming Various Prepayment Speeds

Prepayment Rate (PSA)	PAC Bonds					
	P-A	P-B	P-C	P-D	P-E	P-F
0	8.46	14.61	16.49	19.41	21.91	23.76
50	3.58	6.82	8.36	11.30	14.50	18.20
90	2.58	4.72	5.78	7.89	10.83	16.92
100	2.58	4.72	5.78	7.89	10.83	16.92
150	2.58	4.72	5.78	7.89	10.83	16.92
165	2.58	4.72	5.78	7.89	10.83	16.92
200	2.58	4.72	5.78	7.89	10.83	16.92
250	2.58	4.72	5.78	7.89	10.83	16.92
300	2.58	4.72	5.78	7.89	10.83	16.92
350	2.58	4.72	5.94	6.95	9.24	14.91
400	2.57	4.37	4.91	6.17	8.33	13.21
450	2.50	3.97	4.44	5.56	7.45	11.81
500	2.40	3.65	4.07	5.06	6.74	10.65
700	2.06	2.82	3.10	3.75	4.88	7.51

is still unchanged. From Exhibit 9.11, it can also be seen that the degree of protection against extension risk increases the shorter the PAC. Thus, while the initial collar may be 90 to 300 PSA, the *effective collar* is wider for the shorter PAC tranches.

Effective Collars and Actual Prepayments

As we have emphasized, the creation of a mortgage-backed security cannot make prepayment risk disappear. This is true for both a passthrough and a CMO. Thus, the reduction in prepayment risk (both extension risk and contraction risk) that a PAC offers must come from somewhere.

Where does the prepayment protection come from? It comes from the support bonds. The support bonds forego principal payments if the collateral prepayments are slow; support bonds do not receive any principal until the PAC bonds receive the scheduled principal repayment. This reduces the risk that the PAC bonds will extend. Similarly, the support bonds absorb any principal payments in excess of the scheduled principal payments that are made. This reduces the contraction risk of the PAC bonds. Thus, the key to the prepayment protection offered by a PAC bond is the amount of support bonds outstanding. If the support bonds are paid off quickly because of faster-than-expected prepayments, then there is no longer any protection for the PAC bonds. In fact, in CMO-05, if the support bond is paid off, the structure is effectively reduced to a sequential pay CMO. In such cases, the schedule is unlikely to be maintained, and the structure is referred to as a *busted PAC*.

The support bonds can be thought of as bodyguards for the PAC bondholders. When the bullets fly (i.e., prepayments occur), the bodyguards get killed first. The bodyguards are there to absorb the bullets. Once all the bodyguards are killed off (i.e., the support bonds paid off with faster-than-expected prepayments), the PAC bonds must fend for themselves: they are exposed to all the bullets.

With the bodyguard metaphor for the support bonds in mind, let's consider two questions asked by CMO buyers:

1. Will the schedule of principal repayments be satisfied if prepayments are faster than the initial upper collar?
2. Will the schedule of principal repayments be satisfied as long as prepayments stay within the initial collar?

Let's address the first question. The initial upper collar for CMO-04 is 300 PSA. Suppose that actual prepayments are 500 PSA for seven consecutive months; will this disrupt the schedule of principal repayments? The answer is: It depends!

There are two pieces of information we will need to answer this question. First, when does the 500 PSA occur? Second, what has been the actual prepayment experience up to the time that prepayments are 500 PSA? For example, suppose six years from now is when the prepayments reach 500 PSA, and also suppose that for the past six years the actual prepayment speed has been 90 PSA every month. What this means is that there are more bodyguards (i.e., support bonds) around than was expected when the PAC was structured at the initial collar. In establishing the schedule of principal repayments, it was assumed that the bodyguards would be killed off at 300 PSA, but the actual prepayment experience results in them being killed off at only 90 PSA. Thus, six years from now when the 500 PSA is assumed to occur, there are more bodyguards than expected. Thus, a 500 PSA for seven consecutive months may have no effect on the ability of the schedule of principal repayments to be met.

In contrast, suppose that the actual prepayment experience for the first six years is 300 PSA (the upper collar of the initial PAC collar). In this case, there are no extra bodyguards around. As a result, any prepayment speeds faster than 300 PSA, such as 500 PSA in our example, jeopardize satisfaction of the principal repayment schedule and increase contraction risk. This does not mean that the schedule will be "busted"—the term used in the CMO market when a PAC schedule is broken. What it does mean is that the prepayment protection is reduced.

It should be clear from these observations that the initial collars are not particularly useful in assessing the prepayment protection for a seasoned PAC bond. This is most important to understand because it is common for CMO buyers to compare prepayment protection of PACs in different CMO structures and conclude that the greater protection is offered by the one with the wider initial collars. This approach is inadequate because actual prepayment experience determines the degree of prepayment protection going forward, as well as the expected future prepayment behavior of the collateral.

The way to determine this protection is to calculate the effective collar for a PAC bond. An effective collar for a PAC is the lower and the upper PSA that can occur in the future and still allow maintenance of the schedule of principal repayments.

The effective collar changes every month. An extended period over which actual prepayments are below the upper range of the initial PAC collar will result in an increase in the upper range of the effective collar. This is because there will be more bodyguards around than anticipated. An extended period of prepayments slower than the lower range of the initial PAC collar will raise the lower range of the effective collar. This is because it will take faster prepayments to make up the shortfall of the scheduled principal payments not made plus the scheduled future principal payments.

The PAC schedule may not be satisfied even if the actual prepayments never fall outside of the initial collar. This may seem surprising since our previous analysis indicated that the average life would not change if prepayments are at either extreme of the initial collar. However, recall that all of our previous analysis has been based on a single PSA speed for the life of the structure.

If we vary the PSA speed over time rather than keep it constant over the life of the CMO, we can see what happens to the effective collar if the prepayments are at the initial upper collar for a certain number of months. Exhibit 9.12 shows the average life two years from now for the PAC bond in CMO-04, assuming that prepayments are 300 PSA for the first 24 months. Notice that the average life is stable at six years if the prepayments for the following months are between 115 PSA and 300 PSA. That is, the effective PAC collar is no longer the initial collar. Instead, the lower collar has shifted upward. This means that the protection from year 2 on is for 115 to 300 PSA, a narrower band than initially, even though the earlier prepayments did not exceed the initial upper collar.

EXHIBIT 9.12 Average Life Two Years from Now for PAC Bond of CMO-04 Assuming Prepayments of 300 PSA for First 24 Months

PSA from Year 2 on	Average Life
95	6.43
105	6.11
115	6.01
120	6.00
125	6.00
300	6.00
305	5.62

Providing Greater Prepayment Protection for PACs

There are two ways to provide greater protection for PAC bonds: lockouts and reverse PAC structures. One obvious way to provide greater protection for PAC bonds is to issue fewer PAC bonds relative to support bonds. In CMO-05, for example, rather than creating the six PAC bonds with a total par value of $243.8 million, we could use only $158.8 million of the $400 million of collateral to create these bonds by reducing the amount of each of the six PAC bonds. An alternative is not to issue one of the PAC bonds, typically the shorter-term one. For example, suppose that we create only the last five of the six PAC bonds in CMO-05. The $85 million for PAC P-A is then used to create more support bonds. Such a CMO structure with no principal payments to a PAC bond in the earlier years is referred to as a *lockout structure*.

A lockout structure provides greater prepayment protection to all PAC bonds in the CMO structure. One way to provide greater prepayment protection to only some PAC bonds is to alter the principal payment rules for distributing principal once all the support bonds have been paid off.

In CMO-05, for example, once the support bond in this structure is paid off, the structure effectively becomes a sequential pay structure. For PAC P-A this means that while there is protection against extension risk, because this tranche receives principal payments before the other five PAC bonds, there is no protection against contraction. To provide greater protection to PAC P-A, the payment rules set forth in the prospectus can specify that after all support bonds have been paid off, any principal payments in excess of the scheduled amount will be paid to the last PAC bond, P-F in CMO-05. Thus, PAC P-F is exposed to greater contraction risk, which provides the other five PAC bonds with more protection against contraction risk. The principal payment rules would also specify that once the support bonds and PAC P-F bond are paid off, then all principal payments in excess of the scheduled amount to earlier tranches are to be paid to the next-to-the-last PAC bond, PAC P-E in our example.

A CMO structure requiring any excess principal payments to be made to the longer PAC bonds after all support bonds are paid off is called a *reverse PAC structure*.

Other PAC Tranches

Earlier we described how the collateral can be used to create a CMO with accrual bonds and floater and inverse floater bonds. These same types of bond classes can be created from a PAC bond. The difference between the bond classes described and those created from a PAC bond is simply the prepayment protection offered by the PAC structure.

Targeted Amortization Class Bonds

A *targeted amortization class*, or TAC, bond resembles a PAC bond in that both have a schedule of principal repayment. The difference between a PAC bond and a TAC bond is that the former has a wide PSA range over which the schedule of principal repayment is protected against contraction risk and extension risk. A TAC bond, in contrast, has a single PSA rate from which the schedule of principal repayment is protected. As a result, the prepayment protection afforded the TAC bond is considerably less than that for a PAC bond.

The PSA rate used to generate the schedule of principal repayments is such that it results in protection against contraction risk but not extension risk. Thus, while PAC bonds are said to have two-sided prepayment protection, TAC bonds have one-sided prepayment protection. Such a bond would not be acceptable to an investor who seeks protection against extension risk.

Some investors are interested in protection against extension risk but are willing to accept contraction risk. This is the opposite protection from that sought by the buyers of TAC bonds. A TAC structure can be created to provide such protection. The TAC created is called a *reverse TAC bond*.

Very Accurately Determined Maturity Bonds

Accrual or Z-bonds have been used in CMO structures as support for bonds called *very accurately determined maturity* (VADM) or *guaranteed final maturity bonds*. In this case, the interest accruing (i.e., not being paid out) on a Z-bond is used to pay the interest and principal on a VADM bond. This effectively provides protection against extension risk even if prepayments slow down, since the interest accruing on the Z-bond will be sufficient to pay off the scheduled principal and interest on the VADM bond. Thus, the maximum final maturity can be determined with a high degree of certainty. However, if prepayments are high, resulting in the supporting Z-bond being paid off faster, a VADM bond can shorten.

A VADM is similar in character to a reverse TAC. For structures with similar collateral, however, a VADM bond offers greater protection against extension risk. Moreover, most VADMs will not shorten significantly if prepayments speed up. Thus, they offer greater protection against contraction risk compared to a reverse TAC with the same underlying collateral. Compared to PACs, VADM bonds have greater absolute protection against extension risk. While VADM bonds do not have as much protection against contraction risk, the structures that have included these bonds are such that contraction risk is generally not significant.

Notional IOs

In our previous illustrations, we used a CMO structure in which all the tranches have the same coupon rate (7.5%) and that coupon rate is the same as the collateral. In practice, the same coupon rate would not be given to each tranche. Instead, the coupon rate would depend on the term structure of interest rates and the average life of the tranche, among other things.

In the earlier CMO deals, all of the excess interest between the coupon rate on the tranches and the coupon interest on the collateral was paid to an equity class referred to as the CMO residual. This is no longer the practice today. Instead, a tranche is created that receives the excess coupon interest. This tranche is called a *notional interest-only class*, *notional IO* or *structured IO*.

To see how a notional IO is created, consider the CMO structure shown in Exhibit 9.13, CMO-06. This is the same structure as CMO-02 except that the coupon rate varies by tranche and there is a class denoted "IO," which is the class of interest to us.

Notice that for this structure the par amount for the IO class is shown as $52,566,667, and the coupon rate is 7.5%. Since this is an IO class there is no par amount. The amount shown is the amount upon which the interest payments will be determined, not the amount that will be paid to the holder of this bond. Therefore, it is called a *notional amount*.

Let's look at how the notional amount is determined. Consider first tranche A. The par value is $194.5 million and the coupon rate is 6%. Since the collateral's coupon rate is 7.5%, the excess interest is 150 basis points (1.5%). Therefore, an IO with a 1.5% coupon rate and a notional amount of $194.5 million can be created from tranche A. But this is equivalent to

EXHIBIT 9.13   CMO-06 A Hypothetical Five-Tranche Sequential Pay with an Accrual Tranche, an Interest-Only Tranche, and a Residual Class

Tranche	Par Amount	Coupon Rate (%)
A	$194,500,000	6.00
B	36,000,000	6.50
C	96,500,000	7.00
Z	73,000,000	7.25
IO	52,566,667 (Notional)	7.50
Total	$400,000,000	

Payment rules:

1. *For payment of periodic coupon interest:* Disburse periodic coupon interest to tranches A, B, and C on the basis of the amount of principal outstanding at the beginning of the period. For tranche Z, accrue the interest based on the principal plus accrued interest in the previous period. The interest for tranche Z is to be paid to the earlier tranches as a principal pay down. Disburse periodic interest to the IO tranche based on the notional amount at the beginning of the period.
2. *For disbursement of principal payments:* Disburse principal payments to tranche A until it is completely paid off. After tranche A is completely paid off, disburse principal payments to tranche B until it is completely paid off. After tranche B is completely paid off, disburse principal payments to tranche C until it is completely paid off. After tranche C is completely paid off, disburse principal payments to tranche Z until the original principal balance plus accrued interest is completely paid off.
3. *No principal is to be paid to the IO tranche:* The notional amount of the IO tranche declines based on the principal payments to all other tranches.

an IO with a notional amount of $38.9 million and a coupon rate of 7.5%. Mathematically, this notional amount is found as follows:

$$\text{Notional amount for 7.5\% IO} = \frac{\text{Tranche's par value} \times \text{Excess interest}}{0.075}$$

where

Excess interest = Collateral coupon rate - Tranche coupon rate

For example, for tranche A:

Excess interest = 0.075 − 0.060 = 0.015

Tranche's par value = $194,500,000

$$\text{Notional amount for 7.5\% IO} = \frac{\$194,500,000 \times 0.015}{0.075} = \$38,900,000$$

Similarly, from tranche B with a par value of $36 million, the excess interest is 100 basis points (1%), and therefore an IO with a coupon rate of 1% and a notional amount of $36 million can be created. But this is equivalent to creating an IO with a notional amount of $4.8 million and a coupon rate of 7.5%. This procedure is shown below for all four tranches:

Tranche	Par Amount	Excess Interest (%)	Notional Amount for a 7.5% Coupon Rate IO
A	$194,500,000	1.50	$38,900,000
B	36,000,000	1.00	4,800,000
C	96,500,000	0.50	6,433,333
Z	73,000,000	0.25	2,433,334
	Notional amount for 7.5% IO		$52,566,667

Support Bonds

The support bonds—or bodyguards—are the bonds that provide prepayment protection for the PAC tranches. Consequently, support tranches expose investors to the greatest level of prepayment risk. Because of this, investors must be particularly careful in assessing the cash flow characteristics of support bonds to reduce the likelihood of adverse portfolio consequences due to prepayments.

The support bond typically is divided into different bond classes. All the bond classes we have discussed earlier are available, including sequential pay support bond classes, floater and inverse floater support bond classes, and accrual support bond classes.

The support bond can even be partitioned to create support bond classes with a schedule of principal payments. That is, support bond classes that are PAC bonds can be created. In a structure with a PAC bond and a support bond with a PAC schedule of principal payments, the former is called a *PAC I bond* or *Level I PAC bond* and the latter a *PAC II bond* or *Level II PAC bond*. While PAC II bonds have greater prepayment protection than the support bond classes without a schedule of principal repayments, the prepayment protection is less than that provided PAC I bonds.

To illustrate this concept, the CMO structure shown in Exhibit 9.14 was created, CMO-07, for the par amounts shown. There is the same PAC bond as in CMO-04 with an initial PAC collar of 90 PSA to 300 PSA. That bond is now labeled P-I, and it is called a PAC I. The support bond in

EXHIBIT 9.14   CMO-07 CMO Structure with a PAC I Bond, a PAC II Bond, and a Support Bond Class without a Principal Repayment Schedule

Initial PAC collar for the PAC I: 90 PSA to 300 PSA
Initial PAC collar for the PAC II: 100 PSA to 225 PSA

Tranche	Par Amount ($)	Coupon Rate (%)
P-I (PAC I)	$243,800,000	7.50
P-II (PAC II)	50,330,000	7.50
S	105,870,000	7.50
Total	$400,000,000	

Payment rules:

1. *For payment of periodic coupon interest:* Disburse periodic coupon interest to each tranche based on the amount of principal outstanding at the beginning of the period.

2. *For disbursement of principal payments:* Disburse principal payments to tranche P-I based on its schedule of principal repayments. Tranche P-I has priority with respect to current and future principal payments to satisfy the schedule. Any excess principal payments in a month over the amount necessary to satisfy the schedule for tranche P-I are paid to tranches P-II and S. Priority is given to tranche P-II to satisfy its schedule of principal repayments. Any excess principal payments in a month are paid to tranche S. When tranche S is completely paid off its original balance, then any excess is to be paid to tranche P-II regardless of its schedule. After tranche P-II is completely paid off its original mortgage balance, any excess is paid to tranche P-I regardless of its schedule.

CMO-04 has been split into a support bond with a schedule, labeled P-II, and a support bond without a schedule, labeled S. P-II is a PAC II bond that was created with an initial PAC collar of 100 PSA to 225 PSA.

Exhibit 9.15 indicates the average life for all the bond classes in CMO-07 under various prepayment scenarios. Also shown in the exhibit is the average life for the support bond in CMO-04. The PAC I enjoys the same prepayment protection in the structure with a PAC II as it does in the structure without a PAC II. The PAC II has considerably more average life variability than the PAC I but less variability than the support bond class S. Comparison of the support bond class S in CMO-07 with the support bond in CMO-04 shows that the presence of a PAC II increases the average life variability. Now the support bond class is providing protection for not only a PAC I but also a support bond with a schedule.

There is more that can be done with the PAC II bond. A series of PAC IIs can be created just as we did with the PACs in CMO-05. PAC IIs can also be used to create any other type of bond class, such as a PAC II inverse floater or accrual bond, for example.

EXHIBIT 9.15 Average Life for CMO-07 for Various Assumed Prepayment Rates

Prepayment Rate	Average Life			
	PAC I Bond	PAC II Bond	Bond S	Support Bond in CMO-04
0	15.973	25.44	28.13	27.26
50	9.44	20.32	25.77	24.00
90	7.26	15.69	22.14	20.06
100	7.26	13.77	20.84	18.56
150	7.26	13.77	12.00	12.57
165	7.26	13.77	9.91	11.16
200	7.26	13.77	5.82	8.38
225	7.26	13.77	3.42	6.75
250	7.26	10.75	2.81	5.37
300	7.26	5.07	2.20	3.13
350	6.56	3.85	1.88	2.51
400	5.92	3.24	1.66	2.17
450	5.38	2.85	1.51	1.94
500	4.93	2.58	1.39	1.77
700	3.70	1.99	1.08	1.37

The support bond without a principal repayment schedule can be used to create any type of bond class. In fact, a portion of the non-PAC II support bond can be given a schedule of principal repayments. This bond class would be called a *PAC III bond* or a *Level III PAC bond*. While it provides protection against prepayments for the PAC I and PAC II bonds and is therefore subject to considerable prepayment risk, such a bond class has greater protection than the support bond class without a schedule of principal repayments.

YIELDS

The cash flow yield for a CMO is calculated in the same way as that for a mortgage passthrough security. Consequently, the cash flow yield depends on the prepayment speed assumed.

The offered yield on a particular CMO tranche depends on the market's perceived prepayment risk for that tranche. For a given CMO deal, a PAC tranche would be offered at a lower yield than that of a support bond. In a PAC I/PAC II/support without a schedule CMO deal, the PAC II would be offered at a yield that is greater than the PAC I but less than the support bond without a schedule.

Financial Instruments and Concepts Introduced in this Chapter (in Order of Presentation)

Collateralized mortgage obligations
Tranches
Agency CMOs
Sequential pay CMOs
Principal pay down window
Accrual tranche
Z bond
Coupon leverage
Planned amortization class
Support bonds
Companion bonds
Initial PAC collars
Initial PAC bands
Effective collar
Busted PAC
Lookout structure

Reverse PAC structure
Targeted amortization class
Reverse TAC bond
Very accurately determined maturity
Guaranteed final maturity bonds
Notional interest-only class
Notional IO
Structured IO
Notional amount
PAC I bond
Level I PAC bond
PAC II bond
Level II PAC bond
PAC III bond
Level III PAC bond

CHAPTER 10

Structured Credit Products

We described the securitization of residential mortgage loans in the previous two chapters, showing how a pool of residential mortgage loans can be used to create a mortgage-backed security (MBS). The tranching procedure as explained in the previous chapter demonstrated how one can obtain tranches or bond classes with different risk-return characteristics. However, our discussion of MBS in the two previous chapters ignored the issue of credit risk because we restricted our description to agency passthrough securities and collateralized mortgage obligations (CMOs).

The securitization technology can be applied to a pool of assets where the resulting tranches created are subject to varying degrees of credit risk as well as prepayment risk (if applicable). The securitization process involves the owner of assets selling a pool of assets to a bankruptcy remote vehicle called a *special purpose vehicle* (SPV) or *special purpose entity* (SPE). The SPV obtains the proceeds to acquire the asset pool, referred to as the collateral, by issuing debt instruments. The cash flow of the asset pool is used to satisfy the obligations of the debt instruments issued by the SPV. To be able to create securities with different degrees of credit risk, securitization uses credit enhancement mechanisms.

We refer to the generic term for the debt obligations or securities issued in a securitization where the investor is exposed to credit risk as *structured credit products*. In turn, these products can be further classified as mortgage-backed securities, asset-backed securities, and collateralized debt obligations.

A mortgage-backed security backed by residential real estate loans is referred to as a *residential MBS* (RMBS). An MBS backed by commercial real estate loans is called a *commercial MBS* (CMBS). An *asset-backed security* (ABS) is backed by a pool of assets for non-real estate loans. The classification we have just provided, however, is not universally adopted. In Europe, an ABS refers all to securitized products regardless of whether the pool of loans consists of real estate loans or any type of loan or receivable. In the United States, the market convention is to refer to RMBS as either MBS or

ABS. The classification depends on the credit quality of the borrowers. As we will explain later in this chapter, loans can be classified as prime loans and subprime loans. An MBS backed by prime loans is classified as an MBS while an MBS backed by subprime loans is referred to as an ABS. In turn, the ABS market is divided into the mortgage-related ABS market and non-mortgage-related MBS market.

Although a collateralized debt obligation (CDO) employs the securitization technology, the resulting securities are quite different from that of an ABS or MBS. This is because unlike in an MBS or ABS, in a CDO there is active management of the collateral pool.

In this chapter, we describe RMBS, CMBS, non-mortgage-ABS, and CDOs.

PRIVATE LABEL RESIDENTIAL MBS

RMBS can be classified as agency RMBS and private-label (or nonagency) RMBS. Agency RMBS are those issued by three government-related entities that we described in the previous chapter (Ginnie Mae, Fannie, and Freddie Mac) and is by far the largest sector of the investment-grade bond market (more than 35%). Private-label RMBS are issued by any other entity.

Because of the credit risk associated with private-label RMBS, they require credit enhancement to provide some form of credit protection against default on the pool of assets backing a transaction. Credit enhancement mechanisms are typical in ABS transactions. In the case of agency RMBS, the credit enhancement is either a government guarantee or the guarantee of a government-sponsored enterprise.

Private-label RMBS are further classified based on the credit quality of the mortgage loans in the pool: prime loans and subprime loans. Deals backed by prime loans are referred to as *prime RMBS*. Subprime loans are loans made to borrowers with impaired credit ratings and RMBS backed by them are referred to as *subprime RMBS*. The market classifies prime loans as part of the nonagency RMBS market and those backed by subprime loans as part of the ABS market.

Prime RMBS

Aside from the presence of credit enhancement decribed below, prime RMB deals share many features and structuring techniques with agency CMOs.

The first step in structuring the credit enhancement for a prime RMB deal is to split the face value of the loans into senior and subordinated interests. The senior bonds have higher priority with respect to both the receipt of interest and principal and the allocation of realized losses, and are generally created with enough subordination to be rated AAA by the credit rating agencies. In most cases, the subordinate interests are subdivided (or tranched) into a series of bonds that decline sequentially in priority. The subordinate classes normally range from AA in rating to an unrated first loss piece. These securities are often referenced as the "six-pack" because there are six broad rating grades generally issued by the rating agencies. In the investment-grade category, bonds range from AA to BBB; noninvestment grade ratings decline from BB to the unrated first-loss piece. The structure (or "splits") of a hypothetical deal is shown in Exhibit 10.1, while a schematic detailing how and losses are allocated within the structure is contained in Exhibit 10.2.

Internal credit enhancement requires two complimentary mechanisms. The cash flows for deals are allocated through the mechanism of a *waterfall*, which dictates the allocation of principal and interest payments to tranches with different degrees of seniority. At the same time, the allocation of realized losses is also governed by a separate prioritization schedule, with the subordinates (subs) typically being impacted in reverse order of priority.

While the original subordination levels are set at the time of issuance (or, more precisely, at the time the attributes of the deal's collateral are finalized), deals with internal credit enhancement are designed such that the amount of credit enhancement grows over time. Private-label structures generally use a so-called *shifting interest mechanism*, in which the classes of subordinates do not receive principal prepayments for a period of time after issuance (usually five years). After the lockout period expires, the subs begin to receive prepayments on an escalating basis. It is only after 10 years that the subs receive a pro rata allocation of prepayments. Locking out the subs means that as the collateral experiences prepayments, the face value of the subs grows in proportion relative to the senior classes; the senior classes receive all the collateral prepayments during the lockout period and hence decline proportionately over time.

Subprime RMBS

Subprime loans are riskier than those in prime deals, either because the loans are granted to borrowers with impaired credit (which greatly increases their expected defaults and losses) or are in an inferior lien position (which creates high-loss severities). Investors have become painfully aware of this sector of the RMBS market due to the poor performance and loss of liquidity that occurred in the summer of 2007, popularly referred to as the "subprime mortgage crisis."

EXHIBIT 10.1   Measuring Subordination by Percentage of Deal Size and Credit Support for a Hypothetical $400 million Deal with 3.5% Initial Subordination

A. Tranche Size as a Percentage of the Total Deal

	Face Value	Percent of Deal
AAA	$386,000,000	96.50%
AA	6,000,000	1.50%
A	2,600,000	0.65%
BBB	1,800,000	0.45%
BB	1,200,000	0.30%
B	1,200,000	0.30%
First Loss (nonrated)	1,200,000	0.30%
Total Subordination	14,000,000	3.50%

B. Tranche Size Measured by Percentage of Subordination for Each Rating Level (i.e., credit support)

	Face Value	Credit Support (%)[a]
AAA	$386,000,000	3.50%
AA	6,000,000	2.00%
A	2,600,000	1.35%
BBB	1,800,000	0.90%
BB	1,200,000	0.60%
B	1,200,000	0.30%
First Loss (nonrated)	1,200,000	0.00%

[a]Calculated by summing the deal percentages of all tranches junior in priority.
Note: As an example, if cumulative losses on the deal were 0.40%, the First Loss and rated B tranches would be fully exhausted, but the tranches rated BB and above would not be affected.

The challenge in structuring subprime RMBS is to create cash flow protection and credit enhancement for the senior securities in the most efficient possible way. The optimal form of credit enhancement for deals backed by risky loans with high interest rates is the *overcollateralization* (OC) structure. This structure allows the higher loan rates associated with these riskier loans to be converted into credit enhancement. In addition to the utilization of excess spread as credit enhancement, deals securitizing these types

EXHIBIT 10.2 Schematic of Hypothetical Structure with Cash Flow and Loss Allocations

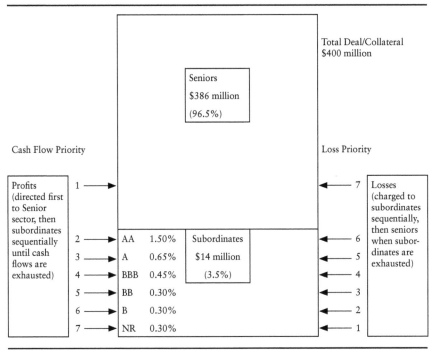

of risky loans must have higher levels of subordination than in the prime sector. The mechanisms associated with the OC structure are more complex than the traditional shifting interest structures utilized in prime RMBS.

Subprime RMBS deals have various forms of credit enhancement, which is higher than that associated with prime RMBS deals. In the prime sector, credit enhancement levels (i.e., the credit support) for the senior, AAA tranches) vary depending on the type of loan securitized, but typically do not exceed 10% for the most risky loan categories. In contrast, subprime RMBS deals generally have initial enhancement levels in excess of 20%.

A challenge with subprime RMBS deals is also to efficiently utilize the incrementally higher loan rate of the underlying loans in providing credit support, effectively converting interest cash flows into principal. Understanding this requires the introduction of two concepts. One is *excess spread*, which is the difference between interest received from borrowers on the loans and interest paid to the investors in the securities. While all deals technically have excess spread, it is not large enough in prime RMBS deals to supplement credit enhancement. However, due to the high loan

EXHIBIT 10.3   Normal Cash Flow Allocation and Allocation with Turboing to Create Overcollateralization

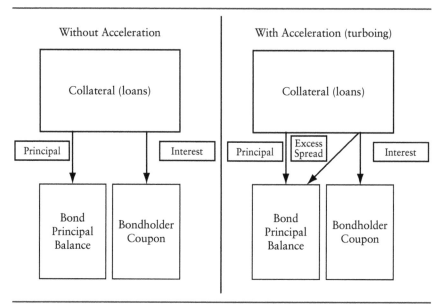

rates associated with risky loans, the amount of excess spread in a typical subprime RMBS deal is relatively high.

The other concept is overcollateralization, or OC, which refers to the fact that the face value of loans collateralizing the deal is greater than the amount of bonds. OC is created through two mechanisms. One way is to structure a smaller number of bonds at issuance, which is referenced as initial OC. The other mechanism is to utilize some or all of the excess spread to pay down bonds faster than simply through the return of principal. This is called *acceleration* or *turboing*. A depiction of the allocation of cash flows with and without turboing is shown in Exhibit 10.3.

COMMERCIAL MORTGAGE-BACKED SECURITIES

Commercial mortgage-backed securities (CMBSs) are backed by a pool of commercial mortgage loans on income-producing property—multifamily properties (i.e., apartment buildings), office buildings, industrial properties (including warehouses), shopping centers, hotels, and health care facilities (i.e., senior housing care facilities). The basic building block of the CMBS transaction is a commercial loan that was originated either to finance a commercial purchase or to refinance a prior mortgage obligation.

Commercial mortgage loans are nonrecourse loans. This means that the lender can only look to the income-producing property backing the loan for interest and principal repayment. If there is a default, the lender looks to the proceeds from the sale of the property for repayment and has no recourse to the borrower for any unpaid balance. Basically, this means that the lender must view each property as a stand-alone business and evaluate each property using measures that have been found to be useful in assessing credit risk.

Regardless of the property type, the two measures that have been found to be key indicators of the potential credit performance are the *debt-to-service coverage* (DSC) *ratio* and the *loan-to-value* (LTV) *ratio*. The DSC ratio is the ratio of the property's *net operating income* (NOI) divided by the debt service. The NOI is defined as the rental income reduced by cash operating expenses (adjusted for a replacement reserve). A ratio greater than one means that the cash flow from the property is sufficient to cover debt servicing. The higher the ratio, the more likely it is that the borrower will be able to meet debt servicing from the property's cash flow. In computing the LTV, "value" in the ratio is either market value or appraised value. In valuing commercial property, there can be considerable variation in the estimates of the property's market value. The lower the LTV, the greater the protection afforded the lender.

Another characteristic of the underlying loans that is used in gauging the quality of a CMBS deal is the prepayment protection provisions. We review these provisions later. Finally, there are characteristics of the property that affect quality. Specifically, investors and rating agencies look at the concentration of loans by property type and by geographical location.

As with any securitization transaction, the rating agencies will determine the level of credit enhancement to achieve a desired rating level for each tranche in the structure. For example, if certain DSC and LTV ratios are needed, and these ratios cannot be met at the loan level, then subordination is used to achieve these levels.

Call Protection

The degree of call protection available to a CMBS investor is a function of the following two characteristics: (1) call protection available at the loan level and (2) call protection afforded from the actual CMBS structure. At the commercial loan level, call protection can take the following forms: (1) prepayment lockout, (2) defeasance, (3) prepayment penalty points, and (4) yield maintenance charges.

A *prepayment lockout* is a contractual agreement that prohibits any prepayments during a specified period of time, called the *lockout period*.

The lockout period at issuance can be from two to five years. After the lockout period, call protection comes in the form of either prepayment penalty points or yield maintenance charges. Prepayment lockout and defeasance are the strongest forms of prepayment protection.

With *defeasance*, rather than prepaying a loan, the borrower provides sufficient funds for the servicer to invest in a portfolio of Treasury securities that replicates the cash flows that would exist in the absence of prepayments. The substitution of the cash flow of a Treasury portfolio for that of the borrower improves the credit quality of the CMBS deal.

Prepayment penalty points are predetermined penalties that must be paid by a borrower wishing to refinance. For example, 5-4-3-2-1 is a common prepayment penalty point structure. That is, if the borrower wishes to prepay during the first year, a 5% penalty for a total of $105 per $100 principal balance outstanding rather than $100 (which is the norm in the residential market) must be paid. Likewise, during the second year, a 4% penalty would apply, and so on.

A *yield maintenance charge*, in its simplest terms, is designed to make the lender indifferent as to the timing of prepayments. The yield maintenance charge, also called the *make-whole charge*, makes it uneconomical to refinance solely to get a lower interest rate.

The other type of call protection available in CMBS transactions is structural. That is, because the CMBS bond structures are sequential pay bonds (by rating), the bonds rated AA cannot pay down until the bonds rated AAA are completely retired, and the bonds rated AA must be paid off before the bonds rated A, and so on. However, principal losses due to defaults are impacted from the bottom of the structure upward.

Balloon Maturity Provisions

Many commercial loans backing CMBS transactions are balloon loans that require substantial principal payment at the end of the term of the loan. If the borrower fails to make the balloon payment, the borrower is in default. The lender may extend the loan, and in so doing may modify the original loan terms. During the workout period for the loan, a higher interest rate will be charged, the "default interest rate."

The risk that a borrower cannot make the balloon payment, because either the borrower cannot arrange for refinancing at the balloon payment date or cannot sell the property to generate sufficient funds to pay off the balloon balance, is called *balloon risk*. Since the term of the loan will be extended by the lender during the workout period, balloon risk is also referred to as *extension risk*.

NONMORTGAGE ASSET-BACKED SECURITIES

In this section, we discuss ABSs for which the collateral is a pool of traditional nonmortgage assets. More specifically, we will describe the largest sectors of the nonmortgage ABS market.

Credit Card Receivable-Backed Securities

Credit cards are issued by banks (e.g., Visa and MasterCard), retailers (e.g., JCPenney and Sears), and travel and entertainment companies (e.g., American Express). For a pool of credit card receivables, the cash flow consists of finance charges collected, fees, and principal. Finance charges collected represent the periodic interest the credit card borrower is charged based on the unpaid balance after the grace period. Fees include late payment fees and any annual membership fees. Interest to security holders is paid periodically (e.g., monthly, quarterly, or semiannually). The interest rate may be fixed or floating.

A *credit card receivable-backed security* is a nonamortizing security. For a specified period of time, referred to as the lockout period or *revolving period*, the principal payments made by credit card borrowers comprising the pool are retained by the trustee and reinvested in additional receivables to maintain the size of the pool. The lockout period can vary from 18 months to 10 years. So, during the lockout period, the cash flow that is paid out to security holders is based on finance charges collected and fees. After the lockout period, the principal is no longer reinvested but paid to investors. This period is referred to as the *principal amortization period.*

Several concepts must be understood in order to assess the performance of the portfolio of receivables and the ability of the issuer to meet its interest obligation and repay principal as scheduled. The *gross portfolio yield* includes finance charges collected and fees. *Charge offs* represent the accounts charged off as uncollectible. *Net portfolio yield* is equal to gross portfolio yield minus charge-offs. The net portfolio yield is important because it is from this yield that the bondholders will be paid. So, for example, if the average yield that must be paid to the various tranches in the structure is 5% and the net portfolio yield for the month is only 4.5%, there is the risk that the bondholder obligations will not be satisfied.

Delinquencies are the percentages of receivables that are past due for a specified number of months, usually 30, 60, and 90 days. They are considered an indicator of potential future charge-offs.

The *monthly payment rate* (MPR) expresses the monthly payment (which includes finance charges, fees, and any principal repayment) of a credit card receivable portfolio as a percentage of credit card debt outstanding in the previous month. For example, suppose a $500 million credit card receivable portfolio in January realized $50 million of payments in February. The MPR would then be 10% ($50 million divided by $500 million).

There are two reasons why the MPR is important. First, if the MPR reaches an extremely low level, there is a chance that there will be extension risk with respect to the principal payments on the bonds. Second, if the MPR is very low, then there is a chance that there will not be sufficient cash flows to pay off principal. This is one of the events that could trigger early amortization of the principal (described next).

There are provisions in credit card receivable-backed securities that require early amortization of the principal if certain events occur. Such provisions, which are referred to as either *early amortization* or *rapid amortization*, are included to safeguard the credit quality of the issue. The only way that principal cash flows can be altered is by triggering the early amortization provision.

AUTO LOAN-BACKED SECURITIES

Auto loan-backed securities are issued by (1) the financial subsidiaries of auto manufacturers (domestic and foreign), (2) commercial banks, and (3) independent finance companies and small financial institutions specializing in auto loans.

In terms of credit, borrowers are classified as either prime, nonprime, or subprime. Each originator employs its own criteria for classifying borrowers into these three broad groups. Typically, prime borrowers are those that have had a strong credit history that is characterized by timely payment of all their debt obligations. The FICO score of prime borrowers is generally greater than 680. Nonprime borrowers have usually had a few delinquent payments. Nonprime borrowers, also called near-prime borrowers, typically have a FICO score ranging from the low 600s to the mid-600s. When a borrower has a credit history of missed or major problems with delinquent loan payments and the borrower may have previously filed for bankruptcy, the borrower is classified as subprime. The FICO score for subprime borrowers typically is less than the low 600s.

The cash flow for auto loan-backed securities consists of regularly scheduled monthly loan payments (interest and scheduled principal repayments) and any prepayments. For securities backed by auto loans, prepayments result from:

1. Sales and trade-ins requiring full payoff of the loan.
2. Repossession and subsequent resale of the automobile.

3. Loss or destruction of the vehicle.
4. Payoff of the loan with cash to save on the interest cost.
5. Refinancing of the loan at a lower interest cost.

While refinancings may be a major reason for prepayments of mortgage loans, they are of minor importance for automobile loans.

Student Loan Asset-Backed Securities

Student loans are made to cover college cost (undergraduate, graduate, and professional programs such as medical school and law school) and tuition for a wide range of vocational and trade schools. Securities backed by student loans are popularly referred to as *SLABS* (*student loan asset-backed securities*). Sallie Mae is a major issuer of SLABS, and its issues are viewed as the benchmark issues.

The student loans that have been most commonly securitized are those that are made under the Federal Family Education Loan Program (FFELP). Under this program, the federal government makes loans to students via private lenders. The decision by private lenders to extend a loan to a student is not based on the applicant's ability to repay the loan. If a default of a loan occurs and the loan has been properly serviced, then the federal government will guarantee 97% of the principal and accrued interest (for loans originated in July 2006 or later).

Loans that are not part of a government guarantee program are called *alternative loans* or *private loans*. These loans are basically consumer loans, and the lender's decision to extend an alternative loan will be based on the ability of the applicant to repay the loan.

SBA Loan-Backed Securities

The Small Business Administration (SBA) is an agency of the U.S. government empowered to guarantee loans made by approved SBA lenders to qualified borrowers. The loans are backed by the full faith and credit of the government. Most SBA loans are variable rate loans where the reference rate is the prime rate. Newly originated loans have maturities between five and 25 years.

Most variable rate SBA loans make monthly payments consisting of interest and principal repayment. The amount of the monthly payment for an individual loan is determined as follows. Given the coupon formula of the prime rate plus the loan's quoted margin, the interest rate is determined for each loan. Given the interest rate, a level payment amortization schedule is determined. This level payment is paid until the coupon rate is reset.

SBA-loan backed securities are backed by a pool of SBA loans. The monthly cash flow that the investor receives consists of (1) the coupon interest based on the coupon rate set for the period; (2) the scheduled principal repayment (that is, scheduled amortization); and (3) prepayments.

Aircraft Lease-Backed Securities

Aircraft financing has gone thorough an evolution over the past 10 or so years. It started with mainly bank financing, then moved to equipment trust certificates, then to enhanced ETCs (EETCs), and finally to aircraft ABS. Today, both EETCs and *aircraft lease-backed securities* are widely used.

EETCs are corporate bonds that share some of the features of structured products, such as credit tranching and liquidity facilities. Aircraft ABS differ from EETCs in that they are not corporate bonds, and they are backed by leases to a number of airlines instead of being tied to a single airline. The rating of aircraft ABS is based primarily on the cash flow from their pool of aircraft leases or loans and the collateral value of that aircraft, not on the rating of lessee airlines.

One of the major characteristics that sets aircraft ABS apart from other forms of aircraft financing is their diversification. ETCs and EETCs finance aircraft from a single airline. An aircraft ABS is usually backed by leases from a number of different airlines, located in a number of different countries and flying a variety of aircraft types. This diversification is a major attraction for investors. In essence, they are investing in a portfolio of airlines and aircraft types rather than a single airline—as is the case of an airline corporate bond. Diversification also is one of the main criteria that rating agencies look for in an aircraft securitization. All else being equal, the greater the diversification is, the higher the credit rating.

Although there are various forms of financing that might appear in an aircraft ABS deal—including operating leases, financing leases, loans or mortgages—to date, the vast majority of the collateral in aircraft deals has been operating leases. This does not mean that a diversified finance company or an airline itself might not at some point bring a lease-backed or other aircraft ABS deal. It just means that so far, aircraft ABS have been mainly the province of leasing companies. Airlines, on the other hand, are active issuers of EETCs.

Aircraft leasing differs from general equipment leasing in that the useful life of an aircraft is much longer than most pieces of industrial or commercial equipment. In a typical equipment lease deal, cash flow from a particular lease on a particular piece of equipment only contributes to the ABS deal for the life of the lease. There is no assumption that the lease will be renewed. In aircraft leasing, the equipment usually has an original useful life of 20+ years, but leases run for only around four to five years. This means that the aircraft will have to be re-leased on expiration of the original lease. Hence, in the rating agencies' review, there is a great deal of focus on risks associated with re-leasing the aircraft.

The risk of being able to put the plane back out on an attractive lease can be broken down into three components: (1) the time it takes to re-lease the aircraft; (2) the lease rate; and (3) the lease term. Factors that can affect re-leasing include the general health of the economy, the health of the airline industry, obsolescence, and type of aircraft.

Franchise Loan-Backed Securities

Franchise loan-backed securities are a hybrid between the CMBS and ABS markets. They are often backed by real estate, as in CMBS, but the deal structures are more akin to ABS. In a pool of 100 to 200 loans (typical franchise loan group sizing) each loan is significant. By contrast, within the consumer sector, any individual loan from a pool of 10,000 loans (as in RMBS) does not represent as large a percentage, thus is not considered quite as important.

Franchise loans are similar to SBA loans in average size, maturity, and end use. But whereas most SBA loans are floating rate loans indexed to the prime rate, most securitized franchise loans are fixed rate; if they are floating, they are likely to be LIBOR linked.

The typical securitized deal borrower owns a large number of units, as opposed to being a small individual owner of a single franchise unit. However, individual loans are usually made on a single unit, secured either by the real estate, the building, or the equipment in the franchise.

A "concept" is simply another name for a particular franchise idea. This is because each franchise seeks to differentiate itself from its competitors. Hence, even though Burger King and Wendy's are both quick-service restaurants specializing in sandwiches, their menu and style of service are sufficiently different that each has its own business/marketing plan—or "concept." For example, Wendy's has long promoted the "fresh" market because the firm mandated fresh (not frozen) beef patties in their hamburgers, and helped pioneer the industry's salad bars. Burger King is noted for its "flame-broiled" burgers, and doing it "your way."

The vast majority of franchise operations consist of three types of retail establishments: restaurants, specialty retail stores (e.g., convenience stores, Blockbuster, 7-11s, Jiffy Lube, and Meineke Muffler), and retail gas stations (e.g., Texaco and Shell). The restaurant category has three major subsectors: quick-service restaurants (e.g., McDonald's, Burger King, Wendy's, and Pizza Hut), casual restaurants (e.g., T.G.I. Fridays, Red Lobster, and Don Pablo's), and family restaurants (e.g., Denny's, Perkins, and Friendly's).

As in all ABS sectors, a primary risk factor is the degree of diversification. In a franchise loan deal, important areas for diversification include franchise owner, concept, and geographical location.

Rate Reduction Bonds

The concept of *rate reduction bonds* (RRBs) grew out of the movement to deregulate the electric utility industry and bring about a competitive market environment for electric power. Deregulating the electric utility market was complicated by large amounts of "stranded assets" already on the books of many electric utilities. These stranded assets were commitments that had been undertaken by utilities at an earlier time with the understanding that they would be recoverable in utility rates to be approved by the states' utility commissions. However, in a competitive environment for electricity, these assets would likely become uneconomic, and utilities would no longer be assured that they could charge a high enough rate to recover the costs. To compensate investors of these utilities, a special tariff was proposed. This tariff, which would be collected over a specified period of time, would allow the utility to recover its stranded costs.

This tariff, which is commonly known as the *competitive transition charge* (CTC), is created through legislation. State legislatures allow utilities to levy a fee, which is collected from its customers. In order to facilitate the securitization of these fees, legislation typically designates the revenue stream from these fees as a statutory property right. These rights may be sold to an SPV, which may then issue securities backed by future cash flows from the tariff. The result is a structured security similar in many ways to other ABS products, but different in one critical aspect: The underlying asset in a RRB deal is created by legislation, which is not the case for other ABS products.

State regulatory commissions decide how much, if any, of a specific utility's stranded assets will be recaptured via securitization. They will also decide on an acceptable time frame and collection formula to be used to calculate the CTC. When this legislation is finalized, the utility is free to proceed with the securitization process.

The basic structure of an RRB issue is straightforward. The utility sells its rights to future CTC cash flows to an SPV created for the sole purpose of purchasing these assets and issuing debt to finance this purchase. In most cases, the utility itself will act as the servicer because it collects the CTC payment from its customer base along with the regular electric utility bill. Upon issuance, the utility receives the proceeds of the securitization (less the fees associated with issuing a deal), effectively reimbursing the utility for its stranded costs immediately.

RRBs usually have a "true-up" mechanism. This mechanism allows the utility to recalculate the CTC on a periodic basis over the term of the deal. Because the CTC is initially calculated based on projections of utility usage and the ability of the servicer to collect revenues, the actual collection experience may differ from initial projections. In most cases, the utility can reexamine actual collections, and if the variance is large enough, the utility will be allowed to revise the CTC charge. This true-up mechanism provides cash flow stability as well as credit enhancement to the bondholder.

Credit enhancement levels required by the rating agencies for RRB deals are very low relative to other ABS asset classes. Although exact amounts and forms of credit enhancement may vary by deal, most transactions require little credit enhancement because the underlying asset (the CTC) is a statutory asset and is not directly affected by economic factors or other exogenous variables. Furthermore, the true-up mechanism virtually assures cash flow stability to the bondholder.

COLLATERALIZED DEBT OBLIGATIONS

A *collateralized debt obligation* (CDO) is debt instrument backed by a diversified pool of one or more classes of debt. These classes can include corporate loans, corporate bonds, emerging market bonds, asset-backed securities, residential mortgage-backed securities, commercial mortgage-backed securities, real estate investment trusts, and tranches of other CDOs.

Because of the problems in the CDO market, little issuance of these securities have been issued in recent years. Nevertheless, there is considerable volume of this product outstanding. Consequently, in this chapter we provide the basics of CDOs.[1]

Attributes of CDOs

A CDO issues debt tranches and equity and uses the money it raises to invest in a portfolio of financial assets. It distributes the cash flows from its asset portfolio to the holders of its various liabilities in prescribed ways that take into account the relative seniority of those liabilities.

Any CDO can be well described by focusing on its four important attributes: assets, liabilities, purposes, and credit structures. Like any company, a CDO has assets. With a CDO, these are financial assets. And like any company, a CDO has liabilities. With a CDO, these run the gamut of preferred

---

[1]For a more detailed discussion, see Douglas J. Lucas, Laurie S. Goodman, and Frank J. Fabozzi, *Collateralized Debt Obligations: Structures and Analysis*, 2nd ed. (Hoboken, N.J.: John Wiley & Sons, 2006).

shares to AAA-rated senior debt. Beyond the seniority and subordination of CDO liabilities, CDOs have additional structural credit protections, which fall into the category of either cash flow or market value protections. Finally, every CDO has a purpose that it was created to fulfill.

Here we describe the different types of assets CDOs hold, the different types of liabilities CDOs issue, the purposes for which CDOs are created, and the different credit structures CDOs employ.

Assets

A CDO is primarily identified by its underlying assets. The first CDOs created in 1987 owned high-yield bond portfolios. In fact, before the term "CDO" was invented to encompass an ever-broadening array of assets, the term in use was "collateralized bond obligation" or "CBO." In 1989, corporate loans were used in CDOs for the first time, causing the term "collateralized loan obligation" or "CLO" to be coined. Generally, CLOs are comprised of performing high-yield loans, but a few CLOs targeted distressed and nonperforming loans.

Loans and bonds issued by corporations in emerging markets and bonds issued by sovereign governments were first used as CDO collateral in 1994, thus creating the "emerging-market CDO" or "EM CDO." In 1995, CDOs comprised of RMBS were first issued. CDOs comprised of CMBSs and ABSs, or combinations of RMBS, CMBS, and, ABS followed, commonly referred to as "structured finance CDOs," "SF CDOs," or "resecuritizations."

Liabilities

A company that has assets typically also has liabilities. In the case of a CDO, these liabilities have a detailed and strict ranking of seniority, going up the CDO's capital structure as equity or preferred shares, subordinated debt, mezzanine debt, and senior debt. These tranches of notes and equity are commonly labeled Class A, Class B, Class C, and so forth, going from the top to bottom of the capital structure. They range from the AAA-rated tranche with the greatest amount of subordination beneath it, to the most levered, unrated equity tranche. Most CDO debt is floating rate where the reference rate is LIBOR (London Interbank Offered Rate), but sometimes a fixed-rate tranche is structured.[2]

---

[2]When there is a mismatch between the nature of the cash flow of the portfolio assets (i.e., fixed vs. floating) and that of the liabilities, the rating agencies will require that the asset manager hedge this risk with interest rate derivatives (i.e., interest rate swaps or interest rate caps).

Special purposes entities such as CDOs are said to be "bankrupt remote." One aspect of the term is that they are new entities without previous business activities. They therefore cannot have any legal liability for sins of the past. Another aspect of their "remoteness from bankruptcy" is that the CDO will not be caught up in the bankruptcy of any other entity, such as the manager of the CDO's assets, or a party that sold assets to the CDO, or the banker that structured the CDO.

Another very important aspect of a CDO's bankruptcy remoteness is the absolute seniority and subordination of the CDO's debt tranches to one another. Even if it is a certainty that some holders of the CDO's debt will not receive their full principal and interest, cash flows from the CDO's assets are still distributed according to the original game plan dictated by seniority. The CDO cannot go into bankruptcy, either voluntarily or through the action of an aggrieved creditor. In fact, the need for bankruptcy is obviated because the distribution of the CDO's cash flows, even if the CDO is insolvent, has already been determined in detail at the origination of the CDO.

Within the stipulation of strict seniority, there is great variety in the features of CDO debt tranches. The driving force for CDO structurers is to raise funds at the lowest possible cost. This is done so that holder's of the CDO's equity tranche, who are at the bottom of the chain of seniority, can get the most residual cash flow.

Prior to the difficulties with monoline insurers, sometimes a financial guaranty insurer will wrap a CDO tranche. Usually this involved a AAA-rated insurer and the most senior CDO tranche. To meet the needs of particular investors, sometimes the AAA tranche is divided into senior AAA and junior AAA tranches.

Cash vs. Synthetic CDOs

A CDO that invests in financial assets by acquiring the securities for the portfolio is called a *cash CDO*. There are CDOs where instead of the assets being purchased, exposure to those assets is acquired by entering into a derivative transaction. More specifically, a credit default swap is used to obtain credit exposure to an asset or portfolio of assets. A CDO that uses credit default swaps in this way is called a *synthetic CDO*. Our focus in this section is on cash CDOs although the principles regarding the investment characteristics and risk apply equally to synthetic CDOs. The additional risk with a synthetic CDO is that the counterparties to the credit default swap transactions may default. Hence the investor in a synthetic CDO is exposed to counterparty risk.

Balance Sheet vs. Arbitrage CDOs

CDOs are classified as balance sheet CDOs or arbitrage CDOs. The classification depends on the purpose for which the CDO was created.

In a *balance sheet CDO*, a holder of assets desires to remove those assets from its balance sheet. The classic example of this is a bank that has originated loans over months or years and now wants to remove them from its balance sheet and finds that there is an economic advantage to doing so

In an *arbitrage CDO*, an asset manager wishes to gain assets under management and management fees while at the same time investors wish to have the expertise of an asset manager. Assets are purchased by the asset manager in the marketplace from many different sellers and put into the CDO. CDOs are another means, along with mutual funds and hedge funds, for an asset management firm to provide its services to investors. The difference is that instead of all the investors sharing the fund's return in proportion to their investment (i.e., change in net asset value), investor returns are determined by the seniority of the CDO tranches they purchase and the performance of those tranches.

From the point of view of CDO investors, however, all CDOs have a number of common purposes. One purpose is the division and distribution of the risk of the CDO's assets to parties that have different risk appetites. Thus, a AAA investor can invest in speculative-grade assets on a loss-protected basis. Or a BB investor can invest in AAA assets on a levered basis.

For CDO equity investors, the CDO structure provides a leveraged return without some of the severe adverse consequences of borrowing from a bank. CDO equity holders own stock in a company and are not liable for the losses of that company. Equity's exposure to the CDO asset portfolio is therefore capped. Instead of short-term bank financing, financing via the CDO is locked in for the long term at fixed spreads to LIBOR.

Parties to a CDO

A number of parties and institutions contribute to the creation of a CDO.

A CDO is a distinct legal entity, usually incorporated in the Cayman Islands. Its liabilities are called CDOs, so one might hear the seemingly circular phrase "the CDO issues CDOs."

Asset managers (or collateral managers) select the initial portfolio of an arbitrage CDO and manage it according to prescribed guidelines contained in the CDO's indenture. Sometimes an asset manager is used in a balance sheet CDO of distressed assets to handle their workout or sale. A variety of firms offer CDO asset management services including hedge fund managers, mutual fund managers, and firms that specialize exclusively in CDO management.

Investment bankers and structurers work with the asset manager or asset seller to bring the CDO to fruition. They set up corporate entities, shepherd the CDO through the debt-rating process, place the CDO's debt and equity with investors, and handle other organizational details. A big part of this job involves structuring the CDO's liabilities: their size and ratings, the cash diversion features of the structure, and, of course, debt tranche coupons. Another part of the structurer's job is to negotiate an acceptable set of eligible assets for the CDO. These tasks obviously involve working with and balancing the desires of the asset manager or seller, different debt and equity investors, and rating agencies.

Historically, monoline bond insurers or financial guarantors typically only guarantee the senior-most tranche in a CDO. Often, insurance is used when a CDO invests in newer asset types or is managed by a new CDO manager. Rating agencies approve the legal and credit structure of the CDO, perform due diligence on the asset manager and the trustee, and rate the various seniorities of debt issued by the CDO. Usually two or three of the major rating agencies rate the CDO's debt. Trustees hold the CDO's assets for the benefit of debt and equity holders, enforce the terms of the CDO indenture, monitor and report upon collateral performance, and disburse cash to debt and equity investors according to set rules.

Cash Flow CDOs

Arbitrage can be divided into two types depending on what the primary source of the proceeds from the underlying assets is to come from to satisfy the obligation to the tranches. If the primary source is the interest and maturing principal from the underlying assets, then the transaction is referred to as a *cash flow CDO*. If instead the proceeds to meet the obligations depend heavily on the total return generated from the portfolio (i.e., interest income, capital gain, and maturing principal), then the transaction is referred to as a *market value CDO*. Since the latter structures have been rarely issued in recent years, we limit our discussion to cash flow CDOs. Specifically, we look at the distribution of the cash flows, restrictions imposed on the asset manager to protect the noteholders, and the key factors considered by rating agencies in rating tranches of a cash flow transaction.

In a cash flow transaction, the cash flows from income and principal are distributed according to rules set forth in the prospectus. The distribution of the cash flows is described in the waterfall.

Distribution of Income

Income is derived from interest income from the underlying assets and capital appreciation. The income is then used as follows. Payments are first made to the trustee and administrators and then to the senior asset manager. There are other management fees that are usually made based on performance, but these fees are made after payments to the mezzanine tranches and hence referred to as subordinated fees.

Once these fees are paid, then the senior tranches are paid their interest. At this point, before any other payments are made, certain tests must be passed. These tests are called *coverage tests* and are discussed later. If the coverage tests are passed, then interest is paid. In contrast, if the coverage tests are not passed, then payments are made to protect the senior tranches. The remaining income after paying the fees and senior tranche interest is used to redeem the senior tranches (i.e., pay off principal) until the coverage tests are brought into compliance. If the senior tranches are paid off fully because the coverage tests are not brought into compliance, then any remaining income is used to redeem the mezzanine tranches. Any remaining income is then used to redeem the subordinate/equity tranche.

Distribution of Principal Cash Flow

The principal cash flow is distributed as follows after the payment of the fees to the trustees, administrators, and senior managers. If there is a shortfall in interest paid to the senior tranches, principal proceeds are used to make up the shortfall. Assuming that the coverage tests are satisfied, during the reinvestment period the principal is reinvested. After the reinvestment period or if the coverage tests are failed, the principal cash flow is used to pay down the senior tranches until the coverage tests are satisfied. If all the senior tranches are paid down, then the mezzanine tranches are paid off and then the subordinate/equity tranche is paid off.

After all the debt obligations are satisfied in full and if permissible, the equity investors are paid. Typically, there are also incentive fees paid to management based on performance. Usually, a target return for the equity investors is established at the inception of the transaction. Management is then permitted to share on some prorated basis once the target return is achieved.

Restrictions on Management: Safety Nets

Noteholders have two major protections provided in the form of tests. They are coverage tests and quality tests.

Coverage Tests   Coverage tests are designed to protect noteholders against a deterioration of the existing portfolio. There are actually two categories of tests—*overcollateralization tests* and *interest coverage tests*. The overcollateralization or O/C ratio for a tranche is found by computing the ratio of the principal balance of the collateral portfolio over the principal balance of that tranche and all tranches senior to it. The higher the O/C ratio is the greater protection for the note holders. This is based on the principal or par value of the assets, hence, an O/C test is also referred to as a *par value test*. An O/C ratio is computed for specified tranches subject to the O/C test. The O/C test for a tranche involves comparing the tranche's O/C ratio to the tranche's required minimum ratio as specified in the CDO's guidelines. The required minimum ratio is referred to as the *overcollateralization trigger*. The O/C test for a tranche is passed if the O/C ratio is greater than or equal to its respective O/C trigger.

The interest coverage or I/C ratio for a tranche is the ratio of scheduled interest due on the underlying collateral portfolio to scheduled interest to be paid to that tranche and all tranches senior to it. The higher the I/C ratio is the greater the protection. An I/C ratio is computed for specified tranches subject to the I/C test. The I/C test for a tranche involves comparing the tranche's I/C ratio to the tranche's I/C trigger (that is, the required minimum ratio as specified in the guidelines). The I/C test for a tranche is passed if the computed I/C ratio is greater than or equal to its respective interest coverage trigger.

Quality Tests   After the tranches of a CDO deal are rated, the rating agencies are concerned that the composition of the collateral portfolio may be adversely altered by the asset manager over time. Tests are imposed to prevent the asset manager from trading assets so as to result in a deterioration of the quality of the portfolio and are referred to as *quality tests*. These tests deal with maturity restrictions, the degree of diversification, and credit ratings of the assets in the collateral portfolio.

Call Provisions in CDO Transactions

The commonly used optional redemption features in CDO transactions is where the deal is callable at par by the equity holders, after a prespecified lockout. The call is generally exercised when the deal is doing very well, and the collateral can be liquidated at a healthy net profit. The deal is more apt to be called when the spreads on the debt tranches have narrowed. That is, the equity holders are looking at the possibility of liquidating the deal, paying off the debt holders, and putting the collateral into a new deal where the debt holders are paid a smaller spread. When evaluating CDOs that have been outstanding for a few years and are being traded in the secondary market, call provisions can be important to their valuation.

Financial Instruments and Concepts Introduced in this Chapter (in Order of Presentation)

Special purpose vehicle
Special purpose entity
Structured credit products
Residential MBS
Commercial MBS
Asset-backed security
Prime RMBS
Subprime RMBS
Waterfall
Shifting interest mechanism
Overcollateralization
Acceleration
Turboing
Debt-to-coverage ratio
Loan-to-value ratio
Net operating income
Payment lockout
Lockout period
Defeasance
Prepayment penalty points
Yield maintenance charge
Make-whole charge
Balloon risk
Extension risk
Credit card receivable-backed security
Revolving period
Principal amortization period
Gross portfolio yield
Charge offs

Net portfolio yield
Delinquencies
Monthly prepayment rate
Early amortization
Rapid amortization
Auto loan-backed securities
SLABS (Student loan asset-backed securities)
Alternative loans
Private loans
SBA loan-backed securities
Aircraft lease-backed securities
Franchise loan-backed securities
Rate reduction bonds
Competitive transition charge
Collateralized debt obligation
Cash CDO
Synthetic CDO
Balance sheet CDO
Arbitrage CDO
Cash flow CDO
Market value CDO
Coverage tests
Overcollateralization tests
Interest coverage tests
Par value test
Overcollateralization trigger
Quality tests

Investment-Oriented Life Insurance

Insurance and investments are distinct concepts. This distinction leads to the development of various insurance and investment products. In practice, however, there is an overlap between some types of insurance products and investment products. This overlap occurs due partially to specific tax advantages provided to investment-oriented life insurance products. In this chapter, we do not consider any of the pure life insurance products. Rather, we consider only various types of investment-oriented life insurance products.

CASH VALUE LIFE INSURANCE

With *cash value life insurance*, each year's premium is segregated into two components by the insurance company. The first is the amount needed to pay for the pure insurance, which, as indicated, increases each year. The second goes into the insured's investment account, which is the cash value of the life insurance contract. An investment return is earned on this cash value, which further increases the cash value. The buildup of this *cash value* and the ability to borrow against it both have tax advantages, as discussed below. Two important observations can be made here.

First, a common marketing or sales advantage attributed to cash value life insurance is that the higher premium paid will "force" the individuals to save, whereas if they did not pay the higher insurance premium, they would use their income for consumption rather than savings. According to this rationale, the higher insurance premium is, thus, forced savings.

Whether or not this first observation has merit, the second observation unequivocally does. The federal government encourages the use of cash value life insurance by providing significant tax advantages. Thus the second advantage of cash value life insurance is tax-advantaged savings.

There are several tax advantages to cash value life insurance. The first and major tax advantage is called *inside buildup*. This means that the returns on the investment component of the premium, both income and capital gains, are not subject to taxation (income or capital gains) while held in the insurance contract. Inside buildup is a significant advantage to "saving" via a cash value life insurance policy rather than, for example, saving via a mutual fund.

The second tax advantage of a cash value life insurance policy relates to borrowing against the policy. In general, an amount equal to the cash value of the policy can be borrowed. However, there are some tax implications. The taxation of life insurance is covered in more detail in a following section. In addition to the above, the *death benefit*, that is the amount paid to the beneficiary of the life insurance contract at the death of the insured, is exempt from income taxes, although it may be subject to estate taxes. This benefit applies both to cash value and pure life insurance.

Term insurance has become much more of a commodity product and, in fact, there are websites that provide premium quotes for term life insurance for various providers. Cash value life insurance, due to its complexity and multiple features, is not, however, a commodity.

Obviously, the cost of annual term life insurance is much lower than that of whole life insurance, particularly for the young and middle-aged. For example, while there is a wide range of premiums for both term and whole life insurance, for a 35-year-old male, the annual cost of $500,000 of annual term insurance may be $400 and the cost of whole life insurance may be $5,000.

STOCK AND MUTUAL INSURANCE COMPANIES

There are two major forms of life insurance companies, stock and mutual. A stock insurance company is similar in structure to any corporation (also called a public company). Shares (of ownership) are owned by independent shareholders and may be traded publicly. The shareholders care only about the performance of their shares, that is the stock appreciation and the dividends over time. Their holding period and, thus, their view may be short term or long term. The insurance policies are simply the products or businesses of the company in which they own shares.

In contrast, mutual insurance companies have no stock and no external owners. Their policyholders are their owners. The owners, that is the policyholders, care primarily or even solely about the performance of their insurance policies, notably the company's ability to eventually pay on the policy and to, in the interim, provide investment returns on the cash value of the policy, if any. Since these payments may occur considerably into the future, the policyholders' view will be long term. Thus, while stock insurance companies have two constituencies, their stockholders and their policyholders, mutual insurance companies only have one since their policyholders and their owners are the same. Traditionally, the largest insurance companies have been mutual, but recently there have been many demutualizations, that is, conversions by mutual companies to stock companies. Currently several of the largest life insurance companies are stock companies.

The debate on which is the better form of insurance company, stock or mutual, is too involved to be considered in any depth here. However, consider selected comments on this issue. First, consider this issue from the perspective of the policyholder. Mutual holding companies have only one constituency, their policyholder or owner. The liabilities of many types of insurance companies are long term, particularly the writers of whole life insurance. Thus, mutual insurance companies can appropriately have a long time horizon for their strategies and policies. They do not have to make short-term decisions to benefit their shareholders, whose interests are usually short term, via an increase in the stock price or dividend, in a way that might reduce their long-term profitability or the financial strength of the insurance company. In addition, if the insurance company earns a profit, it can pass the profit onto its policyholders via reduced premiums. (Policies that benefit from an increased profitability of the insurance company are called participating policies, as discussed later.) These increased profits do not have to accrue to stockholders because there are none.

Finally, mutual insurance companies can adopt a longer time frame in their investments, which will most likely make possible a higher return. Mutual insurance companies, for example, typically hold more common stock in their portfolios than stock companies. However, whereas the long time frame of mutual insurance companies may be construed an advantage over stock companies, it may also be construed as a disadvantage. Rating agencies and others assert that, due to their longer horizon and their long time frame, mutual insurance companies may be less efficient and have higher expenses than stock companies. Empirically, rating agencies and others assert that mutual insurance companies have typically significantly reduced their expenses shortly before and after converting to stock companies.

Overall, it is argued, mutual insurance companies have such long planning horizons that they may not operate efficiently, particularly with respect to expenses. Stock companies, on the other hand, have very short planning horizons and may operate to the long-term disadvantage of their policyholders to satisfy their stockholders in the short run. Recently, however, mutual insurance companies have become more cost conscientious.

GENERAL ACCOUNT VS. SEPARATE ACCOUNT PRODUCTS

The general account of an insurance company refers to the overall resources of the life insurance company, mainly its investment portfolio. Products "written by the company itself" are said to have a "general account guarantee," that is, they are a liability of the insurance company. When the rating agencies (Moody's, Standard & Poor's, Fitch) provide a credit rating, these ratings are on products written by or guaranteed by the general account, specifically on the "claims-paying ability" of the company. Typical products written by and guaranteed by the general account are whole life, universal life, and fixed annuities (including GICs). Insurance companies must support the guaranteed performance of their general account products to the extent of their solvency. These are called *general account products.*

Other types of insurance products receive no guarantee from the insurance company's general account, and their performance is based, not on the performance of the insurance company's general account, but solely on the performance of an investment account separate from the general account of the insurance company, often an account selected by the policyholder. These products are called *separate account products.* Variable life insurance and variable annuities are separate account products. The policyholder selects specific investment portfolios to support these separate account products. The performance of the insurance product depends almost solely on the performance of the portfolio selected, adjusted for the fees or expenses of the insuring company (which do depend on the insurance company). The performance of the separate account products, thus, is not affected by the performance of the overall insurance company's general account portfolio.

Most general account insurance products, including whole life insurance, participate in the performance of the company's general account performance. For example, whereas a life insurance company provides the guarantee of a minimum dividend on its whole life policies, the policies' actual dividend may be greater if the investment portfolio performs well. This is called the "interest component" of the dividend. (The other two components of the dividend are the expense and mortality components.) Thus, the performance of the insurance policy participates in the overall company's performance. Such a policy is called a *participating policy*, in this case a participating whole life insurance policy.

In addition, the performance of some general account products may not be affected by the performance of the general account portfolio. For example, disability income insurance policies may be written on a general account, and while their payoff depends on the solvency of the general account, the policy performance (for example, its premium) may not participate in the investment performance of the insurance companies' general account investment portfolio.

Both stock and mutual insurance companies write both general and separate account products. However, most participating general account products tend to be written in mutual companies.

OVERVIEW OF CASH VALUE WHOLE LIFE INSURANCE

The details of *cash value whole life insurance* (CVWLI) are very complex. This section provides a simple overview of CVWLI, partially by contrasting it with term life insurance.

As discussed above, in annual term life insurance, the owner of the policy, typically also the insured, pays an annual premium that reflects the actuarial risk of death during the year. The premium, thus, increases each year. If the insured dies during the year, the death benefit is paid to the insurer's beneficiary. If the insured does not die during the year, the term policy has no value at the end of the year.

The construction and performance of CVWLI and term life insurance are quite different. Primarily, the owner of the CVWLI policy pays a constant premium. This premium on the CVWLI policy is initially much higher than the initial premium on a term policy (the pure insurance cost) because the constant premium must cover not only lower insurance risk early in the policy but also higher insurance risk later in the policy when the insured has a higher age and the annual cost of the pure insurance exceeds the level premium. However, assuming the same interest and mortality assumptions on both products, the CVWLI premium should be lower than the average of the term premium over time. This is because in the early years, the excess of the level CVWLI premium over the term premium can earn interest, which lowers the overall premium needed to fund the policy; and some CVWLI policy holders paying the level premium die in the early years, leaving funds (from the excess of the level premium over the early life insurance cost) available to the remaining policy holders, which can be used to decrease the CVWLI premium.

In the early years of the policy, the excess of the premium over the pure insurance cost is invested by the insurance company in its general account portfolio. In the later years, there is a shortfall in the premiums relative to the pure insurance cost and the previous cash value buildup is used to fund this shortfall. This portfolio generates a return that accrues to the policy owner's cash value. Typically, the insurance company guarantees a minimum increase in cash value, called the *guaranteed cash value buildup*. The insurance company, however, may provide an amount in excess of the guaranteed cash value buildup based on earnings for participating policies. What happens to this excess? Assume that the insurance company has a mutual structure, that is, it is owned by the policyholders. In this case, with no stockholders, the earnings accrue to the policyholders as dividends.

The arithmetic of the development of the cash value in a life insurance contract follows:

+ Premium
− Cost of insurance (mortality) (denoted by M)
− Expenses (denoted by E)
+ Guaranteed (minimum) cash value buildup
+ (Participating) dividend
_____
= Increase (buildup) in cash value

Note that the overall dividend is calculated from the investment income, the cost of paying the death benefit (the mortality expense denoted by M), and the expense of running the company (denoted by E). The latter two together are called the *M&E charges*.

If the insurance company is owned by stockholders, some or all of the earnings might go to the stockholders as dividends.

The returns to the insurance company and, therefore, the dividends to the policyholder can increase if: (1) investment returns increase; (2) company expenses decrease; or (3) mortality costs decrease (that is, the life expectancy of the insured increases).

The dividends can be "used" by the policyholder in either of two ways. The first is to decrease the annual premium. In this case, the death benefit remains constant. The second is to increase the death benefit and the cash value of the policy. Such increases are called *paid-up additions* (PUAs). In this case, the annual premium remains constant. Most policies are written in the second way.

The intended way for the life insurance policy to terminate is for the insured to die and the life insurance company to pay the death benefit to the beneficiary. There are other ways, however. First, the policy can be *lapsed* (alternatively called *forfeited* or *surrendered*). In this case, the owner of the policy withdraws the cash value of the policy and the policy is terminated.

There are also two *nonforfeiture options*—that is methods whereby an insurance policy for the insured remains. The owner can use the cash value of the policy to buy *extended term insurance* (the amount and term of the resulting term insurance policy depends on the cash value). In addition, the cash value of the policy can be used to buy a reduced amount of fully paid (that is, no subsequent premiums are due) whole life insurance—this is called *reduced paid up*.

In addition to the forfeiture option and the two non-forfeiture options of terminating the CVWLI policy, the policy could be left intact and borrowed against. This is called a *policy loan*. An amount equal to the cash value of the policy can be borrowed. There are two effects of the loan on the policy. First, the dividend is paid only on the amount equal to the cash value of the policy minus the loan. Second, the death benefit of the policy paid is the policy death benefit minus the loan.

The taxation of the death benefit payout, a policy lapse, and borrowing against the loan are considered next. For taxation of life insurance, it is important to recall that the insurance premium is paid by the policy owner with after-tax dollars (this is often called the *cost of the policy*). But the cash value is allowed to build up inside the policy with taxes deferred (or usually tax-free), often called the *return on the policy*.

TAXABILITY OF LIFE INSURANCE

A major attraction of life insurance as an investment product is its taxability. Consider the four major tax advantages of life insurance.

The first tax advantage is that when the death benefit is paid to the beneficiary of the insurance policy, the benefit is free of income tax. If the life insurance policy is properly structured in an estate plan, the benefit is also free of estate taxes.

The second tax advantage is the inside buildup—that is, all earnings (interest, dividend, and realized capital gains) are exempt from income and capital gains taxes. Thus, these earnings are tax deferred (and when included in the death benefit become income tax free, and in some cases also estate tax free).

The third relates to the lapse of a policy. When the policy is lapsed, the owner receives the cash value of the policy. The amount taxed is the cash value minus the cost of the policy (the total premiums paid plus the dividends, if paid in cash). That is, the tax basis of the policy is the cost (accumulated premiums) of the policy. The cost, thus, increases the basis and is recovered tax-free. (Remember, however, that these costs were paid with after-tax dollars.) And, the remainder was allowed to accumulate without taxation but is taxed at the time of the lapse.

The fourth tax issue relates to borrowing against the policy—that is, a policy loan. The primary tax issue is the distinction between the cost (accumulated premium) and the excess of the policy cash value over the cost (call it the excess). When a policy loan is made, the cost is deemed to be borrowed first.[1] The amount up to the cash value of the policy can be borrowed and not be subject to the ordinary income tax.[2]

Although CVWLI has both insurance and investment characteristics, Congress provided insurance policies tax advantages because of their insurance, not their investment, characteristics. And Congress does not wish to apply these insurance-directed tax benefits to primarily investment products. In this regard, in the past some activities related to borrowing against insurance policies were considered abuses by Congress and tax law changes were made to moderate these activities. These abuses originated with a product called *single-premium life insurance*. This policy is one in which only a single premium is paid for a whole life insurance policy. The premium creates an immediate cash value. This cash value and the resulting investment income earned are sufficient to pay the policy's benefits. The excess investment income accumulates tax-free.

PRODUCTS

The major investment-oriented insurance products can be divided into two categories—cash value life insurance and annuities. Each has several types, which are listed in Exhibit 11.1. These products are described in the following sections.

Cash Value Life Insurance

Cash value life insurance was introduced above. There are two dimensions of cash value life insurance policies. The first is whether the cash value is guaranteed (called whole life) or variable (called variable life). The second is whether the required premium payment is fixed or flexible, that is whether it has a universal (flexible) feature or not. They can be combined in all ways.

EXHIBIT 11.1 Types of Life Insurance by Premium

Premium	Guaranteed	Variable
Fixed	Whole life	Variable life
Flexible	Universal life	Variable universal life

[1]That is, FIFO—first in-first out—accounting is employed.
[2]An exception to this practice is for a Modified Endowment Contract (MEC). If the loan is outstanding at the time of the policy lapse, the loan is treated on a FIFO basis whereby the cost basis is assumed to be borrowed first and is not taxable, and when the cost basis is exhausted by the loan, the remainder of the loan—up to the cash value of the policy—is taxable.

Thus, there are four combinations, which we discuss next. The broad classification of cash value life insurance, called *whole life insurance*, in addition to providing pure life insurance (as does term insurance), builds up a cash value or investment value inside the policy.

Traditional cash value life insurance, usually called whole life insurance, has a *guaranteed buildup* of cash value based on the investment returns on the general account portfolio of the insurance company. That is, the cash value in the policy is guaranteed to increase by a specified minimum amount each year. This is called the *cash value buildup*.[3] The cash value may grow by more than this minimum amount if a dividend is paid on the policy. Dividends, however, are not guaranteed. There are two types of dividends, participating and nonparticipating. Participating dividends depend on (that is, participate in) the investment returns of the general account of the insurance company portfolio (the insurance company M&E charges also affect the dividend).

The participating dividend may be used to increase the cash value of the policy by more than its guaranteed amount. Actually, there are two potential uses of the dividend. The first is to reduce the annual premium paid on the policy. In this case, while the premium decreases, the cash value of the policy increases by only its guaranteed amount (and the face value the death benefit remains constant).

The second use is to buy more life insurance with the premium, the paid-up additions (PUA). In this case, the cash value of the entire policy increases by more than the guaranteed amount on the original policy (and the face value of the current policy is greater than the face value of the original policy).

In either case, the performance of the policy over time may be substantially affected by the participating dividends.

Contrary to the guaranteed or fixed cash value policies based on the general account portfolio of the insurance company, variable life insurance polices allow the policyowners to allocate their premium payments to and among several separate investment accounts maintained by the insurance company, and also to be able to shift the policy cash value among these separate accounts. As a result, the amount of the policy cash value depends on the investment results of the separate accounts the policyowners have selected. Thus, there is no guaranteed cash value or death benefit. Both depend on the performance of the selected investment portfolio.

The types of separate account investment options offered in their variable life insurance policies vary by insurance companies. Typically, the insurance company offers a selection of common stock and bond fund investment opportunities, often managed by the company itself and also

---

[3]The guaranteed cash value buildup of many U.S. CVWLI policies tend to be in the range of 3%–4%.

by other investment managers. If the investment options perform well, the cash value buildup in the policy will be significant. However, if the policyholder selects investment options that perform poorly, the variable life insurance policy will perform poorly. There could be little or no cash value buildup, or, in the worst case, the policy could be terminated because there is not enough value in the contract to pay the mortality charge. This type of cash value life insurance is called *variable life insurance.*

The key element of *universal life* is the flexibility of the premium for the policyowner. The flexible premium concept separates the pure insurance protection (term insurance) from the investment (cash value) element of the policy. The policy cash value is set up as a cash value fund (or accumulation fund) to which the investment income is credited and from which the cost of term insurance for the insured (the mortality charge) is debited. The policy expenses are also debited.

This separation of the cash value from the pure insurance is called the "unbundling" of the traditional life insurance policy. Premium payments for universal life are at the discretion of the policyholder, that is, are flexible with the exceptions that there must be a minimum initial premium to begin the coverage, and there must also be at least enough cash value in the policy each month to cover the mortality charge and other expenses. If not, the policy will lapse. Both guaranteed cash value and variable life can be written on a flexible premium or fixed premium basis.

The universal feature—flexible premiums—can be applied to either guaranteed value whole life (called simply universal life) or to variable life (called variable universal life). These types are summarized in Exhibit 11.1. Variable universal life insurance combines the features of variable life and universal life policies—that is, the choice of separate account investment products and flexible premiums.

Over the last decade, term and variable life insurance have been growing at the expense of whole life insurance. The most common form of variable life is variable universal.

Most whole life insurance policies are designed to pay death benefits when one specified insured dies. An added dimension of whole life policies is that two people (usually a married couple) are jointly insured, and the policy pays the death benefit not when the first person dies, but when the second person (the "surviving spouse") dies. This is called *survivorship insurance* or *second-to-die insurance.* This survivorship feature can be added to standard cash value whole life, universal life, variable life, and variable universal life policies. Thus, each of the four policies discussed could also be written on a survivorship basis.

In general, the annual premium for a survivorship insurance policy is lower than for a policy on a single person because, by construction, the second of two people to die has a longer life span than the first. Survivorship insurance is typically sold for estate planning purposes.

Exhibit 11.2 provides a summary of the various types of cash value life insurance, with (annual renewable) term insurance included for contrast.

Whole Life Insurance and Wealth Management

Some wealth managers consider whole life insurance an asset class and include it in their bond portfolio as a tax-efficient bond. As discussed above, whole life insurance has some of the characteristics of fixed income instruments. Whole life insurance pays annual dividend payments, some part of which is guaranteed (the guaranteed (minimum) cash value buildup) and another part not guaranteed (the participating) dividend). Both parts increase the cash value.

Based on the assumed life expectancy, the premium paid until the assumed life expectancy, and the death benefit payable at the assumed life expectancy, the *internal rate of return* (IRR) on a policy can be calculated. These IRR are competitive with other high-quality fixed income instruments such as bonds or saving accounts.[4]

There are also several tax efficiencies of whole life insurance. First, the inside buildup, both income and capital gains, on life insurance is not taxed when generated. Second, the death benefit, that is the amount paid to the beneficiary of the policy at the death of the insured, is not subject to income taxes. Wealth managers also observe that the payment to the beneficiary has no correlation to any other financial asset. Third, the death benefit of the insurance policy, if the ownership of the insurance policy is properly structured (that is, in an *irrevocable life insurance trust* (ILIT)) may not be subject to estate taxes or generation-skipping taxes. Finally, as cash value accumulates in the policy, the cash value may be borrowed (with no tax), used as collateral for other loans, cashed out (canceled) or converted into another product (such as an annuity), all in a tax-efficient manner. Of course, in the early years of a whole life insurance policy there may be no cash value which can be used by the policyholder in these ways. These tax advantages increase the IRR of the whole life insurance policy.

Obviously, whole life insurance adds liquidity to a portfolio as collateral for borrowing or in the other ways mentioned above when the owner is still

---

[4]See Richard L. Harris, "Life Insurance and Wealth Management: A Perfect Combination for the Ultra-Affluent," *Journal of Wealth Management* 11, no. 4 (Spring 2009): 115–118; Isabelle Sender, "Life Insurance with Life-Long Benefits," *Standard & Poors' The Outlook,* December 2, 2009, p. 4, and; Leslie Scism, "Whole Life Insurance, Long Derided, Gets New Lease," *Wall Street Journal*, February 26–28, 2010, p. B8.

EXHIBIT 11.2 Life Insurance Comparison (by type and element)

Type	Description	Death Benefit	Premium	Cash Value (CV)	Advantages to Owner	Disadvantages to Owner
Annual renewable term	"Pure" life insurance with no cash value; initially, the highest death benefit for the lowest premium; premium increases exponentially	Fixed, constant	Increases exponentially	None	Low premium for coverage	Increasing premium; most term insurance is lapsed
Whole life	Known maximum cost and minimum death benefit; dividends may: reduce premiums; pay-up policy; buy paid-up additions; accumulate at interest; or be paid in cash	Fixed, constant	Fixed, constant	Fixed	Predictable; forced savings and conservative investment	High premiums given death benefit
Variable life	Whole life contract; choice of investment assets; death benefits depend on investment results	Guaranteed minimum; can increase based on investment performance	Fixed, constant	Based on investment performance; not guaranteed	Combines life insurance and investments on excess premiums	All investment risk is to the owner
Universal life	Flexible premium, current assumption adjustable death benefit policy; policy elements unbundled	Adjustable; Two options: (1) like ordinary life; (2) like ordinary life plus term rider equal to cash value	Flexible at option of policyowner	Varies depending on face amount and premium; minimum guaranteed interest; excess increases cash value	Flexibility	Some investment risk to owner
Variable universal life	Features of universal and variable life	Adjustable	Flexible at option of policyowner	Varies depending on face amount, premium, and investment performance; not guaranteed	Flexibility and choice of investments	All investment risk is to owner

alive; or to provide funds to pay estate taxes, or to estates when some assets being bequeathed are illiquid and indivisible when the owner is deceased.

Overall, whole life insurance can be an important addition to an investor's overall bond portfolio that provides liquidity, is very tax efficient, and is a flexible asset which satisfies existing limitations in some financial plans.

Annuities

By definition, an *annuity* is simply a series of periodic payments. Annuity contracts have been offered by insurance companies and, more recently, by other types of financial institutions such as mutual fund companies.

There are two phases to annuities according to cash flows, the accumulation period and the liquidation period. During the accumulation period, the investor is providing funds, or investing. Annuities are considered primarily accumulation products rather than insurance products. During the liquidation period, the investor is withdrawing funds, or liquidating the annuity. One type of liquidation is annuitization, or withdrawal via a series of fixed payments, as discussed below. This method of liquidation is the basis for the name of annuities.

There are several ways to classify annuities. One is the method of paying premiums. Annuities are purchased with single premiums, fixed periodic premiums, or flexible periodic premiums during the accumulation phase. All three are used in current practice.

A second classification is the time the income payments commence during the liquidation phase. An *immediate annuity* is one in which the first benefit payment is due one payment interval (month, year or other) from the purchasing date. Under a *deferred annuity*, there is a longer period before the benefit period begins. While an immediate annuity is purchased with a single premium, a deferred annuity may be purchased with a single, fixed periodic, or flexible periodic payments, although the flexible periodic payment is most common.

An important basis for annuities is whether they are fixed or variable annuities. Fixed annuities, as discussed in more detail below, are expressed in a fixed number of dollars, while variable annuities are expressed in a fixed number annuity units, each unit of which may have a different and changing market value. Fixed versus variable annuities is the key distinction between annuities currently provided.

Now we will look at the various types of annuities. The most common categories are variable annuities and fixed annuities.

While cash value life insurance has the appearance of life insurance with an investment feature, annuities, in contrast, have the appearance of an investment product with an insurance feature. The major advantage of an annuity is its inside buildup, that is, its investment earnings are tax deferred. However, unlike life insurance where the death benefit is not subject to income taxes, withdrawals from annuities are taxable. There are also restrictions on withdrawals. Specifically, there are IRS requirements for the taxability of early withdrawals (before age 59.5) and required minimum withdrawals (after age 70.5). These requirements and the other tax issues of annuities are very complex and considered only briefly here.

The most common types of annuities, variable and fixed annuities, are discussed below.

Variable Annuities

Variable annuities are, in many ways, similar to mutual funds. Given the above discussion, variable annuities are often considered to be "mutual funds in an insurance wrapper." The return on a variable annuity depends on the return of the underlying portfolio. The returns on annuities are, thus, in a word, "variable." In fact, many investment managers offer similar or identical funds separately in both a mutual fund and an annuity format. Thus, variable annuity offerings are approximately as broad as mutual fund offerings. For example, consider a large capitalization, blended stock fund. The investment manager may offer this fund in both a mutual fund and annuity format. But, of course, the two portfolios are segregated. The portfolios of these two products may be identical and, thus, the portfolio returns will be identical.

Before considering the differences, however, there is one similarity. Investments in both mutual funds and annuities are made with after-tax dollars; that is, taxes are paid on the income before it is invested in either a mutual fund or an annuity.

But there are important differences to investors in these two products. First, all income (dividend and interest) and realized capital gains generated in the mutual fund are taxable, even if they are not withdrawn. On the other hand, income and realized capital gains generated in the annuity are not taxable until withdrawn. Thus, annuities benefit from the same inside buildup as cash value life insurance.

There is another tax advantage to annuities. If a variable annuity company has a group of annuities in its family (called a "contract"), an investor can switch from one annuity fund to another in the contract (for example from a stock fund to a bond fund) and the switch is not a taxable event. However, if the investor shifts from a stock fund in one annuity company to a bond fund in another annuity company, it is considered a withdrawal and a reinvestment, and the withdrawal is a taxable event (there are exceptions to this, however, as will be discussed). The taxation of annuity withdrawals will also be considered.

While the inside buildup is an advantage of annuities, there are offsetting disadvantages. For comparison, there are no restrictions on withdrawals from (selling shares of) a mutual fund. Of course, withdrawals from a mutual fund are a taxable event and will generate realized capital gains or losses, which will generate long-term or short-term gains or losses and, thus, tax consequences. There are, however, significant restrictions on withdrawals from annuities. First, withdrawals before age 59.5 are assessed a 10% penalty (there are, however, some "hardship" exceptions to this). Second, withdrawals must begin by age 70.5 according to the IRS *required minimum distribution rules* (RMD). These mandatory withdrawals are designed to eventually produce tax revenues on annuities to the IRS. Mutual funds have no disadvantages to withdrawing before 59.5 nor requirements to withdraw after 70.5.

There is an exception to the taxation resulting from a shift of funds from one variable annuity company to another. Under specific circumstances, funds can be so moved without causing a taxable event. Such a shift is called a *1035 exchange* after the IRS rule that permits this transfer.

Another disadvantage of annuities is that all gains on withdrawals, when they occur, are taxed as ordinary income, not capital gains, whether their source was income or capital gains. For many investors, their income tax rate is significantly higher than the long-term capital gains tax rate and this form of taxation is therefore a disadvantage.

The final disadvantage of annuities is that the heirs of a deceased owner receive them with a cost basis equal to the purchase price (which means that the gains are taxed at the heir's ordinary income tax rate) rather than being stepped up to a current market value as with most investments.

Why has the IRS given annuities the same tax advantage of inside buildup that insurance policies have? The answer to this question is that annuities are structured to have some of the characteristics of life insurance, commonly called "features." There are many such features. The most common feature is that the minimum value of an annuity fund that will be paid at the investor's death is the initial amount invested. Thus, if an investor invests $100 in a stock annuity, the stock market declines such that the value of the fund is $90, and the investor dies, the investor's beneficiary will receive $100, not $90. This is a life insurance characteristic of an annuity.

The above feature represents a *death benefit* (DB), commonly called a return of premium. However, new, and often more complicated, death benefits have been introduced, including a periodic lock-in of gains (called a *stepped-up DB*); a predetermined annual percentage increase (called a *rising floor DB*); a percentage of earnings to offset estate taxes; and other death expenses (called an *earnings enhancement DB*). In addition to these death benefit features, some *living benefit features* have also been developed, including premium enhancements and minimum accumulation guarantees.

Obviously these features have value to the investor and, as a result, a cost to the provider. The value of a feature depends on its design and can be high or approximately worthless. And the annuity company will charge the investor for the value of these features.

The cost of the features relates to another disadvantage of annuities, specifically their expenses. The insurance company will impose a charge for the potential death benefit payment (called *mortality*) and other expenses, overall called M&E charges, as discussed previously for insurance policies. These M&E charges will be in addition to the normal investment management, custody, and other expenses experienced by mutual funds. Thus, annuity expenses will exceed mutual fund expenses by the annuity's M&E charges. The annuity investor does, however, receive the value of the insurance feature for the M&E charge.

Thus, the overall trade-offs between mutual funds and annuities can be summarized as follows. Annuities have the advantages of inside buildup and the particular life insurance features of the specific annuity. But annuities also have the disadvantages of higher taxes on withdrawal (ordinary income versus capital gains), restrictions on withdrawals, and higher expenses. For short holding periods, mutual funds will have a higher after-tax return. For very long holding periods, the value of the inside buildup will dominate and the annuity will have a higher after-tax return.

What is the breakeven holding period, that is, the holding period beyond which annuities have higher after-tax returns? The answer to this question depends on several factors, such as the tax rates (income and capital gains), the excess of the expenses on the annuity, and others.

Fixed Annuities

There are several types of fixed annuities but, in general, the invested premiums grow at a rate—the credited rate—specified by the insurance company in each. This growth is accrued and added to the cash value of the annuity each year (or more frequently, such as monthly) and is not taxable as long as it remains in the annuity. Upon liquidation, it is taxed as ordinary income (to the extent that is represents previously untaxed income).

The two most common types of fixed annuities are the *flexible premium deferred annuity* (FPDA) and the *single-premium deferred annuity* (SPDA). The FPDA permits contributions that are flexible in amount and timing. The interest rate paid on these contracts—the credited rate—varies and depends on the insurance company's current interest earnings and its desired competitive position in the market. There are, however, two types of limits on the rate. First, the rate is guaranteed to be no lower than a specified contract guaranteed rate, often in the range 3% to 4%. Second, these contracts often have *bail-out provisions*, which stipulate that if the credited rate decreases below a specified rate, the owner may withdraw all the funds (lapse the contract) without a surrender charge. Bail-out credited rates are often set at 1% to 3% below the current credited rate and are designed to limit the use of a "teaser rate" (or "bait and switch" practices), whereby an insurance company offers a high credited rate to attract new investors and then reduces the credited rate significantly, with the investor limited from withdrawing the funds by the surrender charges.

An initial credited rate, a minimum guaranteed rate, and a bailout rate are set initially on the contract. The initial credited rate, thus, may be changed by the insurance company over time. The *reset period* (or *renewal period*) must also be specified—this is, the frequency with which the credited rate can be changed.

Another important characteristic of annuities is the basis for the valuation of withdrawals prior to maturity. The traditional method has been book value, that is, withdrawals are paid based on the purchase price of the bonds (bonds rather than stocks are used to fund annuities). Thus, if yields have increased, the insurance company will be paying the withdrawing investor more than the bonds are currently worth. And at this time, there is an incentive for the investor to withdraw and invest in a new higher yielding fixed annuity. Thus, book value fixed annuities provide risk to the insurance company. Surrender charges, discussed next, mitigate this risk. Another way to mitigate this risk is via *market value-adjusted* (MVA) *annuities*, whereby early withdrawals are paid on the basis of the current market value of the bond portfolio rather than the book value. This practice eliminates the early withdrawal risk to the insurance company. (Obviously, all variable annuities are paid on the basis of market value rather than bonds value.)

Another characteristic of both variable and fixed annuities relates to one aspect of their sales charges. These charges are very similar for annuities and mutual funds. Mutual funds and annuities were originally provided with front-end loans, that is, sales charges imposed on the initial investment. For example, with a 5% front-end load of a $100 initial investment, $5 would be retained by the firm for itself and the agent, and $95 invested in the fund for the investor.

More recently, back-end loads have been used as an alternative to front-end loads. With a back-end load, the fixed percentage charge is imposed at the time of withdrawal. Currently, the most common form of back-end load is the contingent deferred sales charge, also called a *surrender charge*. This approach imposes a load which is gradually declining over time. For example, a common CDSC is a "7%/6%/5%/4%/3%/2%/1%/0%" charge according to which a 7% load is imposed on withdrawals during the first year, 6% during the second year, 5% during the third year, and so forth. There is no charge for withdrawals after the seventh year.

Finally, there are level loads, which impose a constant load (1% for example) every year. Currently on annuities, a front-end load is often used along with a CDSC surrender charge.

Annuities have become very complex instruments. This section provides only an overview.

Guaranteed Investment Contracts

The first major investment-oriented product developed by life insurance companies, and a form of fixed annuity, was the *guaranteed investment contract* (GIC). GICs were used extensively for retirement plans. With a GIC, a life insurance company agrees, in return for a single premium, to pay the principal amount and a predetermined annual crediting rate over the life of the investment, all of which are paid at the maturity date of the GIC. For example, a $10 million five-year GIC with a predetermined crediting rate of 10% means that at the end of five years, the insurance company pays the guaranteed crediting rate and the principal. The return of the principal depends on the ability of the life insurance company to satisfy the obligation, just as in any corporate debt obligation. The risk that the insurer faces is that the rate earned on the portfolio of supporting assets is less than the guaranteed rate.

The maturity of a GIC can vary from 1 year to 20 years. The interest rate guaranteed depends on market conditions and the rating of the life insurance company. The interest rate will be higher than the yield on U.S. Treasury securities of the same maturity. These policies are typically purchased by pension plan sponsors as a pension investment.

A GIC is a liability of the life insurance company issuing the contract. The word guarantee does not mean that there is a guarantor other than the life insurance company. Effectively, a GIC is a zero-coupon bond issued by a life insurance company and, as such, exposes the investor to the same credit risk. This credit risk has been highlighted by the default of several major issuers of GICs. The two most publicized defaults were Mutual Benefit, a New Jersey-based insurer, and Executive Life, a California-based insurer, which were both seized by regulators in 1991.

The basis for these defaults is that fixed annuities are insurance company general account products and variable annuities are separate account products. For fixed annuities, the premiums become part of the insurance company, are invested in the insurance company's general account (which are regulated by state laws), and the payments are the obligations of the insurance company. Variable annuities are separate account products, that is, the premiums are deposited in investment vehicles separate from the insurance company, and are usually selected by the investor. Thus fixed annuities are general account products and the insurance company bears the investment risk, while variable annuities are separate account products and the investor bears the investment risk.

SPDAs and GICs

SPDAs and GICs with the same maturity and crediting rate have much in common. For example, for each the value of a $1 initial investment with a five-year maturity and a fixed crediting rate for the five years at $r\%$ would have a value at maturity of $(1 + r)^5$.

However, there are also significant differences. SPDAs have elements of an insurance product and so its inside buildup is not taxed as earned (it is taxed as income at maturity). SPDAs are not qualified products, that is, they must be paid for in after tax-dollars. GICs are not insurance products. GICs, however, are typically put into pension plans (defined benefit or defined contribution), which are qualified. In this case, thus, the GIC investments are paid for in after-tax dollars and receive the tax deferral of inside buildup. SPDAs are also put into qualified plans. Specifically, banks often sell IRAs funded with SPDAs.

Another difference between SPDAs and GICs is that since SPDAs are annuities, they usually have surrender charges, typically the 7%/6%/5%/4%/3%/2%/1%/0%, mentioned previously. Thus, if a five-year SPDA is withdrawn after three years, there is a 4% surrender charge. GICs do not have surrender charges and can be withdrawn with no penalty (under benefit responsive provisions).

Another feature of SPDAs is the reset period, the period after which the credited rate can be changed by the writer of the product. For example, a five-year SPDA may have a reset period after three years, at which time the credited rate can also be increased or decreased. For SPDAs, there can also be an interaction between the reset period and the surrender charge. For example, a five-year SPDA with a three-year reset period could be liquidated after three years due to a lowered crediting rate, but only with a 4% surrender charge. GICs have no reset period, that is, the credited rate is constant throughout the contract's life. Early withdrawals of GICs are at book value; they are interest rate insensitive.

SPDAs typically have a reset period of one year but with an initial M-year minimum guarantee ($M = 1, 2, 3, 5, 7, 9$). SPDAs typically have a maturity based on the age of the annuitant (such as age 90 or 95), not a fixed number of years. Thus, while SPDAs typically have a maturity greater than the guarantee period, for GICs the maturity period equals the guarantee period. Common maturities for GICs and SPDAs are one, three, five, and seven years.

Financial Instruments and Concepts Introduced in this Chapter (in Order of Presentation)

Cash value life insurance	Survivorship insurance
Cash value	Second-to-die insurance
Inside buildup	Internal rate of return
Death benefit	Irrevocable life insurance trust
General account products	Annuity
Separate account products	Immediate annuity
Participating policy	Deferred annuity
Cash value whole life insurance	Variable annuities
Guaranteed cash value buildup	Fixed annuities
M&E charges	Required minimum distribution rules
Paid-up additions	1035 exchange
Lapsed	Death benefit
Forfeited	Stepped up DB
Surrendered	Rising floor DB
Nonforfeiture options	Earnings enhancement DB
Extended term insurance	Living benefit features
Reduced paid up	Mortality
Policy loan	Flexible predeferred annuity
Cost of the policy	Single premium deferred annuity
Return on the policy	Bail-out provisions
Single-premium life insurance	Reset period
Whole life insurance	Renewal period
Guaranteed buildup	Market value-adjusted annuities
Cash value buildup	Surrender charge
Variable life insurance	Guaranteed investment contract
Universal life	

CHAPTER 12

Investment Companies

Investment companies include open-end mutual funds, closed-end funds, and unit trusts. Shares in investment companies are sold to the public and the proceeds invested in a diversified portfolio of securities. The value of a share of an investment company is called its net asset value. The two types of costs borne by investors in mutual funds are the shareholder sales charge or loads and the annual fund operating expense. Two major advantages of the indirect ownership of securities by investing in mutual funds are (1) risk reduction through diversification; and (2) reduced cost of contracting and processing information because an investor purchases the services of a presumably skilled financial advisor at less cost than if the investor directly and individually negotiated with such an advisor. There is a wide-range of investment companies that invest in different asset classes and with different investment objectives.

TYPES OF INVESTMENT COMPANIES

There are three types of investment companies: open-end funds, closed-end funds, and unit trusts. A closely related product—exchange-traded funds (ETFs)—is discussed in the next chapter.

Open-End Funds (Mutual Funds)

Open-end funds, commonly referred to simply as *mutual funds*, are portfolios of securities, mainly stocks, bonds, and money market instruments. There are several important aspects of mutual funds. First, investors in mutual funds own a pro rata share of the overall portfolio. Second, the investment manager of the mutual fund manages the portfolio, that is, buys some securities and sells others (this characteristic is unlike unit investment trusts, discussed later).

Third, the value or price of each share of the portfolio, called the *net asset value* (NAV), equals the market value of the portfolio minus the liabilities of the mutual fund divided by the number of shares owned by the mutual fund investors. That is,

$$NAV = \frac{Market\ value\ of\ portfolio - Liabilities}{Number\ of\ shares\ outstanding}$$

For example, suppose that a mutual fund with 20 million shares outstanding has a portfolio with a market value of $315 million and liabilities of $15 million. The NAV is

$$NAV = \frac{\$315,000,000 - \$15,000,000}{20,000,000} = \$15$$

Fourth, the NAV or price of the fund is determined only once each day, at the close of the day. For example, the NAV for a stock mutual fund is determined from the closing stock prices for the day. Business publications provide the NAV each day in their mutual fund tables. The published NAV's are the closing NAV's.

Fifth, and very importantly, all new investments into the fund or withdrawals from the fund during a day are priced at the closing NAV (investments after the end of the day or on a nonbusiness day are priced at the next day's closing NAV).

The total number of shares in the fund increases if there are more investments than withdrawals during the day, and vice versa. This is the reason such a fund is called an "open-end" fund. For example, assume that at the beginning of a day a mutual fund portfolio has a value of $1 million, there are no liabilities, and there are 10,000 shares outstanding. Thus, the NAV of the fund is $100. Assume that during the day $5,000 is deposited into the fund, $1,000 is withdrawn, and the prices of all the securities in the portfolio remain constant. This means that 50 shares were issued for the $5,000 deposited (since each share is $100) and 10 shares redeemed for $1,000 (again since each share is $100). The net number of new shares issued is then 40. Therefore, at the end of the day there will be 10,040 shares and the total value of the fund will be $1,004,000. The NAV will remain at $100.

If, instead, the prices of the securities in the portfolio change, both the total size of the portfolio and, therefore, the NAV will change. In the previous example, assume that during the day the value of the portfolio doubles to $2 million. Since deposits and withdrawals are priced at the end-of-day NAV, which is now $200 after the doubling of the portfolio's value, the $5,000 deposit will be credited with 25 shares ($5,000/$200) and the $1,000 withdrawn will reduce the number of shares by 5 shares ($1,000/$200). Thus, at the end of the day there will be 10,020 shares in the fund with an NAV of $200, and the value of the fund will be $2,004,000. (Note that 10,020 shares × $200 NAV equals $2,004,000, the portfolio value.)

Overall, the NAV of a mutual fund will increase or decrease due to an increase or decrease in the prices of the securities in the portfolio, respectively. The number of shares in the fund will increase or decrease due to the net deposits into or withdrawals from the fund, respectively. And the total value of the fund will increase or decrease for both reasons. To repeat, the NAV of mutual funds is determined only once a day, at the day's close of trading.

Closed-End Funds

The shares of *closed-end funds* are very similar to the shares of common stock of a corporation. The new shares of a closed-end fund are initially issued by an underwriter for the fund. And after the new issue, the number of shares remains constant. This is the reason such a fund is called a "closed-end" fund. After the initial issue, there are no sales or purchases of fund shares by the fund company as there are for open-end funds. The shares are traded on a secondary market, either on an exchange or in the over-the-counter market.

Investors can buy shares either at the time of the initial issue (as discussed below), or thereafter in the secondary market. Shares are sold only on the secondary market. The price of the shares of a closed-end fund are determined by the supply and demand in the market in which these funds are traded. Thus, investors who transact closed-end fund shares must pay a brokerage commission at the time of purchase and at the time of sale.

The NAV of closed-end funds is calculated in the same way as for open-end funds. However, the price of a share in a closed-end fund is determined by supply and demand, so the price can fall below or rise above the net asset value per share. Shares selling below NAV are said to be "trading at a discount," while shares trading above NAV are "trading at a premium." Newspapers list quotations of the prices of these shares under the heading "Closed-End Funds." Some sources also list the NAV and the discount or premium of the shares.

Consequently, there are two important differences between open-end funds and closed-end funds. First, the number of shares of an open-end fund varies because the fund sponsor will sell new shares to investors and buy existing shares from shareholders. Second, by doing so, the share price is always the NAV of the fund. In contrast, closed-end funds have a constant number of shares outstanding because the fund sponsor does not redeem shares and sell new shares to investors (except at the time of a new underwriting). Thus, the price of the fund shares will be determined by supply and demand in the market and may be above or below NAV, as discussed above.

Although the divergence of the price from NAV is often puzzling, in some cases the reasons for the premium or discount are easily understood. For example, a share's price may be below the NAV because the fund has a large built-in tax liability and investors are discounting the share's price for that future tax liability. (We discuss this tax liability issue later in this chapter.) A fund's leverage and resulting risk may be another reason for the share's price trading below NAV. Many bond closed-end funds borrow against their holdings. A fund's shares may trade at a premium to the NAV because the fund offers relatively cheap access to, and professional management of, stocks in another country about which information is not readily available to or transactions are difficult or expensive for small investors. The premiums and discounts of closed-end funds can be significant. Individual funds may have either premiums or discounts exceeding 50%. And the aggregate closed-end fund market frequently has a discount of 10% to 20%.

Under the Investment Company Act of 1940, closed-end funds are capitalized only once. They make an initial public offering (IPO) and then their shares are traded on the secondary market, just like any corporate stock, as discussed earlier. The number of shares is fixed at the IPO; closed-end funds cannot issue more shares. In fact, many closed-end funds become leveraged to raise more funds without issuing more shares.

An important feature of closed-end funds is that the initial investors bear the substantial cost of underwriting the issuance of the funds' shares. The proceeds that the managers of the fund have to invest equals the total paid by initial buyers of the shares minus all costs of issuance. These costs, which average around 7.5% of the total amount paid for the issue, normally include selling fees or commissions paid to the retail brokerage firms that distribute them to the public. The high commissions are strong incentives for retail brokers to recommend these shares to their retail customers, and also for investors to avoid buying these shares on their initial offering.

As explained later in the next chapter, exchange-traded funds pose a threat to both mutual funds and closed-end funds. Exchange-traded funds (ETFs) are essentially hybrid closed-end vehicles, which trade on exchanges but which typically trade very close to NAV.

Since closed-end funds are traded like stocks, the cost to any investor of buying or selling a closed-end fund is the same as that of a stock. The obvious charge is the stock broker's commission. The bid-offer spread of the market on which the stock is traded is also a cost.

Exhibit 12.1 summarizes the differences between mutual funds and closed-end funds.

EXHIBIT 12.1   Mutual Funds (open-end funds) vs. Closed-End Funds

Characteristics	Mutual Fund	Closed-End Fund
1. Share Price (SP) vs. NAV	Always Equal (SP = NAV)	Can Differ: (SP > NAV: Premium) (SP < NAV: Discount)
2. Number of Shares Outstanding	Varies (open-end)	Constant (closed-end)
3. Determination of NAV	Once a day at close of trading day	All during trading day, trade on exchange
4. Exchange of Shares	Buyers and sellers separately exchange via Mutual Fund Company	Between buyers and sellers via exchange
5. Issuance of Shares	Continuously (issuance and retirement) via Mutual Fund Company	Once, at initial public offering

Unit Trusts

A *unit trust* is similar to a closed-end fund in that the number of unit certificates is fixed. Unit trusts typically invest in bonds. They differ in several ways from both mutual funds and closed-end funds that specialize in bonds. First, there is no active trading of the bonds in the portfolio of the unit trust. Once the unit trust is assembled by the sponsor (usually a brokerage firm or bond underwriter) and turned over to a trustee, the trustee holds all the bonds until they are redeemed by the issuer. Typically, the only time the trustee can sell an issue in the portfolio is if there is a dramatic decline in the issuer's credit quality. As a result, the cost of operating the trust will be considerably less than costs incurred by either a mutual fund or a closed-end fund. Second, unit trusts have a fixed termination date, while mutual funds and closed-end funds do not. (There are, however, exceptions. Target term closed-end funds have a fixed termination date.) Third, unlike the mutual fund and closed-end fund investor, the unit trust investor knows that the portfolio consists of a specific portfolio of bonds and has no concern that the trustee will alter the portfolio. While unit trusts are common in Europe, they are not common in the United States.

All unit trusts charge a sales commission. The initial sales charge for a unit trust ranges from 3.5% to 5.5%. In addition to these costs, there is the cost incurred by the sponsor to purchase the bonds for the trust that an investor indirectly pays. That is, when the brokerage firm or bond underwriting firm assembles the unit trust, the price of each bond to the trust also includes the dealer's spread. There is also often a commission if the units are sold.

In the remainder this chapter of our primary focus chapter is on open-end (mutual) funds.

FUND SALES CHARGES AND ANNUAL OPERATING EXPENSES

There are two types of costs borne by investors in mutual funds. The first is the *shareholder fee*, usually called the *sales charge* or *load*. For securities transactions, this charge is called a *commission*. This cost is a "one-time" charge debited to the investor for a specific transaction, such as a purchase, redemption or exchange. The type of charge is related to the way the fund is sold or distributed. The second cost is the annual fund operating expense, usually called the *expense ratio*, which covers the funds' expenses, the largest of which is for investment management. This charge is imposed annually. This cost occurs on all funds and for all types of distribution. We discuss each cost next.

Sales Charges or Loads

Sales charges on mutual funds are related to their method of distribution. The current menu of sales charges and distribution mechanisms has evolved significantly and is now much more diverse than it was a decade ago. To understand the current diversity and the evolution of distribution mechanisms, consider initially the circumstances of a decade ago. At that time, there were two basic methods of distribution, two types of sales charges, and the type of the distribution was directly related to the type of sales charge.

The two types of distribution were sales force and direct. Sales-force distribution occurred via an intermediary, that is via an agent, a stockbroker, insurance agent, or other entity who provided investment advice and incentive to the client, actively "made the sale," and provided subsequent service. This distribution approach is active, that is the fund is typically sold, not bought.

The other approach is direct (from the fund company to the investor), whereby there is no intermediary or salesperson to actively approach the client, provide investment advice and service, or make the sale. Rather, the client approaches the mutual fund company, most likely by a "1-800" telephone contact, in response to media advertisements or general information, and opens the account. Little or no investment counsel or service is provided either initially or subsequently. With respect to the mutual fund sale, this is a passive approach, although these mutual funds may be quite active in their advertising and other marketing activities. Funds provided by the direct approach are bought, not sold.

There is a *quid pro quo*, however, for the service provided in the sales-force distribution method which is a sales charge borne by the customer and paid to the agent. The load is the sales charge for the agent-distributed fund. Agent-distributed funds are typically called *load mutual funds*. The traditional type of load is called a *front-end load* since the load is deducted initially or "up-front." That is, the load is deducted from the amount invested by the client and paid to the agent/distributor. The remainder is the net amount invested in the fund in the client's name. For example, if the load on the mutual fund is 5% and the investor invests $100, the $5 load is paid to the agent and the remaining $95 is the net amount invested in the mutual fund at NAV. Importantly, only $95, not $100, is invested in the fund. The fund is, thus, said to be "purchased above NAV" (i.e., the investor pays $100 for $95 of the fund). The $5 load compensates the sales agent for the investment advice and service provided to the client by the agent. The load to the client, of course, represents income to the agent.

Let's contrast this with directly placed mutual funds. There is no sales agent and, therefore, there is no need for a sales charge. Funds with no sales charges are called *no-load mutual funds*. In this case, if the client provides $100 to the mutual fund, $100 is invested in the fund in the client's name. This approach to buying the fund is called buying the fund "at NAV," that is, the whole amount provided by the investor is invested in the fund.

Previously, many observers speculated that load funds would become obsolete and no-load funds would dominate because of the sales charge. Increasingly financially sophisticated individuals, the reasoning went, would make their own investment decisions and not need to compensate agents for their advice and service. But the actual trend has been quite different.

Why has the trend not been away from the more costly agent-distributed funds as many expected? There are two reasons. First, many investors have remained dependent on the investment counsel and service, and perhaps more importantly, the initiative of the sales agent. Second, sales-force distributed funds have shown considerable ingenuity and flexibility in imposing sales charges, which both compensate the distributors and are acceptable to the clients. Among the recent adaptations of the front-end sales load are the back-end load and level load. While the front-end load is imposed at the time of the purchase of the fund, the *back-end load* is imposed at the time fund shares are sold or redeemed. Level loads are imposed uniformly each year. These two alternative methods both provide ways to compensate the agent. However, unlike with the front-end load, both of these distribution mechanisms permit the client to buy a fund at NAV—that is, not have any of their initial investment debited as a sales charge before it is invested in their account.

The most common type of back-end load currently is the *contingent deferred sales charge* (CDSC). This approach imposes a gradually declining load on withdrawal. For example, a common "3,3,2,2,1,1,0" CDSC approach imposes a 3% load on the amount withdrawn within one year, 3% within the second year, 2% within the third year, and so on. There is no sales charge for withdrawals after the sixth year. Thus, the sales charge is postponed or deferred, and it is contingent upon how long the investment is held.

The third type of load is neither a front-end load at the time of investment nor a (gradually declining) back-end load at the time of withdrawal, but a constant load each year (e.g., a 1% load every year). This approach is called a *level load*. Most mutual fund families are strictly either no-load (direct) or load (sales-force).

Many load type mutual fund families offer their funds with all three types of loads—that is, front-end loads (usually called "A shares"); back-end loads (often called "B shares"); and level loads (often called "C shares"). These families permit the distributor and its client to select the type of load they prefer.[1] These different types of load shares are called *share classes*. A recent type of share class is the F share. F shares have no front, level or back loads. In this way they are like C shares. But F shares have considerably lower annual expenses than C shares, as will be seen below. F shares are designed for financial planners who charge annual fees (called fee-based financial planners) rather than sales charges such as commissions or loads. F shares of a fund family may only be sold by financial planners and their representatives which have an arrangement with the fund family.

According to the National Association of Securities Dealers (NASD), the maximum allowable sales charge is 8.5%, although most funds impose lower charges.

The sales charge for a fund applies to most, even very small, investments (although there is typically a minimum initial investment). For large investments, however, the sales charge may be reduced. For example, a fund with a 4.5% front-end load may reduce this load to 3.0% for investments over $1 million. There may be in addition further reductions in the sales charge at greater investments at some level of investment the front-end load will be 0%. The amount of investment needed to obtain a reduction in the sales charge is called a *breakpoint*—the breakpoint is $1 million in this example. There are also mechanisms whereby the total amount of the investment necessary to qualify for the breakpoint does not need to be invested up front, but only over time (according to a "letter of intent" signed by the investor).[2]

---

[1]Edward S. O'Neal, "Mutual Fund Share Classes and Broker Incentives," *Financial Analysts Journal* 55, no. 5 (September–October 1999): 76–87.
[2]See D. C. Inro, C. X. Jaing, M. Y. Ho, and W. Y. Lee, "Mutual Fund performance: Does Fund Size Matter?" *Financial Analysts Journal* 55, no. 3 (May–June 1999): 74–87.

Fund returns are calculated without subtracting sales charges since different individual investors have different sales charges (e.g., may have different breakpoints).

The sales charge is, in effect, paid by the client to the distributor. How does the fund family, typically called the sponsor or manufacturer of the fund, cover its costs and make a profit? This is the topic of the second type of "cost" to the investor, the fund annual operating expense.

Annual Operating Expenses (Expense Ratio)

The *operating expense*, also called the *expense ratio*, is debited annually from the investor's fund balance by the fund sponsor. The three main categories of annual operating expenses are the management fee, distribution fee, and other expenses.

The *management fee*, also called the *investment advisory fee*, is the fee charged by the investment advisor for managing a fund's portfolio. If the investment advisor is part of a company separate from the fund sponsor, some or all of this investment advisory fee is passed on to the investment advisor by the fund sponsor. In this case, the fund manager is called a *subadvisor*. The management fee varies by the type of fund, specifically by the risk of the asset class of the fund. For example, the management fee as well as the risk may increase from money market funds to bond funds, to U.S. growth stock funds, to emerging market stock funds, as illustrated by examples to come.

In 1980, the SEC approved the imposition of a fixed annual fee, called the *12b-1 fee*, which is, in general, intended to cover *distribution costs*, also including continuing agent compensation and manufacturer marketing and advertising expenses. Such 12b-1 fees are now imposed by many mutual funds. By law, 12b-1 fees cannot exceed 1% of the fund's assets per year. The 12b-1 fee may also include a service fee of up to 0.25% of assets per year to compensate sales professionals for providing services or maintaining shareholder accounts. The major rationale for the component of the 12b-1 fee which accrues to the selling agent is to provide an incentive to selling agents to continue to service their accounts after having received a transaction-based fee such as a front-end load. As a result, a 12b-1 fee of this type is consistent with sales-force sold, load funds, not with directly sold, no-load funds. The rationale for the component of the 12b-1 fee that accrues to the manufacturer of the fund is to provide incentive and compensate for continuing advertising and marketing costs. This continuing service fee is called a *trail commission*. Fund returns are calculated after annual expenses are deducted but before sales charges are deducted.

Other expenses include primarily the costs of (1) custody (holding the cash and securities of the fund); (2) the transfer agent (transferring cash and securities among buyers and sellers of securities and the fund distributions, etc.); (3) independent public accountant fees; and (4) directors' fees.

The sum of the annual management fee, the annual distribution fee, and other annual expenses is called the expense ratio or annual operating expense. All the cost information on a fund, including selling charges and annual expenses, are included in the fund prospectus. In addition to the annual operating expenses, the fund prospectus provides the sales charge which may be imposed at the time of a fund transaction.

As we explained earlier, many agent-distributed funds are provided in different forms, typically the following: (1) A shares: front-end load; (2) B shares: back-end load (contingent deferred sales charge); (3) C shares: level load; and (4) F shares: fee-based program. These different forms of the same fund are called share classes. Exhibit 12.2 provides an example of hypothetical sales charges and annual expenses of funds of different classes for an agent-distributed stock mutual fund. The sales charge accrues to the sales agent. The management fee accrues to the mutual fund manager. The 12b-1 fee accrues to the sales agent and the fund sponsor. Other expenses, including custody and transfer fees and the fees of managing the fund company, accrue to the fund sponsor to cover expenses. All of these expenses are deducted from fund returns on an annual basis.

Often, as is the case in this example, the expense ratio is lower for A shares than for B shares. For this reason, after the period during which back-end charges are imposed expires for B shares, B shares revert to A shares; that is, their expense ratio declines to that of A shares

Many financial firms provide expense analyzers for judging the effects of sales charges and annual expense on performance. In addition, the SEC provides a "Mutual Fund Cost Calculator" (at www.sec.gov).

EXHIBIT 12.2 Hypothetical Sales Charges and Annual Expenses of Funds of Different Classes for an Agent-Distributed Stock Mutual Fund

	Sales Charge			Annual Operating Expenses			
	Front	Back	Level	Management Fee	Distribution (12b-1 fee)	Other Expenses	Expense Ratio
A	4.5%	0	0%	0.90%	0.25%	0.15%	1.30%
B	0	a	0%	0.90%	1.00%	0.15%	2.05%
C	0	0	1%	0.90%	1.00%	0.15%	2.05%
F	0	0	0	0.90%	0.25%	0.15%	1.30%

a 3%, 3%, 2%, 2%, 1%, 0%.

Multiple-Share Classes

Share classes were first offered in 1989 following the SEC's approval of multiple-share class. Initially, share classes were used primarily by sales-force funds to offer alternatives to the front-end load as a means of compensating brokers. Later, some of these funds used additional share classes as a means of offering the same fund or portfolio through alternative distribution channels in which some fund expenses varied by channel. Offering new share classes was more efficient and less costly than setting up two separate funds.[3]

ADVANTAGES OF INVESTING IN MUTUAL FUNDS

There are several advantages of the indirect ownership of securities by investing in mutual funds. The first is risk reduction through diversification. By investing in a fund, an investor can obtain broad-based ownership of a sufficient number of securities to reduce portfolio risk. While an individual investor may be able to acquire a broad-based portfolio of securities, the degree of diversification will be limited by the amount available to invest. By investing in an investment company, however, the investor can effectively achieve the benefits of diversification at a lower cost even if the amount of money available to invest is not large.

The second advantage is the reduced cost of contracting and processing information because an investor purchases the services of a presumably skilled financial advisor at less cost than if the investor directly and individually negotiated with such an advisor. The advisory fee is lower because of the larger size of assets managed, as well as the reduced costs of searching for an investment manager and obtaining information about the securities. Also, the costs of transacting in the securities are reduced because a fund is better able to negotiate transactions costs; and custodial fees and record keeping costs are less for a fund than for an individual investor. For these reasons, there are said to be economies of scale in investment management.

Third, and related to the first two advantages, is the advantage of the professional management of the mutual fund. Fourth is the advantage of liquidity. Mutual funds can be bought or liquidated any day at the closing NAV. Fifth is the advantage of the variety of funds available, in general, and even in one particular funds family, as discussed later.

Finally, money market funds and some other types of funds provide payment services by allowing investors to write checks drawn on the fund, although this facility may be limited in various ways.

---

[3]Brian Reid, "The 1990s: A Decade of Expansion and Changes in the U.S. Mutual Fund Industry," *Perspectives: Investment Company Institute* 6, no. 3 (2000): 1–20.

TYPES OF FUNDS BY INVESTMENT OBJECTIVE

Mutual funds have been provided to satisfy the various investment objectives of investors. In general, there are stock funds, bond funds, money market funds, and others. Within each of these categories, there are several subcategories of funds. There are also U.S.-only funds, international funds (no U.S. securities), and global funds (both U.S. and international securities). There are also passive and active funds. Passive (or indexed) funds are designed to replicate an index, such as: the S&P 500 Stock Index; the Barclay's Aggregate Bond Index; or the Morgan Stanley Capital International EAFE Index (Europe, Australasia, and the Far East). Active funds, on the other hand, attempt to outperform an index by actively trading the fund portfolio. While the holdings of passive funds are known, managers of active funds are very proprietary about their holdings. In this regard, the SEC requires that institutional investors, including mutual funds, report their holdings on a quarterly basis, within 45 days after the end of the quarter. These reports are the so-called *13F disclosures*.

There are also many other categories of funds, as discussed below. Each fund's objective is stated in its prospectus, as required by the SEC and the "1940 Act," as discussed next.

Stock funds differ by:

- Average market capitalization ("market cap") (large, mid, and small) of the stocks in the portfolio.
- Style (growth, value, and blend).
- Sector—"sector funds" specialize in one particular sector or industry, such as technology, healthcare or utilities.

With respect to style, stocks with high price-to-book value and price/earnings ratios are considered growth stocks, and stocks with low price-to-book value and price/earnings ratios are considered value stocks, although other variables may also be considered. There are also blend stocks with respect to style.

Bond funds differ by the creditworthiness of the issuers of the bonds in the portfolio (for example, U.S. government and investment-grade and high-yield corporates) and by the maturity (or duration) of the bonds (long, intermediate, and short.) There is also a category of bond funds called municipal bond funds whose interest income is exempt from federal income taxes. Municipal funds may be single state (that is, all the bonds in the portfolio were issued by issuers in the same state) or multistate or national.

There are also other categories of funds such as asset allocation, hybrid, and balanced funds (all of which hold both stocks and bonds), and convertible bond funds. Until 1997, mutual funds were not permitted to short securities. The expanded ability to short in 1997 augmented the strategies mutual funds could employ to strategies such as long-short, bear market, and market-neutral funds.

Another subcategory of the stock/bond hybrid category that is a recent addition to the types of mutual funds is the *target-date fund*. This type of fund, popularly referred to as a *life-cycle fund*, establishes its asset allocation on a specific date, the assumed retirement date for the investor, and then rebalances to a more conservative allocation as that date approaches.[4] The first generation of target-date funds had fairly simple asset allocations. For example, in 2010 a 30-year old investor who planned to retire at 65 would invest in a 2045 target date fund. A specific target date fund might specify a 70%/30% U.S. stocks/bonds allocations. Such an allocation prompts two types of questions. First is whether 70%/30% is the optimal asset mix. This issue could never be resolved in a "one size fits all" product such as a target date fund. To better address this issue, the risk tolerance on an individual investor basis should be considered. The second question relates to the overall asset allocation. What proportion of international stocks should be in the allocation? Of this, what is the share of emerging markets? Should there be real estate, commodities, or other inflation-protected assets in the portfolio? Again, these issues cannot be resolved on a one-size-fits-all basis. Although target-date funds are superior to an extreme portfolio allocation such as 100% to one asset class, they are inferior to an individually designed portfolio for an investor. Target-date funds at least provide some diversification and become more conservative as retirement approaches. Currently, there are significant differences with respect to both stock and bond mix and degree of diversification for target-date funds with the same retirement date.

Although not as popular as the target-date fund, a related type of fund is the *target-risk fund*. This type of mutual fund determines its asset allocation around pre-specified levels of risk (such as aggressive, moderate, or conservative) and subsequently rebalances the fund's portfolio to maintain this risk level.

There is also a category of money market funds (maturities of one year or less) which provide protection against interest rate fluctuations. These funds may have some degree of credit risk (except for the U.S. government money market category). Many of these funds offer check-writing privileges. In addition to taxable money market funds, there are also tax-exempt municipal money market funds.

---

[4]Target-date funds are actually "funds of funds," whereby the overall target-date fund is a combination of stock funds, bond funds and, in some cases, other funds. These individual funds can be either active or passive funds.

Among the other fund offerings are index funds and funds of funds. Index funds, as discussed above, attempt to passively replicate an index. Funds of funds invest in other mutual funds not in individual securities.

Several organizations provide data on mutual funds. The most popular ones are *Morningstar* and *Lipper*. These firms provide data on fund expenses, portfolio managers, fund sizes, and fund holdings. But perhaps most importantly, they provide performance (that is, rate of return and risk) data and rankings among funds based on performance and other factors. To compare fund performance on an "apples to apples" basis, these firms divide mutual funds into several categories which are intended to be fairly homogeneous by investment objective. Many of the categories of these two services are shown and compared in Exhibit 12.3. Thus, the performance of one Morningstar "large-cap blend" fund can be meaningfully compared with another fund in the same category, but not with a "small-cap value" fund. The categories provided by Morningstar and Lipper are similar but not identical. Morningstar's performance ranking system whereby each fund is rated on the basis of return and risk from one-star (the worst) to five-stars (the best) relative to the other funds in its category is well known.

Mutual fund data are also provided by the Investment Company Institute, the national association for mutual funds.

THE CONCEPT OF A FAMILY OF FUNDS

A concept that revolutionized the fund industry and benefitted many investors is what the mutual fund industry calls a *family of funds*, a group of funds or a complex of funds. That is, many fund management companies offer investors a choice of numerous funds with different investment objectives in the same fund family. In many cases, investors may move their assets from one fund to another within the family at little or no cost, and with only a phone call. Of course, if these funds are in a taxable account, there may be tax consequences to the sale. While the same policies regarding loads and other costs may apply to all the funds in a family, a management company may have different fee structures for transfers among different funds in its family.

Large fund families usually include money market funds, U.S. bond funds of several types, global stock and bond funds, broadly diversified U.S. stock funds, U.S. stock funds which specialize by market capitalization and style, and stock funds devoted to particular sectors such as healthcare, technology or gold companies. Well-known management companies, such as Vanguard, American Funds, and Fidelity the three largest fund families, sponsor and manage varied types of funds in a family. Fund families may

EXHIBIT 12.3 Fund Categories: Morningstar vs. Lipper

	Morningstar			Lipper	
LG	Large Growth		LG	Target-Cap Growth	
LV	Large Value		LV	Large-Cap Value	
LB	Large Blend		LC	Large-Cap Core	
MG	Mid-Cap Growth		MG	Mid-Cap Growth	
MV	Mid-Cap Value		MV	Mid-Cap Value	
MB	Mid-Cap Blend		MC	Mid-Cap Core	
SG	Small Growth		SG	Small-Cap Growth	
SV	Small Value		SV	Small-Cap Value	
SB	Small Blend		SC	Small-Cap Core	
—			XG	Multi-Cap Growth	
—			XV	Multi-Cap Value	
—			XC	Multi-Cap Core	
MA	Moderate Allocation		BL	Balanced	
CA	Conservative Allocation		MP	Stock/Bond Blend	
TA	Target—Date 2004–2014		—		
TB	Target—Date 2015–2029		—		
TC	Target—Date 2030+		—		
DH	Domestic Hybrid		EI	Equity Income	
			SP	S&P 500 Funds	
			SQ	Specialty Diversified Equity	
			TK	Science & Technology	
ST	Technology		UT	Utility	
SU	Utilities		HB	Health/Biotech	
SH	Health		SC	Telecommunications	
SC	Communication		—		
SF	Financial		NR	Natural Resources	
SN	Natural Resources		AU	Gold Oriented	
SP	Precious Metals		—		
SR	Real Estate		—		
BM	Bear Market		RE	Real Estate	
LO	Long-Short		SQ	Special Equity	
—			SE	Sector	
—			IL	International Stock (non-U.S.)	
FS	Foreign Stock		GL	Global Stock (inc. U.S.)	
—			EU	European Region	

EXHIBIT 12.3 (Continued)

Morningstar		Lipper	
WS	World Stock	EM	Emerging Markets
ES	Europe Stock		
EM	Diversified Emerging Mkt.	PR	Pacific Region
DP	Diversified Pacific Asia		
PJ	Pacific ex-Japan		
JS	Japan Stock	LT	Latin American
LS	Latin America Stock		
IH	International Hybrid	SB	Short-Term Bond
CS	Short-Term Bond—General	SU	Short-Term U.S. Govt.
GS	Short Government		
CI	Interm.-Term Bond—General		
GI	Interm.-Term Government	IB	Intermediate Bond
MT	Mortgage	IG	Intermediate U.S. Govt.
CL	Long-Term Bond—General	MT	Mortgage
GL	Long Government	AB	Long-Term Bond
IP	Inflation-Protected Bond	LU	Long-Term U.S. Govt.
CV	Convertibles	GT	General U.S. Taxable
UB	Ultrashort Bond		
HY	High-Yield Bond		
MU	Multisector Bond	HC	High-Yield Taxable
IB	World Bond	—	
EB	Emerging Market Bond		
BL	Bank Loan		
ML	Muni National Long	WB	World Bond
MI	Muni National Interm.	GM	General Muni Debt
MS	Muni National Short	IM	Interm. Muni Debt
HM	High Yield Muni	SM	Short-Term Muni Debt
SL	Muni Single St. Long	HM	High-Yield Muni
SI	Muni Single St. Interm.	NM	Insured Muni
SS	Muni Single St. Short	SS	Single-State Muni
MY	Muni New York Long		
MC	Muni California Long		
MN	Muni New York Interm./Sht		
MF	Muni California Interm./Sht		

also use external investment advisers (called subadvisors) along with their internal advisers in their fund families.

Fund data provided in newspapers group the various funds according to their families. For example, all the American Funds are listed under the American Fund heading, all the funds of Vanguard are listed under their name, and so on. Some fund families are very large (for example 100 funds) and others may specialize in one or two strategies (called *niche funds*).

TAXATION OF MUTUAL FUNDS

Mutual funds must distribute at least 90% of their net investment income earned (bond coupons and stock dividends) exclusive of realized capital gains or losses to shareholders (along with meeting other criteria) to be considered a *regulated investment company* (RIC) and, thus, not be required to pay taxes at the fund level prior to distributions to shareholders. Consequently, funds always make these distributions. Taxes, if this criterion is met, are then paid on distributions only at the investor level, not the fund level. Even though many mutual fund investors choose to reinvest these distributions, the distributions are taxable to the investor, either as ordinary income or capital gains (long term or short term), whichever is relevant.

Capital gains distributions must occur annually, and typically occur late during the calendar year. The capital gains distributions may be either long-term or short-term capital gains, depending on whether the fund held the security for a year or more. Mutual fund investors have no control over the size of these distributions and, as a result, the timing and amount of the taxes paid on their fund holdings is largely out of their control. In particular, withdrawals by some investors may necessitate sales in the fund, which in turn cause realized capital gains and a tax liability to accrue to investors who maintain their holding.

New investors in the fund may assume a tax liability even though they have no gains. That is, all shareholders as of the date of record receive a full year's worth of dividends and capital gains distributions, even if they have owned shares for only one day. This lack of control over capital gains taxes is regarded as a major limitation of mutual funds. In fact, this adverse tax consequence is one of the reasons suggested for a closed-end company's price selling below par value. Also, this adverse tax consequence is one of the reasons for the popularity of exchange-traded funds to be discussed later.

Of course, the investor must also pay ordinary income taxes on distributions of income. Finally, when the fund investors sell the fund, they will have long-term or short-term capital gains, taxes, depending on whether they held the fund for a year or less.

STRUCTURE OF A FUND

A mutual fund organization is structured as follows:

- A board of directors (also called the fund trustees), which represents the shareholders who are the owners of the mutual fund.
- The mutual fund, which is an entity based on the Investment Company Act of 1940.
- An investment advisor, which manages the fund's portfolios and is a registered investment advisor (RIA) according to the Investment Advisor's Act of 1940.
- A distributor or broker-dealer, which is registered under the Securities Act of 1934.
- Other service providers, both external to the fund (the independent public accountant, custodian, and transfer agent) and internal to the fund (marketing, legal, reporting, etc.).

The role of the board of directors is to represent the fund shareholders. The board is composed of both "interested" (or "inside") directors who are affiliated with the investment company (current or previous management) and "independent" (or "outside") directors who have no affiliation with the investment company. Currently, regulations require that more than half of the board be composed of independent directors and that the chairperson can be either an interested or independent director.

The mutual fund enters into a contract with an investment advisor to manage the fund's portfolios. The investment advisor can be an affiliate of a brokerage firm, an insurance company, a bank, an investment management firm, or an unrelated company.

The distributor, which may or may not be affiliated with the mutual fund or investment advisor, is a broker-dealer.

The role of the custodian is to hold the fund assets, segregating them from other accounts to protect the shareholders' interests. The transfer agent processes orders to buy and redeem fund shares, transfers the securities and cash, collects dividends and coupons, and makes distributions. The independent public accountant audits the fund's financial statements.

Financial Instruments and Concepts Introduced in this Chapter (in Order of Presentation)

Open-end funds	Closed-end funds
Mutual funds	Unit trust
Net asset value	Shareholder fee

Sale charge   Investment advisory fee
Load   Subadvisor
Commission   12b-1 fee
Load mutual funds   Distribution costs
Expense ratio   Trail commission
Front-end load   13F disclosures
No-load mutual funds   Target-date fund
Back-end load   Life-cycle fund
Contingent deferred sales charge   Target-risk fund
Level load   Morningstar
Share classes   Lipper
Breakpoint   Family of funds
Operating expense   Niche funds
Expense ratio   Regulated investment company
Management fee

CHAPTER 13

Exchange-Traded Funds

Two types of managed portfolios valued relative to their net asset value (NAV) (the value of the assets in the portfolio less its liabilities) were discussed in Chapter 12. They are mutual funds (MF) and closed-end funds (CEFs). The structure of both of these investment vehicles has some practical defects.

MFs as an investment vehicle are often criticized for two major reasons. First, the shares of MFs are priced at and can be transacted (purchased and sold) only at the end of the trading day ("at the close"). That is, transactions cannot be made at intraday prices. The second criticism relates to taxes and investors' control over taxes. As explained later in this chapter, withdrawals by some fund shareholders can cause taxable realized capital gains (or losses) for the other shareholders who have maintained their positions. CEFs, in contrast to MFs, trade throughout the trading day on stock exchanges. However, there is often a significant difference between the NAVs of the underlying portfolios and the price of a share of a CEF that is bought and sold.

In this chapter, a third type of managed funds, exchange-traded funds which overcome the practical defects of MFs and CEFs described above is the subject of this chapter.

REVIEW OF MUTUAL FUNDS AND CLOSED-END FUNDS

Overall, both MFs and CEFs are similar in that they are financial instruments whose share value depends on the portfolio's NAV. But unlike MFs, CEFs are transacted continuously throughout the day because they are traded on an exchange. For this reason, CEFs can be shorted, traded on margin, and limit orders and stop loss orders can be used. However, because the quantity of CEFs is fixed (that is why they are called "closed-end funds"), the price at which the CEF trades throughout the day can be greater than or less than the NAV of the underlying portfolio. That is, the price of the CEF is determined in a different market and semi-independently from the markets on which the prices of the securities which comprise the NAV are determined. Consequently, a share of a CEF can trade at either a premium, discount, or a value equal to the portfolio's NAV.

MF shares, on the other hand, are always exchanged at a price equal to the portfolio's NAV because the MF sponsor will always issue new fund shares or redeem outstanding fund shares at NAV on a daily basis. Thus, the quantity of fund shares outstanding can increase or decrease. Of course, this is why MFs are referred to as "open-end funds."[1] But because the MF sponsor cannot quickly and accurately value the portfolios of most MF shares continuously throughout the trading day, they can redeem the shares of MF only once a day, at the closing price for the day. Even then for many portfolios, the 4:00 P.M. price is available only with a significant delay after 4:00 P.M. In fact, for portfolios containing very illiquid securities, this closing price may not be available until the evening. Some portfolios, like that of the S&P 500 Index, can be accurately and quickly valued throughout the day, but they are a limited exception. The 4:00 P.M. EST closing time of the New York Stock Exchange is used as the time for the closing prices of all MFs. Thus, all mutual fund orders received by the fund sponsor during the previous 24 hours are settled at this single closing price.

BASICS OF EXCHANGE-TRADED FUNDS

Would it not be ideal if there were an investment vehicle that embodied a combination of the desirable aspects of both MFs and CEFs? The resolution to this dichotomy would require portfolios which could be traded throughout the day just like stocks but at a price equal to the continuously known NAV (i.e., the price is not at a premium or discount to the portfolio's NAV). Such a vehicle would be, in effect, a portfolio or fund which traded on an exchange, hence called an exchange-traded portfolio or as more commonly referred to as an *exchange-traded fund* (ETF).

At a very basic level, ETFs are easily understood. Most are based on indexes. ETFs are different, however, than conventional index mutual funds in the way they are bought and sold. An ETF is like a CEF and a stock in that it is traded throughout the day on an exchange. This means that investors can execute limit and stop-loss orders for ETFs, just as with individual equities and CEFs. ETFs can also be sold short, and bought on margin (i.e., with borrowed money). Options are also available on many ETFs. Since ETFs trade on exchanges, they have a ticker symbol like stocks, as shown in

---

[1]Economists would point out that CEFs have a fixed quantity and a variable price (relative to NAV) and MFs have a variable quantity and a fixed price (relative to NAV).

Exhibit 13.1. Finally, ETFs are open-end funds like MFs since their number of shares outstanding can change. Just how the number of shares outstanding can change is explained later.

To maintain the equality, or near equality, of the NAV of the securities in the portfolio and the share price of an ETF requires some intervention by a third party. To assure that the price of the ETF on the exchange would be very close to the continuously known NAV, an agent is commissioned to arbitrage between the price of the ETF and the value of the underlying portfolio and keep their values equal. The agent is commissioned to conduct an arbitrage as follows. Suppose that the price of the ETF is less than the portfolio's NAV of the portfolio. The agent would purchase the cheap ETF and sell the expensive underlying portfolio at NAV. This would be a profitable arbitrage for the agent since it buys the cheap ETF and sells the expensive portfolios. If, instead, the price of the ETF exceeds the portfolio's NAV, the agent would sell the expensive ETF and buy the cheap underlying portfolio, thereby generating a profitable arbitrage.

These actions by an agent to capture the potential arbitrage would tend to cause the price of the ETF to trade very close (or equal) to that of the NAV. The agent who keeps the price of the ETF equal to (or close to) the portfolio's underlying NAV is, thus called, an *arbitrageur*. This agent is retained by the sponsor of the ETF, as discussed below.

The requirement for making this arbitrage process feasible is that the composition and the NAV of the underlying portfolio be known accurately and the securities in the portfolio be continuously traded throughout the trading day. An obvious example of such a portfolio would be the S&P 500 Index portfolio. The 500 stocks in the Index are very liquid and their prices and the value of the Index are quoted continuously throughout the trading day.

Thus, it is no coincidence that the first ETF was based on the S&P 500 Index. This ETF began trading on the American Stock Exchange on January 1, 1993. The ETF sponsor was State Street Global Advisers (SSgA) as its sponsor. Because its and ticker symbol was SPY, it quickly became known as the "Spider." As shown in Exhibit 13.1, it remains the largest ETF. On the other hand, this process would not be feasible for the typical actively managed mutual fund because the composition of the portfolio and the prices of the securities comprising the portfolio are not known throughout the trading day. This is because mutual fund sponsors are required to make the composition of their funds public only four times a year and even then only 45 days after the date of portfolio report.

So ETFs are feasible for indexes on broad liquid security indexes but not on typical actively managed mutual funds. How far from the former to the latter can the ETF industry proceed?

EXHIBIT 13.1 Largest United States Exchange-Traded Funds (June 3, 2010)

Name	Ticker	Broad Category Group	Morningstar Category	Net Assets-Share Class Base Currency	Annual Report Net Expense Ratio	Inception Date	Avg. Daily Volume (3 mos.)
SPDR S&P 500	SPY	Equity	ETF Large Blend	70,563,692,820.00	0.09	01/93	241,190,220
SPDR Gold Shares	GLD	—	ETF Commodities Precious Metals	50,041,100,299.00	0.40	11/04	17,154,253
iShares MSCI Emerging Markets Index	EEM	Equity	ETF Diversified Emerging Mkts	33,142,075,630.00	0.72	04/03	86,312,163
iShares MSCI EAFE Index	EFA	Equity	ETF Foreign Large Blend	31,443,064,971.00	0.35	08/01	25,764,754
Vanguard Emerging Markets Stock ETF	VWO	Equity	ETF Diversified Emerging Mkts	23,579,652,685.00	0.27	03/05	16,489,153
iShares S&P 500 Index	IVV	Equity	ETF Large Blend	21,655,254,747.00	0.09	05/00	4,469,955
iShares Barclays TIPS Bond	TIP	Fixed Income	ETF Inflation-Protected Bond	20,048,459,991.00	0.20	12/03	1,085,360
PowerShares QQQ	QQQQ	Equity	ETF Large Growth	18,060,393,603.00	0.20	03/99	98,281,596
Vanguard Total Stock Market ETF	VTI	Equity	ETF Large Blend	13,467,164,126.00	0.07	05/01	2,098,514
iShares Russell 2000 Index	IWM	Equity	ETF Small Blend	13,401,119,990.00	0.20	05/00	76,252,267
iShares iBoxx $ Invest Grade Corp Bond	LQD	Fixed Income	ETF Long-Term Bond	12,389,598,931.00	0.15	07/02	838,692
iShares Barclays Aggregate Bond	AGG	Fixed Income	ETF Intermediate-Term Bond	11,458,651,807.00	0.20	09/03	790,721
iShares Russell 1000 Growth Index	IWF	Equity	ETF Large Growth	10,660,837,235.00	0.20	05/00	3,338,780
iShares MSCI Brazil Index	EWZ	Equity	ETF Latin America Stock	9,319,509,854.00	0.65	07/00	23,410,402
iShares Russell 1000 Value Index	IWD	Equity	ETF Large Value	8,911,127,697.00	0.20	05/00	2,330,028
SPDR S&P MidCap 400	MDY	Equity	ETF Mid-Cap Blend	8,748,695,459.00	0.25	04/95	3,961,866
iShares Barclays 1-3 Year Treasury Bond	SHY	Fixed Income	ETF Short Government	8,451,453,093.00	0.15	07/02	1,180,547
SPDR Dow Jones Industrial Average	DIA	Equity	ETF Large Value	8,206,955,373.00	0.17	01/98	12,652,807
iShares FTSE/Xinhua China 25 Index	FXI	Equity	ETF Pacific/Asia ex-Japan Stk	7,484,084,047.00	0.73	10/04	32,066,995
Vanguard Total Bond Market ETF	BND	Fixed Income	ETF Intermediate-Term Bond	7,463,456,000.00	0.12	04/07	684,622
Market Vectors Gold Miners ETF	GDX	Equity	ETF Equity Precious Metals	7,307,259,935.00	0.54	05/06	13,218,787
iShares S&P MidCap 400 Index	IJH	Equity	ETF Mid-Cap Blend	7,209,729,851.00	0.20	05/00	1,130,362
Financial Select Sector SPDR	XLF	Equity	ETF Financial	6,718,417,437.00	0.22	12/98	122,503,457
iShares Barclays 1-3 Year Credit Bond	CSJ	Fixed Income	ETF Short-Term Bond	6,237,377,405.00	0.20	01/07	489,584
Energy Select Sector SPDR	XLE	Equity	ETF Equity Energy	6,132,852,187.00	0.22	12/98	23,473,691

Source: Morningstar Direct, June 30, 2010.

Since, their advent in 1993, ETFs have grown rapidly. During early 2010, there were 865 ETFs with assets of $831 billion; 7,617 MFs with assets of $11,224 billion; and 623 CEFs with assets of $233 billion. Exhibit 13.1 provides data on the 25 largest ETFs. Note that they are all based on passive portfolios. Note also the breadth of asset classes covered by these ETFs. These 25 ETFs include primarily U.S stock indexes, international stock indexes, U.S bond indexes, and also some other asset classes.

The size of these ETFs, measured by assets (in billions of dollars), and their average daily trading volume, an important measure of liquidity as discussed below, are also provided in Exhibit 13.1. Their annual expense ratios are provided. These low annual expense ratios are an important feature of ETFs.

ETF MECHANICS: THE ETF CREATION/REDEMPTION PROCESS

When an investor invests in a mutual fund, they (or their advisor) purchase MF shares directly from the fund company at a price equal to the fund's NAV, which is calculated at the end of each trading day based on the market prices of the securities held by the fund. However, buying and selling ETFs works quite differently. Rather than dealing directly with the fund company, the investor buys ETF shares from another individual investor via a securities exchange at a price determined by supply and demand for the ETF, not the ETF's underlying NAV as is the case for MFs. The NAV of the underlying portfolio, however, is dependent on the forces in the underlying securities markets and is calculable.

For ETFs, individuals do not deal directly with the provider or sponsor of the ETF. This privilege is reserved for a few very large investors called *authorized participants* (AP) who are the agents or arbitrageurs referred to above. APs are the only investors who may create or redeem shares of an ETF with the ETF sponsor and then only in large, specified quantities called *creation/redemption units*. These unit sizes range from approximately 50,000 to 100,000 ETF shares. The AP may create new ETF shares by providing the sponsor with a specified basket of stocks (that is, a Creation Unit (CU)) and the sponsor responds by transferring the corresponding number of the ETF shares to the AP. Similarly, an AP can redeem ETF shares by providing the fund with a specific number of ETF shares (a Redemption Unit (RU)), and the fund will transfer to the AP the specific basket of stocks. These transfers are considered "in-kind transfers" of assets and have no net cost or tax impact. No cash changes hands. This tax treatment is the basis for one of the major advantages of ETFs relative to MFs. This "in-kind" creation and redemption process also tends to keep an ETF's market price close to its NAV. If discrepancies arise between a fund's market price and its NAV, this discrepancy opens up a profit-making opportunity for an AP. As explained earlier, the very act of exploiting this opportunity drives the market price of a share of the ETF and the portfolio's NAV closer together.

Consider more specifically the dynamics of the relationship between APs on one hand, and either the markets for the individual stock which determine the NAV of the underlying portfolio or the ETF on the other hand. If there is a large demand for an ETF, the price of the ETF will move above the underlying portfolio's NAV. The APs will then earn an arbitrage profit by buying the basket of stocks, which are cheap relative to the ETF, and then engaging in an in-kind transfer of the cheap stock for the ETF units. There are two outcomes of this transfer. First, there are fewer securities available on the market, making the NAV increase. In addition, there are more ETF units available on the market (i.e., the ETF market has grown), which tends to make the price of the ETF decrease. Both of these changes tend to make the gap between the price of the ETC and the portfolio's NAV disappear. The arbitrage by the AP has eliminated the gap and so the ETF "tracks" the underlying portfolio of securities. Second, the ETF market has grown. That is, there are more ETF units outstanding and the ETF fund has more securities in its portfolio. Thus, when there is more buying of ETFs, their size increases, and vice versa.

The change in the size of the portfolio as measured by the number of ETF units outstanding demonstrates that ETFs are an "open-end" investment structure. "Open-end" means the fund can create new shares or redeem existing shares to meet market demand. Thus, ETFs are like MFs and unlike CEFs in this regard.

The case discussed above where the price of the an ETF share exceeds the NAV, resulting in the creation of new ETF shares, is illustrated in Exhibit 13.2A. The opposite case where the price of an ETF share is less than the NAV, resulting in the redemption of ETF shares, is illustrated in Exhibit 13.2B. Both demonstrate the open-end nature of ETFs.

The role of the AP is critical in meeting investor expectations. Since most ETFs are based on passive indexes where value is represented by the NAV, ETF investors expect their return to be equal to that of the portfolio NAV. This will be the case if the ETF price tracks the NAV perfectly, which is the AP's function. However, if the ETF price does not track the NAV, the return to the ETF investor will be different than the return based on the NAV, either higher or lower, and not meet investor expectations. This difference between the return of the ETF and the return of the NAV is called "tracking error." A large tracking error is negative for ETFs. The tracking error for ETFs based on liquid indexes like the S&P 500 or the EAFE is very small. However, the tracking error of ETFs based on underlying portfolios composed of very large numbers of securities (such as the Wilshire 5000),

EXHIBIT 13.2 The ETF Creation/Redemption Process
A. Creation of New ETF Units

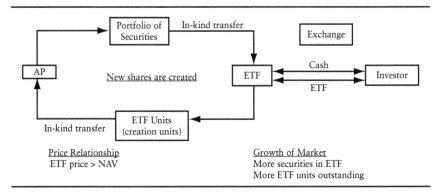

B. Redemption of Outstanding ETF Shares

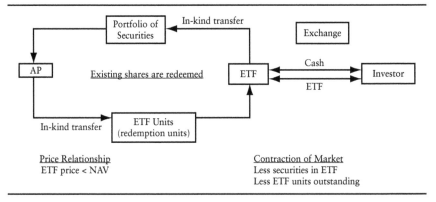

securities which are illiquid and costly to trade, or some bond funds can be significantly larger. Tracking error is highly correlated with the liquidity of the ETF and the underlying securities in the ETF's portfolio. The size of an ETF also relates to its liquidity, that is, bigger ETFs are more liquid. The best measure of liquidity of an ETF is its daily trading volume, which is shown in Exhibit 13.1. Data on the tracking error of ETFs are considered below.

The open end aspect of MFs is direct, that is investors invest funds directly in or withdraw funds directly from the MF. The open end aspect of ETFs is, however, indirect in that the investors buy the ETF in a closed end manner like CEFs and then the AP arbitrages between the ETF and the underlying portfolio, providing the indirect open end aspect of the ETF. For this process via the AP to work effectively, the underlying securities need to be known and they must be traded in a liquid market. If an AP does not know and cannot trade the underlying securities in the exact proportions as they are in the NAV of the portfolios, the share price of an ETF and its NAV can diverge significantly. That is, if the composition of the underlying portfolio is not known exactly throughout the trading day, the arbitrage will be imperfect and the tracking error could be significant.

Institutional investors are constantly monitoring the ETF market to take advantage of discounts and premiums when they develop. A high degree of transparency is required to make this process possible.

ETF SPONSORS

Like MFs, ETFs require a company to sponsor them. These companies are called *sponsors* or *providers* of ETFs. As of May 2010, the five major ETF sponsors according to *Morningstar ETF Investor* were as follows (assets in billions and market share shown in parentheses):

iShares BGI (BlackRock Global Investors) ($397; 47.2%)
State Street Global Advisors, SSgA ($200; 23.8%)
Vanguard ($109; 12.9%)
PowerShares ($50; 5.9%)
ProShares ($25; 3.0%)

The ETF sponsor is responsible for the following:

- Select the index.
- Develop the ETF.
- Register the ETF.
- Select, retain and monitor the APs.
- Provide seed capital to initiate the ETF.
- Advertise and market the ETF to develop a customer base.
- Engage in other related activities.

The APs are typically large, financial institutions. Each ETF must have at least one AP; some have more than one. The APs have contractual agreements with the sponsor. Retaining the APs is essential because if the arbitrage between the ETF price and portfolio's NAV of the portfolio is not effective, the ETF price will not track the portfolio's NAV and the ETF will not have the same return as the underlying portfolio. This tracking error depends on the liquidity of the underlying portfolio and the ability of the ETF's AP, that is, the quality of their arbitrage. The investor expects a return based on the underlying portfolio but due to tracking error the actual return based on the ETF price may be different than the return of the underlying portfolio.

The variation of the tracking errors of outstanding ETFs is illustrated by recent data. On average, ETFs missed their indexes by an average of 1.25% in 2009 relative to 0.52% in 2008.[2] During 2009, 54 ETFs showed tracking errors of more than 3% versus four ETFs in 2008. To a large extent, these increases were due to an increase in ETFs based on less liquid securities and an increase of more active ETFs. With respect to specific funds during 2009:

- The iShares MSCI Emerging Markets Index ETF (EEM) returned 71.8%, 6.7% below its index.
- The SPDR Barclays Capital High Yield Bond ETF (JNK) returned 50.5%, 13% below its index.
- The Vanguard Telecom securities ETF (VOX) returned 29.6%, 17% above its index.

On the other hand, some of the larger ETFs that follow broad market indexes based on liquid securities follow their indexes much more closely:

- The return of the SPDR (SPY), the largest ETF, was within 0.19% of its index.
- Large stock stock funds of Barclays Capital's iShares and Vanguard were even closer.

There are competing issues with respect to the tracking error resulting from managing an ETF. On one hand, for ETFs based on broad indexes, some ETFs managers hold every or most of the securities in the index, which increases transactions costs, particularly for indexes which contain small, illiquid securities, such as emerging market stocks or noninvestment grade bonds. On the other hand, some ETFs hold only a small subset of the securities in the index to reduce trading costs. But then the performance of the fund can deviate from that of the index due to the dispersion of the returns of the securities in the index and which securities are left out of the arbitrage portfolio. This choice creates a balancing act, particularly for indexes with small, less liquid securities. The new active ETFs exhibit greater tracking errors than the early passive ETFs.

Many ETFs employ an index which has been previously developed by another company. The index providers are paid a commission by the sponsor for the use of their index. For example, BGI uses indexes supplied by Dow Jones, FTSE, BlackRock Global Investors, Morgan Stanley Capital International (MSCI), Morningstar, Russell, Standard & Poor's and others.

---

[2]Ian Salisbury, "ETFs Were Wider Off the Mark in 2009," *Wall Street Journal*, February 19, 2010, p. C9.

MUTUAL FUNDS VS. ETFS: RELATIVE ADVANTAGES

MFs have been available for several decades and had $11,224 billion in assets as of early 2010. ETFs began in 1993 and have grown rapidly to $831 billion in assets during this short period. This growth, of course, suggests that ETFs have proved very attractive to investors. What are the relative advantages and disadvantages of ETFs?

As mentioned earlier, MFs are priced only once a day by being redeemed or offered by the mutual fund company at a price equal to the NAV. On the other hand, ETFs are traded on an exchange and so are priced continuously throughout the day. For MFs, the price of the fund is exactly the NAV of the underlying portfolio. For ETFs, there may be a discrepancy, although for actively traded funds, the discrepancy is very small. ETFs also, since they are traded on an exchange, can also be shorted, leveraged and limit and stop orders can be used. This is not the case for MFs.

Both passive MFs and ETFs have low fees, but ETF fees tend to be somewhat lower. All ETFs trade on an exchange and, thus, incur a commission, ranging from a discount to a full-service commission depending on the broker used. MFs may be either no-load funds or load funds. For frequent, small investments—for example, monthly payroll deductions—MFs would most likely be better since no-load MFs cost nothing to trade and ETFs incur a commission cost. This is the reason that ETFs have not been widely used in employee retirement plans, such as 401(k) plans. For infrequent, large investments, ETFs may be better because of their somewhat lower expenses.

With respect to taxes, MFs, as discussed above, may lead to capital gains taxes for investors who do not even liquidate their fund. This is because the fund has to sell securities in their portfolio to fund the sales of shares of other investors. The sale of these shares may cause capital gains—and a capital gains tax liability—to the remaining shareholders, even though their holdings represent an unrealized loss. Thus, these shareholders incur a tax obligation even though they have not made a transaction. Because of the unique structure of ETFs discussed above, ETFs can fund redemptions by in-kind transfers without selling their holdings which have no tax consequences. ETFs are more tax efficient than MFs in this regard.

MFs may have some other advantages. Although ETFs have been exclusively passive or indexes, MF families offer many types of active funds as well as passive funds. In addition, no-load MFs, both active and passive, permit transactions with no loads or commissions.

Exhibit 13.3 provides a comparison of ETFs and MFs. Exhibit 13.4 compares the taxation of MFs and ETFs.

EXHIBIT 13.3 Mutual Funds vs. Exchange-Traded Funds

	Mutual Funds	ETFs
Variety	Wide choice: Active and Passive	Mainly passive/indexes. Active ETFs are being developed
Taxation	Subject to taxation on dividend and realized capital gains. May have gains/losses when other investors redeem funds. May have gains/losses when stocks in index are changed.	Subject to taxation on dividend and realized capital gains. No gains/losses when other investors redeem funds. May have gains/losses when stocks in index are changed.
Valuation	NAV, based on actual price of underlying portfolio. Transactions via mutual fund company.	Creations and redemptions at NAV. Transactions via an exchange. Market price may be valued somewhat above or below NAV, but the deviation is typically small due to arbitrage.
Pricing	End-of-day.	Continuous.
Transaction cost (initial)	None for no-load funds; Sales charge for load funds.	Commission or brokerage charge.
Management fee (annual)	Depends on fund: Low for index funds; higher for active funds.	Depends on ETF: Low and, in some cases, even lower than for index mutual funds. Higher for more active, less liquid underlying portfolios.

EXHIBIT 13.4 Taxes: Mutual Funds vs. Exchange-Traded Funds

	Mutual Funds	ETFs
Holding/Maintaining	—	—
Dividends, income and realized capital gains	Fully taxable.	Fully taxable.
Withdrawal by other investors	May necessitate portfolio sales and realized capital gains for holder.	Does not cause portfolio sales and, thus, no realized capital for holder.
Disposition	—	—
Withdrawal of investment	Capital gains tax on difference between sales and purchase price.	Capital gains tax on difference between sales and purchase price.

USES OF ETFs

The uses of ETFs depend on their characteristics:

- They can be executed on an intraday basis on an exchange.
- They are inexpensive:
  - Low commissions are available for both individuals and institutions.
  - Annual expense ratios are low.
- They are based on passive indexes, including:
  - Aggregate asset classes, including U.S. and international equities and bonds.
  - Sub assets classes based on size (market cap), style (value and growth) and sectors.
  - Niche areas such as real estate, water and indexes with various weighting methodologies.

As a result, ETFs can be used for:

- Long-term portfolio management or short-term trading.
- Long/short arbitrage strategies since ETFs can be shorted.
- Short-term asset reallocation by using long/short transactions.
- Many niche asset types.

All of these strategies can be effectively conducted via ETFs because they are inexpensive and can be executed quickly. One disadvantage of ETFs is that heretofore they have been mostly passive. Therefore, they can be used for beta strategies only, not alpha-generating strategies. The reason they are inexpensive is that they are based on passive indexes. If, and when, active ETFs become successful, they will be more expensive than the existing passive ETFs and are likely to have higher tracking errors.

THE NEW GENERATION OF MUTUAL FUNDS

The original ETFs were based on well-known stock and bond indexes, both U.S and international. These included the S&P 500, Dow Jones Industrial Average, Russell 2000, Barclays Aggregate Bond Index, MSCI EAFE, and MSCI Emerging Markets. These were followed by ETFs based on narrower sector indexes covering financial, health care, industrial, natural resources, precious metals, technology, utilities, real estate, and others. These were, in turn, followed by ETFs based on new and often narrower indexes that were specifically designed for ETFs.

During this development period, it was thought that the "holy grail" of ETFs would be ETFs based on actively managed funds. Considerable research was devoted to this effort during the mid-to-late 2000s. Investors wanted not only the "pure beta" returns offered by passive ETFs, but "alpha" returns as well.

ETFs require SEC approval. The fundamental issue in the design of an active ETF is the requirement for transparency by the SEC and by the AP who needs the portfolio composition to conduct their arbitrage versus the preference for privacy by the fund managers. The SEC requires that ETFs provide investors with the transparency equivalent to stocks. In addition, the arbitrageurs must know the composition of its portfolios to arbitrage the ETF against it. For passive ETFs, the composition of the portfolio is known and transparent throughout the trading day. But for active ETFs, the portfolio managers do not want to disclose their portfolios because other traders could step in front of their trades, a practice referred to as "front running," or investors could take a "free ride" on their research. Of course, the less well known the composition of the underlying portfolio, the less effective the arbitrage can be and the greater the tracking error will be. The main obstacle to active ETFs has been finding an acceptable compromise between transparency and confidentiality.

On March 25, 2008, the first active ETF was launched at the American Stock Exchange. This ETF was the Bear Stearns Current Yield ETF (ticker symbol: YYY). According to the fund's statement:

> The fund differs from an index fund since it is actively managed by its portfolio manager who has the discretion to choose securities for the fund's portfolio consistent with its investment objective.

The fund employed a disciplined investment strategy, adding value through sector allocation, security selection, yield-curve positioning, and duration management. This is an unusual description for an ETF. This fund was short-lived, partly because of the demise of Bear Stearns. Other active funds have been developed and are trading. Some have very high expense ratios. As of yet, however, no active ETFs have proved to be the holy grail.

It remains to be seen how successful active ETFs will be in attracting investors and in providing returns. It is certain, however, that they will be more expensive and will track indexes less well, which will make them more like active mutual funds and other alpha generators.

Financial Instruments and Concepts Introduced in this Chapter (in Order of Presentation)

Exchange-traded funds
Arbitrageur
Authorized participants

Creation/Redemption units
Sponsors
Providers

CHAPTER 14

Investing in Real Estate

In this chapter we explore real estate as an investment in a diversified portfolio. In this regard, the chapter focus is more on the economics of real estate and less on the difficulties in measuring its value. We also explore other investment strategies beyond *real estate investment trusts* (REITs) that we described in Chapter 15 and core real estate portfolios. Specifically, we review core, value-added, and opportunistic real estate investing, comparing and contrasting their styles and return expectations.

THE BENEFITS OF REAL ESTATE INVESTING

Real estate is a valuable part of any well-diversified portfolio. There are five goals for adding real estate to an investment portfolio:[1]

1. To achieve absolute returns above the risk-free rate.
2. To provide a hedge against inflation.
3. As a portfolio diversification tool that provides exposure to a different type of systematic risk and return than stocks and bonds.
4. To constitute an investment portfolio that resembles the global investment opportunity set.
5. To deliver strong cash flows to the portfolio through lease and rental payments.

When assessing exposure to real estate, the extent to which these five goals are accomplished should be kept in mind.

---

[1]See Susan Hudson-Wilson, Jacques N. Gordon, Frank J. Fabozzi, Mark J.P. Anson, and S. Michael Giliberto, "Why Real Estate? And ... How? Where? And When?" *Journal of Portfolio Management* 32, Special Issue on Real Estate (2005): 12–22.

REAL ESTATE PERFORMANCE

Exhibit 14.1 compares the returns for real estate to the returns for other asset classes. The objective of the exhibit is simply to see how real estate stacks up compared to other asset classes on a risk-adjusted basis. The real estate indexes used to represent the real estate sector are the *National Council of Real Estate Investment Fiduciaries* (NCREIF) Property Index (NPI) and four of its components, and the *NAREIT Index* that represents returns on REITs that we describe in Chapter 15. The indexes for the other asset classes are explained in the exhibit.

First, looking at risk-adjusted returns as measured by the Sharpe ratio, we can see that the NPI's performance compares very well to stocks, bonds, and credit. In fact, the highest Sharpe ratios are scored by the NCREIF Apartment index at 0.41, investment-grade bonds at 0.40, and the NCREIF Retail index at 0.41. These Sharpe ratios are diminished by the volatility that was experienced in the financial markets and real estate markets during 2008–2009.

Another observation that is apparent from Exhibit 14.1 is the nature of lagged returns associated with real estate. Real estate is one of the least liquid asset classes. Simply, it takes time to sell an office building, retail shopping center, or apartment complex. As a result, valuations of real estate are based on appraisals, which in turn are based on prior sales. As a consequence, it takes time for real estate values to reflect what is happening in the broader financial markets. Notice that all of the NCREIF NPI and all of its sub-categories recorded negative returns in 2009 while the publicly traded markets (including REITs) all gathered positive returns.

Also, we compare the NPI, smoothed and unsmoothed, to REIT returns. We use the NAREIT index as well as the mutual fund of actively managed returns. The NAREIT index provides an average annual total return of 12% but it has a much larger standard deviation, reflective of the fact that REITs are publicly traded and therefore pick up a significant amount of systematic risk from the stock market. This leads to a higher level of volatility than for direct real estate investing, and a lower Sharpe ratio. In fact, the NAREIT index has just about the same level of volatility as small-cap stocks (in fact, a little higher), not surprising since the market cap of most REITs is in the $500 million to $4 billion range, which is the market-capitalization range for small companies and the smaller segment of mid-cap companies.

Interestingly, when we turn to the actively managed REIT mutual fund, we find the lowest Sharpe ratio of all asset classes in Exhibit 14.1. The actively managed REIT product produces one of the lowest average returns (6.06%) with one of the largest measures of volatility (20.66%). The result is a lower Sharpe ratio. The conclusion is that while REITs provide a valuable

EXHIBIT 14.1 Returns to Real Estate and Other Asset Classes

	NCREIF Composite	NCREIF Unsmoothed	NCREIF Apts.	NCREIF Offices	NCREIF Retail	NCREIF Industrial	NAREIT	FRESX	Ru1000	Ru2000	Inv. Grade	High Yield	10-Year T-Bond	1-Year T-Bill	Inflation
1990	2.29%	5.73%	5.79%	−1.06%	5.96%	1.96%	−15.35%	−13.87%	−7.50%	−21.45%	9.09%	−7.04%	6.56%	4.25%	5.70%
1991	−5.59%	−16.78%	−1.36%	−11.44%	−1.85%	−3.86%	35.70%	32.45%	28.83%	43.68%	15.98%	34.22%	6.86%	4.37%	−0.10%
1992	−4.26%	−1.95%	1.72%	−8.05%	−2.25%	−4.47%	14.59%	15.17%	5.89%	16.36%	7.58%	18.35%	6.80%	3.56%	1.60%
1993	1.38%	10.87%	8.72%	−3.95%	4.84%	−0.77%	19.65%	7.70%	7.33%	17.00%	9.92%	17.37%	5.89%	3.59%	0.20%
1994	6.38%	13.62%	12.07%	3.92%	6.01%	7.63%	3.17%	−2.73%	−2.42%	−3.18%	−2.85%	−0.82%	7.95%	6.92%	1.70%
1995	7.53%	9.03%	11.66%	7.18%	3.98%	12.30%	15.27%	5.15%	34.44%	26.21%	18.53%	19.23%	5.61%	5.22%	2.30%
1996	10.30%	13.79%	11.54%	13.56%	4.85%	13.57%	35.27%	29.90%	19.72%	14.76%	3.62%	10.85%	6.41%	5.62%	2.80%
1997	13.90%	18.20%	12.90%	17.87%	8.53%	15.94%	20.26%	13.42%	30.49%	20.52%	9.64%	13.10%	5.74%	5.62%	−1.20%
1998	16.25%	18.86%	14.12%	19.62%	12.91%	15.86%	−17.50%	−24.01%	25.12%	−3.45%	8.71%	4.43%	4.63%	4.58%	0.00%
1999	11.36%	6.15%	11.73%	12.22%	9.55%	11.65%	−4.62%	−5.41%	19.46%	19.62%	−0.83%	0.84%	6.42%	6.14%	2.90%
2000	12.25%	13.29%	12.99%	14.11%	7.76%	14.02%	26.37%	25.85%	−8.84%	−4.20%	11.59%	−4.41%	5.06%	5.47%	3.60%
2001	7.28%	1.57%	9.37%	6.20%	6.74%	9.30%	13.93%	0.11%	−13.59%	1.03%	8.52%	6.92%	5.02%	2.03%	−1.60%
2002	6.75%	6.07%	8.76%	2.78%	13.74%	6.70%	3.82%	−0.70%	−22.94%	−21.58%	10.09%	−0.58%	3.85%	1.20%	1.20%
2003	9.00%	11.88%	8.90%	5.67%	17.15%	8.23%	37.13%	28.93%	27.54%	45.37%	4.20%	29.36%	4.22%	1.21%	4.00%
2004	14.49%	21.21%	13.04%	12.02%	22.95%	12.07%	31.58%	24.59%	9.49%	17.00%	4.48%	10.51%	4.26%	2.79%	4.20%
2005	20.06%	26.20%	21.15%	19.46%	19.98%	20.31%	12.16%	5.48%	4.37%	3.32%	2.57%	2.07%	4.40%	4.42%	5.40%
2006	16.60%	13.14%	14.63%	19.16%	13.35%	16.96%	35.06%	17.68%	13.34%	17.00%	4.33%	11.71%	4.72%	4.00%	1.10%
2007	15.85%	15.05%	11.36%	20.51%	13.51%	14.95%	−15.69%	−29.15%	3.86%	−2.75%	7.22%	1.91%	4.14%	3.29%	6.20%
2008	−14.70%	−16.10%	−16.40%	−16.30%	−9.50%	−14.10%	−37.50%	−38.21%	−37.60%	−33.80%	−12.40%	−24.68%	22.81%	2.30%	0.10%
2009	−15.70%	−14.30%	−17.50%	−19.10%	−10.90%	−17.90%	27.45%	28.86%	26.40%	27.20%	10.46%	58.21%	−12.90%	0.45%	2.70%
Average	6.57%	7.78%	7.76%	5.72%	7.37%	7.02%	12.04%	6.06%	9.70%	8.93%	6.52%	10.08%	5.42%	3.85%	2.14%
Volatility	10.04%	12.06%	9.67%	12.31%	8.80%	10.45%	21.15%	20.66%	16.54%	20.63%	6.74%	17.31%	5.90%	1.77%	2.25%
Sharpe Ratio	0.28	0.33	0.41	0.16	0.41	0.31	0.39	0.11	0.36	0.25	0.40	0.36	0.27		

EXHIBIT 14.1 (Continued)

The following asset classes are included:

- Real estate: the NCREIF Property Index both smoothed and unsmoothed as well as the four (unsmoothed) indexes of the NPI.
- REITs as represented by the NAREIT index and a mutual fund that actively buys and sells REITs to add value (FRESX).
- Large-cap stocks represented by the Russell 1000 stock index.
- Small-cap stocks represented by the Russell 2000 stock index.
- Investment-grade bonds.
- High-yield bonds.
- Credit risk–free bonds represented by 10-year U.S. Treasury bonds.
- Cash equivalent, represented by one-year U.S. Treasury bills (used as the risk-free rate for our Sharpe ratio calculations).
- Inflation, not as an asset class but for historical perspective on real returns.

Sources: NCREIF, www.ncreif.com; NAREIT, www.reit.com; and Bloomberg Finance, L.P.

---

way to access the real estate market, this actively managed REIT fund did not add value. Further, it is worth reminding the reader that each REIT is, in fact, an actively managed pool of real estate assets. Therefore, an actively managed REIT fund is simply an overlay of active management on top of active real estate management. The results do not bear out that a second layer of active management added value. Finally, on an inflation-adjusted basis, real estate offers a significant return premium over inflation, leading to excellent real returns. The real returns (in excess of the inflation rate) for the NPI both smoothed and unsmoothed are 4.43% and 5.64%, respectively. In addition, the NAREIT index provided a real return of 9.90%. Clearly, over this time period, real estate provided an excellent premium over the inflation rate. A better demonstration of the inflation hedging properties is provided later in this chapter.

REAL ESTATE RISK PROFILE

Exhibit 14.2 reports statistics on the quarterly return distribution from 1990 through June 2009 for the NPI index (smoothed and unsmoothed), four components of that index (apartments, offices, retail, and industrial), and REITS. For statistics for the NPI index and its components, both the smoothed and unsmoothed return series are shown.

Based on a risk-adjusted basis for the NPI smoothed index, the returns to real estate are very favorable risk and return profile. However, the negative skew indicates a bias to the downside; that is, that there are more large negative returns than large positive returns. The large value of kurtosis of

EXHIBIT 14.2   Quarterly Return Distributions: 1990 through June 2009

Index	Mean (%)	Standard Deviation (%)	Skew	Kurtosis	Sharpe Ratio
NPI Smoothed	2.06%	2.19%	−2.22	7.59	0.51
NPI Unsmoothed	2.03%	3.67%	−2.56	13.5	0.29
NPI Apartments	2.29%	3.30%	−2.43	14.74	0.41
NPI Offices	1.78%	4.60%	−1.71	7.55	0.18
NPI Retail	2.28%	3.55%	−0.53	4.43	0.38
NPI Industrial	2.13%	3.29%	−2.16	12.89	0.36
REITs	3.03%	8.94%	−1.10	5.25	0.23

Sources: NPI and its sectors obtained from NCREIF, www.ncreif.com; REITs obtained from Bloomberg Finance L.P.

7.59 indicates fatter tails than a normal distribution or a greater exposure to outlier events. In general, we would like to see a positive skew with fat tails—indicating a bias toward large positive outlier returns. For the NPI smoothed index, we see a return pattern that demonstrates a large negative downside tail. This means that there can be significant losses in real estate during short periods of time that can have a significantly negative impact on an investment portfolio.

Looking at the NPI unsmoothed index, we observe a higher expected return than the smoothed index but also a much larger volatility. This leads to a much lower Sharpe ratio. Simply, once we unsmooth the NPI, the risk-adjusted returns decline, primarily as a result of higher volatility that is otherwise masked by the lagged effect of appraisal values in the NPI. We also see a negative skew similar to the smoothed index, but a much larger value for kurtosis. The negative skew combined with the large value of kurtosis indicates a large downside tail associated with the unsmoothed NPI. Consequently, once we unsmooth the NPI data, we find that the returns to real estate exhibit much more risk than otherwise thought as measured by a larger value of volatility and by a larger downside tail risk.

For the individual sectors of the NPI, we find similar statistics. Quarterly returns are consistently positive in the 2% range. All Sharpe ratios are positive. Each of the sectors also has a negative skew and a large value of kurtosis, indicating risk to the downside, or "fat tail" risk. These results are consistent with the broader NPI. We do note that the negative skew and large values of kurtosis are influenced by the brutal year for real estate of 2008 and which also spilled over to the values for real estate in 2009.

Overall, if we picked sectors based solely on the statistics reported in Exhibit 14.2, the Apartments sector would be our first choice because it had the best risk versus return trade-off with a positive bias to upside returns, while the Offices sector had the lowest risk versus return trade-off with the greatest exposure to downside fat tails. However, it should be noted that Apartments had the largest negative value of skew and the largest value of kurtosis, indicating the greatest amount of downside risk.

As for REITs, valuations are observed without the appraisal lag that infects the NPI. Consequently, there is no need to unsmooth the data. The distribution of returns for REITs demonstrates the smallest (but still negative) skew reported in Exhibit 14.2 (in absolute value) but still exhibits a reasonably large value of kurtosis of 4.7. REITs are also exposed to downside fat tails; again, these statistics are influenced by the very difficult year of 2008 as well as the strong positive year of 2009, which contributed to large outlier returns that, in turn, contributed to the skew and kurtosis of the return distribution. Average returns are much higher for REITs but so is volatility as the lack of smoothing reveals the riskiness of the real estate market. The Sharpe ratio of 0.23 is lower compared to the NPI and its individual sectors, with the exception of the Office sector. Much of the lower Sharpe ratio can be explained by the much higher quarterly volatility for REITs of 8.94% compared to the appraisal-based NPI and its sectors.

REAL ESTATE AS PART OF A DIVERSIFIED PORTFOLIO

When we think about real estate as part of a diversified portfolio, the first thing we need to consider is the correlation of returns for real estate with other asset classes. The lower the correlation coefficient, the greater the diversification benefits of combining real estate with stocks, bonds, and other asset classes.

Exhibit 14.3 displays the correlation coefficients for the NPI, its sectors, and REITs with other asset classes. We include both the smoothed and unsmoothed NPI numbers and use the unsmoothed numbers primarily for our discussion. First, we can see that the NPI is highly correlated with its sector components. The correlation coefficients of the NPI with its four sectors are all 0.85 or greater. This is what we would expect given that these four sectors should be driven by common factors that drive the returns of all four sectors of real estate that comprise the composite NPI.

Next we compare the unsmoothed NPI to the NAREIT index. Somewhat surprisingly, we find a very low correlation of 0.12. However, the answer lies with respect to how these two indexes track with small-cap stocks. REITs are publicly traded on an exchange, just like stocks. Furthermore, most REITs are in the market capitalization range described as small-

EXHIBIT 14.3 Correlation Coefficients for the NPI, NPI Sectors, REITs with Other Asset Classes

	NCREIF Composite	NCREIF Unsmoothed	NCREIF Apts.	NCREIF Offices	NCREIF Retail	NCREIF Industrial	NAREIT	FRESX	RU1000	RU2000	Inv. Grade	High Yield	10-Year T-Bond	1-Year T-Bill	Inflation
NCREIF Composite	1.00														
NCREIF Unsmoothed	0.92	1.00													
NCREIF Apartments	0.95	0.90	1.00												
NCREIF Offices	0.98	0.88	0.89	1.00											
NCREIF Retail	0.89	0.85	0.84	0.81	1.00										
NCREIF Industrial	0.98	0.88	0.95	0.98	0.83	1.00									
NAREIT	0.13	0.12	0.19	0.07	0.16	0.14	1.00								
FRSEX	-0.01	0.00	0.06	-0.07	0.04	0.01	0.97	1.00							
RU1000	0.21	0.18	0.20	0.21	0.10	0.22	0.53	0.50	1.00						
RU2000	0.03	-0.03	0.07	-0.01	0.04	0.03	0.77	0.74	0.85	1.00					
Investment grade	0.09	0.02	0.17	0.04	0.02	0.12	0.44	0.42	0.49	0.42	1.00				
High yield	-0.29	-0.27	-0.27	-0.31	-0.23	-0.30	0.68	0.69	0.71	0.82	0.54	1.00			
10-Year T-bond	-0.04	-0.07	0.00	-0.02	-0.06	0.01	-0.48	-0.50	-0.50	-0.44	-0.55	-0.76	1.00		
1-Year T-bill	0.41	0.40	0.52	0.45	0.11	0.49	-0.04	-0.04	0.24	0.02	-0.03	-0.32	0.29	1.00	
Inflation	0.27	0.34	0.21	0.25	0.38	0.22	-0.05	0.00	0.01	-0.06	-0.05	-0.08	-0.22	0.01	1.00

Sources: NCREIF, www.ncreif.com; NAREIT, www.reit.com; and Bloomberg Finance, L.P.

cap stocks. In fact, most REITs are contained in the Russell 2000, an index of 2,000 small-cap stocks traded in the United States. Therefore, it is not surprising to see that the NAREIT index, as a market-traded index, has a large positive correlation with the Russell 2000 of 0.77. Conversely, the NPI has almost a zero correlation with small-cap stocks of –0.03. This negative correlation may reflect the diversification benefits of direct investing in unique real estate properties compared to the stock market, or it may be caused by the use of appraisals.

Also, when we compare the unsmoothed NPI or smoothed NPI to large-cap stocks, represented by the Russell 1000, we find very low correlations of 0.18 and 0.21, respectively. We find a very low correlation between the Russell 2000 and either the smoothed or unsmoothed NPI, demonstrating that direct real estate investing has very good diversification properties with small-cap stocks in addition to large-cap stocks. We also see that direct real estate investing is an excellent diversifier with respect to investment-grade, high-yield, and U.S. Treasury bonds. The correlation coefficients of the composite NCREIF unsmoothed index with these three bond classes are very consistent at 0.02, –0.27, and –0.07, respectively. Combined with the low or negative correlation coefficients observed between real estate and stocks, we would expect real estate to be an excellent diversifying asset class for a traditional stock and bond portfolio.

Note that the unsmoothed NPI has a positive correlation with the inflation rate. This strongly suggests that real estate may be a good inflation hedge. The reason is that real estate properties can adjust their rental and lease rates to take into account higher inflationary costs. There is inevitably some lag in the ability to increase lease/rental rates with inflation, which is a reason why the NPI is not perfectly correlated with the inflation rate. We can also see that each of the four NPI sectors is also positively correlated with the inflation rate, with the Retail sector having the best inflation hedging properties. This simply demonstrates the ability of shopping centers and strip malls to adjust their lease rates more quickly in tune with higher inflation.

Turning to the other asset classes—small-cap stocks, investment-grade bonds, high-yield bonds, U.S. Treasury bonds, and even REITs—we can see that these asset classes have uniformly negative correlation coefficient switch inflation (large-cap stocks have a 0.01 correlation with the inflation rate). Simply, these asset classes form poor inflation hedges. For investment-grade bonds, high-yield bonds, and U.S. Treasury bonds, this is not surprising because higher inflation rates mean higher interest rates and lower bond prices. In sum, it is clear that direct real estate investing provides excellent diversification properties for a variety of asset classes. In addition, direct real estate investing also provides an excellent hedge against inflation.

CORE, VALUE-ADDED, AND OPPORTUNISTIC REAL ESTATE

We conclude this chapter on real estate investing with a description of core, value-added, and opportunistic real estate. Office, apartment, retail, and industrial properties are what most investors consider to be the core of any real estate portfolio. As large institutional investors have become more sophisticated they have expanded beyond the four sectors that make up the NPI. These opportunities, ranging from hotels to nursing homes, can provide a return boost beyond what core properties can offer.

Here we explore other styles of real estate investing. Investment styles provide investors with a convenient way to categorize an investment such that return and risk expectations can be established. While "style boxes" have been used for many years in equity and fixed income investing, real estate investment styles are relatively new. There are three main reasons for introducing styles into real estate portfolio analysis:

1. *Performance measurement.* Investors continually look for tools that can provide them with a better understanding of an investment sector's objectives. This includes identifying peer groups, return objectives, range of risk taking, return attribution, and peer performance.

2. *Monitoring style drift.* It is a fact of investment life that portfolio managers occasionally drift from their stated risk, return, or other objectives. Classifying different styles of real estate investments allows an investor to measure the overlap among investment products and to gain a better understanding of the risk level at any given point of time. Tracking style drift is another factor in monitoring and evaluating performance. The better the categorization of real estate, the better an investor can track the resulting risk and return of the portfolio relative to its stated style.

3. *Style diversification.* The ability to determine the risk and return profile of a manager relative to its style will allow for a better diversification of the portfolio since an investor can construct a portfolio that has a more robust risk and return profile if there is a better understanding of a real estate manager's style location.

Style boxes are essentially locators. Style investing is all about identifying the space in which the investment manager operates. Styles identify where and how an investment manager invests. Consequently, they identify dimensions in addition to simply risk and return.

The NCREIF Style Boxes

In 2003, the NCREIF took it upon itself to define style boxes within the real estate investment industry.[2] Specifically, NCREIF identified three styles that apply at the underlying asset level for direct real estate investing: core, value-added, and opportunistic. These styles may be thought of as a way to classify the individual real estate investment. In addition, NCREIF identified eight attributes to distinguish the three types of real estate asset styles:

1. Property type
2. Life cycle
3. Occupancy
4. Rollover concentration
5. Near-term rollover
6. Leverage
7. Market recognition
8. Investment structure/control

Exhibit 14.4 defines the three NCREIF real estate styles along with discussing the attributes that help to identify the type of property. The following discussion provides a summary to help distinguish core properties from value-added and opportunistic properties.

Core

Core properties are the most liquid, most developed, least leveraged, and most recognizable properties in a real estate portfolio. These properties have the greatest amount of liquidity but still are not sold quickly relative to traditional investments. Core properties tend to be held for a long period of time to take full advantage of the lease and rental cash flows that they provide. The majority of their returns come from the cash flows instead of value appreciation, and very little leverage is applied.

Value-Added

Value-added properties begin to get off the beaten path. This can include hotels, resorts, assisted care living, low-income housing, outlet malls, hospitals, and the like. These properties tend to require a subspecialty within the real estate market to manage well and can involve repositioning, renovation, and redevelopment of existing properties. Relative to core properties,

---

[2]See John Baczewski, Kathleen Hands, and Charles R. Lathem, "Real Estate Investment Styles: Trends from the Catwalk," NCREIF white paper, October 2, 2003.

EXHIBIT 14.4 NCREIF Style Boxes for Real Estate Assets

Core Definition	Value-Added Definition	Opportunistic Definition
Real estate assets that achieve a relatively high percentage of their return from income and are expected to have low volatility.	Real estate assets that exhibit one or more of the following attributes: (1) achieve a significant portion of their return from appreciation in value, (2) exhibit moderate volatility, and/or (3) are not considered to be core type properties.	A real estate asset that is expected to derive most of its return from property appreciation and that may exhibit significant volatility in returns. This may be due to a variety of characteristics such as exposure to development risk, significant leasing risk, or high leverage, but may also result from a combination of more moderate risk factors that in total create a more volatile risk profile.

Core Attributes	Value-Added Attributes	Opportunistic Attributes
1. The major property types only: Offices, Apartments, Retail, Industrial.	Major property types plus specialty retail, hospitality, senior/assisted care housing, storage, and low-income housing.	Nontraditional property types, including speculative development for sale or rent and undeveloped land.
2. Life cycle: fully operating.	Life cycle: operating and leasing.	Life cycle: development and newly constructed.
3. High occupancy.	Moderately to well leased and/or substantially preleased development.	Low economic occupancy.
4. Low rollover concentration; this means that core assets tend to be held for a long period of time—they form the central component of the real estate portfolio, which is geared toward generating income and not sales appreciation.	Moderate rollover concentration—a higher percentage of the assets are held for a short- to intermediate-term sale and rollover into new assets.	High rollover concentration risk—most of these assets are held for appreciation and resale.
5. Low total near-term rollover.	Moderate total near-term rollover.	High total near-term rollover.
6. Low leverage.	Moderate leverage.	High leverage.
7. Well-recognized institutional properties and locations.	Institutional and emerging real estate markets.	Secondary and tertiary markets and international real estate.
8. Investment structures with significant or direct control.	Investment structures with moderate control but with security or a preferred liquidation position.	Investment structures with minimal control; usually in a limited partnership vehicle and with unsecured positions.

these properties tend to produce less income and rely more on property appreciation to generate the total return. These properties can also include new properties that might otherwise be core properties except that they are not fully leased, such as a new apartment complex or a new shopping center. A value-added property could also be an existing property that needs a new strategy like a facelift, new tenants, or a new marketing campaign. These properties tend to use more leverage and generate a total return from both capital appreciation and income.

For example, the Pennsylvania Public School Employees' Retirement System (PSERS) identifies value-added real estate as:

Value-added real estate investing typically focuses on both income and growth appreciation potential, where opportunities created by dislocation and inefficiencies between and within segments of the real estate capital markets are capitalized upon to enhance returns. Investments can include high-yield equity and debt investments and undervalued or impaired properties in need of repositioning, redevelopment, or leasing. Modest leverage is generally applied in value added portfolios to facilitate the execution of a variety of value creation strategies.[3]

Opportunistic

Opportunistic real estate moves away from a core/income approach to a capital appreciation approach. Often, opportunistic real estate is accessed through real estate opportunity funds, sometimes called *private equity real estate* (PERE). PERE funds invest in real estate with a high risk and return profile, particularly those properties that require extensive development or are turnaround opportunities.[4]

Consistent with our description of opportunistic real estate in Exhibit 14.4, the majority of the return from these properties comes from value appreciation over a three- to five-year period of time. Rollover risk is high because total return is based on value appreciation. Compare this to core properties where sales of the underlying real estate are infrequent and core properties are held for a long period of time to harness their income-producing attributes. Due to their high focus on value appreciation, opportunistic real estate managers tend to resemble traders and value enhancers compared

---

[3]See Pennsylvania Public School Employees' Retirement System, Investment Policy Statement, Objectives and Guidelines for Closed End Opportunistic and Value Added Real Estate Investments, Addendum U, June 22, 2007.

[4]See Thea C. Hahn, David Geltner, and Nori Gerardo-Lietz, "Real Estate Opportunity Funds," *Journal of Portfolio Management* 31, no. 5 (2005): 143–153.

to core managers, who are operators of properties. Therefore, opportunistic managers tend to pursue some event that will result in the real estate being quickly and dramatically revalued. This can come from development of raw property, redevelopment of property that is in disrepair, or the purchase of property in an area that is undergoing significant urban renewal.

Using an example from PSERS again, its investment policy identifies opportunistic real estate as follows:

> Opportunistic real estate investing is the financing, acquisition, or investment in real estate assets, real estate companies, portfolios of real estate assets, private and public REITs that do not have access to traditional public equity or debt financing. Opportunistic real estate investing consists of strategies that seek to exploit market inefficiencies with an emphasis on total return. Opportunistic investments require specialized expertise and the flexibility to respond quickly to market imbalances or changing market conditions. Investments may include non-traditional property types and/or assets that involve development, redevelopment, or leasing risks. Leverage is typically incorporated into this strategy to further enhance total returns.

Last, opportunistic real estate investing is often the way institutional investors expand their property holdings outside their domestic country. Often, institutional investors access international property opportunities through a PERE limited partnership. For example, over the past five years, public companies in Germany have been selling their investment holdings of apartment housing to private investors, as these real estate properties represent investments outside the core expertise of the operating companies. The properties were held to house the workers of the operating companies. The workers still reside there but the properties are now in the hands of professional property managers. In addition to defining style boxes for individual real estate assets, NCREIF also identified style boxes at the portfolio level. In other words, NCREIF defined the attributes of portfolios that could be described as core, value-added, or opportunistic. Thus, while each real estate property is unique, the combination of the unique attributes of each property form a portfolio that can resemble a core, value-added, or opportunistic style. Exhibit 14.5 provides these real estate style definitions at the portfolio level.

Return Expectations

The unique nature of each real estate property and the general lack of liquidity make tracking real estate returns more difficult than tracking other

EXHIBIT 14.5 Real Estate Portfolio Style Definitions

Core Portfolio Definition	Value-Added Portfolio Definition	Opportunistic Portfolio Definition
A portfolio that includes a preponderance of core attributes. As a whole, the portfolio will have low lease exposure and low leverage. A low percentage of noncore assets is acceptable. Such portfolios should achieve relatively high income returns and exhibit relatively low volatility. The portfolio attributes should reflect the return versus risk profile of the NPI.	A portfolio that generally includes a mix of core real estate with other real estate investments that have a less reliable income stream. The portfolio as a whole is likely to have moderate lease exposure and moderate leverage. Such portfolios should achieve a significant portion of the return from the appreciation of real estate property values and should exhibit moderate volatility. A risk and return moderately greater than the NPI is expected.	A portfolio preponderantly of noncore investments that is expected to derive most of its return from the appreciation of real estate property values and that may exhibit significant volatility in total return. The increased volatility and appreciation risk may be due to a variety of factors, such as exposure to development risk, significant leasing risk, high degree of leverage, or a combination of moderate risk factors. The risk and return profile is significantly greater than the NPI.

asset classes. The most difficult part of the real estate market is estimating returns for the value-added and opportunistic segments of the real estate investing market. A paper by the Center for International Securities and Derivatives Markets (CISDM) shows that there are reported data only for publicly traded REITs, exchange-traded funds that track REITs, and the NPI indexes.[5] However, it is important in utilizing style boxes to have some range of risk and return expectations, in order to determine how a real estate property or investment manager should be monitored and evaluated.

Style Box Return Objectives

Exhibit 14.6 provides a range of returns for the three style boxes. There is no exact specification for the returns and risks associated with real estate style boxes. Instead, general ranges are used. Some investors define their return expectations in absolute returns, citing an exact range of returns for each style box. Other investors define the risk and return ranges for value-added and opportunistic real estate in relation to the returns produced by the NPI.[6]

---

[5]CISDM Research Department, "The Benefits of Real Estate Investment: 2006 Update," May 2006.
[6]See Baczewski, Hands, and Lathem, "Real Estate Investment Styles."

EXHIBIT 14.6 Style Box Return Objectives

Absolute Return Investor	Relative Return Investor
Core Returns: Target total returns of 9% to 10% per year. An expected real return of 5% to 7% per year. High percentage of total return from cash flows.	Core Returns: Stable current income and market-level returns commensurate with a low to moderate level of risk. Income is expected to make up the majority of returns, and total return performance is expected to mirror the composite NPI.
Value-Added: Target returns of 10% to 13% per year. Volatility expected to be in the same range.	Value-Added: Income is still a significant portion of total return, but value appreciation may be the source of the majority of the returns. Expected to outpace the NPI by 200 basis points.
Opportunistic: Target return of 13% or more. Higher level of volatility that may exceed 13%.	Opportunistic: Returns are primarily from property appreciation. Current income plays only a small role in total return. Returns are expected to exceed the NPI by 500 basis points.

Exhibit 14.6 provides estimations of return expectations for real estate returns. It is really a matter of preferences based on objectives and circumstances as to whether an investor uses an absolute definition of real estate returns or a relative definition in relation to the NPI. The return expectations in Exhibit 14.6 have been dampened in light of the recent turmoil in this asset class over 2007 and 2008. Consequently, these return expectations have been reduced by 1% to 2% compared to estimates for these three styles during the real estate boom of 2000 to mid-2007.

Core Returns

The easiest range of returns to define is the core portfolio. There are sufficient data from the NPI to set well-grounded expectations about core real estate assets. Using our data from Exhibit 14.1, we can see that the NPI had an average return of 7.74% with a volatility of a little more than 8.79% over the time period 1990 to 2008. Using unsmoothed NPI data, the average annual return increases to almost 9% with a volatility of 11.19%. One might expect that this range of data is consistent with what investors can expect from their core portfolios. The period from 1990 to 2008 was filled with two recessions, two Gulf Wars, a technology boom and bust, the Asian contagion, the start of the subprime mortgage crisis, the Russian bond default, and the bailout of Long-Term Capital Management (LTCM), and a global financial meltdown not witnessed by this generation of investors. In short, this time period was diverse in its business cycle development, shocks to the financial markets, and global economic and political crises. Consequently, expected returns derived from this time period should be robust with respect to future economic and political events.

Value-Added Returns

While the range of returns for value-added and opportunistic properties given in Exhibit 14.6 come from NCREIF's definitions, actual institutional investors are a bit more conservative in their return expectations for the different style categories. However, PSERS defines value-added return expectations in total return terms. It cites an absolute return of 9% to 13% for value-added investments.[7] Compared to our return analysis for the NPI core properties in Exhibit 14.1, we can see that PSERS's range of return expectations for value-added real estate is just above the historical return average for core real estate.

---

[7]See Pennsylvania Public School Employees' Retirement System, Investment Policy Statement, 2007.

Opportunistic Returns

PSERS also defines its opportunistic return target in absolute terms. It sets a hurdle rate for opportunistic real estate investing at 13% or greater, depending on the level of risk taken. A return below 13% falls into the value-added real estate style box. As another data point, the California Public Employees' Retirement System (CalPERS) also defines its opportunistic return target in absolute terms. It cites an expected return hurdle rate of 13% or greater.[8] The CalPERS investment policy goes further to note that investment staff may adjust this 13% hurdle rate depending on the characteristics of the individual opportunistic real estate fund or changes in the marketplace, including changes to the inflation rate, capital market risk levels, or levels of available investment opportunities. The CalPERS investment policy for opportunistic real estate provides additional guidance:

> Opportunistic investments shall provide superior returns with acceptable risk levels when compared to direct equity US real estate investments. Additionally, rates of return will reflect the unique strategies associated with the investment opportunities and shall include, but are not limited to, such factors such as relative stages of development and/or redevelopment, targeted property types, entity or debt vehicles, relative control or liquidity or both that are associated with the investment, and other structuring techniques used to mitigate taxes and currency exposure, if any.

The last part of the CalPERS policy statement mentions taxes and currency exposure because many institutional investors look at real estate investing outside of their home country as being opportunistic in nature since it involves a different market where real estate is valued differently, where development issues such as planning and zoning can be much more difficult, and where property management must recognize the peculiar nature of the foreign market. So, for example, when a U.S. institution invests overseas, it loses its U.S. tax-exempt status and must also deal with the conversion of the total return back into U.S. dollars. This raises the currency and tax issues mentioned in the CalPERS investment policy. These are additional risk factors for which additional expected return must compensate.

One of the difficulties of assessing the return expectations for opportunistic real estate is that many of these investments take place through private limited partnerships (i.e., private equity real estate). Unfortunately, there is no voluntary reporting of data for PERE as there is for members of

---

[8] See California Public Employees' Retirement System, Statement of Investment Policy for Opportunistic Real Estate, February 14, 2006.

NCREIF. These private limited partnerships are just that: private. Consequently, data regarding opportunistic real estate investing is limited.

However, one study examined the returns to PERE funds over the time period 1991 to 2001.[9] found that For 68 opportunistic real estate funds over this time period, the researchers found that the arithmetic average of gross returns (e.g. no weighting for the amount of capital/size of the funds), before management and incentive fees, was 20.15%. However, after fees were deducted, net total returns were 14.24%. This is pretty much in line with the absolute hurdle rates of CalPERS and PSERS and just a little less than that cited by NCREIF.

Distribution of the NPI Returns

In Exhibit 14.2, we reported summary statistics for the pattern of real estate returns over time. Let's now look at the dispersion of returns associated with individual real estate properties. This is a cross-sectional analysis. We want to observe the returns to all real estate properties at a point in time rather than examining the returns of a composite basket or real estate asset through time. The purpose of a cross-sectional analysis is to give us a sense of the dispersion of returns across real estate assets in a given year.

Exhibit 14.7 presents a cross-sectional histogram of returns. We draw breakpoints at the 5th percentile range, 25th percentile range, 50th percentile range, 75th percentile range, and 95th percentile range. We can see that the median return for the NPI (at the 50th percentile range) is 15.85%. Despite the beginning of the subprime mortgage crisis in 2007, it was a good year for core real estate returns. But we note that due to the lagged nature of the appraisal process for real estate assets, the returns in Exhibit 14.7 might not have yet fully incorporated the subprime meltdown that began in 2007. Conversely, if we were to plot the distribution of returns from 2008 we would not be plotting the returns from a normal year. The year 2008 was a year of epic upheaval in the financial markets and therefore is inappropriate as a benchmark for real estate return expectations. The year 2007 is a better measure of the expected return distribution for real estate investments.

We introduce a rule of thumb that uses the 5th, 25th, 75th, and 95th percentile ranges around the median as natural breakpoints for determining core, value-added, and opportunistic return expectations. For example, for a portfolio following a core approach in 2007, the rule of thumb suggests that we should expect to earn an average return of 15.85% but have a range of returns mostly ranging from the 25th to the 75th percentiles. Thus, a core portfolio could have a range of returns between 8.3% and 19.1% with an average of 15.85%. Core portfolios are not always within these ranges.

[9]See Hahn, Geltner, and Gerardo-Lietz, "Real Estate Opportunity Funds."

EXHIBIT 14.7 Cross-Section Distribution of NPI Component Property Returns in 2007

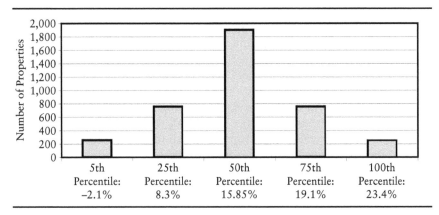

Source: NCREIF, www.ncreif.com.

They can occasionally fall into larger or smaller return ranges as occupancy and lease rates fluctuate, as some core properties are redeveloped or repositioned, or as new management changes its tenant strategies. The key point is that not all core portfolios in 2007 produced a return of 15.8%. This was simply the mean.

We use the ranges from core real estate returns in Exhibit 14.7 from the 5th percentile to the 25th percentile and from the 75th percentile to the 95th percentile to represent value-added portfolios. These are portfolios that deviate significantly from core portfolios in their risk and return profiles in that they fall outside the center mass of core portfolios more often. These properties can involve the gearing up of new leasing, pursuing a new leasing strategy, renovating and repositioning an existing core property, and occasionally redevelopment. Initially, we would expect that reported returns would fall into the 5th percentile to 25th percentile range as the new leasing strategy begins or as the repositioning of the property starts. Therefore, initially, these more risky properties earn a reported return in the –2.1% to 8.3% range. However, after successfully repositioning a property or initiating a new leasing program, we would expect returns to these types of properties to reflect their value appreciation and jump into the 75th to 95th percentile range with a range of returns from 19.1% to 23.4%.

Now let's look at the range of returns in the zero to 5th percentile and top 95th to 100th percentile to represent what we would expect for opportunistic real estate. As Exhibit 14.7 demonstrates, these properties are in the tails of the return distribution. Opportunistic real estate properties will often have negative reported returns early on as capital is deployed for the development, redevelopment, repositioning, restructuring, or ground-up building of the property. However, opportunistic properties would jump into the high end of the return distribution upon successful completion of the development, restructuring, and so on. Therefore, the initial returns can even be below the –2.1% average for the 5th percentile while the positive upside can be greater than the 23.4% average return for the top 95th percentile properties.

Exhibit 14.8 summarizes these return ranges and where core, value-added, and opportunistic properties should fall within these ranges. We can see visually that we would expect core assets to fall within the sweet spot of returns: limited downside, but also limited upside. For those investors willing to take on more risk, the rewards are apparent, but so are the downside risks, and core properties with such relatively extreme return characteristics may be more appropriately considered noncore properties.

Said differently, we can use Exhibits 14.6 and 14.7 to assess the style purity of a real estate manager. Keeping in mind that these returns are produced for the 2007 year only, a manager who professes to pursue a core style of real estate investing would expect to have a large portion of the

EXHIBIT 14.8   Distribution of Real Estate Returns for 2007

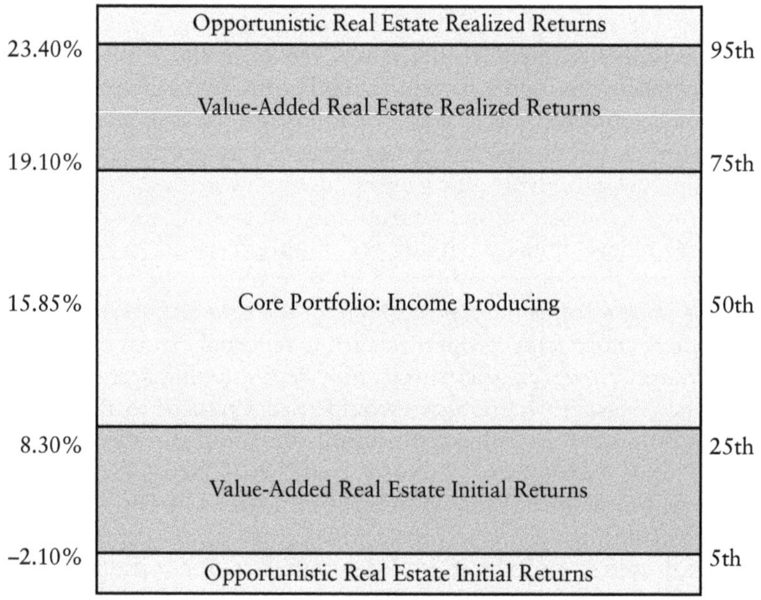

23.40%	Opportunistic Real Estate Realized Returns	95th
19.10%	Value-Added Real Estate Realized Returns	75th
15.85%	Core Portfolio: Income Producing	50th
8.30%		25th
–2.10%	Value-Added Real Estate Initial Returns	5th
	Opportunistic Real Estate Initial Returns	

Source: NCREIF, www.ncreif.com.

properties under management generating a return between the 25th and 75th percentile ranges, 8.3% to 19.1%. If a significant number of these properties produce returns outside of this range, despite what the manager professes, the investor might wish to choose to categorize the real estate manager as a value-added or opportunistic real estate manager.

These ranges can also be used as a way to understand the risk profile of the real estate manager. A value-added manager, for example, would be expected to have a significant number of properties producing lower returns in the –2.1% to 8.3% range, as well as other properties producing very good returns in the 19.1% to 23.4% range. The fact that a value-added manager could have returns in the very low range, as well as the very high range is an indicator of the riskiness of the portfolio. The return range would be even more extreme for an opportunistic real estate manager, reflecting the greater risk of these strategies

Private Equity Real Estate

PERE is a fast-growing part of the real estate market. Leverage is typically used at a very high level in PERE. The capital structure of these investments is generally very complex. Compared to core properties, increased risks include leverage, development risk, zoning and public policy risk, environmental concerns, currency risk, tenant exposure, and property turnarounds. These investment strategies are hard to access, require considerable specialized expertise, and are hard to execute.

A significant problem of PERE investments is valuation. As the market is, by definition, private, transaction and carrying values do not have to be disclosed to anyone except the investors in the private limited partnership, and sometimes, depending on the governance of the private fund, not even to them. A valuation is placed on an asset at the time it is acquired, but often these properties are priced well below their potential. It is the redevelopment, repositioning, or restructuring that will add the value, and these are hard to value quantitatively. Appraisers try to assign interim values to opportunistic properties, but appraising redevelopment/repositioning/restructuring efforts is even more difficult than appraising core properties. Plus, there is a distinct lag in valuation with the NPI.

Valuations can also be subject to selection bias because opportunistic real estate investments change hands depending on the underlying market cycle. For example, in a cyclical downturn, prices may remain artificially high. The reason is that the buyers' bids may be below the sellers' asking prices. This leads to fewer transactions and means that the most recently reported price is the price the seller originally paid for the property, which, in a market downturn, is often higher than what buyers are bidding.

Finally, we note that PERE investments are not exclusive to opportunistic properties. PERE is being used more and more for value-added and even core properties.[10] Core properties are only a small portion of the overall PERE market, with value-added and opportunistic properties combining for the major part of the market. PERE structures are being used more and more for opportunistic as well as value-added and core properties.

Financial Instruments and Concepts Introduced in this Chapter (in Order of Presentation)

Real estate	Core properties
Real estate investment trusts	Value-added properties
NCREIF Property Index	Opportunistic real estate
NAREIT Index	Private equity real estate

---

[10]See "Can Bumper Fundraising Be Sustained?" Preqin Real Estate Feature Article, *Real Estate Spotlight* 1, no. 2 (July 2007).

CHAPTER 15

Investing in Real Estate Investment Trusts

In this chapter, we discuss *real estate investment trusts* (REITs), a simple and liquid way to bring real estate into an investor's portfolio. REITs are stocks listed on major stock exchanges that represent an interest in an underlying pool of real estate properties. Effectively, REITs operate much in the same fashion as mutual funds. They pool investment capital from many small investors, and invest the larger collective pool in real estate properties that would not be available to the small investor. The key advantage of REITs is that they provide access to an illiquid asset class for investors who would not otherwise invest in real property. For now, consider an investment in a REIT as providing a broad exposure to real estate properties that the investor would not otherwise be able to obtain.

ADVANTAGES AND DISADVANTAGES OF REITs

The benefits of REITs are several. One of the biggest advantages is the pass-through tax status of a REIT. Subject to the several requirements discussed later, a REIT avoids double taxation that comes with paying taxes at both the corporate and individual levels and instead is able to avoid corporate income taxation by passing all of its income and capital gains to its shareholders (where the distributions may be subject to taxation at the individual level).

A second advantage is that investors in REITs can freely trade the shares of a REIT (e.g., in the United States they are traded on the New York, Nasdaq, or other stock markets), making REIT investing both convenient and liquid. Consequently, an investor can add to or trim her exposure to real estate quickly and easily through REITs. In fact, a REIT is a marginable security, which means that investors can typically borrow from their broker (up to 50%) to purchase shares in a REIT.

EXHIBIT 15.1   The NAREIT Market, 2009

Sector	($ in billions)
Retail	$56.0
Office	31.3
Residential	34.0
Healthcare	32.4
Industrial	18.0
Speciality	16.2
Storage	16.0
Diversified	16.0
Hotel	13.5

Source: FTSE Group and National Association of Real Estate Investment Trusts at www.reit.com, January 31, 2010. Reprinted with permission.

Another advantage of REITs is in facilitating asset allocation. This comes at two levels. First, an investor can use REITs as part of a strategic asset allocation to real estate as an asset class. Second, investors can use tactical asset allocation by tilting their real property exposure to certain parts of the real estate market. For example, an investor can choose different categories of REITs such as office building REITs, health care REITs, shopping center REITs, apartment REITs, and so on.

Exhibit 15.1 demonstrates the size and diversity of the REIT market as represented by the NAREIT U.S. Real Estate Total Return Index, the benchmark index for the return of publicly traded REITs. The exhibit represents the market as of January 2010 at which time the REIT market had recovered dramatically from the downturn of 2008.

A fourth benefit of REITs is the professional asset management of real estate properties by the REIT executives. These are real estate professionals who know how to acquire, finance, develop, renovate, and negotiate lease agreements with respect to real estate properties to get the most return for their shareholders.

A fifth advantage is that REITs provide a consistent dividend yield for their shareholders. This is particularly important for retirees and others living on a fixed income. Having a dependable cash flow stream is a necessity to pay bills, medical expenses, and so on. Exhibit 15.2 shows the dividend yields for most categories of REITs. The cash flows from REITS can be quite generous. For example, the categories of Healthcare, Industrial, Specialty, Residential, and Diversified all had dividend yields over 4% in January 2010. Compare this to the dividend yield on the S&P 500 of less than 2%.

Finally, REITs are also overseen by an independent board of directors that is charged with seeing to the best interests of the REIT's shareholders.

EXHIBIT 15.2 REIT Annual Yields

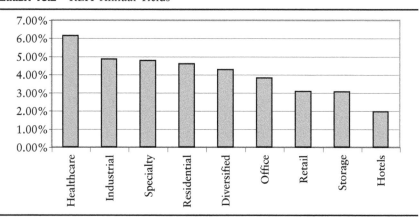

Data source: FTSE Group and National Association of Real Estate Investment Trusts at www.reit.com, January 31, 2010. Reprinted with permission.

This provides a level of corporate governance protection similar to that employed for other public companies.

The major disadvantage of REITs comes from being listed on a stock exchange or on Nasdaq. As a result, their prices pick up some of the systematic risk associated with the broader stock market. This reduces their diversification benefits, as an investor in a REIT obtains both real estate and stock market exposure. Therefore, REITs are less of a pure play in real estate. They are an imperfect substitute or proxy for direct real estate investing.

Most REITs fall into the capitalization range of $500 million to $5 billion—a range typically associated with small-cap stocks and the smaller half of mid-cap stocks. Therefore, they are more highly correlated with small-cap stocks than with large-cap stocks. This is demonstrated later in this chapter where REITs' correlation coefficient with small-cap stocks is 0.70, much higher than with large-cap stocks.

The beta of REITs with the Russell 2000 small-cap stock index is about 0.75. The size of the beta is relatively large, indicating that there is still a substantial amount of stock market risk embedded within REITs, which tends to reduce some of their diversification benefit.

Another disadvantage of REITs is that their dividend distributions are taxed at ordinary income rates. This is in contrast to dividends from most other public companies that are eligible for a 15% qualified dividend tax rate. The reason is that a REIT is a pass-through investment pool of underlying real estate properties. As a result the dividend tax advantages that apply to most public companies are not extended to REITs. Simply, REITs are less tax efficient for high-tax-bracket investors.

DIFFERENT TYPES OF REITS

REITs can differ by investment philosophy, type of structure, and the markets in which they invest.

Investment Philosophy

There are three basic investment types of REITs: equity REITS, mortgage REITs, and hybrid REITs.

An *equity REIT* uses the pooled capital from investors to purchase property directly. The REIT is the equity owner of the properties underlying the REIT portfolio. An equity REIT will also manage, renovate, and develop real estate properties. An equity REIT produces revenue for its investors from the rental and lease payments it receives as the landlord of the properties it owns. An equity REIT also benefits from the appreciation in value of the properties that it owns as well as an increase in rents. In fact, one of the benefits of equity REITs is that their rental and lease receipts tend to increase along with inflation, making REITs a potential hedge against inflation.

A *mortgage REIT* derives its value from financing the purchase of real estate properties. A mortgage REIT invests in loans that are used to purchase real estate such as mortgages, mortgage-backed securities, subprime loans (we have more to say about this later), or some other securitization of real property values. Mortgage REITs are lenders to owners, developers, and purchasers of real estate. Pure mortgage REITs, however, do not own any real estate property directly. They generate returns for their shareholders from the interest earned on the financing they provide.

A *hybrid REIT* invests in both the equity interests and the debt interests of real estate properties. They provide lending for the acquisition and development of real estate properties as well as purchase and develop real estate properties themselves. Some hybrid REITs are explicit as to the amount of equity ownership and mortgage financing they may provide (e.g., a 50–50 split). Other hybrid REITs are flexible as to the amount of ownership versus financing they may provide. As the name implies, hybrids can do an unlimited combination of real estate investing and mortgage financing.

REIT Structures

There are many different ways a REIT can be structured, depending on the type of properties acquired or financed.

A *single-property REIT* accumulates capital to purchase a single large property. Rockefeller Center in New York City is a very large collection of office buildings, shopping promenades, and dining establishments grouped together in the center of Manhattan. The mortgage of the complex used to be owned by a single-property REIT.

A *finite-life REIT* establishes a termination date by which the REIT will sell its underlying properties and wind up its affairs. The typical term is eight to 15 years. This provides sufficient time for the REIT manager, for example, to acquire the properties, renovate them, replace the existing tenants, increase the rents, and ultimately increase the value of the underlying properties upon their sale to new investors.

A *dedicated REIT* is typically established to invest in: (1) one type of property only (e.g. retail strip malls); (2) a single development (e.g. LaSalle Partners developed office buildings); or (3) a geographic region (e.g. Washington, D.C., office buildings). Another development in the dedicated REIT is the health care REIT. These are REITs that specialize in the purchase and sale/leaseback of health care facilities such as nursing homes, hospitals, and outpatient facilities. Dedicated REITs add value by providing a deep specialized knowledge of a small slice of the real estate market. However, they are often more risky because of the narrow focus of their investment universe.

An *umbrella partnership REIT* (an UPREIT) is a REIT where the REIT itself does not own any real estate properties directly but rather holds the properties in an operating partnership. The motivation for the UPREIT is to permit real estate investors to contribute properties in exchange for ownership in a manner such that they can defer built-in capital gains that would have to be recognized if the appreciated real estate properties were contributed directly in exchange for the REIT's stock. The UPREIT has been used since 1992. All of the properties are held through an operating partnership. Investment bankers like the UPREIT structure because it is a way for the REIT to reach a minimum level of capitalization before accessing the public capital markets. Exhibit 15.3 shows the structure of an UPREIT.

In contrast to an UPREIT is a *Down REIT*. A Down REIT is also driven by tax consequences. They were created as a way for property owners to contribute property to a REIT in exchange for stock as a nontaxable exchange of value. Down REITs were created with the same technology that established UPREITs. These vehicles were created out of older REITs as a way to provide growth opportunities. In a Down REIT, an older REIT forms a subsidiary partnership that holds the existing real estate assets. This subsidiary REIT then allows in new partners who contribute new properties for an equity stake in the more diversified REIT. Effectively, in a Down REIT, the REIT downsteams its assets into a new partnership to which other partners can contribute real estate properties in exchange for stock in the Down REIT. Exhibit 15.4 shows the structure for a Down REIT.

EXHIBIT 15.3   An UPREIT

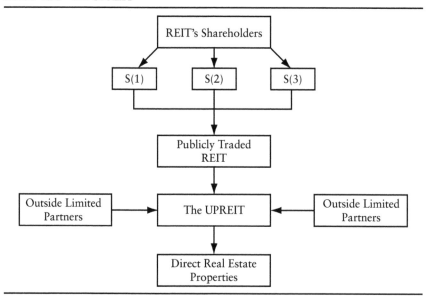

Markets in which REITs Invest

REITs also differ in terms of the markets in which they invest their capital. The primary distinction of markets is the property type (e.g. office, retail, industrial). REITs can also differ by property type subcategories such as by concentrating on upscale properties. The geographic region, or regions, of focus (if any) is another common distinction—along with other potential distinctions such as the typical sizes of portfolio investments.

REIT RULES

As noted earlier, the main advantage of a REIT is its ability to pass on income and capital gains directly to its investors without suffering any tax at the corporate REIT level. However, there are many rules and regulations that must be obeyed for a REIT to obtain this tax-advantaged status.

Corporate Structure

To be structured as a REIT, the following six rules apply:

1. It must be organized as a corporation, a trust, or an association.
2. It must be managed by one or more trustees or directors.

EXHIBIT 15.4 A Down-REIT

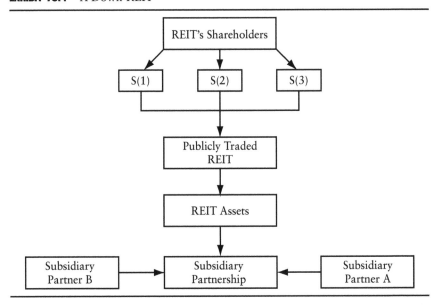

3. Its shares must be transferable, usually accomplished by listing the REIT shares publicly on an exchange.
4. It cannot be a financial institution or an insurance company.
5. It must be owned by 100 or more persons.
6. No more than 50% of the REIT's shares can be owned by five or fewer persons—this must be in the REIT organizational documents as a preventive measure against concentrated ownership.

Tax Structure

To ensure the favorable tax status as a REIT, the following five rules apply:

1. At least 75% of the REIT's assets must be invested in (1) real estate assets, (2) cash and cash equivalents, (3) government securities, or (4) temporary investments (up to one year) while the REIT searches for new properties to purchase with its investment capital.
2. The remaining 25% of the REIT's assets may be held in the securities of other issuers, but they cannot exceed 5% of the total assets of the issuer or 10% of the total outstanding voting shares of the issuer.
3. At least 75% of the REIT's gross income must come from revenue related to real estate: (1) rents from real property, (2) interest from real estate and mortgage loans, (3) gains from the sale of real property,

(4) dividends from ownership of other REIT shares, (5) gains from the sale of other REIT shares, (6) tax abatements from owning real property, (7) income from foreclosure of properties, and (8) commitment fees from investing in real property.

4. As a second income test, at least 95% of the REIT's income must come from: (1) sources that qualify for the 75% test, (2) dividends and interest, and (3) gains from the sale of stock or securities.

5. A REIT must distribute annually to its shareholders at least 95% of its taxable income (excluding capital gains). This test is required to prevent a REIT from being a vehicle for income accumulation.

If a REIT meets these tests, then it receives pass-through tax status where the REIT is not taxed on any gains and income passed through to its shareholders (but which are then potentially taxed at the shareholder level). Income not passed through to shareholders in the form of a distribution (i.e., retained by the REIT) is subject to tax at the corporate (REIT) level.

REIT distributions of income are generally taxed as dividends to the REIT shareholders. But portions of a REIT's distributions that are identified as long-term capital gains resulting from the sale of real estate properties are taxed as long-term capital gains to the REIT shareholders.

ECONOMICS OF REITs

Let's look at the economic benefits of REITs compared to other asset classes. Exhibit 15.5 shows the returns to the S&P REIT index for the past 12 years (since inception, respectively), including the disastrous years of 2007 and 2008. The S&P REIT index contains 100 publicly traded REIT stocks across all of the sectors of REITs listed in Exhibit 15.1. Consequently, it is a well-diversified portfolio of REITs, as well as a good snapshot into the performance of the real estate market generally.

Exhibit 15.5 also contains the average return, standard deviation, and Sharpe ratio for the S&P REIT index (SPREIT) as well as comparative returns for large-cap and small cap stocks (the Russell 1000 and Russell 2000 stock indexes, respectively), high yield bonds (the Salomon Smith Barney Cash Pay High Yield index, SBHYCP), 10-year U.S. Treasury bonds, one-year Treasury bills (a measure of cash returns), and the annual inflation rate for the time period 1997–2009. Keep in mind that 2008 was a brutal year for most asset classes. Every asset class that had some amount of risk attached to it lost value in 2008. The safest of the safe, U.S. Treasury bonds, soared in 2008 while other asset classes deteriorated.

EXHIBIT 15.5 Comparative Financial Performance for REITs

	SPREIT	RIY1000	RTY2000	SBHYCP	10-Year T-Bond	1-Year T-Bill	Inflation
2009	27.45%	28.40%	27.10%	54.10%	−12.90%	0.40%	2.70%
2008	−37.95	−37.60	−33.80	−24.68	22.81	2.30	0.10
2007	−16.21	5.78	−1.51	1.91	9.60	3.28	4.10
2006	35.03	15.38	18.34	11.72	2.04	5.00	2.50
2005	11.18	6.21	4.56	2.07	6.61	4.42	3.40
2004	30.98	11.25	18.28	10.51	7.78	2.79	3.30
2003	34.77	29.55	46.90	29.36	3.29	1.21	1.90
2002	4.12	−21.52	−20.34	−0.58	16.06	1.19	2.40
2001	13.82	−12.22	2.52	6.92	4.53	2.03	1.60
2000	27.97	−7.71	−2.87	−4.41	18.73	5.47	3.40
1999	−5.57	20.77	21.11	0.84	−8.98	6.14	2.70
1998	−19.41	26.56	−2.25	4.42	12.93	4.58	1.60
1997	13.41	32.28	22.06	13.10	14.45	5.62	1.70
Average	7.68%	5.73%	6.08%	4.27%	9.15%	3.67%	2.39%
Std. dev.	23.54%	21.70%	21.23%	12.68%	8.59%	1.76%	1.09%
Sharpe	0.17	0.09	0.11	0.04	0.62		

Exhibit 15.5 indicates that the Sharpe ratio, a measure of risk-adjusted returns, is higher for REITs than for large-cap or small-cap stocks. U.S. Treasury bonds have the highest Sharpe ratio, and this is due to their higher return and lower volatility. In fact, 10-year Treasury bonds were the best-performing asset class over this time period on a risk-adjusted basis. Part of this is due to the flight to safety during the global market meltdown of 2008 when the total return soared to almost 23% as well as the safe haven they provided after the popping of the tech bubble and the recession years of 2001–2002. We do not calculate a Sharpe ratio for U.S. Treasury bills because this is the risk-free rate that we use as part of the Sharpe ratio calculation for the other asset classes.

During this time period, the average return to REITs was 200 basis points higher than for large-cap stocks, 160 basis points higher for small-cap stocks, almost 340 basis points higher than for high-yield bonds, and even 200 basis points higher than for U.S. Treasury bonds, despite the phenomenal year for Treasury bonds in 2008. Clearly, during the period 1997–2008, REITs delivered a favorable return premium over stocks and bonds. However, this extra return did come with extra risk, as the volatility for REITs was higher than for any other asset class and this volatility hurt

EXHIBIT 15.6   The Subprime Crisis and the Real Estate Market

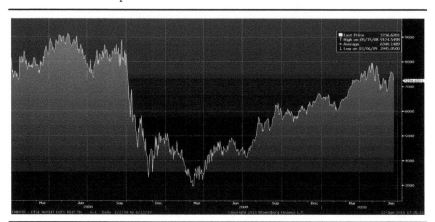

Source: Copyright 2010 Bloomberg Finance, L.P.

REITs in 2008. Still, the extra return from REITs offset this extra risk in that the Sharpe ratio is higher compared to stocks and high-yield bonds. In summary, REITs provided a good total return for investors but not without some additional risk.

However, the risk associated with real estate hit with a vengeance starting in May 2007. At that time, a meltdown in the subprime mortgage market sent a ripple effect—more closely resembling a tsunami—through the financial markets. In its wake, the subprime meltdown severely eroded real estate values across the United States. Exhibit 15.6 shows the recent declines in the S&P REIT index. At its nadir, this index was down 33 percent year over year before recovering slightly as 2008 wore on. However, the message is clear: real estate investing is subject to the risk of liquidity and credit events.[1] Interestingly, although the REIT declines originated from the problems in the subprime mortgage market, most of the REITs in the S&P REIT index had little or no direct involvement with the subprime market. Also, Exhibit 15.6 demonstrates how quickly REITs recovered their value in 2009—almost back to their pre-recession highs of 2008.

Exhibit 15.7 provides a histogram for the monthly returns to the S&P REIT index over the time period 1997 to December 2009. This 13-year period provides us with enough data to draw some conclusions, but not enough observations to produce a full probability distribution. First, we can see that the mass of the distribution is centered around the monthly return range of –4% to 8%. However, the average monthly return is much

---

[1]From its high point in February 2007 through its low point in March 2009, the S&P REIT index lost almost 77% of its value, a dramatic decline for any asset class.

EXHIBIT 15.7   Frequency Distribution for Monthly Return to REITs

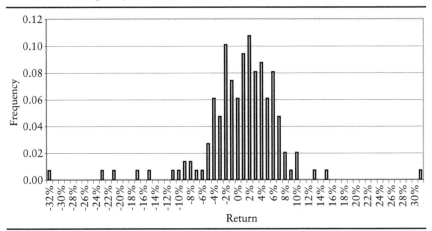

Note: Average 0.22%; Std. dev. 6.53%; Sharpe ratio 0.02; Skew –0.75; Kurtosis 7.47.
Source: Bloomberg Finance, L.P.

lower, only 0.33%, which reflects the fact that there is a wide dispersion of monthly returns. This is confirmed by our estimate of the standard deviation of 6.53% per month, resulting in a monthly Sharpe ratio of 0.02.

Exhibit 15.7 also shows the skew and excess kurtosis[2] of the distribution) for the S&P REIT index. The skew tells us how the distribution of returns is tilted or leans in one direction. Asset classes that produce return distributions with positive skew are to be favored, as this indicates a bias to the upside. Kurtosis is a method to measure the fatness of the tails of the distribution. Return distributions that have large positive measures of kurtosis are called "leptokurtic" and have exposure to large outlier events that deviate greatly from the mean return.

Exhibit 15.7 shows a negative skew of –0.75. This demonstrates a bias toward the downside—that there is a larger number of extreme negative returns than extreme positive returns. The value of kurtosis is a positive 7.47. This is the value measured compared to a normal distribution. This tells us that REITs have more exposure to outlier events than what would be predicted by a normal distribution. The combination of a large negative skew value and a large value of kurtosis demonstrates that REITs are exposed to large downside risks. This is a way of saying that REITs produce a return stream with a large or fat downside tail. The results in Exhibit 15.7 are skewed themselves because they are greatly influenced by the returns

---

[2]The normal distribution has a kurtosis value of 3. Excess kurtosis is therefore defined as kurtosis minus 3. For simplicity, kurtosis in this chapter means excess kurtosis.

EXHIBIT 15.8 Correlation Analysis: 1997–2008

	S&P REIT	RU1000	RU2000	SBHYCP	10-Year T-Bond	1-Year T-Bill	Inflation
S&P REIT	1.00						
RIY1000	0.42	1.00					
RTY2000	0.70	0.85	1.00				
SBHYCP	0.64	0.71	0.78	1.00			
10-year T-note	−0.56	−0.57	−0.55	−0.88	1.00		
1-year T-bill	−0.10	0.22	0.01	−0.43	0.33	1.00	
Inflation	0.39	0.26	0.26	0.22	−0.49	0.18	1.00

Data Source: Bloomberg Finance, L.P.

achieved by REITs in 2008 and 2009, which were distinctly large and negative in 2008 and then large and positive in 2009.

Exhibit 15.8 reviews the portfolio diversification properties of REITs. As we discussed earlier, REITs provide both good access to real estate and diversification. We test the diversification abilities of REITs by calculating the correlation between REIT returns and the returns to other major asset classes. The results are in the Exhibit 15.8. When two asset classes have a correlation less than 1.0 there is the ability to diversify the investor's portfolio by blending the two asset classes together in the portfolio. A negative correlation indicates that the two asset classes tend to move in the opposite direction from one another—when the first asset class is up, the second is down and vice versa. This is an extreme example of diversification—return streams that do not track together but go their different ways to produce a portfolio that will tend to exhibit stability at all points of the business cycle.

The correlations reported in Exhibit 15.8 indicate that REITs offer very good diversification properties to large-cap stocks, Treasury bonds, and Treasury bills. In fact, the correlation between REITs and Treasury bonds is negative, indicating excellent diversification potential. With respect to stocks, REITs have a much lower correlation to large-cap stocks than to small-cap stocks. This is not surprising since most REITs have a market capitalization range closer to small-cap stocks than large-cap stocks. It is rare for a REIT to have a large-cap market capitalization (more than $10 billion). More precisely, there are only 14 REITs in the S&P 500 index, which contains the stocks which are among the largest in the United States. These 14 REITs have an average market capitalization of only $14 billion. Also, REITs have the highest correlation with high-yield bonds. This reflects the credit risk that can creep into the REIT market that we discussed previously. During the credit and liquidity meltdown of 2008, REITs and high-yield bonds declined in value precipitously.

In summary, most REITs would be classified as small- to mid-cap rather than large-cap. Therefore, it is not surprising that the S&P REIT index would have moderately high correlation (0.70) to the small-cap Russell 2000 stock index and a lower correlation with the large-cap-dominated Russell 1000 stock index.

In the last row, we look at the correlation of REITs with the U.S. inflation rate. REITs are often considered to be a hedge against inflation. The reason is that as inflation rises, REIT managers can raise the lease rates to keep pace. Although there is a lag between inflation and higher lease rates, REITs would appear able to maintain some pace with inflation. Exhibit 15.8 shows a positive correlation coefficient of 0.39 with inflation. This demonstrates a good ability of REITs to hedge against inflation.

REITs tend to be a good hedge against inflation for two reasons. First, rental/lease payments are typically adjusted upward during times of inflation. Thus, properties with shorter term leases such as multifamily housing or even hotels can adjust their rental rates quickly in line with inflation. For multiyear commercial leases, there is often a clause to adjust the rent upward over the course of the lease for increases in inflation. Second, REIT values tend to increase during periods of inflation as investors shift their portfolios away from financial assets to real assets. However, there is a negative relationship between REIT dividend yields and inflation. The reason is that dividends often lag increases in lease rates and lease rates react to inflation. As a result, it may take one or two periods to adjust the dividends associated with a REIT after lease rates have already been adjusted. Exhibit 15.9 compares dividend yields from REITs and the rate of inflation.

Recent academic research continues to support the notion that REITs are good inflation-hedging assets. Simpson, Ramchander, and Webb reviewed prior studies that did not find a positive relationship between REITs and inflation and concluded that there is an asymmetric response of REIT returns to inflation.[3] Specifically, they proposed that the reason REITs may be potentially negatively correlated with inflation is that REIT returns increase in periods of both rising and declining inflation. They found that the negative correlation between REIT values and declining inflation leads to an overall negative correlation between REITs and inflation. Similarly, Chatrah and Liang found that while REIT returns may be negatively correlated with inflation over small periods of time, REITs provide a good inflation hedge over the long run.[4]

---

[3]Marc Simpson, Sanjay Ramchander, and James Webb, "The Asymmetric Response of Equity REIT Returns to Inflation," *Journal of Real Estate Finance and Economics* 34, no. 4 (2007): 301–317.
[4]Arjun Chatrah and Youguo Liang, "REITs and Inflation: A Long-Run Perspective," *Journal of Real Estate Research* 16, no. 3 (1999): 311–326.

EXHIBIT 15.9   REIT Dividends and CPI Correlation is –0.13

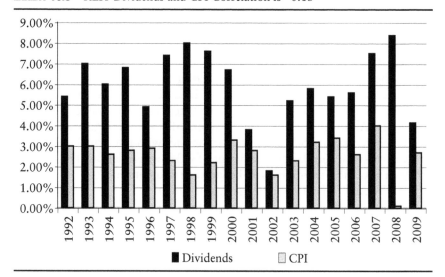

Data Source: Bloomberg Finance, L.P.

In summary, REITs have demonstrated very good diversification potential with stocks, bonds, and Treasury bills. In addition, REITs may be positively correlated with the inflation rate, especially in the long run, and therefore may possess some ability to retain real value as inflation creeps ahead. Combining these correlations with the favorable Sharpe ratio from Exhibit 15.5, it is clear why REITs are a popular investment choice for many investors.

Financial Instruments and Concepts Introduced in this Chapter (in Order of Presentation)

Real estate investment trusts
Equity REIT
Mortgage REIT
Hybrid REIT
Single-property REIT

Finite-life REIT
Dedicated REIT
Umbrella partnership REIT
Down REIT

CHAPTER 16

Introduction to Hedge Funds

The phrase *hedge fund* is an artful term. It is not defined in the Securities Act of 1933 or the Securities Exchange Act of 1934. Additionally, "hedge fund" is not defined by the Investment Company Act of 1940, the Investment Advisers Act of 1940, the Commodity Exchange Act, or, finally, the Bank Holding Company Act. Even though the Securities and Exchange Commission (SEC) has attempted (unsuccessfully) to regulate hedge funds, it has yet to define the term "hedge fund" within its security regulations. So what is this investment vehicle that every investor seems to know but for which there is scant regulatory guidance?

As a starting point, we turn to the *American Heritage Dictionary*, 3rd edition, which defines a hedge fund as: "An investment company that uses high-risk techniques, such as borrowing money and selling short, in an effort to make extraordinary capital gains." This is a good start; however, many hedge fund strategies use tightly controlled, low-risk strategies to produce consistent but conservative rates of return and do not "swing for the fences" to earn extraordinary gains.

We define hedge fund as a privately organized investment vehicle that manages a concentrated portfolio of public and private securities and derivative instruments on those securities, that can invest both long and short and can apply leverage.

In this chapter, we discuss the various types of hedge funds according to the investment strategies that they pursue. In the next chapter, we focus on considerations in investing in hedge funds.

HEDGE FUNDS VS. MUTUAL FUNDS

Within this definition there are six key elements of hedge funds that distinguish them from their more traditional counterpart, the mutual fund.

First, hedge funds are private investment vehicles that pool the resources of sophisticated investors. One of the ways that hedge funds avoid the regulatory scrutiny of the SEC or the Commodity Futures Trading Commission (CFTC) is that they are available only for high-net-worth investors. Under SEC rules, hedge funds cannot have more than 100 accredited investors in the fund. An accredited investor is defined as an individual that has a minimum net worth in excess of $1 million, or income in each of the past two years of $200,000 ($300,000 for a married couple) with an expectation of earning at least that amount in the current year. Additionally, hedge funds may accept no more than 500 "qualified purchasers" in the fund. These are individuals or institutions that have a net worth in excess of $5 million.

There is a penalty, however, for the privacy of hedge funds. They cannot raise funds from investors via a public offering. Additionally, hedge funds may not advertise broadly or engage in a general solicitation for new funds. Instead, their marketing and fund-raising efforts must be targeted to a narrow niche of very wealthy individuals and institutions. As a result, the predominant investors in hedge funds are family offices, foundations, endowments, and, to a lesser extent, pension funds.

Second, hedge funds tend to have portfolios that are much more concentrated than their mutual fund brethren. Most hedge funds do not have broad securities benchmarks. One reason is that most hedge fund managers claim that their style of investing is "skill based" and cannot be measured by a market return. Consequently, hedge fund managers are not forced to maintain security holdings relative to a benchmark; they do not need to worry about "benchmark" risk. This allows them to concentrate their portfolio on only those securities that they believe will add value to the portfolio.

Another reason for the concentrated portfolio is that hedge fund managers tend to have narrow investment strategies. These strategies tend to focus on only one sector of the economy or one segment of the market. They can tailor their portfolio to extract the most value from their smaller investment sector or segment. Furthermore, the concentrated portfolios of hedge fund managers generally are not dependent on the direction of the financial markets, in contrast to long-only managers.

Third, hedge funds tend to use derivative strategies much more predominantly than mutual funds. Indeed, in some strategies, such as convertible arbitrage, the ability to sell or buy options is a key component of executing the arbitrage. The use of derivative strategies may result in nonlinear cash flows that may require more sophisticated risk management techniques to control these risks.

Fourth, hedge funds may go both long and short securities. The ability to short public securities and derivative instruments is one of the key distinctions between hedge funds and traditional money managers. Hedge fund managers incorporate their ability to short securities explicitly into their investment strategies. For example, equity long/short hedge funds tend to buy and sell securities within the same industry to maximize their return but also to control their risk. This is very different from traditional money managers that are tied to a long-only securities benchmark.

Fifth, many hedge fund strategies invest in nonpublic securities, that is, securities that have been issued to investors without the support of a prospectus and a public offering. Many bonds, both convertible and high yield, are issued as what are known as "144A securities." These are securities issued to institutional investors in a private transaction instead of a public offering. These securities may be offered with a private placement memorandum (ppm), but not a public prospectus. In addition, these securities are offered without the benefit of an SEC review as would be conducted for a public offering. Bottom line: with 144A securities it is buyer beware. The SEC allows this because, presumably, large institutional investors are more sophisticated than that average, small investor.

Finally, hedge funds use leverage, sometimes, large amounts. In fact, a lesson in leverage is described in this chapter with respect to Long-Term Capital Management. Mutual funds, for example, are limited in the amount of leverage they can employ; they may borrow up to 33% of their net asset base. Hedge funds do not have this restriction. Consequently, it is not unusual to see some hedge fund strategies that employ leverage up to 10 times their net asset base.

We can see that hedge funds are different than traditional long-only investment managers.

GROWTH OF THE HEDGE FUND INDUSTRY

The hedge fund industry experienced huge growth during the decade of 2000–2009. A key driver of this growth was the performance of hedge funds at the beginning of the decade.

Recall back to March 2000. This was the official popping of the "Tech Bubble." There was a time when the world believed that technology stocks would take over the world and that the "clicks" would dominate the "bricks." Certainly, in certain industries (media, newspapers, and books, for example) it does appear that the clicks are surpassing the bricks, but in many other industries, technology has not had the dominant influence that was expected.

As a result, the technology boom that drove stock returns in the late 1990s died in early 2000 sending the stock market into a three-year bear market. During 2000–2002, every developed stock market index declined by double digit returns each year. However, hedge funds produced positive performance over this time period.

EXHIBIT 16.1   Returns to Hedge Funds and the S&P 500, 2000–2009

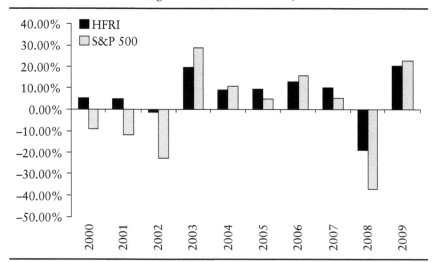

Exhibit 16.1 tracks the annual performance of hedge funds and the S&P 500 over the time period 2000–2009. Notice, that from 2000 to 2002, hedge funds lived up to their name and hedged the decline in value of the stock market. Hedge funds became bear market heros.

This led to tremendous growth in hedge fund assets. In 2000, assets under management in the hedge fund industry were only $300 billion. This amount surged to $1.8 trillion by 2007, at the peak of the hedge fund market. Hedge fund assets declined significantly in 2008 during the financial market meltdown that impacted all asset classes. However, hedge fund growth rebounded in 2009 back to $1.6 trillion in assets under management. The cumulative annual growth rate over this time period for hedge funds was close to 22% per year.

CATEGORIES OF HEDGE FUNDS

It seems like everyone has their own classification scheme for hedge funds.[1] This merely reflects the fact that hedge funds are a bit difficult to "box in"— a topic we will address further when we examine a number of the hedge fund index providers. For purposes of this book, we try to break down hedge funds into broad categories, as depicted in Exhibit 16.2. We classify

---

[1]See Francois-Serge L'habitant, *Hedge Funds: Quantitative Insights* (Chichester, U.K.: John Wiley & Sons, 2004); and Joseph G. Nicholas, *Market Neutral Investing* (Princeton, N.J.: Bloomberg Press, 2000).

EXHIBIT 16.2 Hedge Fund Styles and Risk Exposures

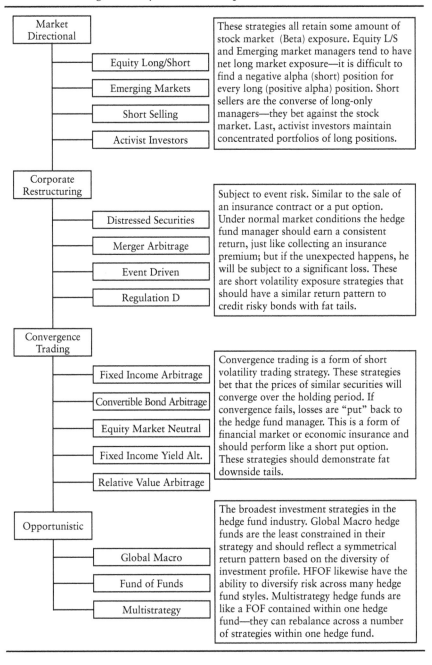

These strategies all retain some amount of stock market (Beta) exposure. Equity L/S and Emerging market managers tend to have net long market exposure—it is difficult to find a negative alpha (short) position for every long (positive alpha) position. Short sellers are the converse of long-only managers—they bet against the stock market. Last, activist investors maintain concentrated portfolios of long positions.

Subject to event risk. Similar to the sale of an insurance contract or a put option. Under normal market conditions the hedge fund manager should earn a consistent return, just like collecting an insurance premium; but if the unexpected happens, he will be subject to a significant loss. These are short volatility exposure strategies that should have a similar return pattern to credit risky bonds with fat tails.

Convergence trading is a form of short volatility trading strategy. These strategies bet that the prices of similar securities will converge over the holding period. If convergence fails, losses are "put" back to the hedge fund manager. This is a form of financial market or economic insurance and should perform like a short put option. These strategies should demonstrate fat downside tails.

The broadest investment strategies in the hedge fund industry. Global Macro hedge funds are the least constrained in their strategy and should reflect a symmetrical return pattern based on the diversity of investment profile. HFOF likewise have the ability to diversify risk across many hedge fund styles. Multistrategy hedge funds are like a FOF contained within one hedge fund—they can rebalance across a number of strategies within one hedge fund.

hedge funds into four broad buckets: market directional, corporate restructuring, convergence trading, and opportunistic.

Market directional hedge funds are those that retain some amount of systematic risk exposure. For example, *equity long/short hedge funds* (or, as it is sometimes called, *equity hedge funds*) are hedge funds that typically contain some amount of net long market exposure. For example, they may leverage up the hedge fund to go 150% long on stocks that they like while simultaneously shorting 80% of the fund value with stocks that they think will decline in value. The remaining net long market exposure is 70%. Thus, they retain some amount of systematic risk exposure that will be affected by the direction of the stock market.

Corporate restructuring hedge funds take advantage of significant corporate transactions like mergers, acquisitions, or bankruptcies. These funds earn their living by concentrating their portfolios on a handful of companies where it is more important to understand the likelihood that the corporate transaction will be completed than it is to determine whether the corporation is under or overvalued.

Convergence trading hedge funds are the hedge funds that practice the art of arbitrage. In fact, the specialized subcategories within this bucket typically contain the word "arbitrage" in their description, such as statistical arbitrage, fixed income arbitrage, or convertible arbitrage. In general, these hedge funds make bets that two similar securities but with dissimilar prices will converge to the same value over the investment holding period.

Finally, we have the *opportunistic hedge funds*. We include *global macro hedge funds* as well as *fund of funds* (FOF) in this category. These funds are designed to take advantage of whatever opportunities present themselves, hence the term "opportunistic." For example, FOF often practice tactical asset allocation among the hedge funds contained in the FOF based on the FOF manager's view as to which hedge fund strategies are currently poised to earn the best results. This shifting of the assets around is based on the FOF manager's assessment of the opportunity for each hedge fund contained in the FOF to earn a significant return.

HEDGE FUND STRATEGIES

Hedge funds invest in the same equity and fixed income securities as traditional long-only managers. Therefore, it is not the alternative "assets" in which hedge funds invest that differentiates them from long-only managers, but rather, it is the alternative investment strategies that they pursue. In this section we provide more detail on the types of strategies pursued by hedge fund managers.

Market Direction Hedge Funds

The strategies in this bucket of hedge funds either retain some systematic market exposure associated with the stock market such as equity long/short or are specifically driven by the movements of the stock market such as market timing or short selling.

Equity Long/Short

Equity long/short managers build their portfolios by combining a core group of long stock positions with short sales of stock or stock index options and futures. Their net market exposure of long positions minus short positions tends to have a positive bias. That is, equity long/short managers tend to be long market exposure. The length of their exposure depends on current market conditions. For instance, during the bear market of 2000–2002, these managers decreased their market exposures as they sold more stock short or sold stock index options and futures, whereas during the bull stock market of 2003–2006 these managers tended to have much longer equity exposure.

For example, consider a hedge fund manager who at the beginning of 2008 went long by 150% of the portfolio value in the SPDR XME, an exchange-traded fund (ETF) that passively replicates exposure to the metals and mining sector of the S&P 500. Simultaneously, the hedge fund manager went short by 50% of the portfolio value in the SPDR XLF, an exchange-traded fund that passively replicates exposure to the financial sector in the S&P 500. The beta of the XME is 0.99 and the beta of the XLF is 0.98. The weighted average beta of this equity long/short portfolio is

$$(1.5 \times 0.99) - (0.5 \times 0.98) = 0.995$$

Therefore, this long/short equity portfolio is just about beta neutral to the S&P 500 benchmark.[2]

According to the capital asset pricing model (CAPM), the hedge fund manager has a portfolio that has just about the same systematic risk as the S&P 500. In 2008, the return on the market, represented by the S&P 500 was –13.64% through August 2008, while the risk-free rate was about 2.25%. Given the realized return on the market portfolio and beta of the hedge fund, the realized return on this portfolio, according to the model, should be:

---

[2]As explained in Chapter 3, beta is a measure of market exposure (or systematic risk). A portfolio with a beta of 1.0 is beta neutral with respect to S&P 500 and therefore has the same stock market exposure or risk as a broad-based stock index such as the S&P 500.

$$\text{Return} = 2.25\% + 0.995(-13.6\% - 2.25\%) = -13.52\%$$

However, from January to August 2008, the return on the XLF was −33% while the return on the XME was +23%. This beta-neutral portfolio would have earned the following return:

$$(1.5 \times 23\%) + (-0.5 \times -33\%) = 51\%$$

This is a much higher return than that predicted by the CAPM.

This example serves to highlight two points. First, the ability to go both long and short in the market is a powerful tool for earning excess returns. The ability to fully implement a strategy not only about stocks and sectors that are expected to increase in value but also stocks and sectors that are expected to decrease in value allows the hedge fund manager to maximize the value of her market insights.

The ability to go both long and short in the market is a powerful tool for earning excess returns. The ability to fully implement a strategy not only about stocks and sectors that are expected to increase in value but also stocks and sectors that are expected to decrease in value allows the hedge fund manager to maximize the value of her market insights.

Equity long/short hedge funds essentially come in two flavors: fundamental or quantitative. Fundamental long/short hedge funds conduct traditional economic analysis on a company's business prospects compared to its competitors and the current economic environment. These shops will visit with management, talk with Wall Street analysts, contact customers and competitors and essentially conduct bottom-up analysis. The difference between these hedge funds and long-only managers is that they will short the stocks that they consider to be poor performers and buy those stocks that are expected to outperform the market. In addition, they may leverage their long and short positions.

Fundamental long/short equity hedge funds tend to invest in one economic sector or market segment. For instance, they may specialize in buying and selling Internet companies (sector focus) or buying and selling small market capitalization companies (segment focus). In contrast, quantitative equity long/short hedge fund managers tend not to be sector or segment specialists. In fact, quite the reverse, quantitative hedge fund managers like to cast as broad a net as possible in their analysis. These managers are often referred to as statistical arbitrageurs because they base their trade selection on the use of quantitative statistics instead of fundamental stock selection.

Emerging Markets

Emerging markets have become an increasingly important part of asset allocation for institutional investors and, as a result, has seen the risk of hedge funds investing in this section—*emerging market hedge funds*. In addition, the maturity and sophistication of hedge fund investing is now extensive in the emerging markets.

Emerging markets have performed significantly better than the S&P 500 and U.S. Treasury bonds, particularly during the current decade. This is partly due to a higher beta (systematic risk) associated with emerging compared to developed markets, and this was a period of good economic growth for emerging market economies. In addition, hedge funds became much more sophisticated investors in emerging markets during this time.

Note, however, that in the global bear market of 2008, the return for this strategy declined significantly. This reflects the long bias to stock market exposure that is retained in emerging market strategies. The MSCI Barra Emerging Markets index was down around 55% through 2008, a more precipitous decline than the 37% drop in the S&P 500. However, emerging markets rebounded an amazing 80% in 2009. Together, 2008 and 2009 demonstrate the much higher volatility associated with emerging markets—a land of great opportunity and risk for hedge fund managers.

Short Selling

Short selling hedge funds have the opposite exposure of traditional long-only managers. In that sense, their return distribution should be the mirror image of long-only managers: they make money when the stock market is declining and lose money when the stock market is gaining.

These hedge fund managers may be distinguished from equity long/short managers in that they generally maintain a net short exposure to the stock market. However, short selling hedge funds tend to use some form of market timing. That is, they trim their short positions when the stock market is increasing and go fully short when the stock market is declining. When the stock market is gaining, short sellers maintain that portion of their investment capital not committed to short selling in short-term interest rate–bearing accounts.

Activist Investors

Corporate governance can be used as an alpha-driven investment strategy. Data from the California Public Employees' Retirement System (CalPERS) and well-identified market benchmarks demonstrate that corporate governance can generate returns in excess of the stock market while providing excellent return diversification.

The corporate governance style of investing has grown in importance. Essentially, this is the same type of corporate governance investing pursued by CalPERS, the California State Teachers Retirement System, Hermes Pensions Management, and other activist investors. Essentially, it entails building a very concentrated portfolio of only 5 to 15 equity positions in publicly traded corporations. These positions are large, anywhere from 1% to 10% of the outstanding stock of the company. The activist investor then demands a meeting with the public company's board of directors and chief executive officer (CEO). The purpose is to impose better governance techniques on the board of directors (e.g., to be less cozy with the CEO and to act in shareholders' interests). In addition, activist investors work with the CEO to implement a better business plan and even remove the CEO if he or she is ineffective. This manner of investing is also called *corporate engagement,* as the activist investor pursues a direct dialogue with the management and board of directors. The success of investors such as CalPERS and Hermes has encouraged many other investors to enter this form of equity investing to reap the rewards of better corporate governance. This strategy is included under market directional because these funds tend to take long-only positions. Even though their portfolios are very concentrated, there is still a considerable amount of stock market risk embedded in their portfolios.

Using a large hand-collected dataset from 2001 to 2006, Brav, Jiang, Partnoy, and Thomas find that target firms in the United States experience increases in operating performance, payout, and higher CEO turnover after activism from hedge funds.[3]

Corporate Restructuring Hedge Funds

In the literature, the strategies used by corporate restructuring hedge funds are referred to as "event driven" or "risk arbitrage" strategies. However, that does not really describe what is at the heart of each of these type of strategies. The focal point is some form of corporate restructuring such as a merger, acquisition, or bankruptcy. Companies that are undergoing a significant transformation generally provide an opportunity for trading around that event. These strategies are driven by the deal, not by the market.

---

[3]Furthermore, they also calculate that the abnormal stock return upon announcement of activism is around 7%. Alon Brav, Wei Jiang, Frank Partnoy, and Randall Thomas, "Hedge Fund Activism, Corporate Governance, and Firm Performance," *Journal of Finance* 63, no. 4 (2008): 1729–1773.

Distressed Securities

Distressed debt hedge funds invest in the securities of a corporation that is in bankruptcy, or is likely to fall into bankruptcy.[4] Companies can become distressed for any number of reasons such as too much leverage on their balance sheet, poor operating performance, accounting irregularities, or even competitive pressure. Some of these strategies can overlap with private equity strategies that we discuss in Chapter 18. The key difference here is that hedge funds are less concerned with the fundamental value of a distressed corporation and, instead, concentrate on trading opportunities surrounding the company's outstanding stock-and-bond securities.

There are many different variations on how to play a distressed situation, but most fall into three categories. In its simplest form, the easiest way to profit from a distressed corporation is to sell its stock short. This requires the hedge fund manager to borrow stock from its prime broker and sell in the marketplace stock that it does not own with the expectation that the hedge fund manager will be able to purchase the stock back at a later date and at a cheaper price as the company continues to spiral downward in its distressed situation. This is nothing more than "sell high and buy low."

However, the short selling of a distressed company exposes the hedge fund manager to significant risk if the company's fortunes should suddenly turn around. Therefore, most hedge fund managers in this space typically use a hedging strategy within a company's capital structure.

A second form of distressed securities investing is called capital structure arbitrage. Consider Company A, which has four levels of outstanding capital: senior secured debt, junior subordinated debt, preferred stock, and common stock. A standard distressed security investment strategy would be to (1) buy the senior secured debt and short the junior subordinated debt and (2) buy the preferred stock and short the common stock.

In a bankruptcy situation, the senior secured debt stands in line in front of the junior subordinated debt for any bankruptcy-determined payouts. The same is true for the preferred stock compared to Company A's common stock. Both the senior secured debt and the preferred stock enjoy a higher standing in the bankruptcy process than either junior debt or common equity, respectively. Therefore, when the distressed situation occurs or progresses, senior secured debt should appreciate in value relative to the junior subordinated debt. In addition, there should be an increase in the spread of prices between preferred stock and common stock. When this happens, the hedge fund manager closes out her positions and locks in the profit that occurs from the increase in the spread.

---

[4]Investing in distressed debt securities is described in Chapter 21.

Finally, distressed securities hedge funds can become involved in the bankruptcy process to find significantly undervalued securities. This is where an overlap with private equity firms can occur. To the extent that a distressed securities hedge fund is willing to learn the arcane workings of the bankruptcy process and to sit on creditor committees, significant value can be accrued if a distressed company can restructure and regain its footing. In a similar fashion, hedge fund managers do purchase the securities of a distressed company shortly before it announces its reorganization plan to the bankruptcy court with the expectation that there will be a positive resolution with the company's creditors.

Merger Arbitrage

Merger arbitrage is perhaps the best-known corporate restructuring investment among investors and hedge fund managers. Merger arbitrage generally entails buying the stock of the firm that is to be acquired and selling the stock of the firm that is the acquirer. Merger arbitrage managers seek to capture the price spread between the current market prices of the merger partners and the value of those companies upon the successful completion of the merger.

The stock of the target company usually trades at a discount to the announced merger price. The discount reflects the risk inherent in the deal; other market participants are unwilling to take on the full exposure of the transaction-based risk. Merger arbitrage is then subject to event risk. There is the risk that the two companies will fail to come to terms and call off the deal. There is the risk that another company will enter into the bidding contest, ruining the initial dynamics of the arbitrage. There is finally regulatory risk. Various U.S. and foreign regulatory agencies may not allow the merger to take place for antitrust reasons. Merger arbitrageurs specialize in assessing event risk and building a diversified portfolio to spread out this risk.

Merger arbitrageurs conduct significant research on the companies involved in the merger. They will review current and prior financial statements, SEC electronic data gathering analysis and retrieval (EDGAR) filings, proxy statements, management structures, cost savings from redundant operations, strategic reasons for the merger, regulatory issues, press releases, and competitive position of the combined company within the industries in which it competes. Merger arbitrageurs will calculate the rate of return that is implicit in the current spread and compare it to the event risk associated with the deal. If the spread is sufficient to compensate for the expected event risk, they will execute the arbitrage.

Once again, the term "arbitrage" is used loosely. As discussed earlier, there is plenty of event risk associated with a merger announcement. The profits earned from merger arbitrage are not riskless. Consider the saga of the purchase of MCI Corporation by Verizon Communications. Throughout 2005, Verizon was in a bidding war against Qwest Communications for the purchase of MCI. On February 3, 2005, Qwest announced a $6.3 billion merger offer for MCI. This bid was quickly countered by Verizon on February 10 that matched the $6.3 billion bid established by Qwest. The bidding war raged back and forth for several months before Verizon finally won the day in October 2005 with an ultimate purchase price of $8.44 billion.

To see the vicissitudes of merger arbitrage at work, we follow both the successful Verizon bid for MCI as well as the unsuccessful bid by Qwest. Starting with Verizon: at the announcement of its bid for MCI, its stock was trading at $36.00, while MCI was trading at $20. Therefore, the merger arbitrage trade was:

- Sell 1,000 shares of Verizon at $36 (short proceeds of $36,000).
- Buy 1,000 shares of MCI at $20 (cash outflow of $20,000).

While for the Qwest bid, the trade was:

- Sell 1,000 shares of Qwest at $4.20 (short proceeds of $4,200).
- Buy 1,000 shares of MCI at $20 (cash outflow of $20,000).

Throughout the spring and summer of 2005, Qwest and Verizon battled it out for MCI, with Verizon ultimately winning in October 2005. At that time, MCI's stock had increased in value to $25.50, while Verizon's stock had lost value and was trading at $30, and finally Qwest was trading unchanged at $4.20.

Total return for theMCI/Verizon merger arbitrage trade:

Gain on MCI long position:	$1,000 \times (\$25.50 - \$20) =$	$5,500
Gain on Verizon short position:	$1,000 \times (\$36 - \$30) =$	$6,000
Interest on short rebate:	$4\% \times 1,000 \times \$36 \times 240/360 =$	$960
Total		$12,460

The return on invested capital is: $12,460 ÷ $20,000 = 62.3%.

If the merger arbitrage manager had applied 50% leverage to this deal and borrowed half of the net outflow, the return would have been (ignoring financing costs):

$$\$12,460 \div \$10,000 = 124.6\% \text{ total return}$$

Turning to the MCI/Qwest merger arbitrage trade, the total return was:

Gain on MCI long position:	$1,000 \times (\$25.50 - \$20) =$	$5,500
Gain on Qwest short position:	$1,000 \times (\$4.20 - \$4.20) =$	$0
Gain on short rebate:	$4\% \times 1,000 \times \$4.20 \times 240/360 =$	$112
Total		$5,612

The return on invested capital is: $5,612 ÷ $20,000 = 28.06%. With 50% leverage the return would be: $5,612 ÷ $10,000 = 56.12%.

While both merger arbitrage trades made money, clearly, it made more sense to bet on the Verizon/MCI merger than the Qwest/MCI merger. This is where merger arbitrage managers make their money, by assessing the likelihood of one bid over another. Also, in a situation where there are two bidders for a company, there is a very high probability that there will be a successful merger with one of the bidders. Consequently, many merger arbitrage hedge fund managers will play both bids. This is exactly what happened in the MCI deal—many merger arbitrage managers bet on both the MCI/Verizon deal and the MCI/Qwest deal, expecting that one of the two suitors would be successful in winning the hand of MCI. Some merger arbitrage managers invest only in announced deals. However, other hedge fund managers will put on positions on the basis of rumor or speculation. The deal risk is much greater with this type of strategy, but so too is the merger spread (the premium that can be captured).

To control for risk, most merger arbitrage hedge fund managers have some risk of loss limit at which they will exit positions. Some hedge fund managers concentrate only on one or two industries, applying their specialized knowledge regarding an economic sector to their advantage. Other merger arbitrage managers maintain a diversified portfolio across several industries to spread out the event risk.

Merger arbitrage is deal driven rather than market driven. Merger arbitrage derives its return from the relative value of the stock prices between two companies as opposed to the status of the current market conditions. Consequently, merger arbitrage returns should not be highly correlated with the general stock market.

Event Driven

Event-driven hedge funds are very similar, in their approach to investing, to distressed securities and merger arbitrage. The only difference is that their mandate is broader than the other two corporate restructuring strategies. Event-driven transactions include mergers and acquisitions, spin-offs, tracking stocks, accounting writeoffs, reorganizations, bankruptcies, share buybacks, special dividends, and any other significant market event. Event-driven managers are nondiscriminatory in their transaction selection.

By their very nature, these special events are nonrecurring. Therefore, the financial markets typically do not digest the information associated with these transactions in a timely manner. The financial markets are simply less efficient when it comes to large, isolated transactions. This provides an opportunity for event-driven managers to act quickly and capture a premium in the market. Additionally, most of these events may be subject to certain conditions such as shareholder or regulatory approval. Therefore, there is significant deal risk associated with this strategy for which a savvy hedge fund manager can earn a return premium. The profitability of this type of strategy is dependent on the successful completion of the corporate transaction within the expected time frame.

Regulation D Hedge Funds

Strategies employed by *Regulation D hedge funds* relate to the regulatory environment of the United States. Regulation D (Reg D) hedge funds invest in privately issued securities of public companies. Regulation D is a securities law under the Securities Act of 1933 that allows public companies to issue stock or debt in an offering other than to the public. Under Reg D, the securities must be offered to only the most sophisticated of investors and there cannot be any marketing materials. Corporations often raise capital by selling securities directly to sophisticated investors without the need for the lengthy public offering and registration process. The advantage is speed of completing the offering. The disadvantage is that the offering is made to a smaller pool of investors.

Hedge funds purchase Reg D offerings for two reasons. First, Reg D securities might be priced more cheaply than the similar, but publicly traded, securities of the issuer. This is just a value play where the hedge fund uses leverage to boost the returns of buying privately issued securities at a discount to their publicly traded counterparts. Second, Reg D hedge funds can perform a form of arbitrage where they buy the privately issued securities and short similar but publicly traded securities. It is a case of buying cheap and selling rich. This makes the Reg D strategy sound like more of an arbitrage strategy, but we include it within the corporate restructuring category because Reg D securities have an impact on the capital structure of a public company. Also, many Reg D offerings are made in debt form but are convertible to equity after a certain period of time. This allows a Reg D hedge fund manager to buy equity at a cheaper price than the publicly traded stock of the company. Alternatively, the hedge fund manager can buy the Reg D convertible debt of the issuer and short the publicly traded stock of the issuer to end up owning a cheap bond. However, if the hedge fund manager uses Reg D offerings, they have an impact on the capital structure of the issuing corporation.

Convergence Trading Hedge Funds

As we have emphasized, hedge fund managers tend to use the term arbitrage somewhat loosely. *Arbitrage* is defined simply as riskless profits. It is the purchase of a security for cash at one price and the immediate resale for cash of the same security at a higher price. Alternatively, it may be defined as the simultaneous purchase of security A for cash at one price and the selling of identical security B for cash at a higher price. In both cases, the arbitrageur has no risk. There is no market risk because the holding of the securities is instantaneous. There is no basis risk because the securities are identical, and there is no credit risk because the transaction is conducted in cash.

Instead of riskless profits, in the hedge fund world, arbitrage is generally used to mean low-risk investments. Instead of the purchase and sale of identical instruments, there is the purchase and sale of similar instruments. The securities also may not be sold for cash, so there may be credit risk during the collection period. Finally, the purchase and sale may not be instantaneous. The arbitrageur may need to hold onto its positions for a period of time, exposing him to market risk.

Fixed Income Arbitrage

Fixed income arbitrage involves purchasing one fixed income security and simultaneously selling a similar fixed income security with the expectation that over the investment holding period, the two security prices will converge to a similar value. Hedge fund managers search continuously for these pricing inefficiencies across all fixed income markets. This is nothing more than buying low and selling high and waiting for the undervalued security to increase in value or the overvalued security to decline in value, or wait for both to occur.

The sale of the second security is done to hedge the underlying market risk contained in the first security. Typically, the two securities are related either mathematically or economically such that they move similarly with respect to market developments. Generally, the difference in pricing between the two securities is small, and this is what the fixed income arbitrageur hopes to gain. By buying and selling two fixed income securities that are tied together, the hedge fund manager hopes to capture a pricing discrepancy that will cause the prices of the two securities to converge over time.

However, because the price discrepancies can be small, the way hedge fund managers add more value is to leverage their portfolio through direct borrowings from their prime broker, or by creating leverage through swaps and other derivative securities. Bottom line: They find pricing anomalies, then "crank up the volume" through leverage. Fixed income arbitrage does not need to use exotic securities. For example, it can be nothing more than buying and selling U.S. Treasury bonds. As explained in Chapter 5, in the bond market, the most liquid securities are the on-the-run Treasury bonds. These are the most currently issued bonds issued by the U.S. Treasury Department. However, there are other U.S. Treasury bonds outstanding that have very similar characteristics to the on-the-run Treasury bonds. The difference is that off-the-run bonds were issued at an earlier date, and are now less liquid than the on-the-run bonds. As a result, price discrepancies occur. The difference in price may be no more than one-half or one quarter of a point ($25) but can increase in times of uncertainty when investor money shifts to the most liquid U.S. Treasury bond. During the Russian bond default crisis, for example, on-the-run U.S. Treasuries were valued as much as $100 more than similar, off-the-run U.S. Treasury bonds of the same maturity.

Nonetheless, when held to maturity, the prices of these two bonds will converge to the same value. Any difference will be eliminated by the time they mature, and any price discrepancy may be captured by the hedge fund manager. Fixed income arbitrage is not limited to the U.S. Treasury market. It can be used with corporate bonds, municipal bonds, sovereign debt, or mortgage-backed securities.

Another form of fixed income arbitrage involves trading among fixed income securities that are close in maturity. This is a form of yield curve arbitrage. These types of trades are driven by temporary imbalances in the term structure of interest rates.

Exhibit 16.3 is a snapshot of the term structure in the U.S. Treasury bond market in October 2008. Instead of a smooth yield curve, there are kinks in the term structure between the three-month and five-year time

EXHIBIT 16.3   U.S. Treasury Bond Yield Curve, October 2008

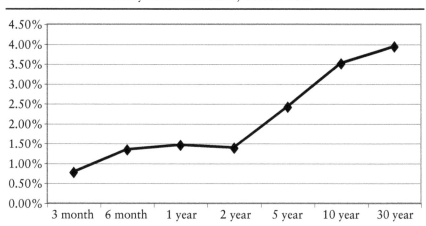

horizons. Kinks in the yield curve can happen at any maturity and usually reflect an increase (or decrease) in liquidity demand around the focal point. These kinks provide an opportunity to profit by purchasing and selling Treasury securities that are similar in maturity.

Consider the kink that bottoms at the two-year maturity. The holder of the five-year Treasury bond profits by rolling down the yield curve toward the two-year rate. In other words, if interest rates remain static, the five-year Treasury note will age into a lower-yielding part of the yield curve. Moving down the yield curve will mean positive price appreciation. Conversely, Treasury bonds maturing in the two-year to three-month range will roll up the yield curve to higher yields. This means that their prices are expected to depreciate.

An arbitrage trade would be to purchase the five-year Treasury bond and short a two-year bond. As the two-year bond rolls up the yield curve, its value should decline, while the five-year Treasury bond should increase in value as it rolls down the yield curve. This arbitrage trade will work as long as the kinks remain in place. However, this trade does have its risks. First, shifts in the yield curve up or down can affect the profitability of the trade because the two securities have different maturities and duration. To counter this problem, the hedge fund manager would need to purchase and sell securities in proper proportion to neutralize the differences in duration. Also, liquidity preferences of investors could change and the kink could reverse itself or flatten out. In either case, the hedge fund manager would lose money. Conversely, should liquidity preferences increase, the trade will become even more profitable.

Still another subset of fixed income arbitrage uses mortgage-backed securities (MBSs). As explained in Chapters 8 and 9, MBSs represent an ownership interest in an underlying pool of individual mortgages loaned by banks and other financial institutions. Therefore, an MBS is a fixed income security with underlying prepayment options. MBS hedge funds seek to capture pricing inefficiencies in the U.S. mortgage-backed market.

MBS arbitrage can be between fixed income markets, such as buying MBS and selling U.S. Treasuries. This investment strategy is designed to capture credit spread inefficiencies between U.S. Treasuries and MBSs. MBSs trade at a credit spread over U.S. Treasuries to reflect the uncertainty of cash flows associated with MBSs compared to the lack of credit risk associated with U.S. Treasury bonds.

During a flight to quality, investors tend to seek out the most liquid markets such as the on-the-run U.S. Treasury market. This is exactly what happened in 2008. Mortgage-backed securities of all types and levels of credit rating declined dramatically in value while the U.S. Treasury bond market rallied dramatically. The hedge fund trade would have been to short investment-grade MBS and to buy Treasuries. This trade would then be reversed once the market stabilized as it did in 2009 when credit risky securities of all types rallied dramatically compared to Treasury bonds.

MBS arbitrage can be quite sophisticated. MBS arbitrage can be quite sophisticated. MBS hedge fund managers use proprietary models to rank the value of MBSs by their option-adjusted spread (OAS). The hedge fund manager evaluates the present value of an MBS by explicitly incorporating assumptions about the probability of prepayment options being exercised. In effect, the hedge fund manager calculates the option-adjusted price of the MBS and compares it to its current market price. The OAS reflects the MBS's average spread over U.S. Treasury bonds of a similar maturity, taking into account the fact that the MBS may be liquidated early from the exercise of the prepayment option by the underlying mortgagors. The MBSs that have the best OAS compared to U.S. Treasuries are purchased, and then their interest rate exposure is hedged to zero. Interest rate exposure is neutralized using Treasury bonds, options, swaps, futures, and caps. MBS hedge fund managers seek to maintain a duration of zero. This allows them to concentrate on selecting the MBSs that yield the highest OAS.

There are many risks associated with MBS arbitrage. Chief among them are duration, convexity, yield curve rotation, prepayment risk, credit risk, and liquidity risk. Hedging these risks may require the purchase or sale of other MBS products such as interest-only strips and principal-only strips, U.S. Treasuries, interest rate futures, swaps, and options.

What should be noted about fixed income arbitrage strategies is that they do not depend on the direction of the general financial markets. Arbitrageurs seek out pricing inefficiencies between two securities instead of making bets on market direction.

Convertible Bond Arbitrage

Convertible bonds combine elements of both stocks and bonds in one package. A convertible bond is a bond that contains an embedded option to convert the bond into the underlying company's stock.

Convertible bond arbitrage funds build long positions of convertible bonds and then hedge the equity component of the bond by selling the underlying stock or options on that stock. Equity risk can be hedged by selling the appropriate ratio of stock underlying the convertible option.

This hedge ratio is known as the "delta" and is designed to measure the sensitivity of the convertible bond value to movements in the underlying stock. Convertible bonds that trade at a low premium to their conversion value tend to be more correlated with the movement of the underlying stock. These convertibles then trade more like stock than they do a bond.

Consequently, a high hedge ratio, or delta, is required to hedge the equity risk contained in the convertible bond. Convertible bonds that trade at a premium to their conversion value are highly valued for their bond-like protection. Therefore, a lower delta hedge ratio is necessary.

However, convertible bonds that trade at a high conversion act more like fixed income securities and therefore have more interest rate exposure than those with more equity exposure. This risk must be managed by selling interest rate futures, interest rate swaps, or other bonds. Furthermore, it should be noted that the hedging ratios for equity and interest rate risk are not static; they change as the value of the underlying equity changes and as interest rates change. Therefore, the hedge fund manager must continually adjust his hedge ratios to ensure that the arbitrage remains intact.

If this all sounds complicated, it is, but that is how hedge fund managers make money. They use sophisticated option-pricing models and interest rate models to keep track of all of the moving parts associated with convertible bonds. Hedge fund managers make arbitrage profits by identifying pricing discrepancies between the convertible bond and its component parts, and then continually monitoring these component parts for any change in their relationship.

Consider the following example. A hedge fund manager purchases 10 convertible bonds with a par value of $1,000, a coupon of 7.5%, and a market price of $900. The conversion ratio for the bonds is 20. The conversion ratio is based on the current price of the underlying stock, $45, and the current price of the convertible bond. The delta, or hedge, ratio for the bonds is 0.5. Therefore, to hedge the equity exposure in the convertible bond, the hedge fund manager must short the following shares of underlying stock:

10 Bonds × 20 Conversion ratio × 0.5 Hedge ratio = 100 Shares of stock

To establish the arbitrage, the hedge fund manager purchases 10 convertible bonds and sells 100 shares of stock. With the equity exposure hedged, the convertible bond is transformed into a traditional fixed income instrument with a 7.5% coupon.

Additionally, the hedge fund manager earns interest on the cash proceeds received from the short sale of stock. This is known as the "short rebate." The cash proceeds remain with the hedge fund manager's prime broker, but the hedge fund manager is entitled to the interest earned on the cash balance from the short sale (a rebate). (The short rebate is negotiated between the hedge fund manager and the prime broker. Typically, large, well-established hedge fund managers receive a larger short rebate.) We assume that the hedge fund manager receives a short rebate of 4.5%.

Therefore, if the hedge fund manager holds the convertible arbitrage position for one year, he expects to earn interest not only from his long bond position, but also from his short stock position.

The catch to this arbitrage is that the price of the underlying stock may change as well as the price of the bond. Assume the price of the stock increases to $47 and the price of the convertible bond increases to $920. If the hedge fund manager does not adjust the hedge ratio during the holding period, the total return for this arbitrage will be

Appreciation of bond price:	10 × ($920 – $900) =	$200
Appreciation of stock price:	100 × ($45 – $47) =	–$200
Interest on bonds:	10 × $1,000 × 7.5% =	$750
Short rebate:	100 × $45 × 4.5% =	$202.50
Total:		$952.50

If the hedge fund manager paid for the 10 bonds without using any leverage, the holding period return is

$$\$952.50 \div \$9,000 = 10.58\%$$

Suppose the underlying stock price declined from $45 to $43, and the convertible bonds declined in value from $900 to $880. The hedge fund manager would then earn

Depreciation of bond price:	10 × ($880 – $900) =	–$200
Depreciation of stock price:	100 × ($45 – $43) =	$200
Interest on bonds:	10 × $1,000 × 7.5% =	$750
Short rebate:	100 × $45 × 4.5% =	$202.50
Total		$952.50

What this example demonstrates is that with the proper delta or hedge ratio in place, the convertible arbitrage manager should be insulated from movements in the underlying stock price so that the expected return should be the same regardless of whether the stock price goes up or goes down.

However, suppose that the hedge fund manager purchased the convertible bonds with $4,500 of initial capital and $4,500 of borrowed money. We further assume that the hedge fund manager borrows the additional investment capital from his prime broker at a prime rate of 6%.

Our analysis of the total return is then

Appreciation of bond price:	$10 \times (\$920 - \$900) =$	$200
Appreciation of stock price:	$100 \times (\$47 - \$45) =$	−$200
Interest on bonds:	$10 \times \$1,000 \times 7.5\% =$	$750
Short rebate:	$100 \times \$45 \times 4.5\% =$	$202.5
Interest on borrowing:	$6\% \times \$4,500 =$	−$270
Total:		$682.5

And the total return on capital is $682.5 ÷ $4,500 = 15.17%.

The amount of leverage used in convertible arbitrage will vary with the size of the long positions and the objectives of the portfolio. Yet, in the preceding example, we can see how using a conservative leverage ratio of 2:1 in the purchase of the convertible bonds added almost 500 basis points of return to the strategy and earned a total return equal to twice that of the convertible bond coupon rate.

It is easy to see why hedge fund managers are tempted to use leverage. Hedge fund managers earn incentive fees on every additional basis point of return they earn. Furthermore, even though leverage is a two-edged sword—it can magnify losses as well as gains—hedge fund managers bear no loss if the use of leverage turns against them. In other words, hedge fund managers have everything to gain by applying leverage, but nothing to lose.

Leverage is also inherent in the shorting strategy because the underlying short equity position must be borrowed. Convertible arbitrage leverage can range from two to six times the amount of invested capital. This may seem significant, but it is lower than other forms of arbitrage.

Convertible bonds earn returns for taking on exposure to a number of risks such as (1) liquidity (convertible bonds are typically issued as private securities); (2) credit risk (convertible bonds are usually issued by less than investment-grade companies); (3) event risk (the company may be downgraded or declare bankruptcy); (4) interest rate risk (as a bond it is exposed to interest rate risk); (5) negative convexity (most convertible bonds are callable); and (6) model risk (it is complex to model all of the moving parts associated with a convertible bond). These events are magnified only when leverage is applied.

Since convertible bond managers hedge away the equity risk through delta-neutral hedging, we should see little impact from the U.S. stock market. In addition, for undertaking all of the risks listed above, convertible bond arbitrage managers should earn a return premium to U.S. Treasury bonds.

Market Neutral

Market-neutral hedge funds also go long and short the market. The difference is that they maintain integrated portfolios, which are designed to neutralize market risk. This means being neutral to the general stock market as well as having neutral risk exposures across industries. Security selection is all that matters.

Market-neutral hedge fund managers generally apply the rule of one alpha.[5] This means that they build an integrated portfolio designed to produce only one source of alpha. This is distinct from equity long/short managers that build two separate portfolios: one long and one short, with two sources of alpha. The idea of integrated portfolio construction is to neutralize market and industry risk and concentrate purely on stock selection. In other words, there is no beta risk in the portfolio with respect to either the broad stock market or any industry. Only stock selection, or alpha, should remain.

Market-neutral hedge fund managers generally hold equal positions of long and short stock positions. Therefore, the manager is dollar neutral; there is no net exposure to the market either on the long side or on the short side. Additionally, market-neutral managers generally apply no leverage because there is no market exposure to leverage. However, some leverage is always inherent when stocks are borrowed and shorted. Nonetheless, the nature of this strategy is that it does not have credit risk.

Generally, market-neutral managers follow a three-step procedure in their strategy. The first step is to build an initial screen of "investable" stocks. These are stocks traded on the manager's local exchange, with sufficient liquidity so as to be able to enter and exit positions quickly, and with sufficient float so that the stock may be borrowed from the hedge fund manager's prime broker for short positions. Additionally, the hedge fund manager may limit his universe to a capitalization segment of the equity universe such as the midcap range.

Second, the hedge fund manager typically builds factor models. These models are often known as "alpha engines." Their purpose is to find those financial variables that influence stock prices. These are bottom models that concentrate solely on corporate financial information as opposed to macroeconomic data. This is the source of the manager's skill—his stock-selection ability.

The last step is portfolio construction. The hedge fund manager will use a computer program to construct his portfolio in such a way that it is neutral to the market as well as across industries. The hedge fund manager may use a commercial "optimizer"—computer software designed to measure exposure to the market and produce a trade list for execution based on a manager's desired exposure to the market—or he may use his own computer algorithms to measure and neutralize risk.

---

[5] See Bruce Jacobs and Kenneth Levy, "The Law of One Alpha," *Journal of Portfolio Management* 21, no. 4 (Summer 1995): 78–79.

Most market-neutral managers use optimizers to neutralize market and industry exposure. However, more sophisticated optimizers attempt to keep the portfolio neutral to several risk factors. These include size, book to value, price/earnings ratios, and market price to book value ratios. The idea is to have no intended or unintended risk exposures that might compromise the portfolio's neutrality.

We have more to say about transparency in our discussion later in this chapter regarding the selection of hedge fund managers and whether the hedge fund industry should be institutionalized. For now, it is sufficient to point out that black boxes tend to be problematic for investors.

We would expect market-neutral managers to produce returns independent of the general market (they are neutral to the market).

Fixed Income Yield Alternatives

The *fixed income yield alternatives* category includes many of the strategies discussed earlier with respect to fixed income arbitrage but also includes other strategies that are tied to fundamental value selection, both long and short. This exposes yield alternatives to the same problems of convergence as traditional fixed income arbitrage. This strategy works best in stable markets such as the low volatility markets that existed through 2006. However, starting in 2007 into 2008, these strategies declined significantly as the credit and liquidity markets dried up and virtually every security other than U.S. Treasury bonds was penalized. As a result, there was a rapid decline in value from these strategies as the financial crisis of 2007–2008 unfolded.

Relative-Value Arbitrage

Relative-value arbitrage might be better named the smorgasbord of arbitrage. This is because relative-value hedge fund managers are catholic in their investment strategies; they invest across the universe of arbitrage strategies. The best known of these managers was Long-Term Capital Management. Once the story of LTCM unfolded, it was clear that their trading strategies involved merger arbitrage, fixed income arbitrage, volatility arbitrage, stub trading, and convertible arbitrage.

In general, the strategy of relative value managers is to invest in spread trades: the simultaneous purchase of one security and the sale of another when the economic relationship between the two securities (the "spread") has become mispriced. The mispricing may be based on historical averages or mathematical equations. In either case, the relative arbitrage manager purchases the security that is "cheap" and sells the security that is "rich." It is called relative-value arbitrage because the cheapness or richness of a security is determined relative to a second security. Consequently, relative-value managers do not take directional bets on the financial markets. Instead, they take focused bets on the pricing relationship between two securities.

Relative-value managers attempt to remove the influence of the financial markets from their investment strategies. This is made easy by the fact that they simultaneously buy and sell similar securities. Therefore, the market risk embedded in each security should cancel out. Any residual risk can be neutralized through the use of options or futures. What is left is pure security selection: the purchase of those securities that are relatively cheap and the sale of those securities that are relatively rich. Relative-value managers earn a profit when the spread between the two securities returns to normal. They then unwind their positions and collect their profit.

We have already discussed fixed income arbitrage, convertible arbitrage and statistical arbitrage. Two other popular forms of relative-value arbitrage are stub trading and volatility arbitrage.

Stub trading is an equity-based strategy. Frequently, companies acquire a majority stake in another company, but their stock price does not fully reflect their interest in the acquired company. As an example, consider Company A, whose stock is trading at $50. Company A owns a majority stake in Company B, whose remaining outstanding stock, or stub, is trading at $40. The value of Company A should be the combination of its own operations, estimated at $45 a share, plus its majority stake in Company B's operations, estimated at $8 a share. Therefore, Company A's share price is undervalued relative to the value that Company B should contribute to Company A's share price. The share price of Company A should be about $53, but instead, it is trading at $50. The investment strategy would be to purchase Company A's stock and sell the appropriate ratio of Company B's stock.

Let us assume that Company A's ownership in Company B contributes to 20% of Company A's consolidated operating income. Therefore, the operations of Company B should contribute one fifth to Company A's share price. A proper hedging ratio would be four shares of Company A's stock to one share of Company B's stock.

The arbitrage strategy is

Buy four shares of Company A stock at 4 × $50 = $200
Sell one share of Company B stock at 1 × $40 = $40

The relative-value manager is now long Company A stock and hedged against the fluctuation of Company B's stock. Let us assume that over three months, the share price of Company B increases to $42 a share, the value of Company A's operations remains constant at $45, but now the shares of

Company A correctly reflect the contribution of Company B's operations. The value of the position will be

Value of Company A's operations:	4 × $45 =	$180
Value of Company B's operations:	4 × $42 × 20% =	$33.6
Loss on short of Company B stock:	1 × ($40 – $42) =	–$2
Short rebate on Company B stock:	1 × $40 × 4.5% × 3/12 =	$0.45
Total:		$212.05

The initial invested capital was $200 for a gain of $12.05 or 6.02% over three months. Suppose the stock of Company B had declined to $30, but Company B's operations were properly valued in Company A's share price. The position value would be

Value of Company A's operations:	4 × $45 =	$180
Value of Company B's operations:	4 × $30 × 20% =	$24
Gain on short of Company B's stock:	1 × ($40 – $30) =	$10
Short rebate on Company B's stock:	1 × $40 × 4.5% × 3/12 =	$0.45
Total:		$214.45

The initial invested capital was $200 for a gain of $14.45 or 7.22% over three months. Stub trading is not arbitrage. Although the value of Company B's stock has been hedged, the hedge fund manager must still hold its position in Company A's stock until the market recognizes its proper value.

Volatility arbitrage involves options and warrant trading. Option prices contain an implied number for volatility. That is, it is possible to observe the market price of an option and back out the value of volatility implied in the current price using various option pricing models. The arbitrageur can then compare options on the same underlying stock to determine if the volatility implied by their prices are the same.

The implied volatility derived from option pricing models should represent the expected volatility of the underlying stock that will be realized over the life of the option. Therefore, two options on the same underlying stock should have the same implied volatility. If they do not, an arbitrage opportunity may be available. Additionally, if the implied volatility is significantly different from the historical volatility of the underlying stock, then relative-value arbitrageurs expect the implied volatility will revert back to its historical average.

Volatility arbitrage generally is applied in one of two models. The first is a mean reversion model. This model compares the implied volatility from current option prices to the historical volatility of the underlying security with the expectation that the volatility reflected in the current option price will revert to its historical average and the option price will adjust accordingly.

A second volatility arbitrage model applies a statistical technique called generalized autoregressive conditional heteroskedasticity (GARCH). GARCH models use prior data points of realized volatility to forecast future volatility. The GARCH forecast is then compared to the volatility implied in current option prices.

Both models are designed to allow hedge fund managers to determine which options are priced "cheap" versus "rich." Once again, relative-value managers sell those options that are rich based on the implied volatility *relative* to the historical volatility and buy those options with cheap volatility relative to historical volatility.

Opportunistic Hedge Fund Strategies

Along the lines of the smorgasbord comment for relative-value hedge funds, these strategies have the broadest mandate across the financial, commodity, and futures markets. These all-encompassing mandates can lead to specific bets on currencies or stocks as well as a well-diversified portfolio.

Global Macro

As their name implies, global macro hedge funds take a macroeconomic approach on a global basis in their investment strategy. These are top-down managers who invest opportunistically across financial markets, currencies, national borders, and commodities. They take large positions depending on the hedge fund manager's forecast of changes in interest rates, currency movements, monetary policies, and macroeconomic indicators.

Global macro managers have the broadest investment universe. They are not limited by market segment or industry sector, nor by geographic region, financial market, or currency. Global macro also may invest in commodities. In fact, a fund of global macro hedge funds offers the greatest diversification of investment strategies.

Global macro hedge funds tend to have large amounts of investor capital. This is necessary to execute their macroeconomic strategies. In addition, they may apply leverage to increase the size of their macro bets. As a result, global macro hedge funds tend to receive the greatest attention and publicity in the financial markets.

The best known of these hedge funds was the Quantum Hedge Fund managed by George Soros. It is well documented that this fund made significant gains in 1992 by betting that the British pound would devalue (which it did). This fund was also accused of contributing to the "Asian Contagion" in the fall of 1997 when the government of Thailand devalued its currency, the baht, triggering a domino effect in currency movements throughout Southeast Asia.

In recent times, however, global macro hedge funds have fallen on hard times. One reason is that many global macro hedge funds were hurt by the Russian bond default in August 1998 and the bursting of the technology bubble in March 2000. These two events caused large losses for the global macro hedge funds.

A second reason, as indicated above, is that global macro hedge funds had the broadest investment mandate of any hedge fund strategy. The ability to invest widely across currencies, commodities, financial markets, geographic borders, and time zones is a two-edged sword. On the one hand, it allows global macro hedge funds the widest universe in which to implement their strategies. On the other hand, it lacks focus. As more institutional investors have moved into the hedge fund marketplace, they have demanded greater investment focus as opposed to free investment rein.

Fund of Funds

Finally, we come to hedge fund of funds. These are hedge fund managers that invest their capital in other hedge funds. These managers practice tactical asset allocation; reallocating capital across hedge fund strategies when they believe that certain hedge fund strategies will do better than others. For example, during the bear market of 2000 to 2002, short-selling strategies performed the best of all hedge fund categories. Not surprisingly, fund of fund managers allocated a significant portion of their portfolios to short sellers during the recent bear market. Other strategies that are popular in fund of funds are global macro, fixed income arbitrage, convertible arbitrage, statistical arbitrage, equity long/short, and event driven.

One drawback on fund of funds is the double layer of fees. Investors in hedge fund of funds typically pay a management fee plus profit-sharing fees to the hedge fund of funds managers in addition to the management and incentive fees that must be absorbed from the underlying hedge fund managers. This double layer of fees makes it difficult for fund of fund managers to outperform some of the more aggressive individual hedge fund strategies. Brown, Goetzmann, and Liang document that individual hedge funds outperform funds of funds on an after-tax return or Sharpe ratio basis and argue that the nature of the FOF's fee arrangement (the fees on fees) is partly responsible for this result.[6] However, the trade-off of investing in funds of funds is better risk control from a diversified portfolio. In this regard, Fung

---

[6]Stephen J. Brown, William N. Goetzmann, and Bing Liang, "Fees on Fees in Fund of Funds," *Journal of Investment Management*, 2(4) (2004), pp. 1–18.

and Hsieh contend that FOF returns are a better reflection of the actual investment experience in hedge funds, as these returns are netting out the cost of due diligence, portfolio construction, and so on.[7]

Multistrategy Hedge Funds

Agarwal and Kale document the recent rapid growth in both FOFs and multistrategy hedge funds.[8] *Multistrategy* (MS) *hedge funds* have the ability to invest in different strategies, shifting capital among them according to their expected profitability, thus potentially benefiting from greater investment flexibility and from the ability to invest in less liquid investments because of longer lockup periods. In sum, a MS hedge fund acts like a "mini" FOF. Most MS hedge funds have equity long/short as a core position and then add other strategies such as convertible arbitrage, event driven, activist investing, and so on. Generally, MS hedge funds grow out of a once core strategy and then the hedge fund manager adds new strategies as either capacity constraints or new investment opportunities present themselves.

A study by Reddy, Brady, and Patel suggests that most multistrategy managers generally concentrate on two to four strategies and typically do not make significant shifts in investment allocation in the short run.[9] According to Agarwal and Kale, FOFs and MS hedge funds should yield similar risk-adjusted performances, as they represent similar forms of investments. However, they find that multistrategy funds outperform FoFs by 2.6% to 4.8% per annum in gross of fees alphas and by 3.0% to 3.6% on a net of fees basis, thus suggesting that the higher fees charged by FoFs cannot explain the differences in performance. They propose that the explanation for this result lies is that rational investors anticipate the additional agency risk that arises from investing in MS funds relative to FOFs and demand a higher return from them. This greater agency risk is the result of MS funds' investments being more opaque and their managers being constrained to invest in strategies in which they do not have sufficient skill.

Reddy, Brady, and Patel make the case for investing in FOFs when compared to MS funds. First, they argue, similar to Ineichen,[10] that manager

---

[7] William Fung and David A. Hsieh, "Hedge Funds: An Industry in its Adolescence," *Federal Reserve Bank of Atlanta Economic Review*, Fourth Quarter (2006): 1–34.

[8] Vikas Agarwal and Jayant R. Kale, "On the Relative Performance of Multi-Strategy and Funds of Hedge Funds," *Journal of Investment Management* 5, no. 3 (2007): 41–63.

[9] Girish Reddy, Peter Brady, and Kartik Patel, "Are Funds of Funds Simply Multi-Strategy Managers with Extra Fees," *Journal of Alternative Investments* 10, no. 3 (Winter 2007): 49–61.

[10] Alexander M. Ineichen, *Absolute Returns* (Hoboken, N.J.: John Wiley & Sons, 2002).

selection is a source of likely advantage for FOFs because these funds can choose managers from a large pool of hedge funds, whereas an MS fund manager is restricted by its capability to recruit skillful teams within each strategy in which it invests. Second, these authors also contend that FOFs generally provide greater diversification than MS funds and point to the case of the implosion of the large MS manager Amaranth Advisors, where institutions that invested directly in Amaranth experienced, by being undiversified, much higher losses than FOFs that invested in that same fund among others, which had an average investment of around 6% and recognized losses of close to 4%. Third, the potential effect of manager selection is greater than strategy allocation, something that tends to benefit FOFs relative to MS hedge funds. Fourth, while investors in MS hedge funds must bear the business and operational risks of the MS fund manager, an FOF diversifies these risks as it invests in different managers, each having its own risk management policy.

Finally, FOFs offer an additional level of monitoring and due diligence. In spite of all this, Reddy, Brady, and Patel caution that FOFs and MS hedge funds are simply manifestations of different investment approaches, and that institutions may choose to invest in both investment vehicles.

Financial Instruments and Concepts Introduced in this Chapter (in Order of Presentation)

Hedge fund	Distressed hedge funds
Market directional hedge funds	Merger arbitrage
Equity long/short hedge funds	Event-driven hedge funds
Equity hedge funds	Regulation D hedge funds
Corporate restructuring hedge funds	Regulation D
Convergence trading hedge funds	Arbitrage
Opportunistic hedge funds	Fixed income arbitrage
Global macro hedge funds	Convertible bond arbitrage funds
Fund of funds	Market-neutral hedge funds
Emerging market hedge funds	Fixed income yield alternatives
Short selling hedge funds	Relative-value arbitrage
Corporate governance	Volatility arbitrage
Corporate engagement	Multistrategy hedge funds

CHAPTER 17

Considerations in Investing in Hedge Funds

In the previous chapter, we discussed the fundamentals of hedge funds and the various types of hedge fund strategies. In this chapter, we discuss the factors that investors should consider in making hedge funds part of an investment program.

HEDGE FUND PERFORMANCE

A considerable amount of research has been dedicated to examining the return potential of several hedge fund styles. Additionally, a number of studies have considered hedge funds within a portfolio context, that is, hedge funds blended with other asset classes.

In the top panel of Exhibit 17.1, we update the prior research by examining the returns to hedge funds over the period 1990 through 2008 for the HFRI Hedge Fund Composite Index as well as the HFRI FOF index (both of these indexes report returns to hedge fund investors net of fees) compared to large-capitalization stocks (measured by the returns of the S&P 500 index); small-capitalization stocks (measured using the Nasdaq Composite index returns, an index that is highly correlated to the returns on small stocks); U.S. Treasury bond returns; EAFE (a measure of returns on international stocks); and cash. As can be seen in the exhibit, the returns for the HFRI Composite index compare favorably with large-cap stocks but with much less volatility. The FOF index earns less than large-cap and small-cap stocks but significantly more than EAFE, and has significantly less volatility than any of the stock categories. Both the HFRI Composite and FOF indexes earn premiums significantly in excess of a cash rate. Also, the HFRI FOF index has a volatility that is even lower than that of U.S. Treasury bonds. These findings are consistent with the prior research cited earlier.

EXHIBIT 17.1 Expected Return, Standard Deviations and Sharpe Ratios for the HFRI Hedge Fund Composite Index, 1990–2008

Using Annual Returns

Asset Class	Expected Return	Standard Deviation	Sharpe Ratio
S&P 500	9.92%	13.98%	0.43
10-Year U.S. Treasury	6.93%	6.82%	0.44
Nasdaq	11.74%	33.96%	0.23
EAFE	4.00%	16.17%	0.01
HFRI Composite	12.83%	6.85%	1.30
HFRI FOF	8.97%	5.78%	0.88
Cash	3.90%	0.47%	n/a

Correlation Matrix, Annual Returns, 1990–2008

Asset Class	S&P 500	10 Year UST	Nasdaq	EAFE	HFRI Comp.	HFRI FOF
S&P 500	1.00					
10-Year U.S. Treasury	0.14	1.00				
Nasdaq	0.85	−0.10	1.00			
EAFE	0.74	−0.15	0.74	1.00		
HFRI Composite	0.75	0.05	0.77	0.67	1.00	
HFRI FOF	0.58	0.00	0.57	0.53	0.89	1.00

Another benefit of hedge funds is that they provide good diversification benefits. In other words, hedge funds do, in fact, hedge other financial assets. Correlation coefficients with the S&P 500 range from –0.7 for short selling hedge funds to 0.83 for opportunistic hedge funds investing in the U.S. markets. The less than perfect positive correlation with financial assets indicates that hedge funds can expand the efficient frontier for asset managers.

The bottom panel of Exhibit 17.1 presents the correlation of the HFRI Composite Index and HFRI Fund of Funds Index with large-cap stocks, Treasury bonds, small-cap stocks, and international stocks over the time period from 1990 through 2008. The relatively low correlation coefficients of funds of hedge funds that can be observed in the exhibit reinforce the conclusion that funds of hedge funds provide good diversification benefits. In the case of the HFRI Composite Index, the correlations with stocks are somewhat higher, but the benefits of diversification are still present. In our discussion of funds of hedge funds later in this chapter, we come back to this point and illustrate, using a numerical example, the potential benefits of diversification that can be provided by funds of hedge funds.

In summary, research on hedge funds indicates consistent, positive performance with low correlation with traditional asset classes. The conclusion is that hedge funds can expand the investment opportunity set for investors, offering both return enhancement as well as diversification benefits. Nonetheless, there are several caveats to keep in mind with respect to the documented results for hedge funds. First, research provides clear evidence that shocks to one segment of the hedge fund industry can be felt across many different hedge fund strategies.[1]

Second, most of the research to date on hedge funds has still not factored in the tremendous growth of this industry over the past 10 years. The impact on returns of this explosive growth has yet to be fully documented. Third, some form of bias (survivorship bias, self-selection bias, or catastrophe bias) exists in the empirical studies. All of the cited studies make use of a hedge fund database. The building of these databases results in certain biases becoming embedded in the data. These biases, if not corrected, can unintentionally inflate the documented returns to hedge funds. It has been estimated that these three biases can add from 100 to 400 basis points to the estimated total return of hedge funds.

IS HEDGE FUND PERFORMANCE PERSISTENT?

The persistence of hedge fund performance is the age-old question with respect to all asset managers, not just hedge funds: Can the manager repeat her good performance? This issue, though, is particularly acute for the hedge fund marketplace for two reasons. First, hedge fund managers often claim that the source of their returns is "skill based" rather than dependent on general financial market conditions. Second, hedge fund managers tend to have shorter track records than traditional money managers.

Unfortunately, the evidence regarding hedge fund performance persistence is mixed. The few empirical studies that have addressed this issue have provided inconclusive evidence whether hedge fund managers can produce enduring results. Part of the reason for the mixed results is the short track records of most hedge fund managers. A three-year or five-year track record is too short a period of time to be able to estimate an accurate expected return or risk associated with that manager.

In addition, the skill-based claim of hedge fund managers makes it more difficult to assess their performance relative to a benchmark. Without

---

[1]See Mark Anson, "Financial Market Dislocations and Hedge Fund Returns," *Journal of Alternative Assets* 5, no. 4 (2002): 78–88.

a benchmark index for comparison, it is difficult to determine whether a hedge fund manager has outperformed or underperformed her performance "bogey." One way to measure performance persistence is to measure the serial correlation among the returns to hedge funds. Serial correlation measures the correlation of the return in the current year to the return performance of the previous year. If performance persistence is present, we should expect to see positive serial correlation, that is, good years followed by more good years. Exhibit 17.2 shows the serial correlation for large-cap stocks, small-cap stocks, EAFE, U.S. Treasury bonds, the cash return, and various hedge fund strategies.

As can be seen, the FOF index has negative serial correlation. This means that a good year tended to be followed by a year with lower returns, and

EXHIBIT 17.2   Serial Correlations of Hedge Fund Returns, 1990–2008

Asset Class	Serial Correlation
S&P 500	0.19
10-Year U.S. Treasury	−0.60
Nasdaq	−0.10
EAFE	−0.05
Cash	0.33
HFRI Composite	−0.07
Market Directional	
Equity Long/Short	0.13
Emerging Markets	−0.50
Short Selling	−0.28
Activist Investors	0.32
Corporate Restructuring	
Distressed Securities	0.06
Merger Arbitrage	0.11
Event Driven	−0.05
Regulation D	0.56
Convergence Trading	
Fixed Income Arbitrage	−0.03
Convertible Bond Arbitrage	0.11
Equity Market Neutral	0.32
Yield Alternatives	0.19
Relative Value Arbitrage	−0.03
Opportunistic	
Global Macro	−0.64
Fund of Funds	−0.30

a lower-returning year tended to be followed by a year with better returns. In other words, past performance was no indication of future results. In the case of HFRI, the serial correlation was only slightly negative. The two asset classes that had positive serial correlation were large-cap stocks and cash. Here good years tended to be followed by even better years and past performance was a reasonable indication of future performance.

Examining the performance of the different categories of hedge funds, we can see that the convergence trading strategies generated positive serial correlation, with the exception of fixed income arbitrage and relative value hedge fund managers. That is, these managers demonstrated the greatest affinity for performance persistence. In the case of market directional strategies, whereas equity long/short and activist investors showed positive serial correlations, emerging markets and short selling exhibited negative serial correlations. In the case of corporate restructuring, whereas distressed securities and merger arbitrage showed small but positive serial correlations, Regulation D strategies exhibited a higher level of serial correlation, and event driven had a slightly negative serial correlation. Finally, in the case of opportunistic strategies, both global macro funds and funds of funds showed negative serial correlations.

It is difficult to reconcile the varying conclusions regarding hedge fund performance persistence. The different conclusions could be due to different databases used or different time periods tested. This emphasizes all the more the need to conduct individual due diligence on each hedge fund manager.

As a result, the persistence of hedge fund manager performance will remain an open issue until manager databases with longer performance track records can be developed.

A HEDGE FUND INVESTMENT STRATEGY

The discussion thus far in this chapter suggests that hedge funds can expand the investment opportunity set for investors. The question now becomes: What is to be accomplished by the hedge fund investment program? The strategy may be simply a search for an additional source of return. Conversely, it may be for risk management purposes. Whatever its purpose, an investment plan for hedge funds may consider one of three strategies. Hedge funds may be selected on an opportunistic basis, as a hedge fund of funds, or as an absolute-return strategy. A fourth possible strategy is a joint venture where an investor provides seed capital and investment capital for a new hedge fund manager. The investor receives professional hedge fund management plus a "piece of the action."

Opportunistic Hedge Fund Investing

The term hedge fund can be misleading. Hedge funds do not necessarily have to hedge an investment portfolio. Rather, they can be used to expand the investment opportunity set. This is the opportunistic nature of hedge funds—they can provide an investor with new investment opportunities that she cannot otherwise obtain through traditional long-only investments.

There are several ways hedge funds can be opportunistic. First, many hedge fund managers can add value to an existing investment portfolio through specialization in a sector or in a market strategy. These managers do not contribute portable alpha. Instead, they contribute above market returns through the application of superior skill or knowledge to a narrow market or strategy.

Consider a portfolio manager whose particular expertise is the biotechnology industry. She has followed this industry for years and has developed a superior information set to identify winners and losers. On the long-only side, the manager purchases those stocks that she believes will increase in value and avoids those biotech stocks she believes will decline in value. However, this strategy does not utilize her superior information set to its fullest advantage. The ability to go both long and short biotech stocks in a hedge fund is the only way to maximize the value of the manager's information set. Therefore, a biotech hedge fund provides a new opportunity: the ability to extract value on both the long side and the short side of the biotech market. These are known as *sector hedge funds*.

The goal of this strategy is to identify the best managers in a specific economic sector or specific market segment that complements the existing investment portfolio. These managers are used to enhance the risk and return profile of an existing portfolio, rather than hedge it.

Sector hedge funds tend to have well-defined benchmarks. Take the example of the biotech long/short hedge fund. An appropriate benchmark would be the AMEX Biotech Index that contains 17 biotechnology companies. Alternatively, if the investor believed that the biotech sector will outperform the general stock market, she could use a broad-based stock index such as the S&P 500 for the benchmark. The point is that sector hedge funds are not absolute-return vehicles (discussed later). Their performance can be measured relative to a benchmark.

All traditional long-only managers are benchmarked to some passive index. The nature of benchmarking is such that it forces the manager to focus on his benchmark and the tracking error associated with that benchmark. This focus on benchmarking leads traditional active managers to commit a large portion of their portfolios to tracking their benchmark. Oftentimes, the long-only manager will identify these positions as being utilized for risk management purposes. The necessity to consider the impact of every trade on the portfolio's tracking error relative to its assigned benchmark reduces the flexibility of the investment manager.

In addition, long-only active managers are constrained in their ability to short securities. They may short a security only up to its weight in the benchmark index. If the security is only a small part of the index, the manager's efforts to short the stock will be further constrained. For example, the median weight in the Russell 1000 stock index is only 0.04%. The inability to short a security beyond its benchmark weight deprives an active manager of the opportunity to take full advantage of the mispricing in the marketplace. Furthermore, not only are long-only managers unable to take advantage of overpriced securities, but they also cannot fully take advantage of underpriced securities because they cannot generate the necessary short positions to balance the overweights with respect to underpriced securities. The long-only constraint is a well-known limitation on the ability of traditional active management to earn excess returns.

In summary, opportunistic (sector) hedge fund investing does not have to hedge the portfolio. Instead, it can lead to more efficient investing, a broader investment universe, and the freedom to allow managers to trade on an expanded information set. More to the point, opportunistic hedge fund managers can build a long/short market neutral portfolio based on biotech stocks if that is where they have the expertise to add value.

As another example, most institutional investors have a broad equity portfolio. This portfolio may include an index fund, external value and growth managers, and possibly, private equity investments. However, along the spectrum of this equity portfolio, there may be gaps in its investment lineup. For instance, many hedge funds combine late-stage private investments with public securities. These hybrid funds are a natural extension of an institution's investment portfolio because they bridge the gap between private equity and index funds. Therefore, a new opportunity is identified: the ability to blend private equity and public securities within one investment strategy.

Alternative "assets" are really alternative investment strategies, and these alternative strategies are used to expand the investment opportunity set rather than hedge it. In summary, hedge funds may be selected not necessarily to reduce the risk of an existing investment portfolio, but instead, to complement its risk and return profile. Opportunistic investing is designed to select hedge fund managers that can enhance certain portions of a broader portfolio. In other words, hedge funds can be used to expand the investment opportunity set with respect to an asset class rather than hedge it.

Constructing an opportunistic portfolio of hedge funds will depend on the constraints under which such a program operates. For example, if an investor's hedge fund program is not limited in scope or style, then

EXHIBIT 17.3   Implementing an Opportunistic Hedge Fund Strategy

Diversified Hedge Fund Portfolio	Equity-Based Hedge Fund Portfolio
Equity long/short	Equity long/short
Short selling	Short selling
Market neutral	Market neutral
Merger arbitrage	Merger arbitrage
Event driven	Event driven
Convertible arbitrage	Convertible arbitrage
Global macro	Activist Investing
Fixed income arbitrage	
Relative-value arbitrage	

diversification across a broad range of hedge fund styles would be appropriate. If, however, the hedge fund program is limited in scope to, for instance, expanding the equity investment opportunity set, the choices will be less diversified across strategies. Exhibit 17.3 demonstrates these two choices.

Hedge Fund of Funds

A *hedge fund of funds* is an investment in a group of hedge funds, from 10 to more than 20. The purpose of a hedge fund of funds is to reduce the idiosyncratic risk of any one hedge fund manager. In other words, there is safety in numbers. This is simply modern portfolio theory applied to the hedge fund marketplace. Diversification is one of the founding principles of modern portfolio theory, and it is as applicable to hedge funds as it is to stocks and bonds.

The success to any fund of hedge funds relies on manager selection. Typically, this is a winnowing process from the large universe of existing hedge funds down to a manageable pool that forms the FOF. Exhibit 17.4 demonstrates how the selection process works. Typically, a FOF starts with the total universe of hedge funds, which was estimated at close to 10,000 at the end of 2009. However, databases such as that of Hedge Fund Research, Inc. and others cover only about 6,000 managers. From there, the list gets narrowed down further by quantitative screens and hedge fund styles to a list of 500 to 1,000 hedge funds that an FOF manager may do further analysis on (returns, risk profile, style bias, capacity limits, and other limiting criteria).

The list gets further narrowed down to approximately 100 to 200 managers that are considered prospective and for which the FOF manager will conduct due diligence through actual on-site visits, interviews, reference checks, checking of trading programs and service providers, and so on. Finally, from this list the FOF manager selects 10 to 50 individual hedge funds for the pool.

EXHIBIT 17.4

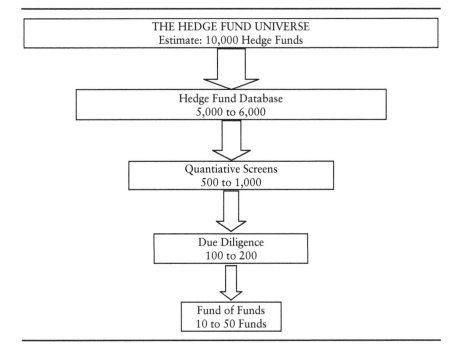

Absolute Return

Hedge funds are often described as *absolute-return products*. This term comes from the skill-based nature of the industry. Hedge fund managers generally claim that their investment returns are derived from their skill at security selection rather than that of broad asset classes. This is due to the fact that most hedge fund managers build concentrated portfolios of relatively few investment positions and do not attempt to track a stock or bond index. One study suggests shows that hedge funds generate a return distribution that is very different from mutual funds.[2]

Furthermore, given the generally unregulated waters in which hedge fund managers operate, they have greater flexibility in their trading style and execution than traditional long-only managers. This flexibility provides a greater probability that a hedge fund manager will reach his return targets. As a result, hedge funds have often been described as absolute-return vehicles that target a specific annual return regardless of what performance might be

---

[2]William Fung and David A. Hsieh, "Empirical Characteristics of Dynamic Trading Strategies: The Case of Hedge Funds," *Review of Financial Studies* 10, no. 2 (Summer 1997): 275–302.

found among market indexes. In other words, hedge fund managers target an absolute return rather than determine their performance relative to an index.

All traditional long-only managers are benchmarked to some passive index. The nature of benchmarking is such that it forces the manager to focus on his benchmark and his tracking error associated with that benchmark. This focus on benchmarking leads traditional active managers to commit a large portion their portfolios to tracking their benchmark. The necessity to consider the impact of every trade on the portfolio's tracking error relative to its assigned benchmark reduces the flexibility of the investment manager.

The flexibility of hedge fund managers allows them to go both long and short without benchmark constraints. This allows them to set a target rate of return or an "absolute return."

Specific parameters must be set for an absolute-return program. These parameters will direct how the hedge fund program is constructed and operated and should include risk and return targets as well as the type of hedge fund strategies that may be selected. Absolute-return parameters should operate at two levels: that of the individual hedge fund manager and for the overall hedge fund program. The investor sets target return ranges for each hedge fund manager but sets a specific target return level for the absolute return program. The parameters for the individual managers may be different than that for the program. For example, acceptable levels of volatility for individual hedge fund managers may be greater than that for the program.

The program parameters for the hedge fund managers may be based on such factors as volatility, expected return, types of instruments traded, leverage, and historical drawdown. Other qualitative factors may be included such as length of track record, periodic liquidity, minimum investment, and assets under management. Liquidity is particularly important because an investor needs to know with certainty her time frame for cashing out of an absolute return program if hedge fund returns turn sour.

Exhibit 17.5 demonstrates an absolute-return program strategy. Notice that the return for the portfolio has a specific target rate of 10%, while for the individual hedge funds the return range is 8% to 15%. In the lower return environment of 2010, these returns are a reasonable alternative U.S. stock and investment grade bond market. Also, the absolute-return portfolio has a target level for risk and drawdowns, while for the individual hedge funds, a range is acceptable.

However, certain parameters are synchronized. Liquidity, for instance, must be the same for both the absolute-return portfolio and that of the individual hedge fund managers. The reason is that a range of liquidity is not acceptable if the investor wishes to liquidate her portfolio. She must be able to cash out of each hedge fund within the same time-frame as that established for the portfolio.

EXHIBIT 17.5   An Absolute-Return Strategy

Absolute-Return Portfolio	Individual Hedge Fund Manager
Target return: 10%	Expected return: 8% to 15%
Target volatility: 7%	Target volatility: 5% to 15%
Largest acceptable draw-down: 10%	Largest drawdown: 10% to 20%
Liquidity: Semiannual	Liquidity: Semiannual
Hedge fund style: equity based	Hedge fund style: equity L/S, market neutral, merger arbitrage, short selling, event driven, convertible arbitrage
Target correlation to stock and bond market: 0.0	Target correlation to stock market and investment grade bond market: 0.6
Length of track record: 3 years	Minimum track record: 3 years

Bond Substitute

Exhibit 17.1 shows that hedge funds of funds have significantly lower risk than large-cap, small-cap, or foreign stocks. In fact, the HFRI FOF index generates a lower risk profile than even U.S. Treasury bonds while generating greater return. This has led some researchers to consider whether hedge funds can replace bonds in an efficient portfolio. One research paper studied the issue of hedge funds as a cash substitute.[3] That study combined hedge funds with stocks and bonds in an efficient frontier analysis, and found that hedge funds enter efficient frontiers across all risk levels because of their superior risk-adjusted returns. More importantly, the study found that hedge funds entered efficient portfolios largely at the expense of bonds. That is, hedge funds primarily displaced cash and bonds in efficient portfolios. This finding suggests that hedge funds may be used as a cash substitute.

We note that in Exhibit 17.1 the FOF index has a superior Sharpe ratio compared to U.S. Treasury bonds. In addition, the correlation coefficients between FOFs and the different categories of stocks are positive, and relatively low. This also contributes to the ability of hedge funds to be a bond substitute. However, we do note that the correlation of U.S. Treasury bonds with small-cap, large-cap, and international stocks is either close to zero or negative, so that FOFs are a close but not perfect substitute for Treasury bonds.

---

[3]See R. McFall Lamm Jr., "Portfolios of Alternative Assets: Why Not 100% Hedge Funds?" *Journal of Investing* 8, no. 4 (1999): 87–97.

SELECTING A HEDGE FUND MANAGER

The hedge fund industry is still relatively new. Most of the academic research on hedge funds only began in the 1990s. As a result, for most hedge fund managers, a two- to three-year track record is considered long term. In fact, a study by Park, Brown, and Goetzmann finds that the attrition rate in the hedge fund industry is about 15% per year and that the half-life for hedge funds is about 2.5 years.[4] A study by Liang documents an attrition rate of 8.54% per year for hedge funds.[5] Weisman and Abernathy indicate that relying on a hedge fund manager's past performance history can lead to disappointing investment results. Consequently, performance history, while useful, cannot be relied upon solely in selecting a hedge fund manager.[6]

Beyond performance numbers, there are three fundamental questions that every hedge fund manager should answer during the initial screening process. The answers to these three questions are critical to understanding the nature of the hedge fund manager's investment program. The three questions are:

1. What is the investment objective of the hedge fund?
2. What is the investment process of the hedge fund manager?
3. What makes the hedge fund manager so smart?

A hedge fund manager should have a clear and concise statement of its investment objective. Second, the hedge fund manager should identify its investment process. For instance, is it quantitatively or qualitatively based? Last, the hedge fund manager must demonstrate that he or she is smarter than other money managers. The questions presented are threshold issues.

These questions are screening tools designed to reduce an initial universe of hedge fund managers down to a select pool of potential investments. They are not, however, a substitute for a thorough due diligence review.

Investment Objective

The question of a hedge fund manager's investment objective can be broken down into three questions:

---

[4]James M. Park, Stephen J. Brown, and William Goetzmann, "Careers and Survival: Competition and Risk in the Hedge Fund and CTA Industry," *Journal of Finance* 56, no. 5 (2001): 1869–1886.

[5]Bing Liang, "Hedge Fund Performance: 1990–1999," *Financial Analysts Journal* 57, no. 1 (January–February 2001): 11–18.

[6]Andrew B. Weisman and Jerome Abernathy, "The Dangers of Historical Hedge Fund Data," *Risk Budgeting*, edited by Leslie Rahl, pp. 65–81 (London, Risk Books, 2000).

1. In which markets does the hedge fund manager invest?
2. What is the hedge fund manager's general investment strategy?
3. What is the hedge fund manager's benchmark, if any?

Although these questions may seem straightforward, they are often surprisingly difficult to answer. Consider the following language from a hedge fund disclosure document:

> The principal objective of the Fund is capital appreciation, primarily through the purchase and sale of securities, commodities and other financial instruments including without limitation, stocks, bonds, notes, debentures, and bills issued by corporations, municipalities, sovereign nations or other entities; options, rights, warrants, convertible securities, exchangeable securities, synthetic and/or structured convertible or exchangeable products, participation interests, investment contracts, mortgages, mortgage and asset-backed securities, real estate and interests therein; currencies, other futures, commodity options, forward contracts, money market instruments, bank notes, bank guarantees, letters of credit, other forms of bank obligations; other swaps and other derivative instruments; limited partnership interests and other limited partnership securities or instruments; and contracts relating to the foregoing; in each case whether now existing or created in the future.

Let's analyze the above statement in light of our three investment objective questions.

Question 1: In which markets does the hedge fund manager invest?
Answer: In every market known to exist.

By listing every possible financial, commodity, or investment contract currently in existence (or to exist in the future), the hedge fund manager has covered all options, but has left the investor uninformed. Unfortunately, the unlimited nature of the hedge fund manager's potential investment universe does not help to narrow the scope of the manager's investment objective.

Question 2: What is the hedge fund manager's general strategy?
Answer: Capital appreciation.

This answer too, is uninformative. Rarely does any investor invest in a hedge fund for capital *depreciation*. Generally, hedge funds are not used as tax shelters. Furthermore, many institutional investors are tax exempt so that taxes are not a consideration. Capital appreciation is assumed for most investments, including hedge funds. The preceding language is far too general to be informative.

> *Question 3:* What is the manager's benchmark, if any?
> *Answer:* There is no effective benchmark. The manager's investment universe is so widespread as to make any benchmark useless. In fact, given the extensive laundry list of financial instruments that the hedge fund manager lists in the offering document, the most suitable benchmark for this hedge fund manager is the Intergalactic Investable Universe!

Unfortunately, the preceding disclosure language, while very detailed, discloses very little. It does cover all of the manager's legal bases, but it does not inform the investor. It is nothing more than a laundry list of financial instruments, which obfuscates the true strategy of the hedge fund manager.

Where does this manager fall within the hedge fund spectrum? The very broad nature of this hedge fund's investment objective places it in the global macro category. Its investment universe is far too broad to be an arbitrage fund. By the same token, its strategy is too expansive to be considered an equity long/short program. Its only appropriate category is global macro.

By contrast, consider the following language from a second hedge fund disclosure document:

> The Fund's investment objective is to make investments in public securities that generate a long-term return in excess of that generated by the overall U.S. public portfolio through selective short positions.

This one sentence answers all three investment objective questions. First, the manager identifies that it invests in the U.S. public equity market. Second, the manager discloses that it uses a long/short investment strategy. Finally, the manager states that its objective is to outperform the overall U.S. equity market. Therefore, a suitable benchmark might be the S&P 500, the Russell 1000, or a sector index.

In summary, long-winded disclosure statements are not necessary. A well-thought-out investment strategy can be summarized in one sentence.

Investment Process

Most investors prefer a well-defined investment process that describes how an investment manager makes its investments. The articulation and documentation of the process can be just as important as the investment results generated by the process. Consider the following language from another hedge fund disclosure document:

The manager makes extensive use of computer technology in both the formulation and execution of many investment decisions. Buy and sell decisions will, in many cases, be made and executed algorithmically according to quantitative trading strategies embodied in analytical computer software running the manager's computer facilities or on other computers used to support the Fund's trading activities.

This is a "black box." A black box is the algorithmic extension of the hedge fund manager's brain power. Computer algorithms are developed to quantify the manager's skill or investment insight.

For black box managers, the black box itself is the investment process. It is not that the black boxes are bad investments. In fact, the hedge fund research indicates that proprietary quantitative trading strategies can be quite successful. Rather, the issue is whether good performance results justify the lack of a clear investment process.

Black box programs tend to be used in arbitrage or relative-value hedge fund programs. Hedge fund managers use quantitative computer algorithms to seek out pricing discrepancies between similar securities or investment contracts. They then sell the investment that appears to be "expensive" and buy the investment that appears to be "cheap." The very nature of arbitrage programs is to minimize market risk. Leverage is then applied to extract the most value from their small net exposure to market risk.

A black box is just one example of process versus investment results. The hedge fund industry considers itself to be "skill based." However, it is very difficult to translate manager skill into a process. This is particularly true when the performance of the hedge fund is dependent on the skill of a specific individual. Let's consider another, well-publicized skill-based investment process. In the spring of 2000, the hedge funds headed by George Soros stumbled, leading to the departure of Stanley Druckenmiller, the chief investment strategist for Soros Fund Management. The *Wall Street Journal* documented the concentrated skill-based investment style of this hedge fund group:[7]

> For years, [Soros Fund Management] fostered an entrepreneurial culture, with a cadre of employees battling wits to persuade Mr. Druckenmiller to invest.

> "[Mr. Druckenmiller] didn't scream, but he could be very tough. It could be three days or three weeks of battling it out until he's convinced, or you're defeated."

---

[7]*Wall Street Journal*, May 1, 2000, p. C1.

The preceding statement does not describe an investment process. It is a description of an individual. The hedge fund manager's investment analysis and decision making is concentrated in one person. This is a pure example of "skill-based" investing. There is no discernible process. Instead, all information is filtered through the brain of one individual. In essence, the institutional investor must trust the judgment of one person.

Mr. Druckenmiller compiled an exceptional track record as the manager of the Soros Quantum Fund and as the manager of his own hedge fund Duquense Capital Management. However, the concentration of decision-making authority is not an economic risk, it is a process risk.

Investors should accept economic risk but not process risk. Soros Fund Management is a well-known global macro hedge fund manager. The fundamental risks of an investment in a global macro fund are credit risk and market risk. Investors are generally unwilling to bear risks that are not fundamental to their tactical and strategic asset allocations. Process risk is not a fundamental risk. It is an idiosyncratic risk of the hedge fund manager's structure and operations.

Generally, process risk is not a risk that investors wish to bear. Nor is it a risk for which they expect to be compensated. Furthermore, how would an investor go about pricing the process risk of a hedge fund manager? It can't be quantified, and it can't be calibrated. Therefore, there is no way to tell whether an institutional investor is being properly compensated for this risk. For example, Park and Staum demonstrate that idiosyncratic process risks can largely be eliminated through a diversified fund of funds program.[8] They indicate that a portfolio of 15 to 20 hedge funds can eliminate much of the idiosyncratic risk associated with hedge fund investments.

Process risk also raises the ancillary issue of lack of transparency. Skill-based investing usually is opaque. Are the decisions of the key individual quantitatively based? Qualitatively based? There is no way to really tell. This is similar to the problems discussed earlier with respect to black boxes.

To summarize, process risk cannot be quantified and it is not a risk that investors are willing to bear. Process risk also raises issues of transparency. Investors want clarity and definition, not opaqueness and amorphousness.

What Makes the Hedge Fund Manager so Smart?

Before investing money with a hedge fund manager, an investor must determine one of the following. The hedge fund manager must be able to demonstrate that he or she is smarter than the next manager. One way to be smarter than another hedge fund manager is to have superior skill in

---

[8]James M. Park and Jeremy C. Staum, "Fund of Funds Diversification: How Much is Enough?" *Journal of Alternative Investments* 1, no. 3 (1998): 39–42.

filtering information. That is, the hedge fund manager must be able to look at the same information set as another manager but be able to glean more investment insight from that dataset.

Alternatively, if the hedge fund manager is not smarter than the next manager, he must demonstrate that he has a better information set; his competitive advantage is not filtering information but gathering it. To be successful, a hedge fund manager must demonstrate one or both of these competitive advantages. Generally speaking, quantitative, computer-driven managers satisfy the first criterion. That is, hedge fund managers that run computer models access the same information set as everyone else, but have better (smarter) algorithms to extract more value per information unit than the next manager. These managers tend to be relative-value managers.

Relative-value managers extract value by simultaneously comparing the prices of two securities and buying and selling accordingly. This information is available to all investors in the marketplace. However, it is the relative-value managers that are able to process the information quickly enough to capture mispricings in the market. These arbitrage strategies expose an investor to credit risk.

Alternatively, hedge fund managers that confine themselves to a particular market segment or sector generally satisfy the second criterion. They have a larger information set that allows them to gain a competitive edge in their chosen market. Their advantage is a proprietary information set accumulated over time rather than a proprietary data filtering system. Consider the following statement from a hedge fund disclosure document: "The Adviser hopes to achieve consistently high returns by focusing on small and mid-cap companies in the biotechnology market." The competitive advantage of this type of manager is his or her knowledge not only about a particular economic sector (biotechnology), but also, about a particular market segment of that sector (small and mid-cap). This type of manger tends to take more market risk exposure than credit risk exposure and generally applies equity long/short programs.

Identifying the competitive advantage of the hedge fund manager is the key to determining whether the hedge fund manager can sustain performance results. We indicated earlier that the issue of performance persistence is undecided.

Therefore, an investor cannot rely on historical hedge fund performance data as a means of selecting good managers from bad managers. Furthermore, every hedge fund disclosure document contains some variation of the following language: "Past performance is no indication of future results." Essentially, this statement directs the investor to ignore the hedge fund manager's performance history.

To assess the likelihood of performance persistence, the investor must then determine whether the hedge fund manager is an information gatherer or an information filterer. Consider the following language from a hedge fund disclosure document:

> The General Partner will utilize its industry expertise, contacts, and databases developed over the past 11 years to identify company investment ideas outside traditional sources and will analyze these investment opportunities using, among other techniques, many aspects of its proven methodology in determining value.

This hedge fund manager has a superior information set that has been developed over 11 years. He is an information gatherer. This manager applies an equity long/short program within a specific market sector.

Finally, consider the following disclosure language from a merger arbitrage hedge fund manager:

> [The] research group [is] staffed by experienced M&A [merger and acquisition] lawyers with detailed knowledge of deal lifecycle, with extensive experience with corporate law of multiple U.S. states, U.S. and foreign securities laws regarding proxy contests, and antitrust laws (both of the United States and EU), and who have made relevant filings before regulators and have closed a wide variety of M&A transactions.

This hedge fund manager is an information filterer. His expertise is sifting through the outstanding legal and regulatory issues associated with a merger and determining the likelihood that the deal will be completed.

To summarize, a good lesson is that successful hedge fund managers know the exact nature of their competitive advantage, and how to exploit it.

Financial Instruments and Concepts Introduced in this Chapter (in Order of Presentation)

Multistrategy hedge funds	Hedge fund of funds
Sector hedge funds	Absolute-return products

CHAPTER 18

Investing in Capital Venture Funds

The private equity sector purchases the private stock or equity-linked securities of nonpublic companies that are expected to go public or provides the capital for public companies (or their divisions) that may wish to go private. The key component in either case is the private nature of the securities purchased. Private equity, by definition, is not publicly traded. Therefore, investments in private equity are illiquid. Investors in this marketplace must be prepared to invest for the long haul—investment horizons may be as long as five to 10 years.

Private equity is a generic term that encompasses the following four distinct strategies in the market for private investing:

1. Venture capital, the financing of start-up companies.
2. Leveraged buyouts (LBOs) where public companies repurchase all of their outstanding shares and turn themselves into private companies.
3. Mezzanine financing, a hybrid of private debt and equity financing.
4. Distressed debt investing, private equity investments in established (as opposed to start-up) but troubled companies.

Private equity is as old as Columbus' journey to America. Queen Isabella of Spain sold her jewelry to finance Columbus' small fleet of ships in return for whatever spoils Columbus could find in the New World. The risks were great, but the potential rewards were even greater. This in a nutshell summarizes the private equity market: a large risk of failure but the potential for outstanding gains.

More generally, private equity provides the long-term equity base of a company that is not listed on any exchange and therefore cannot raise capital via the public stock market. Private equity provides the working capital that is used to help private companies grow and succeed. It is a long-term investment process that requires patient due diligence and hands on monitoring.

In this chapter and the three to follow, we discuss private equity. Our focus in this chapter is on the best known of the private equity categories: venture capital. *Venture capital* is the supply of equity financing to start-up companies that do not have a sufficient track record to attract investment capital from traditional sources (e.g., the public markets or lending institutions). Entrepreneurs that develop business plans require investment capital to implement those plans. However, these start-up ventures often lack tangible assets that can be used as collateral for a loan. In addition, start-up companies are unlikely to produce positive earnings for several years. Negative cash flows are another reason why banks and other lending institutions as well as the public stock market are unwilling to provide capital to support the business plan.

It is in this uncertain space where nascent companies are born that venture capitalists operate. *Venture capitalists* finance these high-risk, illiquid, and unproven ideas by purchasing senior equity stakes while the firms are still privately held. The ultimate goal is to make a buck. Venture capitalists are willing to underwrite new ventures with untested products and bear the risk of no liquidity only if they can expect a reasonable return for their efforts. Often venture capitalists set expected target rates of return of 33% or more to support the risks they bear. Successful start-up companies funded by venture capital money include Google, Cisco Systems, Cray Research, Microsoft, and Genentech.

THE ROLE OF A VENTURE CAPITALIST

Venture capital firms have two roles within the industry:

- Raising money from investors.
- Investing the funds raised with start-up companies.

Venture capital firms are not passive investors. Once they invest in a company, they take an active role either in an advisory capacity or as a director on the board of the company. They monitor the progress of the company, implement incentive plans for the entrepreneurs and management, and establish financial goals for the company.

Besides providing management insight, venture capital firms usually have the right to hire and fire key managers, including the original entrepreneur. They also provide access to consultants, accountants, lawyers, investment bankers, and most importantly, other businesses that might purchase the start-up company's product.

In this section, we focus on the relationship between the venture capital firms and its investors. In the next section, we consider the process by which a the management of venture funds selects investments.

The Relationship of the Venture Capital Firm to Its Investors

Before a venture capital firm can invest money with start-up ventures, it must go through a period of fund raising with outside investors. Most venture capital funds are structured as limited partnerships, where the venture capital firm is the general partner and the investors are limited partners. Each venture capital fund first goes through a period of fund raising before it begins to invest the capital raised from the limited partners.

The venture capital firm is the general partner of the venture capital fund. All other investors are limited partners. As the general partner, the venture capital firm has full operating authority to managed the fund as it pleases, subject to restrictions placed in the covenants of the fund's documents.

As the venture capital industry matured, sophisticated investors such as pension funds, endowments, foundations, and high-net-worth individuals began to demand contractual provisions be placed in the documents and subscription agreements that establish and govern a private equity fund. These covenants ensure that the venture capital firm operates in the best interest of the limited partners who have invested in the venture capital fund.

These *protective covenants* can be broken down into three broad classes of investor protections:[1]

- Covenants relating to the overall management of the fund.
- Covenants that relate to the activities of the general partners.
- Covenants that determine what constitutes a permissible investment.

Restrictions on the Management of the Venture Capital Fund

Typically, the most important covenant is the size of an investment by the venture capital fund in any one start-up venture. This is typically expressed as a percentage of the capital committed to the venture capital fund. The purpose is to ensure that the venture capitalist does not bet the fund on any single investment. In any venture capital fund, there will be start-up ventures that fail to generate a return. This is expected. By diversifying across several venture investments, this risk is mitigated.

---

[1]See Josh Lerner, *Venture Capital and Private Equity* (New York: John Wiley & Sons, 2000).

Other covenants may include a restriction on the use of debt or leverage by the venture capital fund's management. Venture capital investments are risky enough without management leveraging the fund through borrowing.

In addition, there may be a restriction on co-investments with prior or future funds controlled by the venture capital firm. If a venture capital firm has made a poor investment in a prior fund, the investors in the current fund do not want management to throw more good money after bad. Finally, there is usually a covenant regarding the distribution of profits. It is optimal for investors to receive the profits as they accrue. Furthermore, distributed profits reduce the amount of committed capital in the venture fund, which in turn reduces the fees paid to the venture capital firm. It is in the venture capital firm's economic interest to hold onto profits, while investors prefer to have them distributed as they accrue.

Restrictions on the Activities of the General Partner

Primary among these is a limit on the amount of private investments management of the venture capital firm can make in any of the firms funded by the venture capital fund. If the venture capital firm makes private investments on its own in a select group of companies, these companies may receive more attention than the remaining portfolio of companies included in the venture fund.

In addition, general partners are often limited in their ability to sell their general partnership interest in the venture fund to a third party. Such a sale would likely reduce the general partner's incentive to monitor and produce an effective exit strategy for the venture fund's portfolio companies.

Two other covenants are related to keeping the venture capital fund's management eye on the ball. The first is a restriction on the amount of future fund raising. Fund raising is time consuming and distracting—less time is spent managing the investments of the fund. Also, the limited partners typically demand that the general partner spend substantially all of his time on managing the investments of the fund—outside interests are limited or restricted.

Restrictions on the Type of Investments

Generally, covenants that restrict the type of investments serve to keep the venture capital firm's management focussed on investing in those companies, industries and transactions where she has the greatest experience. So, for instance, there may be restrictions or prohibitions on investing in leveraged buyouts, other venture capital funds, PIPES, foreign securities, or companies and industries outside the realm of the venture capitalists' expertise.

Venture Capital Fees

Venture capital firms earn two types of fees:

- Management fee
- Profit sharing/incentive fee

Management Fee   The management fee can range anywhere from 1% to 3.5%, with most venture capital funds in the 2% to 2.5% range. This fee is used to pay the expenses of the venture capital firm while it looks for attractive investment opportunities for the venture fund.

A key point is that the management fee is assessed on the amount of committed capital, not invested capital. Consider the following example: the venture capitalist raises $100 million in committed capital for her venture fund. The management fee 2.5%. To date, only $50 million dollars of the raised capital has been invested. The annual management fee that the venture capitalist collects is $2.5 million—2.5% × $100 million—even though not all of the capital has been invested. Investors pay the management fee on the amount of capital they have agreed to commit to the venture fund whether or not that capital has actually been invested.

Consider the implications of this fee arrangement. The venture capital firm collects a management fee from the moment that an investor signs a subscription agreement to invest capital in the venture fund—even though no capital has actually been contributed by the limited partners yet. Furthermore, the venture capital firm then effectively has a call option to demand—according to the subscription agreement—that the investors contribute capital when the venture capital firm finds an appropriate investment for the fund. This is a great deal for the venture capital firm—it is paid a large fee to have a call option on the limited partners' capital. Not a bad business model. We will see in the next chapter that this has some keen implications for leveraged buyout funds.

Profit Sharing/Incentive Fee   The second part of the remuneration for a venture capital firm is the *profit sharing* or *incentive fee*. This is really where the venture capital firm makes its money. The incentive fee provides the venture capital firm with a share of the profits generated by the venture fund. The typical incentive fee is 20%, but the better known venture capital funds can charge up to 35%.

Similar to our discussion of hedge fund incentive fees in Chapter 16, the incentive fee for venture capital funds are a free option. If the venture capital firm generates profits for the venture fund, it can collect a share of these profits. If the venture fund loses money, the venture capital firm does not collect an incentive fee. This binary fee payout can be described as

$$\text{Payout on incentive fee} = \text{Max}[i \times \text{Profits}, 0]$$

where

i = the percent of profit sharing by the venture capitalist, e.g., 20%
Profits = the profits generated by the venture fund

The above equation is the basic equation for the payout on a call option. Similar to hedge fund incentive fees, this option has significant value to the venture capitalist. Furthermore, valued within an option context, venture capital profit sharing fees provide some interesting incentives to the venture capital firm.

For example, one way to increase the value of a call option is to increase the volatility of the underlying asset. This means that the management of the venture fund is encouraged to make riskier investments in order to maximize the value of its incentive fee. This increased risk may run counter to the desires of the limited partners to maintain a less risky profile. It is also fascinating to realize that this incentive fee is costless to the venture capital firm—it does not pay any price for the receipt of this option. Indeed, the venture capital firm gets paid a management fee in addition to this free call option on the profits of the venture fund. As we noted previously, this is not a bad business model for the venture capital firm.

Fortunately, there is a check and balance on incentive fees in the venture capital world. Most, if not all, venture capital limited partnership agreements include some restrictive covenants on when incentive fees may be paid to the venture capital firm. There are three primary covenants that are used.

First, most venture capital partnership agreements include a *clawback provision*. This covenant allows the limited partners to clawback previously paid incentive fees to the venture capital firm if, at the end/liquidation of the venture fund, the limited partners are still out of pocket some costs or lost capital investment. This prevents the venture capital firm from making money if the limited partners do not earn a profit.

Second, there is often an *escrow agreement* where a portion of the venture capital firm incentive fees are held in a segregated escrow account until the fund is liquidated. Again this ensures that the venture capital firm does not walk away with any profit unless the limited partners also earn a profit. If a profit is earned by every limited partner, the escrow proceeds are released to the venture capital firm.

Finally, there is often a prohibition on the distribution of profit sharing fees to the venture capital firm until all committed capital is paid back to the limited partners. In other words, the limited partners must first be paid back their invested capital before profits may be shared in the venture fund. Sometimes this covenant also provides that all management fees must also be recouped by the limited partners before the venture capital firm can collect its incentive fees.

Just as a side observation: It is interesting to note that these types of profit-sharing covenants are not used in hedge fund limited partnership agreements.

THE BUSINESS PLAN

The venture capital firm has two constituencies: investors on the one hand, and start-up portfolio companies on the other. In the prior section, we discussed the relationship between the venture capital firm and its investors. In this section, we discuss how the management of a venture fund selects its investments.

The most important document upon which a venture fund's management will base her decision to invest in a start-up company is the *business plan*. The business plan must be comprehensive, coherent, and internally consistent. It must clearly state the business strategy, identify the niche that the new company will fill, and describe the resources needed to fill that niche.

The business plan also reflects the start-up management team's ability to develop and present an intelligent and strategic plan of action. The business plan not only describes the business opportunity but also provides management of the venture fund with an insight to the viability of the start-up management team.

Finally, the business plan must be realistic. One part of every business plan is the assumptions about revenue growth, cash-burn rate, additional rounds of capital injection, and expected date of profitability and/or IPO status. The financial goals stated in the business plan must be achievable. Additionally, financial milestones identified in the business plan can become important conditions for the vesting of management equity, the release of deferred investment commitments, and the control of the board of directors.

In this section, we review the key elements of a business plan for a start-up venture. This is the heart and soul of the venture capital industry—it is where new ideas are born and capital is committed.

Executive Summary

The *executive summary* is the opening statement of any business plan. In this short synopsis, it must be clear what is the unique selling point of the start-up venture. Is it a new product, distribution channel, manufacturing process, chip design, or consumer service? Whatever it is, it must be spelled out clearly for a nontechnical person to understand.[2]

The executive summary should quickly summarize the eight main parts of the business plan:

1. The market
2. The product/service
3. Intellectual property rights
4. The start-up management team
5. Operations and prior operating history
6. Financial projections
7. Amount of financing
8. Exit opportunities

We next discuss briefly each part of the business plan.

The Market

With respect to the market, the key issue is whether there is a viable commercial opportunity for the start-up venture. The first question is whether there is an existing market already. If the answer is yes, this is both good and bad. It is good because the commercial opportunity has already been demonstrated by someone else. It is bad because someone else has already developed a product or service to meet the existing demand.

This raises the issue of competition. Virtually every new product already has some competition at the outset. It is most unlikely that the product or service is so revolutionary such that there is no form of competition. Even if the start-up venture is first to market, there must be an explanation on how this gap in the market is currently being filled with existing (but deficient) solutions.

An existing marketplace makes a prima facie case for market demand, but then the start-up venture must describe how its product/service improves upon the existing market solution. Furthermore, if there is an existing product, the start-up venture should make a direct product comparison including price, quality, length of warranty, ease of use, product distribution, and target audience.

In addition to a review of the competition, the start-up venture must describe its market plan. The marketing plan must include three elements: pricing, product distribution, and promotion.

---

[2]See British Venture Capital Association, "A Guide to Private Equity," White paper, October 2004.

Pricing is clear enough. If the product is first to market, it can command a price premium. Furthermore, in today's electronic markets, prices erode rapidly. The start-up venture must describe its initial margins, but also how those margins will be affected as technology advances are made.

Product distribution is simply a way to describe how the start-up venture will get its product to the market. Will it use wholesalers, retailers, the internet, or direct sales? Is a sales force needed? Is a 24-hour help desk required? Also, different distribution channels may require different pricing. For example, wholesalers will need price discounts to be able to make a profit when they sell to retailers. Conversely, the start-up company may wish to offer a discount to those that order the product directly from the start-up venture.

Finally, the start-up venture must describe its promotion strategy. A discussion of trade shows, the Internet, mass media and tie-ins to other products should be described. The start-up venture should indicate whether its product should be marketed to a targeted audience or whether it has mass appeal. The cost of promotional materials and events must also be evaluated as part of the business plan.

The Product/Service

A description of the product or service should be done along every dimension, which establishes the start-up venture's unique selling point. Furthermore, this discussion must be done in plain English without the psychobabble or jargon that normally creeps into the explanation of technology products.

In fact, the key part of this section of the business plan is to cement the unique selling point of the product or service. Is it new to the market, available at a lower price, constructed with better quality, constructed in a shorter timeframe, provided with better customer service, smaller in size, easier to operation, and so on? Each of these points can provide a competitive advantage upon which to build a new product or service.

One-shot, single products are a concern for a venture capital firm. The upside will be inevitably limited as competition is drawn into the market. Therefore, business plans that address a second generation of products are generally preferred.

Intellectual Property Rights

The third essential part of the business plan is a discussion of intellectual property rights. Often, the industries to which venture capital flow are technology related such as computer software, telecom, biotech, and semiconductors. Most start-ups in the technology and other growth sectors base their business opportunity on the claim to proprietary technology. It is very important that a start-up's claim and rights to that intellectual property be absolute. Any intellectual property owned by the company must be clearly and unequivocally assigned to the company by third parties (usually the entrepreneur and management team). A structure where the entrepreneur still owns the intellectual property but licenses it to the start-up company are disfavored by venture capital firms because license agreements can expire or be terminated leaving the venture capital firm with a shell of a start-up company.

Generally, before a venture capital firm invests with a start-up company, it will conduct patent and trademark searches, seek the opinion of a patent counsel, and possibly ask third parties to confidentially evaluate the technology owned by the start-up company.

Additionally, the venture capital firm may ask key employees to sign noncompetition agreements, where they agree not to start another company or join another company operating in the same sector as the start-up for a reasonable period of time. Key employees may also be asked to sign nondisclosure agreements because protecting a start-up company's proprietary technology is an essential element to success.

The Start-Up Management Team

Venture capital firms invest in ideas and people. Once the manager of a venture fund has reviewed the start-up venture's unique selling point, it will turn to the start-up management team. Ideally, the start-up management team should have complementary skill sets: marketing, technology, finance, and operations. Every management team has gaps. The business plan must carefully address how these gaps will be filled.

The venture capital firm will closely review the resumes of every member of the start-up management team. Academic backgrounds, professional work history, and references will all be checked. Most important to the venture capital firm will be the professional background of the start-up management team. In particular, a management team that has successfully brought a previous start-up company to the IPO stage will be viewed most favorably.

In general, a great start-up management team with a good business plan is viewed more favorably than a good management team with a great business plan. The best business plan in the world can still fail from inability to execute. Thus a management team that has demonstrated a previous ability to follow and execute a business plan gets a greater chance of success than an unproven management team with a great business opportunity.

However, this is where a venture capital firm can add value. Recognizing a great business opportunity but a weak management team, the venture capital firm can bring its expertise to the start-up company as well as bring in other, more seasoned management professionals. While this often creates some friction with the original entrepreneur, the ultimate goal is to make money. Egos often succumb when there is money to be made.

In addition to filling in the gaps that may exist in the start-up management team, the venture capital firm will need to round out the board of directors of the start-up venture. One seat on the board will be filled by a member of the venture capital firm's own management team. However, other directors may be added to fill in some of the gaps found among the management team. In addition, the venture capital firm may ask an executive from an established company to sit on the board of the start-up company to provide contacts within the industry when the start-up is ready to look for a strategic buyer. A seasoned board member from a successful company can lend credibility to a start-up venture when it decides to go public.

Last, the start-up management team will need a seasoned chief financial officer (CFO). This will be the person primarily responsible for bringing the start-up company public. The CFO will work with the investment bankers to establish the price of the company's stock at the initial public offering. Since the IPO is often the exit strategy for the venture capital firm as well as some of the founders and key employees, it is critical that the CFO have IPO experience.

Operations and Prior Operating History

The operations section of the business plan discusses how the product will be built or the service delivered. This will include a discussion of production facilities, labor requirements, raw materials, tax incentives, regulatory approvals, and shipping.

If a prototype has not yet been developed, then the business plan must lay out a time line for its production as well as its cost. Cost of production must be discussed because this will feed into the gross margin discussion as part of the financial projections (discussed next).

Barriers to entry should be described. While there might be a higher cost of production at the outset, it will also prevent competition from entering the market later.

Venture capital firms are not always the first investors in a start-up company. In fact, they may be the third source of financing for a company. Many start-up companies begin by seeking capital from friends, family members, and business associates. Next they may seek a so called "angel investor": a wealthy private individual or an institution that invests capital with the company but does not take an active role in managing or directing the strategy of the company. Then come the venture capital firms.

As a result, a start-up company may already have a prior history before presenting its business plan to a venture capital firm. At this stage, venture capital firms ensure that the start-up company does not have any unusual history such as a prior bankruptcy or failure.

The venture capital firm will also closely review the equity stakes that have been previously provided to family, friends, business associates, and angel investors. These equity stakes should be clearly identified in the business plan and any unusual provisions must be discussed. Equity interests can include common stock, preferred stock, convertible securities, rights, warrants, and stock options. There must still be sufficient equity and upside potential for the venture capital firm to invest. Finally, all prior security issues must be properly documented and must comply with applicable securities laws.

The venture capital firm will also check the company's articles of incorporation to determine whether it is in good legal standing in the state of incorporation. Furthermore, the venture capital firm will examine the company's bylaws, and the minutes of any shareholder and board of directors meetings. The minutes of the meetings can indicate whether the company has a clear sense of direction or whether it is mired in indecision.

Financial Projections

In light of the discussion on operations and cost of projections, this information leads right into the financial projections. A comprehensive set of financial statements are required including income statement, balance sheet, and cash flow projections. These projections must be realistic but at the same time, entice the venture capital firm that there is a sufficient return to be earned to warrant the investment of capital.

First, the income statement must show in which year a breakeven point will be achieved. Most business plans show a profit being turned by the third year after initial financing. The income statement should include realistic sales forecasts, allowances for discounts, clear numbers for the cost of goods sold, and reasonable estimates of marketing and other overhead costs. Gross margins and net margins must meet the return requirements of the venture capital firm.

The balance sheet is important to determine at what point debt and other forms of financing should be added to the capital structure of the start-up venture. Also, the balance sheet should reflect the receivables received from the sale of the product as well as reasonable assumptions about the timing and collection of those receivables.

Finally, the cash flow statement provides the venture capital firm with a realistic burn rate on the cash on hand. Initially, all firms require infusions of capital to fund their working capital. However, at some point of time, the start-up venture must become self financing such that its operating and expansion needs can draw from the money raised from the sale of its products.

For all of these financial projections, different scenarios must be included. What happens if a new competitor comes to the market quickly or the economy experiences a period of recessionary growth? Generally, the forecasts should include a base case of sales growth, a pessimistic case, and an optimistic case.

Amount of Financing

This section of the business plan gets down to brass tacks: how much money is the start-up venture requesting? This ties in neatly from the financial projections. As part of the assessment of cash flows, the start-up company needs to estimate its burn rate. The *burn rate* is simply the rate at which the start-up venture uses cash on a monthly basis. The amount of financing requested must be equal to the burn rate over the time horizon expected by the start-up venture.

Exit Plan

Eventually, the venture capital firm must liquidate its investment in the start-up company to realize a gain for the fund and its investors. When the management of a venture fund reviews a business plan it will keep in mind the timing and probability of an *exit strategy*.

An exit strategy is another way the venture capital firm can add value beyond providing start-up financing. Venture capital firms often have many contacts with established operating companies. An established company may be willing to acquire the start-up company for its technology as part of a strategic expansion of its product line. Alternatively, venture capital firms maintain close ties with investment bankers. These bankers will be necessary if the start-up company decides to seek an IPO. In addition, a venture capital firm may ask other venture capital firms to invest in the start-up company. This helps to spread the risk as well as provide additional sources of contacts with operating companies and investment bankers.

Venture capital firms almost always invest in the convertible preferred stock of the start-up company. There may be several rounds (or series) of financing of preferred stock before a start-up company goes public. Convertible preferred shares are the accepted manner of investment because these shares carry a priority over common stock in terms of dividends, voting rights, and liquidation preferences. Furthermore, venture capital firms have the option to convert their shares to common stock to enjoy the benefits of an IPO.

Other investment structures used by venture capital firms include convertible notes or debentures that provide for the conversion of the principal amount of the note or bond into either common or preferred shares at the option of the venture capital firm. Convertible notes and debentures may also be converted upon the occurrence of an event such as a merger, acquisition, or IPO. Venture capital firms may also be granted warrants to purchase the common equity of the start-up company as well as stock rights in the event of an IPO.

Other exit strategies used by venture capital firms are redemption rights and put options. Usually, these strategies are used as part of a company reorganization. *Redemption rights* and *put options* are generally not favored because they do not provide as large a rate of return as an acquisition or IPO. These strategies are often used as a last resort when there are no other viable alternatives. Redemption rights and put options are usually negotiated at the time the venture capital firm makes an investment in the start-up company (often called the *registration rights agreement*).

Usually, venture capital firms require no less than the minimum return provided for in the liquidation preference of a preferred stock investment. Alternatively, the redemption rights or put option might be established by a common stock equivalent value that is usually determined by an investment banking appraisal. Last redemption rights or put option values may be based on a multiple of sales or earnings. Some redemption rights take the highest of all three valuation methods: the liquidation preference, the appraisal value, or the earnings/sales multiple.

In sum, there are many issues a venture capital firm must sort through before funding a start-up company. These issues range from identifying the business opportunity to sorting through legal and regulatory issues. Along the way, the venture capital must assess the quality of the management team, prior capital infusions, status of proprietary technology, operating history (if any) of the company, and timing and likelihood of an exit strategy.

VENTURE CAPITAL INVESTMENT VEHICLES

Venture capital investments include limited partnerships, limited liability companies, corporate venture funds, and venture capital fund of funds. We discuss each in this section.

Limited Partnerships

The predominant form of venture capital investing in the United States is the *limited partnership*. Recall our discussion with respect to the regulation of hedge funds in Chapter 16. In that chapter we indicated that hedge funds operated either as "3(c)(1)" or "3(c)(7)" funds to avoid registration as an investment company under the Investment Company Act of 1940. The same regulatory exemptions apply to venture capital funds.

As a limited partnership, all income and capital gains flow through the partnership to the limited partner investors. The partnership itself is not taxed. Limited partnerships are generally formed with an expected life of 10 years with an option to extend the limited partnership for another one to five years. The limited partnership is managed by a general partner who has day to day responsibility for managing the venture capital fund's investments as well as general liability for any lawsuits that may be brought against the fund. Limited partners, as their name implies, have only a limited (investor) role in the partnership. They do not partake in the management of the fund and they do not bear any liability beyond their committed capital.

All partners in the fund will commit to a specific investment amount at the formation of the limited partnership. However, the limited partners do not contribute money to the fund until it is called down or "taken down" by the general partner. Usually, the general partner will give one to two months notice of when it intends to make additional capital calls on the limited partners. Capital calls are made when the general partner has found a start-up company in which to invest. The general partner can make capital calls up to the amount of the limited partners' initial commitments.

An important element of limited partnership venture funds is that the general partner/venture capital firm has also committed investment capital to the fund. This assures the limited partners of an alignment of interests with the venture capital firm. Typically, limited partnership agreements specify a percentage or dollar amount of capital that the general partner must commit to the partnership.

Limited Liability Companies

Another financing vehicle in the venture capital industry is the *limited liability company* (LLC). Similar to a limited partnership, all items of net income or loss as well as capital gains are passed through to the shareholders in the LLC. Also, like a limited partnership, an LLC must adhere to the safe harbors of the Investment Company Act of 1940. In addition, LLCs usually have a life of 10 years with possible options to extend for another one to five years.

The managing director of an LLC acts like the general partner of a limited partnership. She has management responsibility for the LLC including the decision to invest in start-up companies the committed capital of the LLC's shareholders. The managing director of the LLC might itself be another LLC or a corporation. The same is true for limited partnerships; the general partner need not be an individual, it can be a legal entity like a corporation.

In sum, LLCs and limited partnerships accomplish the same goal—the pooling of investor capital into a central fund from which to make venture capital investments. The choice is dependent upon the type of investor sought. If the venture capital firm wishes to raise funds from a large number of passive and relatively uninformed investors, the limited partnership vehicle is the preferred venue. However, if the venture capital firm intends to raise capital from a small group of knowledgeable investors, the LLC is preferred.

The reason is twofold. First, LLCs usually have more specific shareholder rights and privileges. These privileges are best utilized with a small group of well-informed investors. Second, an LLC structure provides shareholders with control over the sale of additional shares in the LLC to new shareholders. This provides the shareholders with more power with respect to the twin issues of increasing the LLC's pool of committed capital and from whom that capital will be committed.

Corporate Venture Capital Funds

Corporate venture capital funds are typically formed only with the parent company's capital, outside investors are not allowed to join. Corporate venture funds include Microsoft, Xerox Venture Capital, Hewlett-Packard Co. Corporate Investments, Intel Capital, and Amoco Venture Capital. Investments in start-up companies are a way for large public companies to supplement their research and development budgets. In addition to accessing to new technology, corporate venture capital funds also gain the ability to generate new products, identify new or diminishing industries, acquire a stake in a future potential competitor, derive attractive returns for excess cash balances, and learn the dynamics of a new marketplace.

Perhaps the best reason for corporate venture capital funds is to gain a window on new technology. Consider the case of Supercomputer Systems of Wisconsin. Steve Chen, the former CEO of Cray Research left Cray to start his own super computer company. Cray Research is a supercomputer company that was itself a spin-off from Control Data Corp., which in turn was an outgrowth of Sperry Corporation. When Mr. Chen founded his new company, IBM was one of his first investors even though IBM had shifted its focus from large mainframe computers to laptop computers, personal computers, and service contracts.[3]

---

[3] W. Keith Schilit, "Structure of the Venture Capital Industry," *Journal of Private Equity* 1, no. 3 (Spring 1998): 60–67.

There are, however, several potential pitfalls to a corporate venture capital program. These may include conflicting goals between the venture capital subsidiary and the corporate parent. In addition, the 5- to 10-year investment horizon for most venture capital investments may be a longer horizon than the parent company's short-term profit requirements. Furthermore, a funded start-up company may be unwilling to be acquired by the parent company. Still, the benefits from corporate venture capital programs appear to outweigh these potential problems.

Another pitfall of corporate venture capital funds is the risk of loss. Just as every venture capital firm experiences losses in her portfolio of companies, so too will the corporate venture capital firm. This can translate into significant losses for the parent company. Take the case of Dell Computers. Dell took a charge of $200 million in the second quarter of 2001 as a result of losses from Dell Ventures, the company's venture capital fund. Additionally, in June 2001, Dell reported that its investment portfolio has declined in value by more than $1 billion.[4] Eventually, Dell decided to exit the venture capital business all together. It sold the remainder of its venture capital portfolio to Lake Street Capital, a San Francisco private equity firm, for $100 million in 2005.

Venture Capital Fund of Funds

A *venture capital fund of funds* is a venture pool of capital that, instead of investing directly in start-up companies, invests in other venture capital funds. The general partner of a fund of funds does not select start-up companies in which to invest. Instead, the general partner selects the best venture capital firms with the expectation that they will find appropriate start-up companies to fund.

A venture capital fund of funds offers several advantages to investors. First, the investor receives broad exposure to a diverse range of venture capital firms, and in turn, a wide range of start-up investing. Second, the investor receives the expertise of the fund of funds manager in selecting the best venture capital firms with whom to invest money. Last, a fund of funds may have better access to popular, well-funded venture capital firms whose funds may be closed to individual investors. In return for these benefits, investors pay a management fee (and, in some cases, an incentive fee) to the fund of funds manager. The management fee can range from 0.5% to 2% of the net assets managed.

Fund of fund investing also offers benefits to the venture capital firms. First, the venture capital firm receives one large investment (from the venture

---

[4]See Joseph Menn, "Tech Giants Lose Big on Start-Up Ventures," *Los Angeles Times,* June 11, 2001.

fund of funds) instead of several small investments. This makes fund raising and investor administration more efficient. Second, the venture capital firm interfaces with an experienced fund of funds manager instead of several (potentially inexperienced) investors.

THE LIFE CYCLE OF A VENTURE CAPITAL FUND

A venture capital fund is a long-term investment. Typically, investors' capital is locked up for a minimum of 10 years—the standard term of a venture capital limited partnership. During this long investment period, a venture capital fund will normally go through five stages of development.

The first stage is the fund raising stage where the venture capital firm raises capital from outside investors. Capital is committed—not collected. This is an important distinction noted above. Investors sign a legal agreement (typically a subscription) that legally binds them to make cash investments in the venture capital fund up to a certain amount. This is the committed, but not yet drawn, capital. The venture capital firm/general partner will also post a sizeable amount of committed capital. Fundraising normally takes six months to a year. However, the more successful venture funds typically fund raise over a much shorter time priod.

The second stage consists of sourcing investments, reading business plans, preparing intense due diligence on start-up companies and determining the unique selling point of each start-up company. This period begins the moment the fund is closed to investors and normally takes up the first five years of the venture fund's existence. During the second stage, no profits are generated by the venture capital fund. In fact, quite the reverse, the venture capital fund generates losses because the venture capital firm continues to draw annual management fees (which can be up to 3.5% a year on the total committed capital). These fees generate a loss until the venture capital firm begins to extract value from the investments of the venture fund.

The investment of capital is the third stage. During this stage, the venture capital firm determines how much capital to commit to each start-up company, at what level of financing, and in what form of investment (convertible preferred shares, convertible debentures, and so on). At this stage the venture capital firm will also present capital calls to the investors in the venture fund to draw on the capital of the limited partners. Note that because no positive cash flow is generated yet, the venture fund is still in a deficit.

The fourth stage begins after the funds have been invested and lasts almost to the end of the term of the venture capital fund. During this time, the management team of the venture capital firm works with the companies

EXHIBIT 18.1   The Life Cycle of a Venture Capital Fund

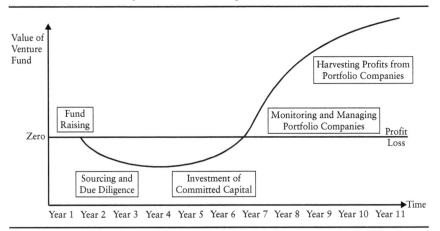

in which the venture capital fund has invested. The venture capital firm may help to improve the start-up management team, establish distribution channels for the new product, refine the prototype product to generate the greatest sales, and generally position the start-up company for an eventual public offering or sale to a strategic buyer. It is also during this time period that the venture capital firm will begin to generate profits for the venture fund and its limited partner investors. These profits will initially offset the previously collected management fees until a positive net asset value is established for the venture fund.

The last stage of the venture capital fund is its windup and liquidation. At this point, all committed capital has been invested and now the venture capital firm is in the harvesting stage. Each portfolio company is either sold to a strategic buyer, brought to the public markets in an IPO, or liquidated through a Chapter 7 bankruptcy liquidation process. Profits are distributed to the limited partners and the general partner/venture capital firm now collects its incentive/profit sharing fees.

These stages of a venture capital fund lead to what is known as the *J-curve effect*. Exhibit 18.1 demonstrates the J curve. We can see that during the early life of the venture capital fund, it generates negative revenues (losses) but eventually, profits are harvested from successful companies and these cash flows overcome the initial losses to generate a net profit for the fund. Clearly, given the initial losses that pile up during the first four to five years of a venture capital fund, this type of investing is only for patient, long-term investors.

SPECIALIZATION WITHIN THE VENTURE CAPITAL INDUSTRY

The growth of the venture capital industry has created the need for venture capital specialists. The range of new business opportunities is now so diverse that it is simply not possible for a single venture capital firm to stay on top of all opportunities in all industries. Therefore, by necessity, venture capital firms have narrowed their investment domain to concentrate on certain niches within the start-up universe. The trend towards specialization in the venture capital industry exists on several levels: by industry, geography, stage of financing, and "special situations."

Specialization by Industry

Specialization by entrepreneurs is another reason why venture capital firms have tailored their investment domain. Just as entrepreneurs have become more focused in their start-up companies, venture capital firms have followed suit. The biotechnology industry is a good example.

The biotech industry was born on October 14, 1980, when the stock of Genentech, Inc. went public. On that day, the stock price went from $39 to $85 and a new industry was born. Today, Genentech is a Fortune 500 company with a market capitalization of almost $100 billion. Other successful biotech start-ups include Cetus Corp., Biogen, Inc., Amgen Corp., and Centacor, Inc.

The biotech paradigm has changed since the days of Genentech. Genentech was founded on the science of gene mapping and slicing to cure diseases. However, initially it did not have a specific product target. Instead, it was concerned with developing its gene-mapping technology without a specific product to market.

Compare this situation to that of Applied Microbiology, Inc. of New York. It has focused on two products with the financial support of Merck and Pfizer, two large pharmaceuticals.[5] One of its products is an antibacterial agent to fight gum disease contained in a mouthwash to be marketed by Pfizer.

Specialized start-up biotech firms have led to specialized venture capital firms. For example, Domain Associates of Princeton, New Jersey, focuses on funding new technology in molecular engineering. However, specialization is not unique to the biotech industry. Other examples include Communication Ventures of Menlo Park, California. This venture firm provides financing primarily for start-up companies in the telecommunications industry. Another example is American Health Capital Ventures of Brentwood, Tennessee, that specializes in funding new health care companies.

---

[5]See W. Keith Schilit, "The Nature of Venture Capital Investments," *The Journal of Private Equity* 1, no. 2 (Winter 1997): 59–75.

Specialization by Geography

With the boom in technology companies in Silicon Valley, Los Angeles, and Seattle, it is not surprising to find that many California-based venture capital firms concentrate their investments on the west coast of the United States. Not only are there plenty of investment opportunities in this region, it is also easier for the venture capital firms to monitor their investments locally. The same is true for other technology centers in New York, Boston, and Texas.

As another example, consider Marquette Ventures based in Chicago. This venture capital company invests primarily with start-up companies in the Midwest. Although it has provided venture capital financing to companies outside of this region, its predominate investment pattern is with companies located in the midwestern states.[6] Similarly, the Massey Birch venture capital firm of Nashville, Tennessee, has provided venture financing to a number of companies in its hometown of Nashville as well as other companies throughout the southeastern states.

Regional specialization has the advantage of easier monitoring of invested capital. Also, larger venture capital firms may overlook viable start-up opportunities located in more remote sections of the United States. Regional venture capital firms step in to fill this niche.

The downside of regional specialization is twofold. First, regional concentration may not provide sufficient diversification to a venture capital portfolio. Second, a start-up company in a less-exposed geographic region may have greater difficulty in attracting additional rounds of venture capital financing. This may limit the start-up company's growth potential as well as exit opportunities for the regional venture capital firm.

Special Situation Venture Capital

In any industry, there are always failures. Not every start-up company makes it to the IPO stage. However, this opens another specialized niche in the venture capital industry: the turnaround venture deal. Turnaround deals are as risky as seed financing because the start-up company may be facing pressure from creditors. The turnaround venture capital firm exists because mainstream venture capital firms may not be sufficiently well-versed in restructuring a turnaround situation.

Consider the following example.[7] A start-up company is owned 50% by early and midstage venture capital firms and 50% by the founder. Product delays and poor management have resulted in $10 million in corporate assets and $15 million in liabilities. The company has a negative net worth and is technically bankrupt.

[6]Schilit, "The Nature of Venture Capital Investments."
[7]A similar example is in Schilit, "The Nature of Venture Capital Investments."

The turnaround venture capital firm offers the founder/entrepreneur of the company $1 million for his 50% ownership plus a job as an executive of the company. The turnaround venture capital firm then offers the start-up company's creditors 50 cents for every one dollar of claims. The total of $8.5 million might come from a $1 million dollar contribution from the turnaround venture capital firm and $7.5 million in bank loans secured by the $10 million in assets. Therefore, for $1 million the turnaround venture capital firm receives 50% of the start-up company and restores it to a positive net worth.

The founder of the company is happy because he receives $1 million for a bankrupt company plus he remains as an executive. The other venture capital firms are also happy because now they will be dealing with another venture specialist plus the company has been restored to financial health. With some additional hard work the company may proceed on to an IPO. The creditors, however, will not be as pleased, but may make the deal anyway because 50 cents on the dollar may be more than they could expect to receive through a formal liquidation procedure.

An example of such a turnaround specialist is Reprise Capital Corp. of Garden City, New Jersey. In 1997, this company raised $25 million for turnaround venture capital deals.

STAGE OF FINANCING

While some venture capital firms classify themselves by geography or industry, by far the most distinguishing characteristic of venture capital firms is the stage of financing. Some venture capital firms provide first stage, or "seed capital" while others wait to invest in companies that are further along in their development. Still other venture capital firms come in at the final round of financing before the IPO. A different level of due diligence is required at each level of financing because the start-up venture has achieved another milestone on its way to success. In all, there are five discrete stages of venture capital financing: angel investing, seed capital, first stage capital, second state/expansion capital, and mezzanine financing. We discuss each in this section.

Angel Investing

Angel investors often come from "F & F": Friends and Family. (Sometimes, venture capital firms include a third "F" for Fools.) At this stage of the new venture, typically there is a lone entrepreneur who has just an idea—possibly sketched out at the kitchen table or in the garage. There is no formal business plan, no management team, no product, no market analysis—just an idea.

In addition to family and friends, angel investors can also be wealthy individuals who "dabble" in start-up companies. This level of financing is typically done without a private placement memorandum or subscription agreement. It may be as informal as a "cocktail napkin" agreement. Yet without the Angel Investor, many ideas would wither on the vine before reaching more traditional venture capital firms.

At this stage of financing, the task of the entrepreneur is to begin the development of a prototype product or service. In addition, the entrepreneur begins the draft of his business plan, assesses the market potential, and may even begin to assemble some key management team members. No marketing or product testing is done at this stage.

The amount of financing at this stage is very small—$50,000 to $500,000. Any more than that would strain family, friends, and other angels. The funds are used primarily to flush out the concept to the point where an intelligent business plan can be constructed.

Seed Capital

Seed capital is the first stage where venture capital firms invest their capital. At this stage, a business plan is completed and presented to a venture capital firm. Some parts of the start-up management team have been assembled at this point, a market analysis has been completed, and other points of the business plan as discussed previously in this chapter are addressed by the entrepreneur and his small team. Financing is provided to complete the product development and, possibly, to begin initial marketing of the prototype to potential customers. This phase of financing usually raises $1 to $10 million.

At this stage of financing, a prototype may have been developed and the testing of a product with customers may have begun. This is often referred to as "beta testing," and is the process where a prototype product is sent to potential customers free of charge to get their input into the viability, design, and user friendliness of the product.

Very little revenue has been generated at this stage, and the company is definitely not profitable. Venture capital firms invest in this stage based on their due diligence of the management team, their own market analysis of the demand for the product, the viability of getting the product to the market while there is still time and not another competitor, the additional management team members that will need to be added, and the likely timing for additional rounds of capital from the same venture capital firm for from other venture capital funds.

Seed capital venture capital firms tend to be smaller firms because large venture capital firms cannot afford to spend the endless hours with an entrepreneur for a small investment, usually that may be no greater than $1 to $10 million.

Early Stage Venture Capital

At this point the start-up company should have a viable product that has been beta tested. Alpha testing may have already begun. This is the testing of the second generation prototype with potential end users. Typically, a price is charged for the product or a fee for the service. Revenues are being generated and the product/service has now demonstrated commercial viability. *Early stage venture capital financing* is usually $5 million and more.

Early stage financing is typically used to build out the commercial scale manufacturing services. The product is no longer being produced out of the entrepreneur's garage or out of some vacant space above a grocery store. The company is now a going concern with an initial, if not complete management team. At this stage, there will be at least one venture capital firm sitting on the board of directors of the company.

The goal of the start-up venture is to achieve market penetration with its product. Some of this will have already been accomplished with the beta and alpha testing of the product. However, additional marketing must now be completed. In addition, distribution channels should be identified by now and the product should be established in these channels. Reaching a break-even point is the financial goal.

Late Stage/Expansion Venture Capital

At this point the start-up company may have generated its first profitable quarter, or be just at the breakeven point. Commercial viability is now established. Cash flow management is critical at this stage, as the company is not yet at the level where its cash flows can self sustain its own growth.

Last stage/expansion venture capital financing fills this void. This level of venture capital financing is used to help the start-up company get through its cash crunch. The additional capital is used to tap into the distribution channels, establish call centers, expand the manufacturing facilities, and to attract the additional management and operational talent necessary to the make the start-up company a longer-term success. Because this capital comes in to allow the company to expand, financing needs are typically greater than for seed and early stage. Amounts may be in the $5 million to $20 million range.

At this stage, the start-up venture enjoys the growing pains of all successful companies. It may need additional working capital because it has focussed on product development and product sales, but now finds itself with a huge backload of accounts receivable from customers upon which it must now collect. Inevitably, start-up companies are very good at getting the product out of the door but very poor at collecting receivables and turning sales into cold hard cash.

Again, this is where expansion capital can help. Late stage venture financing helps the successful start-up get through its initial cash crunch. Eventually, the receivables will be collected and sufficient internal cash will be generated to make the start-up company a self-sustaining force. Until then, one more round of financing may be needed.

Mezzanine Stage

Mezzanine venture capital is the last stage before a start-up company goes public or is sold to a strategic buyer. At this point a second generation product may already be in production if not distribution. The management team is together and solid, and the company is working on managing its cash flow better. Manufacturing facilities are established, and the company may already be thinking about penetrating international markets. Amounts vary depending on how long the bridge financing is meant to last but generally is in the range of $5 to $15 million.

The financing at this stage is considered "bridge" or mezzanine financing to keep the company from running out of cash until the IPO or strategic sale. The start-up company may still have a large inventory of uncollected accounts receivable that need to be financed in the short term. Profits are being recorded, but accounts receivable are growing at the same rate of sales.

Mezzanine financing may be in the form of convertible debt. In addition the company may have sufficient revenue and earning power that traditional bank debt may be added at this stage. This means that the start-up company may have to clean up its balance sheet as well as its statement of cash flows. Commercial viability is more than just generating sales, it also requires turning accounts receivable into actual dollars.

The J Curve for a Start-Up Company

Exhibit 18.2 presents the J curve for a start-up company. Similar to the J curve for a venture capital fund, the initial years of a start-up company generate a loss. Money is spent turning an idea into a prototype product and from there beta testing the product with potential customers. Little or no revenue is generated during this time. It is not until the product goes into alpha testing that revenues may be generated and the start-up becomes a viable concern.

EXHIBIT 18.2   The Life Cycle of a Start-Up Company

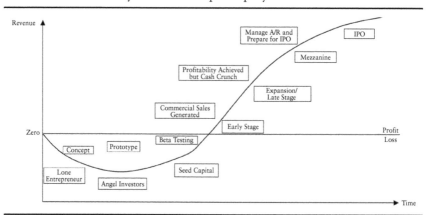

Once a critical mass is generated—where sales are turned into profits and accounts receivable is turned into cash—then it becomes a matter of timing until the start-up company achieves a public offering. Additional rounds of financing may be needed to get the company to its IPO nirvana. At this point commercial viability is established, but managing the cash crunch becomes critical.

HISTORICAL PERFORMANCE

In this last section, we provide a brief review of the performance of venture capital compared to the S&P 500 stock index and the Nasdaq Composite stock index. We use these two indexes to provide a comparison of the performance of the public stock markets to the venture capital/private stock transactions.

The S&P 500 is often used as a reference for the broad stock market in the United States. However, this index is limited to the 500 largest capitalized stocks in the United States. Consequently, it may not be the best comparison for venture capital performance because venture capital firms that eventually become public through an IPO tend to have a smaller market capitalization at their outset. As a result, we also include the Nasdaq Composite, which includes many companies of smaller market scale. Also, the Nasdaq index contains only companies listed in the over-the-counter market—consistent with the public offering of many start-up companies.

Exhibit 18.3 shows the 1-, 3-, 5-, 10-, and 20-year compounded annual returns through the end of 2009. Looking at the 1-year returns, the S&P 500

EXHIBIT 18.3   Returns to Venture Capital

	1 Year	3 Years	5 Years	10 Years	20 Years
Seed capital	5.40%	2.10%	0.70%	–1.90%	11.80%
Early stage	0.60%	–1.10%	0.90%	–0.20%	24.10%
Late stage	9.30%	5.60%	7.60%	1.70%	15.00%
S&P 500	27.11%	–5.59%	0.41%	–0.99%	8.23%
Nasdaq Composite	28.92%	–5.37%	1.32%	–4.30%	8.86%

Data source: Thomson Venture Economics.

and the Nasdaq returns dominate venture capital returns. 2009 was a strong year for all publicly traded stock markets globally. However, venture capital returns lagged behind the public stock market returns. This is exactly what we should expect with respect to venture capital. This is because it may take a year or more before the tailwinds that are felt in the public stock markets wash over into the private equity world of venture capital and start up firms. As a case in point, venture capital returns did not decline until after the popping of the public traded tech bubble stocks in 2000.

On a longer term basis—20 years—we see that all forms of venture capital earn a large premium over the public stock markets. However, a word of warning: This premium is earned but only after a long period of investing in venture capital. Even when we look at a 10-year basis, there is no clear conclusion as to whether venture capital provides a consistent premium over the public stock markets.

Finally, when we look at the various stages of venture capital, we see that over the long term (20 years), early stage venture capital is the most successful category of venture financing—even better than seed capital. In fact, surprisingly, seed capital—perhaps the most risky of all venture financing—earns the least return compared to the other stages of venture capital. However, it does outperform public equities.

What are our takeaways from Exhibit 18.3? There are several. Venture capital is a long-term illiquid investment. To gain returns in excess of the public markets, one must invest for the long haul. However, the returns are worth it. Every stage of venture capital investing earns a significant premium to the public markets over the 20-year horizon. Although early stage venture capital provides the greatest long-term return, if lower risk is sought, then late stage venture capital provides a good risk premium over the public markets while taking less risk in the venture capital space.

Financial Instruments and Concepts Introduced in this Chapter (in Order of Presentation)

Private equity
Venture capital
Venture capitalists
Protective covenants
Management fee
Profit sharing or incentive fee
Clawback provision
Escrow agreement
Business plan
Executive summary
Burn rate
Exit strategy
Redemption rights

Put options
Regististration rights agreement
Limited partnership
Limited liability company
Corporate venture capital funds
Venture capital fund of funds
J-curve effect
Angel investing
Seed capital
Early stage venture capital financing
Late stage/expansion venture capital
   financing
Mezzanine venture capital

Investing in Leveraged Buyouts

A *leveraged buyout* (LBO) is a way to take a company with publicly traded stock private, or a way to put a company in the hands of the current management (sometimes referred to as a *management buyout* or MBO). An LBO uses the assets or cash flows of the company to secure debt financing either in bonds issued by the corporation or bank loans, to purchase the outstanding equity of the company. In either case, control of the company is concentrated in the hands of the LBO firm and management, and there is no public stock outstanding.

LBOs represent a mechanism to take advantage of a window of opportunity to increase the value of a corporation. Leverage buyouts can be a way to unlock hidden value or exploit existing but underfunded opportunities.

A THEORETICAL EXAMPLE OF A LEVERAGED BUYOUT

In a perfect world, everyone makes money, and no one is unhappy. We will discuss some spectacular LBO failures below. In the meantime, we describe how a theoretical LBO should work.

Imagine a company that is capitalized with a market value of equity of $500 million and a face value of debt of $100 million. The company generates an earnings before interest, taxes, depreciation, and amortization (EBITDA) of $80 million. EBITDA represents the free cash flow from operations that is available for the owners and debtors of the company. This is a 13.3% return on capital for the company's shareholders and debtholders.

An LBO firm offers $700 million to purchase the equity of the company and to pay off the outstanding debt. The debt is paid off at face value of $100 million and $600 million is offered to the equity holders (a 20% premium over the market value) to entice them to tender their shares to the LBO offer.

The $700 million LBO is financed with $600 million in debt (with a 10% coupon rate) and $100 million in equity. The company must pay yearly debt service of $60 million to meet its interest payment obligations.

After the LBO, the management of the company improves its operations, streamlines its expenses, and implements better asset utilization. The result is that the cash flow of the company improves from $80 million a year to $120 million a year.[1] By foregoing dividends and using the free cash flow to pay down the existing debt, the management of the company can own the company free and clear in about seven years.

This means that, after seven years, the LBO firm can claim the annual cash flow of $120 million completely for itself. Using a long-term growth rate of 2% per year and a discount rate of 12%, this cash flow is worth

$$\$120 \text{ million}/(0.12 - 0.02) = \$1.2 \text{ billion}$$

Therefore, the total return on the investment for the LBO transaction is

$$[\$1.2 \text{ billion}/\$100 \text{ million}]^{1/2} - 1 = 42.6\%$$

The amount of 42.6% represents the annual compounded return for this investment. Notice the impact that leverage has on this transaction. The company is financed with a 6:1 debt to equity ratio. This is a very high leverage ratio for any company.

However, the cash flows generated by the company are used to pay down the debt to a point where the company is completely owned by the equity holders. The equity holders receive a very high return because the debt used to finance the transaction is locked in at a 10% coupon rate. This means that any operating efficiencies and capital gains generated from the business accrue to the benefit of the equity holders. This is a keen incentive for the equity holders to improve the operations of the company.

As the above example demonstrates, the returns to LBO transactions can be quite large, but the holding period may also be commensurately long. At the end of seven years, the management of the company can reap the $1.2 billion value through one of four methods:

1. The management can sell the company to a competitor or another company that wishes to expand into the industry.
2. Through an initial public offering. Consider the example of Gibson Greetings. This company was purchased from RCA for $81 million with all but $1 million financed by bank loans and real estate leasebacks.

---

[1]Studies of LBOs indicate that corporate cash flows increase 96% from the year before the buyout to three years after the buyout. See Michael Jensen, "The Modern Industrial Revolution, Exit, and the Failure of Internal Control Systems," *The New Corporate Finance*, 2nd ed., edited by Donald H. Chew, Jr. (New York: Irwin/McGraw Hill, 1999).

When Gibson Greetings went public, the 50% equity interest owned by the LBO firm was worth about $140 million, equal to a compound annual rate of return of over 200%.

3. Another LBO. The management of the company doubled its value from $600 million to $1.2 billion. They can now refinance the company in another LBO deal where debt is reintroduced into the company to compensate management for their equity stake. In fact, the existing management may even remain as the operators of the company with an existing stake in the second LBO transaction, providing them with the opportunity for a second go round of leveraged equity appreciation.

4. Straight refinancing. This is similar to method 3, where a company reintroduces debt into its balance sheet to pay out a large cash dividend to its equity owners.

Consider United Defense Industries Inc. This company is the main contractor on the U.S. Army's Bradley fighting vehicle and in the development of the Crusader field artillery system. The Carlyle Group, an LBO firm operating out of Washington D.C., purchased United Defense in 1997 from the FMC Corp and Harsco Corp. for $850 million with $173 million in equity and the rest in debt. By July 2001, United Defense had paid down its debt to $235 million. At that point, the Carlyle Group added more debt to United Defense's balance sheet by arranging for a loan of $850 million. Of the $850 million refinancing, The Carlyle Group used $400 million to pay a dividend to its investors, which include pension funds, endowments, and wealthy individuals.

The Appeal of an LBO

LBOs have a number of appealing characteristics to corporate management and investors alike. From the perspective of corporate management, the benefits of a buyout are:

- The use of leverage whose interest payments are tax deductible.
- Less scrutiny from public equity investors.
- Freedom from a distracted corporate parent.
- The ability of the management of the company to become significant equity holders and to enjoy in the upside of building the business.

From the shareholders' side of the equation, they typically respond favorably to a leveraged buyout because the bid price for their shares is typically at a large premium compared to the market price. Consequently, they also share in a portion of the upside potential of the LBO when they tender their shares at a premium to initiate the buyout transaction.

More to the point, leveraged buyout firms often target company's that have a depressed stock price. This is one of the leading criteria for an LBO target (which we will discuss in more detail below). Consequently, shareholders often welcome an LBO bid because it typically reflects superior pricing to what they can currently receive for their shares in the market place.

Financing a Leveraged Buyout

As our simple example demonstrated above, a leveraged buyout will be financed with a combination of debt and equity, with debt being the large majority of the financing. Generally, in every LBO deal, there are three tranches of financing: senior debt, mezzanine debt, and equity. *Senior debt* is typically bank financing along with credit/finance companies and insurance companies. *Mezzanine debt* is purchased by *mezzanine debt funds* (another form of private equity that we will discuss in the next chapter), insurance companies, and other institutional investors. Last is the *equity tranche*, which will be held by the LBO firm that has taken the company private, the management of the company, and some "equity kickers" from the mezzanine debt tranche. Exhibit 19.1 lays out the layers of LBO financing.

As an example of a financing for a large buyout deal, Exhibit 19.2 details the financing for the $11.5 billion leveraged buyout of SunGard Data Systems in 2005. SunGard provides trade clearing and data processing for stock, option, and future exchanges. This transaction was financed with $6 billion in bank loans, $2 billion in mezzanine debt, and $3.5 billion of equity from several LBO firms. The 30% equity contribution of the LBO firms is a bit lower than the current average equity contribution, but SunGard's dominant position in the trade clearing business demonstrated strong cash flows to support a higher level of debt financing.

HOW LBOs CREATE VALUE

The theoretical example given in the previous section is a good starting point for describing an LBO transaction; but there is no standard format for a buyout, each company is different, and every LBO deal has different motivations. However, there are five general categories of LBOs that illuminate how these transactions can create value.

LBOs that Improve Operating Efficiency

A company may be bought out because it is shackled with a noncompetitive operating structure. For large public companies with widespread equity

EXHIBIT 19.1 Tranche Financing for a Leveraged Buyout

Financing Tranche	Percentage of Transaction	Expected Return	Financing Parameters	Source of Funding
Senior debt	40% to 60%	4% to 5% over LIBOR	4 to 6 year payback 2x to 3x EBITDA	Commercial Banks Finance Companies Insurance Companies
Mezzanine debt	20% to 30%	10% to 16% Coupon 17% to 20% Total Return	5 to 7 year payback 1x to 2x EBITDA Equity Kickers to boost Total Return	Mezz Debt Funds Insurance Companies Instutitional Investors Investment Banks
Equity	20% to 40%	25% to 40%	5 to 7 year exit	LBO Firm Management of Company Equity Kickers for Mezz Debt

EXHIBIT 19.2 Financing Tranches for the SunGard Data Systems Buyout

Financing Tranche	Dollar Amount	Percentage of Transaction	Financing Parameters	Source of Funding
Senior bank loans	$4 billion	34.80%	7-year term loan at LIBOR + 2.5%	5 bank consortium led by JPMorgan Chase
	$1 billion	8.70%	Bridge loan	
	$1 billion	8.70%	Revolving credit facility	
Total bank loans	$6 billion	52.20%		
Mezzanine debt	$1.6 billion	13.90%	7 year, fixed coupon at 9.125%	CDO Funds and Mezzanine Debt Funds
	$400 million	3.50%	Floating rate at LIBOR + 4.5%	Insurance Companies
Total mezzanine debt	$2 billion	17.40%	Both offerings rated "junk" by S&P	
Equity	$3.5 billion	30.40%	Collects the benefits of any capital gains and residual cash flows	Club Deal of 7 LBO Firms
Total	$11.5 billion	100.00%		

ownership, the separation of ownership and management can create agency problems with ineffective control mechanisms. Management may have little incentive to create value because it has a small stake in the company, and monitoring of management's actions by a diverse shareholder base is likely to be just as minimal.

Under these circumstances, management is likely to be compensated based on revenue growth. This may result in excess expansion and operating inefficiencies resulting from too much growth. These examples often occur in mature industries with stable cash flows. Consider the following case history.

Safeway Corporation

In 1986, KKR took Safeway, a grocery/supermarket chain, private at a cost of $4.8 billion. The transaction was financed with 86% debt financing. At the time Safeway had an expensive cost structure that was not competitive with the rest of the supermarket food industry. Its employees earned wages that were 33% above the industry average. In sum, Safeway had stores that were losing money, inefficient inventory controls, and other poor operating procedures. Safeway's managers were compensated based on revenue growth, not profitability.

Drastic measures were implemented: renegotiations with unions, employee layoffs, and store closings. For example, Safeway sold its poorest performing division in Salt Lake City to Borman's Supermarkets for $75 million, and sold all 121 stores in its Dallas division to different grocery chains. Within two years, all divisions lacking wage parity with Safeway's competitors had been divested. This resulted in a reduction of over 1,000 stores and a 40% reduction in employees.

In addition, regional managers were compensated not by how much they generated in sales (the prior incentive scheme), but instead, on how well their operations earned a return on the market value of capital employed. As a result, managers worked harder to keep costs in line, closed underperforming stores, and expanded the business only when it appeared profitable.

The freedom to cut costs and the necessity to meet high-debt service forced the management of Safeway to think of profits first, and expansion second. It worked, and KKR eventually took public again the company after it had improved its operations and profitability. The LBO investors earned an annualized return of almost 43%.

Safeway is an example where value creation came not from entrepreneurial input, but rather from greater operating efficiencies. The grocery chain industry is a mature industry. New innovations are rare; it is a high-volume, low-margin business. Margin expansion comes not from brilliant insights into new strategies, but rather, from increasing operating efficiencies. As a result, Safeway is best categorized as an efficiency buyout.[2] Efficiency buyouts often result in a reduction in firm assets and revenue, but eventually, an increase in firm profits.

Such a buyout introduces more concentrated ownership and a better incentive scheme to mitigate agency problems. Management is given a stake in the company with an incentive scheme tied not to increasing revenues, but to increasing operating margins and equity value. In addition, a high leverage ratio is used to ensure that management has little discretion to pursue inefficient projects. Last, the LBO firm replaces the diverse shareholder base and provides the active oversight that was lacking by the prior (widespread) equity owners.

Unlocking an Entrepreneurial Mindset

Another way an LBO can create value is by helping to free management to concentrate on innovations. Another frequent LBO strategy is the unwanted (or neglected) operating division. Often an operating division of a conglomerate is chained to its parent company and does not have sufficient freedom to implement its business plan. An LBO can free the operating division as a new company, able to control its own destiny.

Duracell Corporation

Duracell was a division of Kraft Foods, a consumer products company, but its batteries were very different from the consumer foods (cookies, macaroni and cheese, etc.) primarily produced by Kraft. Duracell was too small and too different from its parent company to warrant much attention. The buyout of Duracell was led by its management in a MBO because they felt that they could increase the value of the company if they were freed from a bureaucratic parent company.

Duracell was taken private in 1988. The goal of management was not to sell assets and shrink the company (although it did consolidate its production by eliminating small plants). Instead, the company increased its budget for research and development, producing batteries that were not only longer lived, but also were more environmentally friendly. Additionally, management pursued an overseas expansion plan, to become a dominant supplier around the globe. Finally, management implemented an aggressive marketing and advertising campaign.

---

[2]See Robert Hoskisson, Mike Wright, and Lowel W. Busenitz, "Firm Rebirth: Buyouts as Facilitators of Strategic Growth and Entrepreneurship," *Academy of Management Executive* 15, no. 1 (February 2001): 111–125.

In short, once unshackled from a corporate parent, Duracell was free to pursue its expansion plans with the capital that it previously did not receive from its corporate parent. However, this capital was costly, and more than ever, the management of Duracell had to focus on cash flows and efficient use of existing assets—there was no corporate parent with deep pockets to bail it out.

In response to the pressure to manage its debt service and increase the value of equity, Duracell adopted the concept of economic value added (EVA). EVA is a method for evaluating projects and performance by including a charge against profits for the cost of capital that a company employs.[3] The capital charge under EVA measures the return that investors could expect to earn by investing their money in a portfolio of stocks with similar risk as the company.

The EVA approach to value creation has gained popular attention because it reflects economic reality rather than accounting conventions such as earnings per share or return on equity. Accounting-based measures can be distorted by noncash charges, early revenue recognition, and other accounting conventions. This may lead to a temptation by management to manipulate accounting-based performance measures such as earnings per share. Conversely, EVA measures the opportunity cost of capital based on the risk undertaken to achieve a revenue stream. As a result, EVA redirects management's focus from accounting numbers to equity value creation.

Duracell was a success story. It managed to increase its cash flows from operations at an annual rate of 17% from 1989 through 1995. Eventually, KKR negotiated the sale of Duracell to the Gillette corporation, resulting in a compound annual return of 40%. Management's shares were valued in excess of $45 at the time compared to the price of $5 a share at the time of the buyout.[4]

Duracell is a prime example of an entrepreneurial LBO. Once freed from Kraft Foods, Duracell could implement new innovations such as mercury-free alkaline batteries. Not only was the production process cheaper, its new environmentally friendly batteries appealed to the public. Additionally, Duracell developed rechargeable nickel-metal hydride (NiMH) batteries

---

[3]The formula for EVA is: Net Operating Profits after Tax – (Cost of Capital) × (Total Capital Employed). See Al Ehrbar, *EVA: The Real Key to Creating Wealth* (New York: John Wiley & Sons, Inc., 1998). Many firms have adopted EVA as a way to measure their performance including Coca-Cola, Briggs & Stratton, and Boise Cascade.

[4]For more details on the Safeway and Duracell buyouts, see George Baker and George David Smith, "Leveraged Management Buyouts at KKR: Historical Perspectives on Patient Equity, Debt Discipline and LBO Governance," in Rick Lake and Ronald Lake (eds.), *Private Equity and Venture Capital: A Practical Guide for Investors and Practitioners* (London: Euromoney Books, 2000).

for use in laptop personal computers. And rather than build new production facilities as it had done previously, Duracell formed manufacturing joint ventures in Germany, Japan, India, and China. This helped Duracell to expand internationally while deploying its capital most efficiently under the principles of EVA.

It is important to note that in an entrepreneurial LBO, the leverage ratio cannot be as high as for an operating efficiency LBO. The reason is that there must be sufficient flexibility for the managers/entrepreneurs to pursue their new initiatives. Whereas in the Safeway example management's actions needed to be restricted, in the Duracell example management's actions needed to be indulged. A moderate amount of leverage is usually required (50% to 70%), which provides sufficient discipline, but still allows for innovative flexibility.

The Overstuffed Corporation

One of the mainstream targets of many LBO firms are conglomerates. Conglomerate corporations consist of many different operating divisions or subsidiaries, often in completely different industries. Wall Street analysts are often reluctant to follow or "cover" conglomerates because they do not fit neatly into any one industrial category. As a result, these companies can be misunderstood by the investing public and therefore undervalued. Consider the following case history.

Beatrice Foods

In yet another KKR deal, Beatrice Foods (a food-processing conglomerate) was bought out in an LBO in 1986 for $6.2 billion. This was a 45% premium over the company's market value one month earlier.

Over the next two years, the management of the company, with KKR's assistance, sold off $7 billion of assets, reaping an $800 million gain over the initial LBO price. This is a clear demonstration of how the market and Wall Street analysts can undervalue a company. The LBO transaction paid for itself in the asset sales alone. This is all the more impressive when we recall that when KKR purchased the company for $6.2 billion, this price was at a 45% premium to the company' current stock price. Beatrice Foods is an excellent example of an undervalued conglomerate.

As might be expected, sales for the streamlined company declined from $11.4 billion to $4.2 billion after the $7 billion of asset sales. Yet, profits increased from about $300 million to almost $1 billion. Finally, after the sale of assets, the total debt of Beatrice Foods rose only slightly from $300 million to $376 million. The annual compounded return on this transaction was in excess of 40%.

Beatrice Foods is similar in some respects to the Safeway example. In each case, entrepreneurial insight was not required. Instead, strong operating management was the key to a successful LBO. In Safeway's case, management's job was to eliminate inefficient and unprofitable divisions. Safeway sold off these divisions and made them someone else's problem.

Similarly, Beatrice Food's management also pared down its assets, not necessarily to improve operations, but instead, to give the company a better focus and identity. Beatrice was "overstuffed" in that it had too many products across too many markets, resulting in a lack of coverage by the investment community and a lack of understanding of its core value.

What Safeway and Beatrice needed was strong monitoring by their shareholders. In their public form this was difficult to do for both companies because of their widespread shareholder base. However, in the LBO format, the equity of both companies was concentrated in the hands of the LBO fund. This resulted in close monitoring of their operations. What these companies needed was not more growth, but rather, a business plan that focussed on streamlining and improving core divisions.

Buy and Build Strategies

Another LBO value creation strategy involves combining several operating companies or divisions through additional buyouts. The LBO firm begins with one buyout and then acquires more companies and divisions that are strategically aligned with the initial LBO portfolio company. The strategy is that there will be synergies from combining several different companies into one. In some respects, this strategy is the reverse of that for conglomerates. Rather than strip a conglomerate down to its most profitable divisions, this strategy pursues a "buy and build" approach. This type of strategy is also known as a "leveraged build-up."

Berg Electronics

The buyout firms of Hicks, Muse, Tate & Furst and Mills & Partners jointly purchased Berg Electronics from the DuPont Corporation in 1993 for a purchase price of $335 million. At that time, DuPont's evaluation of Berg indicated that it generated about $18 million in profit on revenue of $380 million. Berg manufactured computer connectors as well as socket and cable assembly products for the telecommunications industry.

Berg Electronics was used as a platform for further leveraged transactions in the same industry. Over the next five years, Berg Electronics made eight acquisitions under the direction of Hicks, Muse and Mills & Partners including the acquisition of AT&T's connector business and Ericsson AB's connector division. By 1997, Berg had sales of $785 million and profits of over $180 million and employed 7,800 workers in 22 countries.

In early 1998, the buyout firms distributed shares in Berg to their investment partners and retained 20% of the firm for themselves. In August 1998, Framatome Connectors International, based in France and the third largest maker of electrical connectors, purchased Berg Electronics for $35 a share, for a total of $1.85 million, a 41% gain in purchase price before including the effects of leverage. Based on the initial equity contributed, the Berg Electronics transaction earned an estimated return in excess of 1,000%.[5]

LBO Turnaround Strategies

The U.S. economic recession of 2001 to 2002 highlighted another form of LBOs: the turnaround LBO. Unlike traditional buyout firms that look for successful, mature companies with low debt to equity ratios and stable management, turnaround LBO funds look for underperforming companies with excessive leverage and poor management. The targets for turnaround LBO specialists come from two primary sources: (1) ailing companies on the brink of Chapter 11 bankruptcy and (2) underperforming companies in another LBO fund's portfolio.

One LBO firm that pursues such a strategy is Questor Management Co. This company was founded in 1995 and has specialized in turnaround and distressed investments of troubled companies in other LBO firm's portfolios.

Aegis Communications Group

Aegis Communications Group is a teleservices company that offers integrated marketing services including customer acquisition, customer care, high volume outbound database telemarketing, and marketing research. Aegis started as the result of a buy and build strategy but subsequently morphed into a turnaround strategy.

In December 1996, Thayer Capital Partners, through its buyout fund, Thayer Equity Investors III, purchased majority stakes in two teleservice companies, Edward Blank Associates and LEXI International Inc. In 1997, these two companies were combined with a third company in Thayer Capital's portfolio to build IQI, Inc. Thayer Capital then used IQI, Inc. as a merger partner with ATC Communications Group in July 1998 to form Aegis Communications Group. The plan was to build a national call center

---

[5]See Hoskisson, Wright, and Busenitz, "Firm Rebirth: Buyouts as Facilitators of Strategic Growth and Entrepreneurship."

servicing company for other companies that wished to outsource their customer service lines for efficiency purposes. This was a classic buy-and-build strategy. After the merger, Thayer Capital became Aegis Communications' largest shareholder.

Unfortunately, the Aegis buy-and-build strategy was not a success story. From a high price of $19 in 1996, Aegis stock quickly dropped to $1 at the beginning of 1999. In August 1999, Thayer Capital brought in Questor to help revive the company. Aegis was suffering from high employee turnover, and an over leveraged balance sheet. Questor purchased $46.75 million in Series F senior voting convertible preferred stock in Aegis that was used to repay about $43 million in existing bank debt. As a result of its capital infusion, Questor was able to control approximately 47% of Aegis' voting stock.

Initially, Aegis' stock price increased to $1.875 a share in 2000, but then drifted to below $1 in 2001. In March 2001, Questor and Thayer Capital acquired the remaining outstanding shares of Aegis that they did not already at an offer price of $1, which was a 45% premium over the current price of 68 cents. The total cost was about $30 million (of which $10 million went back to other Thayer Capital funds).

However, Aegis fortunes continued to erode as it racked up losses of $19 million and $22 million in 2003 and 2004. Its stock price tumbled to pennies on the dollar, even trading below 1 cent a share in 2003. To try and salvage some portion of its value, Questor and Thayer Capital initially agreed to sell Aegis to AllServe Systems of England for $22.7 million in September 2003. This deal however, fell through.

However, Questor and Thayer were rescued by a second offer from Essar Group of India and Deutsche Bank who bid $28 million to acquire 80% of the equity of Aegis. Eventually, in 2005, Aegis converted a significant amount of its debt outstanding to common stock to satisfy three promissory notes held by another investor, World Focus. The approximately $100 million that Questor and Thayer had invested was wiped out. Since that time, Aegis has prospered. It transformed itself into one of the largest business processing outsourcing in India. In January 2010 Essar and Aegis announced plans for an initial public offering for Aegis. It's estimated value in January 2010 was $1.6 billion.

LBO Club Deals

A newer phenomenon in the buyout world is the *LBO Club Deal*. This is where a number of leveraged buyout firms come together to form a "club" to purchase a large public company. Typically, club deals are organized to take private very large public companies. The reason for taking the public

EXHIBIT 19.3   LBO Club Deals

Club	Company Acquired	Price	Year
KKR and Texax Pacific Group	TXU Energy Holdings	$45 billion	2007
Apollo and Texas Pacific Group	Harrah's Entertainment	$30.7 billion	2008
Texas Pacific Group and Goldman Sachs Private Equity Partners	AllTel	$23 billion	2007
Bain Capital and TH Lee	Clear Channel Communications	$17.9 billion	2008
Silverlake Partners, KKR, Bain Capital, GS Private Equity Partners, Providence Equity Partners, Blackstone Group, Texas Pacific Group	SunGard Services	$11.3 billion	2005

company private can be for any number of the reasons listed above. However, the reason that we mention club deals is that this makes any public company a potential leveraged buyout target when several buyout firms come together to combine their investment capital.

The best example of a club deal was the 2005 purchase of SunGard Data Services for $11.3 billion. SunGard is an information technology company that specializes in electronic data storage, data security, records management, and disaster recovery. It was taken private by seven private equity firms. This club put up $3.5 of equity capital and the rest was financed with debt. Exhibit 19.3 shows some of the larger club deals in recent years.

LBO FUND STRUCTURES

In this section we discuss how LBO funds are structured as well as discuss their fees. While LBO funds are very similar to venture capital funds in design, they are much more creative in fee generation.

Fund Design

Almost all LBO funds are designed as limited partnerships. This is very similar to the way hedge funds and venture capital funds are established. In fact many LBO funds have the name "partners" in their title.

Every *LBO fund* is run by a general partner. The general partner is typically the LBO firm, and all investment discretion as well as day-to-day operations vest with the general partner. Limited partners, as their name applies, have a very limited role in the management of the LBO fund. For the most part, limited partners are passive investors who rely on the general partner to source, analyze, perform due diligence, and invest the committed capital of the fund.

Some LBO funds have advisory boards comprised of the general partner and a select group of limited partners. The duties of the advisory board are to advise the general partner on conflicts of issue that may arise as a result of acquiring a portfolio company or collecting fees, provide input as to when it might be judicious to seek independent valuations of the LBO fund's portfolio companies, and to discuss whether dividend payments for portfolio companies should be in cash or securities.

Similar to hedge funds and venture capital funds, LBO funds must be aware of the regulatory restrictions that apply to the offering of interests in their fund. To avoid being deemed an investment company, LBO funds take advantage of the 3(c)(1) and 3(c)(7) provisions of the Investment Company Act of 1940.

Fees

If there was ever an investment structure that could have its cake and eat it too, it would be an LBO firm. LBO firms have any number of ways to make their money.

First, consider the annual management fees charged by LBO firms. These range from 1.25% to 3%. Consider the recent Blackstone Fund that raised $12 billion. The management fee on this fund is reported at around 2%. Two percent times $12 billion equals $240 million in annual management fees. And these fees are collected before any profits are recorded, indeed, even before any investments are made.

In addition, LBO firms share in the profits of the investment pool. These incentive fees usually range from 20% to 30%. Incentive fees are profit sharing fees. For instance, an incentive fee of 20% means that the LBO firm keeps one dollar out of every five earned on LBO transactions. Also, this incentive fee is a "free option" just as we discussed with respect to the incentive fees for venture capital funds and hedge funds.

LBO firms also may charge fees to the corporation that it is taken private of up to 1% of the total selling price for arranging and negotiating the transaction. As an example, KKR earned $75 million for arranging the buyout of RJR Nabisco, and $60 million for arranging the buyout of Safeway Stores. These transaction fees are divided up differently by LBO firm; there is no standard practice. Some LBO firms keep all of these fees for the LBO firm itself and do not share the transaction fees with their limited partner investors. Some LBO firms split the transaction fees with the percentage kept by the LBO firm ranging from 75% to 25%. Still other LBO firms include all of these fees as part of the profits to be split up between the general partner and the limited partners.

Not only do LBO firms earn fees for arranging deals, they can earn breakup fees if a deal craters. Consider the Donaldson, Lufkin & Jenrette LBO of IBP Inc. This $3.8 billion buyout deal, first announced in October, 2000 was subsequently topped by a $4.1 billion takeover bid from Smithfield Foods Inc. in November, 2000. This bid was in turn topped by a $4.3 billion takeover bid from Tyson Foods Inc. in December 2000. Despite losing out on the buyout of IBP, as part of the LBO deal terms, DLJ received a $66.5 million breakup fee from IBP because it was sold to another bidder.

In addition to earning fees for arranging the buyout of a company or for losing a buyout bid, LBO firms may also charge a divestiture fee for arranging the sale of a division of a private company after the buyout has been completed. Furthermore, an LBO firm may charge director's fees to a buyout company if managing partners of the LBO firm sit on the company's board of directors after the buyout has occurred. In fact, there are any number of ways for an LBO firm to make money on a buyout transaction.

In summary, LBO firms are "Masters of the Universe" when it comes to fee structures. It is no wonder that they have become such popular and profitable investment vehicles.

The J-Curve Effect

In our coverage of venture capital in the previous chapter, we described the J-curve effect for a venture capital fund. The same effect applies to leveraged buyout funds. LBO funds go through the same stages as a venture capital fund: fund raising, due diligence, investment, and harvesting of profits.

Recall from our discussion in the previous chapter, that initially, a private equity fund will provide negative returns in the early part of its life. This is because the LBO firm draws management fees from its investor limited partners to finance the sourcing of deals, to conduct due diligence of potential LBO candidates, and to monitor the portfolio companies once an investment is made. Therefore, in the early part of the LBO fund's life, the fund will generate a negative cash flow reflecting the cost of management fees. However, as the fund matures, and portfolio companies are sold to generate the fund's investment returns, it is expected that the investment profits should more than compensate for the initial management fees charged, and eventually, the private equity fund generates positive cash flows for its investors.

Exhibit 19.4 demonstrates the J-curve effect from another angle. In this exhibit, we introduce the concept of "vintage year." Vintage year is a way to compare private equity funds based on their year of formation.

EXHIBIT 19.4   Vintage Year Returns for Leveraged Buyouts

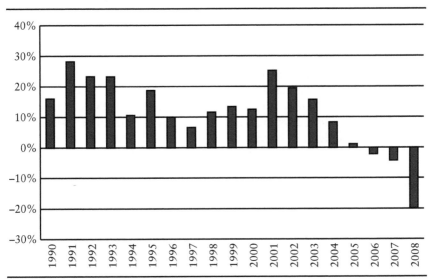

Data source: Cambridge Associates, LLC.

For example, it would be unfair to compare an LBO fund in its first year of operations with an LBO fund it its eighth year of operations because in the former fund, it is just getting started with the sourcing of private equity deals and due diligence, while in the latter fund, it is in the profit harvesting stage. Therefore, to make an "apples to apples" comparison, it is only fair to compare a fund of one vintage year to other funds of the same vintage year—these funds have all left the starting gate at the same time.

Exhibit 19.4 shows the return (as measured by the internal rate of return, IRR) by vintage year (year of formation). Notice that the most recent years show the most negative returns. This is an application of the J-curve effect. More recent vintage year funds are still in their sourcing, due diligence, investment, and monitoring phases. They tend to have lower rates of return because they have not had sufficient time to implement their business plan and harvest profits from their portfolio companies. As Exhibit 19.4 shows, returns to LBO funds are positive through vintage year 2005. Then the returns turn negative in vintage years 2006–2008. These vintage years reflect younger funds that are still putting their investment capital to work and have not had a chance to harvest profits yet. Given the difficult financial markets in 2008, it may take longer for these vintage years to return a profit to their investors.

PROFILE OF AN LBO CANDIDATE

We now turn to how LBO firms find good buyout candidates. Or, another way to consider the question is: What makes a good LBO candidate? In this section, we examine the profile of a public company that has been bandied about as a potential candidate.

Lexmark International Inc., one of the largest office machine companies in the United States, was identified as a potential LBO candidate in a credit report published by the Bank of America in May 2010.[6] When looking for LBO candidates, buyout firms look at both financial characteristics and operating characteristics. Not surprisingly, the financial characteristics focus on cash flows and the ability to support large amounts of debt on the balance sheet. Specifically, LBO firms look for:

- A history of profitability with steady profit margins.
- Strong free cash flows to service additional debt levels.
- A balance sheet this is not already overburdened with a high debt level.
- A strong balance sheet with a large cash/current asset balance.
- Opportunities for synergies with other companies in the same industry—looking for future strategic buyers.
- A weak stock price.

Exhibits 19.5 and 19.6 demonstrate many of the financial characteristics that LBO firms look for. Lexmark has been successful, although its operating and net margins are low, 7.4% and 3.8%, respectively. Although the printer business is competitive, the low margins indicate some room for improvement in the operations of Lexmark. Also, Lexmark has a relatively high debt ratio—70% debt/30% equity.

On the operating side of the equation, LBO firms look for:

- A mature firm with a strong brand name and competitive market position.
- Products that are not subject to technological obsolescence.
- A diversified customer base that generates recurring revenues.
- A management team that might need some improvement to increase operating efficiency.

Lexmark was spun off from IBM 19 years ago and competes against Hewlett-Packard, Xerox, Ricoh, and Canon. Lexmark maintains a strong position in the market for laser printers and copiers. It has carved out a living in producing office copiers and desktop laser printers—the bread and butter of every day office life.

---

[6]Steve Hannaford, "Lexmark: A Buyout Target?" *DocuCrunch.com*, May 21, 2010.

EXHIBIT 19.5 Financial Data for Lexmark (in $ millions)

Income Statement for Lexmark		Balance Sheet for Lexmark	
Net sales	$3,880	Current assets	$2,141
Less: Cost of goods sold	$2,570	Long-term assets	$1,214
Less selling, general, administrative	$1,023		
		Total assets	$3,355
Operating income	$287		
Less: Interest expense	$39	Current liabilities	$1,192
Less: Nonoperating losses	$60	Long-term liabilities	$1,148
Less: Income taxes	$41	Shareholders' equity	$1,015
			$3,355
Net income	$147		
Free cash flow for lexmark			
Net income	$147		
Plus:			
Depreciation & amortization	$213.70		
Other noncash adjustments	$23		
Changes in noncash capital	$19.30		
Cash from operating activities	$403		

EXHIBIT 19.6 Lexmark Share Price

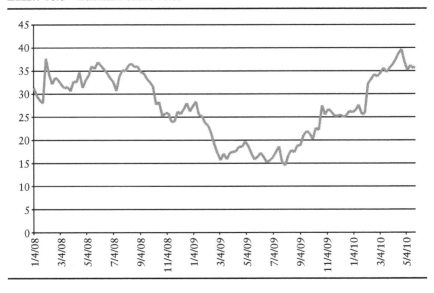

Exhibit 19.6 shows the stock price of Lexmark. While it declined significantly during 2008, its price has rebounded to its pre-2008 levels in the mid-30s range. While this shows the resiliency of Lexmark, buyout firms might like to see its stock price languish down in the $30 range before bidding on the company.

While its operating margins seem low, the printer business is very competive. Perhaps the most attractive aspect of Lexmark as a buyout candidate is that there are several strategic partners to whom Lexmark could be later sold after taking it private. So the simple game plan for a buyout firm would be to take Lexmark private, improve operating margins, and then sell Lexmark to the competitor in the industry. One way to improve margins in a competitive industry like the printer/copier industry is to build scale. Mergers are a great way to build scale quickly, and Lexmark could have several suitors in a few years if its margins are improved.

VENTURE CAPITAL VS. LEVERAGED BUYOUTS

Venture capital and LBOs are two sides of the capital markets coin. While venture capital funds nascent, start-up companies, leveraged buyouts target established mature companies. They operate at opposite ends of the life cycle of a company. Every corporation experiences three stages in its life: a start-up stage, a growth stage, and a stable or mature stage. Different financing needs are required for these different stages and different product technology is found in each stage. For example, as a start-up, venture capital is necessary to get a prototype product or service out the door. Whereas in a leveraged buyout the capital is necessary not for product development but to take the company private so that it can concentrate on operating efficiencies.

A summary of the differences between start-up companies and the venture capital they need compared to the companies targeted by LBO firms is presented in Exhibit 19.7.

In terms of company characteristics, start-up companies generally have a new or innovative technology that can be exploited with the right amount of capital. The management of the company is typically idea driven rather than operations driven. There may not even be a proven revenue model yet and the capital consumption is high.

Conversely, with an LBO, there is an established product, if not, in fact, an established industry. The management of the company is driven not by idea generation but by operating efficiency. Revenues are established, recurring, and fairly predictable. Also, a mature company generally has self-sustaining cash flows that allows it to fund its growth internally.

EXHIBIT 19.7 Venture Capital vs. Leveraged Buyouts: Start-Up vs. Mature

Company Characteristics	Start-Up	Mature
Market environment	Developing	Developed
Product demand	Undiscovered	Established
Customer base	Early adopter	Widespread acceptance
Management type	Entrepreneur	Seasoned
Management skills	Idea generation	Operations management
Revenues	Just beginning	Recurring and predictable
Capital consumption	Ravenous	Conservative
Competitive advantage	New technology	Distribution, marketing, production
Financing characteristics	Venture capital	Leveraged buyout
Target IRR	40% to 50%	20% to 30%
Shareholder position	Minority	Control of company
Board seats	One or two	All
Valuation	Compare to other companies	Discounted cash flow model
Use of debt	Non existent	Majority of financing
Investment strategy	Finance innovation	Improve operating efficiency
Time to exit	2 to 5 year	4 to 7 years
Exit options	IPO, acquistion	IPO, acquisition or recapitalization

It is also interesting to note the equity stake venture capitalists acquire versus that of leveraged buyout firms. A venture capital firm will typically acquire a significant, but minority position in the company. Control is not absolute. Conversely, in a leveraged buyout all of the equity is acquired and control is absolute. In addition, venture capitalist and LBO firms have different target IRRs that they wish to achieve. While both are quite high, not surprisingly, venture capital target IRRs are higher. The reason is simple: There is more risk funding a nascent company with brand new technology than an established company with regular and predictable cash flows.

The last significant difference between venture capital and LBOs is the investment strategy. Venture capital finances new, but unproven technology. The technology may even be disruptive in that it is so radical that it defines a new industry like the Sony Walkman of the early 1980s or revolutionizes an existing industry like the Apple iPod in the early 2000s. Conversely, leveraged buyouts look to see where they can add operating efficiencies or expand product distribution. New technology or innovation is not the cornerstone of their investment philosophy. They take an existing product and redefine it through better production processes, new marketing to a new audience, or an expansion of existing distribution channels. The product is established; LBO firms seek only to improve it.

RISKS OF LBOs

LBOs have less risk than venture capital deals for several reasons. First, the target corporation is already a seasoned company with public equity outstanding. Indeed, many LBO targets are mature companies with undervalued assets.

Second, the management of the company has an established track record. Therefore, assessment of the key employees is easier than a new team in a venture capital deal.

Third, the LBO target usually has established products or services and a history of earning profits. However, management of the company may not have the freedom to fully pursue their initiatives. An LBO transaction can provide this freedom.

Finally, the exit strategy of a new IPO in several years time is much more feasible than a venture capital deal because the company already had publicly traded stock outstanding. A prior history as a public company, demonstrable operating profits, and a proven management team make an IPO for a buyout firm much more feasible than an IPO for a start-up venture.

The obvious risk of LBO transactions is the extreme leverage used. This will leave the company with a high debt to equity ratio and a very large debt service. The high leverage can provide large gains for the equity owners, but it also leaves the margin for error very small. If the company cannot generate enough cash flow to service the coupon and interest payments demanded of its bondholders, it may end up in bankruptcy, with little left over for its equity investors. "Leveraged Fallouts" are an inevitable fact of life in the LBO marketplace.

Consider the example of Robert Campeau's buyout of the department store chain Allied Stores in December 1986. Campeau bid $3.6 billion for the stores, a 36% premium over the common share price at that time. With such a high offer, shareholders quickly tendered their shares and the company became private. The deal was highly leveraged. Of the $3.6 billion, $3.3 billion was financed by callable senior and subordinated notes.

Upon completion of the LBO, Campeau quickly sold a large portion of Allied Stores' assets for $2.2 billion and paid down the outstanding debt.

As a result, sales of Allied Stores declined from $4.2 billion in 1986 to $3.3 billion in 1988. In addition to asset sales, employment declined significantly from 62,000 employees in 1986 to 27,000 in 1988. As a result, the Allied Stores, which lost $50 million in 1986, turned a profit in 1988.

Unfortunately, the debt-to-equity ratio of Allied Stores remained high, and the company could not generate sufficient cash flow to meet its debt service. The chain filed for bankruptcy in 1990.

Another example of a retailing LBO is the management buyout of Macy's Department Stores in 1986. Unlike the Allied Stores example, the management of Macy's attempted to keep the company intact rather than sell off chunks of assets. Macy's was purchased for $3.5 billion, about a 20% premium over the existing stock price at that time. Over the next two years, sales increased from $4.7 billion to $5.7 billion as Macy's management pursued a course of expansion rather than contraction. Unfortunately, the cost of expansion as well as the high debt service turned Macy's from a profitable company to a money losing venture. By 1988, Macy's debt service was $570 million.[7] That is, its interest payments (not the face value of debt) totaled almost $600 million. By the end of 1991, Macy's had over $5.4 billion dollars of debt on its balance sheet. The large debt ratio plus the recession of 1991 forced Macy's into Chapter 11 bankruptcy protection in January 1992.

Although high debt levels eventually forced Allied Stores and Macy's into bankruptcy, there are several advantages to using large leverage ratios. First, high levels of debt financing allows equity investors with only a small amount of capital to realize large gains as debt levels are paid down. Second, a high debt level means a small equity level and this allows the management of a buyout company to purchase a significant equity stake in the company. This "carrot" provides for a proper alignment of management's interests with that of the LBO investment firm. Finally, high debt levels and debt service payments are a useful "stick" to keep management operating at peak levels of efficiency to ensure that the debt is paid down at timely intervals.

Financial Instruments and Concepts Introduced in this Chapter (in Order of Presentation)

Leveraged buyout	Mezzanine debt funds
Management buyout	Equity tranche
Senior debt	LBO club deal
Mezzanine debt	LBO fund

---

[7]See W. Keith Schilit, "The Nature of Venture Capital Investments," *The Journal of Private Equity* 1, no. 2 (Winter 1997): 59–75.

CHAPTER 20

Investing in Mezzanine Debt

In this chapter, we discuss a form of private equity that appears as debt on an issuer's balance sheet. Mezzanine debt is closely linked to the leveraged buyout (LBO) market, and investing in this form of debt can result in a significant equity stake in a target company. In addition, like venture capital and LBOs, mezzanine debt provides an alternative investment strategy within the equity asset class.

It is important to recognize that mezzanine debt investing can be distinguished from traditional long-only investing. The reason is that this form of private equity attempts to capture investment returns from economic sources that are mostly independent of the economy's long-term macroeconomic growth. While the direction of the stock market and the health of the overall economy may have some influence on a company, it is more likely that the fortunes of the company will be determined by its capital structure.

OVERVIEW OF MEZZANINE DEBT

Mezzanine debt is often hard to classify because the distinction between debt and equity can blur at this level of financing. Oftentimes, mezzanine debt represents a hybrid, a combination of debt and equity. Mezzanine financing gets its name because it is inserted into a company's capital structure between the "floor" of equity and the "ceiling" of senior, secured debt. It is from the in between nature of this type of debt that mezzanine derives its name.

Mezzanine debt is a hybrid security that has features of both debt and equity. Typically, *mezzanine financing* is constructed as a intermediate term bond with some form of equity participation, or "kicker" thrown in as additional enticement to the investor. The equity portion provides the investor with an interest in the upside of the company while the debt component provides a level of high cash payments.

The most common form of mezzanine financing is an intermediate term note, typically unsecured, coupled with stock warrants to purchase the stock of the acquiring company. The coupon payments on the note may be in cash or as *payment in kind* (PIK). Payment in kind means that instead of paying cash on the mezzanine debt, the company distributes more notes to the investor. This increases the company's leverage as well as the investor's equity stake in the company (through the receipt of more warrants).

Mezzanine financing does not have to be in the form of debt, sometimes it is in the form of preferred stock. In such circumstances, the preferred stock generally has a set dividend payment as well as a conversion right into the common stock. The main point is that mezzanine finance provides the filler between the senior debt of the company and its bottom line common equity holders.

Exhibit 20.1 provides a general view of the capital structure of a company. This exhibit demonstrates that mezzanine financing can take several forms between senior debt and common equity. Therefore, the gap that mezzanine finance might provide can be quite large, and include several tranches of junior debt or preferred equity.

Mezzanine financing is not used to provide cash for the day-to-day operations of a company. Instead, it is used during transitional periods in a company's life. Frequently, a company is in a situation where its senior creditors (banks) are unwilling to provide any additional capital and the company does not wish to issue additional stock. Mezzanine financing can fill this void.

Mezzanine financing is a niche market, operating between "story credits" and the junk bond market. Story credits are private debt issues that have a good "story" to sell them. Generally, these are senior secured financings with good credit and an interesting story to spin. However, not all firms have good credit or interesting stories. Mezzanine debt may be their best source of financing.

EXHIBIT 20.1   Overview of Corporate Capital Structure

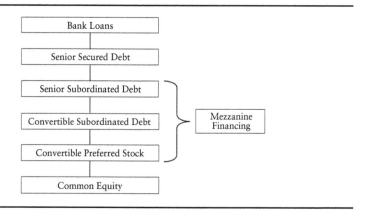

Mezzanine financing is often described as a "middle market" vehicle. This refers to companies that are not as large as those companies who have ready access to the financial markets and larger than companies that have a need for venture capital. Companies in this middle market category form the broad backbone of any economy, generally in the range of $200 million to $2 billion of market capitalization.

Some investors, such as insurance companies, view mezzanine as a traditional form of debt. Insurance companies are concerned with the preservation of capital, the consistency of cash flows, and the ability to make timely interest payments. Other investors, such as mezzanine limited partnerships, LBO firms, and commercial banks, focus on the capital appreciation, or equity component of mezzanine debt. Often these firms demand an equity "kicker" be attached to the mezzanine debt. This kicker is usually in the form of equity warrants to purchase stock at a discounted strike price.

Return Expectations for Mezzanine Financing

Mezzanine financing provides a greater risk profile to an investor than senior debt because of its unsecured status, lower credit priority, and equity kicker. Typically, the total return sought by investors in mezzanine financing is in the rage of 15% to 20%.

However, this return range is significantly below that for venture capital and leveraged buyouts. The reduced return reflects a lower risk profile compared to other forms of private equity. The reason is twofold. First, mezzanine financing does not translate into control of the company compared to a leveraged buyout. Mezzanine financing is much more passive than that of an LBO. Second, mezzanine financing is appropriate for those companies that have a reliable cash flow. This is in contrast to venture capital where the start-up company does not have sufficient cash flows to support debt.

The largest piece of the total return is the coupon rate on the mezzanine security; usually 10% to 16%. Furthermore, this coupon payment may be divided between cash payment and payment in kind. The reminder of the upside comes from the equity kicker—either warrants of some other equity conversion.

Mezzanine Debt and the J Curve

In the two previous chapters, we discussed the J-curve effect for private equity. Essentially, in the early years of a private equity fund, the fund experiences a negative return because it incurs management fees while investing the fund's capital. It generally takes up to four to five years before the general partner for the private equity fund begins to harvest profits from its initial investments. Until then, the fund experiences a negative cash flow to pay for the assessed management fees.

However, with a mezzanine fund, the J-curve effect is not a factor. One of the distinct advantages of mezzanine financing is its immediate cash on cash return. Mezzanine debt bears a coupon that requires twice yearly interest payments to investors. As a result, mezzanine financing funds can avoid the steep negative returns associated with venture capital or leveraged buyout funds.

Mezzanine Compared to Other Forms of Financing

Not only does mezzanine financing fill a gap in a company's capital structure, it also fills a gap in the capital markets. Increasingly, high-yield financing is not available to middle-market companies. High-yield issues now tend to start at $400 million and up. The same is true for leveraged loans. Generally, it is large public companies that tap the high-yield or leveraged loan market. Conversely, mezzanine financing can operate in any range of financing including smaller amounts below $400 million.

Mezzanine financing is highly negotiated, and can be tailored to any company's situation. The flipside is that the level of tailoring makes mezzanine debt illiquid. Any trading usually involves a lengthy negotiated process between the company that issued the mezzanine debt to buy back its securities or with a secondary private equity investor. In both cases, mezzanine debt is often sold at a large discount in the secondary market.

In Exhibit 20.2, we compare mezzanine debt to leveraged loans and high-yield debt. Notice that leveraged loans have the most strict debt covenants, which leads to greater protection from default but also a lower return. Furthermore, leveraged loans do not contain any type of equity kicker, so they do not share in any upside of the company. A credit rating is also required before a bank will lend credit through a leveraged loan while this is not necessary for mezzanine debt. In addition, leveraged loans typically have a floating interest rate tied to LIBOR while mezzanine debt has a fixed coupon. Finally, mezzanine financing typically has some PIK provision with respect to its coupon payments while leveraged loans never have such a provision.

These are just some of the differences between leveraged loans and mezzanine debt. High-yield debt falls somewhere in between these two forms of financing. Exhibit 20.2 shows the differences between these three types of financing.

EXHIBIT 20.2 A Comparison of Leveraged Loans, Mezzanine Debt and High-Yield Bonds

	Leveraged Loans	High-Yield Bonds	Mezzanine Debt
Seniority	Most senior	Contractual and structural subordination	Lowest priority
Type of security	First lien on assets	Unsecured	Unsecured
Credit rating	Required	Required	Not required
Loan covenants	Extensive	Less Comprehensive	Minimal—typically related only to payment of coupons
Term	5 years	7 to 10 years	4 to 6 years
Amortization	Installments	Bullet Payment	Bullet payment
Coupon type	Cash/Floating	Cash/Fixed	Cash/PIK/Fixed
Coupon rate	LIBOR + 300 to 450	8% to 12%	10% to 16%
Prepayment penalty	Usually none	High—usually the company must pay a call premium	Moderate—sometimes equity conversion is forced
Equity kicker	None	Sometimes	Almost always—usually equity warrants
Recovery if default	60% to 100%	40% to 50%	20% to 30%
Liquidity	High	Low	Minimial

417

EXAMPLES OF MEZZANINE FINANCING

As noted above, mezzanine financing fills either a gap in a company's financial structure or a gap in the supply of capital in the financial markets. This makes mezzanine financing extremely flexible. The examples below demonstrate this flexibility. Note that while mezzanine financing is mostly the domain of smaller companies in the middle market, large companies are not excluded from its use, as the Hertz Company example demonstrates in this section.

Mezzanine Financing to Bridge a Gap in Time

Mezzanine financing has three general purposes. First, it can be financing used to bridge a gap in time. This might be a round of financing to get a private company to the IPO stage. In this case, mezzanine financing can either be subordinated debt convertible into equity, or preferred shares, convertible into common equity upon the completion of a successful IPO.

Examples of this time-gap financing include Extricity, Inc. a platform provider for business-to-business relationship management. In May 2000, Extricity raised $50 million in mezzanine financing from a broad group of corporate and financial investors. Within a matter of days after its mezzanine round, Extricity also filed a registration statement for an IPO, but subsequently withdrew its registration statement as the market for IPOs cooled off. However, the mezzanine round of financing was sufficient to get Extricity through the next 10 months until March 2001, when the company was purchased for $168 million by Peregrine Systems Inc., a business-software maker.

Similarly, the Internet company iComs, Inc. raised $20 million in mezzanine financing while awaiting its IPO window of opportunity. The mezzanine debt was structured as subordinated convertible debt plus warrants. This financing was later supplemented by a sale of 14% of the company to Lycos, Inc.

The above examples demonstrate a common use of mezzanine financing in an uncertain economy. The global economic recession during the 2007–2008 slowdown led to a substantial decrease in IPOs. IPOs declined 90% from the first quarter of 2007 to the first quarter of 2009. The delay in many IPOs drove private companies to seek a mezzanine round of financing, to bridge the time until the company can launch a successful IPO.

Mezzanine financing may also be used to fill a gap in time associated with project finance. Project finance focuses on the completion of a specific corporate project as opposed to general growth or production. For instance, a real estate developer needs to finance the construction of a new office building. Upon completion of the office building, the developer can execute a first mortgage using the completed building as collateral for the loan. However, the bank is unwilling to bear the construction risk and will not provide the mortgage financing until the building is completed. In order to complete the construction process, the developer will seek mezzanine financing to bride the gap of time while the office building is under construction. Then the long-term financing will be received and the mezzanine debt retired.

An example is the $235 million high-yield issue for the construction of an 800 room Hilton Hotel Corporation hotel in Austin, Texas. The construction of this hotel had been delayed several times until financing was finalized in March 2001. U.S. Bancorp Piper Jaffray underwrote the financing for the project that consisted of $100 million in Series A senior debt and $135 million in Series B mezzanine debt. The senior bonds will mature in 2015, 2020, and 2030 and the mezzanine debt can be called sooner.

Mezzanine financing that is used to bridge a gap in time for project financing is usually deployed quickly. There may be less time in which to complete the deal, and due diligence may not be as rigorous. As a result, time-gap mezzanine financing bears more risk and will be priced accordingly, usually with a coupon rate of 12% to 14% with equity kickers that bring the total return up to the 20% to 30% range.[1] Alternatively, mezzanine debt used to finance another round of private capital before an IPO may have more time to complete the due diligence process, but will still be priced expensively commensurate with the considerable risk of a private company.

Mezzanine Financing to Bridge a Gap in the Capital Structure

A second and more common use of mezzanine financing is to bridge a gap in the capital structure of a company. In this case, mezzanine financing is used not because of time constraints but rather because of financing constraints between senior debt and equity. Mezzanine financing provides the layer of capital beyond what secured lenders are willing to provide while minimizing the dilution of a company's outstanding equity.

Mezzanine debt is used to fill the gap between senior debt represented by bank loans, mortgages and senior bonds, and equity. Consequently, mezzanine debt is junior, or subordinated, to the debt of the bank loans, and is typically the last component of debt to be retired.

Under this definition, mezzanine financing is used to fund acquisitions, corporate recapitalizations, or production growth. More generally, mezzanine financing is used whenever the equity component of a transaction is too low to attract senior lenders such as banks and insurance companies.

---

[1]See Bailey S. Barnard, "Mezzanine Financing Demystified," *Mergers & Acquisitions Insights,* April 2000.

Senior lenders may require a lower debt-to-equity ratio than the borrower is willing to provide. Most borrowers dislike reducing their equity share price through offerings that dilute equity ownership.

As an example of how mezzanine financing can be used to plug a gap in a company's capital structure, consider the recapitalization of Elis Group. The company was originally bought out by the LBO firm BC Partners in 1997. In 2000, Goldman Sachs, BNP Paribas, and Credit Agricole Indosuez arranged the €1.13 billion refinancing of the buyout that was split into five tranches: a €400 million seven-year term loan at 200 basis points over LIBOR, a €50 million seven-year term loan at 250 basis points over LIBOR, a €400 million eight-year term loan at 250 basis points over LIBOR, a €50 million seven-year revolver, and a USD 130 million 10-year mezzanine tranche that was priced at 450 basis points over LIBOR. To demonstrate the flexibility of mezzanine financing, this layer of debt was priced in U.S. dollars to encourage U.S. mezzanine investors to participate.

To illustrate the equity-like nature of mezzanine financing, in a subsequent IPO of Elis Group stock, the mezzanine tranche was taken out before any of the senior €1 billion senior debt. Simply stated, one form of equity (mezzanine) was replaced with another (common shares).

Mezzanine Financing to Bridge a Gap in an LBO

The third popular use of mezzanine debt is a tranche of financing in many LBO deals. For instance, LBO target companies may not have the ability to access the bond markets right away, particularly if the target company was an operating division of a larger entity. It may not have a separate financial history to satisfy the Securities and Exchange Commission (SEC) requirements for a public sale of its bonds. Consequently, a mezzanine tranche may be necessary to complete the financing of the buyout deal. Alternatively, a buyout candidate may not have enough physical assets to provide the necessary collateral in a buyout transaction. Finally, bank lenders may be hesitant to lend if there is not sufficient equity committed to the transaction. Mezzanine debt is often the solution to solve these LBO financing problems.

The mezzanine tranche often reflects a layer of quasi-equity to banks in an LBO deal. Usually, the mezzanine tranche receives an equity kicker to solidify its status as "equity."

Bridge Financing

Another key element in leveraged buyouts is the use of bridge financing. *Bridge financing*, as its name suggests, is a form of temporary financing to bridge a gap in the capital structure of a company. It operates much like mezzanine financing in its gap-filling nature. The difference is that bridge financing is temporary in nature. The expectation is that it will be rolled into permanent financing, typically, within one year. Often this permanent financing turns out to be mezzanine debt.

MEZZANINE FUNDS

Similar to venture capital and leveraged buyout funds, certain private equity managers specialize in buying mezzanine debt. They set up limited partnerships to buy mezzanine debt from LBO transactions and other sources. The general partner of a *mezzanine fund* will pool the capital of limited partners and invest their capital in the mezzanine debt issued by LBO firms, banks, and individual financing projects.

Mezzanine funds must pay attention to the same securities laws as hedge funds, venture capital funds, and buyout funds. This means that mezzanine funds must ensure that they fall within either the 3(c)(1) or the 3(c)(7) exemptions of the Investment Company Act of 1940. These "safe harbor" provisions ensure that mezzanine funds do not have to adhere to the filing, disclosure, record keeping, and reporting requirements as do mutual funds.

There are two key distinctions between venture capital funds and mezzanine funds. The first is the return expectations. Mezzanine funds seek total rates of return in the 15% to 20% range. Compare this to LBO funds that seek returns in the mid-to-high twenties and venture capital funds that seek returns in excess of 30%. This puts mezzanine funds at the lower end of the private equity risk spectrum.

Exhibit 20.3 shows the risk and return spectrum for the four basic forms of private equity: venture capital, leveraged buyouts, distressed debt (discussed in the next chapter) and mezzanine financing. Mezzanine financing is the least risky of the private equity strategies. Part of this comes from the fact that mezzanine debt is not subject to J-curve effect unlike venture capital or leveraged buyouts, and is not faced with a distressed situation like distressed debt.

For example, senior bank debt in a private equity transaction is usually priced at 200 to 250 basis points over LIBOR, while mezzanine financing usually bears a coupon rate of 400 to 600 basis points over LIBOR. In addition, mezzanine financing will contain some form of equity appreciation such as warrants or the ability to convert into common stock that raises the total return towards 20%.

Mezzanine financing is the most expensive form of debt because it is the last to be repaid. It ranks at the bottom of the creditor totem pole, just above equity. As a result, it is expected to earn a rate of return only slightly less

EXHIBIT 20.3   Risk-and-Return Spectrum for Private Equity

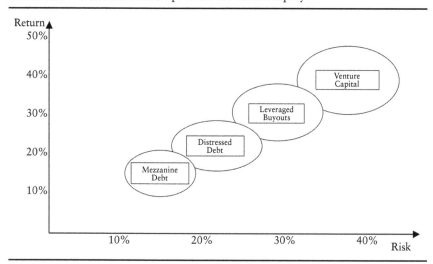

than common equity. Given the highly leveraged nature of companies that use mezzanine debt, the return can, in fact, resemble that of equity returns.

Second, mezzanine funds are staffed with different expertise than a venture capital fund. Most venture capital funds have staff with heavy technology-related experience including former senior executives of software, semiconductor, and Internet companies. In contrast, mezzanine funds tend to have financial professionals, experienced in negotiating "equity kickers" to be added on to the mezzanine debt offering as well as trying to ensure the most favorable credit terms to get any shot at the assets on the balance sheet of the creditor.

Mezzanine funds have begun to attract the types of fund flows typically seen in leveraged buyout funds. Consider Goldman Sachs Mezzanine Partners. Goldman Sachs has been raising investor capital and investing in mezzanine debt since 1996. It has raised five mezzanine funds in total, with its most recent fund, in 2007, raising $13 billion in capital.

However, mezzanine financing has not attracted as much investor capital as leveraged buyouts. One reason is that mezzanine financing tends to be small, generally in the $20 million to $300 million range. Another reason is that mezzanine debt, while it yields greater returns than high-yield bonds, cannot compete with the returns earned by venture capitalists and leveraged buyout funds.

Mezzanine funds look for businesses that have a high potential for growth and earnings, but do not have a sufficient cash flow to receive full funding from banks or other senior creditors. Banks may be unwilling to lend because of a short operating history or a high debt to equity ratio. Mezzanine funds look for companies that, over the next four to seven years, can repay the mezzanine debt through a debt refinancing, an initial equity offering, or an acquisition.

Mezzanine funds are risk lenders. This means that in a liquidation of the company, mezzanine investors expect little or no recovery of their principal. Mezzanine debt is rarely secured. As the last rung of the financing ladder (see the Hertz example, above) it is often viewed as a form of equity by the more senior lenders. Consequently, mezzanine investors must assess investment opportunities outside of conventional banking parameters. Existing collateral and short-term cash flow are less of a consideration. Instead, mezzanine investors carefully review the management team and its business plan to assess the likelihood that future growth will be achieved by the issuing company. In sum, similar to stockholders, mezzanine debt investors assume the risk of the company's success or failure.

Investors in mezzanine funds are generally pension funds, endowments, and foundations. These investors do not have the internal infrastructure or expertise to invest directly in the mezzanine market. Therefore, they enter this alternative investment strategy as limited partners through a mezzanine fund. Mezzanine funds also tend to reflect a similar fee structure as venture capital and LBO funds: a management fee in the 1% to 2% range and generally, a profit sharing fee of 20%.

Similar to hedge funds, venture capital funds and LBO funds, mezzanine funds are managed by a general partner who has full investment discretion. Many mezzanine funds are managed by merchant banks who have experience with gap financing or by mezzanine professionals who previously worked in the mezzanine departments of insurance companies and banks.

VENTURE CAPITAL AND THE DISTINCTION BETWEEN MEZANNINE FINANCING AND DIFFERENT FORMS OF PRIVATE EQUITY

As the economy has softened, venture capital firms have looked for ways to maintain their stellar returns. Additionally, the large flows of capital into venture funds have created the need for venture capital funds to expand their investment horizons. As a result, there has been a greater interest in mezzanine financing.

Consider the example of Metrika Inc, a privately owned developer and manufacturer of quantitative medical devices. In April 2001, this company raised $26 million in mezzanine financing to scale up production and market Metrika's quantitative testing device of hemoglobin A1c, a measure of long-term glucose control for people with diabetes. The financing was led by Oak Hill Capital Partners, L.P., a private equity partnership founded by Robert M. Bass and Sutter Hill Ventures. Oak Hill Capital invests across a wide variety of private equity transactions. However, Sutter Hill Ventures is one of Silicon Valley's original venture capital firms. Founded in 1962, Sutter Hill Ventures generally provides venture capital financing for technology and health care based start-up companies.

As the example above demonstrates, the lines between mezzanine financing and different forms of private equity can become blurred. With respect to pre-IPO companies, it is difficult to distinguish where venture capital ends and mezzanine financing begins. Also, as we noted already, mezzanine financing can be used as the last leg in the capital structure of a start-up company before it goes public. This bridge financing allows the company to clean up its balance sheet before its IPO.

ADVANTAGES OF MEZZANINE DEBT TO THE INVESTOR

Mezzanine debt is a hybrid. It has debtlike components but usually provides for some form of equity appreciation. This appeals to investors who are more conservative but like to have some spice in their portfolios.

The high returns to mezzanine debt compared to senior debt appeals to traditional fixed income investors who look for a little extra yield. Mezzanine debt typically has a coupon rate that is 200 to 300 basis points over that of senior secured debt (in the Hertz example it was 167.5 basis points above the senior bonds). Additionally, given an insurance company's long-term investment horizon, it may be less concerned with short-term earnings fluctuations. Furthermore, mezzanine debt often has an equity kicker, typically in the form of warrants. These warrants may have a strike price as low as $0.01 per share. The amount of warrants included is inversely proportional to the coupon rate. The higher the coupon rate, the fewer the warrants that need to be issued. Nonetheless, the investor receives both a high coupon payment plus participation in the upside of the company should it achieve its growth potential. The equity component can be significant, representing up to 5% to 20% of the outstanding equity of the company. For this reason, mezzanine debt is often viewed as an investment in the company as opposed to an unsecured lien on assets.

Although mezzanine debt is generally not secured by collateral, it still ranks higher than equity and other unsecured creditors. Therefore, mezzanine debt is senior to trade creditors. Like senior secured debt, mezzanine debt usually has a repayment schedule. This schedule may not start for several years as senior debt is paid off, but it provides the certainty of when a return of capital is expected. Unlike other forms of private equity, mezzanine debt provides instant returns through the coupon payment on the debt. This provides investors with a high level of current return instead of waiting for returns along the J curve.

A subordinated lender generally expects to be considered an equity partner. In some cases, mezzanine lenders may request board observation rights. However, in other cases, the mezzanine lender may take a seat on the board of directors with full voting rights.

Although mezzanine debt is typically unsecured, it still may come with restrictions on the borrower. The mezzanine lender may have the right to approve or disapprove of additional debt, acquisitions made by the borrower, changes in the management team, and the payment of dividends.

ADVANTAGES TO THE COMPANY/BORROWER

Mezzanine debt is a tool for plugging holes in a company's business plan. It can be shaped and molded to meet the company's business needs. Its malleability appeals to corporate issuers.

There are no set terms to mezzanine financing. Subordinated debt comes in all shapes, maturities, and sizes. The structure of mezzanine debt can be as flexible as needed to accommodate the parties involved. For example, the repayment of principal is usually deferred for several years and can be tailored to fit the borrowers cash flow projections.

Mezzanine lenders focus on the total return of the investment over the life of the debt. Therefore, they are less concerned with collateral or short-term earnings fluctuations. In fact, subordinated unsecured debt resembles a senior class of equity, and most senior lenders consider a company to have strengthened its balance sheet by adding this layer of capital.

The borrower can improve its cash flow by lengthening the maturity of the debt repayment associated with mezzanine financing. This is because the payback of the mezzanine debt is often delayed until the fifth or sixth year, and is usually paid with a bullet payment. The borrower does not have to pledge any collateral for mezzanine debt.

As discussed previously, mezzanine debt coupons are often structured so that some form of the coupon is not required to be paid in cash but can be paid in kind. This means that the holder of the mezzanine debt receives additional issuances of debt as part of the coupon payment on the debt. This can provide the issuer of the mezzanine debt considerable flexibility if there is a crunch on the cash flows of the company.

The borrower has not immediately diluted the equity of its outstanding shares when it uses mezzanine debt. True, mezzanine debt almost always

EXHIBIT 20.4   Hypothetical Terms for a Mezzanine Debt Offering

Company	Company XYZ
Debt amount	$50 million
Security on debt	None
Interest rate	12% coupon with up to 4% of coupon as PIK
Maturity	6 years
Amortization	Six-year bullet
Subordination	Subordinated to bank loans and senior notes
Conversion rights	None
Warrants	10 warrants per $1,000 face value detachable and exercisable at $0.50
Exercise period	3 years from the date of issuance until maturity
Tag-along rights	Holders of warrants have the right to participate in any sale of common stock by the issuer
Drag-along rights	Company may require debt holders to sell their warrants in the sale of a controlling interest of the company
Board representation	None
Registration	None—sold as an exempt offering under Rule 144A of the Securities Act of 1933

comes with some form of equity kicker that will eventually dilute the number of outstanding common shares. However, this "kicker" may not kick in for several years, affording the company a chance to implement its business plan and improve its share price before it is subject to dilution. Additionally, the company can refinance the mezzanine debt at a later date with traditional bonds before the equity kickers kick in.

Even though senior lenders may consider mezzanine financing to be a form of equity, it does not carry all the risks of equity. Therefore, it does not need to yield the same total return as expected by shareholders.

Exhibit 20.4 shows a typical term sheet for a mezzanine debt offering.

NEGOTIATIONS WITH SENIOR CREDITORS

The subordination of mezzanine debt is typically accomplished in an agreement with the company's existing creditors. The agreement, usually called an *intercreditor agreement*, may be negotiated separately between the senior creditors and the mezzanine investor, or it may be incorporated directly into the loan agreement between the mezzanine investor and the company. In either case, this agreement places certain restrictions on both the senior creditor and the mezzanine investor.

Subordination

The subordination may be either a blanket subordination or a springing subordination.[2] A *blanket subordination* prevents any payment of principal or interest to the mezzanine investor until the senior debt is fully repaid. A *springing subordination* occurs when the mezzanine investor receives payments while the senior debt is outstanding. However, if a default occurs or a covenant is violated, the subordination "springs" up to stop all payments to the mezzanine investor until the default is cured or fully repaid.

Acceleration

The violation of any covenant may result in the senior debt lender accelerating the senior loan. This means that the senior lender can declare the senior debt due and payable immediately. This typically forces a default and allows the senior lender to enforce the collateral security.

Drawdown

The order of drawdown is important to senior lenders. Because senior lenders often view mezzanine capital as a form of equity financing, they will require that mezzanine debt be fully drawn before lending the senior debt.

Restrictions to Amending Credit Facility Documents

Intercreditor agreements usually restrict amendments to the credit facility so that the terms of the intercreditor agreement cannot be circumvented by new agreements between the individual lenders and the borrower.

Assignment

Senior lenders typically restrict the rights of the mezzanine investor to assign its interests to a third party. Generally, senior lenders will allow an assignment providing the assignee signs a new intercreditor agreement with the senior lender.

---

[2]See Chapman Tripp and Sheffield Young, "Mezzanine Finance: One Person's Ceiling is Another Person's Floor," *Finance Law Focus*, November 1998.

Insurance Proceeds

Mezzanine lenders typically want any insurance proceeds to be deployed to purchase new assets for the borrower and not to repay senior debt. The reason is the equity-like nature of mezzanine financing. Mezzanine investors consider their debt to be a long-term investment in the company where a significant return component depends upon the operations of the company appreciating in value.

Takeout Provisions

A *takeout provision* allows the mezzanine investor to purchase the senior debt once it has been repaid to a certain level. This is one of the most important provisions in an intercreditor agreement and goes to the heart of mezzanine investing. By taking out the senior debt, the mezzanine investor becomes the most senior level of financing in the company, and in fact, can take control of the company. At this point, the mezzanine investor usually converts its debt into equity (either through convertible bonds or warrants) and becomes the largest shareholder of the company.

From the above discussion, it can be seen that intercreditor agreements are a matter of give and take between senior secured lenders and mezzanine investors. Mezzanine investors are willing to grant senior lenders certain provisions that protect the capital at risk of the senior lenders. In return, mezzanine investors have the ability to buyout the senior debt and then assert their equity rights in the company.

MARKET PERFORMANCE

Exhibit 20.5 shows the returns to mezzanine debt on a 1-, 3-, 5-, 10-, and 20-year basis. Let's compare these returns through December 2009 to public equity market benchmarks. The year 2009 was a good year for the equity markets, but mezzanine debt did not recover to the same extent as public equities. However, over a 3-, 5-, and 10-year period, mezzanine debt outperformed public equities.

EXHIBIT 20.5   Returns to Mezzanine Debt

	1 Year	3 Years	5 Years	10 Years	20 Years
Mezzanine debt	–4.80%	0.70%	2.80%	2.90%	6.80%
S&P 500	27.11%	–5.59%	0.41%	–0.99%	8.23%
Nasdaq composite	28.92%	–5.37%	1.32%	–4.30%	8.86%

Source: Thomson Venture Economics.

This demonstrates the debt-like nature of mezzanine debt. Although mezzanine debt often contains some equity kickers, it is still a financing liability to the company and, as a result, ranks superior to equity in the payment scale. The large coupons associated with mezzanine debt also provided some return protection that was not enjoyed by the equity markets over the decade of 2000–2009.

Finally, on a long-term basis—20 years—the public equity markets outperformed mezzanine debt. We would expect equities to outperform debt on a long-term basis, but one has to wonder whether mezzanine debt funds are worth their "2 and 20" fee structure over the long haul.

Financial Instruments and Concepts Introduced in this Chapter (In Order of Presentation)

Mezzanine debt	Intercreditor agreement
Mezzanine financing	Blanket subordination
Payment-in-kind	Springing subordination
Bridge financing	Takeout provision
Mezzanine fund	

Investing in Distressed Debt

Investing in *distressed debt* involves purchasing the debt of troubled companies. These companies may have already defaulted on their debt or may be on the brink of default. Additionally, distressed debt may be that of a company seeking bankruptcy protection. Now a company seeking protection from its creditors does not seem like a very tasty investment, but beneath the distress of the company investment opportunities exist. Like the other forms of private equity previously discussed, this form of investing requires a longer-term horizon and the ability to accept the lack of liquidity for a security where no trading market may exist.

Similar to mezzanine debt discussed in the previous chapter, the returns to distressed debt are less dependent upon the overall performance of the stock market. This is because the value of the debt of a distressed or bankrupt company is more likely to rise and fall with the fortunes of the individual company. In particular, the company's negotiations with its creditors will have a greater impact on the value of the company's debt than with the movement of the general economy.

The key to distressed debt investing is to recognize that the term "distressed" has two meanings. First, it means that the issuer of the debt is troubled—its liabilities may exceed its assets—or it may be unable to meet its debt service and interest payments as they become due. Therefore, distressed debt investing almost always means that some workout, turnaround, or bankruptcy solution must be implemented for the bonds to appreciate in value.

Second, "distressed" refers to the price of the bonds. Distressed debt often trades for pennies on the dollar. This affords a savvy investor the opportunity to make a killing if she can identify a company with a viable business plan but a short-term cash flow problem.

VULTURE INVESTORS AND HEDGE FUND MANAGERS

Distressed debt investors are often referred to as "vulture investors," or just "vultures" because they pick the bones of underperforming companies. They buy the debt of troubled companies including subordinated debt, junk bonds, bank loans, and obligations to suppliers. Their investment plan is to buy the distressed debt at a fraction of its face value and then seek improvement of the company.

Sometimes this debt is used as a way to gain an equity investment stake in the company as the vultures agree to forgive the debt they own in return for stock in the company. Other times, the vultures may help the troubled company to get on its feet, thus earning a significant return as the value of their distressed debt recovers in value. Still other times distressed debt buyers help impatient creditors to cut their losses and wipe a bad debt off their books. The vulture, in return, waits patiently for the company to correct itself and for the value of the distressed debt to recover.

There is no standard model for distressed debt investing, each distressed situation requires a unique approach and solution. As a result, distressed debt investing is mostly company selection. There is a low covariance with the general stock market.

DISTRESSED DEBT IS AN INEFFICIENT AND SEGMENTED MARKET

One reason that the distressed debt market is attractive to vulture and other investors is that it is an inefficient market. First, distressed debt is not publicly traded like stocks. Furthermore, most distressed bonds were issued in a private offering under Rule 144A of the Securities Act of 1933, which allows companies to sell their bonds directly to institutional investors instead of retail investors. These bonds lack liquidity from the outset, and what little liquidity exists dries up even more when the company becomes distressed. The lack of liquidity leads to bonds trading at steep discounts to their true value.

A second reason that the distressed debt market is inefficient is that it is a segmented market. Segmented markets occur when certain classes of investors "deselect" themselves from the market. For example, many pension funds are banned by their charters from investing in below investment grade debt. So when a company becomes distressed, the fund must sell the bonds regardless of their true value, often at depressed prices. Another form of segmentation occurs with banks. Banks are in the business of lending credit, not the tedious work out process of a bankruptcy situation.

Consequently, they may sell their nonperforming loans at prices that offer a considerable discount to vulture investors who have greater experience at working out a plan of reorganization for a company. Finally, trade creditors are in the business of producing goods, not managing a distressed debt portfolio. They also may sell their claims at discount prices.

Take the example of Barney's clothing stores. This is one of the most successful brand names in retail clothing with shops that sell high-end merchandise beyond most people's pocketbook. In the late 1990s, Barney's expanded rapidly leading to a distressed situation in which the clothing retailer had overextended itself. Subsequently, Barney's filed for bankruptcy under Chapter 11. At that point, its trade claims sold for as little as 30 cents on the dollar. Barney's was and is a solid business that experienced a temporary distress situation. Barney's survived and its trade claims subsequently doubled in value.

Another way to consider the distressed debt market is to examine recovery rates. Once a company becomes distressed or declares bankruptcy it does not mean that the value of the debt is completely wiped out. In almost all instances, there is some amount of recovery value. Not the full face value of the debt, to be sure, but some amount is typically offered to the debt holder.

Exhibit 21.1 demonstrates the cumulative default rate and recovery rates for both bonds and bank loans for the years 2006–2008, as well as the recovery rates for 1998–2008. Bank loans are typically senior to bond financing in a company's capital structure. This is reflected in the recovery rate for bank loans compared to corporate bonds—the recovery rate is generally twice as great for bank loans as corporate bonds.

EXHIBIT 21.1 Standard and Poor's Recovery Rates for Loans and Bonds

Average Annual Recovery Rates	2006	2007	2008
Senior secured bank loan	84%	92%	99%
Senior unsecured bank loan	71%	83%	69%
Subordinated debt	30%	47%	46%
Mean Recovery Rates 1998–2008			
Senior secured bank loan	82%		
Senior unsecured bank loan	45%		
Subordinated debt	17%		

Data source: Standard & Poor's, based on recovery rates as of November 8, 2008.

DISTRESSED DEBT AND BANKRUPTCY

Distressed debt investing and the bankruptcy process are inextricably intertwined. Many distressed debt investors purchase the debt while the borrowing company is currently in the throes of bankruptcy. Other investors purchase the debt before a company enters into bankruptcy proceedings with the expectation of gaining control of the company. In either case, a brief summary of Chapter 11 Bankruptcy is appropriate to understanding distressed debt investing.

Overview of Chapter 11

Chapter 11 of the U.S. Bankruptcy Code recognizes the corporation as a going concern.[1] It affords a troubled company protection from its creditors while the company attempts to work through its operational problems. Only the debtor company can file for protection under Chapter 11.

Generally, under a Chapter 11 bankruptcy, the debtor company proposes a plan of reorganization that describes how creditors and shareholders are to be treated under the new business plan. The claimants in each class of creditors are entitled to vote on the plan. If all impaired classes of security holders vote in favor of the plan, the bankruptcy court will conduct a confirmation hearing. If all requirements of the bankruptcy code are met, the plan is confirmed and a newly reorganized company will emerge from bankruptcy protection.

The process of Chapter 11 Bankruptcy is illustrated in Exhibit 21.2.

Classification of Claims

Under the bankruptcy code, a reorganization plan may place a claim in a particular class only if such claim is substantially similar to the other claims in that class. For instance, all issues of subordinated debt by a company would constitute one class of creditors under a bankruptcy plan. Similarly, all secured bank loans (usually the most senior of creditor claims) are usually grouped together as one class of creditors. Finally, at the bottom of the pile is common equity, the last class of claimants in a bankruptcy.

Plan of Reorganization

The debtor has an exclusive right to file a *plan of reorganization* within 120 days of seeking Chapter 11 bankruptcy protection.[2] If the debtor company files a plan during this 120-day window, it has another 60 days to lobby its

---

[1] See 11 U.S.C. sections 101 and sequence.
[2] See 11 U.S. C., section 1121(b).

EXHIBIT 21.2 An Overview of the Chapter 11 Bankruptcy Process

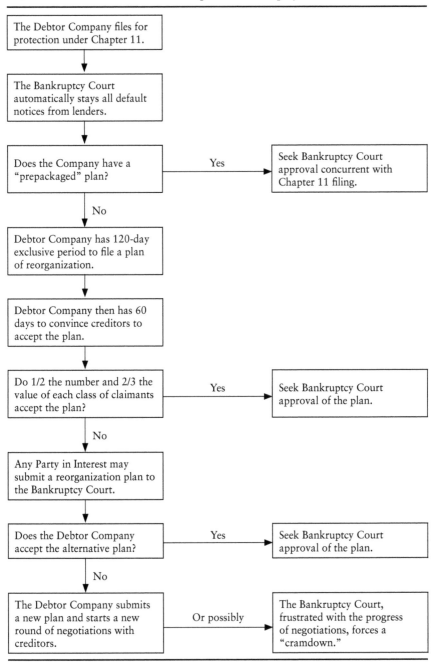

creditors to accept the plan. During this time (120 days plus 60 days) no other party in interest may file a competing reorganization plan.[3]

After the exclusive period ends, any claimant may file a reorganization plan with the bankruptcy court. At this point the gloves come off and senior and subordinated creditors can petition the bankruptcy court to have their reorganization plan accepted.

This is the interesting part of a bankruptcy process and it can become very acrimonious. In the Federated/Macy's case discussed below, the negotiations became so intense that the bankruptcy court appointed Cyrus Vance, the former U.S. Secretary of State, to mediate the discussions.

A plan is accepted when all classes of claimants vote in favor of the plan. This is an important point because any one class of creditors can block a debtor's plan of reorganization.

Prepackaged Bankruptcy Filing

Sometimes a debtor company agrees in advance with its creditors on a plan of organization before it formerly files for protection under Chapter 11. Creditors usually agree to make concessions up front in return for equity in the reorganized company. The company then files with the bankruptcy court, submits its already negotiated plan of reorganization, and quickly emerges with a new structure. The discussion of Loews Cinemas later in this chapter is an example of a prepackaged Chapter 11 filing.

Voting within a Class

To constitute an acceptance of a plan of reorganization either (1) the class must be completely unimpaired by the plan (i.e., the class will be paid in full) or (2) one half in number and two-thirds in dollar amount of claims in the class must vote in favor of the reorganization plan.

All claims within a class must receive the same treatment. If the members of a class vote in favor of a reorganization less than unanimously, and any dissenting claimants in the class receive at least what they would have obtained in a Chapter 7 liquidation plan, the dissenters are bound to receive the treatment under the reorganization plan. The reason is that the dissenters are no worse off than they would be under a liquidation of the company, and may be better off if the reorganized company is successful.

Blocking Position

A single creditor can block a plan of reorganization if it holds one-third of the dollar amount of any class of claimants. Recall, that acceptance of a

---

[3]However, the bankruptcy court may increase or reduce this exclusive period "for cause."

plan is usually predicated on a vote of each class of security holders, which requires support of two-thirds of the dollar amount of the claims in each class of creditors. Therefore, a single investor can obtain a blocking position by purchasing one-third of the debt in any class. A blocking position will force the debtor company to negotiate with the blocking creditor.

The Cramdown

Under Section 1129(b) of the bankruptcy code, a reorganization plan may be confirmed over the objection of any impaired class that votes against it so long as the plan (1) does not unfairly discriminate against the member of that class, and (2) is fair and equitable with respect to the members of that class.[4] This provision of the bankruptcy court is called the *cramdown* because it empowers the bankruptcy court judge to confirm a plan of reorganization over the objections of an impaired class of security holders. (The plan is "crammed down" the throat of the objecting claimants.)

Cramdowns are usually an option of last resort if the debtor and creditors cannot come to agreement. Bankruptcy courts have considerable discretion to determine what constitutes "unfair discrimination" and "fair and equitable" treatment for members of a class. In practice cramdown reorganizations are rare. Eventually, the debtor and creditors come to some resolution.

Absolute Priority

A plan of reorganization must follow the *rule of priority* with respect to its security holders. Senior secured debtholders, typically bank loans, must be satisfied first. The company's bondholders come next. These may be split between senior and subordinated bondholders. The company's shareholders get whatever remains. As the company pie is split up it is usually the case that senior secured debt is made whole and that subordinated debt receives some payment less than its face value with the remainder of its obligation is transformed into equity in the reorganized company. Finally, the original equity holders often receive nothing. Their equity is replaced by that converted from the subordinated debt.

It may seem unfair that the original equity holders are wiped out, but this is the residual risk that is born by every shareholder in every company. As the U.S. Supreme Court has stated, "one of the painful facts of bankruptcy is that the interests of shareholders become subordinated to the interests of creditors."[5]

---

[4] See 11 U.S.C., section 1129(b)(1).
[5] See Commodity Futures Trading Commission v. Weintraub, 471 U.S. 343, at 355 (1985).

Also, throughout the bankruptcy process, the debtor company's outstanding debt may be freely bought and sold. This allows distressed debt investors the opportunity to purchase undervalued debt securities with the anticipation that the debtor company will implement a successful reorganization.

The ability in the bankruptcy process to wipe out the ownership of existing shareholders and to transform the debt of senior and subordinated creditors into the company's new equity class is a key factor in distressed debt investing. The examples below demonstrate how distressed debt investors may gain control of a company through Chapter 11 Bankruptcy proceedings.

Chapter 7 Bankruptcy

If a plan of reorganization cannot be accepted by the creditors for the company, the company may liquidate its assets. This is a *Chapter 7 bankruptcy* process. Under Chapter 7, the company is no longer considered a going concern. Chapter 7 results in a liquidation of the company's assets for the benefit of its debt holders. Essentially it shuts down its operations and parcels out its assets to its creditors.

DISTRESSED DEBT INVESTMENT STRATEGIES

There are three broad categories of investing in distressed debt securities. The first approach is an active approach with an intent to obtain control of the company. In this strategy, the investors intend to assume an active role in the management and direction of the company. These investors typically purchase distressed debt to gain control through a blocking position in the bankruptcy process with a subsequent conversion into the equity of the reorganized company. Often, these investors purchase the more junior debt that is most likely to be converted into the equity of the reorganized company—these are sometimes called "fulcrum securities."

This strategy will also seek seats on the board of directors, and even, the chairmanship of the board. This is the most risky and time intensive of the distressed investment strategies. Returns are expected in the 20% to 25% range, consistent with those for leveraged buyouts—where control of a company is also sought.

The second general category of distressed debt investing seeks to plan an active role in the bankruptcy and reorganization process but stops short of taking control of the company. Here the principals may be willing to swap their debt for equity or for another form of restructured debt. Again an equity conversion is not required because control of the company is not sought. These investors participate actively in the creditors' committee to ensure the most beneficial outcome for their of debt. They may accept equity kickers such as warrants with their restructured debt. Their return target is in the 15% to 20% range—very similar to mezzanine debt investors.

There are passive or opportunistic investors. They often do not take an active role in the reorganization and rarely seek to convert their debt into equity. These investors buy debt securities that no one else wants. These investors might be the purest of the vulture investors because they have no goal other than to pick at the scraps that other investors wish to leave behind. These vultures receive their "scraps" from several sources:

- Banks and other financial institutions that do not have the time or inclination to participate in the bankruptcy reorganization.
- High-yield mutual funds that are restricted in their ability to hold distressed securities—there may be limits as to the amount of distressed securities that they can hold in their portfolios.
- Investors that invested in high-yield bonds for their high coupon payments, but do not want to convert a high cash yield into an equity position in the company.

Exhibit 21.3 provides an overview of these strategies. In the following sections, we examine specific examples of distressed debt investment strategies both active and passive.

Using Distressed Debt to Recycle Private Equity

LBO firms are a great source for distressed debt. "Leveraged fallouts" occur frequently, leaving large amounts of distressed debt in their wake. However, this provides an opportunity for distressed debt buyers to jump in, purchase cheaply nonperforming bank loans and subordinated debt, eliminate the prior private equity investors, and assert their own private equity ownership.

Consider Regal Cinemas Inc., the largest U.S. theater chain. Regal was originally taken private in 1998 in a combined effort of Hicks, Muse, Tate & Furst and KKR. The two buyout firms each put up about $500 million in equity to purchase the firm for $1.5 billion. Over the next two years, Regal added $1.2 billion to its balance sheet in bank debt and subordinated notes.

Unfortunately, over capacity of movie theaters, a slowing U.S. economy, and fewer blockbuster movies resulted in a loss of $167 million for Regal in the first nine months of 2000. In December 2000, bank lenders refused to let the company pay interest to its subordinated bondholders because it would violate loan covenants. Regal's debt officially became distressed.

EXHIBIT 21.3   Distressed Debt Investment Strategies

Active, Seeking Control	Active, Not Seeking Control	Passive
Often seeks one-third of a class of debt to block and control the Chapter 11 bankruptcy process.	May seek one-third of a debt class to obtain a blocking position.	Goal is to purchase debt securites that are undervalued and trading significantly below their face value.
Control of the company is expressly sought through an equity for debt conversion.	Will take an active role in the restructuring process.	Various strategies may include credit arbitrage among different levels of seniority or fire sale purchases.
Control is also sought through board seats and even the chairmanship.	Will be an active participant in the creditors's committee.	
Investors play a direct role in restrucruting both the capital structure of the company as well as its business plan.	Typically, will not seek control but may be willing to accept an equity for debt conversion. If not a full conversion, may seek equity kickers.	Buy securities from more risk averse investors who cannot commit the time required for a bankruptcy reorganization.
Additional equity infusions might be made after the equity for debt conversion.	Exit timeframe is 1 to 3 years.	Holding period is up to one year.
Exit timeframe is two to four years	Return expectation is 15% to 20%	Return Expecation is 12% to 15%.
Return expectation is 20% to 25%		

In stepped distressed debt buyers Philip Anschutz and Oaktree Capital Management. Together, they purchased 82% of Regal's outstanding bank debt and 95% of its subordinated debt paying 70 to 75 cents on the dollar. In September 2001, Regal announced a prepackaged bankruptcy plan where holders of Regal's bank debt would receive all of the equity in the reorganized company. In effect, Anschutz and Oaktree Capital replaced the private equity ownership of KKR and Hicks, Muse in Regal Cinemas with their own private equity stake. In fact, in May 2001, KKR had already written off its $492 million investment in Regal Cinemas. However, for Philip Anschutz and Oaktree, their prospects improved. Regal Cinemas went public in May 2002. Fourteen percent of the company was sold for $342 million, for a total market value of the company of $2.5 billion —significantly more than what Philip Anschutz and Oaktree paid for the distressed debt.

Distressed Buyouts

Even as leveraged buyout firms create distress situations, they also actively invest in this arena that is referred to as distressed buyouts. After all, bankruptcy court and creditor workouts provide opportunities to purchase undervalued assets. Often, creditors are sufficiently worried about receiving any recovery that they bail out of their positions when possible, opening up the door for buyout firms to scoop up assets on the cheap. This is another form of active control in the distressed area. Consider the following example.

Vlasic Foods International Inc., the maker of Vlasic pickles[6] and Swanson and Hungry Man frozen dinners, filed for Chapter 11 bankruptcy in early 2001, listing $458 million in assets and $649 million in debts, including almost $200 million in outstanding junk bonds. Vlasic was originally purchased by Campbell Soups in 1978. Twenty years later, Campbell Soup spun out Vlasic to a group of senior managers. A group of 22 banks lent Vlasic $560 million to pay Campbell as part of the split off. Vlasic incurred additional debt over the next two years to finance its operations.

In June 2001, the U.S. Bankruptcy Court in Delaware agreed to a cash bid by Hicks, Muse, Tate & Furst of $370 million for the assets of Vlasic. Following the strict priority of bankruptcy proceedings, the $370 million was first used to pay secured creditors in full. The remainder, about $70 million, was used to pay unsecured creditors approximately 35 to 40 cents on the dollar. Existing equity shareholders received no payment; their value was wiped out by the bankruptcy.

Consider the advantages to Hicks, Muse of the Vlasic deal. First, the buyout firm acquires for $370 million, assets that have a book value of $458 million. This does not take into account the productive ability of those assets to generate a market value in excess of their book value.

Second, Hicks, Muse acquired several well-known brand names. In fact, the A.J. Heinz & Co. had initially bid $195 million for Vlasic's pickle and barbecue sauce divisions while the company was in bankruptcy. It is possible that Hicks, Muse could negotiate a better deal with Heinz or another packaged food company for the sale of those assets.

Third, Hicks, Muse acquired the company free and clear of any outstanding debt. This was all wiped out through the bankruptcy proceedings. This allows for the opportunity to refinance the company with new debt while keeping the company out of bankruptcy proceedings.

Last, all shareholder equity was wiped out in the bankruptcy proceedings. Hicks, Muse became the sole owner of Vlasic Foods. Once purchased, Hicks, Muse pursued the same business plan that it used for many buyouts:

---

[6]Remember the TV commercials with the cartoon stork that talked like Groucho Marx?

streamline operations, sell unrelated business units to generate cash, provide stronger management, and promote Vlasic's well-known brand names.

Compare this example of Hicks, Muse to the one previous with respect to Regal Cinemas. LBO firms can be both suppliers and acquirers of distressed assets. It might be fair to say that "what goes around, comes around." Better yet, private equity firms specialize in seeking undervalued companies. However, not every private equity deal succeeds, and these underperforming companies, through distressed debt, can become another source of private equity investing.

Shortly after the Vlasic acquisition by Hicks Muse, the name of the company was changed to Pinnacle Foods Corp. Hicks Muse sold Pinnacle to J.P. Morgan Partners (the private equity arm of J.P. Morgan) in 2003 for $485 million for a gain of $115 million, or 31% over two years time. J.P. Morgan Partners, in turn, sold Pinnacle in 2007 to the Blackstone Group in another buyout-to-buyout deal worth $2.16 billion. This represented a 345% gain on J.P. Morgan's investment.

Converting Distressed Debt to Private Equity in a Prepackaged Bankruptcy

In February 2001, Loews Cineplex Entertainment Corp., the largest publicly traded U.S. movie theater chain, and one of the largest movie theater chains in the world, filed for Chapter 11 Bankruptcy. At the same time, it signed a letter of intent with Oaktree Capital Management, LLC and the Onex Corporation to sell Loews Cineplex and its subsidiaries to the investor group. This was a *prepackaged bankruptcy* where the debtor agrees in advance to a plan of reorganization before formerly filing for Chapter 11 Bankruptcy.

The letter agreement proposed that Onex and Oaktree convert their distressed debt holdings of about $250 million of senior secured bank debt and $180 million of unsecured company bonds into 88% of the equity of the reorganized company. Unsecured creditors, including subordinated debtholders, would receive the other 12% of equity.[7] All existing equity interests would be wiped out by the reorganization. Last, the remaining holders of bank debt would receive new term loans as part of the bankruptcy process equal in recovery to about 98% of the face amount of current debt.

In this prepackaged example, Onex and Oaktree became the majority equity owners of Loews by purchasing its bank and subordinated debt. Furthermore, their bank debt was converted to a private equity stake because all public shares of Loews were wiped out through the bankruptcy proceedings. Loews two largest shareholders, Sony Corporation (40% equity ownership) and Vivendi Universal SA (26%) lost their complete equity stake

---

[7]Oaktree Capital also owned about 60% of Loews' senior subordinated notes.

in Loews. In effect, the bankruptcy proceeding transformed Loews from a public company to a private one.

Loews was subsequently sold to another group of private equity investors including Bain Capital, The Carlyle Group and Spectrum Equity Partners in June 2004. The sale price was $1.5 billion of which 88%—$1.32 billion—went to Onex and Oaktree. Based on their original investment of $430 million, this was a profit of $890 million for an internal rate of return of 45%. In 2005, the group led by Bain Capital merged Loews into AMC Entertainment, another movie theater chain. This combined company was targeted to compete with Regal Cinemas (see our prior discussion). AMC listed itself for a $750 million IPO in December 2006 but this was cancelled. AMC again tried to have an IPO in 2008 but this was pulled once again. As of June 2010, AMC remains a private company.

Using Distressed Debt for a Takeover

As a good example of how a corporation can use distressed debt to take control of another company, consider the merger of Federated Department Stores and R.H. Macy & Co. Federated was able to gain control of Macy's with an initial investment in distressed debt of only $109 million.

Federated itself was a victim of the leveraged fallouts of the late 1980s and early 1990s. Federated was taken private in an LBO by Robert Campeau in 1988, the same gentleman that took Allied Department Stores private in 1986. Campeau's vision was to create a huge retailing empire anchored by two separate retailing chains: Allied and Federated. Unfortunately, the high debt burden of both buyouts forced both companies into Chapter 11 bankruptcy in January 1990.

Federated Department Stores emerged from bankruptcy in February 1992 after creditors agreed to swap $4.8 billion in claims for equity in the reorganized company. This helped to reduce Federated's debt from $8.3 billion to $3.5 billion, and reduced its interest payments from $606 million to $259 million. The connection to Robert Campeau was severed. In an ironic twist of fate, Federated emerged from bankruptcy just nine days after Macy's filed for Chapter 11 bankruptcy protection. Macy's was another victim of a leveraged fallout.

Soon after the Macy's bankruptcy filing, Federated made overtures to acquire its long-time rival. This was another twist of fate because Macy's had bid against Robert Campeau in 1988 for control of Federated. Macy's rebuffed Federated's inquiries because it believe that the company could be better served if it remained independent.[8]

---

[8]See Richard Siklos, "Macy's Holiday Revival," *Financial Post,* December 24, 1994, pp. 46–47.

With Macy's mired in negotiations with its senior creditors regarding a plan of reorganization and a takeover out of the question (there was no equity to takeover), Federated decided to become one of Macy's creditors. In January 1994, Federated purchased one half of Macy's most senior secured debt from Macy's largest creditor: the Prudential Insurance Co. of America. Prudential held a senior loan of $832.5 million that was secured by 70 of Macy's best stores. With accrued interest, the total of the distressed debt was $1 billion, representing one-sixth of Macy's total debt.[9]

Federated paid $109.3 million for one half of this loan with a promissory note to pay the remainder in three years. In addition, Federated received an option from Prudential to purchase the remaining half of Prudential's senior loan within three years. Overnight, Federated became Macy's largest and most senior creditor.

Given its new standing as a senior secured creditor, Federated received standing from the bankruptcy court to (1) challenge Macy's plan of reorganization (Federated now had a blocking position within the senior secured class of creditors); (2) propose a competing plan to the bankruptcy court; and (3) obtain nonpublic financial information regarding Macy's business prospects.

Federated proposed converting its bank debt into equity and assuming Macy's existing liabilities. Macy's continued to resist. Specifically, Macy director Laurence A. Tisch teamed up with counsel for bondholders holding $1.2 billion in subordinated debt and demanded a reorganization plan valued at least $4 billion.[10] Meanwhile Federated received support from Fidelity Management & Research Co., which signed a "lock-up letter" stating that it would only support a plan that gave the banks full recovery in return for the banks support of Federated's plan.[11] The lock-up letter worked and Federated was able to merge the two companies in December 1994 when it agreed to convert its senior loan to equity and to assume $4.1 billion in outstanding Macy's debts.[12]

In a more recent example, during 2009 and 2010, Texas Pacific Group and Apollo Management, the owners of Harrah's Entertainment began to purchase the debt of Palm's Casino in a systematic strategy to acquire Palm's through the acquisition of its distressed debt. Specifically, TPG and Apollo

---

[9]See "Federated Buys Large Share of Macy Debt," *Facts on File World News Digest,* January 6, 1994.

[10]See Karen Donovan, "Macy Merger Squeezes out Weil Gotshal; Bankruptcy Judge Approves Federated's Takeover Plan," *National Law Journal,* December 19, 1994.

[11]Donovan, "Macy Merger Squeezes out Weil Gotshal; Bankruptcy Judge Approves Federated's Takeover Plan."

[12]There was significant legal maneuvering before the deal was completed including the appointment of Cyrus R. Vance, the former U.S. Secretary of State, to mediate the discussions between Macy's, Federated, and other outstanding creditors.

purchased a $140 million stake in Palm's junior debt at a large discount to its par value—reported as priced at around 40 cents on the dollar.[13] TPG and Apollo had executed a similar strategy in 2009 when acquiring Planet Hollywood Hotel and Casino through the purchase of its distressed debt.

Distressed Debt as an Undervalued Security

Distressed debt is not always an entrée into private equity; it can simply be an investment in an undervalued security. In this instance, distressed debt investors are less concerned with an equity stake in the troubled company. Instead, they expect to benefit if the company can implement a successful turnaround strategy.

Consider the bankruptcy of Montgomery Ward & Co. in July 1997. Founded in 1872, Montgomery Ward was the first mail-order merchant (Sears was second) and became a successful and savvy mass merchandiser throughout most of the 1900s.[14] However, it failed to ride the wave of the post–World War II economic boom and was eventually eclipsed by other large retailers such as Sears and J.C. Penney's.

As a result, Montgomery Ward went through several owners in the 1970s and 1980s including Marcor Inc., Mobil Oil Corporation, and a senior management buyout. Despite its varied ownership, Montgomery Ward could not turn itself around. Its lack of brandname goods, dingy stores, and out-of-date image kept customers away and led to its July 1997 Chapter 11 bankruptcy filing.[15]

Montgomery Ward's bankruptcy provided an opportunity for distressed investors, vendors, and bank lenders alike. By October 1997, Ward's unsecured debt was trading around 35 cents on the dollar. At that price, distress debt investors such as the Third Avenue Value Fund, bought $17 million of Ward's debt from its vendors.[16] In addition, secured lender New York Life accepted an unsolicited bid from Merrill Lynch & Co. for its entire senior Montgomery Ward debt of $40 million. Nationwide Insurance Cos. also sold $31.5 million of its secured debt.

---

[13]See Jon Berke and Andrew Ragsly, "TPG Buys Palms Loans," *Financial Times*, February 24, 2010.

[14]In fact, it was a Montgomery Ward copywriter who invented the character and illustrated poem "Rudolph the Red-Nosed Reindeer" for Santa Claus to give to children in Montgomery Ward department stores. Rudolph was an instant hit and helped to draw large crowds to Montgomery Ward stores.

[15]See Jef Feeley, "Wards Emerges From Bankruptcy Court to Clouded Future," *Bloomberg News,* August 2, 1999.

[16]See Rekha Balu, "Debt Traders Capitalize on Vendor Uncertainty; Buying, Selling Ward's Stakes could Affect Proceedings," *Crain's Chicago Business,* October 6, 1997.

From a distressed investor's point of view the Montgomery Ward's bankruptcy provided a good opportunity because GE Capital Inc. already owned more than 50% of Ward's. Additionally, it was one of its largest creditors having provided $1 billion in financing for the retailer's previous reorganization plan. It seemed reasonable to believe that GE Capital would provide additional relief to get the company out of bankruptcy. In fact, GE Capital did step up to the plate and paid $650 million for the remainder of the company (plus its Signature Group direct marketing arm) as well as wiping clean the $1 billion in debt. Montgomery Ward emerged from bankruptcy in August 1999.

However, GE Capital did not step up as much as some distressed debt investors had hoped. Secured creditors were paid in full, but unsecured creditors received only 26 to 28 cents on the dollar. Those distressed debt investors who purchased senior claims at a discount profited nicely. However, those who purchased vendor claims (unsecured debt) lost money.

As an unfortunate postscript, Montgomery Ward still could not make a go of it and filed for bankruptcy again in December 2000. This time there was no reorganization. The company went out of business.

However, the name "Wards" lives on. Through the bankruptcy liquidation process, a Chicago-based multititle retail mailer, Direct Marketing Services Inc., acquired the marketing rights to use the Montgomery Wards name in June 2004 and resurrected the Montgomery Wards catalog in September 2004. Although there are no longer any Montgomery Ward stores, the name lives on through online retailing.

Distressed Debt in a Fire Sale

In American parlance, a "fire sale" is a liquidation of inventory at prices far below their normal value. The term comes from the fact that after a devastating fire to a business, what inventory remains is sold at distressed prices. This is the best example of distressed debt as an opportunistic investment strategy.

An excellent example of a fire sale is Refco, Inc. In October 2005, a spectacular fraud was uncovered at Refco, Inc., a leading broker in the futures industry. It was revealed that Refco's Chief Executive Officer, Phillip Bennett had allegedly hidden from investors a $430 million receivable that he owed to Refco and that Refco's 2002–2005 financial statements could not be relied upon. He was subsequently indicted by a grand jury in New York for violating U.S. securities laws.[17]

---

[17]See "Former Refco CEO Phillip Bennett Indicted for Securities Fraud," *Bloomberg News*, November 11, 2005.

EXHIBIT 21.4   Stock Price of Refco from IPO to Bankruptcy

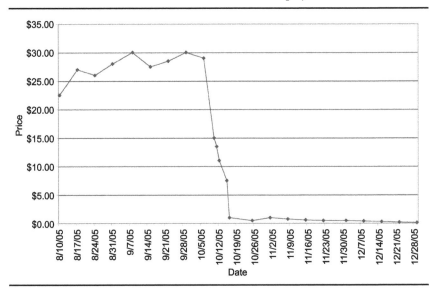

What is fascinating about Refco is that this was a private equity deal to begin with. The large buyout firm Thomas H. Lee had purchased a large private equity stake in Refco and subsequently had taken the company public in an initial public offering in August of 2005. Refco stock was sold at $22 a share in a $670 million IPO. Only two short months later, the fraud was uncovered and Refco's stock price spiralled down. Exhibit 21.4 shows the rapid decline of Refco's common stock price.

Refco quickly entered into bankruptcy liquidation proceedings under Chapter 7 of the Bankruptcy Code to pay off its creditors. At the time of its bankruptcy filing, Refco had one bond issue outstanding, 9% notes due 2012. Vulture investors quickly swooped down on these bonds.

Before the discovery of the fraud, the Refco bonds were well received by the market and were trading at close to 110 with a yield of 7%. Once the fraud was discovered, these bonds dropped as precipitously as Refco's stock price, falling from 110 down to 40 (40 cents on the dollar), a drop of 63% of value in the first few days of Refco's fraud revelation. However, these were senior securities and therefore had considerably more protection than stockholders or other unsecured creditors. Investors who sold these bonds did so in a panicked fire sale—willing to part with them at severely depressed prices But distressed and vulture investors made out like bandits. Exhibit 21.5 shows the steep decline of the Refco bonds along with a strong

EXHIBIT 21.5   Price of Refco 9% Bond due 2012

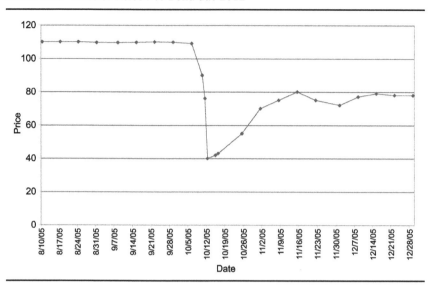

recovery in market value. After the initial fire sale, Refco bonds doubled in value from 40 to 80.

The key to this vignette is that distressed debt investing must take advantage of opportunities. The Refco fire sale took place quickly with traditional investors bailing out of Refco's bonds without a rational analysis of their value in the bankruptcy liquidation. Also, traditional investors were not ready for the rigors of the bankruptcy process, and so they sold their bonds for whatever they could get for them.

This example of distressed debt investing also demonstrates another useful principle about this market: there is always something left for creditors in a bankruptcy. Compare Exhibit 21.4 with Exhibit 21.5. The former exhibit shows that the price of Refco's stock declined precipitously once the fraud was uncovered, and it never recovered. Effectively, Refco's stock is worth zero. This highlights that the equity owners of the company really do bear the final losses associated with the company—Refco's shareholders had their investment wiped out.

Conversely, Exhibit 21.5 shows the value of Refco's bonds. While the bond prices declined just as steeply as Refco's stock price upon the discovery of the fraud, their value subsequently recovered. And while the bond prices did not reach their prefraud valuations, there was still 80 cents on the dollar worth of value left. A much better situation than losing everything as a stockholder. This is the added value of debt: Creditors come first, equityholders come last.

Distressed Debt in a Prepackaged Bankruptcy

The CIT group filed for bankruptcy in November 2009. At that time it was the fifth largest bankruptcy filing in U.S. history. CIT started out in 1908 financing horse-drawn carriages. Over the years it expanded into the financing of receivables for small businesses—it accounted for 70% of the factoring in the United States. However, during the deep recession of 2007–2009, many small businesses defaulted and ceased operations, leaving CIT with many worthless assets. In addition, during the last decade, CIT had expanded aggressively into student loans, construction loans, and industrial and equipment financing—all hit hard by the economic recession of 2007–2009.

As a result, by the summer of 2009, CIT was in deep financial trouble and began negotiations with its creditors for a prepackaged bankruptcy. As discussed previously, a prepackaged bankruptcy allows a company to reach an agreement with the majority of its creditors before making a Chapter 11 Bankruptcy Reorganization filing.

CIT formally filed for bankruptcy on November 1, 2009. Senior bank loans received 100 cents on the dollar. Unsecured and subordinated debt received 70 cents on the dollar plus over 90% of the equity in the company. Preferred stockholders and common equity were virtually wiped out—they only got to share a 2.5% equity stake in the new company.

However, for distressed debt investors, there was a great opportunity. Given the high probability that CIT would be able to restructure its balance sheet, there was a good chance that recovery on its existing subordinated debt would be sufficient to compensate for the risks of buying CIT's distressed debt. Exhibit 21.6 shows the price of CIT's 5.65% bonds due 2014 over the time period 2007–2009. A distressed debt investor could have purchased CIT's notes at 40 cents on the dollar in the summer of 2009 and received 70 cents on the dollar plus equity in December 2009.

CIT emerged from bankruptcy just 38 days after its initial filing on December 9, 2009. At the same time, it floated new stock. So far, CIT's strategy seems to have worked. As of June 2010, its stock price was trading above $36.

Distressed Debt Arbitrage

If there is any way to skin an arbitrage, hedge fund managers will think of it. While *distressed debt arbitrage* is not a private equity form of investing, it is a form of equity arbitrage best suited for hedge fund managers.

The arbitrage is constructed as follows. A hedge fund manager purchases distressed debt, which she believes is undervalued. At the same time, she shorts the company's underlying stock. The idea is that if the bonds are going

EXHIBIT 21.6   CIT 5.65% Notes

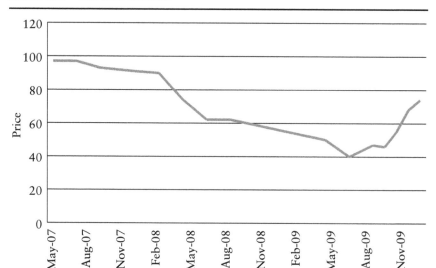

to decline in value, the company's stock price will decline even more dramatically because equity holders have only a residual claim behind debtholders.

Conversely, if the company's prospects improve, both the distressed debt and equity will appreciate significantly. The difference then will be between the coupon payment on the debt versus dividends paid on the stock. Since a company coming out of a workout or turnaround situation almost always conserves its cash and does not pay cash stock dividends, the hedge fund manager should earn large interest payments on the debt compared to the equity.

Hedge fund managers might very well be called active/passive managers. The key to their dual nature is that while the hedge fund manager actively trades the securities of the distressed company, she has no interest in an active role in the future direction of the company. Hedge fund managers typically do not participate in the restructuring of the company. Their goal is to make a play on the relative value of the distressed companies securities. Their holding period is typically six months to one year—much less than the time period needed to exert control and influence.

RISKS OF DISTRESSED DEBT INVESTING

There are two main risks associated with distressed debt investing. First, business risk still applies. Just because distressed debt investors can purchase the debt of a company on the cheap does not mean it cannot go lower.

EXHIBIT 21.7   Corporate Defaults, 2007–2009 (in $ billions)

	2007	2008	2009
1st Quarter	$1.50	$3.10	$18.50
2nd Quarter	$0.70	$12.10	$41.80
3rd Quarter	$3.80	$147.50	$5.20
4th Quarter	$17.70	$4.40	$42.10
Total	$23.70	$167.10	$107.60

Source: Distressed Debt Securities Newsletter Income Securities Advisor, January 2010.

This is the greatest risk to distressed debt investing, a troubled company may be worthless and unable to pay off its creditors. While creditors often convert their debt into equity, the company may not be viable as a going concern. If the company cannot develop a successful plan of reorganization, it will only continue its spiral downwards.

Consider Exhibit 21.7. This shows the amount of defaulted corporate debt in 2007–2009 for which there was no company reorganization and distressed debt investors had to wait in line for whatever assets they could get. As this exhibit demonstrates, there was a big jump in corporate defaults in 2008 and 2009.

The biggest jump came in the third quarter of 2008 with the bankruptcy and liquidation of Lehman Brothers. Lehman Brothers was the largest bankruptcy in U.S. history with over $600 billion of assets at the time. Although Lehman closed its subprime mortgage lender, BNC Capital in 2007, it retained significant positions in subprime and lower rated mortgages on its balance sheet. Coupled with a leverage ratio of 31 to 1 by 2007, Lehman was greatly exposed to any downturn in the housing market. As a result, Lehman was forced into bankruptcy and its empire broken up as Barclays, HSBC, J.P. Morgan, and other large banks purchased large pieces of Lehman's business at distressed prices.

It may seem strange, but creditworthiness has only a small impact on the distressed investment decision. The reason is that the debt is already distressed because the company may already be in default and its debt thoroughly discounted. Consequently, failure to pay interest and debt service has already occurred.

Instead, vulture investors consider the business risks of the company. They are concerned not with the short-term payment of interest and debt service, but rather, the ability of the company to execute a viable business plan. From this perspective, it can be said that distressed debt investors are truly equity investors. They view the purchase of distressed debt as an investment in the company as opposed to a lending facility.

Consider the case of Iridium LLC, a satellite telephone system with $1.5 billion in high-yield debt. Motorola Inc. started Iridium in 1997, and owned 18% of the company. Iridium launched a network of 66 satellites to build a global telephone network. After Iridium went public in 1997, its market capitalization reached almost $11 billion.

However, Iridium's business plan eventually fell apart as it failed to attract enough customers to make the business viable. Iridium's phones were too bulky, about the size of a brick, much larger than the small, pocket-sized cellular phones to which consumers had become accustomed. In addition, service was unreliable, the satellite phones worked poorly in buildings and cars. Instead of the 600,000 subscribers that Iridium had projected, it could only muster 20,000.

As a consequence, Iridium could not meet the interest payments on $800 million of senior bank debt. Still, in May 1999, distressed debt investors jumped to buy Iridium's 14% subordinated notes for 26 cents on the dollar when it appeared that Iridium would be able to restructure its senior bank loans. However, the restructuring failed, and with over $3 billion in debt Iridium filed for Chapter 11 bankruptcy in August 1999.

At the time of its bankruptcy, Iridium's subordinated notes were trading at 14.5 cents on the dollar. Unfortunately, Iridium's financial woes continued as the company sank further and further into losses and debt. By March 2000, Iridium's subordinated bonds were trading at 2 to 3 cents on the dollar. Iridium was finally put out of its misery in November 2000 when the bankruptcy court liquidated the company for a paltry $25 million. Its bonds were worthless.

The second main risk is the lack of liquidity. The distressed debt arena is a fragmented market, dominated by a few players. Trading out of a distressed debt position may mean selling at a significant discount to the book value of the debt. For example, at the time of the Loews bankruptcy filing, its senior subordinated notes were trading at an offer of 15, but with a bid of 10, a gap of 5 cents or $50 dollars for every $1000 face value bond.

In addition, purchasers of distressed debt must have long-term investment horizons. Workout and turnaround situations do not happen overnight. The example of CIT, cited earlier, is rare in that its bankruptcy and reorganization process lasted only a month. It may be several years before a troubled company can correct its course and appreciate in value.

MARKET PERFORMANCE

The returns for distressed debt investing can be very rewarding. Distressed debt obligations generally trade at levels that yield a total return of 20%

EXHIBIT 21.8   Returns to Distressed Debt[a]

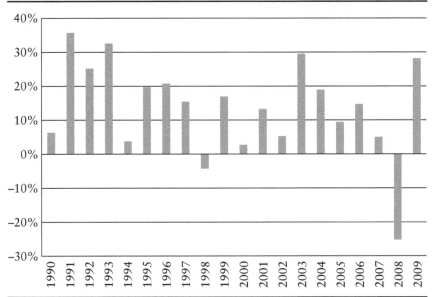

[a]Average = 13.71%, Std Dev = 14.20%, Sharpe = 0.68.
Data source: Hedge Fund Research, Inc.

or higher. Exhibit 21.8 shows the returns to the Hedge Fund Research Inc., distressed debt index. These are hedge funds that trade in distressed debt because of the inefficient nature of this market. We can see that for the past 20 years, the returns to distressed debt were mostly in the high teens to over 20%. Of course, in a bad credit year like 2008, the returns were very negative—a –25%. Still, the long-term average return to distressed debt investing is over 13% with a very positive Sharpe ratio of 0.68.

Financial Instruments and Concepts Introduced in this Chapter (in Order of Presentation)

Distressed debt
Chapter 11 of the U.S. Bankruptcy Code
Plan of reorganization
Cramdown
Rule of priority
Chapter 7 bankruptcy
Distressed buyouts
Prepackaged bankruptcy
Distressed debt arbitrage

CHAPTER 22

Investing in Commodities

In Chapter 1 we discussed how most alternative asset classes are really alternative investment strategies within an existing asset class. This statement applies to hedge funds and private equity, for example. However, it does not apply to commodities. Investment in this asset class can be achieved through various products. Some investors will take passive positions in physical commodities and earn the risk premium that is associated with this asset class. Other investors will use other products to actively trade both physical commodities and commodity derivatives and generate a rate of return that is both a function of the risk premium embedded in this asset class and the trading skills of the manager.

It is important to note that capital assets such as stocks and bonds can be valued on the basis of the present value of the expected cash flows. Expected cash flows and discount rates are prime ingredients used to determine the value of capital assets. Conversely, *commodities* do not provide a claim on an ongoing stream of revenue in the same fashion as stocks and bonds.[1] For this reason, they cannot be valued using discounted value techniques, and interest rates have only a small impact on their value. Commodities generally fall into the category of consumable or transformable assets. You can consume a commodity such as corn either as feedstock or as food stock. Alternatively, you can transform commodities like crude oil into gasoline and other petroleum products. Consequently, they have economic value, but they do not yield an ongoing stream of revenue.

Another distinction between capital assets and commodities is the global nature of commodity markets. Worldwide, commodities markets are mostly dollar-denominated. However, as other economies such as China and India grow and become the major source of demand for most commodities, other currencies may become increasingly important in determining the value of these commodities. Regardless, the value of a particular commodity is dependent on global supply and demand imbalances rather than regional

---

[1]An exception to this rule is precious metals such as gold, silver, and platinum, which can be lent out at a market lease rate

EXHIBIT 22.1   Correlation Coefficients, 2000–2009

	S&P 500	FTSE	New York Crude	London Crude
S&P 500	1.00	0.86	0.00	0.06
FTSE	0.86	1.00	0.10	0.08
New York Crude	0.00	0.10	1.00	0.94
London Crude	0.06	0.084	0.94	1.00

imbalances. Consequently, commodity prices are determined globally rather than regionally. This is very different from the equity markets, where, for instance, you have the U.S. stock market, foreign developed stock markets, and emerging markets. Foreign stock markets will reflect economic developments within their own regions compared to the United States.

Exhibit 22.1 shows the correlation coefficients between changes in the S&P 500 and the FTSE 100 stock indexes for the period 2000 to 2009. As can be seen, stock price changes in the two countries are less than perfectly correlated, with a correlation coefficient of 0.86. Compare this to the correlation coefficient associated with the change in prices of crude oil listed on the New York Mercantile Exchange and the International Petroleum Exchange in London.[2] The correlation is 0.94. The changes in crude oil prices in London and New York move in closer lockstep than stock prices in London and New York. This is because crude oil prices are determined by global economic factors, whereas stock markets, despite the ease of moving capital around the globe, still retain regional factors.[3] Note also that the changes in the U.S. and UK stock market indexes have very low correlations with changes in the price of crude oil. These low correlations demonstrate that crude oil prices are driven by economic fundamentals different from the systematic risk factors for the stock market.

In this chapter, we provide an introduction to the commodity markets, the methods by which investors access those markets, and the strategic reasons for investing in commodity futures. We begin by developing the

---

[2]In order to make a fair comparison of the correlation coefficients associated with the stock market returns of the United States and the United Kingdom, and the crude oil markets in the same two countries, we converted FTSE prices into dollars. This removes any currency effects that might confound our analysis. Therefore, the correlation coefficients presented in Exhibit 22.1 are based on changes in dollar-denominated prices.

[3]Of course, another reason is that the FTSE and the S&P 500 do not represent the same companies or even the same industries. The high correlation between oil prices in the United States and the United Kingdom is due to the fact that the global market for some energy products is highly integrated (e.g., natural gas, by contrast, is less integrated because it is expensive to move and store).

economic case for commodity futures. At the end of this chapter we examine several investable benchmarks that have been developed for the commodity futures markets.

GAINING EXPOSURE TO COMMODITIES

There are six ways to obtain economic exposure to commodity assets: through the commodity itself, shares in a commodity-related firm, futures contracts, commodity swaps/forward contracts, commodity-linked notes, or exchange-traded funds (ETFs).

Purchase of the Underlying Commodity

An investor can purchase the underlying commodity to gain economic exposure. Actual ownership of physical commodities can be problematic, however. Storage and transportation costs associated with direct investments in commodities make this an unattractive alternative for most investors. Most investors are unfamiliar with the storage issues of physical commodities, let alone willing to bear the storage costs of ownership associated with physical commodities.

However, there are parts of the world where physical ownership of commodities is still the major form of economic wealth. India, for example, is the second largest consumer of precious metals in the world, after the United States. The reason is that many parts of India are geographically remote, far removed from the financial services and products that are commonplace in the United States. Stocks, bonds, mutual funds, and even bank savings accounts are the exception, not the rule. Consequently, some of the people in these remote regions may denominate their wealth in gold, silver, and platinum.

Position in Natural Resource Companies

Another way to gain exposure to commodities is to own the securities of a firm that derives a significant part of its revenues from the purchase and sale of physical commodities. For instance, purchasing shares of Exxon Mobil Corporation might be considered a pure play on the price of oil since three-fourths of Exxon Mobil's revenues are derived from the exploration, refining, and marketing of petroleum products.

However, there are several reasons why this pure play might not work. First, part of the value of the stock in Exxon Mobil is dependent on the movement of the general stock market. As a result an investment in the stock of any company will result in exposure to systematic (market) risk

EXHIBIT 22.2 Beta Coefficients and Correlation Coefficients, 2000–2009

	Stock Market		Crude Oil	
	Beta	Correlation Coefficient	Beta	Correlation Coefficient
ExxonMobil	0.82	0.57	0.17	0.28
Chevron/Texaco	0.80	0.53	0.22	0.33
Conoco/Phillips	0.84	0.49	0.32	0.40
BP Amoco	0.80	0.53	0.20	0.31

as measured by the stock's beta, as well as firm-specific risk. Exhibit 22.2, which lists correlation coefficients and the betas associated with the stock returns of four large petroleum companies compared to the S&P 500 (the proxy for the stock market in the beta estimation). We also include correlation coefficients and betas for the stock returns of the four oil companies compared to the changes in the price of crude oil.

First, we can see that the oil companies all have high betas with respect to the S&P 500. This indicates that oil companies have significant stock market risk. Furthermore, the correlation coefficients between the stock returns of these four companies and the S&P 500 are very large. We can conclude that oil companies have considerable exposure to the general stock market. The analysis changes when we examine the returns of these four companies compared to the prices of crude oil. Exhibit 22.1 shows that the betas associated with crude oil prices are very low. In this case we define the market as the current price of crude oil traded in New York City. In addition, the correlation coefficients between the oil company stock prices and crude oil stock prices are all lower than their correlation with the stock market. We can conclude that the stock prices of oil companies are much more dependent on the movement of the stock market than they are on the movement of crude oil prices. Therefore, investing in an oil company as a pure play on crude oil prices provides an investor with significant stock market exposure and a relatively low crude oil exposure.

Second, when an investor invests with an oil company (or any company, for that matter) the investor assumes all of the idiosyncratic risks associated with that company. Consider the example of Texaco when in the 1980s it attempted an ill-fated merger with the Getty Oil Company despite the Getty Oil Company having an outstanding bid from Pennzoil. The result was massive litigation resulting in a several-billion-dollar verdict against Texaco, forcing the company to seek Chapter 11 bankruptcy protection. Further, in the 1990s, Texaco was the subject of a race discrimination lawsuit by many of its workers. This litigation cost Texaco several hundred million dollars.

Neither of these lawsuits, however, had anything to do with the price of oil. They were instead part of the idiosyncratic risk associated with the management practices of Texaco. Most investors seeking a pure play on oil would be disappointed to receive lengthy and expensive lawsuit exposure.

In addition, there are other operating risks associated with an investment in any company. A company's financing policies, for example, affect the price of its stock. Exxon Mobil has a debt/equity ratio of about 1.25. This is a little above average for the oil industry. There is also operating leverage (i.e., the ratio of fixed to variable expenses). Oil companies tend to have high variable costs associated with their exploration, refining, and marketing programs. While financial and operating leverage affect the price of a stock, they have nothing to do with the price of oil.

Finally, even if all of the other risks associated with an investment in an oil company are accepted, the investor might find that the oil company has hedged away its oil exposure. Most large oil and energy companies maintain their own trading desks. One main goal of these trading desks is to hedge the risk associated with the purchase and sale of petroleum products in order to reduce variability of corporate earnings. The reason is that oil companies, like most companies, prefer to smooth their annual earnings rather than be subject to large swings due to changes in the price of oil. The same issue arises in the context of mining companies. Many of them may choose to hedge against fluctuations in the price of the commodity they produce, and as a result their equities generally do not provide the same exposure that investments in commodities would provide. The can be seen in Exhibit 22.2, where oil companies have low betas with respect to the price of crude oil. This is consistent with the fact that oil companies hedge away a considerable amount of their exposure to oil price risk.

Position in Commodity Futures Contracts

Perhaps the easiest way to gain exposure to commodities is through *commodity futures contracts*. Futures contracts offer several advantages. First, these contracts are traded on an organized exchange. Therefore, they share the same advantages as stock exchanges: a central marketplace, transparent pricing, clearinghouse security, uniform contract size and terms, and daily liquidity.

Second, the purchase of a futures contract (i.e. taking a long position) does not require automatic delivery of the underlying commodity. An offsetting futures position can be initiated that will close out the position of the initial futures contract. In this way an investor can gain exposure to commodities without worrying about physical delivery. In fact, only about 1% of all commodity futures contracts result in the actual delivery of the underlying commodity.

Third, futures contracts can be purchased without paying the full price for the commodity. When a futures contract is purchased, a deposit is required. This deposit is called the *initial margin*. This margin requirement is a small percentage of the full purchase price of the underlying commodity, usually less than 10%. The initial margin is a good faith deposit to ensure full payment upon delivery of the underlying commodity. In the futures markets, the investor does not need to put up the total price for the underlying commodity unless she takes physical delivery of the commodity.

Futures accounts also have two other margin requirements. On a day-by-day basis, the value of the futures contract will fluctuate. Fluctuation of prices in the futures markets will cause the value of the investor's margin account to increase or decrease. This is called *variation margin*. If the price of the futures contract increases, the holder of a long futures position will accrue positive variation margin. This adds to the equity in the futures margin account and may be withdrawn by the investor. Conversely, for an investor who has a short futures position, the increase in the price of the futures contract will result in a negative variation margin.

Maintenance margin is the minimum amount of equity that a futures margin account may have and is usually set at 75% to 80% of the initial margin. If subsequent variation margins reduce the equity in an investor's account down to the maintenance margin level, the investor will receive a margin call from the futures commission merchant. A *margin call* is a demand for additional cash to be contributed to the account to bring the equity in the account back over the maintenance margin level. If the investor cannot meet the margin call, the futures commission merchant has the right to liquidate the investor's positions in the account.

There can be some disadvantages to taking positions in futures contracts. First, if an investor wishes to maintain her exposure to commodity prices without taking physical delivery of the underlying contract, she will have to continually close out her existing futures position and reestablish a new position by entering into a new futures contract. This rolling of futures contracts can be costly, depending on the term structure of the futures prices. We discuss this in more detail in later in this chapter.

Second, as we noted earlier, once a long futures position is established, there may be ongoing margin calls if the futures contract declines in value. Conversely, if an investor's futures contracts increase in value, she may withdraw the additional equity from her account. Nonetheless, managing the contributions and withdrawals from a futures account may require more activity than is required by a traditional long-only security account. Futures accounts may be opened only with licensed futures commission merchants who are registered with the National Futures Association and the Commodity Futures Trading Commission.

Position in Commodity Swaps and Forward Contracts

Close economic cousins to commodity futures contracts are commodity swaps and forward contracts. *Commodity swaps* and *commodity forward contracts* perform the same economic function as commodity futures contracts. However, there are some key structural differences.

- Commodity swaps and forward contracts are custom made for the individual investor. While this provides precise tailoring of the commodity exposure desired by the investor, it also makes commodity swaps and forward contracts less liquid because what works for one investor will not work for all investors. Typically, if an investor wishes to terminate a commodity swap or forward position prior to maturity, the investor will negotiate with the counterparty who sold the swap or forward contract to the investor.
- Commodity swaps and forward contracts are not traded on an exchange. Again, this impacts liquidity. Exchange-traded products with standardized terms and public pricing provide much greater liquidity than customized commodity swaps or forward contracts.
- Counterbalancing the lack of liquidity, a key advantage is that commodity swaps and forward contracts are private contracts that trade outside the public domain of an exchange. To the extent an investor wishes to be discreet about its investment strategy for commodities, commodity swaps and forward contracts provide a degree of privacy not afforded by the public markets.

Purchase Commodity-Linked Notes

Another way an investor can gain exposure to the commodity markets is through a *commodity-linked note*. This is where financial engineering and the commodities markets intersect. In its simplest form, a commodity-linked note is an intermediate-term debt instrument whose value at maturity will be a function of the value of an underlying commodity futures contract or basket of commodity futures contracts.

Commodity-linked notes have several advantages. First, the investor does not have to worry about the rolling of the underlying futures contracts. This becomes the problem of the issuer of the note who must roll the futures contracts to hedge the commodity exposure embedded in the note. Second, the note is, in fact, a debt instrument. While investors may have restrictions on investing in the commodities markets, they can have access to commodity exposure through a debt instrument. The note is recorded as a liability on the balance sheet of the issuer, and as a bond investment on the balance sheet of the investor. In addition, the note can have a stated coupon rate and maturity just like any other debt instrument. The twist is that the investor accepts a lower coupon payment than it otherwise could receive in exchange for sharing in the upside of the commodity prices. Third, the holder of the note does not have to worry about any tracking error issues with respect to the price of a single commodity or basket of commodities. Once again, this problem remains with the issuer.

In practice, commodity-linked notes are tied to the prices of commodity futures contracts or commodity options. Commodity-linked notes are transparent because these notes utilize exchange-traded commodity futures and options contracts with daily pricing and liquidity or commodity swaps that are tied to the prices of commodity futures. As a result, investors may participate in viable securities that offer transparent exposure to a new asset class without a direct investment in that asset class.

Position in Commodity Exchange-Traded Funds

Another straightforward way to invest in a commodity is through an exchange-traded fund (ETF). As explained in Chapter 13, an ETF is very similar to a passively closed-end fund. The ETF can be purchased through organized exchanges throughout the trading hours.

A *commodity ETF* may provide exposure to one commodity or a group of commodities. For example, USO, the oil ETF traded in the United States, seeks to reflect the performance, less expenses, of the spot price of West Texas Intermediate (WTI) light, sweet crude oil. The fund underlying the ETF invests in futures contracts for WTI light and other petroleum-based fuels that are traded on exchanges. Conversely, an investor may want a broader commodity exposure across the several sectors of the commodities markets. GSG is the iShares ETF that tracks the GSCI Excess Return Index. Similarly, DJP is an exchange-traded note (ETN) that tracks the Dow Jones AIG Total Return Commodity Index. There are now over 30 different commodity ETFs and ETNs traded in the United States and on the London Stock Exchange.

COMMODITY PRICES COMPARED TO FINANCIAL ASSET PRICES

Let's compare commodity prices to financial asset prices. As we stated at the beginning of the chapter, financial asset prices reflect the long-term discounted value of a stream of expected future cash flows. In the case of stock prices, this future revenue stream may be eternal. In the case of a bond, the time is finite but can be very long, 10 to 20 years of expected cash flows. Investors in financial assets are compensated for the risk of fluctuating cash flows, and this risk is reflected in the interest rate used to discount those cash flows.

Thus, long-term expectations and interest rates are critical for pricing financial assets. Conversely, speculators and investors in commodities earn returns for bearing short-term commodity price risk. By bearing the price risk for commodity producers and commodity consumers, commodity investors and speculators receive exposure to the hedger's short-term earnings instead of its long-term cash flows. This short-term exposure to a hedger's earnings is the reason why commodities will be priced very differently from financial assets. Long-term expectations and interest rates have only a minimal impact on commodity prices. Therefore, commodity prices can react very differently from financial asset prices when short-term expectations and long-term expectations diverge. This divergence occurs naturally as part of the course of the business cycle.

For instance, at the bottom of a recession, the short-term expectation of the economy's growth is negative. Commodity prices will decline to reflect this lower demand for raw inputs. However, it is at the bottom of a recession when discount rates are low and when long-term earnings expectations are revised upward that stocks and bonds begin to perform well. The converse is true at the peak of an expansion. Commodity prices are high, but long-term earnings expectations decline.

The different reactions to different parts of the business cycle indicate that commodities tend to move in the direction opposite to that of stocks and bonds. This has important portfolio implications that we discuss in the following chapters. For now it is sufficient to understand that commodity prices follow pricing dynamics different from the pricing dynamics of financial assets.

ECONOMIC RATIONALE

We previously stated that commodities are an asset class distinct from stocks and bonds. Here we clarify that distinction and demonstrate where and why commodity prices react differently from capital asset prices.

Commodities and the Business Cycle

As explained in the previous section, commodity prices are not as directly impacted by changes in discount rates as stocks and bonds are. We also discussed how commodity prices are not determined by the discounted value of future cash flows. Instead, commodity prices are determined by the current supply and demand of the underlying commodity. Since commodity prices are driven by different economic fundamentals than stocks and bonds, they should be expected to have little correlation or even negative correlation with the prices of capital assets.

There are three reasons why commodity prices should, in fact, be negatively correlated with the prices of stocks and bonds. The first is the relationship that commodity futures prices have with inflation. Inflation is well documented to have a detrimental impact on the values of stocks and bonds. However, inflation is expected to have a positive impact on commodity futures prices for two reasons.

First, prices of physical commodities such as oil are an underlying source of inflation. As the cost of raw materials increases, so do the producers' price inflation and the consumers' price inflation. In fact, commodity prices are a component of the producer price index (PPI) and the consumer price index (CPI). Therefore, higher commodity prices mean higher inflation.

Also, higher inflation means higher short-term interest rates. This also has a beneficial impact on commodity futures investments because of their collateral yield. As we discussed in the prior chapter, commodity futures contracts can be purchased with a down payment known as the initial margin. The initial margin can be contributed in the form of cash or U.S. Treasury bills. This means that one component of return from an investment in commodity futures is the interest that is earned on the margin deposit that supports the futures contract.[4] Higher inflation therefore means a higher interest rate on the margin on deposit, and a higher return from investing in commodity futures contracts.

Exhibit 22.3 documents the relationship between inflation, commodity futures, and stocks and bonds for the period 1990 through 2009. This chart plots the correlation of monthly returns between large-cap stocks (the Russell 1000), small-cap stocks (the Russell 2000), international stocks (MSCI EAFE and FTSE indexes) high-yield bonds (the Salomon Smith Barney High Yield Cash Pay Index), U.S. Treasury bonds, and commodities (as represented by the Goldman Sachs Commodity Index[5]) with the rate of inflation. As can be seen, commodity futures prices are positively correlated with inflation. Conversely, capital assets such as stocks and bonds are negatively correlated with inflation. Therefore, throughout the course of the business cycle, as inflation increases, capital asset values decrease, but commodity futures values increase. The reverse is also true, as inflation decreases, capital asset prices increase, but commodity futures prices decrease.

---

[4] If the futures margin is deposited in cash, then the futures broker may pay a higher interest rate on that deposit. Alternatively, if the futures margin is deposited in Treasury bills, as the Treasury bills mature, newer, higher-yielding Treasury bills may be used to replace them.

[5] We use the Goldman Sachs Commodity Index as our proxy for commodity prices. There are, in fact, several commodity indexes that we discuss later in the chapter.

EXHIBIT 22.3 Correlation of Stocks, Bonds, and Commodities with U.S. Inflation, 1990–2009

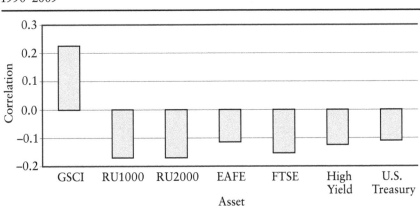

Notice that the Financial Times/Stock Exchange Index (FTSE) of the 100 largest stocks traded on the London Stock Exchange and the MSCI EAFE index (Europe, Australasia, and the Far East) are also negatively correlated with the U.S. inflation rate. This is important to note because an investor seeking international diversification as a means to escape the ravages of domestic inflation does not find it in foreign stocks.

Even more important, commodity futures prices are positively correlated with the change in the inflation rate, whereas capital assets are negatively correlated with changes in the rate of inflation.[6] This is important because changes in the rate of inflation tend to reflect inflation shocks (i.e., unanticipated changes that force investors to revise their expectations about future inflation). A positive change in the inflation rate means that investors' expectations regarding future inflation rates will increase. Stock and bond prices react negatively to such revised expectations, whereas commodity futures prices react positively.

Exhibit 22.4 shows the reaction of capital assets and commodities to changes in the rate of inflation. We see that commodities remain highly correlated with changes in the inflation rate. In fact, commodities have a stronger correlation to changes in the inflation rate than to the absolute inflation rate. Conversely, stocks and corporate bonds do not respond well to changes in inflation, the correlation coefficient is negative (except for MSCI EAFE, where it is close to zero). Last, we note that U.S. Treasury bonds respond positively to changes in inflation.

[6]See Philip Halpern and Randy Warsager, "The Performance of Energy and Non-Energy Based Commodity Investment Vehicles in Periods of Inflation," *Journal of Alternative Assets* 1, no. 1 (Summer 1998): 75–81.

EXHIBIT 22.4   Correlation of Stocks, Bonds, and Commodities with Changes in U.S. Inflation, 1990–2009

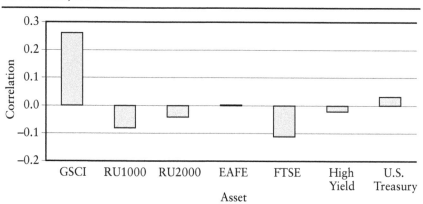

A second reason why commodity price changes may be negatively correlated with the returns to stocks and bonds is that commodity futures prices are impacted by short-term expectations, whereas stocks and bonds are affected by long-term expectations. For example, in a strong economy financial assets may decline over fears of increased inflation or sustainability of economic growth. These are long-term concerns. Conversely, commodity prices will react favorably because they are influenced by the high demand for raw materials under the current market conditions. The result is that commodity futures prices and stock and bond prices can react very differently at different parts of the business cycle. Exhibit 22.5 diagrams these different cyclical price moves.

This countercyclical movement between commodity futures and stocks and bonds is demonstrated by research conducted by Goldman Sachs & Co.[7] When the economy is below capacity (as measured by long-run GDP), equity returns have been at their highest, but commodity prices have been at their lowest. This occurs at the bottom of an economic cycle. As economic growth accelerates, stock prices begin to decline but commodity prices increase. When the economy heats up and exceeds long-run GDP, the return to commodity futures exceeds that for stocks. In sum, rising and falling commodity prices coincide with the current state of the economic cycle, whereas stocks and bonds are priced based on their future cash flows and not the current state of the economy.

---

[7]See Goldman Sachs & Co., "The Strategic Case for Using Commodities in Portfolio Diversification," Goldman Sachs Research Series on Commodities as an Asset Class, July 1996.

EXHIBIT 22.5 The Business Cycle and Stock, Bond, and Commodity Prices

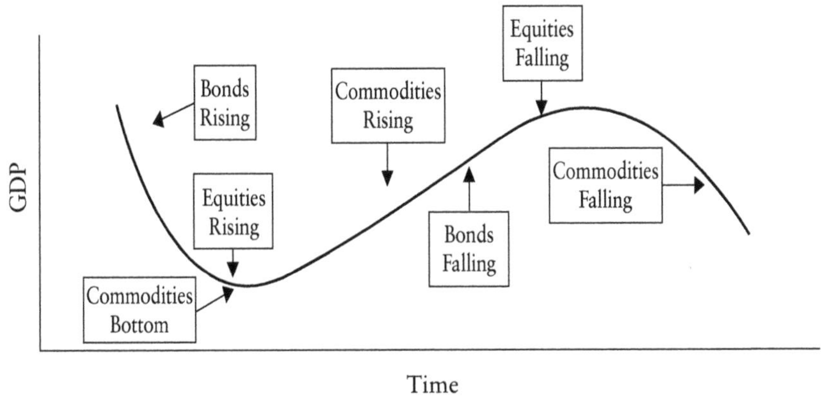

Time

The point of Exhibit 22.6 is that stocks and bonds are anticipatory in their pricing, whereas commodities are priced based on the state of current economic conditions. The value of stocks and bonds is derived from expectations regarding long-term earnings and coupon payments. Consequently, they perform best when the economy appears the worst but the prospects for improvement are the highest.

Real assets, however, show the opposite pattern. Commodity prices are determined not so much by the future prospects of the economy, but by the level of current economic activity. Consequently, commodity prices are at their lowest when economic activity is at its lowest, and at their highest when economic activity is at its highest. Exhibit 22.6 demonstrates that commodity returns are negative when economic activity is negative. The most recent example is the credit crisis and recession of 2008.

A third argument for the negative correlation between commodity prices and capital assets is based on economic production.[8] Consider the three primary inputs to economic production: capital, labor, and raw materials. The returns to these three factors should equal the price of production. In the short to intermediate term, the cost of labor should remain stable. Therefore, for any given price level of production, an increase in the return to capital must mean a reduction in the return to raw materials, and vice versa. The result is a negative correlation between commodity prices and the prices of capital assets.

---

[8]See Robert Greer, "Institutional Use of Physical Commodity Indices," *Commodity Derivatives and Finance*, edited by Kathleen Tener Smith and Pam Kennison (London: Euromoney Books, 1999).

EXHIBIT 22.6 Commodity Returns Are Coincident with the State of the Economic Cycle

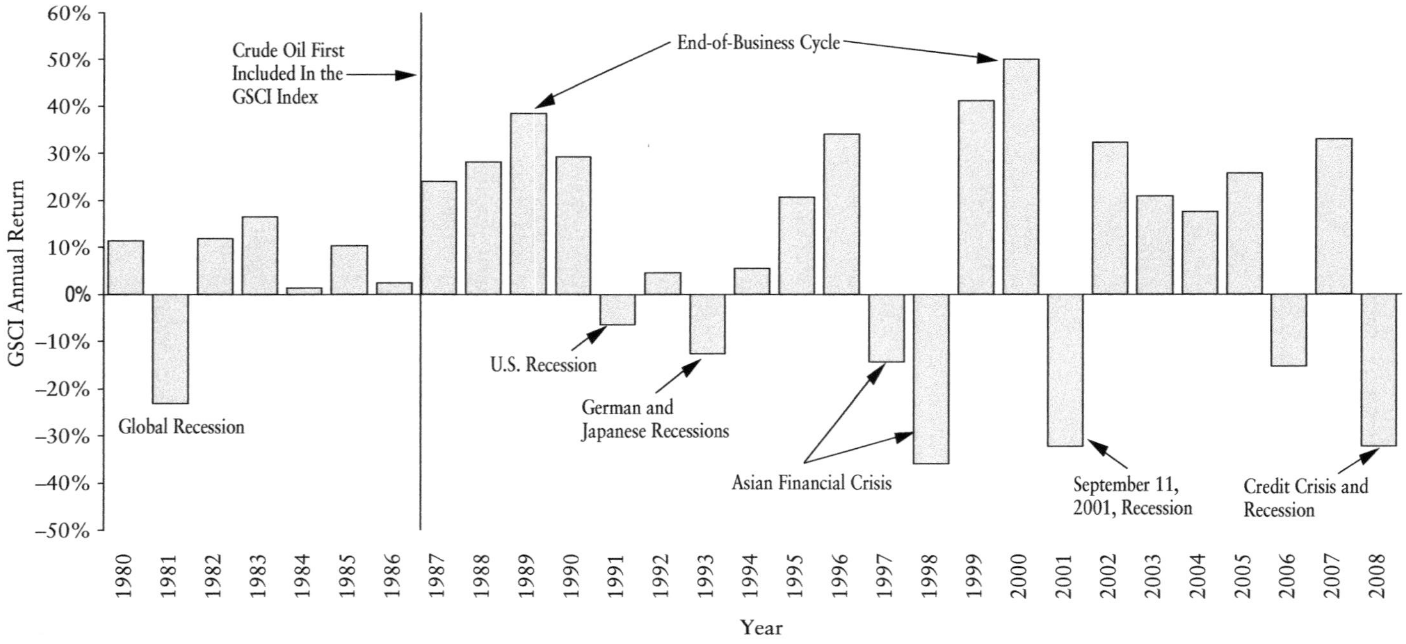

In sum, commodity price changes are expected to be at the very least uncorrelated with the returns to stocks and bonds. Additionally, there are three reasons to expect commodity prices to be negatively correlated with stocks and bonds. First, inflation has a positive impact on commodity prices but a negative impact on stocks and bonds. Second, commodity prices are impacted by a different set of expectations than that for stocks and bonds. Last, in the production process there is a trade-off between the returns to capital and the returns to raw materials.

Event Risk

In our discussion of hedge funds in Chapter 16, we demonstrated how financial assets and hedge fund strategies are exposed to significant event risk. For example, our analysis of the returns to hedge funds around the financial turmoil of 2008 indicated that most hedge fund strategies experienced significant negative returns. Additionally, we demonstrated that most arbitrage strategies have exposure to event risk, which can result in significant negative returns.

Commodities, by contrast, tend to have positive exposure to event risk. The reason is that the surprises that occur in the commodities markets tend to be those that unexpectedly reduce the supply of the commodity to the market. Events such as Organization of Petroleum Exporting Countries (OPEC) agreements to reduce the supply of crude oil, a cold snap in winter, war, or political instability can drive up energy prices. Similarly, events such as droughts, floods, and crop freezes all reduce the supply of agricultural products. Last, strikes and labor unrest can drive up the prices of both precious and industrial metals. Shocks that would unexpectedly reduce demand significantly tend to be rare. However, shocks in terms of unexpectedly large buildups in inventories that may lead to significant price declines do occur. At least historically more commodity prices appear to have a positive exposure to various event risks.

These patterns of unexpected shocks to the commodity prices should provide a pattern of positively skewed returns. In our examination of hedge funds, we demonstrated that many hedge fund strategies have positively skewed distributions, that is, more return observations to the right of the median (positive) than to the left of the median (negative). Positively skewed return distributions will have a beneficial impact to a diversified portfolio because they can provide an upward return bias to the portfolio. We examine the distribution of commodity futures returns later in this chapter. For now, it is sufficient to say that these patterns of returns demonstrate a positive skew to commodity futures prices indicating a bias for upside returns instead of downside returns.

Furthermore, these patterns of commodity shocks are expected to be uncorrelated. For example, OPEC agreements to cut oil production should be uncorrelated with droughts in the agricultural regions around the world[9] or with labor strikes affecting metals mining. The point is that the global supply and demand factors for each individual commodity market that determine the price of each commodity are very different. The primary factors that determine the supply and demand for oil, and the price of oil, are very different from those that affect the price of wheat, gold, or aluminum.[10] Consequently, we would expect the price patterns of commodities to be uncorrelated with each other.

Equally important is that shocks to the commodities markets are expected to be at least uncorrelated with the financial markets, and more likely to be negatively correlated with the financial markets. The reason follows from our prior discussion—most shocks to the commodity markets tend to reduce the supply of raw materials to the market. The sudden decrease of raw materials should have a positive impact on commodity prices, but a negative impact on financial asset prices, whose expected returns will be reduced by the higher cost of production inputs.

Exhibit 22.7 demonstrates several years where there were significant shocks to the supply and demand of physical commodities. Again, we use the GSCI as a benchmark for commodity returns. In the early and mid-1970s there was a series of oil price shocks. This was a boon for commodity prices, but disastrous for financial asset prices. In contrast, 1981 was a year of severe recession for the United States. Financial asset prices declined, but so did prices of commodities, as there was simply insufficient demand both for finished goods and for raw materials to support either financial asset prices or commodity prices. Next, 1990 was the year of the Iraqi invasion of Kuwait. This political instability had a negative impact on financial asset prices, but a positive impact on commodity prices. Conversely, in 1998, there was a glut of cheap crude oil and petroleum products in the market. In late 1997, OPEC voted to increase production just as the Southeast Asian economies were slipping into a steep recession. In addition, under the United Nations Oil-for-Food Program, new oil production came on line from Iraq. Further, an extremely mild winter (recall El Niño) resulted in a buildup of petroleum inventories around the world. The result, in 1998, was plenty of cheap raw materials, which in turn translated to strong stock market gains in the United States.

---

[9]Since oil is a major input to the agricultural sector of the economy in the form of fuel and fertilizers, significant contraction in this sector may have a negative impact on oil prices.

[10]Due to the expansion of ethanol use in recent years, we have since seen an increased correlation between prices of some agricultural products (e.g. corn) and oil prices.

EXHIBIT 22.7 Annual Returns in Years of Market Stress

Year	S&P 500	Commodities
1973	–14.69%	74.96%
1974	–26.47	39.51
1977	–7.16	10.37
1981	–4.92	23.01%
1987	5.25	23.77
Oct. 1987	–21.54	1.05
1990	–3.10	29.08
1998	28.58	–35.75
2000	–9.10	49.74
2001	–11.89	–31.93
2002	–22.10	32.07
2008	–37.98	–32.02

Next came the three-year equity bear market following the bursting of the technology bubble. Note that in 2001 when the economy slid into a brief recession, commodity prices and stock prices moved in the same direction. Another example of when commodity prices and financial prices move in the same direction is during a global financial and economic meltdown. The credit and financial crisis of 2008 led to a deep recession around the world, and commodity prices declined significantly as a result of negative global GDP. Otherwise, commodities have not been correlated with the stock market movements during bear markets. Also, during severe liquidity shocks most commodity prices tend to decline because of lower leverage and availability of capital for commodity trading.

A fair conclusion is that commodity price shocks tend to favor supply disruptions rather than sudden increases in supply. These disruptions provide positive returns for commodities at the same time that they provide negative returns for financial assets. Therefore, the event risk associated with commodities tends to favor investors in the commodity markets while detrimentally impacting investors in the financial markets.

COMMODITY FUTURES INDEXES

In this section, we review several investable commodity futures indexes.

Description of a Commodity Futures Index

A *commodity futures index* should represent the total return that would be earned from holding long-only positions in unleveraged physical commodity futures. Financial futures should not be included because these contracts are economically linked to the underlying financial assets. Therefore, there is no diversification benefit from adding long positions in financial futures to a portfolio of financial assets.

Commodity futures indexes are constructed to be unleveraged. The face value of the futures contracts is fully supported (collateralized) either by cash or by Treasury bills. Futures contracts are purchased to provide economic exposure to commodities equal to the amount of cash dollars invested in the index. Therefore, every dollar of exposure to a commodity futures index represents one dollar of commodity price risk. For example, suppose that the initial margin for gold is $1,500 and that gold is selling at $930 per ounce. Then 100 ounces of gold being the size of the contract, one futures contract has an economic exposure to gold of $93,000. A managed futures account would typically pay the initial margin of $1,500 and receive economic exposure to gold equivalent to $93,000. The percentage of equity capital committed to the futures contract is equal to $1,500/$93,000 = 1.61%. In contrast, a commodity futures index will fully collateralize the gold futures contract. This means $93,000 of U.S. Treasury bills will be held to fully support the face value of the gold futures contract. In fact, the face value of every futures contract included in a commodity index will be fully collateralized by an investment in U.S. Treasury bills. In this way, an unleveraged commodity futures index represents the returns an investor could earn from continuously holding a passive long-only position in a basket of commodity futures contracts. The passive index must reflect all components of return from commodity futures contracts: price changes, collateral yield, and roll yield (this last source of return will be explained later).

Sources of Index Return

The total return from an unleveraged commodity futures index comes from three primary sources: changes in spot prices of the underlying commodity, the interest earned from the Treasury bills used to collateralize the futures contracts, and the roll yield. Each component can be an important part of the return of a commodity index in any given year.

Spot Prices

Spot commodity prices are determined by the supply and demand characteristics of each commodity market as well as the current level of risk aversion between consumers and producers of commodities. We explained, for example, how the price of crude oil plummeted in 1998 due to overproduction by OPEC members, extra production by Iraq, and the slowdown in Southeast Asia due to the Asian contagion of late 1997. This supply imbalance drove crude oil prices down. However, in early 1999, OPEC members reached an agreement to cut production and restrict the supply of crude oil into the marketplace. This changed the supply-and-demand equilibrium from one of excess supply to one of excess demand, and crude oil prices rose significantly.

Other factors remaining equal, it can be demonstrated that when the spot price of the underlying commodity increases in value, so will the futures price. The reverse is also true: as spot prices decline, so will the futures price. Therefore, changes in the current cash price of a commodity flow right through to the futures price.

This is important to understand because, as we discussed already, most of the shocks with respect to physical commodities tend to be events that reduce the current supply. That is, physical commodities have positive event risk. Supply and demand shocks to the physical commodity markets result in positive price changes for both the spot market and the futures market.

Collateral Yield

As we discussed earlier, a commodity futures index is unleveraged. It is unleveraged because the economic exposure underlying the basket of futures contract is fully collateralized by the purchase of U.S. Treasury bills. Therefore, for every $1 invested in a commodity futures index, the investor receives $1 of diversified commodity exposure plus interest on $1 invested in U.S. Treasury bills. The interest earned on the Treasury bills used as collateral is called the *collateral yield*, and it can be a significant part of the total return to a commodity futures index. Further, changes in inflation rates will be reflected in the yield on Treasury bills. This is another way that a commodity futures index can hedge against inflation.

Roll Yield

Roll yield is the least obvious source of return for commodity futures. Roll yield is derived from the shape of the commodity futures term structure. In commodity futures markets the futures prices can either be the spot price for the underlying commodity (a condition referred to as a *backwardation*), or above the current spot price for the underlying commodity (a condition referred to as a *contango*).

When the futures markets are in backwardation, a positive return will be earned from a simple buy-and-hold strategy. The positive return is earned because as the futures contract gets closer to maturity, its price must converge to that of the spot price of the commodity. Since the spot price is greater than the futures price, this means that the futures price must increase in value. This convergence is known as rolling up the yield curve, or simply *roll yield*. A demonstration should help.

Investable Commodity Futures Indexes

It may surprise investors that there are several commodity futures indexes in existence. These indexes have all the benefits of a stock index: They are transparent, they are liquid, you can trade in the underlying component parts of the index, and they are investable. Even if an investor may not be permitted to invest directly into commodity futures indexes, it may still gain exposure through a commodity-linked note of the type described earlier in this chapter.

An investment manager can use commodity futures indexes in two ways. First, a commodity futures index can be used to implement a specific view on the expected returns from commodities as an asset class. This is a tactical bet by the investment manager that commodities will outperform stocks and bonds given the current position of the business cycle. Alternatively, commodity futures indexes can be used to provide passive portfolio diversification. Historically, commodity prices peak and bottom out at different parts of the business cycle than do financial assets. Within this context, commodities have a strategic purpose: to diversify the investment portfolio's risk and return, without any view as to the current state of the business cycle.

Unlike equity stock indexes, where an investor can maintain her positions almost infinitely, commodity futures contracts specify a date for delivery. In order to maintain a continuous long-only position, expiring futures contracts must be sold and new futures contracts must be purchased. This provides the roll yield discussed earlier.

Standard & Poor's Goldman Sachs Commodity Index

The *Standard & Poor's Goldman Sachs Commodity Index* or simply GSCI is designed to be a benchmark for investment in the commodity markets and as a measure of commodity market performance over time. It is also designed to be a tradable index that is readily accessible to market participants. It is a long-only index of physical commodity futures. Not only is the GSCI comprised of physical commodity futures contracts, but a futures contract trades on the index itself. In other words, investors can purchase a futures contract tied to the future expected spot value of the GSCI.

The GSCI was introduced in 1991. Although the GSCI was not published prior to that time, Goldman Sachs has calculated the historical value of the GSCI and related indexes dating back to January 1970, based on historical prices of futures contracts and using the selection criteria and index construction established in 1991. The GSCI has been normalized to a value of 100 on December 31, 1969.

The GSCI is composed only of physical commodity futures. Financial futures contracts (on securities, currencies, or interest rates) are not included. The limitation to only physical commodity futures focuses the construction of the index on real assets that are the inputs to the global production process. Additionally, the GSCI is composed of the first nearby futures contract in each commodity (the futures contract that is closest to maturity).

The GSCI is a production-weighted index that is designed to reflect the relative significance of each of the constituent commodities to the world economy while preserving the tradability of the index by limiting eligible futures contracts to those with adequate liquidity. The use of production weighting is designed as an economic indicator. The GSCI assigns the appropriate weight to each commodity in proportion to the amount of that commodity that flows through the global economic engine. The GSCI is constructed using five-year averages of a particular commodity's contribution to world production. This is done to mitigate the effect of any aberrant year with respect to the production of a commodity.

The GSCI is constructed with 24 physical commodities across five main groups of real assets: precious metals, industrial metals, livestock, agriculture, and energy. As of year-end 2008, energy was the largest component of the index. This reflects the importance of energy products in the global production process, as well as the global surge in energy prices into the first half of 2008. At almost 72% of the total index as of the end of 2008, energy was the most dominant component of the worldwide production cycle. The next largest component of the index was agriculture—not surprising given the need to feed the growing worldwide population. Precious metals, by contrast, represent the smallest component of the GSCI. While precious metals may be held as a store of value, they are a smaller input to global production.

The GSCI physical weights are set once a year (in January) and then the dollar percentage values are allowed to float for the remainder of the year. There is no limit to the weight any one commodity may attain in the index and no minimum weight for any commodity. GSCI and other value-weighted indexes represent a momentum investment strategy because those commodity futures contracts that do well represent an increasing portion of the index.

The distribution of returns associated with the GSCI is shown in Exhibit 22.8 where we plot the monthly return distribution for the GSCI over the period 1990 to 2008. First, note the wide dispersion of monthly returns to

EXHIBIT 22.8 Distribution of Returns for the GSCI

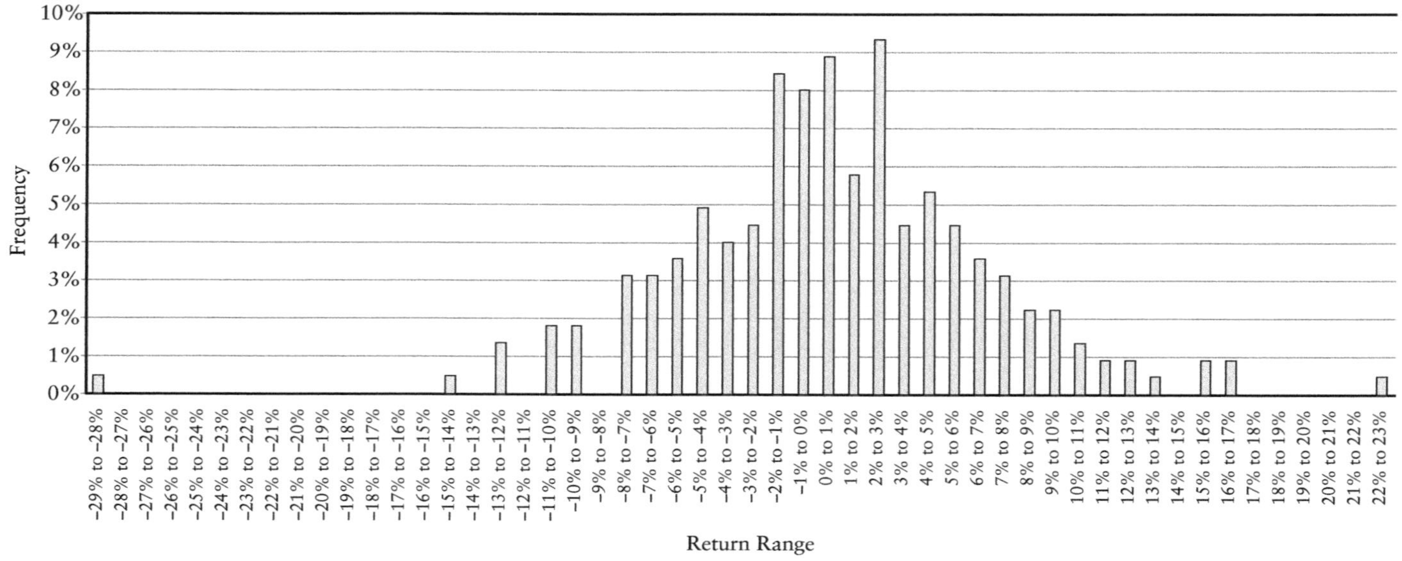

the GSCI. These returns vary from –29% at one end to +23% at the other end of the return distribution. In addition, the mass of the distribution is not concentrated to the same extent as hedge fund returns. For example, the mass of the GSCI return distribution in the 0% to 2% range is only 14.6%. This dispersion is further evidenced by the very high standard deviation of monthly returns of 6.12%. Overall, the average monthly return to the GSCI is 0.65% with a monthly standard deviation of 6.12%. This results in a Sharpe ratio of 0.05.

The GSCI has a slight negative skew of –0.14 and a positive kurtosis of 2.39. This condition of leptokurtosis means that commodity returns experience large outlier returns more frequently than might be expected with a normal distribution. Indeed, when we look at Exhibit 22.8 we can visually discern these outlier data points. This indicates that commodity futures are exposed to event risk: the risk of sudden shocks to the global supply and demand for physical commodities. From our discussion of commodity event risk being mostly shocks that reduce the supply of commodities, we expect that exposure to event risk to have a beneficial impact on commodity returns. Interestingly, we find a slightly negative skew, indicating a small (almost negligible) downward bias to these shocks. The negative skew observed here may be due to the fact that GSCI and other investable commodity indexes are not entirely passive investments; the positions in futures contracts have to be managed, and because of this the return may demonstrate properties not shared by a passive investment in the underlying commodity.

Dow Jones–AIG Commodity Index

The *Dow Jones–AIG Commodity Index* (DJ-AIGCI) is designed to provide both liquidity and diversification with respect to physical commodities.[11] It is a long-only index composed of futures contracts on 20 physical commodities. These include petroleum products (crude oil, heating oil, and unleaded gasoline); natural gas; precious metals (gold and silver); industrial metals (copper, aluminum, zinc, and nickel); grains (wheat, corn, and soybeans); livestock (live cattle and lean hogs); vegetable oil (soybean oil); and the soft commodities (coffee, cotton, cocoa, and sugar).

The DJ-AIGCI is composed of commodities traded on U.S. commodity exchanges and also on the London Metals Exchange (LME). Contracts on the LME provide exposure to industrial metals such as aluminum, nickel, and zinc.

Unlike the GSCI, to determine the weightings of each commodity in the index, the DJ-AIGCI relies primarily on liquidity data. This index considers

---

[11]Information on the DJ-AIGCI can be found at the Dow Jones web site (www.dj.com) and by using the Dow Jones Web links to the DJ-AIGCI.

the relative amount of trading activity associated with a particular commodity to determine its weight in the index. Liquidity is an important indicator of the interest placed on a commodity by financial and physical market participants. The index also relies to a lesser extent on dollar-adjusted production data to determine index weights. Therefore, the index weights depend primarily on endogenous factors in the futures markets (liquidity), and secondarily on exogenous factors to the futures markets (production).

The component weightings are also determined by several rules to ensure diversified commodity exposure. Disproportionate weighting to any particular commodity or sector could increase volatility and negate the concept of a broad-based commodity index. Therefore, the DJ-AIGCI index also applies two important diversification rules:

1. No related group of commodities (e.g. energy products, precious metals, livestock, or grains) may constitute more than 33% of the index weights.
2. No single commodity may constitute less than 2% of the index.

The DJ-AIGCI is reweighted and rebalanced every January. Rebalancing and reweighting are designed to reduce the exposure of the index to commodities that have appreciated in value and to increase the index's exposure to commodities that have underperformed. During the course of the year, commodity weights are free to increase or decrease as their values increase or decrease, subject to the two limits imposed. This represents a momentum type of index.

Exhibit 22.9 presents a frequency distribution of the monthly returns to the DJ-AIGCI over the time period from 1991 to 2008.[12] Similar to the GSCI, this distribution of returns demonstrates a small negative skew of −0.71, indicating that there is a slight bias toward negative returns occurring more frequently than positive returns. In addition, we see a value of kurtosis of 3.52 that is greater than that for the S&P GSCI, indicating a bias toward more outlier events and fatter tails. Visually, like the GSCI, we can see that there are occasionally very large positive and negative returns for the DJ-AIG Commodity Index.

Notice that the dispersion of returns to the DJ-AIGCI is much less than that for the GSCI. At 4.14% the standard deviation of the DJ-AIGCI is about one-third less than the monthly standard deviation for the S&P GSCI. However, the average return is also less at 0.57% per month. This is due to

---

[12]The Dow Jones–AIG Commodity Index has been in operating existence only since 1998. Therefore, to calculate returns prior to 1998, Dow Jones and AIG had to calculate index returns back in time using the index construction rules currently in place. The returns are calculated back to 1991.

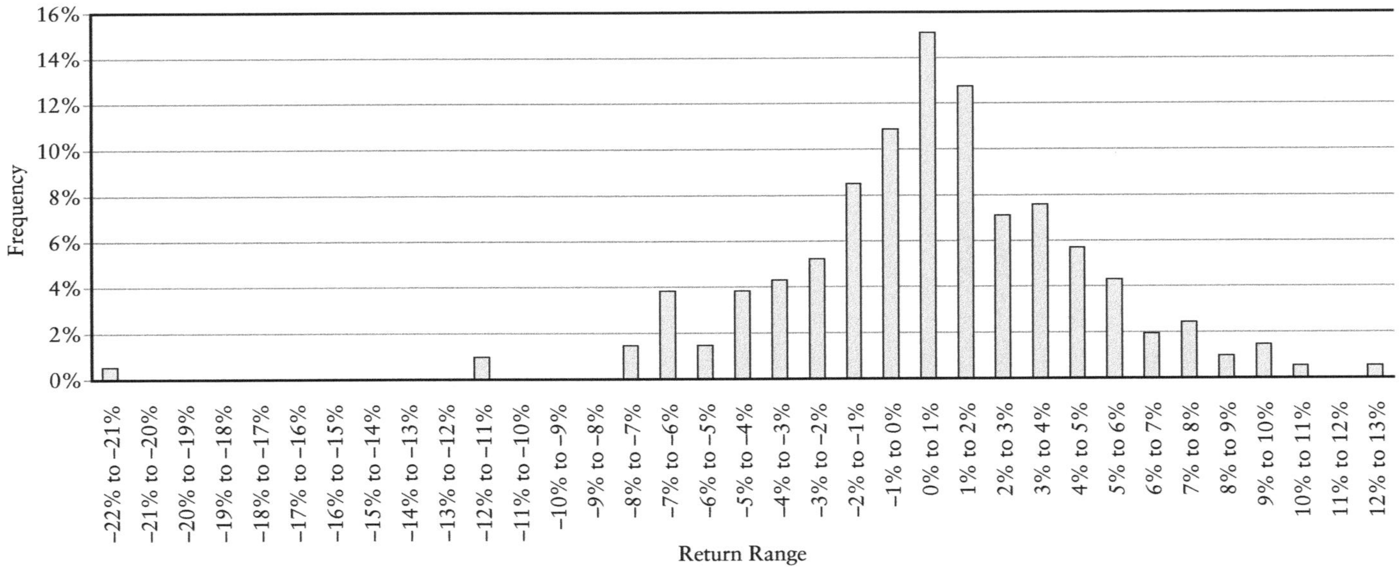

EXHIBIT 22.9 Distribution of Returns for the Dow Jones–AIG Commodity Index

the construction rules for the DJ-AIGCI that expressly limit the exposure to any one commodity group at 33%. Compare this to the exposure of the GSCI to energy at 72%. This limitation ensures broader diversification among the different physical commodities; the index cannot become top-heavy in any one commodity group. However, the S&P GSCI generates a higher monthly average return than the DJ-AIGCI, so the Sharpe ratios for the two indexes are not materially different: 0.05 for the S&P GSCI versus 0.06 for the DJ-AIGCI.

Which is the better commodity index? Like everything else in life, there are pros and cons. On the one hand, the DJ-AIGCI is less volatile. On the other hand, the GSCI provides exposure to the very large price shocks (both positive and negative) that affect commodity prices. The choice of an index is really a matter of preference.

Commodity Research Bureau Index

The *Reuters/Jefferies Commodity Research Bureau Index* (CRB Index) is the oldest of commodity indexes. It was first calculated by Commodity Research Bureau, Inc. in 1957 and has been published since 1958. Originally, the index construction was a simple arithmetic average of a basket of commodity prices. The index was renamed the Reuters/Jefferies CRB Index in 2005 and its index construction changed as well. The index is currently made up of 19 commodities quoted on the New York Mercantile Exchange (NYMEX), Chicago Board of Trade (CBOT), London Metals Exchange (LME), Chicago Mercantile Exchange (CME), and Commodity Exchange of New York (COMEX).

As of this writing, the index uses a four-tiered grouping system of commodities designed to more accurately reflect the significance of each commodity. Tier I has 33% of the index weight and includes only petroleum products: crude oil, heating oil, and unleaded gasoline. These are selected for both their liquidity and their economic importance to global economic development. Tier II commodities represent 42% of the index and consist of markets that are highly liquid: natural gas, corn, soybeans, live cattle, gold, aluminum, and copper. Tier III commodities provide 20% of the index weight and are included to provide diversification and broad representation for the index. Last, Tier IV commodities represent only 5% of the index but provide meaningful diversification for the Reuters/Jefferies CRB Index.

Exhibit 22.10 provides the distribution of returns for the CRB Index. Again, we see a trade-off of risk profiles. For example, the Reuters/Jefferies CRB Index has the lowest monthly standard deviation of the three commodity indexes at 3.48% it also has the most negative skew at −1.23 and the largest value of kurtosis at 8.07. This demonstrates a sizable downside tail associated with this commodity index. Also, the Reuters/Jefferies CRB

EXHIBIT 22.10 Distribution of Returns for the CRB Index

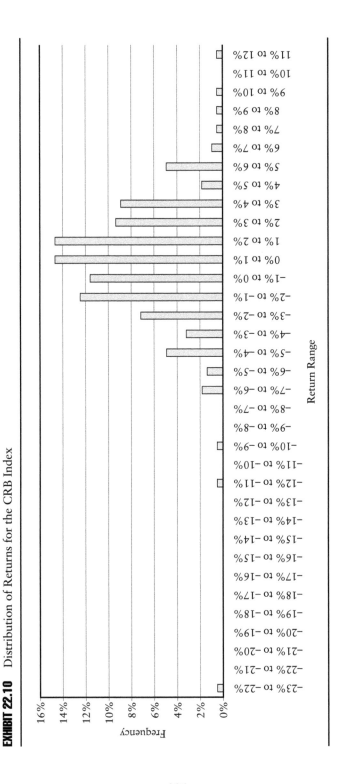

Index has the lowest average monthly return at 0.32%, which leads to a Sharpe ratio of virtually zero.

Mount Lucas Management Index

Mount Lucas Management introduced the *Mount Lucas Management Index* (MLMI) in 1988.[13] It is a passive index designed to capture the returns to active futures investing. The MLMI represents the return to a specific commodity trading strategy and therefore differs significantly from the previously discussed futures indexes in three ways.

First, the MLMI is designed to be a trend-following index. The MLMI uses a 12-month look-back window for calculating the moving average unit asset value for each futures market in which it invests. Once a month, on the day prior to the last trading day, the algorithm examines the current unit asset value in each futures market compared to the average value for the prior 12 months. If the current unit asset value is above the 12-month moving average, the MLMI purchases the futures contract. If the current unit asset value is below the 12-month moving average, the MLMI takes a short position in the futures contract.

This highlights the second difference associated with the MLMI. This index can be both long and short futures contracts, whereas the GSCI, DJ-AIGCI, and CRB Index take only long positions in futures contracts.

The theory behind the MLMI is that the mismatch in commercial firms' futures positions is greatest, and investors can profit the most, when the underlying futures market is moving broadly from one price level to another, either up or down. The object of this index construction is to capture the potential profits represented by such broad market trends.

The last difference with respect to the MLMI is that it invests in physical commodity, financial, and currency futures. There are 22 commodity futures contracts in the three categories.[14] The MLMI has three different categories to the index: commodities at a 25% weighting, currencies at a 32.5% weighting, and global fixed income at 42.5% weighting. Within each category, the physical or financial futures contracts are equally weighted. The purpose of its construction is to capture the pricing trend of each commodity without regard to its production value or trading volume in the market. Therefore, the price trend for each futures contract in the index is

---

[13]Information regarding the MLMI was provided by Raymond Ix at Mount Lucas Management.
[14]There is one additional difference with respect to the MLMI. Two versions of the index are calculated. One version is unleveraged, and one version is three times leveraged.

EXHIBIT 22.11   Distribution of Returns for the MLMI

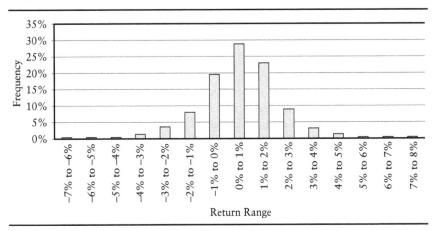

given the same consideration. Given its trend-following design, the MLMI rebalances every month based on the prior 12-month moving average.

In Exhibit 22.11, we present the probability distribution for the returns of the MLMI index. The results are generally better than for the three physical-commodity-only indexes. First, the monthly standard deviation, at 1.73% is much lower than that for the three commodity indexes and the average monthly return is 0.54%, which leads to the highest Sharpe ratio at 0.13. In addition, there is a slight positive skew of 0.06 and a value of kurtosis of 2.76, indicating a slight bias to the upside. Furthermore, in the exhibit we can see that there is a much more symmetrical distribution with fewer outliers than the commodity indexes. Also, a greater portion of the mass (52%) is centered in the 0 to 2% range, demonstrating much more consistent returns compared to the commodity indexes.

Comparison of Commodity Futures Indexes

It is worthwhile to summarize some of the differences between the commodity indexes just discussed. The GSCI, for example, is economically weighted. The weights in the index are determined solely by exogenous economic data (e.g. production values for the global economy). The argument for constructing such an index is analogous to that for the capitalization-weighted S&P 500; the most economically important commodities should influence a portfolio tracking an index.[15] In contrast, the DJ-AIGCI is primarily activity weighted. Those commodities that are most actively traded determine its construction. This index relies on endogenous variables (trading volume

---

[15]See Greer, "Institutional Use of Physical Commodity Indices."

and liquidity) to determine its weights. This approach assures maximum liquidity for portfolios tracking the index.

The Reuters/Jefferies CRB Index provides yet another weighting scheme. It should be noted that for most of its history it was an equally weighted index. This changed in 2005. The R/J CRB Index now follows a hybrid weighting scheme based on a four-tier system. Each tier has a different total weight in the index. However, within each tier, the weights to individual commodities are fixed and the index is rebalanced monthly to maintain the constant weights. We note that the S&P GSCI, the DJ-AIGCI, and the R/J CRB all have negative skews and large positive values of kurtosis. This demonstrates a bias to the downside with large, fat downside tails. While the negative values of skew are small for the S&P GSCI and the DJ-AIGCI, they are larger for the R/J CRB Index. The R/J CRB also has the largest value of kurtosis, demonstrating the largest downside tail. This is different from the situation a few years ago, when small, positive skews were observed for the commodity indexes. The additional three years of commodity futures return data (2006 to 2008) has produced this change in skew.

Conversely, The MLMI is the only futures index that has a positive skew associated with it. This value indicates a positive bias to event risk. In addition, The MLMI has much smaller dispersion in its returns than the other three indexes. The standard deviation of the MLMI returns is 72% less than that for the GSCI, 58% less than that for the DJ-AIGCI, and 50% less than that of the CRB Index. This should be expected given the construction of the MLMI. Its trend-following strategy should reduce its exposure to extreme outlier events. In addition, the MLMI has the largest Sharpe ratio of the four commodity futures indexes. The MLMI not only has the best risk-return trade-off, but it also provides the best exposure to positive outlier events.

The DJ-AIGCI specifically limits the exposures of commodity sectors so the index does not become top-heavy with respect to any particular commodity or sector (particularly the energy sector). This cap may reduce the exposure of outlier events within the DJ-AIGCI compared to the GSCI. This cap, in fact, acts like a short call option position that truncates the distribution of returns above the allowable percentage limit in the index. Truncating a return distribution will reduce an investor's exposure to large outlier returns. This reduces the volatility of the DJ-AIGCI compared to the S&P GSCI, but surprisingly, we get a larger value of kurtosis for the DJ-AIGCI than for the S&P GSCI. Similarly, the monthly rebalancing of the R/J CRB Index reduces the volatility still further compared to the S&P GSCI and the DJ-AIGCI, but the value of kurtosis continues to increase. This is a surprising outcome that we have difficulty explaining. Finally, we note that the MLMI provides a good risk-return trade-off while maintaining a more tightly bunched return distribution (i.e., there are fewer outliers).

Financial Instruments and Concepts Introduced in this Chapter (in Order of Presentation)

Commodities
Commodity futures contracts
Initial margin
Variation margin
Maintenance margin
Commodity swaps
Commodity forward contracts
Commodity-linked note
Commodity ETF
Commodity futures index

Spot commodity prices
Collateral yield
Roll yield
Backwardation
Contango
Standard & Poor's Goldman Sachs
  Commodity Index
Dow Jones-AIG Commodity Index
Mount Lucas Management Index

Arithmetic Mean vs. Geometric Mean

When working with the returns to risky assets, it is sometimes helpful to determine their mean or average return. There are two methods to determine the average return to an asset: the arithmetic mean and geometric mean. The arithmetic mean is simply the sum of the all of the returns divided by the number of periods over which the sum total is calculated. This is also called the average, or average return. For example, if we are interested in the average mean return for some asset, we have

$$\text{Arithmetic mean} = \frac{1}{T} \sum_{t=1}^{T} \text{Asset return}(t)$$

where

$\sum_{t=1}^{T}$ = the summation notation that means that we are adding up all of the observations over T periods

Asset return(t) = the return to the Asset in the tth year

T = the number of periods over which we calculate the average

Consider the returns for Asset X shown in Exhibit A.1 over a 10-year time horizon. We use this data to demonstrate the difference between the arithmetic and geometric mean.

Using the above equation and the data in the exhibit, the arithmetic mean is calculated as:

$$\begin{aligned}
\text{Arithmetic mean} &= [10\% + 14\% + (-7\%) + (-3\%) + 22\% \\
&\quad + 16\% + 8\% + 13\% + 15\% + 12\%]/10 \\
&= 100\%/10 = 10\%
\end{aligned}$$

EXHIBIT A.1   The Returns to Asset X

Year	Return
1	10%
2	14
3	-7
4	-3
5	22
6	16
7	8
8	13
9	15
10	12

This is the average annual return produced by risky asset X over the past 10 years.

The arithmetic mean is the simplest calculation to determine the average return. The average return on an asset, observed over a long period of time, is often used as the expected return for future years. Although the future return is unknown and cannot be predicted with great accuracy, the historical average return is as good a guess as any of what the return will be in the future.

The geometric mean is a bit more complicated. It uses compounding to determine the mean return. For a set of observations related to an asset return stream, the geometric mean is equal to

$$1 + R(G) = \sqrt[T]{[1 + R(1)] \times [1 + R(2)] \times \cdots \times [1 + R(T)]}$$

where

$R(G)$	= the return for the geometric mean
$R(1)$, $R(2)$, $R(T)$	= the returns to asset X in periods 1, 2, all the way to period T
T	= the number of periods over which we calculate the geometric mean
$\sqrt[T]{}$	means that we take the Tth root of our compound return stream to determine $R(G)$

Using the data in Exhibit A.1 and the previous equation, we calculate the geometric mean as:

$$1 + R(G) = \sqrt[10]{\frac{(1+10\%)(1+14\%)(1-7\%)(1-3\%)(1+22\%)(1+16\%)(1+8\%)}{\times(1+13\%)(1+15\%)(1+12\%)}}$$

$$1 + R(G) = 1.0967$$

$$R(G) = 9.67\%$$

We note that the geometric mean is slightly lower than the arithmetic mean. This is the case when the returns are changing through time. In fact, there is an approximate relationship between the two:

$$R(G) \approx R(A) - \frac{1}{2}Var(R)$$

where $Var(R)$ is the variance of the rate of return on asset X. It can be seen that if the annual rate of return on the asset has no volatility, then the geometric mean and arithmetic mean will be equal.

One more observation is appropriate. The geometric mean is also used in the calculation for the cumulative average growth rate (CAGR). CAGR assumes that an asset, cash flow, or some other random variable grows at a constant rate of return compounded over a sample period of time. For example, assume that we purchase a stock of company A at $50 and hold it for three years until it reaches the value of $100. What is our CAGR? The calculation is simple: We combine our holding period return calculation with the equation for the geometric mean.

First, determine the holding period return as

$$\$100/\$50 = 2$$

Then our CAGR is equal to

$$1 + R(G) = \sqrt[3]{2.0} = \sqrt[3]{(1 + CAGR) \times (1 + CAGR) \times (1 + CAGR)}$$

$$1 + R(G) = 1.26 = (1 + CAGR)$$

$$R(G) = 26\% = CAGR$$

Measures of Risk

In this appendix, we introduce the reader to the basic risk measures.

RANGE AND LOCATION

Statisticians often make use of what are known as *quantiles* to divide a ranked (on some chosen statistic) data sample into equal fractions. Quantiles are a way to divide a time series of returns into a descriptive pattern. For example, quartiles (a ranked sample divided into four quantiles) are used most frequently when reviewing data. (For example, are a fund manager's returns in the first quartile of the fund's peer group, in the second quartile, or in the third or fourth?) Dividing the data up into quartiles provides an investor with a quick and convenient way to determine whether a fund manager outperforms the fund's peer group or lags behind. This is another way of determining how a fund manager *ranks* when compared to other hedge fund managers in the same category.

Quantiles divide the data up into fractional units and categorize the return of an asset, fund manager, or return stream into one of the fractions below which a portion of the data population lies. Another way to look at the data is that quantiles divide up the *range* of a data sample into groups based on their ranking within the overall sample. Most popular quantiles are quartiles (four fractional units), quintiles (five fractional units) and deciles (10 fractional units). An example might help.

Exhibit B.1 contains the returns for 32 actual equity long/short hedge fund managers for the year 2007. These managers were selected randomly. We note that the worst hedge fund manager had a return of –16% for 2007 whereas the best had a return of 20%. This is the range of the data: from –16% to +20%.

EXHIBIT B.1 Equity Long/Short Hedge Fund Returns

Hedge Fund	Return
A	−14%
B	7
C	11
D	10
E	8
F	−2
G	−3
H	6
I	12
J	18
K	20
L	13
M	9
N	−12
O	−7
P	9
Q	14
R	3
S	10
T	16
U	−16
V	−2
W	9
X	11
Y	7
Z	2
AA	15
BB	19
CC	8
DD	−4
EE	10
FF	4

The range is a quick way to measure the dispersion, or risk, of a data sample. Simply, the range is calculated as

$$\text{Range} = \text{Highest value in a data sample} - \text{Lowest value}$$

In our hedge fund sample, the range is 20% – (–16%) = 36%.

With 32 hedge fund managers divided up into quartiles, eight hedge fund managers will be in the top quartile of performance, eight in the second quartile, and so forth. Using our quartile rankings, Exhibit B.2 demonstrates how the data can be divided up into a descriptive analysis.

EXHIBIT B.2 Quartile Rankings for Equity Long/Short Hedge Funds

Quartile Ranking	Hedge Funds
Quartile 1	Hedge Fund Manager K = 20%
	Hedge Fund Manager BB = 19%
	Hedge Fund Manager J = 18%
	Hedge Fund Manager T = 16%
	Hedge Fund Manager AA = 15%
	Hedge Fund Manager Q = 14%
	Hedge Fund Manager L = 13%
	Hedge Fund Manager I = 12%
Quartile 2	Hedge Fund Manager C = 11%
	Hedge Fund Manager X = 11%
	Hedge Fund Manager D = 10%
	Hedge Fund Manager S = 10%
	Hedge Fund Manager EE = 10%
	Hedge Fund Manager M = 9%
	Hedge Fund Manager P = 9%
	Hedge Fund Manager W = 9%
Quartile 3	Hedge Fund Manager E = 8%
	Hedge Fund Manager CC = 8%
	Hedge Fund Manager B = 7%
	Hedge Fund Manager Y = 7%
	Hedge Fund Manager H = 6%
	Hedge Fund Manager FF = 4%
	Hedge Fund Manager R = 3%
	Hedge Fund Manager Z = 2%
Quartile 4	Hedge Fund Manager F = –2%
	Hedge Fund Manager V = –2%
	Hedge Fund Manager G = –3%
	Hedge Fund Manager DD = –4%
	Hedge Fund Manager O = –7%
	Hedge Fund Manager N = –12%
	Hedge Fund Manager A = –14%
	Hedge Fund Manager U = –16%

Calculating the average of these hedge fund managers using our methods from Appendix I, the arithmetic average is 6.03%. With the meltdown of the subprime market and the equity markets with it, equity long/short managers had a tough year. We note that the *median* of this cross section of hedge funds is between 8% and 9%. The median is that value for which one-half of the sample population lies above it and one-half of the sample population lies below it. In a normal (bell-shaped) distribution of returns, the mean and the median are equal. The fact that in this case the mean is less than the median indicates that there was significant downside risk associated with equity long/short hedge funds in 2007.

MOMENTS OF THE DISTRIBUTION

Every asset, whether a stock or a bond or a hedge fund, provides a stream of returns. The business of statistics is to provide descriptive numbers that can paint a picture of what these return patterns look like. A distribution of numbers such as a time series of asset returns is often described by its *moments*. The moments of a distribution are calculations that transcribe the pattern of returns into numbers that paint a picture about the return stream.

The first moment of the distribution is one that we discussed thoroughly in Appendix A; it is the mean of the distribution, described as

$$E[X] = \sum_{I}^{N} X_I / N$$

where

X_i = the individual observations in our data population
N = the number of observations in our population
$\sum_{i}^{N}$ = the summation symbol of all of our X observations from i to N

From the cross section of hedge fund returns in Exhibit B.1, we calculate that the value of $E[X] = 6.03\%$. This is the mean of the hedge fund return distribution.

The second moment of the distribution is expressed as

$$E[X^2] = \sum_{i}^{N} X_i^2 / N$$

Using the data in Exhibit B.1, we get a value of 1.208%.

Variance and Semivariance

The first two moments are particularly important because they can be used to determine both the mean and variance of a distribution of returns. Specifically, the *variance* of any sample of returns can be determined by the equation:

$$\text{Variance} = E[X^2] - \{E[X]\}^2$$

Inserting the values obtained for $E[X]$ and $E[X^2]$, we find the variance to be

$$1.208\% - (6.03\%)^2 = 0.008446$$

Taking the square root of the variance gives us the volatility, or standard deviation, of our hedge fund population:

$$\sqrt{0.008446} = 9.19\%$$

Another formula to calculate the variance of a data population is given by

$$\text{Variance} = \sum_{i}^{N} (X_i - E[X])^2 / N$$

Both this equation and the previous one lead us to the same calculation of variance of 0.008446. The variance is often represented by the symbol σ^2, and the volatility, or standard deviation, by the square root of σ^2 (which is simply σ).

In many instances of data examination, we can observe only a subset of the overall data population. In such a case, both the mean and the variance have to be estimated. Because of this, it turns out that the estimated value of the variance will be unbiased if the sum of squared differences is divided by $(N - 1)$. Therefore, the formula for the variance is

$$\sigma^2 = \sum_{i}^{N} (X_i - E[X])^2 / (N - 1)$$

Another risk measure is the *semivariance*. Variance is a symmetrical calculation; it measures the negative and positive dispersion around the mean. However, investors are more concerned with the downside than the upside. Therefore, another measure, the semivariance, is used to determine the risk of the downside. The semivariance is calculated as:

$$\text{Semivariance} = \sum_{i}^{N} (X_i - E[X])^2 / N$$

for all $X_i < E[X]$.

In other words, we calculate the dispersion below the mean value of only those values that are less than the mean. This gives us a sense of how much variability exists for those observations that fall below the mean. Using the above equation, the semivariance for the hedge fund manager returns is to equal 0.01435.

Another use of the semivariance is to calculate a *target* semivariance. The difference is that in the formula for the semivariance we substitute a target rate of return (e.g., 5%) instead of the mean return of 6.03%.

Skewness

Two other calculations are very important to the analysis of alternative assets: *skewness* and *kurtosis*. For a normal distribution, which is represented by the normal distribution (i.e., the classic bell-curve pattern) of returns, the mean and the variance are all that is needed to describe the pattern of returns associated with an investment. That is because a normal distribution is perfect in its symmetry; each side of the curve, centered at the mean of the return distribution, is a mirror imagine of the other side of the curve. For example, under a normal distribution, if the mean were 0%, we would expect that losses in the 0% to –1% range would occur with same frequency as gains from 0% to 1%, and so forth. The distribution would be perfectly balanced on each side of the mean. Under these rare circumstances, the mean and the variance can describe perfectly the shape of the return distribution.

Note that there are many other distributions that are perfectly described by only two parameters (e.g., the lognormal distribution is described by only two parameters). However, most return distributions have not been observed to be symmetrical. They have shapes and return patterns that cannot be described fully by just the mean and the variance. Because gains and losses around the mean are not symmetrical, investors need to have further calculations to fully understand the return pattern. We see these patterns most distinctly when we examine hedge funds, commodities, private equity, and the like.

A distribution that is not symmetrical is said to be *skewed* and its return distribution is described by its *skewness*. A skewed distribution leans either to the right toward more positive gains or to the left toward more negative returns. For example, a positively skewed distribution demonstrates a small number of very large positive gains with small but more frequent losses. Conversely, a negatively skewed distribution has infrequent but very large negative returns combined with frequent but small positive returns. Generally, negatively skewed distributions are to be avoided because they demonstrate the risk of large downside losses. The normal distribution has a skew of 0.

Skewed distributions are referred to in terms of *tails* and *mass*. A positively skewed distribution has a long tail to the right, indicating the probability of large upside returns associated with the return pattern. Sometimes this is described as greater mass located in the right-hand (positive) tail of the distribution. This is a good thing because it demonstrates an asset that has the ability to deliver on occasion large positive returns. For a positively skewed distribution, the median is less than the mean.

For a distribution with a negative skew, the mean is less than the median. This demonstrates an asset that has the potential to deliver large negative returns. Negatively skewed return distributions are to be avoided if possible because they demonstrate a risk of large downside returns.

The skew of a distribution is measured by the third moment of the distribution as follows:

$$\text{Skew} = (1 \, / \, N) \times \sum_{i}^{N} (X_i - E[X])^3 \, / \, \sigma^3$$

Applying this equation, we find the skew of our hedge fund distribution to be –0.80.

Kurtosis

The last moment of the distribution, called the fourth moment, measures the *kurtosis* of the distribution. Kurtosis is a way to measure the thickness of the tails of the distribution. Often, the return distribution associated with an asset has a significant amount of the return observations that are at the extreme ends of the range of the distribution. These outlier returns add to the mass in the tails of the distribution, increasing the value of kurtosis.

Kurtosis is often measured relative to the normal distribution. For a normal distribution, the value of kurtosis is 3. *Leptokurtosis* refers to the condition that more return observations are contained in the tails of the distribution than for a normal distribution. Sometimes this is described as a distribution with *fat tails*. This simply means that there are more large return deviations from the mean than are associated with a normal distribution. The term *platykurtosis* refers to the condition where the tails of the return distribution are thinner than for a normal distribution; that is, there are fewer large deviations from the mean than are observed for a normal distribution. In this book, we measure kurtosis relative to a normal distribution.

So a positive value of kurtosis indicates fatter tails than a normal distribution (leptokurtosis), and a negative value of kurtosis indicates thinner tails than a normal distribution (platykurtosis).

Kurtosis is measured by

$$\text{Kurtosis} = 1 / N \times \sum_{i}^{N} (X_i - E[X])^4 / \sigma^4 - 3$$

This expression is also referred to as excess kurtosis because it is measured in excess of the kurtosis of a normal distribution. In this book we use the term kurtosis to refer to the above equation.

Index

Lightning Source UK Ltd.
Milton Keynes UK
UKHW021530231119
353999UK00003B/80/P